*Children's Literature*
*An Anthology* 1801–1902

# BLACKWELL ANTHOLOGIES

## Children's Literature: An Anthology 1801–1902
### Edited by Peter Hunt

*Rosemary Ashton, University of London; Gillian Beer, University of Cambridge; Gordon Campbell, University of Leicester; Terry Castle, Stanford University; Margaret Ann Doody, Vanderbilt University; Richard Gray, University of Essex; Joseph Harris, Harvard University; Karen L. Kilcup, University of North Carolina, Greensboro; Jerome J. McGann, University of Virginia; David Norbrook, University of Maryland; Tom Paulin, University of Oxford; Michael Payne, Bucknell University; Elaine Showalter, Princeton University; John Sutherland, University of London; Jonathan Wordsworth, University of Oxford.*

Blackwell Anthologies are a series of extensive and comprehensive volumes designed to address the numerous issues raised by recent debates regarding the literary canon, value, text, context, gender, genre, and period. While providing the reader with key canonical writings in their entirety, the series is also ambitious in its coverage of hitherto marginalized texts, and flexible in the overall variety of its approaches to periods and movements. Each volume has been thoroughly researched to meet the current needs of teachers and students.

BRITISH LITERATURE

Victorian Women Poets: An Anthology
*edited by Angela Leighton and Margaret Reynolds*

Romanticism: An Anthology. Second Edition
*edited by Duncan Wu*

Romantic Women Poets: An Anthology
*edited by Duncan Wu*

British Literature 1640–1789: An Anthology
*edited by Robert DeMaria, Jr*

Chaucer to Spenser: An Anthology of writings in English 1375–1575
*edited by Derek Pearsall*

Renaissance Drama: An Anthology of Plays and Entertainments
*edited by Arthur Kinney*

Old and Middle English: An Anthology
*edited by Elaine Treharne*

Restoration Drama: An Anthology
*edited by David Womersley*

The Victorians: An Anthology of Poetry and Poetics
*edited by Valentine Cunningham*

Medieval Drama: An Anthology
*edited by Greg Walker*

Children's Literature: An Anthology 1801–1902
*edited by Peter Hunt*

*Forthcoming*
Renaissance Literature: An Anthology
*edited by Michael Payne and John Hunter*

Gothic Novels: An Anthology
*edited by Nicola Trott*

Modernism: An Anthology
*edited by Lawrence Rainey*

AMERICAN LITERATURE

Nineteenth-Century American Women Writers: An Anthology
*edited by Karen L. Kilcup*

Nineteenth-Century American Women Poets: An Anthology
*edited by Paula Bernat Bennett*

American Gothic: An Anthology 1787–1916
*edited by Charles L. Crow*

Native American Women Writers: An Anthology of Works c. 1800–1924
*edited by Karen L. Kilcup*

*Forthcoming*
Early African-American Literature: An Anthology
*edited by Phillip M. Richards*

# CHILDREN'S LITERATURE

## AN ANTHOLOGY 1801-1902

EDITED BY **PETER HUNT**

BLACKWELL Publishers

Copyright © Blackwell Publishers Ltd, 2001
Editorial matter, selection and organization Copyright © Peter Hunt 2001

First published 2001
2 4 6 8 10 9 7 5 3 1

Blackwell Publishers Ltd
108 Cowley Road
Oxford OX4 1JF
UK

Blackwell Publishers Inc.
350 Main Street
Malden, Massachusetts 02148
USA

*British Library Cataloguing in Publication Data*
A CIP catalogue record for this book is available from the British Library.

*Library of Congress Cataloging-in-Publication Data*

LOC data applied for.

ISBN 0631210482 (hdbk)
ISBN 0631210490 (pbk)

Typeset in Garamond on 9.5/11 pt by
Kolam Information Services Pvt. Ltd, Pondicherry India
Printed in Great Britain by T.J. International, Padstow, Cornwall
This book is printed on acid-free paper

# Contents

# List of Plates

# Acknowledgements

To explore the nineteenth century without the published work of the real experts, Brian Alderson, Gillian Avery, Sheila Egoff, Betty Gilderdale, Anne Scott MacLeod and Maurice Saxby, would be a hopeless task. I am also much indebted to my collaborators on *Children's Literature: An Illustrated History*, Dennis Butts, Tony Watkins, Margaret Evans and the late and much missed Ethel Heins.

For the selections from Australian children's literature, I am deeply indebted to Juliana Bayfield of the State Library of South Australia, Adelaide, for sharing some of her remarkable knowledge of the subject; to Sieta and Pieter van der Hoeven for making that visit to Australia possible; to Dr Rosemary Ross Johnston of University of Technology Sydney; to Maurice Saxby for his hospitality and wisdom; and to Sue Mansfield and the staff at The University of Surrey-Roehampton for making microfiche material available.

For American materials, I owe a similar debt to friends and colleagues at Texas A&M University: Lynne Vallone and Howard Marchitello and Larry Mitchell of the English Department; Johnnique Love of the Sterling C. Evans Library; and Donald H. Dyal, Director, and Stephen Smith, Special Collections Librarian, of the Cushing Memorial Library and their staff for quite exemplary service. In Carolina and Florida, Chip and Ann Sullivan have been as hospitable and helpful as ever.

As always, Betty Gilderdale has been unstinting in her advice on New Zealand children's literature.

Nearer home, Geoff Fox and John Kirkman have provided their customary expert advice; I owe particular thanks to Dennis Butts, who gave me a great deal of general encouragement, and a great deal of specific help with Henty and Hofland, and to Mary Butts, expert book-finder.

I am grateful to David Knott and the staff at the University of Reading Library Special Collections for helping to plug gaps in the anthology with unfailing courtesy.

My most extensive debt is to my colleagues in the School of English at Cardiff University for shouldering my share of the teaching burden during my research leave, and to the remarkably patient and persistent Inter-Library Loan team at Cardiff University Humanities Library.

The publishers gratefully acknowledge the following for permission to reproduce copyright material. Every effort has been made to trace copyright holders, but in some cases it has proved impossible. The publishers would be happy to hear from any copyright holder that has not been acknowledged.

Extract from *Moonfleet* by J. M. Faulkner, reprinted by permission of the Society of Authors as the literary representative of the Estate of J. M. Faulkner.

Extracts from *Stalky & Co* and *The Jungle Book* by Rudyard Kipling. Reprinted by permission of A. P. Watt Limited on behalf of the National Trust for Places of Historic Interest or Natural Beauty.

Extract from *Wild Animals I Have Known* by Ernest Thompson Seton, courtesy of Pamela C. Forcey and Clemency C. Coggins, granddaughters of Ernest Thompson Seton.

Extract from *Seven Little Australians* by Ethel Turner, published by Penguin Books, Australia. Reprinted by permission of Penguin Australia and Philippa Poole.

# Introduction

The most entertaining thing about nineteenth-century children's literature is not its huge variety, nor its attempts to define and react to changing childhood – it is its sheer readability. The evangelical tales of parental retribution for childhood misconduct (as parents 'stood in place of God' to their children) may seem savage at a distance of two hundred years, but they touch a spot of profound, visceral, satisfaction; the stories of pious children doing good in the city slums may be formulaic, but they grip with their intensity and unashamed pathos; and even the chunks of history in boys' adventure stories are carried along by a remarkable pace and verve. Whatever the political, religious or educational motivations of the writers, their work bubbles with energy.

This anthology is also a record of quite spectacular change. At the end of the eighteenth century, the market for children's books in the English-speaking world (and elsewhere), which had been firmly in the grip of the religious and educational Right, was beginning to be affected by a more romantic view of childhood. Frivolous materials were kept in their place – or remained as part of the subversive ground swell of popular culture – or were used, sparingly enough, as weapons in the evangelical war. Charles Lamb famously complained to S. T. Coleridge, in 1802, of the influence of writers like Anna Laetitia Barbauld: 'Mrs Barbauld's stuff has banished all the old classics of the nursery.... Think what you would have been now, if instead of being fed with tales and old wives' fables in childhood, you had been crammed with geography and history.' (To be fair to Barbauld, her *Hymns in Prose for Children* (1781) were a far cry from the hell-fire work of James Janeway and others, a century before – although those books were still in print.) Fundamentally, in what was then regarded as children's literature, adults were in control, and the tone of voice, the narrative stance, and the behaviour and fate of the characters in the fictions all acknowledged this.

In contrast, by the end of the nineteenth century, partly because of the influence of the romantics, partly because of radical changes in the publishing industry, in child health, and in education, and partly because the very concept of childhood (notably in the middle classes) had changed, children's books would have been scarcely recognizable to a Mrs Barbauld. They were a richly varied, established part of the cultural scene, incorporating fairy-tale and fantasy, exploring family relationships, ranging the world in adventures, discussing politics and, most liberatingly, containing moral *ambiguity*. While it can be argued that it is impossible to write for children without exercising control or didacticism of some kind, that didactic element was generally extremely muted; religious or moral education was, if present there at all, implied rather than stated.

The streams of adults' and children's writing had grown together (although they were soon to separate again), and many children's books were shared by adults: Burnett and Henty and Fenimore Cooper were read by everyone; it is only possible to 'classify' some of the work of Christina Rossetti, for example, by closely analysing her point of view. There was also a genuine international dialogue; Australian writers were no longer imitating British writers; Burnett and Alcott were bestsellers on both sides of the Atlantic.

But, most of all, in writers like Carroll, Kipling, Nesbit and Stevenson, a new way of addressing the child reader was being developed – a new attitude, a new narrative stance, and the concept of the new *empowered* child was emerging. For the best writers, children were peers, not inferiors, and the twentieth century would see these characteristics develop into a *separate* literature.

And between 1800 and 1900? In between is a vastly intricate forest of literature which has scarcely been researched. The maps of it – of which this anthology is one version – are constructed, as it were, from those trees that have grown prominent by the quirks of literary weeding and canonical fertilizing. Most were, certainly, bestsellers, but the development of a canon does not necessarily lie with popularity; it lies, complexly enough, with people who were, rather than are, the intended readership. (This is made the more complex, of course, by the fact that the audience for *this* volume is adult.) Literary obscurity is a notoriously undiscriminating disease and the fact that children's literature has been, until very recently, marginalized as a subject of research and literary study, has meant that there are vast resources in libraries worldwide which are untapped. If other literary areas are any guide, further research will almost certainly change the gender-balance and the international, colonial/postcolonial flavour of the 'visible' texts. Equally, the under-representation of the ex-colonial English-speaking world, especially of Canada and New Zealand, might be seen as yet another act of neo-colonialism; there was, it is true, a very small output of indigenous children's books, but the status of even these is, of course, judged imperialistically.

A broad, canonical history is simple enough to outline, but a reading of this anthology will demonstrate how clumsy such formulations are. As the century progressed, evangelicals lost their grip on the market (although a writer as late as Rossetti is scarcely distinguishable in tone from Mary Martha Sherwood). Boys' stories tended towards action and adventure – stories of the sea, exploration and empire – slowly losing their primarily religious–moral thrust (although Henty sometimes seems more preachy than Ballantyne). Girls' stories had a domestic turn, some taking on social problems, albeit by emphasizing the religious and social status quo, others absorbing the fashionable folk- and fairy-tale. In both cases the religious focus gradually diffused (although ideas of strict behaviour survive into the twentieth century). Some critics have seen a Victorian (male) preoccupation with children's bodies emerging as a sub-text in Carroll and Kingsley (although it might equally be detected in Martha Finlay). Overall, through the century, child behaviour, as portrayed, became freer, partly because of actual changes in society, and partly because the fundamental urge of writers for children to portray society as it should be, rather than as it was, became moderated.

Readers may wish to trace other streams. Folk- and fairy-tales became fashionable for adults, and were, naturally enough, in a utilitarian society, 'relegated to the nursery'. Children's verse, here represented by a sample of the most popular, spends a century moving from admonition to a tacit debate as to what can constitute children's poetry. The way in which adult writers approached fantasy – using it as allegory or parody or comedy – is a fascinating study. Fantasy develops many forms and it is interesting to note that, in broad terms, the major fantasists have been men, and the major realistic writers, women. Perhaps most striking of all is the interdependence of children's literature: time and again, books appeared that were modifications or even parodies of their predecessors (compare *Seven Little Australians* with *Little Women*, or *The Little Colonel* with *Little Lord Fauntleroy*).

The chronological structure of this anthology allows, more than anything, the complexity of the history to demonstrate itself: if, for example, 1869 can see both *Mopsa the Fairy* and *The Story of a Bad Boy*, or 1888 *The Happy Prince* and *Two Little Confederates*, then we might be discouraged from being simplistic.

Any history, and any anthology, can (and should) be challenged at virtually every point. History is not, although it has been made out to be, a matter of neat influences and coherent developments; it is an immensely complex matrix of which our current view is necessarily tentative and partial. The temporal boundaries of this anthology are consequently more arguable than most. My own view, that there are relatively few texts before 1800 which have more than antiquarian interest, is likely to provoke forceful protests from supporters of Sarah Fielding, Mary Wollstonecraft, or even (it is possible) of James Janeway. I would not question the interest or importance of the earliest printed versions of nursery rhymes, of chapbooks, catechisms, or of the growth of the children's book market, or even of the straightforward moral tales; but I would argue that from around the turn of the century, particularly with the influence of romanticism, there was a shift which makes the texts included here more accessible to the modern reader. The flavour of eighteenth-century writing lingers, and readers may be encouraged to explore earlier works.

As to where to end the anthology, we could enter even livelier debate. It could be argued that *The Story of the Treasure Seekers* (1899) is essentially a twentieth-century text, whereas *Winnie-the-Pooh* (1926) is essentially of the nineteenth century: that *Rebecca of Sunnybrook Farm* (1903) is a more forward-looking text than *Anne of Green Gables* (1908). Ultimately, such decisions have to be arbitrary.

That said, an anthologist should explain her or his principles, beginning with a belief in the value of anthologies. In a famous discussion of plagiarism, Henry Fielding, in *Tom Jones*, makes some remarks that the anti-anthologists amongst us may relish: 'To fill up a work with these scraps may indeed be considered as a downright cheat on the learned world, who are by such means imposed upon to buy a second time in fragments and by retail what they already have . . . on their shelves' (XII, I, 'Shewing what is to be deemed Plagiarism in a modern Author, and what is to be considered as lawful Prize'). Of course, there may be scholars who have on their shelves the one hundred or so books from which I have anthologized these scraps, or universities that have them in their libraries, and it is increasingly likely that readers will have electronic access to databases which may contain these texts. That being so, what need is there for an anthology? In any case, the anti-anthology lobby would argue that presenting gobbets of books is, *per se*, a bad practice: it saves people the trouble (or delight) of reading the complete texts, it is no substitute for reading the complete texts, it distorts history by validating certain texts, and, ultimately, it reduces the chances of those texts being reprinted.

As an ardent anthologist, of course, I believe the opposite. We live in the real world, where, whether you are reading for a qualification or not, reading time is finite; it would be nice to be able to read a hundred books. If we can't, an anthology provides a rich sampler menu, which is more likely to encourage readers to explore further than if they didn't know the books existed. In any case, well over 50 per cent of the books represented here are not merely out of print, they are available only in specialist libraries. Having an enthusiastic, inquisitive readership might well ease them back into print.

As to the principles of selection, it is a truism that an anthologist cannot get it 'right'; given the hundreds of thousands of items that might have been included, it seems to be inevitable that no two readers will agree on balance and significance. I have, however, adopted four principles (although it has not always been easy to stick to them). The first is that the extracts should give a reasonable representation of what was written for and read widely by English-speaking children in the nineteenth century. The second is that these extracts should be either historically significant, or good examples of their kind. Thus *Through the Looking Glass* and *Just-So Stories* seem to be unique achievements; *Treasure Island* and *Little Women* are masterpieces which sum up a whole genre and point in a new direction. Others are outstanding examples of their type: *Moonfleet* represents, for example, adventure writing; Henty's *Winning His Spurs* stands not only for Henty, but for a whole genre of writing for boys; *Jessica's First Prayer* might have stood aside for a hundred other girls' stories. *The Adventures of Two Dutch Dolls and a 'Golliwogg'* marks the entry of a controversial figure into literature; *Two Little Confederates* and *The Little Colonel* are fascinating political documents, and so on.

However, both these judgements – representation and significance – are infinitely debatable, and the selection I have made has many clear political and sociological implications. The establishment of a canon for children's literature is – probably more so than for any other form of literature – an exceedingly questionable occupation. We live in revisionist times, and I am an ardent revisionist. However, with children's literature it seems to me that we are still starting out on the task of informing readers: children's books are, as I have said, unexplored territory. To give a wide sample of what has most *visibly* been influential should lead not to an atrophy of interest in other books, nor to a further marginalization of texts, but to a stimulation of research. Thus, in the headnotes, I have tried to point out the context of each extract, and how it relates to the various cultural, historical and literary influences swirling around it.

The third principle is that the extract should be readable today. This is a very personal judgement, and I was prepared at the outset to make no apology for excluding texts which may be representative of their period, but which were scarcely approachable now. In practice, however, I found very few writers who fell into that category in the nineteenth century. Thus, however theoretically untenable, my heaviest emphasis is on texts that appeal to a romantic and post-romantic view of childhood; that is, on books that 'entertain' rather than instruct (although it is, I think, obvious that the most uncompromising eighteenth-century moralists entertained their audiences, although perhaps not in a way that is readily recognizable now).

The fourth principle is that the extracts should be comprehensible. The most obvious consequence of that principle was the temptation to include a hundred opening chapters, otherwise what convolutions of explanation would be necessary? Equally, providing a texture of climaxes might well defeat the aim of moving the reader forward. I have therefore taken the general principle of taking coherent episodes; occasionally, as in the case of *Black Beauty* and *The Five Little Peppers and How they Grew*, I have taken chapters from different parts of the book. I have avoided shortening extracts by medial cuts (with the exception of *The Bee Man of Orn*), preferring to lop the beginnings or ends of stories (as in *The Jungle Book* and *Stalky and Co*). Anthologizing is a continuous trade-off between breadth and depth, and I can only apologize to purists (with whom I sympathize) for thus slightly misrepresenting the authors. Occasionally, as in the case of Juliana Ewing's *Mrs Overtheway's Remembrances* (1869), I have had to exclude what some writers see as a key text, simply because my editorial ingenuity could not produce a comprehensible, free-standing extract.

There are some obvious omissions and borderline cases, most of which are discussed in the headnotes. Despite their great importance, Beatrix Potter's books are not here because they are both readily available (in a bewildering number of editions and variants) and because they were designed as complete experiences, of a certain size, shape and texture (like Helen Bannerman's *Little Black Sambo*, also absent). Equally, some of the most influential texts that are also translations – Hans Andersen's *Eventyr* (trans. 1846), *Heidi* (trans. 1884), *Struwwelpeter* (trans. 1948) and *The Swiss Family Robinson* (trans. 1814) – have been arbitrarily excluded on linguistic grounds; similarly, retellings of myth, legend and folklore, such as Nathaniel Hawthorne's *A Wonder Book* (1852), Howard Pyle's *The Merry Adventures of Robin Hood* (1883) and Cornelius Matthews' *The Indian Fairy Book* (1869), have given place to 'original' work. (The exception, discussed in the headnotes, is Joel Chandler Harris's 'Uncle Remus' stories.)

But, most of all, I have tried to confine my selection to books written *for* children, not *to* children, or *about* children or (these being very rare cases) *by* children. The considerable difficulty involved in this (especially towards the end of the century, ironically enough) will be seen in the headnote discussions. The definition of children's literature is an immensely complex and variable one, and generally rests upon authorial intention (however deduced), or the reader 'implied' in the text (however deduced), rather than a factual examination of which books were or are marketed for, adopted by, or imposed upon children. As if that were not tricky enough, as childhood changes, books that were once for adults are read by children and vice versa.

At this point, the role of the anthologist becomes increasingly idiosyncratic and contentious. Blake is not here because in my view Blake wrote *about* childhood (or a version of childhood); Kenneth Grahame's *The Golden Age* and *Dream Days*, Richard Jefferies' *Bevis*, and Rossetti's 'Goblin Market' are not here because they were (or a good case could be made that they were) actually for adults. And there are a few that are here, like *Black Beauty* and *The Adventures of Tom Sawyer*, because they are so overwhelmingly regarded as being children's books.

There could, equally, be a section of material taken specifically from the very rich plantations of children's magazines, but many of the narratives included here (such as *Treasure Island* and *Hans Brinker*) first appeared in magazines, and with space at a premium it seemed better to omit what is at present judged to be more ephemeral matter.

I stress 'at present'. A glance at the bibliography will show how far interest in historical children's literature has tended to shift from the historical and bibliographical to the theoretical and critical. The present anthology, taken in the context of the vast nineteenth-century numbers of children's books and magazines lying unread and unresearched, might well help in changing the emphasis of research in future.

# Maria Edgeworth (1767–1849)

Maria Edgeworth and her father Richard Lovell Edgeworth were 'rational moralists', following the ideas of Rousseau and Locke: children should learn by experience, guided by adults who were in turn guided by reason. They collaborated on *Practical Education* (1798) in which the 'basis of our plan of education' was that 'we should associate pleasure with whatever we wish our pupils should pursue, and pain with whatever we wish they should avoid'.

At first sight, Maria's stories for children, based on these principles, have the same leaden adult-dominated attitudes of the eighteenth-century evangelists. Her most famous story, 'The Purple Jar', in which Rosamond chooses a pretty jar rather than a pair of shoes, only to find that it is a plain jar filled with coloured liquid, ends with her mother and father saying, in effect (and in what might now be regarded as an unfeeling manner), 'we told you so'. However, Rosamond's final comment, 'I am sure – no, not quite sure – but, I hope, I shall be wiser another time', demonstrates Edgeworth's ability to introduce fallible children into the moral framework.

This humanizing of the adult-dominated world of the children's story can be found in many of the contemporary religious tracts, such as those by Mrs Barbauld. Edgeworth's blend of fiction and non-sectarian instruction was particularly influential in the USA, notably on Jacob Abbott's 'Rollo' Books.

Maria was also a not inconsiderable novelist for adults: her *Castle Rackrent* (1801) in particular, has minor-classic status, and she was admired by Scott and Austen.

*Early Lessons* was published in ten parts in 1801, and followed by further stories about its principal characters, Rosamond, Frank, and Harry and Lucy in 1821–5. The booklets were intended to help in reading, and the title (like that of Maria's *The Parent's Assistant*, 1796) clearly implies the adult-centred nature of the text. The preface, however, shows some sensitivity to the needs of the 'real' child: 'The intention of the writers is to prepare the mind for more difficult studies, and the end which they have in view will be completely frustrated if this little book is *crammed* into the minds of children. It is intended to be used in very short portions, and not to be formed into necessary tasks, but to be read when the child's mind has been prepared, by what it has already seen and heard, to wish to hear and see more.' This sensitivity was also extended to the parents: 'This view of what is expected from parents may alarm many, even of those who have much zeal and ability in education', but the Rousseauean attentive parent survived well into the Victorian period, as in Mary Martha Sherwood's *The Fairchild Family*.

Frank has sometimes been dismissed as the most pious and quiescent of Edgeworth's fictional children, but his low-key adventures and the way, in this extract, in which his mother *refrains* from giving him a lesson even when the opportunity presents itself, demonstrate subtly the changes that were beginning to take place in children's literature.

## *Early Lessons* (1801)

### from 'Frank' Part V

Frank was very fond of playing at battledore and shuttlecock; but he could not always play when he liked, nor as long as he liked, because he had no battledore or shuttlecock of his own. He determined to try to make a shuttlecock for himself; but he had no cork for the bottom of it, and he had only five feathers, which had once belonged to an old worn-out shuttlecock, and these were ruffled and bent. His mother was very busy, so that he did not like to interrupt her to ask her for more feathers; and his father was out riding, so that Frank could not ask him for a cork. His brother Edward advised him to put off trying to make his shuttlecock till his mother was not busy, and till his father should return from riding; but Frank was so impatient, that he did not take this prudent advice. He set to work immediately, to make the bottom of his shuttlecock of one end of the handle of his pricker, which he sawed off, because he thought that it resembled the bottom of a shuttlecock in shape more than any other piece of wood which he possessed. When he tried to make holes in it for the feathers he found that the wood was extremely hard; he tried and tried in vain; and, at last, snap went the end of the pricker. It broke in two; and Frank was so sorry, he began to cry; recollecting that his tears would not mend his pricker, he dried his eyes, and resolved to bear the loss of it like a man. He examined the stump of the pricker, which he held in his hand, and he found that there was enough of the steel left to be sharpened again. He began to file it as well as he could; and, after having taken some pains, he sharpened it; but he did not attempt to make any more holes in the hard wood, lest he should break the pricker again. He said to himself, 'Edward gave me good advice, and I will now take it; I will wait till my father comes home, and till my mother is not busy, and then I will ask them for what I want.'

The next day his father gave him a cork, and his mother gave him some feathers; and, after several trials, he at last made a shuttlecock, which flew tolerably well. He was eager to try it, and he ran to his brother Edward, and showed it to him; and Edward liked the shuttlecock, but could not then play, because he was learning his Latin lesson.

'Well! I will have patience till to-morrow, if I can,' said Frank.

It happened, during the same evening, that Frank was present when his brother Edward and three of his cousins were dressing to act a pantomime. They were in a great hurry. They had lost the burnt cork with which they were to blacken their eyebrows. They looked everywhere that they could think of for it, but all in vain; and a messenger came to tell them that everybody was seated, and that they must begin to act the pantomime directly. They looked with still more eagerness for this cork, but it could not be found, and they did not know where to get another.

'I have one! I have one! I have a cork! You shall have it in a minute!' cried the good-natured little Frank. He ran up-stairs directly, pulled all the feathers out of his dear shuttlecock, burnt the end of the cork in the candle, and gave it to his friends. They did not know, at this moment, that it was the cork of Frank's shuttlecock; but when they afterwards found out that this was the case, they were very much obliged to him; and when his father heard this instance of his good nature, he was much pleased. He set Frank upon the table before him, after dinner, when all his friends were present, and said to him:

'My dear little son, I am glad to find that you are of such a generous disposition. Believe me, such a disposition is of more value than all the battledores and shuttlecocks in the world. You are welcome to as many corks and feathers as you please. You who are so willing to help your friends in their amusements, shall find that we are all ready and eager to assist you in yours.'

Close to the garden which Frank's mother had given to him, there was a hut, in which garden tools and watering-pots were once kept; but it had been found to be too small for this purpose, and a larger one had been built in another part of the kitchen garden. Nothing was now kept in that which was near Frank's garden but some old flower-pots and pans. Frank used to like to go into this hut, to play with the flower-pots. They were piled up higher than his head; and one day, when he was pulling out from the undermost part of the pile a large pan, the whole pile of flower pots shook from bottom to top, and one of the upper-most flower-pots fell down. If Frank had not run out of the way in an instant it would have fallen upon his head. As soon as he had recovered a little from his fright he saw that the flower-pot had been broken by the fall, and he took up the broken pieces, and went into the house to his mother, to tell her what had happened. He found his father and mother sitting at the table, writing letters: they both looked up when he came in, and said:

'What is the matter, Frank? You look very pale.'

'Because, mamma, I have broken this flower-pot.'

'Well, my dear, you do rightly to come and tell me that you broke it. It is an accident. There is no occasion to be frightened about it.'

'No, mamma; it was not that which frightened me so much. But it is well that I did not break my own head, and all the flower-pots in the garden house.'

Then he told his mother how he had attempted to pull out the undermost pan, and how 'the great pile shook from top to bottom.'

'It is well you did not hurt yourself, indeed, Frank,' said his mother.

His father asked if there was a key to the door of the hut.

'Papa, there is an old rusty lock, but no key.'

'The gardener has the key; I will go for it directly,' said his father, rising from his seat; 'and I will lock that door, lest the boy should do the same thing again.'

'No, papa,' said Frank; 'I am not so silly as to do again what might hurt me.'

'But, my dear, without doing it on purpose, you might by accident, when you are playing in that house, shake those pots and pull them down upon yourself. Whenever there is any real danger, you know, I always tell you of it. And it is much better to prevent any evil than to be sorry for it afterwards. I will go this minute and look for the key, and lock the door,' continued his father.

'Papa,' said Frank, stopping him, 'you need not go for the key, nor lock the door, for if you desire me not to play in the old garden-house, I will not play there; I will not go in, I promise you; I will never even open the door.'

'Very well, Frank; I can trust to your promise. Therefore, I want no lock and key – your word is enough.'

'But only take care you do not forget, and run in by accident, Frank,' said his mother. 'As you have such a habit of going in there, you might forget.'

'Mamma, I will not forget my promise,' said Frank.

A few days after this time Frank's father and mother were walking in the garden, and they came to the old garden-house, and they stopped and looked at the door, which was a little open. This door could not be blown open by the wind, because it stuck against the ground at one corner, and could not be easily moved.

'I assure you, mamma, I did not forget – I did not open it – I did not go in, indeed, papa,' said Frank.

His father answered, 'We did not suspect you of having opened the door, Frank.'

And his father and mother looked at one another and smiled.

His father called the gardener, and desired that he would not open the door of the old garden-house, and he ordered that none of the servants should go in there.

A week passed, and another week passed, and a third week passed, and again Frank's father and mother were walking in the garden; and his mother said,

'Let us go and look at the old garden-house.'

His father and mother went together, and Frank ran after them, rejoicing that he had kept his promise. He had never gone into that house, though he had often been tempted to do so, because he had left a little boat there of which he was very fond. When his father and mother had looked at the door of the garden-house, they again looked at each other and smiled, and said,

'We are glad to see, Frank, that you have kept your word, and that you have not opened this door.'

'I have not opened the door, papa,' answered Frank; 'but how do you know that by only looking at it?'

'You may find out how we know it, and we had rather that you should find it out than that we should tell you,' said his father.

Frank guessed, first, that they recollected exactly how far open the door had been left, and that they saw it was now open exactly at the same place. But his father answered that this was not the way, for that they could not be certain by this means that the door had not been opened wider, and then shut again to the same place.

'Papa, you might have seen the mark in the dust which the door would have made in opening. Was that the way, papa?'

'No; that is a tolerably good way, but the trace of the opening of the door might have been *effaced* – that is, rubbed out, and the ground might have been smoothed again. There is another circumstance, Frank, which, if you observe carefully, you may discover.'

Frank took hold of the door, and was going to move it; but his father stopped his hand.

'You must not move the door. Look at it without stirring it.'

Frank looked carefully, and then exclaimed, –

'I've found it out, papa! I've found it out! I see a spider's web, with all its fine thin rings and spokes, like a wheel, just at the top of the door, and it stretches from the top of the door to this post, against which the door shuts. Now, if the door had been shut, or opened wider, this spider's web would have been crushed or broken; the door could not have been shut or opened without breaking it. May I try, papa?'

'Yes, my dear.'

He tried to open the door, and the spider's web broke; and that part of it which had been fastened to the door fell down, and hung against the post.

'You have found it out now, Frank, you see,' said his father.

His mother was going to ask him if he knew how a spider makes his web, but she stopped, and did not then ask him this question, because she saw that he was thinking of his little boat.

'Yes, my dear Frank; you may go into the house now,' said his mother, 'and take your little boat.' Frank ran in, and seizing it, hugged it in his arms.

'My dear little boat, how glad I am to have you again!' he cried; 'I wish I might go to the river-side this evening and swim it; there is a fine wind, and it would sail fast.'

Frank was never allowed to go to the river-side to swim this boat, without his father or mother, or eldest brother, could go with him.

'Mamma, will you?' said he; 'can you be so good as to go with me this evening to the river-side, that I may sail my boat?'

His mother told him that she had intended to walk another way, but that she would willingly do what he asked her, as he had done what she desired. His father said the same, and they went to the river-side. His father walked on the banks, looking till he saw a place where he thought it would be safe for Frank to launch his boat. He found a place where the river ran in between two narrow banks of land; such a place, Frank's father told him, in large rivers, is called a *creek*.

The water in this creek was very shallow – so shallow, that you could see the sand and many coloured pebbles at the bottom; yet it was deep enough for Frank's little boat to float upon it. Frank put his boat into the water; he launched it, and set the sail to the wind; that is, turned it so that the wind blew against it, and drove the boat on.

It sailed swiftly over the smooth water, and Frank was happy looking at it and directing it in various ways, by setting or turning the sail in different directions, and then watching which way it would go.

'Mamma,' said he, after his mother had remained a good while, 'you are very good-natured to stay with me so long; but I am afraid you will not have time to come again to-morrow; and, if you cannot, I shall not have the pleasure of swimming my boat. Papa, the water is so very shallow here, and all the way along this creek, that if I was to fall in I could not drown myself; and the banks are so close that I could walk to them, and get on dry land, directly. I wish, papa, you would let me come here whenever I please, without anybody with me; then I should not be obliged to wait till mamma had time, or till my brother Edward had done his lesson; then I could swim my boat so happily, papa, whenever I pleased.'

'But how can I be sure that you will never go to any other part of the river, Frank?'

'You know, papa, I did not open the door, or go into that garden-house, after you had desired me not to do so, and after I had promised that I would not. If I promise that I will not go to any other part of the river, you know you can believe me.'

'Very true, Frank; and therefore I grant your request. I can trust to your doing what I desire you to do; and I can rely upon your promise. You may come here whenever you please; and sail your boat in this creek, from the stump of this willow tree, as far in this way toward the land as you please.'

Frank clapped his hands joyfully, and cried, 'Thank you papa! thank you! Mamma, do you hear that? Papa has given me leave to come to this place, whenever I please to swim my boat; for he trusts to my promise, mamma.'

'Yet, that is a just reward for you, Frank,' said his mother. 'The being believed another time, and the being more and more trusted, is the just reward for having done as you said that you would do, and for having kept your promise.'

'Oh! thank you, mamma; thank you, papa, for trusting to my promise!' said Frank.

'You need not thank me, my dear, for believing you,' said his father; 'for I cannot help believing you, because you speak the truth. Being believed is not only the reward but the necessary consequence, of speaking truth.'

# Ann Taylor (1782–1866), Jane Taylor (1783–1824) and Adelaide O'Keeffe (?1776–1855)

Probably the most imitated poets for children of the century, Ann and Jane Taylor set the tone for children's poetry until Stevenson's *A Child's Garden of Verses*, and were only challenged in popularity (and then only briefly) by Roscoe's *The Butterfly's Ball* and Lear's *A Book of Nonsense*. The blend of small domestic incidents, often in a rural setting, with more than a nod towards a moral consequence marked the beginning of the 'awful warning' school of verse. As a contemporary reviewer in the *Imperial Review* wrote of *Original Poems*: 'The poetry is very superior to what is usually found in books of this kind, and the moral tendency of the whole is excellent.'

Their many imitators, such as Elizabeth Taylor (*The Daisy*, 1807) and Charles and Mary Lamb (*Poetry for Children*, 1809) tended to draw on the puritanism of the eighteenth century, and children being burned to death as a punishment for disobedience became a commonplace. As the century progressed, so the ludicrous possibilities of the form came to be seen: Heinrich Hoffmann's immensely popular *Struwwelpeter* (1845, English translation 1848) was a reaction against it. A hundred years after the Taylors began it, the form was still pervasive enough to warrant the parodies in Harry Graham's *Ruthless Rhymes*

*for Heartless Homes* (1899) and Hilaire Belloc's *Cautionary Tales* (1907).

Of the small selection reprinted here, 'Morning' uses the emblematic technique popularized by John Bunyan in *A Book for Boys and Girls* (1686); 'Never Play with Fire' is obliquely cautionary, and 'The Pin' explicitly so; 'Poor Children' is the forerunner of thousands of philanthropic novels, and 'The Little Husbandman' a romantic rural view (which, incidentally, espouses the *status quo*).

Two poems stand out from the collection: 'The Star' has become absorbed into the culture as a nursery rhyme, while 'My Mother' was probably the most famous poem of the nineteenth century. The first was parodied by Lewis Carroll ('Twinkle, twinkle little bat') probably on the grounds of preciousness; the second, which appealed deeply to the Victorian streak of sentimentality, and which was widely imitated, was unmercifully parodied by Thomas Hood.

Ann and Jane came from a literary family (later known as 'The Taylors of Ongar') and theirs was by far the most influential work in the books. Adelaide O'Keeffe was probably teamed with them by the publishers, Darton and Harvey.

## from *Original Poems for Infant Minds* (two volumes: 1804, 1805)

### MORNING

Awake, little girl, it is time to arise,
  Come shake drowsy sleep from your eye;
The lark is now warbling his notes to the skies,
  And the sun is far mounted on high.

O come, for the fields with gay flowers abound,
  The dewdrop is quivering still,
The lowing herds graze in the pastures around,
  And the sheep-bell is heard from the hill.

O come, for the bee has flown out of his bed,
  Impatient his work to renew;
The spider is weaving her delicate thread,
  Which brilliantly glitters with dew.

O come, for the ant has crept out of her cell,
  And forth to her labour she goes;

She knows the true value of moments too well,
    To waste them in idle repose.

Awake, little sleeper, and do not despise
    Of insects instruction to ask;
From your pillow with good resolutions arise,
    And cheerfully go to your task

                    JANE.

## NEVER PLAY WITH FIRE

My prayers I said, I went to bed,
    And quickly fell asleep;
But soon I woke, my sleep was broke –
    I through my curtains peep.

I heard a noise of men and boys,
    The watchman's rattle too;
And 'Fire!' they cry, and then cried I
    'Alas! what shall I do?'

A shout so loud, came from the crowd,
    Around, above, below,
And in the street the neighbours meet,
    Who would the matter know.

Now down the stairs run threes and pairs,
    Enough their bones to break;
The firemen shout, the engines spout
    Their streams, the fire to slake.

The roof and wall, the stairs and all,
    And rafters tumble in:
Red flames and blaze, now all amaze,
    And make a dreadful din!

And each one screams, when bricks and beams
    Come tumbling on their heads;
And some are smashed, and some are dashed;
    Some leap on feather-beds.

Some burn, some choke with fire and smoke;
    But ah! what was the cause?
My heart's dismayed – last night I played
    With Thomas, lighting straws!

                    ADELAIDE.

## MY MOTHER

Who fed me from her gentle breast,
    And hushed me in her arms to rest,
And on my cheek sweet kisses prest?

                  My Mother.

When sleep forsook my open eye,
Who was it sung sweet hushaby,
And rocked me that I should not cry?
                    My Mother.

Who sat and watched my infant head,
When sleeping on my cradle bed?
And tears of sweet affection shed?
                    My Mother.

When pain and sickness made me cry,
Who gazed upon my heavy eye,
And wept for fear that I should die?
                    My Mother.

Who dressed my doll in clothes so gay,
And taught me pretty how to play,
And minded all I had to say?
                    My Mother.

Who ran to help me when I fell,
And would some pretty story tell,
Or kiss the place to make it well?
                    My Mother.

Who taught my infant lips to pray,
And love GOD's holy book and day,
And walk in wisdom's pleasant way?
                    My Mother.

And can I ever cease to be
Affectionate and kind to thee,
Who was so very kind to me,
                    My Mother?

Ah! no, the thought I cannot bear,
And if GOD please my life to spare,
I hope I shall reward thy care,
                    My Mother.

When thou art feeble, old, and grey,
My healthy arm shall be thy stay,
And I will soothe thy pains away,
                    My Mother.

And when I see thee hang thy head,
'Twill be my turn to watch thy bed,
And tears of sweet affection shed,
                    My Mother.

For GOD, who lives about the skies,
Would look with vengeance in his eyes,
If I should ever dare despise
                    My Mother.[*]

***

[*]  The final verse was emended by Jane, in her old age: For could our father in the skies / Look down with pleased or loving eyes, / If ever I could dare despise / My Mother.

## THE PIN

'Dear me! what signifies a pin!
    I'll leave it on the floor;
My pincushion has others in,
    Mamma has plenty more:
A miser will I never be,'
Said little heedless Emily.

So tripping on to giddy play,
    She left the pin behind,
For Betty's broom to whisk away,
    Or some one else to find;
She never gave a thought, indeed,
To what she might to-morrow need.

Next day a party was to ride,
    To see an air-balloon!
And all the company beside
    Were dressed and ready soon:
But she, poor girl, she could not stir,
For just a pin to finish her.

'Twas vainly now, with eye and hand,
    She did to search begin;
There was not one – not one, the band
    Of her pelisse to pin!
She cut her pincushion in two,
But not a pin had slidden through!

At last, as hunting on the floor,
    Over a crack she lay,
The carriage rattled to the door,
    Then rattled fast away.
Poor Emily! she was not in,
For want of just – a single pin!

from *Rhymes from the Nursery* (1806)

## THE STAR

Twinkle, twinkle, little star,
How I wonder what you are!
Up above the world so high,
Like a diamond in the sky.

When the blazing sun is gone,
When he nothing shines upon,
Then you show your little light,
Twinkle, twinkle, all the night.

Then the traveller in the dark,
Thanks you for your tiny spark!

He could not see which way to go,
If you did not twinkle so.

In the dark blue sky you keep,
And often through my curtains peep,
For you never shut your eye
Till the sun is in the sky.

As your bright and tiny spark
Lights the traveller in the dark,
Though I know not what you are,
Twinkle, twinkle, little star.


## POOR CHILDREN

When I go in the meadows, or walk in the street,
How many poor children I frequently meet,
Without shoes or stockings to cover their feet.

Their clothes are all ragged and let in the cold;
And they have so little to eat I am told,
That indeed 'tis a pitiful sight to behold!

And then I have seen, very often, that they
Are cross and unkind to each other at play;
But they've not been taught better, I've heard mamma say.

But I have kind parents to watch over me,
To teach me how gentle and good I should be,
And to mourn for the poor little children I see.


## THE LITTLE HUSBANDMAN

I'm a little husbandman,
Work and labour hard I can:
I am as happy all the day
At my work as if 'twere play:
Though I've nothing fine to wear,
Yet for that I do not care.

When to work I go along,
Singing loud my morning song,
With my wallet at my back,
Or my waggon-whip to smack;
Oh! I am as happy then
As any idle gentlemen.

I've a hearty appetite,
And I soundly sleep at night,
Down I lie content, and say,
'I've been useful all the day:
I'd rather be a plough-boy than
A useless little gentleman.'

# William Roscoe (1753–1831)

*The Butterfly's Ball* first appeared in *The Gentleman's Magazine* in November 1806, and was issued in book form on 1 January 1807 by the publisher John Harris, who had taken over the Newbery publishing business in 1801, and had begun to produce more light-hearted work. It was immensely popular, becoming the first in a series, *Harris's Cabinet*. With its successor, *The Peacock at Home* by 'A Lady' (Catherine Anne Dorset), *The Butterfly's Ball* is reputed to have sold 40,000 copies in its first year, and was frequently reprinted throughout the century.

William Roscoe was a self-made man, who became a prosperous lawyer and banker, and Member of Parliament for Liverpool. *The Butterfly's Ball*, reputedly written for his son, got off to a very propitious start, being set to music at the request of King George III and Queen Charlotte for the Princesses Elizabeth, Augusta and Mary. It is in some ways a respectable version of the cheerfully unmoralistic chapbook verses, and although it did not displace more purposeful texts, it is generally seen as a landmark in the shift towards entertainment as opposed to didacticism.

This text is from the second, revised edition of 1808.

## The Butterfly's Ball and the Grasshopper's Feast (1807)

Come take up your Hats, and away let us haste
To the *Butterfly's* Ball, and the *Grasshopper's* Feast.
The Trumpeter, *Gad-fly*, has summon'd the Crew,
And the Revels are now only waiting for you.
So said little Robert, and pacing along,
His merry Companions came forth in a Throng.
And on the smooth Grass, by the side of a Wood,
Beneath a broad Oak that for Ages had stood,
Saw the Children of Earth, and the Tenants of Air,
For an Evening's Amusement together repair.
And there came the *Beetle*, so blind and so black,
Who carried the *Emmet*, his Friend, on his Back.
And there was the *Gnat* and the *Dragon-fly* too,
With all their Relations, Green, Orange, and Blue.
And there came the *Moth*, with his Plumage of Down,
And the *Hornet* in Jacket of Yellow and Brown;
Who with him the *Wasp*, his Companion, did bring,
But they promis'd, that Evening, to lay by their Sting.
And the sly little *Dormouse* crept out of his Hole,
And brought to the Feast his blind Brother, the *Mole*.
And the *Snail*, with his Horns peeping out of his Shell,
Came from a great Distance, the Length of an Ell.
A Mushroom their Table, and on it was laid
A Water-dock Leaf, which a Table-cloth made.
The Viands were various, to each of their Taste,
And the *Bee* brought her Honey to crown the Repast.
Then close on his Haunches, so solemn and wise,
The *Frog* from a Corner, look'd up to the Skies.

FRONTISPIECE.

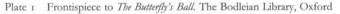

"Come take up your hats & away let us haste."   p.2

Pub.Jan.ᵉ 1808. by J.Harris. 4ᵗᵉ near St. Pauls Church Yd.

Plate 1   Frontispiece to *The Butterfly's Ball*. The Bodleian Library, Oxford

And the *Squirrel* well pleas'd such Diversions to see,
Mounted high over Head, and look'd down from a Tree.
Then out came the *Spider*, with Finger so fine,
To shew his Dexterity on the tight Line.
From one Branch to another, his Cobwebs he slung,
Then quick as an Arrow he darted along,
But just in the Middle, – Oh! shocking to tell,
From his Rope, in an Instant, poor Harlequin fell.
Yet he touch'd not the Ground, but with Talons outspread,
Hung suspended in Air, at the End of a Thread.
Then the *Grasshopper* came with a Jerk and a Spring,
Very long was his Leg, though but short was his Wing;
He took but three Leaps, and was soon out of Sight,
Then chirp'd his own Praises the rest of the Night.
With Step so majestic the *Snail* did advance,
And promis'd the Gazers a Minuet to dance.
But they all laugh'd so loud that he pull'd in his Head,
And went in his own little Chamber to Bed.
Then, as Evening gave Way to the Shadows of Night,
Their Watchman, the *Glow-worm*, came out with a Light.
Then Home let us hasten, while yet we can see,
For no Watchman is waiting for you and for me.
So said little Robert, and pacing along,
His merry Companions returned in a Throng.

# Elizabeth Turner (1775?–1846)

Elizabeth Turner's work is an excellent measure of the difference in general attitudes over two centuries. The first major historian of children's literature, Harvey Darton, could not make up his mind about it: 'Can it be serious?' he mused. Certainly it was parodied; now, perhaps, it scarcely seems to require parody. As Darton (1982) said, her work is so 'defiantly rhythmical' that 'the most sympathetic person today may feel uncertain about it…the sternest moralists of her tribe never leapt so swiftly and surely as she from crime to doom.' But if we compare her work with that of Mary Martha Sherwood, for example, can we be sure that she was anything other than a particularly direct and plain-minded person? It should also be borne in mind that such literalness remains very common today, especially in the work of evangelical censors.

Turner also wrote several other very popular collections, including *The Cowslip* (1811) and *The Crocus* (1844).

## from *The Daisy; or, Cautionary Stories in Verse Adapted to the Ideas of Children from Four to Eight years old* (1807)

### THE CANARY

Mary had a little bird,
  With feathers bright and yellow
Slender legs – upon my word,
  He was a pretty fellow!

Sweetest notes he always sung,
  Which much delighted Mary;
Often where his cage was hung,
  She sat to hear Canary.

Crumbs of bread and dainty seeds
  She carried to him daily,
Seeking for the early weeds,
  She decked his palace gaily.

This, my little readers, learn,
  And ever practice duly;
Songs and smiles of love return
  To friends who love you truly.

### DANGEROUS SPORT

Poor Peter was burnt by the poker one day,
  When he made it look pretty and red;
For the beautiful sparks made him think it fine play,
  To lift it as high as his head.

But somehow it happen'd, his finger and thumb
  Were terribly scorch'd by the heat:

And he scream'd out aloud for his Mother to come,
   And stamp'd on the floor with his feet.

Now if Peter had minded his Mother's command,
   His fingers would not have been sore;
And he promised again, as she bound up his hand,
   To play with hot pokers no more.

# Barbara [Wreaks] Hofland (1770–1844)

Another book from the publisher John Harris, *The History of an Officer's Widow* is essentially a moral tale, but the emphasis has now changed from the often harsh didacticism of the eighteenth century. Barbara Hofland wrote of the puritan work ethic rather than of sectarian religious morality, and her characters obtain prosperity, rather than redemption, through their own efforts (albeit with a little authorial help).

*The History of an Officer's Widow* (she also wrote novels about *A Clergyman's Widow*, 1812 and *The Merchant's Widow* 1814) was the first of her children's books, written shortly after she had been widowed. It was produced for what would now be called the 'teenage' market, and looks forward to two hundred years of children's books in a remarkable number of ways. One of her major themes is the importance of family life, often (as here) in the face of the death or absence of a parent. Although the viewpoint is still essentially an adult one, books like this look forward to more famous examples such as *Little Women* (1868) and *The Railway Children* (1906). Equally, the subtext of the strength and survival of the independent woman (author) is a constantly reiterated theme in nineteenth-century children's books, notably in writers like Alcott, Burnett and Nesbit.

This extract, beginning after the death of Lieutenant Belfield, features another standard feature of the family story, which has survived through Nesbit, to Ransome and beyond: the group of children of contrasting characters. Needless to say, the efforts of the characters (both through hard work and fortuitous rescues) are rewarded by prosperity (partly in the form of a legacy). Commercial, as well as moral virtue, is rewarded.

## from *The History of an Officer's Widow, and Her Young Family* (1809)

### CHAPTER IV

As soon as poor Mrs. Belfield became capable of attending to the advice of her father, she began to consult with him on the means of providing for her family; she was sensible that she ought not to stay any longer with so large a family at the parsonage, which was a very small house, and where so many little children must be very troublesome to her good parents, who were now at a time of life when stillness was absolutely necessary to comfort. Charles, her eldest, had always resided with them, and it was her intention to leave him, as he was very like his dear father, and seemed to be the greatest comfort the old people had now left in the world, except herself. This part of the country was by no means so cheap to live in as some others, and this was a consideration it was indeed very necessary to attend to, as they were now reduced almost to beggary. As soon as Mr. Atkinson saw his dear daughter using every means which a wise and good woman could suggest, for calming her own mind, and fulfilling the awful duties of her widowed situation, he addressed her in the following manner:

'My dear Maria, you are sensible that I have but one wish on this side the grave, that of making up to you, as far as is in my power, the invaluable friend you have lost. I have considered, in every possible way, what will be the best for you to do; and I think, if you were to take a cottage in Lincolnshire, where you can live a great deal cheaper than with us, and which will be within an easy journey of us, it will be the best thing you can do. I have, without saying any thing to you, my love, secured to you the pension allowed by Government; I have likewise, my dear, given you every shilling I have in the world: it is vested in your name in the funds; but I must request, daughter, that you will solemnly promise me not to spend the principal, even if it should be wanting for your boy, on the most promising prospect. Remember, that if I am taken first, your mother has no other fund to look to, and that though you might be willing to give up your own claims, you have no right to subject your aged mother to want the support she so highly merits. Alas! all I have to give you is so little, that even with your pension, it will produce less than sixty pounds a year. But I will charge myself with the education of Charles; I mean to bring him up to the church; I hope to be able to send him to the university, and doubt not but he will do exceedingly well.'

Mrs. Belfield could make no reply but with tears of affectionate gratitude. The scheme of the good old man was soon put in practice; a neat cottage, between Barton and Winteringham, in Lincolnshire, was found suited to her circumstances, and thither the still young and beautiful Maria retired, with her four younger children, whose talents, pursuits, and history, form the principal subject of this little volume.

Charles, the eldest, was now eleven years old; he was in his person remarkably elegant, and of a disposition and manners so mild and conciliating, that he appeared by nature calculated for the pious employment for which his good grandfather had always designed him. Henry, the next boy, was of a very different description; generous, open, and courageous, but violent, impetuous, and headstrong, he was seldom in a medium; always very good, or very naughty: he was praised and scolded ten times a day; but his high spirits were so bounded by the tenderness he felt towards his mother, and the precepts of obedience with which his good father had wisely imbued his infant mind, that a grave look from her would at any time correct his exuberant mirth, or calm his rising passions.

Anna and Maria were two sweet little girls, one seven, the other five years old; the youngest was a boy called Edward, who was just beginning to prattle, and was the darling of them all; when Charles parted with *him* he seemed to suffer more than in leaving all the rest: his mother expressed some surprise at this, saying, 'My dear Charles, why are you so grieved at parting with such a very little boy? you know he is no company for you.' – 'Ah, mother,' replied the sensible child, 'I cry because he is such a very little boy, for I feel somehow as if I ought to be his father.' – It is unnecessary to say what Mrs. Belfield felt at parting with such a child as this, and such parents as she left behind; happily for her she had a great many lesser things, which necessarily occupied her mind. Henry too was all life and spirits; with him the tear was indeed 'forgot as soon as shed,' and in spite of all her sorrows, the prattling rogue drew his mother now and then into a little chat, that beguiled the tedious way.

After they became tolerably settled in their new habitation, Mrs. Belfield applied herself to teaching her little girls to read and to sew; Henry went to a free grammar-school, about two miles off, where he soon became the delight or the terror of the school-boys: who ever was aggrieved Henry undertook their cause, and so completely was he considered the champion of the oppressed, that all the little ones looked up to him as their regular protector, and would say to any one of the great ones who insulted them, 'If you do so and so, Henry Belfield shall knock you down.' In consequence of this pre-eminence, it was but too common to see poor Henry with a black eye or a bloody nose, though it was allowed on all hands that a better-tempered boy never existed; his mother, on these occasions, would often point out to him, in the strongest terms, the impropriety of his conduct; and Henry always listened to her suggestions with the profoundest attention, generally kissed her with tears in his eyes, and promised that he would quarrel with no boys if they did not use some of his friends ill, but that was a thing he could never get over; and as, in every community, there are some spirits which nothing less than the arm of justice can teach obedience, Henry, in spite of his mother's lectures, and his own resolutions, was still subject to the same honours of war, till his prowess became acknowledged, and no one was hardy enough to dispute his right of arbitration.

During the first winter of their abode in this neighbourhood, as Henry was trudging to school one morning, after a night of violent rain, by which the stream he was crossing was prodigiously swelled, he looked over the bridge, and saw a little ragged girl endeavouring to fill her kit* with water; the wind was high, and the child held the vessel in such a manner, that it filled with the wind, and being too strong for her, as she durst not let go, not being aware of her own danger, it took her from her feet, and she was carried away by the current. Henry instantly ran to her assistance, and succeeded in seizing her petticoats, and enabling her to gain the shore; but when the child, still fearful of her treasure, cried out, 'Oh, the kit, the kit, my mammy must have her kit!' Henry laid hold of the ill-fated kit, and was borne away, as the owner had been before, by the rapid current. The grateful girl then besought him to let it go, which he did, but was too much

---

.*    A kit is a pail with a handle on one side. (Author's note)

exhausted to recover the shore: the girl, who screamed and ran on every side, almost distracted, luckily attracted two gentlemen who were riding over the bridge; one of them instantly galloped towards the place, and, directed by the little girl, threw the lash of his whip directly to Henry, who was just able to avail himself of such welcome assistance: the other gentleman arriving at the same moment, they succeeded in extricating him from his perilous situation, and began to inquire how he got into it; a question eagerly answered by the little girl, who told her tale of thankful gratitude in terms of unbounded applause. When Henry was able to speak, he too was eloquent in thanks for his rescue: the gentleman who arrived first, said he was heartily glad he had come in time to save such a noble lad. 'But, (said the other) how happened you to jump into the stream to save this girl and her kit? could you not see your danger? did you know any thing of this girl?'

'Was she not my fellow-creature? was she not a Christian child?' said Henry, looking with surprise and indignation at his interrogator. The first gentleman gave him an approving smile, and said, 'Where shall I take you to, my dear? you shall mount my horse, and I will lead you home.'

'Not for the world, Sir,' said Henry, shaking himself, 'I would not have my mamma see me for the world! she would think of nothing but drowning all night; I know an old woman who will let me lie down in her bed, and dry all my clothes for me, and then poor mamma will know nothing of the matter.'

'Then take this half-crown, and buy yourself some gingerbread with it: you are certainly the most extraordinary boy I ever met with.'

'Half-a-crown!' exclaimed Henry, eyeing the money with transport; 'Oh, sir, I am so much obliged! Here, my girl! here! take this to your mammy to buy a new kit. Yes, Sir,' said he, turning again to the gentleman; 'you are very good; I am sure I shall never forget you, the longest day I have to live. And I would,' said he hesitating, 'I *would* ask you to go to our house, for mamma to thank you, but I am so very, very much afraid of making her unhappy.'

'My charming little fellow, you need say no more,' said the gentleman; 'go and get your clothes off; some time or other I will see you again. Your mother is the richest woman in all England.'

Henry thought the gentleman very much mistaken, but he only thanked him once more, and trudged off to Sally Simpson's, an old woman, who, like the little school-boys, considered herself under great obligations to Henry, for keeping unlucky lads from her little orchard, and likewise for rescuing her fine old cock from destruction about a week before: she instantly set about stripping poor Henry, and gave him a little hot milk to keep him warm, and by her care he sustained no other injury than a slight cold, while his mother happily remained a stranger to the whole transaction.

# Mary Martha [Butt] Sherwood (1775–1851)

In Mary Martha Sherwood we encounter a fiercely dedicated, almost eighteenth-century voice, advocating evangelical values of faith and obedience. *The History of the Fairchild Family* was a great and surprisingly lasting success, with a second part published in 1842 and a third in 1847. It is structured episodically, each section comprising a moral tale, meditations on a biblical text, a prayer and a hymn. The stories have, notoriously, a hard and sometimes brutal edge (and some were moderated in late-Victorian editions) and the book ends with 'A Happy Death' – a feature derived from the puritan writers of a century before, and which remained a standard feature of this kind of work for many more years.

Mrs Sherwood stands firmly in the tradition of Mrs Barbauld and Mrs Trimmer (author of *Fabulous Histories*, 1786), and Mr Fairchild treats his children with stern religious firmness. In one example, 'Story on the Absence of God', the young Henry Fairchild refuses to learn his Latin: he is duly whipped, fed only bread and water, and isolated from the family, having been told (famously) by his father: 'I stand in the place of God to you, whilst you are a child; and as long as I do not ask you to do any thing wrong, you must obey me'. Elsewhere, the children are made to contemplate the rotten remains of a criminal on the gibbet.

Thus described, the book does not seem likely to make inviting reading for the secular twenty-first century reader, but it is one of the surprises of this collection. *The History of the Fairchild Family* is lively and readable, with a great deal of energy, conviction, and narrative skill. Further, as M. Nancy Cutt has pointed out, the children are not neglected – they have the kind of attention from their parents that Edgeworth found it necessary to apologize for. The parents are, in their way, loving, they always explain the reasons for their actions, and at the end of the stories the children are generally comforted and secure.

'Story on Ambition, or the Wish to be Great', reprinted here, is not a sensational text, but concentrates on a child-level situation, rather than one controlled by adults, and, perhaps curiously, contains many of the elements of later family stories in which the morality is assumed or implied. The naughty Miss Augusta receives her due punishment in a later story, 'Fatal Effects of Disobedience to Parents', in which she is burned to death playing with candles (compare the episode in *Holiday House*, p. 49). However, 'The worst part of the whole business' was that 'she had not one moment for . . . repentance; and it is well known that Lady Noble never taught her any thing concerning God and her Redeemer and . . . she was taught to mock at religion and pious people.'

Mrs Sherwood wrote more than 400 books; some, like *The History of Little Henry and his Bearer* (1814), were bestsellers, and her influence was incalculable. Through to the end of the century the genre of domestic fiction still bears traces of her attitudes, although rarely expressed with such power as here.

---

from *The History of the Fairchild Family or, the Child's Manual: being a Collection of Stories Calculated to Shew the Importance and Effects of a Religious Education* (1818)

## STORY ON AMBITION, OR THE WISH TO BE GREAT

Twice every year Sir Charles and Lady Noble used to invite Mr. and Mrs. Fairchild and their children to spend a day with them at their house. Mr. and Mrs. Fairchild did not much like to go, because Sir Charles and his Lady were very proud, and their children were not brought up in the fear of God; yet, as the visit happened only twice in a year, Mr. Fairchild thought it better to go than to have a quarrel with his neighbour. Mrs. Fairchild always had two plain muslin frocks, with white petticoats and mittens, and neat black shoes, for Lucy and Emily to wear when they went to see Lady Noble. As Mr. Fairchild's house was as much as two miles' distance from Sir Charles Noble's, Sir Charles always used to send his carriage for them, and to bring them back again at night.

One morning, just at breakfast-time, Mr. Fairchild came into the parlour, saying to Mrs. Fairchild, 'Here, my dear, is a note from Sir Charles Noble, inviting us to dinner to-morrow, and the children.'

'Well, my dear,' said Mrs. Fairchild, 'as Sir Charles Noble has been so kind as to ask us, we must not offend him by refusing to go.'

The next morning Mr. Fairchild desired his wife and children to be ready at twelve o'clock, which was the time fixed for the coach to be at Mr. Fairchild's door. Accordingly, soon after eleven Mrs. Fairchild dressed Lucy and Emily, and made them sit quietly down on two little stools, till the carriage came. As Lucy and Emily sat in the corner of the room, Lucy looked at Emily, and said, 'Sister, how pretty you look!' 'And how neat you look, Lucy!' said Emily: 'these frocks are very pretty, and make us look very well.'

'My dear little girls,' said Mrs. Fairchild, who overheard what they said to each other, 'do not be conceited because you have got your best frocks on. You now think well of yourselves, because you fancy you are well dressed: by and bye, when you get to Lady Noble's, you will find Miss Augusta much finer dressed than yourselves; then you will be out of humour with yourselves for as little reason as you now are pleased. Do you remember the verses I made you learn, Lucy, concerning one who cometh into the assembly of the Christians in fine clothes?'

*Lucy.* 'Mamma, I remember; they are these: "My brethren, have not the faith of our Lord Jesus Christ, the Lord of glory, with respect of persons; for if there come into your assembly a man with a gold ring, in goodly apparel; and there come in also a poor man, in vile raiment; and ye have respect to him that weareth the gay clothing, and say unto him, Sit thou here, in a good place; and say to the poor, Stand thou there, or sit here under my footstool; are ye not then partial in yourselves, and are become judges of evil thoughts?" ' (James ii. 1–4.)

By the time Lucy had repeated these verses, Henry came, in his Sunday coat, to tell his mamma that Sir Charles Noble's carriage was come. Mrs. Fairchild was quite ready; and Lucy and Emily were in such a hurry, that Emily had like to have tumbled down stairs over her sister, and Lucy was very near slipping down on the step of the hall door: however, they all got into the coach without any accident, and the coachman drove away; and that so fast, that they soon came in sight of Sir Charles Noble's house.

As I suppose you never saw Sir Charles Noble's house, I will give you some account of it. It was a very large house, built all of smooth white stone: it stood in a fine park, or green lawn, scattered over with tall trees and shrubs; but there were no leaves on the trees at that time, because it was winter.

When the carriage drove up to the hall door, a very fine footman came out and opened the carriage door, and shewed Mr. and Mrs. Fairchild the way, through a great many rooms, into a grand parlour, where Lady Noble was sitting upon a sopha, by a large fire, with several other ladies, all of whom were handsomely dressed. Now, as I told you before, Lady Noble was a proud woman: so she did not take much notice of Mrs. Fairchild when she came in, although she ordered the servant to set a chair for her. Miss Augusta Noble was seated on the sopha by her mamma, playing with a very beautiful wax doll; and her two brothers, William and Edward, were standing by her; but they never came forward to Mrs. Fairchild's children, to say that they were glad to see them, or to shew them any kind of civility. If children knew how disagreeable they make themselves when they are rude and ill-mannered, surely they would never be so, but would strive to be civil and courteous to every one, according to the words of the Bible, 'Be kindly affectioned one to another with brotherly love, in honour preferring one another.' (Rom. xii. 10.)

Soon after Mrs. Fairchild was seated, a servant came to say that Miss Noble's and Master William's and Master Edward's dinners were ready. 'Go, Augusta,' said Lady Noble, 'to your dinner, and take Master and Miss Fairchilds with you; and after you have dined, shew them your play-things, and your baby-house.'

Miss Augusta got up; and as she passed by Emily and Lucy, she said, in a very haughty way, 'Mamma says you must come with me.' So Emily and Lucy followed Miss Augusta, and the little boys came after them. She went up a pair of grand stairs, and along a very long gallery full of pictures, till they came to a large room, where Miss Augusta's governess was sitting at work, and the children's dinner set out in great order. In one corner of the room was a baby-house. — Do you know what a baby-house is? If you have not seen such a thing, I will endeavour to describe it to you. It is a small house, fit for dolls, with door and windows, and chimney outside; and inside there is generally a parlour and a kitchen, and a bed-room, with chairs, tables, couches, beds, carpets, and every thing small, just as there is in a real house for people to live in. — Besides the baby-house, were a number of other toys; a large rocking-horse; a cradle, with a big wooden doll lying in it; and tops, and carts, and coaches, and whips, and trumpets, in abundance.

'Governess,' said Miss Augusta, as soon as she opened the door, 'here are Mr. Fairchild's children come to dine with me: this is Lucy, and that is Emily, and that is Henry.'

The governess did not take much notice of Mrs. Fairchild's children, but said, 'Miss Augusta, I wish you would shut the door after you, for it is very cold.'

I do not know whether Miss Augusta heard her governess, but she never offered to go back to shut the door.

The governess then called to Master Edward, who was just coming in, to shut the door after him.

'You may shut it yourself, if you want it shut,' answered the rude boy.

When Lucy heard this, she immediately ran and shut the door: upon which, the governess looked more civilly at her than she had done before, and thanked her for her attention.

Whilst Lucy was shutting the door, Miss Augusta began to stir the fire. 'Miss Augusta,' said the governess, 'has not your Mamma often forbidden you to touch the fire? Some day you will set your frock on fire.'

Miss Augusta did not heed what her governess said this time any more than the last, but went on raking the fire, till at last the governess, fearing some mischief, forced the poker out of her hand. Miss Augusta looked very saucily at her governess; and was going to speak, when her mamma, and the other ladies came into the room to see the children dine. The young ones immediately seated themselves quietly at the table, to eat their dinner.

'Are my children well behaved?' said Lady Noble, speaking to the governess: 'I thought I heard you finding fault with Augusta when I came in.'

'Oh, no! my Lady,' said the governess: 'Miss Augusta is a good young lady: I seldom have reason to find fault with her.'

Lucy and Emily looked at the governess, and wondered to hear her say that Miss Augusta was good; but they were silent.

'I am happy to say,' said Lady Noble, speaking to Mrs. Fairchild, 'that mine are very promising children: Augusta has a good heart.'

'Ah, Lady Noble!' said Mrs. Fairchild, 'I am afraid none of us can say so much of our children: there is no child that can be said to have a good heart.'

Lady Noble looked with surprise at Mrs. Fairchild, but made her no answer. Just at that moment a servant came in, and set a plate of apples on the table.

'Governess,' said Lady Noble, 'take care that Augusta does not eat above one apple: you know that she was unwell yesterday from eating too many.'

The governess promised that Lady Noble should be obeyed: soon after which, all the ladies went out of the room. When the ladies were gone, the governess gave two apples to each of the children, excepting Augusta, to whom she gave only one. The rest of the apples she took out of the plate, and put in her work-bag for her own eating.

When every one had done dinner, and the table-cloth was taken away, Lady Noble's children got up and left the table, and Henry and Emily were following, but Lucy whispered to them to say grace; accordingly they stood still by the table, and, putting their hands together, they said the grace which they had been used to say after dinner at home.

'What are you doing?' said Augusta.

'We are saying grace,' answered Lucy.

'Oh! I forgot,' said Augusta: 'your mamma is religious, and makes you do all these things. Don't you say your prayers four times every day?'

'Sometimes oftener,' said Emily.

'Dear! how tiresome it must be to be so religious!' said Miss Augusta: 'and where's the use of it?'

'Why, don't you know,' said Lucy, 'that if we do not serve God, we shall go to hell when we die; and if we do serve him, we shall go to heaven?'

'But you are not going to die now,' said Miss Augusta: 'you are as young as I am; and young people don't die. It will be time enough to be religious, you know, when we get old, and expect to die.'

'Oh! but,' said little Henry, 'perhaps we may never live to be old: many children die younger than we are.'

Whilst Henry was speaking, William and Edward stood listening to him, with their mouths wide open; and when he had finished his speech, they broke out into a loud fit of laughter.

'When our parson dies, you shall be parson, Henry,' said Edward; 'but I'll never go to church when you preach.'

'No, he sha'n't be parson; he shall be clerk,' said William: 'then he will have all the graves to dig.'

'I'll tell you what,' said Henry; 'your mamma was never worse out in her life than when she said her's were good children.'

'Take that for your sauciness, you little beggar,' said Master William, giving Henry a blow on the side of the head: and he would have given him several more had not Lucy and Emily ran in between.

'If you fight in this room, boys, I shall tell my mamma,' said Miss Augusta. 'Come, go down stairs: we don't want you here: go and feed your dogs.'

William and Edward accordingly went off, and left the little girls and Henry to play quietly. Lucy and Emily were very much pleased with the baby-house and the dolls; and Henry got upon the rocking horse: and so they amused themselves for a while. At length, the governess who had been sitting at work, got up and went to a closet which was within the room. As soon as the governess was out of sight, Miss Augusta, going softly up to the table, took two apples out of the governess's work-bag.

'Oh! Miss Augusta, what are you doing?' said Emily.

'She is stealing,' said Henry.

'Stealing!' said Miss Augusta, coming back into the corner of the room where the baby-house was: 'what a vulgar boy you are! what words you use!'

'You don't like to be called a thief,' said Henry, 'though you are not ashamed to steal, I see.'

'Do, Miss Augusta, put the apples back,' said Emily: 'your mamma said you must have but one, you know, to-day, and you have had one already.'

'Hush, hush!' said Miss Augusta: 'here's my governess coming back: don't say a word.' So saying, she slipped the apples into the bosom of her frock and ran out of the room.

'Where are you going, Miss Augusta?' called out the governess.

'Mamma has sent for me,' answered Augusta: 'I shall be back immediately.'

When Miss Augusta had eaten the apples, she came back quietly, and sat down to play with Lucy and Emily, as if nothing had happened. Soon after, the governess looked into her work-bag, and found that two of the apples were gone. 'Miss Augusta,' she said, 'you have taken two apples: there are two gone.'

'I have not touched them,' said Miss Augusta.

'Some of you have,' said the governess, looking at the other children.

'I can't tell who has,' said Miss Augusta, 'but I know it was not me.'

Lucy and Emily felt very angry, but they did not speak; but Henry would have spoken, if his sister Lucy had not put her hand upon his mouth.

'I see,' said the governess, 'that some of you have taken the apples; and I desire that you Miss Emily, and you Miss Lucy, and you Master Henry, will come and sit down quietly by me, for I don't know what mischief you may do next.'

Now the governess did not believe in her heart that Mrs. Fairchild's children had taken the apples; but she chose to scold them, because she was not afraid of offending their papa and mamma, but she was very much afraid of offending Miss Augusta and her mamma. So she made Lucy and Emily and Henry sit quietly down by her side, before the fire. It was now getting dark, and a maid-servant came in with a candle, and, setting it upon the table, said, 'Miss Augusta, it is time for you to be dressed to go down to tea with the ladies.'

'Well,' said Miss Augusta, 'bring me my clothes, and I will be dressed here by the fire-side.'

The servant then went into the closet I before spoke of, and soon returned with a beautiful muslin frock, wrought with flowers, a rose-coloured sash and shoes, and a pearl necklace. Emily and Lucy had never seen such fine clothes before; and when they saw Miss Augusta dressed in them, they could not help looking at their own plain frocks, and black shoes, and feeling quite ashamed of them; though there was no more reason to be ashamed of their clothes at that time, than there was of their being proud of them when they were first put on.

When Miss Augusta was dressed, she said to the maid-servant, 'Take the candle, and light me down to the door of the drawing-room.' Then, turning to Emily and Lucy, she added, 'Will you come with me? I suppose you have not brought any clean frocks to put on? Well, never mind: when you get into the drawing-room you must keep behind your mamma's chair, and nobody will take any notice of you.'

So Miss Augusta walked first, with the maid-servant, and Henry and Lucy and Emily followed. They went along the great gallery, and down the stairs, and through several fine rooms all lighted up with many lamps and candles, till they came to the door where Sir Charles, and Lady Noble, and Mr. and Mrs. Fairchild, and a great many ladies and gentlemen, were sitting in a circle round a fire. Lucy and Emily and Henry went and stood behind their mamma's chair, and nobody took any notice of them; but Miss Augusta went in among the company, courtseying to one, giving her hand to another, and nodding and smiling to another. – 'What a charming girl Miss Augusta has grown!' said one of the ladies. – 'Your daughter, Lady Noble, will be quite a beauty,' said another. – 'What an elegant frock Miss Augusta has on,' said a third lady. – 'That rose-coloured sash makes her sweet complexion more lovely than ever,' said one of the gentlemen; – and so they went on flattering her, till she grew more conceited and full of herself than ever; and during all the rest of the evening she took no more notice of Mrs. Fairchild's children than if they had not been in the room.

After the company had all drunk tea, several tables were set out, and the ladies and gentlemen began to make parties for playing at cards. As Mr. and Mrs. Fairchild never played at cards, they asked for the coach; and, when it was ready, wished Sir Charles and Lady Noble good night, and came away.

'Well, my dear,' said Mr. Fairchild, when he was got into the coach with his wife and children, 'I am very glad this day is over, and that we are going back to our own comfortable home, where we can serve God in peace.'

'Alas!' said Mrs. Fairchild, 'I am sorry for Lady Noble: she loves the world too well, and all its fine things! though it is written in the Bible, "Love not the world, neither the things that are in the world: if any man love the world, the love of the Father is not in him: for all that is in the world, the lust of the flesh, and the lust of the eye, and the pride of life, is not of the Father, but is of the world; and the world passeth away, and the lust thereof: but he that doeth the will of God abideth for ever."' (I John ii. 15–17.)

'Well,' said little Henry, 'Sir Charles Noble's may be a very fine house, and every thing may be very fine in it; but I like my own little home and garden, and John, and the meadow, and the apple-trees, and the round hill, and the lane, better than all the fine things at Sir Charles's.'

Now all this while Emily and Lucy did not speak a word; and what do you think was the reason? It was this; that the sight of Miss Augusta's fine clothes, and play-things, and beautiful rooms in which she lived, with the number of people she had to attend her, had made them both out of humour with their own humble way of living, and small house and plain clothes. Their hearts were full of the desire of being great, like Miss Augusta, and having things like her; but they did not dare to tell their thoughts to their mamma.

When they got home, Mrs. Fairchild gave a baked apple to each of the children, and some warm milk-and-water to drink: and after they had prayed, she sent them to bed. When Emily and Lucy got into bed, and Betty had taken away the candle, Lucy said, 'Oh, Emily! I wish our papa and mamma were like Sir Charles and Lady Noble. What a beautiful frock that was that Miss Augusta had on! and I dare say that she has a great many more like it – and that sash! – I never saw so fine a colour.'

*Emily.* 'And then the ladies and gentlemen said she was so pretty! and even her governess did not dare to find fault with her!'

*Lucy.* 'But Betty finds fault with us, and John too; and papa and mamma make us work so hard! and we have such coarse clothes! Even our best frocks are not so good as those Miss Augusta wears every morning.'

In this manner they went on talking, till their mamma came up stairs, and into their room. As they had thick curtains round their bed, it being very cold weather, they did not see their mamma come into the room; and so she heard a great deal of what they were talking about, without their knowing it. She came up to the side of their bed, and sat down in a chair which stood near it, and, putting the curtains aside a little, she said; 'My dear little girls, as I came into the room I heard some part of what you were saying, without intending it; and I am glad I heard it, because I can put you in a way of getting rid of these foolish thoughts and desires which you were speaking of to each other. Do not be ashamed, my dears: I am your own mamma, and love you dearly, although I know that you are sinful creatures – and how can my children, who are born in my likeness, be otherwise? Do you remember, Lucy, when Emily got that beautiful doll from Lady Noble, that you said you felt something in your heart which made you very miserable?'

*Lucy.* 'Yes, Mamma, I remember it very well: you told me it was envy; and I have often prayed to God from that time to take envy out of my heart: but I do not feel envy now: I do not wish to take Miss Augusta's things from her, or to hurt her: Emily and I only wish to be like her, and to have the same things she has.'

'What you now feel, my dears,' said Mrs. Fairchild, 'is not exactly envy, though it is very like it: it is what is called Ambition. Ambition is the desire to be greater than we are. Ambition makes people unhappy, and discontented with what they are and what they have. Ambition is in the heart of every man by nature; but, before we can go to heaven, it must be taken out of our hearts, because it is a temper that God hates – though it is spoken of, by people who do not fear God, as a very good thing.'

'I do not exactly understand, Mamma,' said Emily, 'what ambition makes people do.'

'Why, my dear,' said Mrs. Fairchild, 'suppose that Betty was ambitious, she would be discontented at being a servant, and would want to be as high as her mistress: and if I were ambitious, I should strive to be equal to Lady Noble; and Lady Noble would want to be as great as the Duchess, who lives at that beautiful house which we passed by when we went to see your grand-mamma: the Duchess, if she were ambitious, would wish to be like the Queen.'

*Emily.* 'But the Queen could be no higher: so she could not be ambitious.'

*Mrs. Fairchild.* 'My dear, you are much mistaken. When you are old enough to read history, you will find, that when kings and queens are ambitious it does more harm even than when little people are so. When kings are ambitious, they desire to be greater than other kings and then they fight with them, and take their kingdoms from them, and cause many cruel wars and dreadful miseries: and, more than this, it has often happened, that when kings have got all they could get in this world, they have been desirous to be thought more than men, and have caused themselves to be worshipped as God. So, my dear children, you see that there is no end of the mischief which ambition does. – When Satan lived in heaven, and in all the glory of it, he was not content, but he wanted to be equal with God, and rebelled against God: in consequence of which, he was cast down into hell, with his angels. – When Adam and Eve lived in the beautiful garden of Eden, and never knew sorrow, or pain, or sickness, this wicked desire of being great was the cause of their fall: Satan came to them, and told them, that, if they would eat of the tree of the knowledge of good and evil, which was in the midst of the garden, they should be as Gods, knowing good from evil: and they were ambitious, and wished to be like Gods; and so they took the forbidden fruit, and brought sin and death upon themselves and their children. And so you see, my dear children, that wherever this desire to be great comes, it makes us unhappy, and in the end ruins us.'

'Indeed, Mamma,' said Lucy, 'I think it is very true; for I have felt very unhappy ever since the thought came into my head about being as great as Miss Augusta.'

*Emily.* 'But you say, Mamma, that this wish is in every body's heart naturally: then how can we get rid of it?'

*Mrs. Fairchild.* 'In the same manner, my dear, that we master every other sinful inclination; through the help of the Lord Jesus Christ, who came into the world to destroy all sin and all the works of the devil: for "he that committeth sin is of the devil, for the devil sinneth from the beginning: for this purpose, the Son of God was manifested, that he might destroy the works of the devil." (1 John iii. 8.) When you feel in your hearts, my dear children, that wicked desire arise, – O that I was as great as such an one! or as clever as such an one! or as pretty as such an one! – then go into some retired place, if you can, and fall on your knees, and call upon the Lord Jesus Christ, that dear Saviour, who died for you upon the cross, to take this great and dreadful sin of ambition out of your hearts, and to make you humble, and contented with whatever things it may please God to give you in this world. "Let your conversation be without covetousness; and be content with such things as ye have; for He hath said, I will never leave thee nor forsake thee." (Heb. xiii. 5.)'

Then Mrs. Fairchild shewed to her children how much God loves people who do not wish to be great; and how he blesses people who are lowly and humble; and that he will take such people to heaven, as he hath promised – 'For whosoever exalteth himself shall be abased, and he that humbleth himself shall be exalted,' (Luke xiv. 11) – where they will live in the house of God, and in the sight of that dear Saviour who humbled himself for them, 'and, being found in fashion as a man, became obedient unto death, even the death of the cross.' (Phil. ii. 8). Then Mrs. Fairchild kissed her children; for they were beginning to cry to think of their wicked ambition, and how they had been discontented with their dear parents and happy home. And Mrs. Fairchild knelt by the bedside, and prayed that God, for his dear Son's sake, would take the wicked desire to be great out of her dear little girls' hearts. I shall put down Mrs. Fairchild's Prayer in this place, with the Hymn which they sung afterwards: they may both be of use to you when you feel any of the same kind of ambitious desires and thoughts; for, as Mrs. Fairchild said, 'the wish to be great is natural to every man; neither can we conquer our ambition, excepting through Jesus Christ, who died that we might no longer be the slaves of sin.'

### *The Prayer*

O Lord God, Almighty Father! hear the prayer of a poor wicked, proud child! I know that my heart is full of sin, and that my body is corrupt and filthy, and that I must soon die and go down into the dust; and yet I am so foolish and so wicked as to wish to be great in this world. I wish to have a fine house to live in, and a great many servants to wait on me, and to be of great consequence, and to be made a great deal of; and yet I know, that, if I had what I deserved, I should now at this moment be in hell fire. O Thou that resistest the proud, and givest grace to the humble! give me the grace of humility; make me humble and lowly in heart, content and thankful for what I have. O set my sins in order before my eyes, that I may see I have nothing to be proud of, and know that I am not worthy to be set up and made great in the world. I know that thou, O Lord! lovest humble and lowly people; and that thy blessed Son, when in this world, appeared, in the form of a servant, amongst the lowest and poorest of men, and was meek and lowly in his behaviour. O Lord! send thy Holy Spirit to cleanse my heart from all proud thoughts. Teach me to know my sins and hate myself, and to humble myself before men and in thy sight. O give me a clean and a new heart, that I may rather desire to be numbered amongst the saints, and martyrs, and children of God – those holy people, of whom the world was not worthy – than amongst the great and mighty men of the earth.

O holy Father, I am not worthy of myself to make this prayer; but there is One in heaven, even the Lord Jesus Christ, the Lamb who bled and died for me, who has promised to intercede for us before the Throne. For the sake, therefore, of thy beloved Son, O Lord Almighty! be favourable unto my prayer, and send thy Holy Spirit to take all pride from my heart. *Amen.*

'Our Father,' &c. &c.

# Alicia Catherine Mant (?1788–1869)

In the 'Advertisement' to her novel *The Cottage in the Chalk Pit*, Mant wrote: 'The following tale, written for the particular gratification of a young family, in whose pursuits the author feels a strong friendly interest, will, it is hoped, afford a few hours' innocent amusement in many other juvenile circles, besides that to which it is now affectionately presented.' The key words here are 'innocent amusement', for Alicia Mant was an early example of a writer attempting to break away from the explicitly morally serious work of many of her contemporaries, or at least to ameliorate its solemnity by a more warm-hearted approach.

*The Cottage in the Chalk Pit* begins with a familiar situation: the Gardiner family is ruined and father is away, restoring their fortunes. Mrs Gardiner and her children (and two faithful servants) are loaned a cottage by their friend Mrs Montefort. The story is infused by a rigid awareness of English class distinctions, but the textbook responses of the children during educational moments are somewhat more perfunctory than in Mrs Sherwood. One of the themes of the book is the desirability of the rural life; when, at the end of the book, the family's prosperity is renewed, the idyllic cottage is bought as a summer residence.

Alicia Mant is still essentially a writer in the late eighteenth-century mode, but the currents of romantic liberalism are starting to eddy through her work.

In this chapter, the family has just settled into the cottage.

## from *The Cottage in the Chalk Pit* (1822)

### Chapter VII

### The Chalk-Pit

A few days after this, while all the young people were engaged in their separate studies with their mother, their attention was attracted by the sound of voices approaching very near the house. A feeling of curiosity was instantly evident throughout the circle; but none ventured to leave the table but John, who, with an irresistible impulse, started up, and flew to the window which overlooked the wild part of the chalk-pit open to the passing foot-passenger.

'Such nice-looking girls,' said John, as he knelt upon the window-seat; 'and so smart!'

Isabel was on the point of rising to see the smart girls; but Mrs. Gardiner's rather sharp rebuke to John, for allowing his attention to be so idly diverted, prevented her doing so, and brought John back to his place.

'I wish I could make your attention as immovable as Charlotte's and Edward's,' said Mrs. Gardiner, 'while you are engaged with your books. You never will make any progress, while you permit yourselves to be so easily diverted from what you are doing.'

This remark occasioned a general attention, and a dead silence ensued; when, in a few minutes, the party were again disturbed by the noise of hammers and chisels, as if workmen were employed in picking chalk from the rock. Every now and then a collection of stones seemed tumbling down the shelving bank, and peals of laughter accompanied every rattling handful.

The children were all somewhat disturbed, and John and Isabel could scarcely refrain from moving. They watched the countenance of their mother, who was busily employed with her needle, but they could read in it no permission to be idle; and their eyes, therefore, again were fixed upon their lessons.

Presently a louder crash was heard: this was followed by another fit of laughter, and John and Isabel, no longer able to restrain their sympathetic merriment, joined aloud in this hearty expression of gladness.

Mrs. Gardiner again looked up, in order to fix the attention of her children, but she could not herself withhold a smile.

'Do let us go and see what they are doing, mamma,' said Isabel, encouraged by this smile.

'May we just go for a moment to the edge of the underwood,' said John, rising hastily as he spoke, and moving towards the door.

'You may go for five minutes,' said Mrs. Gardiner; 'but do not go near enough to intrude upon the strangers, or interfere with their occupations, whatever they may be.'

John and Isabel were already out of the room. 'Do you wish to go, my love?' said Mrs. Gardiner to Charlotte.

Charlotte was contented with taking a peep at the window, for there was a reserve in her disposition which shrunk from the observation of strangers; and Edward, whose whole attention was then fixed upon a difficult Latin lesson, did not even stir from the table.

John and Isabel rather exceeded their five minutes, and when they did return, it was with a request that the term of their absence might be extended; for 'it was such fun, and they were such nice girls; and Isabel wished she had a hammer and chisel too.'

'They looked up and talked to Isabel, mamma,' said John; 'and I think they admired her very much,' added he, significantly lowering his voice; 'for they whispered to each other about her, and they seemed very anxious she should come down and assist.'

'And what can they be knocking the chalk to pieces for?' said Charlotte, incited to be anxious by Isabel's representation.

'Oh, they are looking for curiosities,' replied Isabel, eagerly; 'and they say there are a great many, and I should so like to go and help them.'

'I am sure they have found one,' said Edward, drily, 'if they have met with you, Isabel.'

'And I am sure they did not think *me* one,' tartly replied Isabel, at the same time throwing her bright hair off her forehead.

'No, that they did not,' said John, who was his sister Isabel's constant companion and admirer: 'I am sure they were very much pleased with her, and' —

'It is not of importance to discover the precise sort of impression made by Isabel,' observed Mrs. Gardiner; 'and I wish, my dear children, you were not so apt to indulge in these little recriminating remarks. You are quite aware, Isabel, that situated as we are, it is not convenient to me to form any new acquaintances; therefore, I hope you will express no dissatisfaction, when I tell you I would rather you did not return to the chalk-pit at present. I had no idea of your doing otherwise than observe the young people at a distance, or should not have allowed you to go out at all.'

Poor Isabel did not receive this disappointment quite as placidly as she might have done; but Mrs. Gardiner took no notice of the transient cloud, which overspread her features during the time she was taking off her tippet and gloves; and a smile of good-humour was restored to her countenance, as she replaced herself by her mother's elbow.

This little strife with inclination was not unnoticed by Mrs. Gardiner: her manner to Isabel was particularly kind and approving; and, when the books were closed, she told the young people all to fetch their bonnets, for it was her intention to take them to Fleetwood.

This information produced general satisfaction; and all were in preparation, when Isabel appeared with a large hand-basket, under the weight of which her slender arm was much inconvenienced.

'And what are you purposing to do with that basket, dear Isabel?' said Mrs. Gardiner, in some surprise.

Isabel was not sorry to take the rest which an answer to this enquiry opened an opportunity for; and placing her basket on the ground, she looked at her sister.

Charlotte blushed. 'I thought, perhaps, mamma,' said she, 'we might also find something curious; so I begged Isabel to prepare a basket.'

'Well, I have no objection to your making geological researches, as well as other young people,' said Mrs. Gardiner, smiling; 'but I must decline the attendance of the basket and implements you have prepared for the purpose: we must get something of a lighter description than this to work with.' And, as she spoke, Mrs. Gardiner took from the basket a very large hammer, which had been begged from James.

'But at present let us proceed in our walk,' said Mrs. Gardiner, 'and Mrs. Montefort may, perhaps, assist you in your preparations; for Captain Montefort has made very large collections of minerals, and she herself is not entirely ignorant on the subject.'

The young people proceeded onwards; but instead of taking the regular path, made a little diversion to the rugged spot, where, a few hours before, the strokes of feeble hammers had so much engaged their attention. The quick eye of John was attracted by the bright shining of some sparkling substance, and he eagerly obtained possession of the treasure.

'What can it be?' exclaimed all the children at once.

'Crystals, of some sort,' replied Mrs. Gardiner; 'but I cannot define it nearer: however, take care of it, and you may learn perhaps, more about it at Fleetwood.'

'What did you mean by *geological*, just now, mamma,' said Edward, who had been thinking it over, ever since his mother had made use of the word some little time before.

'It is an adjective from Geology,' replied Mrs. Gardiner; 'and Geology means that science which 'embraces the study of the earth in general; of its plains, hills, and mountains; and of the relative positions of the masses of which they are composed. I give its definition in the words of a geologist, or a professor of geology, that I may commit no error on a subject in which I am so little conversant. And does this make it intelligible to you?'

'Not quite, mamma,' replied Edward; 'for that seems to make it like geography, and I thought they were different things.'

'Perfectly different, my love,' replied Mrs. Gardiner: 'as different, as the arrangements of art and nature generally are. In geology, you must remember that we mean the natural formations of the earth, or the features it bears unassisted by man; and this will be evident to you, when you bear in mind how impossible it would be for his greatest power to alter, in any manifest degree, the appearance of hills, plains, and mountains: but geography affects more the labours of man; inasmuch as it relates to the situation of country, division of territory, and national distinctions; in all of which, man has been an agent, although a very subordinate one.'

'I understand, mamma,' said Edward, 'and thank you for the explanation. But I have one more question to ask: are Geology and Mineralogy exactly the same?'

'No,' replied Mrs. Gardiner: 'Geology teaches the general construction of the earth; Mineralogy has for its object *the study of mineral bodies in particular*.'

'Now I must thank you for the exact definition of *mineral*, if you please, mamma,' said Edward.

'You understand the meaning of a mine, do you not?' said Mrs. Gardiner.

A general assent was given to this.

'And miner?'

'One that works in a mine,' quickly replied Isabel.

'And what meaning can you, from this, affix to the word mineral, Edward?'

'Any substance coming from a mine.'

'Yes,' replied Mrs Gardiner: 'therefore, generally speaking, all substances dug out of the earth are minerals.'

'I should so like to have a collection of minerals,' said Charlotte.

'I have no other objection,' replied Mrs. Gardiner, 'than a fear that pursuits of this sort might interfere with more necessary occupations. For we must constantly bear in mind, my dear children, that your time is not likely to be at your own disposal; and, therefore, that it will be useless to acquire tastes which may prove to you constant sources of mortification. I object to nothing likely to lead to your admiration of the wonderful works of nature, and, through them, to an increasing reverence for the Creator of so much beauty and variety; but, situated as you are, they must be made subordinate to many other employments.'

The young people all promised that the proposed plan of geological pursuit should never lessen their assiduity in the prosecution of more important objects of attention; and the remainder of the walk to Fleetwood was passed in arrangements relating to the disposition of the quantities of curiosities they expected to gain possession of. Where they were to keep them was a question of some moment; for they had very little room for unnecessary additions, in any part of the house; and Mrs.

Gardiner fairly told them, that any appearance of disorder or untidiness must be paid for by the forfeiture of their valuables.

Many places were suggested, but that of John was most generally approved of, the formation of a little cabinet; and as he had something of a mechanical turn, this was likely to be executed with ease.

'I have not the slightest objection to this,' said Mrs. Gardiner; 'and as I expect that your collection will be some time in gathering, the tardy execution of your piece of furniture will not be of very great importance.'

'Oh, I will begin it this evening, mamma,' said John, eagerly, and studying his mother's countenance, to discover the exact meaning of what she had said.

'And be tired of it before noon to-morrow,' replied Mrs. Gardiner, coolly, 'as you were of the hen-coop, which you undertook to make; which you have neglected, half-finished; and which, perhaps, will be required for the chickens to-morrow morning.'

John blushed and hung his head, as he walked a few paces, in silence, by the side of his mother.

'You more than half finished the coop, I believe,' said Mrs. Gardiner, 'the first morning you commenced it; and, I remember, seemed so interested in your occupation, that none of the entreaties of Isabel could draw you to a game of play: you appeared almost angry, at last, that she should have a wish to claim any of your attention; and told her, as you were employed for me, it was unkind in her to attempt to draw you away. It appears now, however, that it was the delight of something new that engrossed your thoughts, and not any very particular desire to please or assist me.'

'Will you allow me to return and finish it now, mamma?' said John, gently sliding his hand within his mother's arm, a tear at the same time trembling in his eye.

'This facility of execution, but variableness of will, my dear boy,' said Mrs. Gardiner, shaking her head, as she affectionately pressed the hand of her son, 'will prove to you most mortifying inconveniences, as you advance in life: they are even such at present. You are now, I plainly see, uncomfortable, that you have not accomplished what you had promised me you would perform; and you would have been much more so, if, on the appearance of the chickens tomorrow, there had been no shelter provided for them. But of infinitely greater importance will it be to you, as you advance in life, when your credit, nay, even perhaps your bread, may depend, not only in your facility in planning, but on your steadiness in executing the schemes you undertake.'

John attended to all his mother said; and kissing the hand which was pressed on his, promised to exercise a larger share of perseverance.

# Clement Clarke Moore (1779–1863)

There can be very few short poems that have had the impact of 'A Visit from St. Nicholas', written by an academic (Moore was Professor of Latin and Greek at the Protestant Seminary of New York) to amuse his children. The American Christmas tradition was assembled very eclectically, and this poem is a key gene in the development of the cheery, rotund image of Father Christmas – other elements have included the Dutch traditions of 'Sinterk-laas', a soft-drink advertisement of the 1930s, and another poem which completed the sleigh–reindeer motif, Robert L. May's 'Rudolf the Red Nosed Reindeer' (1939).

'A Visit' was published in the *Troy Sentinel* (in New York State) on 23 December 1823. It is quite anomalous in any neat history of children's literature, but demonstrates how popular culture for children can have a powerful effect on culture in general.

## 'A VISIT FROM ST. NICHOLAS' (1823)

'Twas the night before Christmas, when all through the house
Not a creature was stirring, not even a mouse;
The stockings were hung by the chimney with care,
In hopes that St. Nicholas soon would be there;
The children were nestled all snug in their beds,
While visions of sugar-plums danced in their heads;
And mamma in her 'kerchief, and I in my cap,
Had just settled our brains for a long winter's nap—
When out on the lawn there arose such a clatter,
I sprang from my bed to see what was the matter.
Away to the window I flew like a flash,
Tore open the shutters, and threw up the sash.
The moon, on the breast of the new-fallen snow,
Gave the lustre of midday to objects below;
When, what to my wondering eyes should appear,
But a miniature sleigh and eight tiny reindeer,
With a little old driver, so lively and quick,
I knew in a moment it must be St. Nick.
More rapid than eagles his coursers they came,
And he whistled, and shouted, and called them by name:
'Now, *Dasher*! now, *Dancer*! now, *Prancer* and *Vixen*!
On, *Comet*! on, *Cupid*! on, *Donder* and *Blitzen*!
To the top of the porch! to the top of the wall!
Now dash away! dash away! dash away all!'
As dry leaves that before the wild hurricane fly,
When they meet with an obstacle, mount to the sky;
So up to the house-top the courses they flew
With the sleigh full of toys, and St. Nicholas too.
And then, in a twinkling, I heard on the roof
The prancing and pawing of each little hoof—
As I drew in my head, and was turning around,
Down the chimney St. Nicholas came with a bound.
He was dressed all in fur, from his head to his foot,
And his clothes were all tarnished with ashes and soot;
A bundle of toys he had flung on his back,

And he looked like a pedlar just opening his pack.
His eyes – how they twinkled; his dimples, how merry!
His cheeks were like roses, his nose like a cherry!
His droll little mouth was drawn up like a bow,
And the beard of his chin was as white as the snow;
The stump of a pipe he held tight in his teeth,
And the smoke it encircled his head like a wreath;
He had a broad face and a little round belly
That shook, when he laughed, like a bowl full of jelly.
He was chubby and plump, a right jolly old elf,
And I laughed when I saw him, in spite of myself;
A wink of his eye and a twist of his head
Soon gave me to know I had nothing to dread;
He spoke not a word, but went straight to his work,
And filled all the stockings; then turned with a jerk,
And laying his finger aside of his nose,
And giving a nod, up the chimney he rose;
He sprang to his sleigh, to his team gave a whistle,
And away they all flew like the down of a thistle.
But I heard him exclaim, ere he drove out of sight,
*'Happy Christmas to all, and to all a good night!'*

# Mary [Botham] Howitt (1799–1888)

Some poems are better known as proverbs than as actual verses, and the full text of 'The Spider and the Fly' (later published, with no perceptible irony, in *Sketches of Natural History*, 1834) may well give the post-Freudian, let alone feminist reader, pause. Mary Howitt also has an honourable place in the history of children's literature as one of the first translators of Hans Andersen's tales.

## from *The New Year's Gift, and Juvenile Souvenir* (1829)

### THE SPIDER AND THE FLY

'Will you walk into my parlour?' said the Spider to the Fly,
''Tis the prettiest little parlour that ever you did spy;
The way into my parlour is up a winding stair,
And I have many curious things to show when you are there.'
'Oh no, no,' said the little Fly, 'to ask me is in vain,
For who goes up your winding stair can ne'er come down again.'

'I'm sure you must be weary, dear, with soaring up so high;
Will you rest upon my little bed?' said the Spider to the Fly.
'There are pretty curtains drawn around, the sheets are fine and thin;
And if you like to rest awhile, I'll snugly tuck you in!'
'Oh no, no,' said the little Fly, 'for I've often heard it said,
They never, never wake again, who sleep upon your bed!'

Said the cunning Spider to the Fly, 'Dear friend, what can I do,
To prove the warm affection I've always felt for you?
I have within my pantry good store of all that's nice;
I'm sure you're very welcome – will you please to take a slice?'
'Oh no, no,' said the little Fly, 'kind sir, that cannot be,
I've heard what's in your pantry, and I do not wish to see.'

'Sweet creature,' said the Spider, 'you're witty and you're wise;
How handsome are your gauzy wings, how brilliant are your eyes!
I have a little looking-glass upon my parlour shelf,
If you'll step in a moment, dear, you shall behold yourself.'
'I thank you, gentle sir,' she said, 'for what you're pleased to say,
And bidding you good morning now, I'll call another day.'

The Spider turned him round about, and went into his den,
For well he knew the silly Fly would soon come back again;
So he wove a subtle web, in a little corner sly,
And set his table ready, to dine upon the Fly.
Then he came out to his door again, and merrily did sing:
'Come hither, hither, pretty Fly, with the pearl and silver wing;
Your robes are green and purple – there's a crest upon your head;
Your eyes are like the diamond bright, but mine are dull as lead.'

Alas, alas! how very soon this silly little Fly,
Hearing his wily, flattering words, came slowly flitting by;
With buzzing wings she hung aloft, then near and nearer drew,
Thinking only of her brilliant eyes, and green and purple hue;
Thinking only of her crested head – poor foolish thing! At last,
Up jumped the cunning Spider, and fiercely held her fast.
He dragged her up his winding stair, into his dismal den,
Within his little parlour – but she ne'er came out again!

# Sarah Josepha Hale (1788–1879)

One of the industrious widows of children's literature, Sarah Hale edited *The Juvenile Miscellany*, a Boston magazine, in which 'Mary's Lamb' first appeared. Its mixture of sentimentality and moral teaching was characteristic of its period on both sides of the Atlantic. In various modified versions it has become part of the nursery-rhyme stock.

## from *Poems for Our Children* (1830)

### MARY'S LAMB

Mary had a little lamb,
　　Its fleece was white as snow,
And everywhere that Mary went
　　The lamb was sure to go;
He followed her to school one day –
　　That was against the rule,
It made the children laugh and play
　　To see a lamb at school.

And so the teacher turned him out,
　　But still he lingered near,
And waited patiently about,
　　Till Mary did appear.
And then he ran to her and laid
　　His head upon her arm,
As if he said, 'I'm not afraid –
　　You'll shield me from all harm.'

'What makes the lamb love Mary so?'
　　The little children cry;
'Oh, Mary loves the lamb, you know,'
　　The teacher did reply,
'And you each gentle animal
　　In confidence may bind,
And make it follow at your call,
　　If you are always kind.'

# Catharine Maria Sedgwick (1789–1867)

The idea of the (rural) American home, independent and yet, within itself, interdependent, runs through American children's literature, and is celebrated notably in *Little Women* and Laura Ingalls Wilder's 'Little House' series. *Home* was first published as number three of a series 'Scenes and Characters Illustrating Christian Truth', and the story of William Barclay and his wife, Anne, epitomizes an American ideal of self-help. William has firm ideas: 'genteel', he feels, 'is a vulgar word that... ought to be banished from an American's vocabulary'. He goes on: 'It is certainly a false notion in a democratic republic, that a lawyer has any higher claim to respectability... than a tanner, a goldsmith, a printer, or a builder.' But he concedes that 'I fear it will be some time before this new form of society which I anticipate will be seen; before men will seek to consort with men because they are intelligent, accomplished and exemplary, and not because they live in fine houses... and exhaust their resources in extravagant and poisonous eating and drinking.'

William, his home dedicated to God, raises a large family, loses part of his hard-earned money through the fraud of his partner's son John Norton – and eventually the family works its way back to prosperity.

The Nortons represent the modern world, corrupted by wealth. When the Barclay family adopts the homeless Emily, the children all give up something to help house her and eventually come to understand her. She was 'daintily bred and petted from her infancy, had the habits, though not the vicious dispositions, that sometimes grow out of indulgence'. This changes when she joins the family, 'that hive, where every little busy bee did its appointed task'. The book ends with an extended death-bed sequence as the eldest son, Charles, dies, and with an emphasis on Christian acceptance of death. For all its paean to individuality, *Home* is a very traditional book.

In this chapter, we see how parents and children interact, and it is very instructive to compare it with a similar episode in Mary Martha Sherwood's *The Fairchild Family*. In that book, when Henry is wicked, his isolation and punishment are far more strongly stressed; in *Home* the feeling is much more of sorrow than anger, and although there is a Christian element, it is balanced by a rationalism and political awareness. American literature for children is finding its own voice.

Catharine Sedgwick was a Massachusetts philanthropist whose adult novels, such as *A New-England Tale* (1822), praised humble virtues.

## from *Home* (1835)

### Chapter II

### A Glimpse at Family Government

*Pour fourth thy fervors for a healthful mind,*
*Obedient passions, and a will resigned.*
Johnson.

The skilful cultivator discerns in the germination of the bud the perfection, or the disease, that a superficial observer would first perceive in the ripening or the blighted fruit. And the moral observer, if equally skilled, might predict the manhood from the promise of the youth. Few are so skilled, and we seldom turn over ten years of life without surprise at the development of qualities we had not perceived. The happy accidents, – they could not be called virtues, but rather the result of circumstances, – have vanished like the dews of morning. The good-natured, light-hearted, generous youth, as his cares increased and his health abated, has become petulant, gloomy, and selfish; the gay, agreeable girl, moping and censorious. There were many who wondered, that persons who seemed nothing extraordinary in their youth, should turn out as the Barclays had; and they wondered too, how in the world it was that every thing went right with the Barclays; and then the puzzle was solved in the common way, – 'It was their luck.' They did not see that the Barclays had begun right, that they had proposed to themselves rational objects, and had pursued them with all the power of conscience and of an unslacking energy.

That happy, if not happiest portion of married life, when the thousand clustering joys of parents are first felt, when toil is hope without weariness, passed brightly away with them. Twelve years had thus passed; their cares were multiplied, and their enjoyments, a hundred fold. Mr. Barclay's accumulating responsibilities sometimes weighed heavily upon him. He was, like most persons of great sensibility, of an apprehensive temper. The little ailments of his children were apt to disturb his serenity, and, for the time being, it was destroyed by the moral diseases that break out in the healthiest subjects. His wife was of a happier temperament. Her equal, sunny temper soon rectified the disturbed balance of his. She knew that the constitution of weak and susceptible childhood was liable to moral and physical maladies, and that, *if well got through*, it became the more robust and resisting for having suffered them. Her husband knew this too, and was consoled by it, – after the danger was past.

Our friends were now in a convenient house, adapted to their very much improved fortune and increased family. The family were assembled in a back parlor. Mrs. Barclay was at some domestic employment, to facilitate which Martha had just brought in a tub of scalding water. Charles, the eldest boy, with a patience most *unboyish*, was holding a skein of yarn for grandmama to wind; Alice, the eldest girl, was arranging the dinner-table in the adjoining room; Mary, the second, was amusing the baby at the window; Willie was saying his letters to Aunt Betsey; – all were busy, but the busiest was little Haddy, a sweet child of four years, who was sitting in the middle of the room on a low chair, and who, unobserved by the rest, and herself unconscious of wrong, was doing deadly mischief. She had taken a new, unfinished, and very precious kite belonging to her brother Wallace, cut a hole in the centre, thrust into it the head of her pet Maltese kitten, and was holding it by its fore paws and making it dance on her lap; the little animal looking as demure and as formal as one of Queen Elizabeth's maids of honor in her ruff. At this critical juncture Wallace entered in search of his kite. One word of prefatory palliation for Wallace. The kite was the finest he had ever possessed; it had been given him by a friend, and that friend was waiting at the door, to string and fly it for him. At once the ruin of the kite, and the indignity to which it was subjected, flashed on him, and perhaps little Haddy's very satisfied air exasperated him. In a breath he seized the kitten, and dashed it into the tub of scalding water. His father had come in to dinner, and paused at the open door of the next room. Haddy shrieked, – the children all screamed, – Charles dropped grandmama's yarn, and, at the risk of his own hand, rescued the kitten; but seeing its agony, with most characteristic consideration, he gently dropped it in again, and thus put the speediest termination to its sufferings.

The children were all sobbing. Wallace stood pale and trembling. His eye turned to his father, then to his mother, then was riveted on the floor. The children saw the frown on their father's face, more dreaded by them than ever was flogging, or dark closet with all its hobgoblins.

'I guess you did not mean to, did you, Wally?' said little Haddy, whose tender heart was so touched by the utter misery depicted on her brother's face, that her pity for him overcame her sense of her own and pussy's wrongs. Wallace sighed deeply, but spoke no word of apology or justification. The children looked at Wallace, at their father, and their mother, and still the portentous silence was unbroken. The dinner-bell rung. 'Go to your own room, Wallace,' said his father. 'You have forfeited your right to a place among us. Creatures who are the slaves of their passions, are, like beasts of prey, fit only for solitude.'

'How long must Wallace stay up stairs?' asked Haddy, affectionately holding back her brother who was hastening away.

'Till he feels assured,' replied Mr. Barclay, fixing his eye sternly on Wallace, 'that he can control his hasty temper; at least so far as not to be guilty of violence towards such a dear good little girl as you are, and murderous cruelty to an innocent animal; – till, sir, you can give me some proof that you dread the sin and danger of yielding to your passions so much that you can govern them. The boy is hopeless,' he added in a low voice to his wife, as Wallace left the room.

'My dear husband! hopeless at ten years old, and with such a good, affectionate heart as his? We must have patience.'

A happy combination for children is there in an uncompromising father and an all-hoping mother. The family sat down to table. The parents were silent, serious, unhappy. The children caught the infection, and scarcely a word was said above a whisper. There was a favorite dish on the table, followed by a nice pudding. They were eaten, not enjoyed. The children realized that it was not the good things they had to eat, but the kind looks, the innocent laugh, and cheerful voice, that made the pleasure of the social meal.

'My dear children,' said their father, as he took his hat to leave them, 'we have lost all our comfort to-day, have not we?'

'Yes, sir, – yes, sir,' they answered in a breath.

'Then learn one lesson from your poor brother. Learn to dread doing wrong. If you commit sin, you must suffer, and all that love you must suffer with you; for every sin is a violation of the laws of your Heavenly Father, and he will not suffer it to go unpunished.'

If Mr. and Mrs. Barclay had affected their concern, to overawe and impose on their children, they would not have been long deceived; for children, being themselves sincere, are clear-sighted. But they knew that the sadness was real; they felt that it was in accordance with their parents' characters and general conduct. They never saw them ruffled by trifles. Many a glass had been broken, many a greasy knife dropped, many a disappointment and inconvenience incurred, without calling forth more than a gentle rebuke. These were not the things that moved them, or disturbed the domestic tranquillity; but the ill temper, selfishness, unkindness, or any moral fault of the children, was received as an affliction.

The days passed on. Wallace went to school as usual, and returned to his solitude, without speaking or being spoken to. His meals were sent to his room, and whatever the family ate, he ate. For the Barclays took care not to make rewards and punishments out of eating and drinking, and thus associate the duties and pleasures of a moral being with a mere animal gratification. 'But ah!' he thought, as he walked up and down his apartment, while eating his pie or pudding, 'how different it tastes from what it does at table!' and though he did not put it precisely in that form, he felt what it was that 'sanctified the food.' The children began to venture to say to their father, whose justice they dared not question, 'How long Wally has stayed up stairs!' and Charles, each day, eagerly told how well Wallace behaved at school. His grandmother could not resist her desire to comfort him; she would look into his room to see 'if he were well,' 'if he were warm enough,' or 'if he did not want something.' The little fellow's moistening eye and tremulous voice evinced his sensibility to her kindness, but he resolutely abstained from asking any mitigation of his punishment. He overheard his Aunt Betsey (Mrs. Barclay's maiden sister) say, 'It is a sin, and ridiculous besides, to keep Wallace mewed up so, just for a little flash of temper. I am sure he had enough to provoke a saint.'

'We do not keep him mewed up, Betsey,' replied Mrs. Barclay, 'nor does he continue mewed up, for a single flash of temper; but because, with all his good resolutions, his passionate temper is constantly getting the better of him. There is no easy cure for such a fault. If Wallace had the seeds of a consumption, you would think it the extreme of folly not to submit to a few weeks' confinement, if it afforded a means of ridding him of them; and how much worse than a consumption is a moral disease!'

'Well,' answered the sister, 'you must do as you like, but I am sure we never had any such fuss at home; – we grew up, and there was an end on't.'

'But may be,' thought Wallace, 'if there had been a little more fuss when you were younger, it would have been pleasanter living with you now, Aunt Betsey.'

Poor Aunt Betsey, with many virtues, had a temper that made her a nuisance wherever she was. The Barclays alone got on tolerably with her. There was a disinfecting principle in the moral atmosphere of their house.

Two weeks had passed when Mr. Barclay heard Wallace's door open, and heard him say, 'Can I speak with you one minute before dinner, sir.'

'Certainly, my son.' His father entered and closed the door.

'Father,' said Wallace, with a tremulous voice but an open, cheerful face, 'I feel as if I had a right now to ask you to forgive me, and take me back into the family.'

Mr. Barclay felt so too, and kissing him, he said, 'I have only been waiting for you, Wallace; and, from the time you have taken to consider your besetting sin, I trust you have gained strength to resist it.'

'It is not consideration only, sir, that I depend on; for you told me I must wait till I could give you *proof*; so I had to wait till something happened to try me. I could not possibly tell else, for I always do resolve, when I get over my passion, that I never will get angry again. Luckily for me, – for I began to be horribly tired of staying alone, – Tom Allen snatched off my new cap and threw it in the gutter. I had a book in my hand, and I raised it to send at him; but I thought just in time, and I was so glad I had governed my passion, that I did not care about my cap, or Tom, or any thing else. "But one swallow doesn't make a summer," as Aunt Betsey says; so I waited till I should get angry again. It seemed as if I never should; there were provoking things happened, but some-how or other they did not provoke me, – why do you smile, father?'

'I smile with pleasure, my dear boy, to find that one fortnight's resolute watchfulness has enabled you so to curb your temper that you are not easily provoked.'

'But stay, father, you have not yet heard all, yesterday, just as I was putting up my Arithmetic which I had written almost to the end without a single blot, Tom Allen came along and gave my inkstand a jostle, and over it went on my open book; I thought he did it purposely, – I think so still, but I don't feel so sure. I did not reflect then, – I doubled my fist to strike him.'

'O, Wallace!'

'But I did not, father, I did not, – I thought just in time. There was a horrid choking feeling in my throat, and angry words seemed crowding out; but I did not even say, "Blame you." I had to bite my lips, though, so that the blood ran.'

'God bless you, my son.'

'And the best of it all was, father, that Tom Allen, who never before seemed to care how much harm he did you, or how much he hurt your feelings, was really sorry; and this morning he brought me a new blank book nicely ruled, and offered to help me copy my sums into it; so I hope I did *him* some good as well as myself, by governing my temper.'

'There is no telling, Wallace, how much good may be done by a single right action, nor how much harm by a single wrong one.'

'I know it, sir; I have been thinking a great deal since I have been up stairs, and I do wonder why God did not make Adam and Eve so that they could not do wrong.'

'This subject has puzzled older and wiser heads than yours, my son, and puzzled them more than I think it should. If we had been created incapable of sin, there could have been no virtue. Did you not feel happier yesterday after your trial, than if it had not happened?'

'O yes, father; and the strangest of all was, that after the first flash, I had not any bad feelings towards Tom.'

'Then you can see, in your own case, good resulting from being free to do good or evil. You certainly were the better for your victory, and, you say, happier. It is far better to be virtuous than sinless, – I mean, incapable of sin. If you subdue your temper, the exercise of the power to do this will give you a pleasure that you could not have had without it.'

' But if I fail, father?' Wallace looked in his father's face with an expression which showed he felt that he had more than a kingdom to gain or lose.

' You cannot fail, my dear son, while you continue to feel the worth of the object for which you are striving; while you feel that the eye of God is upon you; and that, not only your own happiness, but the happiness of your father, and mother, and brothers, and sisters, – of our *home*, depends on your success.'

' But, father, did you ever know any body that had such a passionate temper, that learned to gov-ern it always?'

' Yes, my child, but not all at once. You are placed in the happiest circumstances to obtain this rule over your own spirit. The Americans are said to be distinguished for their good temper. I believe this is true, not from any natural superiority in them to French, English, or Irish, but because they are brought up among their equals, and compelled from childhood to govern their tempers; one cannot encroach on the rights of another.'

'But it is not so with all Americans, father.'

'No; those in the Southern States unfortunately have not these restraints, – this equal pressure on all sides, and they are esteemed more irascible than the people of the North. This is one of the thousand misfortunes that result from slavery. But we must always remember, my son, that the virtue or vice produced by circumstances is not to be counted to the individual. It is the noble struggle and resistance against them, that makes virtue. It was this that constituted the merit of Washington's subjugation of his temper.'

'Was he, – was General Washington passionate, father?'

'Yes; quite as irascible and passionate naturally, as you are; and yet you know it was his equanimity, his calmness, in the most irritating circumstances, that made him so superior to other men.'

'Was he pious, sir?'

'He had always a strong sense of his responsibility and duty to his Creator.'

'And I guess, too, he had good parents, and a pleasant home, and he hated to make them all unhappy.'

'I guess he had, Wallace,' replied his father, smiling; 'but I can give you another example for your encouragement. Which among the Apostles appears to you to have been the gentlest, – what we should call the sweetest tempered?'

'O, St. John, sir.'

'And yet he appears at one time to have been very impetuous, – what you and I call hasty tempered. He was for calling down fire on the offenders' heads. So you see that even a grown-up person, if he has the love of Christ in him, and lays his precepts to heart, so that he will really strive to be perfect as his Father in heaven is perfect, may, at any age, subdue his temper; though the work is far easier if he begins when a child, as you have, in earnest, my dear boy. You have manifested a virtuous resolution; and you not only have my forgiveness, and my entire sympathy, but I trust you have the approbation of your Heavenly Father. Come, come along to your mother; take her happy kiss, and then to dinner. We have not had one right pleasant dinner since you have been up stairs.'

'Stop one moment, father.' Wallace lowered his voice as he modestly added, 'I don't think I should have got through it alone, but every day I have prayed to God to help me.'

'You have not been alone, my dear son,' replied his father, much moved, 'nor will you ever be left alone in your efforts to obey God; for, you remember, Jesus has said, "If a man keep my words, my Father will love him, and we will come unto him and make our abode with him." God, my son, is present in every dictate of your conscience, in every pure affection and holy emotion of your soul.'

A farmer who has seen a beautiful crop bend under the storm, and after it rise stronger and more promising than ever, can have some feeble conception of Mr. Barclay's satisfaction, while, leaving Wallace with their mother, he assembled the children in the dining-room, and recounted to them as much as he deemed proper of his conversation with their brother.

The dinner-bell sounded, and Wallace was heard running down stairs before his mother, his heels as light as his heart. The children, jumping up behind and before him, shouted out his welcome. Grandmama wiped her eyes, and cleared her voice to say, 'Dear me, Wally, how glad we all are to see you!' Even Aunt Betsey looked smiling, and satisfied, and unprovokable for an hour to come.

Others may think with Aunt Betsey, that Wallace's punishment was out of proportion to his offence; but it must be remembered, that it was not the penalty for a single offence, but for a habit of irascibility that could not be cured without serious and repeated efforts. Mr. Barclay held whipping, and all such summary modes of punishment, on a par with such nostrums in medicine as peppermint and lavender, which suspend the manifestation of the disease, without conducing to its cure. He believed the only effectual and lasting government, – the only one that touches the springs of action, and in all circumstances controls them, is *self*-government. It was this he labored to teach his children. The process was slow but sure. It required judgment, and gentleness, and, above all, patience on the part of the parents; but every inch of ground gained was kept. The children might not appear so orderly as they whose parents are like drill-sergeants, and who, while their eyes are on the fugel-man, appear like little prodigies; but, deprived of external aid or restraint, the self-regulating machine shows its superiority.

# Jacob Abbott (1803–1879)

Jacob Abbott was one of the most important purveyors of fictionalized educational material of the nineteenth century, although he also wrote the 'Franconia' series (1850–4) and other stories, among his 180-plus publications. *The Little Scholar Learning to Talk* is the first of a series (the extract here is reprinted from the 1879 edition, 'revised by the author' as *Rollo Little Scholar Learning to Talk*), which eventually extended to 28 volumes at various reading levels. They are solidly moral, rather than piously insistent, and cover a range of subjects, such as school life, travel and nature study, and provide an insight not only into educational thinking, but to the life of rural New England.

A comparison with Maria Edgeworth's *Frank* shows how far children's books have travelled. Abbott summed up his attitudes in the first edition of *Rollo at Work*:

> Although this little work ... [is] ... intended as a means of entertainment for ... little readers, it is

hoped by the writer that [it] may aid in accomplishing some of the following useful purposes: – 1. In cultivating *the thinking powers* ... 2. In promoting the progress of children in reading and in knowledge of language ... 3. In cultivating the *amiable and gentle qualities of the heart.*

He concluded: 'it is generally better, in dealing with children, to allure them to what is right by agreeable pictures of it, than to attempt to drive them to it by repulsive delineations of what is wrong.'

Perhaps rather against the odds, Rollo emerges as a realistic, likeable character in a realistic setting, and if his activities are studiously mundane they have considerable intrinsic interest, even today.

## from *The Little Scholar Learning to Talk* (1835)

William, William,* – come run here – I have got some pictures to show you. Come and sit up in my lap, and I will show them all to you. Do you not see what an excellent book it is? It has got some good strong covers, and is full of pictures. I shall show them all to you, but not all today. Perhaps I shall let you take the book sometimes. If I do, you must be very careful of it.

### Feeding the Chickens

Here is a picture of a little girl feeding the chickens. Little girl!* Little girl, did you know that you had left the gate open? Little girl, I say, *little girl*, did you know that you had left the gate open? She does not know what I say, she does not hear me; she is nothing but a picture of a girl. She has come out to feed her chickens. I can see the house she lives in. Do you see it? Where is it? Touch it with your finger. It stands back among the trees. I should like to go into that little gate, and walk along under the trees, and go into that house. Who do you think lives there? I think it must be that little girl's father and mother.

She took a little wooden bowl with a handle, and has come out to feed the chickens; and the hens too. There are some large hens. One is running very fast to get some of the corn. I rather think that is corn she is feeding the hens and chickens with. Run, Biddy, run, run, run fast, or you will lose all your corn.

Don't you see the little chickens? How many are there? You may count the chickens. Now you may count the hens. They are all picking up the corn. And there stands the *rooster*, too, opening his mouth to crow. He says, cock-a-doodle-doo, cock-a-doodle-doo!

---

* NOTE TO THE MOTHER. In reading this, use the name of your own child, and so in all similar cases. (Author's note)

* Call 'Little girl!' in the tone you would use if you really expected an answer, and pause a moment for a reply. So in all similar cases. (Author's note)

Do you know why they call him *a roost-er*? It is because he roosts. When it is night do you suppose those hens go to bed, and lie down and cover themselves up with clothes and go to sleep? No indeed; they do not do that. If you should put one of them into a bed in that way, she would jump out and run away as fast as she could. What do you think the hens do when they want to go to sleep? Why, they get up on a long pole and cling to it with their long, sharp claws, and sleep there on a high pole. And that is roosting. So they call the great cock a roost-er. Do you think you could sleep on a high pole?

I can see a beautiful little house in the picture, and that is on a high pole. It is for little birds to live in. The birds are flying all about it. How many birds can you see? What kind of birds do you think they are? They are martins. Martins live in houses like that on the end of a pole.

## from *Rollo at Work* (1837)

### ROLLO'S GARDEN

#### *Farmer Cropwell*

One warm morning, early in the spring, just after the snow was melted off from the ground, Rollo and his father went to take a walk. The ground by the side of the road was dry and settled, and they walked along very pleasantly; and at length they came to a fine-looking farm. The house was not very large, but there were great sheds and barns, and spacious yards, and high wood-piles, and flocks of geese, and hens and turkeys, and cattle and sheep, sunning themselves around the barns.

Rollo and his father walked into the yard, and went up to the end door, a large pig running away with a grunt when they came up. The door was open, and Rollo's father knocked at it with the head of his cane. A pleasant-looking young woman came to the door.

'Is Farmer Cropwell at home?' said Rollo's father.

'Yes, sir,' said she, 'he is out in the long barn, I believe.'

'Shall I go there and look for him?' said he.

'If you please, sir.'

So Rollo's father walked along to the barn.

It was a long barn indeed. Rollo thought he had never seen so large a building. On each side was a long range of stalls for cattle, facing towards the middle, and great scaffolds overhead, partly filled with hay and with bundles of straw. They walked down the barn floor, and in one place Rollo passed a large bull chained by the nose in one of the stalls. The bull uttered a sort of low growl or roar, as Rollo and his father passed, which made him a little afraid; but his attention was soon attracted to some hens, a little farther along, which were standing on the edge of the scaffolding over his head, and cackling with noise enough to fill the whole barn.

When they got to the other end of the barn, they found a door leading out into a shed; and there was Farmer Cropwell, with one of his men and a pretty large boy, getting out some ploughs.

'Good morning, Mr. Cropwell,' said Rollo's father; 'what! are you going to ploughing?'

'Why, it is about time to overhaul the ploughs, and see that they are in order. I think we shall have an early season.'

'Yes, I find my garden is getting settled, and I came to talk with you a little about some garden seeds.'

The truth was, that Rollo's father was accustomed to come every spring, and purchase his garden seeds at this farm; and so, after a few minutes, they went into the house, taking Rollo with them, to get the seeds that were wanted, out of the seed-room.

What they called the seed-room was a large closet in the house, with shelves all around it; and Rollo waited there a little while, until the seeds were selected, put up in papers, and given to his father.

When this was all done, and they were just coming out, the farmer said, 'Well, my little boy, you have been very still and patient. Should not you like some seeds too? Have you got any garden?'

'No, sir,' said Rollo; 'but perhaps my father will give me some ground for one.'

'Well, I will give you a few seeds, at any rate.' So he opened a little drawer, and took out some seeds, and put them in a piece of paper, and wrote something on the outside. Then he did so again and again, until he had four little papers, which he handed to Rollo, and told him to plant them in his garden.

Rollo thanked him, and took his seeds, and they returned home.

## Work and Play

On the way, Rollo thought it would be an excellent plan for him to have a garden, and he told his father so.

'I think it would be an excellent plan myself,' said his father. 'But do you intend to make work or play of it?'

'Why, I must make work of it, must not I, if I have a real garden?'

'No,' said his father; 'you may make play of it if you choose.'

'How?' said Rollo.

'Why, you can take a hoe, and hoe about in the ground as long as it amuses you to hoe; and then you can plant your seeds, and water and weed them just as long as you find any amusement in it. Then, if you have anything else to play with, you can neglect your garden a long time, and let the weeds grow, and not come and pull them up until you get tired of other play, and happen to feel like working in your garden.'

'I should not think that that would be a very good plan,' said Rollo.

'Why, yes,' replied his father; 'I do not know but that it is a good plan enough, – that is, for *play*. It is right for you to play sometimes; and I do not know why you might not play with a piece of ground, and seeds, as well as with anything else.'

'Well, father, how should I manage my garden if I was going to make *work* of it?'

'O, then you would not do it for amusement, but for the useful results. You would consider what you could raise to best advantage, and then lay out your garden; not as you might happen to *fancy* doing it, but so as to get the most produce from it. When you come to dig it over, you would not consider how long you could find amusement in digging, but how much digging is necessary to make the ground productive; and so in all your operations.'

'Well, father, which do you think would be the best plan for me?'

'Why, I hardly know. By making play of it, you will have the greatest pleasure as you go along. But, in the other plan, you will have some good crops of vegetables, fruits, and flowers.'

'And shouldn't I have any crops if I made play of my garden?'

'Yes; I think you might, perhaps, have some flowers, and, perhaps, some beans and peas.'

Rollo hesitated for some time which plan he should adopt. He had worked enough to know that it was often very tiresome to keep on with his work when he wanted to go and play; but then he knew that after it was over, there was great satisfaction in thinking of useful employment, and in seeing what had been done.

That afternoon he went out into the garden to consider what he should do, and he found his father there, staking out some ground.

'Father,' said he, 'whereabouts should you give me the ground for my garden?'

'Why, that depends,' said his father, 'on the plan you determine upon. If you are going to make play of it, I must give you ground in a back corner, where the irregularity, and the weeds, will be out of sight. But if you conclude to have a real garden, and to work industriously a little while every day upon it, I should give it to you there, just beyond the pear-tree.'

Rollo looked at the two places, but he could not make up his mind. That evening he asked Jonas about it, and Jonas advised him to ask his father to let him have both. 'Then,' said he, 'you can work on your real garden as long as there is any necessary work to be done, and then you could go and play about the other with James or Lucy, when they are here.'

Rollo went off immediately, and asked his father. His father said there would be some difficulties about that; but he would think of it, and see if there was any way to avoid them.

The next morning, when he came in to breakfast, he had a paper in his hand, and he told Rollo he had concluded to let him have the two gardens, on certain conditions, which he had written down. He opened the paper, and read as follows: –

'*Conditions on which I let Rollo have two pieces of land to cultivate*; the one to be called his *working-garden*, and the other his *playing-garden*.

'1. In cultivating his working-garden, he is to take Jonas's advice, and to follow it faithfully in every respect.

'2. He is not to go and work upon his playing-garden, at any time, when there is any work that ought to be done on his working-garden.

'3. If he lets his working-garden get out of order, and I give him notice of it; then, if it is not put perfectly in order again within three days after receiving the notice, he is to forfeit the garden, and all that is growing upon it.

'4. Whatever he raises, he may sell to me, at fair prices, at the end of the season.'

## Planting

Rollo accepted the conditions, and asked his father to stake out the two pieces of ground for him, as soon as he could; and his father did so that day. The piece for the working-garden was much the largest. There was a row of currant-bushes near it, and his father said he might consider all those opposite his piece of ground as included in it, and belonging to him.

So Rollo asked Jonas what he had better do first, and Jonas told him that the first thing was to dig his ground all over, pretty deep; and, as it was difficult to begin it, Jonas said he would begin it for him. So Jonas began, and dug along one side, and instructed Rollo how to throw up the spade-fuls of earth out of the way, so that the next spadeful would come up easier.

Jonas, in this way, made a kind of a trench all along the side of Rollo's ground; and he told Rollo to be careful to throw every spadeful well forward, so as to keep the trench open and free, and then it would be easy for him to dig.

Jonas then left him, and told him that there was work enough for him for three or four days, to dig up his ground well.

Rollo went to work, very patiently, for the first day, and persevered an hour in digging up his ground. Then he left his work for that day; and the next morning, when the regular hour which he had allotted to work arrived, he found he had not much inclination to return to it. He accordingly asked his father whether it would not be a good plan to plant what he had already dug, before he dug any more.

'What is Jonas's advice?' said his father.

'Why, he told me I had better dig it all up first; but I thought that, if I planted part first, those things would be growing while I am digging up the rest of the ground.'

'But you must do, you know, as Jonas advises; that is the condition. Next year, perhaps, you will be old enough to act according to your own judgment; but this year you must follow guidance.'

Rollo recollected the condition, and he had nothing to say against it; but he looked dissatisfied.

'Don't you think that is reasonable, Rollo?' said his father.

'Why; I don't know,' said Rollo.

'This very case shows that it is reasonable. Here you want to plant a part before you have got the ground prepared. The real reason is because you are tired of digging; not because you are really of opinion that that would be a better plan. You have not the means of judging whether it is, or is not, now, time to begin to put in seeds.'

Rollo could not help seeing that that was his real motive; and he promised his father that he would go on, though it was tiresome. It was not the hard labour of the digging that fatigued him, for, by following Jonas's directions, he found it easy work; but it was the sameness of it. He longed for something new.

He persevered, however, and it was a valuable lesson to him; for when he had got it all done, he was so satisfied with thinking that it was fairly completed, and in thinking that now it was all ready together, and that he could form a plan for the whole at once, that he determined that for ever after, when he had any unpleasant piece of work to do, he would go on patiently through it, even if it was tiresome.

With Jonas's help, Rollo planned his garden beautifully. He put double rows of peas and beans all around, so that when they should grow up, they would enclose his garden like a fence or hedge, and make it look snug and pleasant within. Then, he had a row of corn, for he thought he should like some green corn himself to roast. Then, he had one bed of beets and some hills of musk-melons, and in one corner he planted some flower seeds, so that he could have some flowers to put into his mother's glasses, for the mantelpiece.

Rollo took great interest in laying out and planting his ground, and in watching the garden when the seeds first came up; for all this was easy and pleasant work. In the intervals, he used to play on his pleasure-ground, planting and digging, and setting out, just as he pleased.

Sometimes he, and James, and Lucy, would go out in the woods with his little wheel-barrow, and dig up roots of flowers and little trees there, and bring them in, and set them out here and there. But he did not proceed regularly with this ground. He did not dig it all up first, and then form a regular plan for the whole; and the consequence was, that it soon became very irregular. He would want to make a path one day where he had set out a little tree, perhaps, a few days before; and it often happened that, when he was making a little trench to sow one kind of seeds, out came a whole parcel of others that he had put in before, and forgotten.

Then, when the seeds came up in his playing-garden, they came up here and there, irregularly; but, in his working-garden, all looked orderly and beautiful.

One evening, just before sundown, Rollo brought out his father and mother to look at his two gardens. The difference between them was very great; and Rollo, as he ran along before his father, said that he thought the working plan of making a garden was a great deal better than the playing plan.

'That depends upon what your object is.'

'How so?' said Rollo.

'Why, which do you think you have had the most amusement from, thus far?'

'Why, I have had most amusement, I suppose, in the little garden in the corner.'

'Yes,' said his father, 'undoubtedly. But the other appears altogether the best now, and will produce altogether more in the end. So, if your object is useful results, you must manage systematically, regularly, and patiently; but if you only want amusement as you go along, you had better do every day just as you happen to feel inclined.'

'Well, father, which do you think is best for a boy?'

'For quite small boys, a garden for play is best. They have not patience or industry enough for any other.'

'Do you think I have patience or industry enough?'

'You have done very well, so far; but the trying time is to come.'

'Why, father?'

'Because the novelty of the beginning is over, and now you will have a good deal of hoeing and weeding to do for a month to come. I am not sure but that you will forfeit your land yet.'

'But you are to give me three days' notice, you know.'

'That is true; but we shall see.'

# James Kirke Paulding (1778–1860)

Fantasy was not greatly regarded in the USA. The legends and myths of the indigenous peoples were not well known, and European fairy-tales did not seem to travel well; the few tales that were produced reflected an inappropriate monarchical society. Paulding's collection, *A Christmas Gift from Fairyland*, provided a corrective.

There are five stories, prefaced by an elaborate introduction by one Sampson Fairlamb of Chicago (dated 1 April!) in which he describes how Simeon Starkweather discovered a birchbark manuscript, left behind by 'a flock of the queerest little varmint women' that he had caught in a trap. Paulding had a pleasantly ironical sense of humour: 'The whole is now published for the joint benefit of the Editor and honest Sim, who not being aware of the liberality, not so say, munificence of our Publishers, modestly anticipates just enough from his share of the profits to buy him a new rifle.'

The stories all make political or philosophical points. In 'The Philosopher and the Fairy Ring' the philosopher exasperates the fairies because he won't believe his eyes; in 'The Hunchback and Beauty', which has echoes of the moral tale, the good fairy rewards 'the youth who essayed to cultivate his mind and his heart, rather than follow the barren paths of vanity and folly'; in 'The Nameless Old Woman' the central character learns, among the Indians, to become a witch, and then plagues her neighbour until she is defeated by St. Nicholas. 'The Fairy Experiment' takes a community of fairies who 'had sought refuge

from the persecutions of science and philosophy, two deadly foes to these playful fantasies, and airy inventions of the imagination'. Unfortunately, they bring with them a despotic rule, and 'despotism cannot exist in our new world'. The quarrelsome king and queen return to the old world, Puck defects to the Indians, and the remaining fairies form a republic.

*A Christmas Gift* was the victim, perhaps, of the broad unfashionableness of fantasy, but as 'Florella, or the Fairy of the Rainbow' shows, fantasy is anything but escapist. It is fascinating to compare this story with *The Wizard of Oz* (see p. 466), to see how far the vision of the New World changed in only 65 years.

Paulding's tactic of turning European fairy-tale structures against themselves as a way of praising the New World is found in the extract reprinted here (from the 1839 edition, retitled *A Gift from Fairyland*). Florella was 'the most beautiful child ever seen and... as usual, had a fairy for her godmother.' To stop her being 'contaminated by low company' she is shut up in a tower, and a marriage is arranged for her with the cowardly Prince of the Sun. While out hunting, she is saved from an attack by a wild boar by a mysterious (handsome) stranger. 'By the law of court etiquette, which was held the most sacred of all the laws of this ancient and mighty kingdom, it was considered a capital crime to touch a princess' and so the young man is arrested. Florella appeals to the little bird who is her fairy godmother's messenger.

## from *A Christmas Gift from Fairyland* (1839)

### 'Florella, or the Fairy of the Rainbow'

'What dost thou require, my princess, that thou callest on me in such tones of sorrow. Speak, that I may carry thy message to thy fairy godmother.'

Florella related her story and her sorrows, apprizing the little bird, that the preserver of her life was, on the morrow, to suffer a cruel death, for having opened his arms to receive her, when she threw herself on his bosom in an agony of terror. She besought him to fly to the fairy, and bid her in the name of her god-daughter to come to her relief, redress her wrongs, and assuage her sorrows, for she felt she could not survive her preserver, if he perished for her sake.

'Be contented, my princess,' answered the little bird. 'Do not despair of the help of Providence, which is ever the shield of the virtuous. Thou art good, and thou art pure, and such have ever a friend in the Giver of all good. Hope for the best, but hope humbly; go to thy rest and sleep soundly to-night, for who knows what to-morrow will bring. Farewell for a while:' and the little bird, flying out at the window, lingered for a few moments on the topmost bough of a neighbouring tree, quavering forth a song so full of triumphant felicity, that Florella became inspired with sweet and balmy hopes. She soon after laid herself quietly down in her bed, and slept so soundly, that she did not awake until the beams of the morning sun, shining full in her face, roused her to the memory of the past, the consciousness of the present, the anticipations of the future.

It was some moments before the princess recalled to mind the circumstances of the preceding day, and the situation of the youth who had saved her life, and already paid, or was about to pay, for conferring that benefit, by the sacrifice of his own. The thought brought with it a gush of tears, at the same time that it roused her to a last effort for his preservation. Starting up, she called her attendants, but none came; and after waiting a few moments in agonizing impatience, she resolved to dress herself. On looking round, however, she could discover no other garments, but such as country-maids are accustomed to wear, and which appeared so coarse and unseemly that she could not find in her heart to put them on, even if she had known how. While standing in this state of perplexity, she cast her eyes around, and was struck with the appearance of her chamber, which was exceedingly small, and furnished in the most plain and simple style. Confounded and alarmed at the change, she remained bewildered and at a loss, until warned by a strange voice without, saying: 'Come, my little damsel, it is high time to get up, and milk the cows; don't you hear them calling to you?' and, sure enough, she heard them lowing close under the window.

'Where am I, and what has happened to me?' exclaimed the princess, and running to the window, looked out on a scene so strange, yet so fair and cheerful, that she paused to gaze on it with delight. A wide range of country spread before her, basking in the bright rays of the sun, and glittering in the jewels of the dewy morning. Cultivated fields, green meadows enamelled with flowers, and woods waving in the summer zephyrs, lay mixed together in all the graceful harmony of nature. Flocks of sheep spread themselves here and there, animating the hills; herds of cattle lay ruminating in lazy luxury under the shady elms; groups of merry children were sporting at the doors of white-washed cottages that dotted the landscape; the birds were singing their morning salutations, the milkmaids their rustic love-ditties, the ploughmen whistling their way to their daily labours, and just at the foot of the hill where stood her new abode, a little winding stream glittered among the grass and trees, lending its murmurs to the universal chorus of nature. Every thing around her seemed free and happy, and for a little while her spirit joined in gentle concert with all these delicious harmonies.

'Do I dream,' at length she said, 'or have I travelled in my sleep to a new and more beautiful world?' She was answered by her little bird, which poured forth one of his most delightful and animated strains, from a bush laden with a thousand moss-roses, some just in the bud, some half expanded, others spread out in all their rich exuberance, sparkling with dew-drops and diffusing more than the fragrance of Araby the blessed, through the surrounding air. When he had finished his song, he bathed his bosom in the dewy sweets, that lingered in the rosy recesses of the flowers, and shivering his feathers in ecstasy, flitted in at the window, greeting her lips with a kiss of his golden bill.

'How likest thou thy new abode, my princess? dost thou think thou canst be happy here, in the enjoyment of repose and liberty, wait on thyself, and be useful to others?'

'What dost thou mean, my little bird?' asked the princess in wonder. 'Where am I, and to what purpose have I been brought hither?'

'To be happy, if thou deservest to be so. Thou art now in the NEW WORLD, far distant from kings and court etiquette, where to be useful is to be dignified; and where, when thy duties are performed to thyself and others, thou mayest, without fear or reproach, enjoy all innocent sports and recreations, relieved from the chains that have fettered thy youthful spirit, and made thee a slave to all those artificial restraints, from which the rest of thy fellow-creatures are free.'

'O happy, happy change!' exclaimed the princess, in ecstasy, 'but the recreant prince of the moon, shall I be free from his odious persecutions?'

'For ever, my princess, if thou performest thy duties in thy new station.'

'But – but – the stranger who saved my life,' said Florella, with blushing hesitation – 'Yet, alas! why do I ask of him? doubtless, before this, he has laid down his life for having given me mine:' and the young princess melted into tears.

'He lives, and thou wilt see him again, on the same conditions which shall free thee for ever from the prince of the moon.'

'And my father?' said Florella, anxiously.

'Seek to know no more, until the period comes. Adieu, my princess, it is time to go forth and milk the cows.' Just then, the same voice was heard calling on her, chiding her delay, but not in anger. 'Go,' said the little bird, 'it is the voice of thy protector, in whose care the fairy hath placed thee, and for whose kindness, thou wilt owe obedience, gratitude, and affection. See that thou payest the debt, or the forfeit will be the loss of thy happiness. Farewell, till I see thee again? Shouldst thou become tired of thy new abode, call on thy godmother, and she will restore thee to the court of thy father.'

The little bird flitted away, and Florella having spent rather a long time arraying herself, for it was an awkward business to one who had heretofore depended on others for assistance, in the most insignificant offices – Florella went forth, and met without the door, a staid and venerable matron, decked in homely yet cleanly weeds, with a countenance full of cheerful benevolence, and eyes that sparkled even among wrinkles.

'Well, my daughter,' said she, 'you have overslept yourself this morning, the cows are waiting for you. But I suppose you are tired with your long journey, and will be earlier to-morrow. Yonder is the milk-pail, and you must bestir yourself, for we shall get no breakfast, except from the cows.'

Florella went forth, ashamed, not that the task of milking alarmed her pride, but that she was conscious of her entire incapacity to fulfil it. The cows snuffed their noses at her appearance, and when she essayed to extract the milky store, sidled away, as if impatient at her awkwardness. In short, she could make nothing of it, and they were likely to have no breakfast if it depended on her. The old woman, who was waiting her progress, at length came up, laughing at her ill success, and saying she was likely to have but an awkward milkmaid. After which, she seated herself on a little bench, and bidding Florella take good notice, finished the milking without any difficulty.

They then went in to breakfast, and the little fatigue Florella had undergone, joined to the wholesome freshness of the morning air, gave her such an appetite, that she ate more than became the daughter of a great king, or than the sacred law of court etiquette allowed, at the court of her father.

When the wholesome morning meal was done, the old woman instructed her in various household duties of a light and cheerful kind, and though Florella failed in some, and performed others in an imperfect manner, the good old soul, instead of scolding or finding fault with her wretched bringing up, encouraged her by the assurance that she could very soon learn to do better. When the cottage was fairly put to rights, she told the princess she might go forth into the fields, and amuse herself in any manner she pleased. Accordingly, Florella, tying on a little straw hat, which she could scarcely feel on her head, went forth on a ramble beside the stream that meandered through the meadows at the foot of the hills. Here she met little children of the neighbouring houses, sporting or fishing, or playing off their various gambols, and such was the smiling welcome she ever bore in her face, that they did not avoid, but approached her, with innocent freedom, asking her name, where she came from, and bringing her bouquets of wild flowers, which grew on the banks of the stream.

There was a playful freedom, devoid of forward impudence, in the words and actions of these little urchins, so different from the fawning servility to which she had been all her life accustomed, that though at first it seemed strange, if not offensive, soon pleased by its native charm, and blithesome hilarity. In a little while, Florella found herself joining in their sportive gambols, associating herself in their rural pursuits, and sharing in all their hopes and fears. When she left them, they told her she must come again, and bring a basket which they would fill with flowers.

The princess returned home pleased and happy, that she had found companions, who were not her slaves, and in whose presence she could follow the impulses of her heart, or the caprices of her fancy, free from the cobweb toils, which had hitherto fettered her on every side. Day after day, week after week, glided away, during which Florella rapidly improved in domestic skill, most especially in milking the cows, who actually seemed now to welcome her coming, until at length the old dame, whom she called her mother, and who deserved the title by her kindness, declared, that she would be a treasure to any farmer's son in twenty miles round, who wanted an industrious, frugal, sweet-tempered wife. The step of the princess became every day more light and elastic; deeper and deeper was the tint of the roses on her cheek, while her waking thoughts – save now and then, a single recollection, that ever brought forth a quivering sigh – were full of happiness, and her nights occupied in balmy rest or happy dreams.

At length, at the expiration of six months from the transformation of Florella, the old woman fell desperately ill, and, for several weeks, lay helpless on her bed of pain. During all this time, the princess attended her with the kindest care, the most gentle, tender, and unabating assiduity. By day, she employed herself in administrating to the pains of sickness, and the infirmities of age; by night, she sat at the bedside, watching, weeping, and praying for the blessing of Heaven on her endeavours. By degrees, her soothing cares, and tender attentions, proved successful. The aged sufferer at length was able to arise from her bed of anguish, and to thank her careful nurse, that she was still in the land of the living. She embraced her with tears of gratitude, blessed her in words of warm sincerity, and over and over predicted that Heaven would reward her for her kindness. The little bird also frequently cheered Florella, with his song, and at length, one day flew in at the window, lighted on her shoulder, and whispered in her ear: –

'Well done, my princess, thy reward is at hand.'

The good old woman insisted that Florella should go forth, that she might, by partaking in the fresh air, recover her activity and spritefulness. Accordingly, she put on her little straw bonnet, and sought her usual walk along the bank of the little twittering stream, where the young children were delighted to see her again, and gathered wreaths of flowers, which they entreated her to wear on her head. In a little while, she was more charming than ever, and more happy, too, in the consciousness of having paid the debt of gratitude to her kind protector.

One bright summer morning, she wandered away to her favourite retreat, a little cascade buried deep in a shady glen, through which the crystal stream had, in the lapse of ages, worn its way, now tumbling over precipices, and anon foaming among the rocks, that were green with moss and clambering vines.

Here, seated on the edge of a little crystal basin, at the foot of the cascade, in which the speckled trout might ever and anon be seen, darting at the little heedless flies that fell upon its surface, Florella sunk into a deep revery, in which the past was reflected on her mind, even as the rocks and trees were reflected in the glassy pool. Mellowed by time and distance, the images of her father, of his court, and of every thing connected with her past existence, appeared and disappeared like the pageants of a dream, and caused neither regret for their absence, or anxiety for their return. One recollection, and one alone, created pain, and that was of the youth in the hunter's suit of green, who had laid her under obligations, she feared he would never give her an opportunity to repay, and whom she longed to see once more, if only to thank him. She sighed deeply at the recollection of the few fleeting moments, when she lay trembling in his arms, felt his heart beat against hers, and in the midst of her terrors, was happier than she ever was before.

While her spirit was thus, as it were, absent from its tenement of clay, expatiating in the past, and seeking to pry into the future, she was awakened to a sense of the present, by the barking of a dog upon the top of the precipice, over which the waters plunged, and looking up, beheld the figure of a man in green, eagerly bending over, as if watching her motions with extreme interest. At first, she felt alarmed, and hastily rising, was about to leave the spot, when a second look revealed to her heart the youth of her contemplations, and caused its pulses to beat with new rapidity.

'Florella,' exclaimed the youth, in a voice trembling with eagerness, 'do not fly. If my presence is painful, I will retire as I came, content with having seen you once more. Fare thee well,' added he, in a saddened tone, as he perceived her going away, 'Fare thee well; I leave you in safety, since there are no ravenous beasts to molest you in these innocent retreats.'

The heart of the princess smote her with a feeling of ingratitude, for the conclusion of his speech had recalled more vividly the obligations she owed him.

'Stay,' cried she, with deep blushes and panting hesitation, 'stay and receive my thanks, for it cannot be a sin against modesty to express our gratitude.'

In a moment, the stranger youth was at her side. Florella thanked him for saving her life, with all the warmth of an innocent heart, and the youth assured her that the obligation was conferred on himself, since it had ever been to him a source of unbounded happiness. Having lightened her bosom of its load of gratitude, one might have thought Florella would have been satisfied and went her way. But some how or other, they had so much to say besides, that neither seemed to think of parting. The princess related her mysterious change from the heiress of a kingdom to the maid of an old peasant woman, and the youth, who announced his name as Armine, declared that their fates seemed united, for he had been delivered from death in the same mysterious manner, by a midnight conveyance to his home. The princess blushed at this allusion to a community of fate, and Armine contemplated her with such speaking looks, that she turned away her face, and seemed gazing at the foaming torrent at her feet.

Florella learned that he was an inhabitant of the neighbourhood, and so significantly looked her wonder at not having seen him before, that he answered her silence, by saying: 'It was forbidden.' Florella blushed ten times redder than before, and rising, turned herself towards home. Armine attempted to follow, and the princess staid him by waving her hand for his departure. But he persisted in following at her side, and such was the roughness of the path, that she was often obliged to let him take her hand, in order to guide her in safety, and if on these occasions he squeezed it too tightly, the princess ascribed it to necessity rather than presumption. The first step is every thing, and Armine, without any farther opposition, accompanied Florella home, where he was welcomed by the dame as an old acquaintance.

From this time, scarcely a day passed, in which they failed to meet by a thousand of those inscrutable accidents which the world calls fate, but which youths and young maidens, learning the first rudiments of love, know full well are the result of a common sympathy, by which they are irresistibly drawn together by the chords of their hearts. Armine had long looked his love, and the princess blushed hers, ere he found words to declare his passion: he received his answer in a silence, more expressive, a thousand times, than all the babbling eloquence of the deceitful tongue. Remembering the wise old saying, that 'silence gives consent,' Armine folded the princess in his arms: the throbbing of their hearts, recalled to her mind, the rescue from the ferocious boar, and as Florella returned the embrace, she persuaded herself it was only a tribute to gratitude.

At this moment, they were startled by the appearance of a little woman, about three feet high riding on a rainbow, and decked in more than its celestial radiance. She sailed towards them, until the beautiful arch, seemed to bend just over their heads, and enclose them within its dazzling semicircle. For a little while they stood in silent wonder, not altogether unmixed with apprehension, when the fairy of the rainbow, who was no other than Florella's godmother, addressed them as follows, in a voice sweeter than that of the sweetest-toned woman:—

'Florella, thou hast tasted of life at both extremes of the fountain. Thou hast learned what wealth, power, and honours can give, and what are the blessings of a life of innocent freedom, joined with the discharge of those duties which all mankind owe to each other. Choose now, and choose for ever, whether thou wilt be a queen, or a free tenant of this land of liberty, where thou and thy posterity for long ages to come, shall enjoy those rights, which, though bestowed by omnipotence, are filched away by his creature, man. Choose now, and for ever.'

'If my father could come and enjoy the same happiness,' replied Florella.

'Thy father,' replied the fairy of the rainbow, 'lives and reigns no more. He died months ago; but the people await thy appearance, and will submit to thy authority. Wilt thou return and reign over them?'

'Never!' replied the princess, firmly. 'When I remember the buoyant health, the cheerful spirits, the innocent freedom I have enjoyed in this land of liberty, and contrast it with the thousand vexatious restràints, the cumbrous splendours, straight-laced etiquette, desperate ennui, and little envious, malignant passions of a court; when I recall all these, my choice is made. I will stay where I am, and share with the rest of my fellow-creatures, what God has given equally to all.'

Armine, who had watched, with breathless impatience, and trembling apprehension, the decision of Florella, at the conclusion of this declaration, threw himself at her feet, and thanked her in words of grateful eloquence that she had not made choice of a station that would have for ever separated his lot from hers. The fairy, too, contemplated her with looks of affectionate approbation, and replied in these encouraging words:—

'Thy choice is wise, my daughter, and thou shalt be rewarded for having learned to administer to the happiness of others, by being happy thyself. Know that thou art the grand-daughter of the old dame under whose protection thou hast lately lived, and that a malignant fairy, being offended with thy mother, stole thee away, and as a punishment, sought to make thee perpetually miserable by passing thee off for the daughter of a king. Thou art now, through thy own wise choice, restored to thy former state, and nothing now remains but to complete thy happiness. Come hither, Armine, and my daughter.'

The youthful pair approached; the fairy bent down, joined their hands, blessed them, and rising on the beams of the rainbow, disappeared in the blue distance of the boundless sky. Florella, with the joyful assent of her grandmother, was soon united to Armine, with whom she passed a life of such joyous freedom, sweetened and mingled with useful occupations, that a thousand times she asked herself, for what unheard-of crimes, Providence should punish people by entailing on them and their posterity, the miseries of kingly power and courtly etiquette.

The prince of the moon, on the disappearance of Florella, returned to his empire, accompanied by the favourite maid-of-honour, and on the death of the emperor, who was called by way of distinction, the man in the moon, played such enormous pranks of tyranny, that the fairy of the rainbow, whose power extended over all that planet, changed him into a vast green cheese, and his people, for one hundred years, were permitted to prey upon him, as he had preyed on them.

# Catherine Sinclair (1800–1864)

*Holiday House* has a reputation as a landmark text, in which the severities of the moral tale, exemplified by *The Fairchild Family* (p. 17) were at last broken. This is a pardonable exaggeration, but the increasing lightness of tone found in Hofland and Mant is now carried much further.

Harry and Laura Graham (whose mother, in the manner of the time, is dead, and their father recovering on a European tour) are left in the hands of the severe Mrs Crabtree, and the more or less irresponsible Uncle David. The interestingly ambivalent position taken by Catherine Sinclair is demonstrated in this authorial intervention:

> In spite of Mrs. Crabtree's admirable 'system' with children, Harry and Laura became, from this time, two of the most heedless, frolicsome beings in the world, and had to be whipped almost every morning; for in those days it had not been discovered that whipping was all a mistake, and that children can be made good without it; though some old-fashioned people still say – and such, too, who take the God of truth for their guide – the old

plan succeeded best, and that those who 'spare the rod will spoil the child'.

Despite this early version of Mary Poppins, then, Harry and Laura career through the book in a way that looks suspiciously like a series of parodies of earlier moralizing. In the chapter reprinted here, the consequences of playing with fire are far removed from those of Mary Martha Sherwood's world.

This is not to say that morals are not drawn, and there is a solid, if understated, underpinning of the virtues of correct behaviour. When Harry loses money gambling, Lady Rockville observes, ' "Look at that poor blind man you could have relieved'; when Uncle David tells the children a 'wonderful story', it is at once balanced by some moralizing. The book also has a very conventional ending, with the protracted death of brother Frank.

But for much of the time *Holiday House* reads more like Nesbit than Sherwood. Fundamentally, Sinclair makes the distinction between thoughtlessness and wickedness and, with some reservations, deserves her revolutionary reputation.

## from *Holiday House* (1839)

### CHAPTER III

### THE TERRIBLE FIRE

*Fire rages with fury wherever it comes,*
*If only one spark should be dropped;*
*Whole houses, or cities, sometimes it consumes,*
*Where its violence cannot be stopped.*

One night, about eight o'clock, Harry and Laura were playing in the nursery, building houses with bricks, and trying who could raise the highest tower without letting it fall, when suddenly they were startled to hear every bell in the house ringing violently, while the servants seemed running up and down stairs as if they were distracted.

'What can be the matter?' cried Laura, turning round and listening, while Harry quietly took this opportunity to shake the walls of her castle till it fell.

'The very house is coming down about your ears, Laura!' said Harry, enjoying his little bit of mischief. 'I should like to be Andrew, now, for five minutes, that I might answer those fifty bells, and see what has happened. Uncle David must be wanting coals, candles, tea, toast, and soda-water, all at once! What a bustle everybody is in! There! the bells are ringing again, worse than ever! Something wonderful is going on! What can it be?'

Presently Betty ran breathlessly into the room, saying that Mrs. Crabtree ought to come downstairs immediately, as Lady Harriet had been suddenly taken very ill, and, till the Doctor arrived, nobody knew what to do; so she must give her advice and assistance.

Harry and Laura felt excessively shocked to hear this alarming news, and listened with grave attention while Mrs. Crabtree told them how amazingly well they ought to behave in her absence, when they were trusted alone in the nursery, with nobody to keep them in order, or to see what they were doing, especially now, as their grandmamma had been taken ill, and would require to be kept quiet.

Harry sat in his chair, and might have been painted as the very picture of a good boy during nearly twenty minutes after Mrs. Crabtree departed; and Laura placed herself opposite to him, trying to follow so excellent an example, while they scarcely spoke above a whisper, wondering what could be the matter with their grandmamma, and wishing for once to see Mrs. Crabtree again, that they might hear how she was. Any one who had observed Harry and Laura at that time would have wondered to see two such quiet, excellent, respectable children, and wished that all little boys and girls were made upon the same pattern; but presently they began to think that probably Lady Harriet was not so very ill, as no more bells had rung during several minutes, and Harry ventured to look about for some better amusement than sitting still.

At this moment Laura unluckily perceived, on the table near where they sat, a pair of Mrs. Crabtree's best scissors, which she had been positively forbid to touch. The long troublesome ringlets were as usual hanging over her eyes in a most teasing manner, so she thought what a good opportunity this might be to shorten them a very little, not above an inch or two; and without considering a moment longer, she slipped upon tiptoe, with a frightened look, round the table, and picked up the scissors in her hand; then hastening towards a looking-glass, she began snipping off the ends of her hair. Laura was much diverted to see it showering down upon the floor, so she cut and cut on, while the curls fell thicker and faster, till at last the whole floor was covered with them, and scarcely a hair left upon her head. Harry went into fits of laughing when he perceived what a ridiculous figure Laura had made of herself, and he turned her round and round to see the havoc she had made, saying, –

'You should give all this hair to Mr. Mills, the upholsterer, to stuff grandmamma's arm-chair with! At any rate, Laura, if Mrs. Crabtree is ever so angry, she can hardly pull you by the hair of the head again! What a sound sleep you will have to-night, with no hard curl-papers to torment you!'

Harry had been told five hundred times never to touch the candles, and threatened with twenty different punishments if he ever ventured to do so; but now he amused himself with trying to snuff one till he snuffed it out. Then he lighted it again, and tried the experiment once more, but again the teasing candle went out, as if on purpose to plague him; so he felt quite provoked. Having lighted it once more, Harry prepared to carry the candlestick with him towards the inner nursery, though afraid to make the smallest noise, in case it might be taken from him. Before he had gone five steps, down dropped the extinguisher, then followed the snuffers with a great crash; but Laura seemed too busy cropping her ringlets to notice what was going on. All the way along upon the floor Harry let fall a perfect shower of hot wax, which spotted the nursery carpet from the table where he had found the candle into the next room, where he disappeared, and shut the door, that no one might interfere with what he liked to do.

After he had been absent some time, the door was hastily opened again, and Laura felt surprised to see Harry come back with his face as red as a stick of sealing-wax, and his large eyes staring wider than they had ever stared before, with a look of rueful consternation.

'What is the matter?' exclaimed Laura, in a terrified voice. 'Has anything dreadful happened?' Why do you look so frightened and so surprised?'

'Oh dear! oh dear! what shall I do?' cried Harry, who seemed scarcely to know how he spoke, or where he was. 'I don't know what to do, Laura!'

'What can be the matter? do tell me at once, Harry,' said Laura, shaking with apprehension. 'Speak as fast as you can!'

'Will you not tell Mrs. Crabtree, nor grandmamma, nor anybody else?' cried Harry, bursting into tears. 'I am so very, very sorry, and so frightened! Laura! do you know, I took a candle into the next room, merely to play with it.'

'Well! go on, Harry! go on! What did you do with the candle?'

'I only put it on the bed for a single minute, to see how the flame would look there. Well! do you know, it blazed away famously, and then all the bedclothes began burning, too! Oh! there is such a terrible fire in the next room! you never saw anything like it! What shall we do? If old Andrew were to come up, do you think he could put it out? I have shut the door, that Mrs. Crabtree may not see the flames. Be sure, Laura, to tell nobody but Andrew.'

Laura became terrified at the way she saw poor Harry in, but when she opened the door to find out the real state of affairs, oh! what a dreadful sight was there! All the beds were on fire, while bright, red flames were blazing up to the roof of the room with a fierce, roaring noise, which it was perfectly frightful to hear. She screamed aloud with terror at this alarming scene, while Harry did all he could to quiet her, and even put his hand over her mouth, that her cries might not be heard. Laura now struggled to get loose, and called louder and louder, till at last every maid in the house came racing upstairs, three steps at a time, to know what was the matter. Immediately upon seeing the flames, they all began screaming too, in such a loud, discordant way, that it sounded as if a whole flight of crows had come into the passages. Never was there such an uproar heard in the house before; for the walls echoed with a general cry of 'Fire! fire! fire!'

Up flew Mrs. Crabtree towards the nursery like a sky-rocket, scolding furiously, talking louder than all the others put together, and asking who had set the house on fire, while Harry and Laura scarcely knew whether to be most frightened for the raging flames or the raging Mrs. Crabtree; but, in the meantime, they both shrank into the smallest possible size, and hid themselves behind a door.

During all this confusion, old Andrew luckily remembered that in the morning there had been a great washing in the laundry, where large tubs full of water were standing, so he called to the few maids who had any of their senses remaining, desiring them to assist in carrying up some buckets, that they might be emptied on the burning beds, to extinguish the flames if possible. Everybody was now in a hurry, and all elbowing each other out of the way, while it was most extraordinary to see how old Andrew exerted himself, as if he had been a fireman all his life, while Mrs. Marmalade, the fat cook, who could hardly carry herself upstairs in general, actively assisted to bring up the great heavy tubs, and to pour them out like a cascade upon the burning curtains, till the nursery floor looked like a duck-pond.

Meantime, Harry and Laura added to the confusion as much as they could, and were busier than anybody, stealing down the back stairs whenever Mrs. Crabtree was not in sight, and filling their little jugs with water, which they brought up, as fast as possible, and dashed upon the flames, till at last, it is to be feared, they began to feel quite amused with the bustle, and to be almost sorry when the conflagration diminished. At one time, Laura very nearly set her frock on fire, as she ventured too near, but Harry pulled her back, and then courageously advanced to discharge a shower from his own little jug, remaining stationary to watch the effect, till his face was almost scorched.

At last the fire became less and less, till it went totally out, but not before the nursery furniture had been reduced to perfect ruins, besides which, Betty had her arm sadly burned in the confusion. Mrs. Marmalade's cap was completely destroyed, and Mrs. Crabtree's best gown had so large a hole burned in the skirt that she never could wear it again.

After all was quiet, and the fire completely extinguished, Major Graham took Laura downstairs to Lady Harriet's dressing-room, that she might tell the whole particulars of how this alarming accident happened in the nursery; for nobody could guess what had caused so sudden and dreadful a fire, which seemed to have been as unexpected as a flash of lightning.

Lady Harriet had felt so terrified by the noise and confusion that she was out of bed, sitting up in an arm-chair, supported by pillows, when Laura entered, at the sight of whom, with her well-cropped head, she uttered an exclamation of perfect amazement.

'Why! who on earth is that? Laura, my dear child! what has become of all your hair? Were your curls burned off in the fire? or did the fright make you grow bald? What is the meaning of all this?'

Laura turned perfectly crimson with shame and distress, for she now felt convinced of her own great misconduct about the scissors and curls; but she had been taught on all occasions to speak the truth, and would rather have died than told a lie, or even allowed any person to believe what was not true. Therefore she answered in a low, frightened voice, while the tears came into her eyes, 'My hair has not been burned off, grandmamma! but – but —'

'Well, child! speak out!' said Lady Harriet impatiently. 'Did some hairdresser come to the house and rob you?'

'Or, are you like the ladies of Carthage, who gave their long hair for bows and arrows?' asked Major Graham. 'I never saw such a little fright in my life as you look now; but tell us all about it.'

'I have been quite as naughty as Harry!' answered Laura, bursting into tears, and sobbing with grief; 'I was cutting off my hair with Mrs. Crabtree's scissors all the time that he was setting the nursery on fire!'

'Did any mortal ever hear of two such little torments!' exclaimed Major Graham, hardly able to help laughing. 'I wonder if anybody else in the world has such mischievous children!'

'It is certainly very strange that you and Harry never can contrive to be three hours out of a scrape!' said Lady Harriet gravely; 'now Frank, on the contrary, never forgets what I bid him do. You might suppose he carried Mrs. Crabtree in his pocket, to remind him constantly of his duty; but there are not two such boys in the world as Frank!'

'No,' added Major Graham; 'Harry set the house on fire, and Frank will set the Thames on fire!'

When Laura saw Uncle David put on one of his funny looks, while he spoke in this way to Lady Harriet, she almost forgot her former fright, and became surprised to observe her grandmamma busily preparing what she called a coach-wheel, which had been often given as a treat to Harry and herself when they were particularly good. This delightful wheel was manufactured by taking a whole round slice of the loaf, in the centre of which was placed a large teaspoonful of jelly, after which long spokes of marmalade, jam, and honey, were made to diverge most tastefully in every direction towards the crust; and Laura watched the progress of this business with great interest and anxiety, wondering if it could be hoped that her grandmamma really meant to forgive all her misconduct during the day.

'That coach-wheel is, of course, meant for me!' said Major Graham, pretending to be very hungry, and looking slyly at Laura. 'It cannot possibly be intended for our little hairdresser here!'

'Yes, it is!' answered Lady Harriet, smiling. 'I have some thoughts of excusing Laura this time, because she always tells me the truth, without attempting to conceal any foolish thing she does. It will be very long before she has any hair to cut off again, so I hope she may be older and wiser by that time, especially considering that every looking-glass she sees for six months will make her feel ashamed of herself. She certainly deserves some reward for having prevented the house to-night from being burned to the ground.'

'I am glad you think so, because here is a shilling that has been burning in my pocket for the last few minutes, as I wished to bestow it on Laura for having saved all our lives; and if she had behaved still better, I might perhaps have given her a gold watch!'

Laura was busily employed in eating her coach-wheel, and trying to fancy what the gold watch would have looked like which she might probably have got from Uncle David, when suddenly the door burst open, and Mrs. Crabtree hurried into the room, with a look of surprise and alarm, her face as red as a poppy, and her eyes fixed on the hole in her best gown, while she spoke so loud and angrily that Laura almost trembled.

'If you please, my lady! where can Master Harry be? I cannot find him in any corner! – we have been searching all over the house, upstairs and downstairs, in vain. Not a garret or a closet but has been ransacked, and nobody can guess what has become of him!'

'Did you look up the chimney, Mrs. Crabtree?' asked Major Graham, laughing to see how excited she looked.

' 'Deed, sir! it is no joke,' answered Mrs. Crabtree sulkily; 'I am almost afraid Master Harry has been burned in the fire! The last time Betty saw him he was throwing a jug of water into the flames, and no one has ever seen or heard of him since! There is a great many ashes and cinders lying about the room, and —'

'Do you think, in sober seriousness, Mrs. Crabtree, that Harry would melt away like a wax-doll, without asking anybody to extinguish him?' said Major Graham, smiling. 'No! no! little boys are not quite so easily disposed of. I shall find Harry in less than five minutes, if he is above ground.'

But Uncle David was quite mistaken in expecting to discover Harry so easily, for he searched and searched in vain. He looked into every possible or impossible place – the library, the kitchen, the garrets, the laundry, the drawing-room – all without success; he peeped under the tables, behind the curtains, over the beds, beneath the pillows, and into Mrs. Crabtree's bonnet-box; he even opened the tea-chest, and looked out at the window, in case Harry had tumbled over; but nowhere could he be found.

'Not a mouse is stirring!' exclaimed Major Graham, beginning now to look exceedingly grave and anxious. 'This is very strange! The house-door is locked; therefore, unless Harry made his escape through the key-hole, he must be here! It is most unaccountable what the little pickle can have done with himself!'

When Major Graham chose to exert his voice, it was as loud as a trumpet, and could be heard half a mile off; so he now called out, like thunder, from the top of the stairs to the bottom, saying, 'Hullo, Harry! Hullo! Come here, my boy! Nobody shall hurt you! Harry! where are you?'

Uncle David waited to listen, but all was still – no answer could be heard, and there was not a sound in the house, except poor Laura at the bottom of the stairs, sobbing with grief and terror about Harry having been lost, and Mrs. Crabtree grumbling angrily to herself on account of the large hole in her best gown.

By this time Lady Harriet nearly fainted with fatigue, for she was so very old, and had been ill all day; so she grew worse and worse, till everybody said she must go to bed, and try if it would be possible to fall asleep, assuring her that Harry must soon be found, as nothing particular could have happened to him, or some person would have seen it.

'Indeed, my lady! Master Harry is just like a bad shilling, that is sure to come back,' said Mrs. Crabtree, helping her to undress, while she continued to talk the whole time about the fire, showing her own unfortunate gown, describing the trouble she had taken to save the house from being burned, and always ending every sentence with a wish that she could lay hands on Harry, to punish him as he deserved.

'The truth is, I just spoil and indulge the children too much, my lady!' added Mrs. Crabtree, in a self-satisfied tone of voice. 'I really blame myself often for being over-easy and kind.'

'You have nothing to accuse yourself of in that respect,' answered Lady Harriet, unable to help smiling.

'Your ladyship is very good to say so. Major Graham is so fond of our young people that it is lucky they have some one to keep them in order. I shall make a duty, my lady, of being more strict than ever. Master Harry must be made an example of this time!' added Mrs. Crabtree, angrily glancing at the hole in her gown. 'I shall teach him to remember this day the longest hour he has to live!'

'Harry will not forget it anyhow,' answered Lady Harriet languidly. 'Perhaps, Mrs. Crabtree, we might as well not be severe with the poor boy on this occasion. As the old proverb says, "There is no use in pouring water on a drowned mouse." Harry has got a sad fright for his pains; and, at all events, you must find him first, before he can be punished. Where can the poor child be hid?'

'I would give sixpence to find out that, my lady!' answered Mrs. Crabtree, helping Lady Harriet into bed; after which she closed the shutters, put out the candles, and left the room, angrily muttering, 'Master Harry cares no more for me than the poker cares for the tongs; but I shall teach him another story soon.'

Lady Harriet now feebly closed her eyes, being quite exhausted, and was beginning to feel the pleasant, confused sensation that people have before going to sleep, when some noise made her suddenly start quite awake. She sat up in bed to listen, but could not be sure whether it had been a great noise at a distance or a little noise in the room; so after waiting two or three minutes, she sank back upon the pillows and tried to forget it. Again, however, she distinctly heard something rustling in the bed-curtains, and opened her eyes to see what could be the matter, but all was dark. Something seemed to be breathing very near her, however, and the curtains shook worse than before, till Lady Harriet became really alarmed.

'It must surely be a cat in the room!' thought she, hastily pulling the bell-rope, till it nearly came down. 'That tiresome little animal will make such a noise, I shall not be able to sleep all night!'

The next minute Lady Harriet was startled to hear a loud sob close beside her; and when everybody rushed upstairs to ask what was the matter, they brought candles to search the room; and there was Harry! He lay doubled up in a corner, and crying as if his heart would break, yet still endeavouring not to be seen; for Harry always thought it a terrible disgrace to cry, and would have concealed himself anywhere rather than be observed weeping. Laura burst into tears also, when she saw what red eyes and pale cheeks Harry had; but Mrs. Crabtree lost no time in pulling him out of his place, being quite impatient to begin her scold and to produce her tawse, though she received a sad disappointment on this occasion, as Uncle David unexpectedly interfered to get him off.

'Come now! Mrs. Crabtree,' said he good-naturedly; 'put up the tawse for this time; you are rather too fond of the leather. Harry seems really sorry and frightened, so we must be merciful. The cataract of tears he is shedding now would have extinguished the fire if it had come in time! Harry is like a culprit with the rope about his neck; but he shall not be executed. Let me be judge and jury in this case; and my sentence is a very dreadful one. Harry must sleep all to-night in the burned nursery, having no other covering than the burned blankets, with large holes in them, that he may never forget

' "THE TERRIBLE FIRE." '

# Charlotte Barton (1797–1862)

The earliest children's books with Australian settings were written in Britain, largely by writers and illustrators who had never been to Australia. Many were adventure stories by writers such as R. M. Ballantyne and W. H. G. Kingston; some, like 'The Happy Grandmother and her Grandchildren who went to Australia', one of the *Amusing and Instructive Tales* by 'Peter Prattle' (published in London by Munday, *c.* 1835) combined domestic felicity with colonial propaganda. That books ends with the grandmother feeling at home 'in this distant land. I have sometimes thought it was rather hard that people willing to work could not get food in England. But I can see the hand of divine providence in this. The clever, industrious and honest people, who are driven from England by poverty, are settling in Asia, Africa and America; and who can calculate the good they will do? I sometimes think', she continues, 'that all the world will become one England –

and that, too, when England is far better than she is now.'

It is in this context that 'the first work written in the Colony expressly for Children' (as the preface claims) should be read. Charlotte Barton was born in London, but was married and brought up her children in Australia (her daughter, Louisa Atkinson, was the first Australian female novelist). *A Mother's Offering* is essentially a didactic work, written on the British model of a dialogue between mother and children. There is a good deal of natural history ('Extraordinary Sounds', 'Sea Shells') and geography, some short instructive stories, and factual accounts of shipwreck and settlement. From our current perspective, perhaps the most interesting material is Mrs Saville's account of the aborigines, reprinted here. Whatever the truth or rumour in the account, it speaks volumes about social attitudes, and of the encounter between two cultures.

## from *A Mother's Offering to her Children: by a Lady, Long Resident in New South Wales* (1841)

### ANECDOTES OF THE ABORIGINES OF NEW SOUTH WALES

*Mrs. S.* – Little Sally the black child has been accidentally killed.

*Clara.* – Oh! Mamma, do you know how?

*Mrs. S.* – She was playing in the barn, which is only a temporary one; and pulled down a heavy prop of wood upon herself. It fell on her temple; and killed her immediately.

*Emma.* – Do you not think her mother will be very sorry, when she hears of it?

*Mrs. S.* – Alas! my dear children, her mother also met with an untimely death. These poor uncivilized people, most frequently meet with some deplorable end through giving way to unrestrained passions.

*Julius.* – Oh! do tell us all you know about little Sally and her mother; if you please, Mamma? It will make the evening pass so pleasantly; and I will be drawing plenty of animals, to fill the little managerie I am making.

*Lucy* (kissing her Mamma). – Do tell us dear Mamma? My sisters are going to work; and may I set your work-box in order; and then we shall all be so happy.

*Mrs. S.* warmly returned the fond embrace of her little Lucy; and after they were all seated, began the following narrative: –

### *History of Nanny and her Children*

The mother of the poor little black girl, who has lately met with so dreadful a death, was called Nanny. I do not know her native name. She was a remarkably fine, well-formed young woman.

Surely Clara and Emma you must remember Nanny coming occasionally, with other blacks? The last time I saw her she had this same little Sally with her; who could just then run alone.

*Clara.* – Oh yes, Mamma! it was a pretty, fat, little brown girl, quite naked.

*Emma.* – And I remember we asked you to give her a little frock: but before you could get one they were gone.

*Mrs. S.* – That was the last time I saw the mother. The child was a half-cast, or brown child, as you call them; and soon after the time you speak of, Jane D . . . . . . . n, a young married woman, who had lost her only child sometime before, took a fancy to little Sally. And her mother agreed to leave the child; as soon as it was weaned. You know the black children are not weaned so soon as white children: most probably from the uncertainty and difficulty in procuring proper food. Though I have remarked that the babies will eat voraciously, at an age when a tender white babe would not touch such food.

*Clara.* – Mamma, I am sure some of the black children are more than four years old, when they are weaned.

*Mrs. S.* – They are my love. But we will continue our narrative.

When little Sally was about two years old, she was weaned; and taken to her future home. It was evening when the child was left; and she was naturally much distressed, when she found herself deserted by her mother. Jane was soon after, going to put her to bed: but she was greatly alarmed at the idea of being put into a bed and said with much eagerness, 'Bail nangarrie waddie' (not sleep in a bed) pointing to the bed 'Nangarrie like-a-that,' (sleep like that,) curling her little body round on the ground floor of the hut. To please her, Jane spread a blanket for her on the floor; and poor little sorrowing Sally covered it about her.

Several times during the night, Jane and her husband heard the poor little girl moaning; as if she were lying lamenting her deserted state.

The man, as was usual, opened the door of the hut very early; and little Sally went and stood outside; looking in all directions; and uttering the most piercing coo-ee-es imaginable. Jane assured me, that she was astonished that such a baby could utter such loud and piercing sounds. The forest echoed and rang with them; and Jane who is a kind-hearted young woman, felt her heart thrill with pity and fear.

*Lucy.* – Oh! Mamma that is just what I should do, if I lost you: cry as loud as ever I could; and be so very, very sorry! What did they do for the poor little girl?

*Mrs. S.* – They tried to console her; for she was very much distressed, when she found her mother did not reply to her coo-ee-es. She would frequently wander about; and call in this wild way; so peculiar to the aborigines: but her mother was far away.

At length time in some degree reconciled poor little Sally to her new parents and altered state of life: when the tribe came again; and with them her mother.

The child immediately recognised her; and you my dear children, can judge, better than I can describe, the joy she felt at again seeing her. The poor little babe rushed into its mother's arms; but the unnatural mother sent her child from her. Poor little Sally screamed and was refractory; when her mother whipt her severely, and left her.

*Emma.* – Oh! Mamma, this is too shocking! to leave her little child among strangers; and then whip it for being so glad to see her again; and for wishing to go with her. Ah! Mamma, I am very sorry for the poor little thing. I wish you had taken it from such a bad mother; and then we would have done all we could to have made it forget, it ever had such a naughty, cruel mother. Why did she go near, to teaze her poor little girl?

*Mrs. S* – I quite agree with you Emma, that she was very blamable to go near the place; to unsettle her child; but she was not in many respects a bad mother; as I will tell you more about soon.

Jane treated her adopted child very kindly and tenderly; dressed it well; and kept it very clean. I saw it when it was about four years old; and it was an interesting child; with large black eyes, black curling hair, a pleasant laughing countenance, fat, and had all the appearance of being happy. Perhaps her mother considered that she was better situated with Jane, than she could be wandering about the forests, in search of precarious food. You know at the best, the women and children are badly off.

*Clara.* – Notwithstanding, Mamma, it seems unnatural for a mother to part with her child. Though I know there is a little boy, who his parents wish you to take: but I think if I were ever so poor, I would not part with my children. Did Nanny ever go again, Mamma?

*Mrs. S.* – More than once, my dear: when the same scenes took place: affection and tears on the part of the child; and severity on that of the mother.

One time when the blacks were encamped in the neighbourhood of Mrs. D . . . . . . . n's hut, they heard a dreadful screaming in the night; and the husband arose and opened the door: he could not see any thing; and concluded the blacks had been drinking; and were fighting. Not wishing to interfere with them, while in that state; he closed the door; and the noise soon ceased: but in the morning they found poor Nanny had been murdered!

It appeared a black man named Woombi (Nanny's half-brother) had been quarrelling with her, and was beating her: she fled for protection near the hut; when he threw a spear after her; which entered the back of her neck; she continued to run, with the spear in her neck: but was soon overtaken by the furious Woombi; who struck her on the head with his tomahawk; and soon dispatched her. I was told she was a dreadful sight in the morning!

*Clara.* – Poor thing! what became of her?

*Mrs. S.* – The blacks dug a grave near the spot; and buried her in a sitting posture; putting her tomahawk, pannikin, net, bangalee, and indeed, *all* her little possessions, with her in the grave.

*Lucy.* – How strange to bury all her things!

*Mrs. S.* – It is their custom, and they appear much shocked at the idea of the clothes, &c., of a deceased person being kept, after their interment. The tribe belonging to the neighbourhood where our property is situated, were very much attached to your dear lamented father. You know they never mention the name of a deceased person; but they were giving me to understand, the regret and sympathy they felt at his loss. I had the locket with me at the time, which has a lock of all our hair in it. I showed this to them, pointing out his (to us) much valued brown curl; when they uttered a piercing cry; and all turned away; holding down their heads a short time: when they looked up I saw they were in tears. One of the women stepped aside; and whispered to me 'Bail you show that to blacks ebber any more missus.' This of course I promised to refrain from. I was much surprised and effected at their manner; having wished to give them pleasure. It was six years after our bereavement.

In a savage state they bury the living infant with its deceased mother: sometimes when several months old!

*Emma.* – How terrible!

*Mrs. S.* – Yes. They place the living child in the grave, by the side of its dead mother; and after covering it with earth, lay heavy stones upon it!

*Clara.* – Poor little creatures, how cruel! Do you think it is ever done now Mamma?

*Mrs. S.* – No doubt it is, far in the interior; where their ancient customs are still kept up. The poor babies, appear to be thought very little about.

*Clara.* – You know Jenny has left three infants to perish in the bush; because, she said, it was too much trouble to rear them: and when our cook asked her if native dogs had eaten them, she replied, 'I believe.' And I am almost sure she killed that little black baby girl, she had sometime ago; for it suddenly disappeared; and when we questioned her about it, she hung down her head and looked very foolish; and at last said, 'Tumble down.' It was buried in one of our paddocks; and some stones laid over the grave: when we were taking a walk, with our nurse, we met one of our men, who opened the grave; and it was evident the body had been burned; for there were remains of burnt bones, ashes, and hair.

*Emma.* – Billy the black man killed one of his little babies.

*Mrs. S.* – Yes, he took it by its feet and dashed its brains out against a tree. Some however, are very kind parents: but I do not think they are in general, to their infants. I remember a tall woman, quite a stranger, coming with a black infant, of less than a month old. It was so ugly and covered with long hair, as not to look like any thing human: but worse than all, the poor little creature had been terribly burned, by the mother putting it too near the fire; and falling asleep. From the ankle to the hip, on one side, it was nearly burned to the bone. It had been done some days; and the fire seemed out. I therefore had it dressed with lard spread on rags: soon after, I heard the bandages were off. The negligent mother had left it; and one of their hungry dogs, attracted by the smell of the lard, had torn off the rags; and dragged them away; notwithstanding they had been tied on carefully. They were replaced; but the cruel mother appeared quite indifferent to the sufferings of her tender babe.

About a week after, I understood it was dead: probably made away with.

*Emma.* – What tribe did she belong to, Mamma?

*Mrs. S.* – I do not recollect: there were a great many tribes collecting; to the number of perhaps 200 blacks on our estate: they were assembling to fight: and we found it a great nuisance. Bullocks and horses are very much frightened at them; and the men found it almost impossible to continue their ploughing.

*Emma.* – It is very odd, that animals should know the difference between black and white people.

*Mrs. S.* – I do not suppose that it is their color altogether. It may be the unpleasant smell which they have; from want of cleanliness: and constantly rubbing themselves with the fat of the animals which they kill.

*Julius.* – Did they fight, Mamma?

*Mrs. S.* – Yes; but their battle will furnish a subject for another evening: we will return to poor Nanny.

*Emma.* – Do you think the women were sorry for poor Nanny, Mamma?

*Mrs. S.* – Yes; I think they are kind to each other.

The son of a cottager residing at Wingelo, saw the ground had been lately dug up in the bush, not far from where they lived: curiosity led him to examine into the cause: when he found the body of a little black infant: he ran home with it, saying, 'Look, mother, I have found a little black baby.' His mother made him take it back instantly; and bury it, as it was before. She then went to look for its mother; she soon found her, sitting with her chin resting between her knees; crouching before a fire: another woman sat near her; who was (according to their ideas on the subject) endeavouring to draw away the pain her friend felt. This was done, by laying a string across the body of the sick woman, where the pain was most violent; the other end was held by her friend; who kept drawing it across her lips, till they were sadly cut; and bled very profusely: while she was doing this, she kept up a mournful monotonous chaunt. The cottager left her to prepare some tea; she returned with it in about a quarter of an hour; when she found the woman was dead; and several black women were preparing her body for interment. They tied her knees to her chest; and her arms to her sides; by passing strips of stringy bark round her. A hole was then dug; and she was put into it; and her dead baby by her side.

*Clara.* – Poor woman! how very soon they buried her. Did they carve the trees about?

*Mrs. S.* – I do not know: but I think the blacks in the civilised parts of the country, are too indolent now to take so much trouble.

The grave on the side of our hill, must have been made at least 23 years ago; and yet the carving in many of the trees is quite visible: though we can only from that circumstance, conjecture where the grave was.

*Lucy.* – Did poor little Sally know her Mother was killed, Mamma?

*Mrs. S.* – I do not think she did my love. I believe it happened about a year after Mrs. D. had adopted her.

*Emma.* – It was very unnatural for her brother to kill her, Mamma: what do you think they quarrelled about?

*Mrs. S.* – The blacks have a great objection to their women living among white people. Nanny was particularly fond of this; and it made the blacks angry. Indeed Nanny would have married an overseer to a Mrs. J. several years ago. The man was very anxious to marry her: but Governor Darling would not allow it. At this time she had a little brown boy, whom she called George. He was a fine little boy; some months older than you, Clara. One day she brought him for me to look at. I admired him very much; and gave her a few clothes for him. Clara was in long petticoats. Nanny asked me to let her see 'piccaninnie's' head: accordingly the cap was put back and the little golden locks exhibited. Nanny was in exstacies; she clapped her hands and exclaimed 'All same Georgey Missus.'

*Emma.* – How droll. I dare say the babies heads were not at all alike: most likely Clara looked like a wax doll beside Georgey.

*Julius.* – What became of him, Mamma?

*Mrs. S.* – When he was about three or four years old, Nanny came one day without him; and told me Mrs. J. had sent for him to Sydney, to put him to school: he remained there some time.

Afterwards, I heard he was acting as a little shepherd at Bombarlowah; over a flock of sheep belonging to the person his mother would have married.

I believe he still lives with the same person; and I heard he had given George some sheep and cattle of his own.

Nanny was very fond and proud of her little George, before he went to school she used to wash him and comb his hair; which was light and curly.

*Julius.* – Where did she get a comb from Mamma?

*Mrs. S.* – She used to carry a broken comb, which had probably been used to comb a horse's mane.

*Clara.* – Not a very fine one then: but better than none; and shewed she wished to keep her little boy clean.

*Mrs. S.* – One day when the tribe was encamped near the house; and Nanny and her child nearer than any of the rest: I went into the store at the back of the house, with the cook and your nurse. Suddenly little George gave a piercing shriek. I sent the nurse to see what had happened; and found Nanny had bitten the child severely on the back of his arm. She looked very much ashamed, when we reproved her for it; and said, piccaninnie wanted to suck.

*Lucy.* – Mamma, that is just what pussy does, when she wishes to wean her kittens.

*Mrs. S.* – It reminded me of a cat Lucy; and I felt quite disgusted with Nanny: but upon the whole her children bore evident signs of her affection and care.

*Clara.* – How curious it is that the black children do not change their teeth, Mamma.

*Mrs. S.* – It is very remarkable. I have taken a great deal of pains to question both parents and children; and they all have told me that they do not. This may account for the large size of their babies' teeth: which we have thought so extraordinary.

Some of the half caste children change their teeth; others do not.

*Emma.* – Jane must have been sadly distressed at poor little Sally's death; she was so much attached to her.

*Mrs. S.* – She was, my dear. She told me she would never take another child. Sally for some time had given her a good deal of trouble and additional work: but for the last few years her love for the child, who was very docile and affectionate, had quite overbalanced any trouble she might have had with her; and she found her a great comfort. I suppose the child was about six years old when the accident happened. Jane was from home; and her husband ran immediately for Dr. A., who told me the man was as much distressed, as if it had been his own child.

*Emma.* – Where was it buried, Mamma?

*Mrs. S.* – They opened poor Nanny's grave, and placed her by her mother.

*Clara.* – If the blacks had been about, they would have been very much terrified at this: you know they are fearful of even going near any place, where any one has been buried.

*Mrs. S.* – Yes, we had an instance of that, when Dr. F. wanted one of the blacks to dig up the bones of a black; who had been interred on our land many years before. The black man looked dreadfully shocked; and exclaimed 'Too much *gerun* me:' (meaning frightened) 'jump up white fellow long time ago.' You know they think the white people have once been black.

*Clara.* – Yes; I have heard of two people, whom they think they recognise as their departed black friends; and call them by their names, when speaking of them.

*Emma.* – How odd: perhaps they think white people have once been black, because they see those who die look pale.

*Mrs. S.* – It would be difficult to ascertain what gave rise to such an idea.

*Julius.* – I wonder Sally was not buried in the Church Yard.

*Mrs. S.* – She was not a Christian, my dear. Jane had neglected to have her christened; though she told me she had intended it.

Another melancholy instance of *procrastination.* Oh! my children! how very, very fatal is this habit of putting off from day to day, what should be done immediately; for we know not the day, nor the hour, when time may cease for us; and we be summoned into eternity.

# Harriet Mozley (1803–1851)

With *The Fairy Bower* British children's books are maturing; the book at once sets out to show the behaviour of children 'realistically...rather than to exhibit moral portraiture for unreserved imitation or avoidance', but also to have a serious moral *debate*. Thus, while it is an early example of the family story for children (containing echoes of Jane Austen, notably *Mansfield Park*), it is also infused with serious matters: Harriet Mozley was the sister of John Henry Newman and was involved with the Oxford Movement, which attempted to steer a middle course between Roman Catholicism and Evangelism. When John Henry became a Roman Catholic, Harriet never spoke to him again, but, equally, her writings (*The Fairy Bower* is a prime example) were intended as a critique of low church attitudes.

At a Twelfth Night party, Mary Anne pretends that the idea for decorating one of the rooms as a bower is hers, rather than Grace's. Her cousin, Emily, eventually exposes the fraud. There is a large cast, generally handled without stereotyping, although the satire is obvious enough. Mary Anne and her siblings have a strict, low-church governess, Miss Newmarsh, whose methods produce children who are sentimental, pious or, in Mary Anne's case, morally suspect. This has seemed to some readers, including Charlotte Yonge, to be negative. A sequel, *The Lost Brooch*, extends the attack.

This extract, in its subtle walking of a line between truth and lies, and Mary Anne's navigation of dangerous conversational waters, demonstrates the depth of the book. The moralizing has to be deduced and formed by the reader, rather than being given, but would almost certainly have been obvious to contemporary readers.

*The Fairy Bower*, then, reacts against the excesses (and perceived self-satisfaction) of the evangelical writers by introducing an alternative religious viewpoint, rather than, as in *Holiday House* (p. 49), either ameliorating or rebelling. Its manner, as novel of character rather than episodic moral tale, moves the children's book into new territory.

## from *The Fairy Bower, or The History of a Month. A Tale* (1841)

### CHAPTER XXV

*The trumpets sound; stand close, the Queen is coming!*
Shakespeare

The fairy bower had abundantly attracted the notice of the elder part of the company. Every body was full of admiration: it was visited and inspected, the flowers examined, and the whole pronounced elegantly devised and executed. A party of the seniors were talking it over in the drawing-room the beginning of the evening, and it was mentioned as entirely the work of the young people – the idea only suggested the night before. It did indeed seem incredible; but a dozen pair of hands, more or less willing, can sometimes effect wonders. Lord and Lady Musgrove were especially pleased, and the latter asked if it was Emily's notion. She was told, No – her cousin Mary Anne Duff's, who was staying in the house.

'Oh,' said Lady Musgrove, 'I have been looking at the Duffs; they are fine girls, and our Isabella has taken a great fancy to one – is that Mary Anne?'

Miss Newmarsh said she rather thought not; she believed Constance was her favourite.

Lady Musgrove said she should like to speak to them some time in the evening, especially to the young designer.

'Well,' said one of the gentlemen, 'it really is a most tasteful plan, and I think the fair *artiste* should receive some honour at our hands – what do you say,' said he, 'to crowning her with her own flowers?'

It was thought a very pretty idea, and some of the party walked into the next room to arrange it. It was near the end of some game, and these gentlemen had a slight conference with Reginald Freemantle. He took to the idea immediately, and undertook the whole management. At a proper moment he stepped forward and made a loud flourish of trumpets, which was an art he excelled in, and having obtained silence, he made a proclamation, demanding in the name of the aristocracy of the other room, that Mary Anne, the fair *artiste* of the Fairy Bower, should be forthwith consigned to his hands; for it was the will and pleasure of the higher powers that more than the praise of words should be awarded to one so accomplished, and that he was the happy herald commissioned to proclaim, that she was to be crowned 'Queen of the Fairy Bower,' in the sight of the assembled multitude. He then summoned all, high and low, to witness the coronation of the Queen of the Fairy Bower, and ended by again demanding the fair Mary Anne to be brought forward. He then closed with his military flourish. Reginald's proclamation was sufficiently clear, yet no one stirred. Emily, Grace, and George were standing near together, as they were on the point of proposing some new arrangement. 'Oh, Emily!' cried Grace, in a low voice, 'then you did not speak to Mary Anne!'

'No,' said Emily, 'she was gone down stairs, and I found them all waiting for me here.'

'Well,' thought Grace, 'then it cannot be helped; we tried to do something – that is a comfort.'

Again came a flourish, and the herald called upon Emily, the lady of the revels, and her lady-in-waiting, the fair Grace, forthwith to conduct Mary Anne, the Queen of the Fairy Bower, to his presence.

There was again a pause. – 'Oh, Emily,' whispered Grace, in great agitation, 'what can we do? we must go!'

'Grace,' said Emily, decidedly, '*I will not*, whatever are the consequences.'

Poor Grace! all fell upon her – what could she do! After waiting due time, the herald repeated his summons. It was really a very solemn scene, and to the three individuals in question must have been, from different causes, a most exciting one. The consequences rushed across Grace's mind; she saw the whole transaction exposed, and Mary Anne publicly degraded, and without another thought she turned to George and asked him to take an answer from them, any thing he chose to say, and to ask permission to depute himself and Campbell to the office proposed for herself and Emily.

George stepped forward, and in due form announced that he had the honour of bearing a message from the ladies Emily and Grace – that they begged to assure the herald it was no disrespect to the higher powers, that they had not immediately hastened to perform their commands; but that their feelings were so excited on the occasion of the unexampled honour, proposed to be conferred on their amiable friend, that they entreated to be allowed to name his unworthy self and his cousin Campbell, as deputies in their place. The herald highly commended the feelings of the young ladies, and assured them they would be equally appreciated by his illustrious employers. Here came another flourish of trumpets, and George withdrew in due form. He sought Campbell, and they conducted Mary Anne between them, across the room, before the herald. – 'Fair maiden,' said he, 'the trumpet of Fame has announced to the puissant powers of the other room, that yon brilliant bower, commonly designated "The Fairy Bower," boasts its origin from the elegant stores of your mind, and is the child of your genius; say, fair maiden, does Fame speak truly?'

Mary Anne said nothing; she hung her head and looked what is called foolish, but her manner and appearance was not any thing unusual, and excited no remark among either friends or strangers. Finding he got no answer, the herald continued, 'Fair maiden, be assured we all respect your modesty and humility, nor shall they be disturbed by the rudeness of forms and of courts. Your maidenly silence shall be accepted as it is meant, and proclamation shall be issued accordingly.' He then in due form announced that the fair Mary Anne, now before them, 'is the true and sole architect of the Fairy Bower, and it is the sovereign will and pleasure of the puissant powers of the other room, that she shall forthwith be crowned Queen of the same: I therefore hereby cite the ladies before mentioned, Emily and Grace, and in the name of my illustrious employers command them, to prepare from the fairest of the wreaths of yon bower, a chaplet for the fair brows of the new Queen.' – And here came another flourish.

Grace again whispered to Emily, and Emily again refused to assist, – 'Oh, Emily!' cried Grace, much distressed, 'is it kind to me?'

'I don't know,' replied the other, 'but don't make me go, I shall throw the chaplet at her head; I cannot go, and so it's no use asking me.'

Grace moved mechanically towards the Bower, and asked one of the young gentlemen to cut her down a certain festoon, which was all white roses and buds. She then approached the group at the other end of the room. – 'Obedient maiden,' said the herald, 'in the name of my puissant employers, I greet you! and command you to weave the purest of chaplets, for the fair brows of the Queen of the Fairy Bower.'

Poor Grace with rather trembling, but not at all ungraceful hands, began to arrange the wreath she held in a suitable garland for the head, having possessed herself of the knife, which her knight, young Thompson, used in her service. As she began, the following words in a fine sonorous tone, dropped slowly from a voice which every one at once recognized as Mr. Everard's: –

> Weave a chaplet, maiden mine,
> Fit for Queen of Fairy line,
> Soft as dew, and pure as snow,
> Let it grace the rightful brow.
> Many a crown is fraught with thorns
> For the brow that it adorns;
> But no thorn, while Grace has power,
> E'er shall mar her roseate dower.
> What high nature should she be,
> Candidate for Queen's degree;
> Not a breath of pride or art
> In her bosom must find part
> Gracious, courteous, gentle, bland,
> Beyond all daughters in the land:
> Yet her steps attended aye,
> By wisdom meek and dignity.
> Weave a chaplet, maiden fair,
> For a royal Fairy's hair:
> Keep the loveliest blossoms, Grace,
> Cast away the mean and base!
> Let the fairy chaplet be,
> Emblem, Grace, befitting thee;
> Pure and simple, firmly blent,
> Modest, sweet, and elegant!
> Fame at best is poor and vain,
> Man's decoy and woman's bane.
> Fame beside is blind and dull,
> Mammon's slave and Error's fool,
> Scarcely right and often wrong,
> Gives what does not all belong:
> Rightful goods she takes away,
> Maidens, watch, lest she betray!
> The woof is wove, the web is spun,
> Herald, see the work is done!

This prompt and apt effusion had a most admirable, and to two of the party, a most startling effect. Grace was so amazed at almost every line, that she did not dare look up. She thought the whole transaction was betrayed to every creature, – how Mr. Everard became acquainted with the history, was however to her a profound mystery. He must have known it some time she felt sure, for so many appropriate lines could never, she thought, have been unpremeditated – what was to come next was now her perplexity. With an outwardly composed demeanour, however, she placed her elegant little garland in the hands of the herald. During the ode, Mary Anne stood where she had been placed, and continued pretty still – only fidgeting now and then with her hands, in a way not quite befitting the candidate for a crown; but this was her usual manner. We have remarked she had not control of either body or mind in any great extent; and indeed, as is usual with those whose thoughts are very much on themselves, she felt most especially awkward when brought into more notice than usual, however much she desired, or as we may unhappily say with truth, *coveted* that sort of distinction. It is the most humble, generally speaking, who are the most self-possessed, and on whom distinction seems to fall naturally without puffing them up. It is doubtful if the unhappy circumstances of Mary Anne's present distinction at all affected her outward manner, or if at this moment they much even affected her mind. She was pleased, and in her sad way satisfied, at being publicly honoured. So blunted were her feelings by self, that she did not even perceive the drift of Mr. Everard's verses, which Grace thought so plain, that no one could mistake. Her mind was confused by vanity and the novelty of her situation; she thought all eyes were upon her, admiring her; and she took Mr. Everard's lines as entirely complimentary to herself; she did not perceive that herself was barely alluded to, and Grace was made much more prominent; nor did she guess, that every eye was fixed on Grace and the chaplet she was dexterously weaving, and that herself was quite secondary in the scene.

Emily was the other individual to whom we alluded, as being amazed at the hints contained in Mr. Everard's effusion. No one else in the room observed them, which is not to be wondered at, as to the uninitiated they contain no more than a moral maxim clothed in poetical language. Many observed he made Grace more the heroine of the scene than Mary Anne: some thought it not fair – others did not wonder. We must however recall the reader to the spectacle, for such it was really becoming. – The herald has the crown in his hand; again he sounds his trumpet, and issues a proclamation for the coronation of the queen of the Fairy Bower; adding, that in the name of his puissant employers, he appointed the fair Grace to the office of placing the crown on the royal head. Grace was bewildered beyond expression at this announcement. She found all was *not* discovered, as at first she supposed; she wished she could hear those verses again, and ended by thinking that she had as Emily said, puzzled herself so that she turned every thing into a meaning of her own. Whatever might be the cause, however, she felt greatly relieved, and proceeded to discharge the office imposed on her without hesitation. Grace had felt no awkwardness in doing any thing that had fallen to her lot. If she had been told beforehand that she would be called on to do such things, she would have felt uncomfortable and anxious – just as she did on a less public occasion in the morning, when she thought of giving George his chain; but her present offices had come upon her naturally and suddenly, and all were things she could easily do. She was bid to do them, and she did them without thinking about it. Before placing the crown, the herald withdrew and cleared a circle before the folding doors; where stood the range of the elders, who had witnessed the whole scene. A cushion was placed, on which the half-created Queen was desired to kneel: she did, upon both knees, – Grace, we think, would have been content with one, – and meanwhile the following coronation chorus fell from the ready lips of the inexhaustible Bard, while Grace had the good sense to wait for the proper moment, according to the verses, for placing the crown on the royal head.

> Gentlest of Graces, and meekest of maids,
> Weaver of garlands whose freshness ne'er fades,
> Thine 'tis to place on the brow of the Queen
> Thine own fairy garland of white and of green.
> Sure if a crown is a hand's worthy prey,
> Fitly that hand may bestow it away!
> Diamonds are brilliant, gold too is rare,
> But crowns of such texture are weighty with care:
> Blossoms are lovely, and lighter than gems,
> But quickly they wither and fall from their stems.
> Grace bears a coronet, wrought by her skill,
> Precious as diamonds, lovelier still;
> Hers is no crown to embarrass with woe,
> Goodness its virtue, kindness its show;
> No sad emotion weighs the head down,
> Heavy and sleepless, that carries her crown.
> Yet – if a bosom is tainted with art,

'Tis not this crown could clear the soiled heart:
No! let us keep the heart safely within,
Then never fear where we end or begin:
All have a friend while their conscience is clear,
Conscience, the monarch of Queen and of Peer.
Gentlest of Graces, and meekest of friends,
Raise now the Crown as the Fairy Queen bends;
Set on her head the pure chaplet of snow,
Let not its honours encumber her brow;
Crowned by a Grace, with leaf and with flower,
Hail her now Queen of the bright Fairy Bower!

It was a very pretty group; the two young gentlemen duly supported the Queen and the attendant, and Grace exactly suited her actions to the words of the ode. It was the same in the former address, – at the line, 'Cast away the mean and the base!' she took care to follow the lead, and the action was followed by plaudits, which, after this burst agreeably interrupted the recital at fitting times. At the conclusion of the whole, the herald blew his trumpet, the multitude cheered, and the ladies waved their handkerchiefs. Many voices were loud in Mary Anne's praises. One lady, a Mrs. Mason, the same that had admired her in a morning call one day, exclaimed, 'A fine young lady indeed Miss Mary Anne is! and how prettily she did her part! just like a little queen!'

'The Grace would have borne such honours more meekly, if not more worthily,' muttered Mr. Everard in reply.

'That little girl is a vast favourite of yours, Mr. Everard,' returned this lady, 'but surely you must think Miss Mary Anne a much finer girl!'

'Not one of my sort,' replied Mr. Everard; 'fine and smooth – smooth and false,' added he, in an almost inaudible tone, as he walked away.

After the acclamations had somewhat subsided, the herald stepped forward and conducted the young Queen into the presence of the elders, especially introducing her to Lord and Lady Musgrove, and saying her Ladyship had expressed a wish to have an audience of the new Queen.

'Indeed,' said Lord Musgrove, 'we are highly honoured by her Majesty's condescension, and we hope the Queen of the Fairy Bower will to-night enjoy the honour she has so richly deserved.'

A few such sentences passed, which Mary Anne received but awkwardly; not that she need have replied much, but her mode of receiving them was any thing but simple – as Grace's would have been, or clever, as Emily's. However she presently fell more into herself, and as she went on, her *manner* rather improved. The reader must judge for himself as to the more important part. Lady Musgrove admired her taste and her skill displayed in the Fairy Bower very much, and asked her how the idea first came into her head – had she been used to such decorations?

Mary Anne answered only, 'No,' and looked sheepish, for she had never before been spoken to by a Lord or a Lady, and she thought it a very great honour; and so it was, but not exactly as Mary Anne felt it.

'How did you plan it, my dear?' said Lady Musgrove, 'by yourself, or did you talk it over with Emily?'

'Emily and I talked of it afterwards,' answered Mary Anne.

'But,' pursued Lady Musgrove, 'was it quite your own idea, or had you ever seen any thing of the sort before?'

'I had never seen any thing of the sort before,' replied Mary Anne, who was beginning to be very much on her guard, or what in her case may be called by the unpleasant word *cunning*.

'Did you,' continued her Ladyship, 'think of the bower for the bird or the bird for the bower?'

'The bower for the bird,' said Mary Anne, obliged to answer, and remembering it rose in that way with Grace.

'Well, that was a very pretty idea,' returned Lady Musgrove, 'and really has a good deal of genius in it; and did anything put it in your head?'

'I think,' said Mary Anne, getting bolder, and thinking now she could afford a little of her fame to her family, 'I think it might be some poetry of my sister Fanny's.'

'Does your sister write poetry?' asked Lady Musgrove, surprised, 'I thought you were the eldest.'

'Yes, I am,' said Mary Anne, proud to recommend her sister, 'Fanny is younger than me.'

'Is it Fanny that Isabella has taken a fancy to?'

'Yes,' returned Mary Anne, 'I believe so.'

Miss Newmarsh felt very much disappointed.

'Well, can you repeat your sister's lines, or say what they were about?'

'They were about a bird – wishing to be like a bird.'

'But was there any thing about a bower?' asked this inquisitive lady.

'Yes, one line,' replied Mary Anne, –

'And live in bowers with thee.'

'Well, it is a very pretty line; and that put it into your head, I suppose?'

'I think so,' said Mary Anne, getting quite hardened.

'Then what made you call it a "fairy bower," and not a bird's bower?' again asked the lady.

'It was not I invented that name,' said Mary Anne, candidly, 'it was done by the rest when the room was finished, and the lights were lit. I had nothing to do with the lighting, Emily and George managed all that – Emily is so very clever.'

Mary Anne now thought she had established her character for taste and genius, she might try at goodness, and introduce her cousin, as she had her sister.

'Oh, yes,' said Lady Musgrove, 'I know Emily is very clever, but she would not have planned such a bower as that; I dare say, however, she helped you in the execution.'

'Oh, yes,' cried Mary Anne, quite in her own manner, 'she and all the rest helped in the flowers, and did a great deal more than I did.'

'Well,' said Lady Musgrove, 'you have passed a very good examination, and have shown that you can be good as well as clever. – True genius has no envy. Now, my dear, I will not keep you from your companions; here is Ellen waiting quite impatiently till I have done with you.'

Mary Anne did not know Ellen or any of the young people were within hearing, and she started to find she was close at her elbow. She could not be sure she had not said some dangerous things before Ellen. She had rather it should have been Grace than Ellen; for though she could not understand Grace, she felt now sure she did not mean to betray her; and as long as Grace kept it all to herself, she did not care for the rest. What a shocking state of mind she must have been in! But Mary Anne's examinations were not at an end: as Ellen was leading her off, Miss Newmarsh stopped them, and said, 'Mary Anne, I am amazed at you for not thinking of these flowers for our Bodstock fair.'

'Oh,' said Mary Anne, 'I did not hear of them till long afterwards.'

'Why, when did you hear of them?'

'Since I have been here,' replied the young lady.

'And who told you?'

Mary Anne all along had the craft or conscience to avoid Grace's name entirely, and if now she announced it, she knew the whole affair was likely to be discovered. She remembered she had in the morning, before Ellen, said simply she heard of them 'since she had been here.' She therefore answered warily, that she could not tell who told her.

'Why, that is very strange,' said her governess, 'you have been here little more than a week, and have been out very little; cannot you remember when it was, or where?'

'It must have been when I first came,' said Mary Anne, thinking it best to put off the time before Grace's arrival, as well as Ellen's.

'When you first came!' said Miss Newmarsh, 'I wonder you did not mention it to your sisters, when they came to see you; you know we are all very busy now upon the drawing-room table stall, and I charged you to look about for any new ideas. But cannot you at all remember who told you? because it is very important to know from what quarter it comes, that we may not be forestalled.'

'It must have been somewhere that I called with Emily,' said Mary Anne, alarmed at committing herself to times and places, for she well knew she had only been to two houses before Grace came, – 'or it might be,' added she, 'somebody calling here.'

'Cannot you tell what room it was in, or whether it was a lady or a child that told you, or any thing at all about it?' pursued her governess.

'No, really I cannot,' said Mary Anne, 'it all passed in a moment.'

'Well,' said Miss Newmarsh, 'it is very unaccountable, Mary Anne, and very unfortunate; but go, my dear child, I am sorry to have kept you, but it is an important subject, and I wish to know whence the idea came.'

The two cousins then returned to the back drawing-room, and mingled in the sports. The Queen was hailed as she joined the young band, and her spirits now rose to an unrestrained height. Every body but Emily and Grace paid her a sort of homage, addressing her by her title, and consulting her with a deference, which, though avowedly mock, was very agreeable to her; and she was the liveliest – perhaps we ought to say the most boisterous – among the throng. Emily, even, wondered at her, though she had seen the same sort of thing at school; but poor Grace was quite aghast; she began to think she was in a dream – she must have made a mistake – that Mary Anne really devised the Fairy Bower – and she ended with believing as a betweenity, that Mary Anne had either persuaded herself that she had, or that she thought so from the very first. This idea restored Grace to herself while it lasted, and accounted for every thing. How else could Mary Anne have gone through all she had that evening? How else stood Mr. Everard's appalling voice, exerted with solemn effect, especially at the word 'conscience,' and the awful pause he made after those two lines? several times it had thrilled herself to her very heart, and that poor little heart at the same time bled for Mary Anne. 'But,' thought she, 'if Mary Anne believes herself the designer, of course she would not notice these things.' Without this persuasion, and the necessity Grace was under of being in constant activity, she would have sat still in a corner, and gazed with surprise all the evening at Mary Anne – full of enjoyment and laughter as she was, her face highly excited with pleasure and notice.

Different amusements filled up the rest of the time, and after the highly popular game of 'mufti,' the whole party adjourned to the supper room.

# Robert Browning (1812–1889)

One of the most famous of all poems for children, *The Pied Piper of Hamelin* is based on a tale that has been traced in various versions to *c.* 1450, and there are many cognate folk-tale versions. Folk-tales and fairy-tales were beginning to be part of the British literary scene (the Grimm brothers' *German Popular Stories* had appeared in 1823) and Browning provides a possibly ironic nod towards the moral tale at the end of his poem. Browning was one of the most intellectually aspiring poets of the nineteenth century, and did not originally intend this uncharacteristic piece, written for a child friend, Willie Macready, for publication. It can be read as a serious, not to say tragic tale, but the ingenuity of the verse has provided a model for light and comic children's poetry ever since its appearance.

## from *Dramatic Lyrics* (1842)

### THE PIED PIPER OF HAMELIN

I

Hamelin Town's in Brunswick,
    By famous Hanover city;
The river Weser, deep and wide,
Washes its wall on the southern side;
A pleasanter spot you never spied;
    But, when begins my ditty,
Almost five hundred years ago,
To see the townsfolk suffer so
    From vermin, was a pity.

II

    Rats!
They fought the dogs and killed the cats,
    And bit the babies in the cradles,
And ate the cheeses out of the vats,
    And licked the soup from the cooks' own ladles,
Split open the kegs of salted sprats,
Made nests inside men's Sunday hats,
And even spoiled the women's chats
    By drowning their speaking
    With shrieking and squeaking
In fifty different sharps and flats.

III

At last the people in a body
    To the Town Hall came flocking:
' 'Tis clear,' cried they, 'our Mayor's a noddy;
    And as for our Corporation – shocking
To think we buy gowns lined with ermine
For dolts that can't or won't determine
What's best to rid us of our vermin!

You hope, because you're old and obese,
To find in the furry civic robe ease?
Rouse up, Sirs! Give your brains a racking
To find the remedy we're lacking,
Or, sure as fate, we'll send you packing!'
At this the Mayor and Corporation
Quaked with a mighty consternation.

### IV

An hour they sat in council,
    At length the Mayor broke silence:
'For a guilder I'd my ermine gown sell,
    I wish I were a mile hence!
It's easy to bid one rack one's brain –
I'm sure my poor head aches again
I've scratched it so, and all in vain.
Oh for a trap, a trap, a trap!'
Just as he said this, what should hap
At the chamber door but a gentle tap?
'Bless us,' cried the Mayor, 'what's that?'
(With the Corporation as he sat,
Looking little though wondrous fat;
Nor brighter was his eye, nor moister
Than a too-long-opened oyster,
Save when at noon his paunch grew mutinous
For a plate of turtle green and glutinous)
'Only a scraping of shoes on the mat?
Anything like the sound of a rat
Makes my heart go pit-a-pat!'

### V

'Come in!' – the Mayor cried, looking bigger:
And in did come the strangest figure!
His queer long coat from heel to head
Was half of yellow and half of red,
And he himself was tall and thin,
With sharp blue eyes, each like a pin,
And light loose hair, yet swarthy skin,
No tuft on cheek nor beard on chin,
But lips where smiles went out and in;
There was no guessing his kith and kin:
And nobody could enough admire
The tall man and his quaint attire.
Quoth one: 'It's as my great-grandsire,
Starting up at the Trump of Doom's tone,
Had walked this way from his painted tombstone!'

### VI

He advanced to the council-table:
And, 'Please your honours,' said he, 'I'm able,
By means of a secret charm, to draw
    All creatures living beneath the sun,
    That creep or swim or fly or run,

After me so as you never saw!
And I chiefly use my charm
On creatures that do people harm,
The mole and toad and newt and viper;
And people call me the Pied Piper.'
(And here they noticed round his neck
   A scarf of red and yellow stripe,
To match with his coat of the self-same cheque;
   And at the scarf's end hung a pipe;
And his fingers, they noticed, were ever straying
As if impatient to be playing
Upon this pipe, as low it dangled
Over his vesture so old-fangled.)
'Yet,' said he, 'poor piper as I am,
In Tartary I freed the Cham,
   Last June, from his huge swarms of gnats;
I eased in Asia the Nizam
   Of a monstrous brood of vampyre-bats:
And as for what your brain bewilders,
   If I can rid your town of rats
Will you give me a thousand guilders?'
'One? fifty thousand!' – was the exclamation
Of the astonished Mayor and Corporation.

VII

Into the street the Piper stept,
   Smiling first a little smile,
As if he knew what magic slept
   In his quiet pipe the while;
Then, like a musical adept,
To blow the pipe his lips he wrinkled,
And green and blue his sharp eyes twinkled,
Like a candle-flame where salt is sprinkled;
And ere three shrill notes the pipe uttered,
You heard as if an army muttered;
And the muttering grew to a grumbling;
And the grumbling grew to a mighty rumbling;
And out of the houses the rats came tumbling.
Great rats, small rats, lean rats, brawny rats,
Brown rats, black rats, grey rats, tawny rats,
Grave old plodders, gay young friskers,
   Fathers, mothers, uncles, cousins,
Cocking tails and pricking whiskers,
   Families by ten and dozens,
Brothers, sisters, husbands, wives –
Followed the Piper for their lives.
From street to street he piped advancing,
And step for step they followed dancing,
Until they came to the river Weser,
   Wherein all plunged and perished!
– Save one who, stout as Julius Cæsar,
Swam across and lived to carry
   (As he, the manuscript he cherished)

To Rat-land home his commentary:
Which was, 'At the first shrill notes of the pipe,
I heard a sound as of scraping tripe,
And putting apples, wondrous ripe,
Into a cider-press's gripe:
And a moving away of pickle-tub-boards,
And a leaving ajar of conserve-cupboards,
And a drawing the corks of train-oil-flasks,
And a breaking the hoops of butter-casks:
And it seemed as if a voice
    (Sweeter far than bý harp or bý psaltery
Is breathed) called out, "Oh rats, rejoice!
    The world is grown to one vast drysaltery!
So munch on, crunch on, take your nuncheon,
Breakfast, supper, dinner, luncheon!"
And just as a bulky sugar-puncheon,
All ready staved, like a great sun shone
Glorious scarce an inch before me,
Just as methought it said, "Come, bore me!"
– I found the Weser rolling o'er me.'

### VIII

You should have heard the Hamelin people
Ringing the bells till they rocked the steeple.
'Go,' cried the Mayor, 'and get long poles!
Poke out the nests and block up the holes!
Consult with carpenters and builders,
And leave in our town not even a trace
Of the rats!' – when suddenly, up the face
Of the Piper perked in the market-place,
With a, 'First, if you please, my thousand guilders!'

### IX

A thousand guilders! The Mayor looked blue;
So did the Corporation too.
For council dinners made rare havoc
With Claret, Moselle, Vin-de-Grave, Hock;
And half the money would replenish
Their cellar's biggest butt with Rhenish.
To pay this sum to a wandering fellow
With a gipsy coat of red and yellow!
'Beside,' quoth the Mayor with a knowing wink,
'Our business was done at the river's brink;
We saw with our eyes the vermin sink,
And what's dead can't come to life, I think.
So, friend, we're not the folks to shrink
From the duty of giving you something for drink,
And a matter of money to put in your poke;
But as for the guilders, what we spoke
Of them, as you very well know, was in joke.
Beside, our losses have made us thrifty.
A thousand guilders! Come, take fifty!'

X

The Piper's face fell, and he cried
'No trifling! I can't wait, beside!
I've promise to visit by dinner time
Bagdat, and accept the prime
Of the Head-Cook's pottage, all he's rich in,
For having left, in the Caliph's kitchen,
Of a nest of scorpions no survivor:
With him I proved no bargain-driver,
With you, don't think I'll bate a stiver!
And folks who put me in a passion
May find me pipe after another fashion.'

XI

'How?' cried the Mayor, 'd'ye think I brook
Being worse treated than a Cook?
Insulted by a lazy ribald
With idle pipe and vesture piebald?
You threaten us, fellow? Do your worst,
Blow your pipe there till you burst!'

XII

Once more he stept into the street;
    And to his lips again
    Laid his long pipe of smooth straight cane;
And ere he blew three notes (such sweet
Soft notes as yet musician's cunning
    Never gave the enraptured air)
There was a rustling that seemed like a bustling
Of merry crowds justling at pitching and hustling,
Small feet were pattering, wooden shoes clattering,
Little hands clapping and little tongues chattering,
And, like fowls in a farm-yard when barley is scattering,
Out came the children running.
All the little boys and girls,
With rosy cheeks and flaxen curls,
And sparkling eyes and teeth like pearls,
Tripping and skipping, ran merrily after
The wonderful music with shouting and laughter.

XIII

The Mayor was dumb, and the Council stood
As if they were changed into blocks of wood,
Unable to move a step, or cry
To the children merrily skipping by,
– Could only follow with the eye
That joyous crowd at the Piper's back.
But how the Mayor was on the rack,
And the wretched Council's bosoms beat,
As the Piper turned from the High Street
To where the Weser rolled its waters
Right in the way of their sons and daughters!
However, he turned from South to West,

And to Koppelberg Hill his steps addressed,
And after him the children pressed;
Great was the joy in every breast.
'He never can cross that mighty top!
He's forced to let the piping drop,
And we shall see our children stop!'
When, lo, as they reached the mountain-side,
A wondrous portal opened wide,
As if a cavern was suddenly hollowed;
And the Piper advanced and the children followed,
And when all were in to the very last,
The door in the mountain-side shut fast.
Did I say, all? No! One was lame,
    And could not dance the whole of the way;
And in after years, if you would blame
    His sadness, he was used to say, —
'It's dull in our town since my playmates left!
I can't forget that I'm bereft
Of all the pleasant sights they see,
Which the Piper also promised me.
For he led us, he said, to a joyous land,
Joining the town and just at hand,
Where waters gushed and fruit-trees grew
And flowers put forth a fairer hue,
And everything was strange and new;
The sparrows were brighter than peacocks here,
And their dogs outran our fallow deer,
And honey-bees had lost their stings,
And horses were born with eagles' wings:
And just as I became assured
My lame foot would be speedily cured,
The music stopped and I stood still,
And found myself outside the hill,
Left alone against my will,
To go now limping as before,
And never hear of that country more!'

XIV

Alas, alas for Hamelin!
    There came into many a burgher's pate
    A text which says, that heaven's gate
    Opes to the rich at as easy rate
As the needle's eye takes a camel in!
The Mayor sent East, West, North and South,
To offer the Piper, by word of mouth,
    Wherever it was men's lot to find him,
Silver and gold to his heart's content,
If he'd only return the way he went,
    And bring the children behind him.
But when they saw 'twas a lost endeavour,
And Piper and dancers were gone for ever,
They made a decree that lawyers never
    Should think their records dated duly

If, after the day of the month and year,
These words did not as well appear,
'And so long after what happened here
   On the Twenty-second of July,
Thirteen hundred and seventy-six:'
And the better in memory to fix
The place of the children's last retreat,
They called it, the Pied Piper's Street –
Where anyone playing on pipe or tabor
Was sure for the future to lose his labour.
Nor suffered they hostelry or tavern
   To shock with mirth a street so solemn;
But opposite the place of the cavern
   They wrote the story on a column,
And on the great church-window painted
The same, to make the world acquainted
How their children were stolen away,
And there it stands to this very day.
And I must not omit to say
That in Transylvania there's a tribe
Of alien people who ascribe
The outlandish ways and dress
On which their neighbours lay such stress,
To their fathers and mothers having risen
Out of some subterraneous prison
Into which they were trepanned
Long time ago in a mighty band
Out of Hamelin town in Brunswick land,
But how or why, they don't understand.

                        XV

So, Willy, let me and you be wipers
Of scores out with all men – especially pipers!
And, whether they pipe us free fróm rats or fróm mice,
If we've promised them aught, let us keep our promise!

# Eliza Lee [Cabot] Follen (1787–1860)

Another of the rhymes that have passed into the oral tradition, it is not clear whether 'Three Little Kittens' was written by Mrs Follen or collected by her. A New Englander, with strong religious and abolitionist views, she was also well known for a didactic novel, *The Well-Spent Hour* (1827).

## from *New Nursery Songs for all Good Children* (1843)

### THREE LITTLE KITTENS

Three little kittens they lost their mittens,
    And they began to cry,
Oh, mother dear, we sadly fear
    Our mittens we have lost.
What! lost your mittens, you naughty kittens!
    Then you shall have no pie.
Mee-ow, mee-ow, mee-ow.
    No, you shall have no pie.

The three little kittens they found their mittens,
    And they began to cry,
Oh, mother dear, see here, see here,
    Our mittens we have found!
Put on your mittens, you silly kittens,
    And you shall have some pie.
    Purr-r, purr-r, purr-r.
    Oh, let us have some pie.

The three little kittens put on their mittens,
    And soon ate up the pie;
Oh, mother dear, we greatly fear
    Our mittens we have soiled.
What! soiled your mittens, you naughty kittens!
    Then they began to sigh.
    Mee-ow, mee-ow, mee-ow.
    Then they began to sigh.

The three little kittens they washed their mittens,
    And hung them out to dry;
Oh! mother dear, do you not hear,
    Our mittens we have washed!
What! washed your mittens, then you're good kittens,
    But I smell a rat close by.
    Mee-ow, mee-ow, mee-ow.
    We smell a rat close by.

# 'William Churne of Staffordshire'
# (Revd Francis Edward Paget) (1806–1882)

*The Hope of the Katzekopfs* usually figures in literary history as a presager of the supposedly far more distinguished *The King of the Golden River* by John Ruskin, *The Rose and the Ring* by W. M. Thackeray and *Prince Prigio* by Andrew Lang; Kipling claimed that his *Rewards and Fairies* (1908) had its roots in this book. Certainly, this perhaps rather sly performance draws on similar several fairy-tale elements, and follows the French style of fairy-tale, but it can stand on its own feet. It has not broken away totally from the moral tale: Prince Eigenwillig ('self-willed') is utterly spoiled by his foolish parents and has to learn how to govern himself. The difference is the often exuberant exaggeration of the characters and situations.

Paget deplored the idea of 'writing down to the intellects of children'. 'Children', he wrote, 'are as capable of understanding deep things as adults.... Many things are *above* a child which are not *beyond* him and it is a wholesome exercise for his intellect when he can be voluntarily induced to grapple with it.' The book was a great success, and in the preface to the second edition in 1847 he wrote that the book 'was an attempt under the guise of a Fairy-tale to lead young minds to a more wholesome train of thought than is commonly found at the present day in popular juvenile literature'. The fairy-tale elements, however, far outweigh the didactic ones.

In this extract, the good fairy Lady Abracadabra has brought the good, noble and unselfish boy Witikind to be a companion to Eigenwillig. Eigenwillig proceeds to bully and abuse him, eventually attacking him with a silver ink-stand. After the dramatic events described here, Eigenwillig is taken to fairyland, where the rule is 'nothing for nothing', and is partly reformed. His pride is then driven from him by a very unpleasant sprite, self-will; and only by self-discipline and self-denial does he win through and become King Katzekopf the Good.

From 1835–82 Paget was Rector of Elford in Staffordshire, the village where the revolutionary novelist, Robert Bage, lived at the end of the previous century. His pseudonym is the name of the servant of Bishop Richard Corbet, author of 'Farewell to the Fairies' (1648), a poem that contains the line 'Farewell rewards and fairies', adopted by Kipling as a book title.

## from *The Hope of the Katzekopfs* (1844)

## from CHAPTER IV

Eigenwillig was in too great a passion to take a deliberate aim, and the consequence was, that the missile, instead of hitting Witikind, struck the centre of a large looking-glass, which it broke to shivers.

The crash of the falling fragments was heard by Queen Ninnilinda, and she immediately entered the apartment, to see what was the matter. The first object which met her eyes was Witikind, who ran against her in his hurry to escape from the Prince.

'Ah,' said she, laying hold of him, 'you need not attempt to run away. I knew I should find you out sooner or later, and now I have caught you. How dared you to break that looking-glass, and spill the ink all over the carpet, you little, good-for-nothing varlet?'

'Please your Majesty, I did not break it.'

'Not break it!' exclaimed the Queen, who was much too angry to observe that her own son was likewise in the room. 'Not break it? Are you not ashamed to utter such falsehoods?' And with that the Queen struck the little boy two or three sharp blows.

'Oh, Mama, Mama,' cried Prince Eigenwillig, rushing forward, and seizing her uplifted arm, 'it was not his doing; it was mine. I don't like him, and I wish he had never come here; but he didn't break the looking-glass. I broke it; do not beat him; he doesn't deserve it. I did the mischief. He put me in such a rage with what he said, that I took up the inkstand and threw it at him; but it struck the glass instead of him.'

The Prince was a spoilt child, and full of faults; but here was an evidence that there were redeeming points in his character. Nothing could have been better than the manner in which he came forward to take the blame on his own shoulders. There was still something to work upon; and had his mother been anything but what she was, the incident might have been turned as much to his advantage as to her own. But her weakness and vanity were excessive. She saw she had been too hasty; but was unwilling to confess herself in the wrong; so she availed herself of an expression of her son, and continued to pour out her wrath on the unfortunate Witikind.

'How dared you offend the Prince?' she cried. 'How could you presume to misbehave yourself in such a manner, as to put him in a rage, as he says you did? And what is the meaning of all these malicious tales you have been carrying to the King?'

'I have carried no tales to the King, Madam,' replied Witikind.

'Yes, you have,' retorted the Queen, 'you have been making him believe that the Prince is cruel to you. And like a little artful, hypocritical wretch, you have been even setting his own attendants against him.'

Witikind was so bewildered with all these charges that he was quite silent.

'Yes,' continued the Queen, 'no wonder you are struck dumb; now you are found out, you have not a word to say for yourself.'

'Will you hear me, Madam, or believe me, when I do speak?' replied Witikind, recovering his self-possession.

'Believe *you*? you little deceitful creature! No, that will I not.'

'Then, since your Majesty says that, when you know I have never deceived you, I had rather say nothing, except that I hope you will confront me with the King, and the Prince's attendants.'

'Leave the room,' said Queen Ninnilinda, in still greater anger, 'I am not going to be argued with by you, I promise you.'

'Mama,' said Prince Eigenwillig, as soon as Witikind had left the room, 'I don't like him, but I don't think he ever tells lies; and I don't think he ever tried to set Nurse Yellowlily against me, though she often praised him, in order to plague me.'

Here again, the boy was getting upon a right path; but his foolish mother, as soon as she perceived it, lost no time in turning him into a wrong one.

'Ah, my sweetest boy,' said she, 'it was no more than I expected from your noble, generous nature, that you should try and find excuses for this odious little brat. You don't know the world as well as I do: if you did, you would find it prudent to consider others less, and yourself more. But I have my own opinion about this Witikind. Everything went on well enough in the palace till he came, and now every thing goes wrong, and I can trace his finger at the bottom of all the mischief. I always misdoubted the intentions of that cross-grained old toad, my Fairy-aunt, ever since she insisted on giving you your horrid name. I was sure her professions of kindliness were a blind, and that she was meaning mischief all the time. And I am quite satisfied now that this creature which she brought here, is not Count Rudolf's son. Count Rudolf is a very respectable man, and would not deceive us, but parents are proverbially blind;' (Yes, indeed, Queen Ninnilinda!) 'and I don't doubt that this Witikind is a changeling, some imp from Fairy-land, hundreds of years old, perhaps, sly, and mischievous, and malicious, who is sent to bring some terrible misfortune on us all.'

Poor Witikind! he little suspected the nature of this fresh accusation against him; and while he was weeping in his chamber over the injustice which he was suffering, and writhing under the indignity of being charged with saying what was not true, he was being subjected to an imputation, at once the most cruel, and (in his case) the most difficult to disprove.

The idea once started, every body had something to say in confirmation of it. All the courtiers discovered that, though they had never mentioned it, they had, from the first, observed something very elvish in his countenance. The Keeper of the Records had been struck with his always being dressed in green and gold, – the fashionable colours in Fairy-land. The Ladies Frigida, Rigida, and Brigida, detected something supernatural in the precocious aptness with which he received their lessons. The Baroness Yellowlily had occasionally found great entanglement in the poor child's sunny ringlets, when she combed them after he had been at play: this was a strong presumption they were elflocks. He was wont to talk with rapture of the happy home he had left; this, in the opinion of the Lord Chamberlain, was proof positive that he had come from Fairy-land, for what but Fairy-land, could be preferable to a palace? Finally, even good-natured King Katzekopf, when he heard all these allegations, was fain to shake his head, and confess that there was something suspicious in the case, and that the circumstance which he had himself observed, namely, Witikind's habit of sitting moping for hours together, by the side of the fountain, was certainly very unlike the habits of other boys.

What was to be done? If they sent him back to his reputed parents, without the Lady Abracadabra's permission, they might bring all kinds of trouble upon themselves. If they kept him longer in the palace, there was no calculating the amount of mischief which might be effected by him. However, it was resolved, that of the two evils, this was the least: and so it was determined, that things should go on as usual, and that Witikind should be kept in ignorance of the nature of the suspicions against him.

Whether all those who contributed to blacken this unlucky boy's character, were sincere in their belief of his elvish origin, may be doubted. To seem so, was to follow the fashion, and a ready method of getting into Queen Ninnilinda's good graces; and that was enough for courtiers.

But, though Witikind knew not of what he was accused, he was not long kept in ignorance of the fact, that he was out of favour with every body. It seemed as if nobody, from the King on his throne, to the scullion in the kitchen, could say a word of kindness to him. Some were ruder than others, in proportion as they desired to pay court to her Majesty; but all made it evident that they wished to have nothing to say to him. A thousand petty mortifications were heaped upon him. He was kept at his lessons for many more hours than heretofore, and his tasks were made doubly difficult. He was allowed, as formerly, to take his meals with the Prince, but those in attendance contrived to give him whatever was likely to be most unpalatable. He was required to be with the Prince, during his play hours, but was not allowed to play with him, but only to wait on him; to run after his ball, or to fetch his hoop out of a ditch, or pick up his arrows which had fallen wide of the mark.

And yet nothing was said or done in such a manner that Witikind could lay hold of it. He felt that every body was against him, though it was their general manner, rather than any particular act, that gave him the impression. It seemed to him, as if his feet had become entangled in a net, and that some unseen hand was preventing his escape. And all this while, Prince Eigenwillig was growing more and more unkind, sometimes not speaking to him at all, and other times, loading him with abuse and reproaches. For weeks and weeks, this state of things continued, and Witikind was nearly broken in spirit, and would have been quite so, had he not been able to cheer himself, by the thought that sooner or later, he would be sent home, and that the Fairy had promised to befriend him.

Yet still as time passed on, and he heard nothing from Taubennest, and his father never came to court to inquire after him, and the Lady Abracadabra failed to appear, he grew more and more downcast. Sometimes he thought of running away; but whither should he run, and how could he find his way home? Sometimes he resolved to entreat the King to dismiss him; but then he remembered the Fairy's commands, that let what would happen, he must not leave the court, without her permission.

However, when things are at the worst, they usually begin to mend; and just as Witikind began to despair, the crisis came, which he feared would never come.

In obedience to his mother, – for sometimes, when he had no temptation the other way, even Eigenwillig could be obedient, – the Prince had carefully abstained from letting fall any expression which should convey to Witikind the knowledge that he was suspected of being an elf in disguise; but at length it happened, as might have been expected, that the boy forgot his secret.

It fell out, upon a summer's evening, that the Prince and Witikind were alone together in one of the apartments of the palace, which opened out of the Queen's sitting-room, and which had a door of communication with the gardens. – The Prince was amusing himself with a game of battledore, and Witikind stood near to pick up the shuttlecock for him as it occasionally fell. But the Prince was expert with his battledore, and would keep the shuttlecock bounding in the air for a long time together. Consequently the services of Witikind were not often needed.

No wonder, therefore, that he crept towards the window to look at the gay flower-beds, and to watch the waters of his favourite fountain as they rose sparkling in the air to a vast height, and then fell into various fantastic basins, from which they issued into the grand reservoir below; and no wonder, as he listened to the soothing plash of the waters, and watched the clouds, painted with all the gorgeous hues which the setting sun threw over them, that his thoughts reverted to Tauben-nest, and that fatal evening when he had expressed a wish to quit it. Surely the error had brought its recompense of punishment! If he had done wrong, he had suffered for it, and had learned a lesson which would last him his life. Oh bitter and sincere was his repentance! What would he not now give to turn his back for ever on the hateful palace! What would he not give to see the towers of Taubennest, and look from its ramparts on the mountains, barren as they were; and the valley, and the winding river! What would he not give, were it but for a few brief minutes, to hear the sweet voices of his sisters, and to be clasped in his mother's arms!

The shuttlecock had fallen, but he heard it not, and remained inattentive to his duties. How could it be otherwise? he was hundreds of miles away.

'Why don't you pick up the shuttlecock?' cried the Prince, in a sharp, impatient tone. – Witikind started, and ran forward in a random way; but he could not see it: tears were blinding his eyes.

'Not there, blockhead!' shouted the Prince, 'look behind the statue.' There were two statues; Witikind went towards the wrong one.

'What a stupid *elf's-brat* you are!' cried the Hope of the Katzekopfs to the child of Countess Ermengarde, when he brought back the shuttlecock.

'What did you call me, Prince?' said Witikind with a look of surprise and anger.

'I called you what you are, – what all the world knows you to be – an elf's-brat: the good-for-nothing, impish son of some malevolent old Fairy, or some old hag of a witch!'

'How dare you call my mother evil names?' exclaimed Witikind, his eyes sparkling with anger, and his whole frame quivering with emotion. His patient endurance and gentleness seemed to have fled from him for ever; his entire character appeared altered on the instant. Anything personal he had long since proved that he could submit to, but the insult to his mother called forth in a moment the long-sleeping energies of his character. 'How DARE you to abuse my mother?' he cried in a still louder tone. 'How dare you utter such a base, cowardly lie?'

The Prince, wholly unprepared for such an outbreak, was too much terrified to answer. He saw that in Witikind's gleaming eye which told him, boy as he was, that Countess Ermengarde's son was not to be trifled with. The Hope of the Katzekopfs turned pale, quailed, and continued retreating towards the corner of the room nearest to his mother's apartments.

'Unsay what you have said,' cried Witikind, following close upon him as he retreated step by step. 'Unsay what you have said, and beg my pardon on your knees for this insult to my mother!'

Down sank the Prince on his knees in the corner of the room, while over him stood Witikind, pale with anger, his arm outstretched, and his fist clenched, repeating in tones hoarse from excitement, but waxing louder, and louder every moment, 'Unsay what you have said, unsay what you have said!'

Such was the sight which presented itself to Queen Ninnilinda's wondering eyes, when she issued from her boudoir to ascertain the cause of the noise which had alarmed her.

'Take him away! take him away!' cried the Prince, as soon as he saw his mother. 'Take him away, or he will kill me!'

'Help! help!' shrieked the Queen, 'or the Prince will be bewitched by this spiteful elf – this Fairy's changeling.'

Her screams brought one of the yeomen of the guard into the room, who instantly seized Witikind.

'Hold him fast!' exclaimed her Majesty. 'Get ropes and tie him hand and foot, and then flog him till he faints. He has been trying to bewitch my son!'

But the Queen's commands were not destined to be obeyed. Even when the hubbub was at its height, a pause ensued, for the well-known whistle of the Fairy at the key-hole, loud and shrill above all other sounds, was heard. Forth from the aperture the Lady Abracadabra sprung, and with a single bound darted into the midst of the group. Her expression was that of the deepest indignation, and her robe seemed glowing with living fire. Throwing her wand down upon the nearest table, she caught hold of Witikind with one hand, and with the other sent the burly yeoman of the guard reeling to the extremity of the apartment, from whence he rushed forth in an agony of terror.

'And this is the way you keep your promises, is it, Queen Ninnilinda? This is the way you treat the poor child whom you engaged to bring up with the same kindness which you exhibit to yonder unhappy boy? Think not that I am not cognizant of all your proceedings! Think not that I have not witnessed the indignities and unkindnesses you have heaped upon him! Think not that I have not overheard your shameless words of ingratitude towards myself. Think not, above all, that I, his friend and protector, have kept Witikind an hour longer than was necessary for his future happiness, in this abode of folly and weakness: think not, that I, your own child's sponsor, will allow him to be longer exposed to your mismanagement, and evil influence. I gave you a fair warning; and you must now take the consequences of having neglected it. You have had your trial. It is over. Now comes your punishment.'

The Queen threw herself on her knees.

'No:' replied the Lady Abracadabra; 'it is too late now. The sooner you take leave of your son the better. But first, Prince Eigenwillig, come here to me.'

'I won't!' cried the Prince doggedly.

'It will be the worse for you if you don't,' said the Fairy.

'I won't, I tell you!' repeated the Prince.

'Oh Eigenwillig,' cried his mother, 'for mercy's sake, do as you are bid; you know not what the consequences of disobedience may be!'

'Come, when I call you!' said Lady Abracadabra calmly, but fixing her eye upon him, 'come here and beg Witikind's pardon for all your abominable conduct towards him.'

Eigenwillig approached Witikind, who had already a smile of reconciliation on his face, expecting that the Prince would now gladly make up for his error. But the Hope of the Katzekopfs had no such intention. He advanced indeed close to Witikind, and stretched out one hand towards him, but with the other he snatched the Fairy's wand off the table, and before she could prevent him, he struck Witikind over the head, and exclaimed, 'Detestable creature! be thou turned into a timid hare! Mays't thou be hunted to death by dogs and men!'

In another instant he was gazing in amazement at what he had done; for such was the portentous power of Abracadabra's wand that, even in his hands, it failed not to work the required transformation. Witikind was crouching before them, a terrified trembling hare!

'Well!' cried the Fairy, 'be it so. You have but anticipated my purpose, evil-minded child that you are!' She opened a door that led into the garden, and said,

> 'Hare! Hare! hurry away!
>     Neither halt nor rest,
>     And at Taubennest
> You shall safely be, by the break of day.
>     No huntsman harm thee!
>     No hound alarm thee!
>     From evil I charm thee!
> Bound forth! away! away!'

She paused a moment to see the little creature safe on its route, and then closed the door.

'And now,' said she to the author of the mischief, 'I come to settle my account with thee. But first surrender my wand.'

'I'll turn you into a toad first,' shouted the Prince, striking at her; but with indecision in his voice and manner; for, in spite of his recent triumph, he was utterly terrified at what he had done, and at what he was doing. He already had a misgiving that Fairies are not to be trifled with.

The Lady Abracadabra was, as may be supposed, in no humour to be turned into a toad. She, therefore, merely stretched out her hand, and caught hold of the extremity of the wand as the Hope of the Katzekopfs struck her with it.

'Give me the wand!' said she.

'I shan't!' cried Eigenwillig.

'Give it me directly!'

'I won't, won't, WON'T!' screamed the naughty boy, clinging fast to one end of the wand, while the Fairy held the other.

'I shall make you glad enough to loose it before I have done with you.'

'Leave it alone, Eigenwillig,' cried his mother, clasping her hands.

'I won't,' exclaimed the boy, 'I won't do anything you tell me. If you had not spoilt me, I shouldn't be in all this trouble now! I *won't* give it up, I say!'

'Then take the consequences!' said the Lady Abracadabra. As she said these words, she darted up into the air, still keeping hold of the wand, and lessening in size, as she rose, made her way towards the keyhole. By the time she had reached it, dragging the Prince after her, she had shrunk to the size which enabled her to go through it. But she paused for a moment before she disappeared, and, standing on the handle of the door, she cried out in a shrill, thin voice, such as might be expected to issue from one of her diminutive size:

'Follow wand,
Follow hand.'

Then she sprung through the keyhole, and in another instant her wand was seen following her.

'Drop it now, my darling!' exclaimed the Queen. 'Let her take her wand, if she'll only take herself off, too!'

All this time the wand, was passing through the keyhole. Less and less of it was left in sight. Now not more than an inch; now not half an inch; now the tips of the Prince's fingers seemed sucked up towards the keyhole.

'Drop it,' cried the Queen, 'why don't you drop it?'

'Oh, mother, mother!' screamed the struggling, breathless boy, in an agony of terror, 'I can't, I CAN'T; it has grown to my fingers; it sticks to them! Oh dear! dear! what shall I do? my fingers are being dragged through the keyhole! they are being stretched into strings! Oh help me! help me!'

The Queen rushed to the door, before which her son was kicking and writhing. But his efforts to escape were fruitless; to her horror, the Queen beheld each joint tapering and elongating itself, till it could pass through the narrow aperture; now the wrists had disappeared; now, in a twinkling the elbows were out of sight; now the upper portion of the arm was gone.

'Surely,' thought Ninnilinda, 'she will never attempt to drag his head through.' But she was wrong; the boy's hair was rapidly sucked through the keyhole, and the head began to lengthen itself out for the purpose of following.

This was too much for endurance. The Queen strove with all her power to open the door; but it was as fast as if it formed part of the original wall. Then, in her dismay, she seized hold of the body of the Prince, for the purpose of dragging him back; but a miserable, elongated drawl from the other side of the door conveyed the boy's entreaty that she would not hurt him.

'Never mind what he says, niece,' cried the voice of the Fairy. 'Hold his legs tight, and in half a minute I shall have finished my work, and wound him up!'

The Queen was so transfixed with dismay, that she stood motionless, watching the receding body of the Prince, till the soles of his feet caught her despairing eyes.

'There! it's done now,' cried the Lady Abracadabra. 'He makes a very compact ball, and will travel well!'

The Queen, in her despair, now rushed to the door leading into the flower-garden; but she was too late.

The Fairy had reached the extremity of the terrace, kicking before her something that seemed like a ball of rope; but which was, in fact, the convoluted form of Prince Eigenwillig.

In another moment, the Lady Abracadabra and the Hope of the Katzekopfs had bounded over the parapet, and were lost to view; and Queen Ninnilinda fell, for the first time in her life, into a real swoon.

# Richard Henry [Hengist] Horne (1802–1884)

A colourful, flamboyant character, with acquaintances ranging from Keats to Dickens and Elizabeth Barrett, Horne was a versatile professional writer. Robert Browning described him as 'an unmistakable genius . . . a fine, honest, enthusiastic, chivalrous fellow'. Among his many activities he was in 1841 an assistant commissioner in a government investigation into child labour, and produced some scathing reports.

With *Memoirs of a London Doll* he claimed to be doing something new; the form itself – the first-person narrative by an inanimate object – was common enough, but the narrative is both undidactic and unsentimental. Maria Poppet, the doll, moves in the course of a year between different owners in London: in the following extract, she has just moved from Ellen Plummy, the pastrycook's daughter

to Lady Flora's house in the rich and fashionable Hanover Square. Horne foregrounds affectionate family life, rather than poverty, but the young reader is left to make social deductions. The key point is that Horne does *not* make a point.

Critics have felt that the uncompromisingly tough, almost sardonic narrative voice makes the *Memoirs* unique in their period, and presages the work of Juliana Ewing (see p. 329). Certainly Maria Poppet's point of view, one of competent innocence, provided Horne with an ideal vehicle for social comment accessible to children.

Horne was not above slipping advertising for his other books into the text: the 'Harriet Myrtle' books referred to in this extract were a series by Horne and the illustrator Mary Gillies; 'The Good-Natured Bear' was by Horne.

## from *Memoirs of a London Doll (written by herself; edited by Mrs Fairstar)* (1846)

### CHAPTER IX

### DOLL'S LETTERS

I had the next day a great joy. It was the arrival of a letter from my dear Ellen Plummy, which her brother Thomas had brought and given to one of the housemaids, saying it was a 'doll's letter'. The housemaid had given it to a page, and the page had given it to the tall footman, and he – after some consideration – had taken it to the governess, who, having opened it, and read it, and shown it to Lady Flowerdale, had asked my little lady mamma if she would allow me to receive a letter, as one had been sent for me by the little girl from whom she had received me. Lady Flora was at first going to say 'No,' but suddenly she recollected the sad face of poor Ellen when she placed me in her hands, and then she said 'Oh yes! – I should so like to read it.' This was the letter. It was addressed on the outside to 'Maria Poppet'.

'My dearest Maria,

'I have never forgotten you, though I have got another doll; and often when I love this other doll, I am thinking of it as if you were this. I have also had a cradle sent me by the kind great lady and little lady both, and some things for the bedding, and a necklace of beads for myself, besides a small painted workbox. We get up at six o'clock to work as usual, and go to bed at nine, after bread and butter. I am so glad to think you are happy and comfortable, and that you have no hard needlework to do, and the little lady is fond of you. Don't you remember the Twelfth-cake my brother Tommy gave for you, and how he laughed all the way we ran home at something that had happened in the doll shop about Bonaparte and Abernethy biscuits? I often think of you. I never forget you, nor all who have been good to me, and whom I love, and I hope we may some day meet again; and I also hope that your happy life among all the riches of the world will not make you quite forget your poor first mamma.

'Your affectionate
'ELLEN PLUMMY.'

The little Lady Flora and the governess were rather amused with this letter of my poor dear Ellen's, but Lady Flowerdale was very much pleased with it, and said that, however simple or foolish it might seem, it showed a good and affectionate nature in the little girl who had sent it; and she was of opinion that the doll should write an answer.

This idea of my writing an answer greatly delighted Lady Flora, and she and her governess sat a whole morning thinking what to say, and writing upon a slate, and then rubbing it out because it would not do. At the same time the governess was obliged to put a pen very often into my hand, and teach me to write, and she often seemed so vexed and tired; but Lady Flora would never let her rest, so that I really had in this manner an excellent lesson in writing.

At last a letter, in answer, was composed on a slate by the governess, with Lady Flora's assistance, and then a pen was put into my hand by the governess, so that I wrote the letter. It was then sent to Lady Flowerdale, to know if she approved of it; but she did not: she said it wanted ease and simplicity, and was not what a nursery letter ought to be, nor like what a doll would say. She then tried herself, but she could not write one to her mind.

That same evening, as she sat at dinner with the earl her husband, they happened to be alone. Lady Flora was gone to bed, but had left me sitting upright in one corner of the room, having forgotten to take me upstairs with her. Her ladyship, observing that Lord Flowerdale, who was a cabinet minister, was troubled with state business, sought to relieve his mind by telling him all about this letter to me, and their difficulty in answering it. The minister at first paid no attention to this triviality, but when her ladyship related how the governess and Lady Flora had tried all the morning to write a proper answer for the doll, and how hard she *herself* had tried, but could not, the minister was amused, and in the end quite laughed, forgot the business of the state, and actually became pleasant. He desired to see the letter. It was brought in by a footman, – placed upon a splendid silver salver, and handed to the minister by the butler with a grave and important face.

The minister read the letter very attentively; then smiled, and laid it by the side of his plate, on which was a slice of currant tart. 'So,' said he, 'Flora and her governess have tried in vain to write a proper reply to this letter from the doll; and your ladyship has also tried in vain. Well, I have a mind to write the reply myself; I need not go down to the house' (meaning, as I afterwards learnt, the House of Lords) 'for ten minutes, and if I do not eat this currant tart, but write instead, I can very well spare that time. Bring me my writing-desk.'

The desk was brought, and placed on a side-table. His lordship sat down, and opening Ellen Plummy's letter, began to write a reply for me.

He sat with his forehead full of lines, frowning and screwing up his mouth, and working very hard at it, and only writing a few words at a time, after studying Ellen's letter, which lay open before him.

Three times a servant came to announce to his lordship that his carriage was at the door; but he had not finished. At last, however, it was done, and he was about to read it, when, hearing the clock strike, he found he had been three quarters of an hour over it, and, jumping up, hurried out of the room, and I heard the carriage drive off at a great rate.

Lady Flowerdale, with a face of smiling curiosity, told one of the footmen to bring her what his lordship had been writing. She cast her eyes over it, laid it down, and then calmly desired all the servants to leave the room. As soon as they were gone she took it up again hastily, and read it aloud, as if to enjoy it more fully. It was as follows:-

'To MISS E. PLUMMY.

'Hanover Square, July 15.

'My dear Madam,

'I have the honour to acknowledge the receipt of your very kind letter, the date of which has been omitted, no doubt by an oversight. You have stated that I still hold a place in your memory, although you have now got another doll, and that your affection for this latter one is only by reason of your thoughts dwelling upon me. You have also stated that you possess various little articles; and I, moreover, notice sundry allusions to needlework and Twelfth-cake, to your brother Master Thomas, and to Bonaparte and Mr Abernethy; the purport of which is not necessary for me to discuss. But I must frankly tell you that, having now become the doll of another, I cannot with propriety reciprocate that solicitude which you are pleased to entertain for me, nor can I, for the same reason, address you in similar terms of affection. At the same time, my dear madam, permit me to add that I cherish a lively sense of all the kindness you once showed me, and I cannot doubt of the sincerity of your present professions of respect and esteem.

'I have the honour to be,<br>
'My dear Madam, very faithfully yours,<br>
'M. P.'

When the countess had concluded this letter she hastily put a cambric handkerchief up to her face, and particularly over her mouth, and laughed to herself for at least a minute. I also laughed to myself. What a polite, unfeeling, stupid reply to a kind, tender-hearted little girl like Ellen Plummy. Whatever knowledge the minister might have had of grown-up men and women, and the world, and the affairs of state, it was certain he was not equal to enter into the mind of a doll who had a heart like mine. It would have been so *much* better if his lordship, instead of writing that letter, had eaten his currant tart, – and then gone to bed.

## CHAPTER X

## PLAYING WITH FIRE

I have now something more than a narrow escape to relate; for though I did really escape, yet it was not without a dreadful accident, and some injury. It was also the occasion of my changing my place of residence and style of living. All, however, shall be told in proper order.

Lady Flora having learnt my name from the address of the letter I had received, she took a sudden fancy to have it engraved upon a little gold bracelet. When the bracelet was sent home she fastened it upon my wrist, but it dropped off once or twice, being rather too large, so we drove to the jeweller's house, which was near Charing cross, and there it was fastened to my wrist by rivets, so that it could not be taken off at all. This was what Lady Flora desired.

On returning through the Haymarket my mamma recollected, as we passed the Opera House, that she had still never seen the dancing there, on account of her sleeping; and at the same time I, for *my* part, only recollected my narrow escape. But the loss of the opera dancing made Lady Flora only think the more about it, and about dancing; and when we arrived at home she ran to her mamma, and begged to be taken to Willis's Rooms – in fact, she wanted to dance herself at 'Almack's,' and to take me with her, as no doubt there would be many other dolls in the room, with whom, after mutual and satisfactory introductions, I could associate.

Lady Flowerdale said she was afraid that Lady Flora, being not yet nine years of age, was too young to be taken to 'Almack's'; she could, however, take her to the Duchess of Guineahen's ball, which was to be given next month. This greatly pleased Flora, and meantime she resolved to take an extra lesson in dancing of Madame Michaud, in order to be the better prepared for the ball.

I was present at all the lessons of dancing, and saw Madame Michaud seated with her gold snuff-box, tapping upon the lid to keep time, and taking an immense pinch of snuff when Lady Flora danced well, and a still more immense pinch when she danced badly, besides scolding the young man who played the violin, as if it had been his fault.

Another thing, however, and a still more important one, was to be done, before this ball occurred, and this was to get ready the ball dresses. A message was immediately sent to a celebrated milliner in Piccadilly to come immediately and take orders for ball dresses, for Lady Flora and her doll.

During all the time these dresses were being made, my mamma was so impatient and restless that it was quite an unhappiness to see her. I often thought what a pity it was she had not learned to make dresses herself, her mind would then have been employed, and she would have been so much more comfortable. Oh, how different was the happy day I spent among the poor little milliners when Ellen Plummy and Nanny Bell sat under the tent made of a sheet, to make me a frock and trousers. How happy were they over the work, and how impatient and cross was Lady Flora, who had no work to do. Her mind was so disturbed that she was quite unable to attend to any of her lessons; she insisted, however, upon her governess giving me lessons instead, by placing the pen in my hand, and directing it till I had copied several pages of a book. By this means I learned to write, – the governess was employed, – and my mamma said it was the same as if she took her usual lessons.

At last the dresses came home. They were beautiful, and both exactly alike. They were made of the thinnest white gauze, to be worn over very full petticoats of the same white gauze; so that they set out very much, and looked very soft and fleecy. They were trimmed with an imitation of lily of the valley, made in white satin and silver. The trousers were of white satin, trimmed with gauze.

Now there was such a trying on and changing, and proposals for alterations, and sending all back to the milliner's, and having all back again two hours afterwards, to try on once more in case they really did *not* need alteration.

The day of the ball was rather cold and windy; so that, although it was the month of August, a fire was ordered in the nursery, and in Lady Flora's bed-room, lest she might take cold. Towards evening the dresses were all laid out ready to put on; but when my mamma saw them, she could not wait, and insisted upon being dressed, although it was five hours before the time. In two hours and a half she was ready; and then I was dressed, which occupied an hour more. Still there was a long time to wait; so Lady Flora took me in her arms, and began to dance from room to room, – that is, from the nursery to her bed-room, from one fire-place to the other. In doing this she observed that each time she turned, her full, gauze frock gave the fire a *puff*, so that a blaze came; and as she was amused by it, she went each time nearer, and whisked round quicker in order to make the blaze greater. 'Oh, Lady Flora!' cried her maid, 'pray take care of your dress; you go too near; wait till I run and fetch the fire-guards.'

Away ran the maid to fetch the fire-guards; and while she was gone Lady Flora determined to dance for the last time still nearer than ever to each fire before she whisked round. The very next time she did it she went just the least bit too near; the hem of her frock whisked against the bars – and her frock was in a blaze in a moment!

She gave a loud scream and a jump, and was going to run, when most fortunately her foot caught one corner of a thick rug, and down she fell. This smothered the blaze, but still her clothes were on fire; and she lay shrieking and rolling and writhing on the floor.

Up ran the nursery maid, and when she saw what had happened, she began screaming too – and up ran the page, and when he saw what had happened he fell down upon his face with fear and confusion – and up ran the very tall footman, and the instant he looked into the room, and smelt the fire, he ran away again as fast as possible – and then up ran the countess herself, and she ran straight to her child, and rolled the thick rug all round her, and carried her in her arms to her own room.

Physicians and surgeons were sent for, and all the burnt things were taken off, and thrown on one side. Among these I lay; my beautiful dress was all black tinder; but I was not really much burnt, nor was Lady Flora. A few weeks might cure her, though the scars would always remain, and spoil her prettiness; but what could cure *me?* I was so scorched and frizzled, that the paint which was on my skin had blistered and peeled off. I was quite black. No notice was taken of me; and in the confusion I was carried out of the room, with the rest of the burnt rags, and thrown by one of the servants, in her haste, out of a back window.

How I escaped utter destruction, in this dreadful fall, I cannot think; unless it was owing to my being wrapped all round in singed clothes, so that I fell softly. I had nearly fainted with fear, when the flames first caught my dress; and when the housemaid threw open the window to fling me out, my senses utterly forsook me.

I fell over a low wall, into a passage leading towards some stables. In the course of a few minutes I recovered my senses, but only to experience a fresh alarm! A fine large Newfoundland dog, who was just passing, thought somebody had thrown him a broiled bone; so he caught me up in his mouth, and away he ran with me, wagging his tail.

## CHAPTER XI

## THE PORTRAIT PAINTER

The Newfoundland dog soon found that the smell of my burnt clothes and scorched skin was not the same as a broiled bone; and that, in fact, I was not good to eat. But he still continued to hold me in his great warm, red mouth, because he was used to fetch and carry; and, as he felt no wish to taste me, he thought he would take me, just as I was, to his young mistress, who was not far off. He had merely wandered about Hanover square to amuse himself, as he knew the neighbourhood very well.

The dog ran through the door-way of some private stables into a passage that led into the square; and turning down, first one street, then another, he soon stopped at a door, upon which was written, 'J. C. Johnson, Portrait Painter.'

The door was shut, but the area gate happened to be open; so down ran the dog into the area, and into the front kitchen, and across that to the stairs, and up the stairs (three flights) till he came to the front room of the second floor, which was a-jar, and in he bounced. There sat a little girl and her aunt; and Mr J. C. Johnson was painting the aunt's portrait, in a great white turban.

The dog ran at once to the little girl, and laying me at her feet, sprang back a step or two, and began wagging and swishing his tail about, and hanging out a long crimson tongue, and breathing very fast, and waiting to be praised and patted, and called a good dog, for what he had brought.

'Oh, Nep!' cried the aunt to the dog, 'what horrid thing *have* you brought? some dirty old bone.'

'It is an Indian idol, I believe,' said Mr Johnson, taking me up from the carpet; 'an Indian image of ebony, much defaced by time.'

'I think,' said the little girl, to whom Mr Johnson handed me, 'I think it looks very like a wooden doll, with a burnt frock and scorched face.'

'Well, so it is, I *do* believe,' said the aunt.

'Let me examine the figure once more,' said the portrait-painter, laying down his palette of colours, but keeping his brush in the other hand. 'Yes, yes, I fancy, madam, your niece is correct. It is not a work of Indian art, nor of Egyptian, nor of Grecian art; it is the work of a London doll-maker.'

I expected he was, of course, about to say, 'by the celebrated Mr Sprat,' but he did not.

'Oh, you poor London doll!' said the little girl, 'what a pity you were not made in India, or somewhere a wonderful way off, then Mr Johnson would have taken pity on you, and painted you all over.'

Mr Johnson laughed at this; and then gave such a droll look at the little girl, and such a good-natured look at me. 'Well,' said he to her, 'well, my little dear, leave this black doll with me; and when you come again with your aunt, you shall see what I have done.'

The aunt thanked Mr Johnson for his pleasant promise, while she was taking off her turban to depart; and away they went, the Newfoundland dog, Nep., leaping down stairs before them, to show them the way. They were from Buckinghamshire, and had lodgings only a few streets distant. The aunt was Mrs Brown, her niece was Mary Hope. Mary Hope's father was a clerk in the Bank; but she chiefly lived with her aunt in the country, as her father had seven other daughters, and a small salary.

As soon as they were gone, Mr Johnson told his son to tear off all my burnt clothes, scrape me all over with the back of a knife, and then wash me well with soap and water. When this was done, the good-natured artist painted me all over from head to foot. When I was dry he again painted me all over with a warmer colour, like flesh; and when that also was dry, he painted my cheeks, and lips, and eyebrows; and finally he gave me a complete skin of the most delicate varnish. My beautiful hair was entirely burned off; and Mr Johnson said this was a sad pity, as he did not know how to supply it. But his son told him there was a doll's wig-shop very near the Temple, where a new head of hair could be got. So the kind Mr Johnson took the measure of my head; and when he went out for his evening walk, he went to the shop and bought me a most lovely dark auburn wig, with long ringlets, and his son glued it on. When all was done, they hung me up in a safe place to dry.

The hanging up to dry immediately reminded me of my infancy in the shop of Mr Sprat, when I first dangled from the beam and looked round upon all my fellow-creature dolls who were dangling and staring and smiling on all sides. The recollection was, on the whole, pleasing. I seemed to have lived a long time since that day. How much I had to recollect! There was the doll-shop in Holborn – and little Emmy, who used to read little books in the back-room – the Marcet books, the Harriet Myrtle books, the Mary Howitt books, and the delightful story of 'The Good-natured Bear' – in short, all the different stories and histories, and voyages, and travels, and fairy-tales she had read – and there was the master of the shop in his brown paper cock'd hat – and Thomas Plummy and the cake – and Ellen Plummy, and Twelfth-night in the pastry-cook's shop – and the different scenes that I had witnessed among the little milliners; and the making of my first frock and trousers under the tent, upon Ellen Plummy's bed; and my life in Hanover square, during which I saw so many great places in great London, and had been taught by Lady Flora's governess to write, and had fallen headlong from a box at the Opera, into a gentleman's hat; and where, after having beautiful ball-dresses made, my little lady mamma and I had both caught fire; and, lastly, there was my tumble over the wall into the passage, where the Newfoundland dog had fancied I was a broiled bone, and caught me up in his mouth. Here was a biography to recollect; while, for the second time in my life, I was hanging up for my paint and varnish to dry.

# Edward Lear (1812–1888)

Edward Lear's *A Book of Nonsense* is commonly seen by literary historians as one of the key texts of nineteenth-century childhood, marking the growing levity and frivolity of children's books. Lear was a painter, and while working for the Earl of Derby, composed a set of limericks for the Earl's grandchildren; with a second collection, they totalled 212.

Lear was a complex character, a friend of the Tennysons, a musician as well as artist and writer, and a depressive, and as 'nonsense' is apt to yield far from nonsensical interpretations by adults of a certain cast, a good deal has been written about him. His later work included *Nonsense Songs, Stories, Botany and Alphabets* (1871), in which the sombre and surreal 'The Jumblies' appeared, and *Laughable Lyrics* (1877) which, it can be argued, is only marginally for children.

The limericks themselves are, in contrast with the ingenuity displayed by many later users of the form, fairly pedestrian: the vast majority employ a crude form of the repetition of the first and last rhymes. This is a selection of the most ingenious, but no selection could avoid the inherent melancholy.

## from *A Book of Nonsense* [by Derry Down Derry] (1846, 1861)

There was an Old Man in a tree,
who was horribly bored by a Bee;
When they said, 'Does it buzz?'
he replied, 'Yes, it does!
It's a regular brute of a Bee!'

There was an Old Man who supposed,
that the street door was partially closed;
But some very large rats,
ate his coats and his hats,
While that futile old gentleman dozed.

There was a Young Lady whose eyes,
were unique as to colour and size;
When she opened them wide,
people all turned aside,
And started away in surprise.

There was an Old Person of Mold,
who shrank from sensations of cold;
So he purchased some muffs,
some furs and some fluffs,
And wrapped himself from the cold.

There was an Old Man of Cape Horn,
who wished he had never been born;
So he sat on a chair,
till he died of despair,
That dolorous Man of Cape Horn,

There was an Old Lady whose folly,
induced her to sit in a holly;

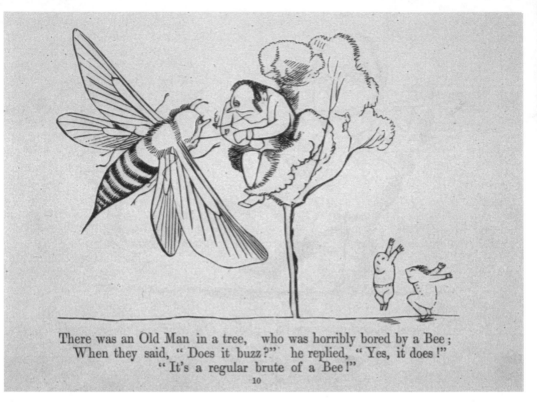

There was an Old Man in a tree, who was horribly bored by a Bee;
When they said, " Does it buzz?" he replied, " Yes, it does !"
" It's a regular brute of a Bee!"
10

Plate 2 'There was an Old Man in a tree...', from *A Book of Nonsense*, illustration by Edward Lear. By permission of the British Library

Whereon by a thorn,
her dress being torn,
She quickly became melancholy.

There was an Old Man of the Coast,
who placidly sat on a post;
But when it was cold,
he relinquished his hold,
And called for some hot buttered toast.

## from *Nonsense Songs, Stories, Botany, and Alphabets* (1871)

### The Jumblies

They went to sea in a Sieve, they did,
In a Sieve they went to sea:
In spite of all their friends could say,
On a winter's morn, on a stormy day,
In a Sieve they went to sea!
And when the Sieve turned round and round,
And everyone cried, 'You'll all be drowned!'
They called aloud, 'Our Sieve ain't big,
But we don't care a button! we don't care a fig!

In a Sieve we'll go to sea!'
    Far and few, far and few,
        Are the lands where the Jumblies live;
      Their heads are green, and their hands are blue,
      And they went to sea in a Sieve.

They sailed away in a Sieve, they did,
  In a Sieve they sailed so fast,
With only a beautiful pea-green veil
Tied with a riband by way of a sail,
  To a small tobacco-pipe mast;
And everyone said, who saw them go,
'O won't they be soon upset, you know!
For the sky is dark, and the voyage is long,
And happen what may, it's extremely wrong
  In a Sieve to sail so fast!'
    Far and few, far and few,
        Are the lands where the Jumblies live;
      Their heads are green, and their hands are blue,
      And they went to sea in a Sieve.

The water it soon came in, it did,
  The water it soon came in;
So to keep them dry, they wrapped their feet
In a pinky paper all folded neat,
  And they fastened it down with a pin.
And they passed the night in a crockery-jar,
And each of them said, 'How wise we are!
Though the sky be dark, and the voyage be long,
Yet we never can think we were rash or wrong,
  While round in our Sieve we spin!'
    Far and few, far and few,
        Are the lands where the Jumblies live;
      Their heads are green, and their hands are blue,
      And they went to sea in a Sieve.

And all night long they sailed away;
  And when the sun went down,
They whistled and warbled a moony song
To the echoing sound of a coppery gong,
  In the shade of the mountains brown.
'O Timballoo! How happy we are,
When we live in a sieve and a crockery-jar,
And all night long in the moonlight pale,
We sail away with a pea-green sail,
  In the shade of the mountains brown!'
    Far and few, far and few,
        Are the lands where the Jumblies live;
      Their heads are green, and their hands are blue,
      And they went to sea in a Sieve.

They sailed to the Western Sea, they did,
  To a land all covered with trees,

And they bought an Owl, and a useful Cart,
And a pound of Rice, and a Cranberry Tart,
   And a hive of silvery Bees.
And they bought a Pig, and some green Jackdaws,
And a lovely Monkey with lollipop paws,
And forty bottles of Ring-Bo-Ree,
   And no end of Stilton Cheese.
      Far and few, far and few,
         Are the lands where the Jumblies live;
      Their heads are green, and their hands are blue,
         And they went to sea in a Sieve.

And in twenty years they all came back,
   In twenty years or more,
And everyone said, 'How tall they've grown!
For they've been to the Lakes, and the Torrible Zone,
   And the hills of the Chankly Bore;
And they drank their health, and gave them a feast
Of dumplings made of beautiful yeast;
And everyone said, 'If we only live,
We too will go to sea in a Sieve,
   To the hills of the Chankly Bore!'
      Far and few, far and few,
         Are the lands where the Jumblies live;
      Their heads are green, and their hands are blue,
         And they went to sea in a Sieve.

# Captain [Frederick] Marryat (1792–1848)

The genre of the adventure story in Britain owed a great deal to the adventurous Captain Marryat, who turned to writing in 1829, but *The Children of the New Forest*, his last book for children, is also important as virtually founding the genre of the historical novel. Marryat's *Masterman Ready* (1841–2) was written in response to the fanciful geography of *The Swiss Family Robinson* and contains a good deal of straightforward moralizing – a tone carried over, although much less overtly, into *The Children of the New Forest*.

Set during the British civil war, it tells the story of the Royalist Beverley children, Edward, Humphrey, Alice and Edith, who hide in the New Forest disguised as the grandchildren of an old forester, Jacob Armitage. The book is a distant relation of *The Swiss Family Robinson*, in that the aristocratic children, their father dead and their home destroyed, learn everyday skills of housekeeping,

farming, hunting and survival. At the end of the book, with the Restoration, the 'children' are prosperously married, and their land returned to them. Although told from the Royalist side, the book is very even-handed politically, and lays some stress on reconciliation: the narrator argues at one point that the children actually had no need to hide, as the Roundheads would not have harmed them.

Despite its occasionally ponderous narrative style, *The Children of the New Forest* is an important book, not only for setting the fashion for the historical novel, but also for its central character, Edward, who has been the model for many thousands of fictional heroes for over a century of children's books.

In this extract, the children are settling into their new life under Jacob's tuition and any didacticism is purely incidental and situational.

## from *The Children of the New Forest* (1847)

### CHAPTER V

As we have before said, time passed rapidly; with the exception of one or two excursions after venison, they remained in the cottage, and Jacob never went to Lymington. The frost had broken up, the snow had long disappeared, and the trees began to bud. The sun became powerful, and in the month of May the forest began again to look green.

'And now, Edward,' said Jacob Armitage, one day at breakfast; 'we will try for vension again to sell at Lymington, for I must purchase Humphrey's cart and harness; so let us get our guns and go out this fine morning. The stags are mostly by themselves at this season, for the does are with their young calves. We must find the slot of a deer, and track him to his lair, and you shall have the first shot if you like; but that, however, depends more upon the deer than upon me.'

They had walked four or five miles when they came upon the slot or track of a deer; but Jacob's practised eye pointed out to Edward that it was the slot of a young one, and not worth following. He explained to Edward the difference in the hoof-marks and other signs by which this knowledge was gained, and they proceeded onwards until they found another slot, which Jacob declared to be that of a warrantable stag – that is, one old enough to kill and to be good venison.

'We must now track him to his lair, Edward.'

This took them about a mile further, when they arrived at a small thicket of thorns about an acre in extent.

'Here he is, you see, Edward; let me now see if he is harboured.'

They walked round the thicket, and could not find any slot or track by which the stag had left the covert, and Jacob pronounced that the animal must be hid in it.

'Now, Edward, do you stay here while I go back to the lee side of the covert: I will enter it with Smoker, and the stag will, in all probability, when he is roused, come out to breast the wind. You will then have a good shot at him. Recollect to fire so as to hit him behind the shoulder; if he is moving quick, fire a little before the shoulders; if slow, take aim accurately; but recollect, if I come upon him in the covert, I shall kill him if I can, for we want the vension, and then we will go after another to give you a chance.'

Jacob then left Edward, and went down to the lee side of the covert, where he entered it with Smoker. Edward was stationed behind a thorn-bush, which grew a few yards clear of the covert, and he soon heard the creaking of the branches.

A short time elapsed, and a fine stag came out at a trot; he turned his head, and was just bounding away, when Edward fired, and the animal fell. Remembering the advice of Jacob, Edward remained where he was, in silence reloading his piece, and was soon afterwards joined by Jacob and the dog.

'Well done, Edward!' said the forester, in a low voice, and covering his forehead to keep off the glare of the sun, he looked earnestly at a high brake between some thorn-trees, about half a mile to windward. 'I think I see something there – look, Edward, your eyes are younger than mine. Is that the branch of a tree in the fern, or is it not?'

'I see what you mean,' replied Edward. 'It is not; it moves.'

'I thought so, but my eyes are not so good as they once were. It's another stag, depend upon it; but how to get near him – we never can get across this patch of clear grass without being seen.'

'No, we cannot get at him from this spot,' replied Edward; 'but if we were to fall back to leeward, and gain the forest again, I think that there are thorns sufficient from the forest to where he lies to creep from behind one to the other, so as to get a shot at him; don't you?'

'It will require care and patience to manage that; but I think it might be done. I will try; it is my turn now, you know. You had better stay here with the dog, for only one can hide from thorn to thorn.'

Jacob, ordering Smoker to remain, then set off. He had to make a circuit of three miles to get to the spot where the thorns extended from the forest, and Edward saw no more of him, although he strained his eyes, until the stag sprung out, and the gun was discharged. Edward perceived that the stag was not killed, but severely wounded, running towards the covert near which he was hid. 'Down, Smoker,' said he, as he cocked his gun. The stag came within shot, and was coming nearer, when, seeing Edward, it turned. Edward fired, and then cheered on the dog, who sprang after the wounded animal, giving tongue as he followed him. Edward, perceiving Jacob hastening towards him, waited for him.

'He's hard hit, Edward,' cried Jacob, 'and Smoker will have him; but we must follow as fast as we can.'

They both caught up their guns and ran as fast as they could, when, as they entered the wood, they heard the dog at bay.

'We shan't have far to go, Edward; the animal is done up, Smoker has him at bay.'

They hastened on another quarter of a mile, when they found that the stag had fallen on his knees, and had been seized by the throat by Smoker.

'Mind, Edward, now how I go up to him, for the wound from the horn of the deer is very dangerous.'

Jacob advanced from behind the stag, and cut his throat with his hunting-knife. 'He is a fine beast, and we have done well to-day; but we shall have two journeys to make to get all this venison home. I could not get a fair shot at him – and see, I have hit him here in the flank.'

'And here is my ball in his throat,' said Edward.

'So it is. Then it was a good shot that you made, and you are master of the hunt this day, Edward. Now, I'll remain, and you go home for White Billy. Humphrey is right about the cart. If we had one, we could have carried all home at once; but I must go now and cut the throat of the other stag which you killed so cleverly. You will be a good hunter one of these days, Edward. A little more knowledge, and a little more practice, and I will leave it all to you, and hang my gun up over the chimney.'

It was late in the evening before they had made their two trips and taken all the vension home, and very tired were they before it was all safely housed. Edward was delighted with his success, but not more so than was old Jacob. The next morning, Jacob set off for Lymington, with the pony loaded with vension, which he sold, as well as two more loads which he promised to bring the next day, and the day after. He then looked out for a cart, and was fortunate in finding a small one just fitted to the size of the pony, who was not tall, but very strong, as all New Forest ponies are. He also procured harness, and then put Billy in the cart to draw him home; but Billy did not admire being put in a cart, and for some time was very restive, and backed and reared, and went every way but the right. But by dint of coaxing and leading, he at last submitted, and went straight on; but then the noise of the cart behind him frightened him, and he ran away. At last, having tired himself out, he thought that he might as well go quietly in harness, as he could not get out of it; and he did so, and arrived safe at the cottage. Humphrey was delighted at the sight of the cart, and said that now he should get on well. The next day, Jacob contrived to put all the remainder of the venison in the cart, and White Billy made no more difficulty; he dragged it all to Lymington, and returned with the cart as quietly and cleverly as if he had been in harness all his life.

'Well, Edward, the venison paid for the cart, at all events,' said Jacob; 'and now I will tell you all the news I collected while I was at Lymington. Captain Burly, who attempted to incite the people to rescue the King, has been hung, drawn, and quartered, as a traitor.'

'They are traitors who condemned him,' replied Edward in wrath.

'Yes, so they are; but there is better news, which is, that the Duke of York has escaped to Holland.'

'Yes, that is good news; and the King?'

'He is still a prisoner in Carisbrook Castle. There are many rumours and talks, but no one knows what is true, and what is false; but depend upon it, this cannot last long, and the King will have his rights yet.'

Edward remained very grave for some time.

'I trust in Heaven we all shall have our rights yet, Jacob,' said he at last. 'I wish I was a man!'

Here the conversation ended, and they went to bed.

This was now a busy time at the cottage. The manure had to be got out of the stable and pig-sties, and carried out to the potato-ground and garden; the crops had to be put in; and the cart was now found valuable. After the manure had been carried out and spread, Edward and Humphrey helped Jacob to dig the ground, and then to put in the seed. The cabbage-plants of last year were then put out, and the turnips and carrots sown. Before the month was over, the garden and potato-field were cropped, and Humphrey took upon himself to weed and keep it clean. Little Edith had also employment now; for the hens began to lay eggs, and as soon as she heard them cackling, she ran for the eggs and brought them in; and before the month was over, Jacob had set four hens upon eggs. Billy, the pony, was now turned out to graze in the forest; he came home every night of his own accord.

'I'll tell you what we want,' said Humphrey, who took the command altogether over the farm; 'we want a cow.'

'Oh, yes, a cow,' cried Alice; 'I have plenty of time to milk her.'

'Whose cows are those which I see in the forest sometimes?' said Humphrey to Jacob.

'If they belong to anybody, they belong to the King,' replied Jacob; 'but they are cattle which have strayed and found their way to the forest, and have remained here ever since. They are rather wild and savage, and you must be careful how you go too near them, as the bulls will run at you. They increase very fast; there were but six a few years ago, and now there are at least fifty in the herd.'

'Well, I'll try and get one, if I can,' said Humphrey.

'You will be puzzled to do that, boy,' replied Jacob; 'and as I said before, beware of the bulls.'

'I don't want a bull,' replied Humphrey; 'but a cow would give us milk, and then we should have more manure for the garden. My garden will then grow more potatoes.'

'Well, Humphrey, if you can catch a cow, no one will interfere; but I think you will not find it very easy, and you may find it very dangerous.'

'I'll look out for one,' replied Humphrey, 'anyhow. Alice, if we only had a cow, wouldn't that be jolly?'

The crops were now all up, and as the days began to be long, the work became comparatively light and easy. Humphrey was busy making a little wheelbarrow for Edith, that she might barrow away the weeds as he hoed them up; and at last this great performance was completed, much to the admiration of all, and much to his own satisfaction. Indeed, when it is recollected that Humphrey had only the handsaw and axe, and that he had to cut down the tree, and then to saw it into plank, it must be acknowledged that it required great patience and perseverance even to make a wheel-barrow; but Humphrey was not only persevering, but was full of invention. He had built up a hen-house with fir poles, and made the nests for the hens to lay and hatch in, and they now had between forty and fifty chickens running about. He had also divided the pig-sty, so that the sow might be kept apart from the other pigs; and they expected very soon to have a litter of young pigs. He had transplanted the wild strawberries from the forest, and had, by manure, made them large and good; and he had also a fine crop of onions in the garden, from seed which Jacob had bought at Lymington; now Humphrey was very busy cutting down some poles in the forest to make a cow-house, for he declared that he would have a cow somehow or another. June arrived, and it was time to mow down grass to make into hay for the winter, and Jacob had two scythes. He showed the boys how to use them, and they soon became expert; and as there was plenty of long grass at this time of the year, and they could mow when they pleased, they soon had White Billy in full employ-ment carrying the hay home. The little girls helped to make it, for Humphrey had made them two rakes. Jacob thought that there was hay enough made, but Humphrey said that there was enough for the pony, but not enough for the cow.

'But where is the cow to come from, Humphrey?'

'Where the venison comes from,' replied he – 'out of the forest.'

So Humphrey continued to mow and make hay, while Edward and Jacob went out for venison. After all the hay was made and stacked, Humphrey found out a method of thatching with fern, which Jacob had never thought of; and when that was done, they commenced cutting down fern for fodder. Here again Humphrey would have twice as much as Jacob had ever cut before, because he wanted litter for the cow. At last it became quite a joke between him and Edward, who, when he brought home more venison than would keep in the hot weather, told Humphrey that the remainder was for the cow. Still Humphrey would not give up the point, and every morn-ing and evening he would be certain to be absent an hour or two, and it was found out he was watching the herd of wild cattle who were feeding: sometimes they were very near, at others a long way off. He used to get up into the trees, and examine them as they passed under him, without perceiving him. One night Humphrey returned very late, and the next morning he was off before daylight. Breakfast was over, and Humphrey did not make his appearance, and they could not tell what was the matter. Jacob felt uneasy, but Edward laughed, and said, –

'Oh, depend upon it, he'll come back and bring the cow with him.'

Hardly had Edward said these words, when in came Humphrey red with perspiration.

'Now then, Jacob and Edward, come with me; we must put Billy in the cart, and take Smoker and a rope with us. Take your guns too, for fear of accident.'

'Why, what's the matter?'

'I'll tell you as we go along; but I must put Billy in the cart, for there is no time to be lost.'

Humphrey disappeared, and Jacob said to Edward, –

'What can it be?'

'It can be nothing but the cow he is so mad about,' replied Edward. 'However, when he comes with the pony, we shall know; let us take our guns and the dog Smoker as he wishes.'

Humphrey now drove up the pony and cart, and they set off.

'Well, I suppose you'll tell us now what we are going for?' said Edward.

'Yes, I will. You know I've been watching the cattle for a long while, because I wanted a cow. I have been in a tree when they have passed under me several times, and I observed that one or two of the heifers were very near calving. Yesterday evening I thought one could not help calving very soon indeed, and as I was watching, I saw that she was uneasy, and that she at last left the herd and went into a little copse of wood. I remained three hours to see if she came out again, and she did not. It was dark when I came home, as you know. This morning I went before daylight and found the herd. She is very remarkable, being black and white spotted; and, after close examination, I found that she was not with the herd, so I am sure that she went into the copse to calve, and that she has calved before this.'

'Well, that may be,' replied Jacob; 'but now I do not understand what we are to do.'

'Nor I,' replied Edward.

'Well, then, I'll tell you what I hope to do. I have got the pony and cart to take the calf home with us, if we can get it – which I think we can. I have got Smoker to worry the heifer and keep her employed while we put the calf in the cart; a rope that we may tie the cow, if we can; and you with your guns must keep off the herd, if they come to her assistance. Now do you understand my plan?'

'Yes, and I think it very likely to succeed, Humphrey,' replied Jacob, 'and I give you credit for the scheme. We will help you all we can. Where is the copse?'

'Not half a mile further,' replied Humphrey. 'We shall soon be there.'

On their arrival, they found that the herd were feeding at a considerable distance from the copse, which was perhaps as well.

'Now,' said Jacob, 'I and Edward will enter into the copse with Smoker, and you follow us, Humphrey. I will make Smoker seize the heifer if necessary; at all events he will keep her at bay – that is, if she is here. First let us walk round the copse and find her *slot*, as we call the track of a deer. See, here is her footing. Now let us go in.'

They advanced cautiously into the thicket, following the track of the heifer, and at last came upon her. Apparently she had not calved more than an hour, and was licking the calf, which was not yet on its legs. As soon as the animal perceived Jacob and Edward she shook her head, and was about to run at them; but Jacob told Smoker to seize her, and the dog flew at her immediately. The attack of the dog drove back the heifer quite into the thicket, and as the dog bounded round her, springing this way and that way to escape her horns, the heifer was soon separated from the calf.

'Now then, Edward and Humphrey,' said Jacob, advancing between the heifer and the calf, 'lift up the calf between you and put it in the cart. Leave Smoker and me to manage the mother.'

The boys put their arms under the stomach of the calf and carried it away. The heifer was at first too busy defending herself against the dog to perceive that the calf was gone; when she did, Jacob called Smoker to him, so as to bring him between the heifer and where the boys were going out of the thicket. At last the heifer gave a loud bellow, and rushed out of the thicket in pursuit of her calf, checked by Smoker, who held on to her ear, and sometimes stopped her from advancing.

'Hold her, Smoker,' said Jacob, who now went back to help the boys. 'Hold her, boy. – Is the calf in the cart?'

'Yes, and tied fast,' replied Edward; 'and we are in the cart, too.'

'That's right,' replied Jacob. 'Now I'll get in too, and let us drive off. She'll follow us, depend upon it. – Here, Smoker! Smoker! let her alone.'

Smoker, at this command, came bounding out of the copse, followed by the heifer, lowing most anxiously. Her lowing was responded to by the calf in the cart, and she ran wildly up to it.

'Drive off, Humphrey,' said Jacob; 'I think I heard the lowing of the heifer answered by some of the herd, and the sooner we are off the better.'

Humphrey, who had the reins, drove off; the heifer followed, at one time running at the dog, at another putting her head almost into the hind part of the cart; but the lowing of the heifer was now answered by deeper tones, and Jacob said, –

'Edward, get your gun ready, for I think the herd is following. Do not fire, however, till I tell you. We must be governed by circumstances. It won't do to lose the pony, or to run any serious risk, for the sake of the heifer and calf. Drive fast, Humphrey.'

A few minutes afterwards they perceived at about a quarter of a mile behind them, not the whole herd, but a single bull, who was coming up at a fast trot with his tail in the air, and tossing his head, lowing deeply in answer to the heifer.

'There's only one, after all,' said Jacob; 'I suppose the heifer is his favourite. Well, we can manage him. – Smoker, come in. Come in, sir, directly,' cried Jacob, perceiving that the dog was about to attack the bull.

Smoker obeyed, and the bull advanced till he was within a hundred yards.

'Now, Edward, do you fire first – aim for his shoulder. Humphrey, pull up.'

Humphrey stopped the pony, and the bull continued to advance, but seemed puzzled whom to attack, unless it was the dog. As soon as the bull was within sixty yards, Edward fired, and the animal fell down on its knees, tearing the ground with its horns.

'That will do,' said Jacob. 'Drive on again, Humphrey; we will have a look at that fellow by-and-by. At present we had better get home, as others may come. He's up again, but he is at a standstill. I have an idea that he is hit hard.'

The cart drove on, followed by the heifer; but no more of the wild herd made their appearance, and they very soon gained the cottage.

'Now, then, what shall we do?' said Jacob. 'Come, Humphrey, you have had all the ordering of this, and have done it well.'

'Well, Jacob, we must now drive the cart into the yard, and shut the gate upon the cow, till I am ready.'

'That's easy done, by setting Smoker at her,' replied Jacob; 'but mercy on us, there's Alice and Edith running out! – the heifer may kill them! Go back, Alice! run quite into the cottage, and shut the door till we come.'

Alice and Edith hearing this, and Edward also crying out to them, made a hasty retreat to the cottage. Humphrey then packed the cart against the paling of the yard, so as to enable Edward to get on the other side of it, ready to open the gate. Smoker was set at the heifer, and, as before, soon engaged her attention; so that the gate was opened and the cart drove in, and the gate closed again, before the heifer could follow.

'Well, Humphrey, what next?'

'Why, now lift the calf out and put it into the cow-house. I will go into the cow-house with a rope and a slip-knot at the end of it, get upon the beam above, and drop it over her horns as she's busy with the calf, which she will be as soon as you let her in. I shall pass the end of the rope outside, for you to haul up when I am ready and then we shall have her fast, till we can secure her properly. When I call out "ready" do you open the gate and let her in. You can do that and jump into the cart afterwards, for fear she may run at you; but I don't think that she will, for it's the calf she wants, and not either of you.'

As soon as Humphrey was ready with the rope, he gave the word, and the gate was opened; the cow ran in immediately, and hearing her calf bleat, went into the cow-house, the door of which was shut upon her. A minute afterwards Humphrey cried out to them to haul upon the rope, which they did.

'That will do,' said Humphrey from the inside: 'now make the rope fast, and then you may come in.'

They went in, and found the heifer drawn close to the side of the cow-house by the rope which was round her horns, and unable to move her head.

'Well, Humphrey, that's very clever; but now what's to be done?'

'First I'll saw off the tips of her horns, and then if she does run at us, she won't hurt us much. Wait till I go for the saw.'

As soon as the ends of her horns were sawed off, Humphrey took another piece of rope, which he fastened securely round her horns, and then made the other end fast to the side of the building, so that the animal could move about a little and eat out of the crib.

'There,' said Humphrey, 'now time and patience will do the rest. We must coax her, and handle her, and soon shall tame her. At present let us leave her with the calf. She has a yard of rope, and that is enough for her to lick her calf, which is all she requires at present. To-morrow we will cut some grass for her.'

They then went out, shutting the cow-house door.

'Well, Humphrey, you've beat us, after all, and have the laugh on your side now,' said Jacob. ' "Where there's a will, there's a way," that's certain; and I assure you, that when you were making so much hay, and gathering so much litter, and building a cow-house, I had no more idea that we should have a cow than that we should have an elephant; and I will say that you deserve great credit for your way of obtaining it.'

'That he certainly does,' replied Edward. 'You have more genius than I have, brother. But dinner must be ready if Alice has done her duty. What think you, Jacob, shall we after dinner go and look after that bull?'

'Yes, by all means. He will not be bad eating, and I can sell all I can carry in the cart at Lymington. Besides, the skin is worth money.'

# John Ruskin (1819–1900)

The popularity of traditional tales had been growing since the first appearance of the Grimm brothers' *German Popular Stories* in 1823, and *The King of the Golden River* was described by its author as 'a fairly good imitation of Grimm'. Ruskin was an enthusiast for the stories, writing an introduction to an 1868 Grimm collection, and observing that properly brought-up children 'have no need of moral fairy tales'.

This was no ordinary recommendation, for Ruskin was an enormously influential Victorian writer and artist, being, among many other things, the first Slade Professor of Fine Art at Oxford University, and a philanthropist and social reformer. Among his most influential works were *Modern Painters* (1843–60) and *Unto This Last* (essays on economics) (1860–2).

He wrote *The King of the Golden River* in 1841 at the request of the twelve-year-old Effie Gray, who later became his wife, and he had no intention of publishing it. The story *does* have an implicit moral, but only of the folk-lore kind, rather than the laboured sectarian kind, and is outstanding for its lucid style.

As with many folk-tales, it centres on a downtrodden but virtuous character, the youngest of the Black brothers, Gluck, and his acts of kindness. The treatment of South-West Wind Esquire by the two elder brothers, described in this extract, leads to drought in the Treasure Valley. The King of the Golden River, who had been imprisoned by a more powerful king, in Gluck's golden mug, is inadvertently released by Gluck, and promises that his river shall turn to gold for anyone who drops three drops of holy water into it. Hans and Schwartz both fail, through selfishness and brutality, and are turned into black stones. Gluck succeeds through kindness, and part of the river flows into the Treasure Valley, restoring his fortunes.

## from *The King of the Golden River or the Black Brothers. A Legend of Stiria* (1851)

### CHAPTER I

### HOW THE AGRICULTURAL SYSTEM OF THE BLACK BROTHERS WAS INTERFERED WITH BY SOUTH-WEST WIND, ESQUIRE

In a secluded and mountainous part of Stiria there was, in old time, a valley of the most surprising and luxuriant fertility. It was surrounded, on all sides, by steep and rocky mountains, rising into peaks, which were always covered with snow, and from which a number of torrents descended in constant cataracts. One of these fell westward, over the face of a crag so high, that, when the sun had set to everything else, and all below was darkness, his beams still shone full upon this waterfall, so that it looked like a shower of gold. It was, therefore, called by the people of the neighbourhood, the Golden River. It was strange that none of these streams fell into the valley itself. They all descended on the other side of the mountains, and wound away through broad plains and by populous cities. But the clouds were drawn so constantly to the snowy hills, and rested so softly in the circular hollow, that in time of drought and heat, when all the country round was burnt up, there was still rain in the little valley; and its crops were so heavy, and its hay so high, and its apples so red, and its grapes so blue, and its wine so rich, and its honey so sweet, that it was a marvel to every one who beheld it, and was commonly called the Treasure Valley.

The whole of this little valley belonged to three brothers, called Schwartz, Hans, and Gluck. Schwartz and Hans, the two elder brothers, were very ugly men, with over-hanging eyebrows and small dull eyes, which were always half shut, so that you couldn't see into *them*, and always fancied they saw very far into *you*. They lived by farming the Treasure Valley, and very good farmers they were. They killed everything that did not pay for its eating. They shot the blackbirds, because they pecked the fruit; and killed the hedgehogs, lest they should suck the cows; they poisoned the crickets for eating the crumbs in the kitchen; and smothered the cicadas, which used to sing all summer in the lime trees. They worked their servants without any wages, till they would not work any more, and then quarrelled with them, and turned them out of doors without paying them. It would have been very odd, if with such a farm, and such a system of farming, they hadn't got very rich; and very rich they *did* get. They generally contrived to keep their corn by them till it was very dear, and then sell it for twice its value; they had heaps of gold lying about on their floors, yet it was never known that they had given so much as a penny or a crust in charity; they never went to mass; grumbled perpetually at paying tithes; and were, in a word, of so cruel and grinding a temper, as to receive from all those with whom they had any dealings, the nick-name of the 'Black Brothers.'

The youngest brother, Gluck, was as completely opposed, in both appearance and character, to his seniors as could possibly be imagined or desired. He was not above twelve years old, fair, blue-eyed, and kind in temper to every living thing. He did not, of course, agree particularly well with his brothers, or rather, they did not agree with *him*. He was usually appointed to the honourable office of turnspit, when there was anything to roast, which was not often; for, to do the brothers justice, they were hardly less sparing upon themselves than upon other people. At other times he used to clean the shoes, floors, and sometimes the plates, occasionally getting what was left on them, by way of encouragement, and a wholesome quantity of dry blows, by way of education.

Things went on in this manner for a long time. At last came a very wet summer, and everything went wrong in the country around. The hay had hardly been got in, when the haystacks were floated bodily down to the sea by an inundation; the vines were cut to pieces with the hail; the corn was all killed by a black blight; only in the Treasure Valley, as usual, all was safe. As it had rain when there was rain no where else, so it had sun when there was sun no where else. Every body came to buy corn at the farm, and went away pouring maledictions on the Black Brothers. They asked what they liked, and got it, except from the poor people, who could only beg, and several of whom were starved at their very door, without the slightest regard or notice.

It was drawing towards winter, and very cold weather, when one day the two elder brothers had gone out, with their usual warning to little Gluck, who was left to mind the roast, that he was to let nobody in, and give nothing out. Gluck sat down quite close to the fire, for it was raining very hard, and the kitchen walls were by no means dry or comfortable looking. He turned and turned, and the roast got nice and brown. 'What a pity,' thought Gluck, 'my brothers never ask any body to dinner. I'm sure, when they've got such a nice piece of mutton as this, and nobody else has got so much as a piece of dry bread, it would do their hearts good to have somebody to eat it with them.'

Just as he spoke, there came a double knock at the house door, yet heavy and dull, as though the knocker had been tied up – more like a puff than a knock.

'It must be the wind,' said Gluck; 'nobody else would venture to knock double knocks at our door.'

No; it wasn't the wind: there it came again very hard, and what was particularly astounding, the knocker seemed to be in a hurry, and not to be in the least afraid of the consequences. Gluck went to the window, opened it, and put his head out to see who it was.

It was the most extraordinary looking little gentleman he had ever seen in his life. He had a very large nose, slightly brass-coloured; his cheeks were very round, and very red, and might have warranted a supposition that he had been blowing a refractory fire for the last eight-and-forty hours; his eyes twinkled merrily through long silky eyelashes, his moustaches curled twice round like a corkscrew on each side of his mouth, and his hair, of a curious mixed pepper-and-salt colour, descended far over his shoulders. He was about four feet six in height, and wore a conical pointed cap of nearly the same altitude, decorated with a black feather some three feet long. His doublet was prolonged behind into something resembling a violent exaggeration of what is now termed a 'swallow tail,' but was much obscured by the swelling folds of an enormous black, glossy-looking cloak, which must have been very much too long in calm weather, as the wind, whistling round the old house, carried it clear out from the wearer's shoulders to about four times his own length.

Gluck was so perfectly paralyzed by the singular appearance of his visitor, that he remained fixed without uttering a word, until the old gentleman, having performed another, and a more energetic concerto on the knocker, turned round to look after his fly-away cloak. In so doing he caught sight of Gluck's little yellow head jammed in the window, with its mouth and eyes very wide open indeed.

Plate 3   Richard Doyle's frontispiece to *The King of the Golden River*. By permission of the British Library

'Hollo!' said the little gentleman, 'that's not the way to answer the door: I'm wet, let me in.'

To do the little gentleman justice, he *was* wet. His feather hung down between his legs like a beaten puppy's tail, dripping like an umbrella; and from the ends of his moustaches the water was running into his waistcoat pockets, and out again like a mill stream.

'I beg pardon, sir,' said Gluck, 'I'm very sorry, but I really can't.'

'Can't what!' said the old gentleman.

'I can't let you in, sir, – I can't, indeed; my brothers would beat me to death, sir, if I thought of such a thing. What do you want, sir?'

'Want?' said the old gentleman, petulantly. 'I want fire, and shelter; and there's your great fire there blazing, crackling, and dancing on the walls, with nobody to feel it. Let me in, I say; I only want to warm myself.'

Gluck had had his head, by this time, so long out of the window, that he began to feel it was really unpleasantly cold, and when he turned, and saw the beautiful fire rustling and roaring, and throwing long bright tongues up the chimney, as if it were licking its chops at the savoury smell of the leg of mutton, his heart melted within him that it should be burning away for nothing. 'He does look *very* wet,' said little Gluck; 'I'll just let him in for a quarter of an hour.' Round he went to the door, and opened it; and as the little gentleman walked in, there came a gust of wind through the house, that made the old chimneys totter.

'That's a good boy,' said the little gentleman. 'Never mind your brothers. I'll talk to them.'

'Pray, sir, don't do any such thing,' said Gluck. 'I can't let you stay till they come; they'd be the death of me.'

'Dear me,' said the old gentleman, 'I'm very sorry to hear that. How long may I stay?'

'Only till the mutton's done, sir,' replied Gluck, 'and it's very brown.'

Then the old gentleman walked into the kitchen, and sat himself down on the hob, with the top of his cap accommodated up the chimney, for it was a great deal too high for the roof.

'You'll soon dry there, sir,' said Gluck, and sat down again to turn the mutton. But the old gentleman did *not* dry there, but went on drip, drip, dripping among the cinders, and the fire fizzed, and sputtered, and began to look very black, and uncomfortable: never was such a cloak; every fold in it ran like a gutter.

'I beg pardon, sir,' said Gluck at length, after watching the water spreading in long, quicksilver-like streams over the floor for a quarter of an hour; 'mayn't I take your cloak?'

'No, thank you,' said the old gentleman.

'Your cap, sir?'

'I am all right, thank you,' said the old gentleman rather gruffly.

'But, – sir, – I'm very sorry,' said Gluck, hesitatingly; 'but – really, sir, – you're – putting the fire out.'

'It'll take longer to do the mutton, then,' replied his visitor drily.

Gluck was very much puzzled by the behaviour of his guest; it was such a strange mixture of coolness and humility. He turned away at the string meditatively for another five minutes.

'That mutton looks very nice,' said the old gentleman at length. 'Can't you give me a little bit?'

'Impossible, sir,' said Gluck.

'I'm very hungry,' continued the old gentleman: 'I've had nothing to eat yesterday, nor to-day. They surely couldn't miss a bit from the knuckle!'

He spoke in so very melancholy a tone, that it quite melted Gluck's heart. 'They promised me one slice to-day, sir,' said he; 'I can give you that, but not a bit more.'

'That's a good boy,' said the old gentleman again.

Then Gluck warmed a plate, and sharpened a knife. 'I don't care if I do get beaten for it,' thought he. Just as he had cut a large slice out of the mutton, there came a tremendous rap at the door. The old gentleman jumped off the hob, as if it had suddenly become inconveniently warm. Gluck fitted the slice into the mutton again, with desperate efforts at exactitude, and ran to open the door.

'What did you keep us waiting in the rain for?' said Schwartz, as he walked in, throwing his umbrella in Gluck's face. 'Ay! what for, indeed, you little vagabond?' said Hans, administering an educational box on the ear, as he followed his brother into the kitchen.

'Bless my soul!' said Schwartz when he opened the door.

'Amen,' said the little gentleman, who had taken his cap off, and was standing in the middle of the kitchen, bowing with the utmost possible velocity.

'Who's that?' said Schwartz, catching up a rolling-pin, and turning to Gluck with a fierce frown.

'I don't know, indeed, brother,' said Gluck in great terror.

'How did he get in?' roared Schwartz.

'My dear brother,' said Gluck, deprecatingly, 'he was so *very* wet!'

The rolling-pin was descending on Gluck's head; but, at the instant, the old gentleman interposed his conical cap, on which it crashed with a shock that shook the water out of it all over the room. What was very odd, the rolling-pin no sooner touched the cap, than it flew out of Schwartz's hand, spinning like a straw in a high wind, and fell into the corner at the further end of the room.

'Who are you, sir?' demanded Schwartz, turning upon him.

'What's your business?' snarled Hans.

'I'm a poor old man, sir,' the little gentleman began very modestly, 'and I saw your fire through the window, and begged shelter for a quarter of an hour.'

'Have the goodness to walk out again, then,' said Schwartz. 'We've quite enough water in our kitchen, without making it a drying house.'

'It is a cold day to turn an old man out in, sir; look at my grey hairs.' They hung down to his shoulders, as I told you before.

'Ay!' said Hans, 'there are enough of them to keep you warm. Walk!'

'I'm very, very hungry, sir; couldn't you spare me a bit of bread before I go?'

'Bread, indeed!' said Schwartz; 'do you suppose we've nothing to do with our bread, but to give it to such red-nosed fellows as you?'

'Why don't you sell your feather?' said Hans, sneeringly. 'Out with you.'

'A little bit,' said the old gentleman.

'Be off!' said Schwartz.

'Pray, gentlemen.'

'Off, and be hanged!' cried Hans, seizing him by the collar. But he had no sooner touched the old gentleman's collar, than away he went after the rolling-pin, spinning round and round, till he fell into the corner on the top of it. Then Schwartz was very angry, and ran at the old gentleman to turn him out; but he also had hardly touched him, when away he went after Hans and the rolling-pin, and hit his head against the wall as he tumbled into the corner. And so there they lay, all three.

Then the old gentleman spun himself round with velocity in the opposite direction; continued to spin until his long cloak was all wound neatly about him; clapped his cap on his head, very much on one side (for it could not stand upright without going through the ceiling), gave an additional twist to his corkscrew moustaches, and replied with perfect coolness: 'Gentlemen, I wish you a very good morning. At twelve o'clock to-night I'll call again; after such a refusal of hospitality as I have just experienced, you will not be surprised if that visit is the last I ever pay you.'

'If ever I catch you here again,' muttered Schwartz, coming, half frightened, out of the corner – but, before he could finish his sentence, the old gentleman had shut the house door behind him with a great bang; and there drove past the window, at the same instant, a wreath of ragged cloud, that whirled and rolled away down the valley in all manner of shapes; turning over and over in the air; and melting away at last in a gush of rain.

'A very pretty business, indeed, Mr. Gluck!' said Schwartz. 'Dish the mutton, sir. If ever I catch you at such a trick again – bless me, why the mutton's been cut!'

'You promised me one slice, brother, you know,' said Gluck.

'Oh! and you were cutting it hot, I suppose, and going to catch all the gravy. It'll be long before I promise you such a thing again. Leave the room, sir; and have the kindness to wait in the coal-cellar till I call you.'

Gluck left the room melancholy enough. The brothers ate as much mutton as they could, locked the rest in the cupboard, and proceeded to get very drunk after dinner.

Such a night as it was! Howling wind, and rushing rain, without intermission. The brothers had just sense enough left to put up all the shutters, and double bar the door, before they went to bed. They usually slept in the same room. As the clock struck twelve, they were both awakened by a tremendous crash. Their door burst open with a violence that shook the house from top to bottom.

'What's that?' cried Schwartz, starting up in his bed.

'Only I,' said the little gentleman.

The two brothers sat up on their bolster, and stared into the darkness. The room was full of water, and by a misty moon-beam, which found its way through a hole in the shutter, they could see in the midst of it, an enormous foam globe, spinning round, and bobbing up and down like a cork, on which, as on a most luxurious cushion, reclined the little old gentleman, cap and all. There was plenty of room for it now, for the roof was off.

'Sorry to incommode you,' said their visitor, ironically. 'I'm afraid your beds are dampish; perhaps you had better go to your brother's room: I've left the ceiling on, there.'

They required no second admonition, but rushed into Gluck's room, wet through, and in an agony of terror.

'You'll find my card on the kitchen table,' the old gentleman called after them. 'Remember, the *last* visit.'

'Pray Heaven it may!' said Schwartz, shuddering. And the foam globe disappeared.

Dawn came at last, and the two brothers looked out of Gluck's little window in the morning. The Treasure Valley was one mass of ruin and desolation. The inundation had swept away trees, crops, and cattle, and left in their stead, a waste of red sand, and grey mud. The two brothers crept shivering and horror-struck into the kitchen. The water had gutted the whole first floor; corn, money, almost every moveable thing had been swept away, and there was left only a small white card on the kitchen table. On it, in large, breezy, long-legged letters, were engraved the words: – SOUTH WEST WIND ESQUIRE.

# Catherine Parr [Strickland] Traill (1802–1899)

Often regarded as the first important children's book written in Canada (Catherine had emigrated there from England in 1832), *Canadian Crusoes* was highly influential for Canadian children's literature. Other examples of survival stories range from James MacDonald Oxley's *Up Among the Ice Flows* (1890; see p. 393, this volume) to Monica Hughes's *Log Jam* (1988). Traill's book reflects the ambivalent relationship of Canadians to the wilderness and, like many Robinsonnades, is at once authentic and romantic.

Three young people, Hector (14), his sister Catharine (12) and their energetic friend Louis (14), get lost while searching for stray cattle, and live alone for two years in what for much of the time seems to be a rural idyll. Their adventures include a forest fire, the rescue of an Indian girl, and Catharine's capture and escape from the Indians. All this happens a mere eight miles from their home, a point which leads Mrs Traill into characteristically reflective territory:

> Little did Hector know that beyond that dark ridge of pine hills lay the home of their childhood.... Thus it is in this life: we wander on, sad and perplexed, our path beset with thorns and briars. We cannot see our way clear ... and we do not know how near we are to our Father's home, where he is waiting to welcome the wanderers of the flock back to the everlasting home, the fold of the Good Shepherd.

The settings are authentic, and there is a good deal of educative natural history slipped into the account (sometimes as footnotes), as well as an attempt, as an early reviewer put it, 'to inculcate the virtues of energy and self-reliance'. Morality has been re-tuned to suit new circumstances.

Catherine Traill may be added to that formidable list of strong women who supported or helped to support their families by writing. After her emigration from England (where she was already an established writer: her books included *Fables for the Nursery*, 1825) she lived the life of a pioneer, with a depressive husband and nine children, and continued to write. Later successes included *The Female Emigrant's Guide, and Hints on Canadian Housekeeping* (1854) and *Lady Mary and Her Nurse: or, A Peep Into the Canadian Forest* (1856).

In this extract, the children approach the task of survival with characteristic insouciance. The text is reprinted from Rupert Schieder's scholarly edition (Carleton University Press, 1986).

## from *Canadian Crusoes, A Tale of Rice Lake Plains* (1852)

### from CHAPTER IV

After they had breakfasted, they all went up towards the high table-land above the ravine, with Wolfe, to look round in hope of getting sight of their friends from Cold Springs, but though they kept an anxious look out in every direction, they returned, towards evening, tired and hopeless. Hector had killed a red squirrel, and a partridge which Wolfe 'treed,' – that is, stood barking at the foot of the tree in which it had perched, – and the supply of meat was a seasonable change. They also noticed, and marked with the axe, several trees where there were beehives, intending to come in the cold weather, and cut them down. Louis's father was a great and successful bee-hunter; and Louis rather prided himself on having learned something of his father's skill in that line. Here, where flowers were so abundant and water plentiful, the wild bees seemed to be abundant also; besides, the open space between the trees, admitting the warm sunbeam freely, was favourable both for the bees and the flowers on which they fed, and Louis talked joyfully of the fine stores of honey they should collect in the fall. He had taught little Fanchon, a small French spaniel of his father's, to find out the trees where the bees hived, and also the nests of the ground-bees, and she would bark at the foot of the tree, or scratch with her feet on the ground, as the other dogs barked at the squirrels or the woodchucks; but Fanchon was far away, and Wolfe was old, and would learn no new tricks, so Louis knew he had nothing but his own observation and the axe to depend upon for procuring honey.

---

1 All these fish are indigenous to the fresh waters of Canada. (Author's note)

The boys had been unsuccessful for some days past in fishing; neither perch nor sunfish, pink roach nor mudpouts[1] were to be caught. However, they found water-mussels by groping in the sand, and cray-fish among the gravel at the edge of the water only; the latter pinched their fingers very spitefully. The mussels were not very palatable, for want of salt; but hungry folks must not be dainty, and Louis declared them very good when well roasted, covered up with hot embers. 'The fish-hawks,' said he, 'set us a good example, for they eat them, and so do the eagles and herons. I watched one the other day with a mussel in his bill; he flew to a high tree, let his prey fall, and immediately darted down to secure it; but I drove him off, and, to my great amusement, perceived the wise fellow had just let it fall on a stone, which had cracked the shell for him just in the right place. I often see shells lying at the foot of trees, far up the hills, where these birds must have left them. There is one large thick-shelled mussel, that I have found several times with a round hole drilled through the shell, just as if it had been done with a small auger, doubtless the work of some bird with a strong beak.'

'Do you remember,' said Catharine, 'the fine pink mussel-shell that Hec. picked up in the little corn-field last year; it had a hole in one of the shells too,' and when my uncle saw it, he said it must have been dropped by some large bird, a fish-hawk possibly, or a heron, and brought from the great lake, as it had been taken out of some deep water, the mussels in our creeks being quite thin-shelled and white.'

'Do you remember what a quantity of large fish bones we found in the eagle's nest on the top of our hill, Louis?' said Hector.

'I do; those fish must have been larger than our perch and sun-fish; they were brought from this very lake, I dare say.'

'If we had a good canoe now, or a boat, and a strong hook and line, we might become great fishermen.'

'Louis,' said Catharine, 'is always thinking about canoes, and boats, and skiffs; he ought to have been a sailor.'

Louis was confident that if they had a canoe he could soon learn to manage her; he was an excellent sailor already in theory. Louis never saw difficulties; he was always hopeful, and had a very good opinion of his own cleverness; he was quicker in most things, his ideas flowed faster than Hector's, but Hector was more prudent, and possessed one valuable quality – steady perseverance; he was slow in adopting an opinion, but when once convinced, he pushed on steadily till he mastered the subject or overcame the obstacle.

'Catharine,' said Louis, one day, 'the huckleberries are now very plentiful, and I think it would be a wise thing to gather a good store of them, and dry them for the winter. See, ma chère, wherever we turn our eyes, or place our feet, they are to be found; the hill sides are purple with them. We may, for aught we know, be obliged to pass the rest of our lives here; it will be well to prepare for the winter when no berries are to be found.'

'It will be well, mon ami, but we must not dry them in the sun; for let me tell you, Mr. Louis, that they will be quite tasteless – mere dry husks.'

'Why so, ma belle?'

'I do not know the reason, but I only know the fact, for when our mothers dried the currants and raspberries in the sun, such was the case, but when they dried them on the oven floor, or on the hearth, they were quite nice.'

'Well, Cath., I think I know of a flat thin stone that will make a good hearthstone, and we can get sheets of birch bark and sew into flat bags, to keep the dried fruit in.'

They now turned all their attention to drying huckleberries (or whortleberries).[2] Catharine and Louis (who fancied nothing could be contrived without his help) attended to the preparing and mak-

---

1  This ingenious mode of cracking the shells of mussels is common to many birds. The crow (*Corvus corone*) has been long known by American naturalists to break the thick shells of the river mussels, by letting them fall from a height on to rocks and stones. (Author's note)

2  From the abundance of this fruit, the Indians have given the name of Whortleberry Plain to the lands on the south shore. During the month of July and the early part of August, large parties come to the Rice Lake Plains to gather huckleberries, which they preserve by drying, for winter use. These berries make a delicious tart or pudding, mixed with bilberries and red-currants, requiring little sugar. (Author's note)

ing of the bags of birch bark; but Hector was soon tired of girl's work, as he termed it, and, after gathering some berries, would wander away over the hills in search of game, and to explore the neighbouring hills and valleys, and sometimes it was sunset before he made his appearance. Hector had made an excellent strong bow, like the Indian bow, out of a tough piece of hickory wood, which he found in one of his rambles, and he made arrows with wood that he seasoned in the smoke, sharpening the heads with great care with his knife, and hardening them by exposure to strong heat, at a certain distance from the fire. The entrails of the woodchucks, stretched, and scraped and dried, and rendered pliable by rubbing and drawing through the hands, answered for a bow-string; but afterwards, when they got the sinews and hide of the deer, they used them, properly dressed for the purpose.

Hector also made a cross-bow, which he used with great effect, being a true and steady marksman. Louis and he would often amuse themselves with shooting at a mark, which they would chip on the bark of a tree; even Catharine was a tolerable archeress with the long-bow, and the hut was now seldom without game of one kind or other. Hector seldom returned from his rambles without partridges, quails, or young pigeons, which are plentiful at this season of the year; many of the old ones that pass over in their migratory flight in the spring, stay to breed, or return thither for the acorns and berries that are to be found in great abundance. Squirrels, too, are very plentiful at this season. Hector and Louis remarked that the red and black squirrels never were to be found very near each other. It is a common belief, that the red squirrels make common cause with the grey, and beat the larger enemy off the ground. The black squirrel, for a succession of years, was very rarely to be met with on the Plains, while there were plenty of the red and grey in the 'oak openings.'[1] Deer, at the time our young Crusoes were living on the Rice Lake Plains, were plentiful, and, of course, so were those beasts that prey upon them, – wolves, bears, and wolverines, besides the Canadian lynx, or catamount, as it is here commonly called, a species of wild-cat or panther. These wild animals are now no longer to be seen; it is a rare thing to hear of bears or wolves, and the wolverine and lynx are known only as matters of history in this part of the country; these animals disappear as civilization advances, while some others increase and follow man, especially many species of birds, which seem to pick up the crumbs that fall from the rich man's board, and multiply about his dwelling; some adopt new habits and modes of building and feeding, according to the alteration and improvement in their circumstances.

While our young people seldom wanted for meat, they felt the privation of the bread to which they had been accustomed very sensibly. One day, while Hector and Louis were busily engaged with their assistant, Wolfe, in unearthing a woodchuck, that had taken refuge in his burrow, on one of the gravelly hills above the lake, Catharine amused herself by looking for flowers; she had filled her lap with ripe May-apples,[2] but finding them cumbersome in climbing the steep wooded hills, she deposited them at the foot of a tree near the boys, and pursued her search; and it was not long before she perceived some pretty grassy-looking plants, with heads of bright lilac flowers, and on plucking one pulled up the root also. The root was about the size and shape of a large crocus, and, on biting it, she found it far from disagreeable, sweet, and slightly astringent; it seemed to be a favourite root with the woodchucks, for she noticed that it grew about their burrows on dry gravelly soil, and many of the stems were bitten, and the roots eaten, a warrant in full of wholesomeness. Therefore, carrying home a parcel of the largest of the roots, she roasted them in the embers, and they proved almost as good as chestnuts, and more satisfying than the acorns of the white oak, which they had often roasted in the fire, when they were out working on the fallow,

---

1  Within the last three years, however, the black squirrels have been very numerous, and the red are less frequently to be seen. The flesh of the black squirrel is tender, white, and delicate, like that of a young rabbit. (Author's note)

2  *Podophyllum peltatum* – May-apple, or Mandrake. The fruit of the May-apple, in rich moist soil, will attain to the size of the magnum bonum, or egg-plum, which it resembles in colour and shape. It makes a delicious preserve, if seasoned with cloves or ginger; when eaten uncooked, the outer rind, which is thick and fleshy, and has a rank taste, should be thrown aside; the fine acid pulp in which the seeds are imbedded alone should be eaten. The root of the Podophyllum is used as a cathartic by the Indians. The root of this plant is reticulated, and when a large body of them are uncovered, they present a singular appearance, interlacing each other in large meshes, like an extensive net-work; these roots are white, as thick as a man's little finger, and fragrant, and spread horizontally along the surface. The blossom is like a small white rose. (Author's note)

at the log heaps. Hector and Louis ate heartily of the roots, and commended Catharine for the discovery. Not many days afterwards, Louis accidentally found a much larger and more valuable root, near the lake shore. He saw a fine climbing shrub, with close bunches of dark reddish-purple pea-shaped flowers, which scented the air with a delicious perfume. The plant climbed to a great height over the young trees, with a profusion of dark green leaves and tendrils. Pleased with the bowery appearance of the plant, he tried to pull one up, that he might show it to his cousin, when the root displayed a number of large tubers, as big as good-sized potatoes, regular oval-shaped; the inside was quite white, tasting somewhat like a potato, only pleasanter, when in its raw state, than an uncooked potato. Louis gathered his pockets full, and hastened home with his prize, and, on being roasted, these new roots were decided to be little inferior to potatoes; at all events, they were a valuable addition to their slender stores, and they procured as many as they could find, carefully storing them in a hole, which they dug for that purpose in a corner of their hut.[1] Hector suggested that these roots would be far better late in the fall, or early in the spring, than during the time that the plant was in bloom, for he knew from observation and experience that at the flowering season the greater part of the nourishment derived from the soil goes to perfect the flower and the seeds. Upon scraping the cut tuber, there was a white floury powder produced, resembling the starchy substance of the potato.

'This flour,' said Catharine, 'would make good porridge with milk.'

'Excellent, no doubt, my wise little cook and housekeeper,' said Louis, laughing, 'but, ma belle cousine, where is the milk, and where is the porridge-pot to come from?'

'Indeed,' said Catharine, 'I fear, Louis, we must wait long for both.'

One fine day, Louis returned home from the lake shore in great haste, for the bows and arrows, with the interesting news that a herd of five deer were in the water, and making for Long Island.

'But, Louis, they will be gone out of sight and beyond the reach of the arrows,' said Catharine, as she handed him down the bows and a sheaf of arrows, which she quickly slung round his shoulders by the belt of skin, which the young hunter had made for himself.

'No fear, ma chère; they will stop to feed on the beds of rice and lilies. We must have Wolfe. Here, Wolfe, Wolfe, Wolfe, – here, boy, here!'

Catharine caught a portion of the excitement that danced in the bright eyes of her cousin, and declaring that she too would go and witness the hunt, ran down the ravine by his side, while Wolfe, who evidently understood that they had some sport in view, trotted along by his mistress, wagging his great bushy tail, and looking in high good humour.

Hector was impatiently waiting the arrival of the bows and Wolfe. The herd of deer, consisting of a noble buck, two full-grown females, and two young half-grown males, were quietly feeding among the beds of rice and rushes, not more than fifteen or twenty yards from the shore, apparently quite unconcerned at the presence of Hector, who stood on a fallen trunk eagerly eyeing their motions; but the hurried steps of Louis and Catharine, with the deep sonorous baying of Wolfe, soon roused the timid creatures to a sense of danger, and the stag, raising his head and making, as the children thought, a signal for retreat, now struck boldly out for the nearest point of Long Island.

'We shall lose them,' cried Louis, despairingly, eyeing the long bright track that cut the silvery waters, as the deer swam gallantly out.

'Hist, hist, Louis,' said Hector, 'all depends upon Wolfe. Turn them. Wolfe; hey, hey, seek them, boy!'

Wolfe dashed bravely into the lake.

'Head them! head them!' shouted Hector.

Wolfe knew what was meant; with the sagacity of a long-trained hunter, he made a desperate effort to gain the advantage by a circuitous route. Twice the stag turned irresolute, as if to face

---

1   This plant appears to me to be a species of the *Psoralea esculenta*, or Indian bread-root, which it resembles in description, excepting that the root of the above is tuberous, oval, and connected by long filaments. The largest tubers are furthest from the stem of the plant. (Author's note)

his foe, and Wolfe, taking the time, swam ahead, and then the race began. As soon as the boys saw the herd had turned, and that Wolfe was between them and the island, they separated, Louis making good his ambush to the right among the cedars, and Hector at the spring to the west, while Catharine was stationed at the solitary pine-tree, at the point which commanded the entrance of the ravine.

'Now, Cathy,' said her brother, 'when you see the herd making for the ravine, shout and clap your hands, and they will turn either to the right or to the left. Do not let them land, or we shall lose them. We must trust to Wolfe for their not escaping to the island. Wolfe is well trained, he knows what he is about.'

Catharine proved a dutiful ally, she did as she was bid; she waited till the deer were within a few yards of the shore, then she shouted and clapped her hands. Frightened at the noise and clamour, the terrified creatures coasted along for some way, till within a little distance of the thicket where Hector lay concealed, the very spot from which they had emerged when they first took to the water; to this place they boldly steered. Louis, who had watched the direction the herd had taken with breathless interest, now noiselessly hurried to Hector's assistance, taking an advantageous post for aim, in case Hector's arrow missed, or only slightly wounded one of the deer.

Hector, crouched beneath the trees, waited cautiously till one of the does was within reach of his arrow, and so good and true was his aim, that it hit the animal in the throat a little above the chest; the stag now turned again, but Wolfe was behind, and pressed him forward, and again the noble animal strained every nerve for the shore. Louis now shot his arrow, but it swerved from the mark; he was too eager, it glanced harmlessly along the water; but the cool, unimpassioned hand of Hector sent another arrow between the eyes of the doe, stunning her with its force, and then, another from Louis laid her on her side, dying, and staining the water with her blood.

The herd, abandoning their dying companion, dashed frantically to the shore, and the young hunters, elated by their success, suffered them to make good their landing without further molestation. Wolfe, at a signal from his master, ran in the quarry, and Louis declared exultingly, that as his last arrow had given the *coup de grace*, he was entitled to the honour of cutting the throat of the doe; but this the stern Highlander protested against, and Louis, with a careless laugh, yielded the point, contenting himself with saying, 'Ah, well, I will get the first steak of the venison when it is roasted, and that is far more to my taste.' Moreover, he privately recounted to Catharine the important share he had had in the exploit, giving her, at the same time, full credit for the worthy service she had performed, in withstanding the landing of the herd. Wolfe, too, came in for a large share of the honour and glory of the chase.

The boys were soon hard at work, skinning the animal, and cutting it up. This was the most valuable acquisition they had yet effected, for many uses were to be made of the deer, besides eating the flesh. It was a store of wealth in their eyes.

During the many years that their fathers had sojourned in the country, there had been occasional intercourse with the fur traders and trappers, and, sometimes, with friendly disposed Indians, who had called at the lodges of their white brothers for food and tobacco.

From all these men, rude as they were, some practical knowledge had been acquired, and their visits, though few and far between, had left good fruit behind them; something to think about and talk about, and turn to future advantage.

The boys had learned from the Indians how precious were the tough sinews of the deer for sewing. They knew how to prepare the skins of the deer for mocassins, which they could cut out and make as neatly as the squaws themselves. They could fashion arrow-heads, and knew how best to season the wood for making both the long and cross-bow; they had seen the fish-hooks these people manufactured from bone and hard wood; they knew that strips of fresh-cut skins would make bow-strings, or the entrails of animals dried and rendered pliable. They had watched the squaws making baskets of the inner bark of the oak, elm, and basswood, and mats of the inner bark of the cedar, with many other ingenious works that they now found would prove useful to them, after a little practice had perfected their inexperienced attempts. They also knew how to dry venison as the Indians and trappers prepare it, by cutting the thick fleshy portions of the meat into strips, from four to six inches in breadth, and two or more in thickness. These strips they strung upon poles supported on forked sticks, and exposed them to the drying action of the sun and wind. Fish they split open, and removed the back and head bones, and smoked them slightly, or dried them in the sun.

Their success in killing the doe greatly raised their spirits; in their joy they embraced each other, and bestowed the most affectionate caresses on Wolfe for his good conduct.

'But for this dear, wise old fellow, we should have had no venison for dinner to-day,' said Louis; 'and so, Wolfe, you shall have a choice piece for your own share.'

Every part of the deer seemed valuable in the eyes of the young hunters; the skin they carefully stretched out upon sticks to dry gradually, and the entrails they also preserved for bow-strings. The sinews of the legs and back, they drew out, and laid carefully aside for future use.

'We shall be glad enough of these strings by-and-by,' said careful Hector; 'for the summer will soon be at an end, and then we must turn our attention to making ourselves winter clothes and mocassins.'

'Yes, Hec., and a good warm shanty; these huts of bark and boughs will not do when once the cold weather sets in.'

'A shanty would soon be put up,' said Hector; 'for even Kate, wee bit lassie as she is, could give us some help in trimming up the logs.'

# Mary Louisa Charlesworth (1819–1880)

*Ministering Children*, which could well have been written by Mary Martha Sherwood, demonstrates how enduring were the ideas of the evangelical writers. A long, episodic work, it ends on a note of homily: 'We have only to ask the children who read this story whether they are also ministering children? This story has been written to show, as in a picture, what ministering children are. There is no child upon earth who may not be a ministering child: because the Holy Spirit of God, even the blessed Comforter Himself, will come to every-one who asks for Him.' The book is a procession of good deeds and pious deaths, although a twenty-first century reader might note that the status quo is maintained: *Ministering Children* and its successors were deeply conservative, indeed, solipsistic in their preoccupation as much with the effect on the ministering child as on the deserving poor. 'Let the truth be borne in mind, that the influence of the giver far exceeds that of the gift on the receiver of it.'

The general tone of the book can be seen in the preface in which Mrs Charlesworth wrote: 'Difficulty being sometimes felt in training children to the exercise of those kindly feelings which have the Poor for their object, it was thought that an illustrative tale might prove a help towards this important end'. The book was very popular (there was a sequel in 1867) and the idea of 'Ministering Children' became embedded in the culture, emerging in a literary genre that lasted half a century, on both sides of the Atlantic. Its influence can be seen strongly in, for example, *Little Women* (p. 205).

However, *Ministering Children* and its followers produced a certain sceptical reaction. In *Good Wives* (1869) Alcott offers a sardonic comment, after Beth's death: 'Now, if she [Jo] had been the heroine of a moral story-book, she ought at this period of her life to have become quite saintly, renounced the world, and gone about doing good in a mortified bonnet, with tracts in her pocket. But, you see, Jo wasn't a heroine; she was only a struggling human girl.'

Along with the temperance movement and the Sunday schools, books like *Ministering Children* scored the concept of middle-class benevolence deep into the nineteenth-century psyche. But it is worth noting that they could not have done so without both dramatic materials and narrative skill, as the opening chapter, reprinted here, demonstrates.

## from *Ministering Children* (1854)

### CHAPTER I

> 'Oh! say not, dream not, heavenly notes
>  To childish ears are vain; –
>  That the young mind at random floats
>  And cannot catch the strain.
>
> Dim or unheard the words may fall,
>  And yet the heaven-taught mind
> May learn the sacred air, and all
>  The harmony unwind.'

'And this is the confidence that we have in Him, that, if we ask anything according to His will, He heareth us.' – 1 *John, v.* 14.

The chimes of a great church-clock in a large old town were playing nine; it was a bright September morning, and the narrow street where the old church stood was filled with merry children, boys and girls, running, racing, shouting, all crowding in at one great door together, to their separate schools, to take their places there before that great church-clock told the last stroke of nine. When the merry children ran breathless to the school, one little girl was there, already seated in her place upon the form, and her lesson-book ready in her hand; her name was Ruth, and she was always in her place at school when that great clock struck nine. Some of the other children lived nearer to the school than little Ruth, and she could not run so fast as they could, but she was always there in time, and often the first of all. She could not run so fast as they did, because she was weak for want of food; her little face was almost as white as the crimped border of the cap that pressed closely round it; she could not learn so fast as some of the stronger children; but she always tried to remember; and, best of all, she remembered the words of the Holy Bible. She had lost her own father; the father she had now was not her own father, and he took no care of her, nor of her little sister, nor yet of his wife, who was their mother. But no hunger or want kept little Ruth from her school. It comforted her to go, because there she learned to know and love that blessed Saviour who has said, 'Suffer the little children to come unto Me, and forbid them not, for of such is the kingdom of Heaven.'

And now that great church-clock had told the last stroke of nine; the good marks were set down in the book for all who were safe in their places at school; then the book was put away and lessons began. Lessons began, but all the children were not there; in a street called 'Ivy Lane,' a poor little school-girl was only then tying on her white apron; she knew that she was very late, but she did not seem to make any haste; she had no kind mother to dress her; she fastened her own little frock, pinned her tippet, tied her little white apron-strings, took her bag of books, and set off for school. Her name was Patience, and her home was a still more unhappy one than that of little Ruth; for poor Patience had never known a mother's love; her mother died when she was an infant; her elder sister was gone quite away to be a servant; she had no brother to be kind to her; and her father had no pity for his child. Poor Patience was not like Ruth; she did not love her school, she found no comfort there, for she seemed as if she could not learn from the Holy Bible, nor remember any thing the lady said who came to the school, to teach the children from the Word of God.

Patience walked slowly on her way, and presently she saw another little school-girl coming up a street near by; this other little girl was a stout and rosy child, and she walked along eating bread and butter, finishing her breakfast on her way to school. The rosy child soon overtook poor Patience, and walked by her side. Patience had had no food that morning, and she longed for some of her little school-fellow's bread and butter, but she did not say a word; and when they reached the school, the rosy child threw all she had not time to eat to a great black goat, at a stable-door near by. The black goat tossed his head, ran to the bread and butter, and soon nibbled it up; little Patience looked wishfully after it, and said, 'O Nancy, how glad I should be of the food you waste!' but Nancy ran into school, and Patience followed slowly after; both children had a bad mark set down against their names for being late, and then they took their places on the forms, and Nancy thought no more of her hungry little school-fellow – for Nancy was not a ministering child.

Another of those bright September mornings came, and little Ruth made haste again to be ready by nine o'clock; she had had no breakfast, but she made no complaint; she had said her morning prayer beside her little bed, and now her poor mother had dressed her for school. 'Good bye, Mother,' said little Ruth; and shutting her mother's door, she came stepping down the long dark staircase at the top of which she lived, her little figure lighting up the gloom. As Ruth came down the stairs she heard a low moan as of some child in pain; she listened and heard it again. A door at the bottom of the stairs stood a little way open; Ruth had often seen a poor widow woman with a sick child who had come to live in that room; so when she heard that moan again, she looked into the room, and there she saw the widow's child lying on her wretched bed.

'Are you ill?' asked Ruth.

'Yes, and my pain is so bad! and I have no one to be with me!'

'Won't your mother come?' asked Ruth.

'No, mother's got a day's work, she won't be home all day! I wish you would stay with me!'

'I must go to school,' said Ruth; 'but I will ask mother, when I come home, to let me stay with you a little.'

'O do! and make haste, do make haste! I don't like to be alone.'

Little Ruth hastened on her way to school, merry boys and girls ran past her, she could not run so fast as they did; but the bright September sun shone warmly on her, and she thought of the lady who would come that day to the school: then the chimes began their cheerful peal, and little Ruth began to run, and so making haste she reached the wide stone steps, and went in at the school-door, and took her seat before the last stroke of nine. Lessons went on till the great church-clock struck ten; lessons went on again till it struck eleven; then Miss Wilson, the lady who visited the school, came in, and called the second class to her. Little Ruth brought the Bibles from the closet, and then took the place that was always hers by that lady's side. Patience was in the same class, but she did not look happy, like little Ruth, when the blessed words were read; neither could she answer any of the questions; she looked upon the ground and seemed to feel no interest in any thing. When the lady went away, she smiled on little Ruth, and said, 'You have answered well to-day!' and Ruth looked up at the face of her friend, and the colour came into her pale cheeks; but Miss Wilson had seen before how pale they were, and she guessed that her little favourite wanted food. Then Miss Wilson turned to Patience and said, 'Oh Patience! will you never love God's Holy Word?' Patience did not look up nor answer, and the lady went away; she did not know that poor Patience also was hungry and weak for want of food – no one on earth seemed to know or feel the sorrows of that poor sorrowful child.

Ruth went home from school at twelve o'clock, but she could not stay with the little sick girl till she had asked her mother's leave; so she only just looked in to tell her she was come back; when the poor sick child saw her again she said,

'Oh, I am so glad you are come! what a long time it was you kept at school! Oh, I want something so bad! I can't eat this bread mother left me; it's so hard – it hurts me when I try!'

'I have not had any food to-day!' said little Ruth.

'Oh dear!' said the sick child, 'what do you do when you have no food?'

'I tell Jesus!' said little Ruth.

'Who do you tell?'

'Jesus!' said little Ruth.

'Who is Jesus?' asked the poor child.

'What! don't you know who Jesus is?' said little Ruth. 'I thought that every body knew that, except the heathen. He is our Saviour!'

'Does he give you some food?' asked the poor child.

'O yes! he often sends us some food when mother has nothing: but I must go to mother now, or she will scold.'

'Do ask her to let you come and stay with me!' said the poor child.

'Yes, I will,' replied little Ruth; and she went up the high staircase to her mother's room. When Ruth went in she saw on the table a can of steaming soup. 'O mother! is that for us?' she asked.

'Yes, to be sure it is – Miss Wilson sent it in this minute!'

Ruth had not told Miss Wilson about their having no food that day; so when she saw this can of hot soup, she knew it was her Saviour who had put it into Miss Wilson's heart to send it to them. The poor babe was asleep on the bed; but Mary, Ruth's little sister, was standing at the table crying to be fed. Then the mother got a bason, and poured it full for Mary. There was meat, and rice, and potato in the nice hot soup; and poor little Mary left off crying directly she had her spoon and began to eat. Then the mother poured out a larger bason for Ruth, who stood quite patient by the table. Ruth waited a minute with her food before her.

'What are you waiting for now?' asked her mother; 'I have nothing more for you.'

'No, mother; but that widow's child is laid in bed; she says her pain is so bad; and her mother's out working, and she wants me to sit with her.'

'Poor thing!' said Ruth's mother; 'well, take your dinner, and then you may go a little while if you like.'

'She has no food, mother, but a hard bit of bread, and she says she can't eat it, because it hurts her.'

'O! and so you want to be after giving her some of yours, do you? here, give me your bason then, and you take this jug.' And Ruth's mother, pouring some more soup into the broken jug she had taken for herself, gave it to Ruth. 'There, take care how you go, that you don't lose it now you have got it!' said the mother. And Ruth, holding the jug in both hands, went slowly and carefully down-stairs. How happy was she now! – in her hands she held the food she so much wanted; and the poor sick child, left all alone, was to share it with her and be happy also! As she got near the bottom of the staircase, she stepped quicker in her haste; then, pushing open the door, she went in, saying, 'See here, Miss Wilson sent us some beautiful soup, and mother's given me some for you!'

'O dear, how nice! – how glad I am!' said the poor child.

'Have you got a bason?' asked Ruth.

'Yes, there's one in that closet, and a spoon too,' said the child.

Ruth found a small yellow bason and spoon; she broke up the child's dry bit of bread in the bason; poured some of the hot soup over it; folded her hands, and asked a blessing in the name of Jesus; and then the two children dined together. The warm nourishment brought the colour to the white cheeks of little Ruth, and soothed the poor sick weary child – 'How good you are to me!' she said to Ruth. 'I feel better now; I think I shall go to sleep.' Ruth put away the bason in the closet again; the sick child had closed her eyes – already almost slumbering; and the little ministering girl went back to her mother.

A day or two after, as Ruth came in from school, the sick child's mother was going out, and she stopped and said to Ruth, 'My Lucy told me how good you were to her; the God above bless you for it! She is always calling out for you; I wish you would stay a bit with her when you can, just to pacify her.'

Ruth's mother gave her leave to take the babe down and nurse it in the poor child's room – where she still lay on her wretched bed, covered with a torn counterpane. Ruth walked up and down to quiet the babe and to get it to sleep; she hushed and hushed it, but that would not do; so at last she began to sing one of her school hymns in a low voice:

'Jesus, refuge of my soul,
Let me to Thy bosom fly.'

The low sweet singing soothed the infant to sleep, and the sick child into quiet feeling. 'Is that Jesus – you sing about – who you ask for food?' said the poor child.

'Yes,' replied Ruth. 'That's Jesus our Saviour! I can sing you something else about our Saviour, if you like?'

'Yes, do,' said the poor dear child. And Ruth sang –

'We read within the Holy Word,
Of how our Saviour died,
And those great drops of blood,
He shed at eventide.'

Over and over again, while she rocked the sleeping baby she sang the same soft words. When she stopped, the sick child said, 'I can't read; I never went to school long enough to learn.'

'What, can't you read the Bible?' asked Ruth.

'No, I can't read any thing; I don't know any thing about it.'

'I can tell you all about it,' said Ruth. 'I know such a number of stories out of the Bible! Miss Wilson tells them to us, and sometimes we tell them to her. And I know a great many verses, and some chapters and Psalms.'

'I like stories best!' said the poor child.

'Well, then, I will tell you one. Let me see, which shall I tell you? O! I know. I will tell you about the little lamb! Once there was a good man, his name was David; he was not at all old, he was quite young; and he didn't live in a town like this, but he lived in beautiful green fields, and on great high hills, where the flowers grow, and the trees, and where the birds sing. He was quite young, but he loved God. And he prayed to God. And when he saw the stars come out in the sky, he thought about Jesus our Saviour, who lives up above the stars in Heaven, and he wrote about Him in the Bible. He lived alone on the great high hills; and God took care of him; and he had a great many sheep and lambs, and they all ate the grass, and were so happy! and he took care of them all. But one day there came a great roaring lion; he came so quiet – he did not make any noise! and he took a little lamb in his great mouth, and ran so fast away! but the little lamb cried out, and David heard the little lamb, and David ran so fast that the great lion could not get away! and he caught the great lion and killed him, and he took the little lamb in his arms, and carried it quite safe back to its mother! Is not that a pretty story? And I know what Miss Wilson tells us about it!'

'What does she tell you?' asked the poor child.

'She tell us that it is just like Jesus our Saviour; when Satan the great roaring lion tries to take us away, if we pray to Jesus, Jesus won't let him have us; but Jesus will take us up safe in His arms, and carry us to Heaven when we die, and then we shall be so happy there!'

'Will He carry me?' asked the poor child.

'Yes, He will if you pray to Him!' said little Ruth.

'I don't know how to pray,' the poor child replied.

'I will teach you my prayer,' said little Ruth.

'O God, my Heavenly Father, give me Thy Holy Spirit to teach me to know and love Thee. Wash me from all my sins in my Saviour's precious blood. Keep me from all evil, and make me ready to live with Thee for ever in Heaven: For the sake of Jesus my Saviour. Amen.'

'That is one of my prayers, and I can teach it to you. I have taught it to our Mary, and she can't read yet!'

The poor child tried to learn it, but she could not remember the words; still it seemed to soothe her, to hear Ruth repeating them; at last the poor child said, 'Wash me from all my sins!' – 'What are SINS?'

'That is when we do wrong,' said little Ruth; 'we can't go with our bad ways to Heaven, but our Saviour can wash them all away in His blood!'

As little Ruth was coming home from school on the last of those bright September days, she saw a poor woman sitting on a door-step with a basket full of small penny nosegays of autumn flowers. Ruth stood still before the basket to look and admire. She had never known what it was to hunt over the meadow banks in spring for violets and primroses, or gather the yellow daffodil and beautiful anemone from the woods, or the sweet and frail wild rose from its thorny stem in the hedge; she had sometimes plucked a daisy from the grass, but this was the only flower that Ruth had ever gathered. And now she stood to look upon the woman's basket full of nosegays of garden flowers. While she stood looking, a mother with her little girl passed by.

'O! mamma,' said the little girl, 'look at these flowers!'

'A penny a nosegay, ma'am; only a penny a nosegay!' said the poor woman, holding out some of her flowers.

'Do you wish for a nosegay, Jane?' asked the mother of her little girl.

'Yes, if you please, mamma!'

Ruth thought how happy that little girl was to have a nosegay of her own! she watched her take it; and then the mother with her little girl went on, and Ruth slowly turned away to her home. But as soon as the little girl had left the basket of flowers, she said, 'Mamma, did you see that poor child who looked so at the flowers?'

'Yes, Jane, do you think she wanted a nosegay?'

'O, mamma! will you buy her one?'

'I have not another penny with me, or I would.'

'Do you think she would like me to give her mine, then, mamma?'

'Yes, suppose you do; I dare say she very seldom has a flower.'

'Then, I will, mamma; shall we go after her?' The little girl looked back, and saw Ruth walking slowly away.

'O, mamma, she will be gone!'

Little Jane did not like to leave her mother's side, so they walked quickly back together, till they overtook Ruth, and then Jane gave her the flowers; the bright colour came into the cheeks of little Ruth as she curtsied and took the flowers; and then she set off to run with them home. And so that ministering child parted with her nosegay for the little girl, who had never gathered any flower but a daisy.

Ruth soon reached home with her flowers; first she went to the poor sick child, and said, 'See what beautiful flowers I have got! A lady bought them in the street, and her little girl gave them all to me! I will give you that beauty!' – And Ruth pulled out the only rose from the nosegay, and put it into the little thin hand of the dying child. 'O how sweet it smells!' said the poor sick child; and she lay on her hard pillow and the rose in her hand – the only gift she had had to gladden her, except food, since she had laid ill in her bed.

'Jesus, our Saviour, made the flowers!' said Ruth. 'Miss Wilson says it was Jesus made every flower to grow out of the ground.'

'How kind He must be!' said the dying child.

Then Ruth took the rest of the flowers up to her mother, and they were put in water to live many days.

Ruth used to go in often to see the poor sick child, and tell her stories from the Bible, and sing her hymns when she had the baby with her. But one cold November day, when she came into the house from school, the poor child's mother came crying from the room, and said to her, 'Oh, I am so glad you are come! I thought I must have come after you; my poor child's dying, and she keeps asking for you!' Ruth went in and stood by the bed, and the dying child said, 'Dear Ruth, I am quite happy! I love you very much; and I want you to sing that about – "Those great drops of blood Jesus shed at even-tide."' Ruth sang it as well as she could, but she was ready to cry.

'I want you to sing it over and over, as you do to the babe,' said the dying child.

Ruth sang it two or three times, and then she stopped; the poor child had shut her eyes and seemed asleep, but she soon opened them again, and said, 'Oh do sing about "Jesus, let me to thy bosom fly!"' and while Ruth sang, and the mother stood weeping by, the little child fell asleep, and died. Ruth cried for her little friend, and missed her very much. But now the child's poor mother said she wanted Ruth to comfort her up, as she had done her dying child; and she begged Ruth to read to her, and tell her those beautiful stories out of the Bible, for she could not read herself. And so Ruth became a ministering child to the poor childless widow.

When we see a child dressed neat and warm in her school-dress, we think she is well taken care of; but it is not always so; and sometimes the little school-girl or boy is much more hungry and faint than the child who begs his food in the streets. We cannot tell how it really is with poor children, or poor men and women, unless we visit them in their homes. Miss Wilson had often been to see little Ruth, so she knew all her sorrows; she comforted and often fed the little girl, and loved her very much. But Miss Wilson thought that poor Patience did not care about anything, and that it would be of no use to go and see a child in her home who never seemed anxious to please her at school; and so she did not know the sorrows of that poor child – she did not know how hungry, and weak, and afraid she was – and so poor Patience as yet had no comforter! We must pray to God that He would be pleased to comfort all sorrowful children, and sorrowful people; and then He will be sure to teach us how we may comfort them also.

# 'Oliver Optic' (William Taylor Adams)
## (1822–1897)

'Oliver Optic' was instrumental in developing the boys' adventure series; his huge output of boys' stories became increasingly sensational, and were widely criticized as being little better than the cheapest mass-market 'dime novels'. They were referred to in Louisa May Alcott's *Eight Cousins* (1875) as *'optical* delusions.... The writers of these popular stories intend to do good, I have no doubt, but it seems to me they fail because their motto is "Be smart, and you will be rich," instead of "Be honest, and you will be happy"'. They can be regarded as part of the gradual process of secularization of American children's books.

Adams edited several children's magazines and was adept at aiming at specific markets. *The Boat Club*, so popular that it grew into a series, is a middle-class book. In the original preface, 'Oliver Optic' made the right gestures:

> The author of the following story pleads guilty of being more than half a boy himself; and in writing a book to meet the wants and tastes of 'Young America' he has had no difficulty in stepping back over the literary waste of years that separates youth from maturity, and entering fully into the spirit of the scenes he describes. He has endeavoured to combine healthy moral lessons with a sufficient amount of exciting interest to render the story attractive to the young; and he hopes he has not mingled these elements of a good juvenile book in disproportionate quantities.

The emphasis on realistic, adventurous boyhood is one of which we shall hear more in American writing for children, although *The Boat Club* begins with a good deal of moralizing. Frank's father, Captain Sedley, gives his sons a boat, the *Zephyr*, which Charles describes as 'a ripper'. He is duly admonished by arguments very similar to those used by Alcott in *Eight Cousins*. 'Not a very elegant word ... I will warrant you cannot find it in the dictionary ... I presume you meant nothing wrong; but such expressions do not add anything to the force of language; and using them may induce a bad habit. If you associated with boys accustomed to use profanities, this desire to use strong words would lead you into the practise.'

The boys and their friends fall into a rivalry with the Bunker gang which, as in this chapter, sometimes erupts into violence. (There is a sub-plot in which Tim Bunker frames Tony Weston, one of the Boat Club members, over the theft of a wallet.) Adams' skilful use of rapid action blended with morality perhaps demonstrates why he was so popular.

---

from *The Boat Club, or the Bunkers of Rippleton* (1855)

### CHAPTER XIII

### THE COLLISION

Joe Braman, the alleged proprietor of the Thunderbolt, was an idle, dissolute fellow, who employed his time in gunning, fishing, and loitering about the dramshops of Rippleton. He lived in a miserable hut on the north shore of the lake. How he obtained his living, it would have been difficult to determine.

Tim Bunker was an especial favorite with Braman, and people said it was because there was a natural sympathy between them. Joe's boat was a long, flat-bottomed affair, not very graceful in its form or construction. With the exception of Captain Sedley's sailboat, and the club boat, it was, perhaps, the only boat on the lake; and small parties occasionally engaged Joe to take them out fishing in it.

The history of its present appearance was sufficiently plain to the Zephyrs. It had been lengthened out, painted, a sharp, false bow attached to it, and such other improvements made as would fit it for the purposes of a club boat.

'Isn't she one of the boats?' laughed Charles.

'Silence, forward!' said Frank, shaking his head as a gesture of warning to the boys not to provoke any ill nature.

'Who you lookin' at!' cried Tim Bunker, as the Thunderbolt came near the Zephyr.

'Good morning, Tim,' said Frank, pleasantly.

'Why don't you pull, you lubbers?' shouted Tim.

'You have a new boat, I see.'

'I'll bet we have,' replied Tim, bringing the Thunderbolt round the stern of the Zephyr.

'Isn't that Joe Braman's boat?' asked Charles.

'No, sir-ee! It's my boat,' answered Tim.

'Did you buy it of him?'

'Didn't do nothin' else.'

'What did you give?'

'Ten dollars, and five for fixin' her up,' replied Tim, with a great deal of importance.

'She looks very well,' continued Charles.

'She'll go some, you better believe.'

Tony Weston could not help smiling at this conversation, and Tim Bunker unfortunately perceived the funny expression on his face. It roused his anger.

'Who stole the wallet?' said he.

This taunt roused a feeling of indignation in the soul of Fred Harper, and he so far forgot the requirements of the constitution as to reply, –

'Tim Bunker.'

'Le's lick 'em,' said one of the Bunkers.

'Pull!' exclaimed Frank, with energy, when he saw the storm brewing.

Mindful of the discipline of the club, every member obeyed the order, and the Zephyr darted away from the belligerent Thunderbolts.

'Pooh! Frank, I wouldn't run away from them,' said Charles.

'I have no desire to quarrel with such fellows,' replied Frank; 'and I hope none of you will say anything to provoke them. That was very thoughtless of you, Fred.'

'I know it; but, somehow, I couldn't help it; the taunt was so mean and contemptible. If I had been on shore, I should have knocked him.'

'Article six,' said Frank.

'Here they come after us,' added Tony.

The boys all laughed involuntarily at the idea of the old 'gundalow,' as Fred called it, chasing them.

'They can't catch us,' continued Frank.

'I guess not,' said Charles.

'But I am sorry we provoked them, for I had a little plan in my head.'

'What is it, Frank?'

'Never mind it now; rest on your oars; we are a quarter of a mile from them, and we can easily keep out of their way.'

'Steady, Frank, we are running too near the shore,' interposed Tony. 'The water is shoal here, you know.'

'Back her!' exclaimed the coxswain. 'I was watching the Bunkers so closely that I did not mind where we were going. Back her, quick!'

But it was too late. The Zephyr darted forward, and buried her keel in the mud at the bottom of the lake.

'By gracious!' exclaimed Charles Hardy; 'we are in for it now.'

'And the Bunkers are upon us,' added Frank, very much perplexed by the difficulties which had so suddenly surrounded them.

'What shall be done?' asked Tony.

'Let them come on,' replied Fred. 'We can't get rid of them now.'

'I don't want to fight with them.'

The Thunderbolt was approaching them, not very rapidly, it was true; but a few minutes would involve them in a quarrel, which Frank and a large majority of the club were very anxious to avoid. Tim Bunker was standing up in the stern sheets of his boat, watching them with malignant interest.

'Hurrah! they are aground!' cried Tim, as soon as he understood the nature of the calamity which had befallen the Zephyr, 'We have them now; they can't run away, the cowardly long faces!'

'Come aft, some of you,' said Frank, when he heard these threatening words. 'The water is deep enough under the stern. We have only run into a mud bank.'

On the starboard side of the boat there was plenty of water, and if they could move her back a rod, they could easily escape.

The boys obeyed the order of the coxswain; but the Zephyr had been forced so deeply into the mud that her bow still stuck fast.

'Half a dozen of you, set your oars in the mud and push!' continued Frank, highly excited by the danger that menaced them.

But it was of no use; they could not start her.

'They are upon us,' said Tony.

'What shall we do?' asked Frank, sadly perplexed.

'We must fight,' said Fred.

'No, I am not willing to do that.'

'Shall we sit here and let them pound us as much as they have a mind to?' replied Fred. 'But you are coxswain, Frank, and I, for one, shall do just what you say.'

'So shall I!' said another.

'And I!'

And so they all said.

Frank was more and more embarrassed as the circumstances multiplied the difficulties around him. He was charged with the direction of the whole club, and the responsibility of his position rested heavily upon his mind. He had been taught at the fireside of his pious home to avoid a quarrel at almost any sacrifice; and he was painfully conscious that the indiscreet words of Fred Harper had provoked the anger of the Bunkers. Poor fellow! What could he do? He could not order them to fight, not even in self-defence, under the circumstances, and he knew that their foes would whip them severely if they did not. The Thunderbolt was within a few rods of them, and five minutes more would decide the question.

'We are in a bad fix!' said Charles, nervously. 'What are you going to do, Frank?'

'Tony, take your boat-hook, and see how deep the water is on the mud bank.'

'Only about a foot,' replied Tony, as he obeyed the order.

'Is the mud deep?'

'Not very,' replied Tony, pushing the boat-hook down.

'I want two volunteers,' said Frank, hurriedly.

'I!' cried Tony.

'I!' repeated half a dozen others.

'Tony and Fred; throw off your pants and jump into the water. You can easily push her off.'

'Agreed!' cried the two volunteers, as they hastened to execute the order.

'Six of you take your oars; back her as they push; the other four stay in the stern sheets to settle her down aft.'

'Ay, ay!' exclaimed the boys.

'Now for it! Pull!'

The effect was instantly perceived; the boat was moved back about a foot.

'Once more, altogether!' said Frank.

Another effort backed her about two feet more, and the case began to look hopeful.

'Again, quick! they are upon us! Leap in, Tony and Fred, when she is free.'

'Heave again!' said Tony.

Their exertions were now crowned with entire success, and the Zephyr darted back into deep water; but an unfortunate occurrence rendered all their labor futile. As the boat slid off the mud bank, Tony and Fred, in their attempt to spring on board, embarrassed each other's movements, so that the foremost lost his hold, and remained standing up to his middle in the mud and water.

At this instant the Thunderbolt reached the spot, and Tim steered directly for poor Tony, whose situation he discovered the moment the Zephyr was free.

'Hit him!' screamed Tim. 'Pound him with your oars! Drownd him!'

Frank's blood seemed to freeze in his veins, as he perceived the imminent peril of his friend. He knew the Bunkers would not spare him, and that even his life was in danger.

Fortunately the Thunderbolt grounded, or Tony would inevitably have been borne under her bottom. Tim seized an oar, and with the ferocity of a madman, sprang forward to execute his vengeance on the helpless boy.

'Let him alone!' shouted Frank, with frantic earnestness. 'Man your oars, boys! Ready – pull!'

Frank was fully roused, and his orders were delivered with rapidity and energy. Seizing the tiller ropes, he steered the boat, as she gathered headway, so that her sharp bow struck the Thunderbolt on her broadside, staving in her gunwale and upsetting her.

The Bunkers thought this was rather sharp practice, as they floundered about in the water. They had not given Frank Sedley credit for half so much determination. They had never seen anything in him that betokened 'spunk' before. He was a peaceable boy, always avoiding a quarrel; but when the very life of his friend was in peril, he was found to be as bold and courageous as the best of them.

The bow of the Zephyr was swung round so that Tony could get in. Washing off the mud from his legs, he resumed his dress.

In the mean time the Bunkers had righted their boat and resumed their places. The bath they had had quite cooled their belligerent heat; though, if it had not, Frank had taken the precaution to back the Zephyr out of their reach.

'You'll catch it for this!' exclaimed Tim Bunker, as his crew were bailing out the Thunderbolt with their hats.

'I am sorry for what has happened, Tim,' replied Frank, 'but I could not help it.'

'Couldn't help it, you – ' I will not soil the pages of my book by writing the expression that Tim made use of. 'Yes, yer could help it. What d'yer run inter me for?'

'You threatened to drown Tony, and if your boat had not got aground you would have run him down.'

'That I would, long face! If ever I catch either of you, I will lick yer within an inch of yer life – mind that!'

'I am sorry for it, Tim.'

'Yer lie, yer ain't!'

'It was all my fault, Tim,' interposed Fred, 'and I will pay for the damage done your boat.'

'I guess yer better.'

'How much will you take, and call it square?'

'Dollar and a half,' growled Tim, glancing at the fractured gunwale.

Fred had not so much money with him, but the sum was immediately raised in the club.

'Now, Tim, we will forget and forgive: what do you say?'

'I don't want nothin' on yer; give me the money, and I don't care what yer do.'

Frank ordered the crew to pull up to the Thunderbolt, and Fred handed Tim the money.

'I'll pay yer for this; see 'f I don't,' said the unforgiving Bunker, as the Zephyr backed away.

# William Makepeace Thackeray (1811–1863)

Perhaps the most famous (and perhaps the best) of the *jeux d'esprit* of major writers of the nineteenth century, *The Rose and the Ring* was written initially as a family story, and later published, under the pseudonym of M. A. Titmarsh, as the last of Thackeray's Christmas stories. (Such stories had a brief vogue in the 1840s and 1850s.) In the same tradition as *The Hope of the Katzekopfs* (see p. 75), but written with a good deal more wit and iconoclasm, it is a cheerful farrago, using elements of the pantomimes which had been growing in popularity through the eighteenth century. Needless to say Prince Giglio marries his Princess Rosalba, and Prince Bulbo marries the Princess Angelica, but not before Thackeray was able to exercise his considerable talents for social satire.

*The Rose and the Ring* having, quite clearly, a dual audience of adults and children, who might be broadly supposed to appreciate different elements of it, is an exemplar of how the live pantomime, as a local and national entertainment, developed over the next hundred years.

Thackeray contributed extensively to the humorous periodical *Punch* and was one of the outstanding Victorian novelists, his most notable works being *Vanity Fair* (1847–8) and *The History of Pendennis* (1848–50).

## *The Rose and the Ring, Or The History of Prince Giglio and Prince Bulbo. A Fireside Pantomime for Great and Small Children* (1855)

### I

### SHOWS HOW THE ROYAL FAMILY SATE DOWN TO BREAKFAST

This is Valoroso XXIV, King of Paflagonia, seated with his Queen and only child at their royal breakfast-table, and receiving the letter which announces to his Majesty a proposed visit from Prince Bulbo, heir of Padella, reigning King of Crim Tartary. Remark the delight upon the monarch's royal features. He is so absorbed in the perusal of the King of Crim Tartary's letter, that he allows his eggs to get cold, and leaves his august muffins untasted.

'What! that wicked, brave, delightful Prince Bulbo!' cries Princess Angelica; 'so handsome, so accomplished, so witty – the conqueror of Rimbombamento, where he slew ten thousand giants!'

'Who told you of him, my dear?' asks his Majesty.

'A little bird,' says Angelica.

'Poor Giglio!' says mamma, pouring out the tea.

'Bother Giglio!' cries Angelica, tossing up her head, which rustled with a thousand curl-papers.

'I wish,' growls the King – 'I wish Giglio was...'

'Was better? Yes, dear, he is better,' says the Queen. 'Angelica's little maid, Betsinda, told me so when she came to my room this morning with my early tea.'

'You are always drinking tea,' said the Monarch, with a scowl.

'It is better than drinking port or brandy-and-water,' replies her Majesty.

'Well, well, my dear, I only said you were fond of drinking tea,' said the King of Paflagonia, with an effort as if to command his temper. 'Angelica! I hope you have plenty of new dresses; your milliners' bills are long enough. My dear Queen, you must see and have some parties. I prefer dinners, but of course you will be for balls. Your everlasting blue velvet quite tires me: and, my love, I should like you to have a new necklace. Order one. Not more than a hundred or a hundred and fifty thousand pounds.'

'And Giglio, dear,' says the Queen.

'GIGLIO MAY GO TO THE–'

'Oh, sir,' screams her Majesty. 'Your own nephew! our late King's only son.'

'Giglio may go to the tailor's, and order the bills to be sent in to Glumboso to pay. Confound him! I mean bless his dear heart. He need want for nothing; give him a couple of guineas for pocket-money, my dear; and you may as well order yourself bracelets, while you are about the necklace, Mrs V.'

Her Majesty, or *Mrs V.*, as the monarch facetiously called her (for even royalty will have its sport, and this august family were very much attached), embraced her husband, and, twining her arm round her daughter's waist, they quitted the breakfast-room in order to make all things ready for the princely stranger.

When they were gone, the smile that had lighted up the eyes of the *husband* and *father* fled – the pride of the *King* fled – the MAN was alone. Had I the pen of a G. P. R. James,* I would describe Valoroso's torments in the choicest language; in which I would also depict his flashing eye, his dis-tended nostril – his dressing-gown, pocket-handkerchief, and boots. But I need not say I have *not* the pen of that novelist; suffice it to say, Valoroso was alone.

He rushed to the cupboard, seizing from the table one of the many egg-cups with which his prin-cely board was served for the matin meal, drew out a bottle of right Nantz or Cognac, filled and emp-tied the cup several times, and laid it down with a hoarse 'Ha, ha, ha! now Valoroso is a man again.

'But oh!' he went on (still sipping, I am sorry to say), 'ere I was a king, I needed not this intox-icating draught; once I detested the hot brandy wine, and quaffed no other fount but nature's rill. It dashes not more quickly o'er the rocks, than I did, as, with blunderbuss in hand, I brushed away the early morning dew, and shot the partridge, snipe, or antlered deer! Ah! well may England's dramatist remark, "Uneasy lies the head that wears a crown!" Why did I steal my nephew's, my young Giglio's –? Steal! said I? no, no, no, not steal, not steal. Let me withdraw that odious expres-sion. I took, and on my manly head I set, the royal crown of Paflagonia; I took, and with my royal arm I wield, the sceptral rod of Paflagonia; I took, and in my out-stretched hand I hold, the royal orb of Paflagonia! Could a poor boy, a snivelling, drivelling boy – was in his nurse's arms but yes-terday, and cried for sugar-plums and puled for pap – bear up the awful weight of crown, orb, sceptre? gird on the sword my royal fathers wore, and meet in fight the tough Crimean foe?'

And then the monarch went on to argue in his own mind (though we need not say that blank verse is not argument) that what he had got it was his duty to keep, and that, if at one time he had entertained ideas of a certain restitution, which shall be nameless, the prospect by a *certain marriage* of uniting two crowns and two nations which had been engaged in bloody and expensive wars, as the Paflagonians and the Crimeans had been, put the idea of Giglio's restoration to the throne out of the question: nay, were his own brother, King Savio, alive, he would certainly will away the crown from his own son in order to bring about such a desirable union.

Thus easily do we deceive ourselves! Thus do we fancy what we wish is right! The King took courage, read the papers, finished his muffins and eggs, and rang the bell for his Prime Minister. The Queen, after thinking whether she should go up and see Giglio, who had been sick, thought 'Not now. Business first; pleasure afterwards. I will go and see dear Giglio this afternoon; and now I will drive to the jeweller's, to look for the necklace and bracelets.' The Princess went up into her own room, and made Betsinda, her maid, bring out all her dresses; and as for Giglio, they forgot him as much as I forget what I had for dinner last Tuesday twelvemonth.

2

## How King Valoroso got the crown, and Prince Giglio
### WENT WITHOUT

Paflagonia, ten or twenty thousand years ago, appears to have been one of those kingdoms where the laws of succession were not settled; for when King Savio died, leaving his brother Regent of

---

* George Paine Raynsford James (1799–1860) was a historical novelist who Thackeray parodied in his 'Novels By Eminent Hands'.

the kingdom, and guardian of Savio's orphan infant, this unfaithful regent took no sort of regard of the late monarch's will; had himself proclaimed sovereign of Paflagonia under the title of King Valoroso XXIV, had a most splendid coronation, and ordered all the nobles of the kingdom to pay him homage. So long as Valoroso gave them plenty of balls at Court, plenty of money and lucrative places, the Paflagonian nobility did not care who was king; and, as for the people, in those early times they were equally indifferent. The Prince Giglio, by reason of his tender age at his royal father's death, did not feel the loss of his crown and empire. As long as he had plenty of toys and sweetmeats, a holiday five times a week, and a horse and gun to go out shooting when he grew a little older, and, above all, the company of his darling cousin, the King's only child, poor Giglio was perfectly contented; nor did he envy his uncle the royal robes and sceptre, the great hot uncomfortable throne of state, and the enormous cumbersome crown in which that monarch appeared from morning till night. King Valoroso's portrait has been left to us; and I think you will agree with me that he must have been sometimes *rather tired* of his velvet, and his diamonds, and his ermine, and his grandeur. I shouldn't like to sit in that stifling robe, with such a thing as that on my head.

No doubt, the Queen must have been lovely in her youth; for though she grew rather stout in after life, yet her features, as shown in her portrait, are certainly *pleasing*. If she was fond of flattery, scandal, cards, and fine clothes, let us deal gently with her infirmities, which, after all, may be no greater than our own. She was kind to her nephew; and if she had any scruples of conscience about her husband's taking the young Prince's crown, consoled herself by thinking that the King, though a usurper, was a most respectable man, and that at his death Prince Giglio would be restored to his throne, and share it with his cousin, whom he loved so fondly.

The Prime Minister was Glumboso, an old statesman, who most cheerfully swore fidelity to King Valoroso, and in whose hands the monarch left all the affairs of his kingdom. All Valoroso wanted was plenty of money, plenty of hunting, plenty of flattery, and as little trouble as possible. As long as he had his sport, this monarch cared little how his people paid for it: he engaged in some wars, and of course the Paflagonian newspapers announced that he gained prodigious victories: he had statues erected to himself in every city of the empire; and of course his pictures placed everywhere, and in all the print-shops: he was Valoroso the Magnanimous, Valoroso the Victorious, Valoroso the Great, and so forth; – for even in these early early times courtiers and people knew how to flatter.

This royal pair had one only child, the Princess Angelica, who, you may be sure, was a paragon in the courtiers' eyes, in her parents', and in her own. It was said she had the longest hair, the largest eyes, the slimmest waist, the smallest foot, and the most lovely complexion of any young lady in the Paflagonian dominions. Her accomplishments were announced to be even superior to her beauty; and governesses used to shame their idle pupils by telling them what Princess Angelica could do. She could play the most difficult pieces of music at sight. She could answer any one of 'Mangnal's Questions'. She knew every date in the history of Paflagonia, and every other country. She knew French, English, Italian, German, Spanish, Hebrew, Greek, Latin, Cappadocian, Samothracian, Aegean, and Crim Tartar. In a word, she was a most accomplished young creature; and her governess and lady-in-waiting was the severe Countess Gruffanuff.

Would you not fancy, from this picture, that Gruffanuff must have been a person of the highest birth? She looks so haughty that I should have thought her a Princess at the very least, with a pedigree reaching as far back as the Deluge. But this lady was no better born than many other ladies who give themselves airs; and all sensible people laughed at her absurd pretensions. The fact is, she had been maid-servant to the Queen when her Majesty was only Princess, and her husband had been head footman; but after his death or *disappearance*, of which you shall hear presently, this Mrs Gruffanuff, by flattering, toadying, and wheedling her royal mistress, became a favourite with the Queen (who was rather a weak woman), and her Majesty gave her a title, and made her nursery governess to the Princess.

And now I must tell you about the Princess's learning and accomplishments, for which she had such a wonderful character. Clever Angelica certainly was, but as *idle as possible*. Play at sight, indeed!

she could play one or two pieces, and pretend that she had never seen them before; she could answer half-a-dozen 'Mangnal's Questions'; but then you must take care to ask the *right* ones. As for her languages, she had masters in plenty, but I doubt whether she knew more than a few phrases in each, for all her pretence; and as for her embroidery and her drawing, she showed beautiful specimens, it is true, but *who did them?*

This obliges me to tell the truth, and to do so I must go back ever so far, and tell you about the FAIRY BLACKSTICK.

## 3

### TELLS WHO THE FAIRY BLACKSTICK WAS, AND WHO WERE EVER SO MANY GRAND PERSONAGES BESIDES

Between the kingdoms of Paflagonia and Crim Tartary, there lived a mysterious personage, who was known in those countries as the Fairy Blackstick, from the ebony wand or crutch which she carried; on which she rode to the moon sometimes, or upon other excursions of business or pleasure, and with which she performed her wonders.

When she was young, and had been first taught the art of conjuring, by the necromancer, her father, she was always practising her skill, whizzing about from one kingdom to another upon her black stick, and conferring her fairy favours upon this Prince or that. She had scores of royal godchildren: turned numberless wicked people into beasts, birds, millstones, clocks, pumps, bootjacks, umbrellas, or other absurd shapes; and in a word was one of the most active and officious of the whole College of fairies.

But after two or three thousand years of this sport, I suppose Blackstick grew tired of it. Or perhaps she thought, 'What good am I doing by sending this Princess to sleep for a hundred years? by fixing a black pudding on to that booby's nose? by causing diamonds and pearls to drop from one little girl's mouth, and vipers and toads from another's? I begin to think I do as much harm as good by my performances. I might as well shut my incantations up, and allow things to take their natural course.

'There were my two young goddaughters, King Savio's wife, and Duke Padella's wife: I gave them each a present, which was to render them charming in the eyes of their husbands, and secure the affection of those gentlemen as long as they lived. What good did my Rose and my Ring do these two women? None on earth. From having all their whims indulged by their husbands, they became capricious, lazy, ill-humoured, absurdly vain, and leered, and languished, and fancied themselves irresistibly beautiful, when they were really quite old and hideous, the ridiculous creatures! They used actually to patronize me when I went to pay them a visit; – *me*, the Fairy Blackstick, who knows all the wisdom of the necromancers, and who could have turned them into baboons, and all their diamonds into strings of onions, by a single wave of my rod!' So she locked up her books in her cupboard, declined further magical performances, and scarcely used her wand at all except as a cane to walk about with.

So when Duke Padella's lady had a little son (the Duke was at that time only one of the principal noblemen in Crim Tartary), Blackstick, although invited to the christening, would not so much as attend; but merely sent her compliments and a silver papboat for the baby, which was really not worth a couple of guineas. About the same time the Queen of Paflagonia presented his Majesty with a son and heir; and guns were fired, the capital illuminated; and no end of feasts ordained to celebrate the young Prince's birth. It was thought the Fairy, who was asked to be his godmother, would at least have presented him with an invisible jacket, a flying horse, a Fortunatus's purse, or some other valuable token of her favour; but instead, Blackstick went up to the cradle of the child Giglio, when everybody was admiring him, and complimenting his royal papa and mamma, and said, 'My poor child, the best thing I can send you is a little *misfortune*'; and this was all she would utter, to the disgust of Giglio's parents, who died very soon after, when Giglio's uncle took the throne, as we read in Chapter I.

In like manner, when CAVOLFIORE, King of Crim Tartary, had a christening of his only child, ROSALBA, the Fairy Blackstick, who had been invited, was not more gracious than in Prince Giglio's case. Whilst everybody was expatiating over the beauty of the darling child, and congratulating its parents, the Fairy Blackstick looked very sadly at the baby and its mother, and said, 'My good woman – (for the Fairy was very familiar, and no more minded a Queen than a washerwoman) – my good woman, these people who are following you will be the first to turn against you; and, as for this little lady, the best thing I can wish her is a *little misfortune.*' So she touched Rosalba with her black wand, looked severely at the courtiers, motioned the Queen an adieu with her hand, and sailed slowly up into the air out of the window.

When she was gone, the Court people, who had been awed and silent in her presence, began to speak. 'What an odious Fairy she is (they said) – a pretty Fairy, indeed! Why, she went to the King of Paflagonia's christening, and pretended to do all sorts of things for that family; and what has happened – the Prince, her godson, has been turned off his throne by his uncle. Would we allow our sweet Princess to be deprived of her rights by any enemy? Never, never, never, never!'

And they all shouted in a chorus, 'Never, never, never, never!'

Now, I should like to know, and how did these fine courtiers show their fidelity? One of King Cavolfiore's vassals, the Duke Padella just mentioned, rebelled against the King, who went out to chastise his rebellious subject. 'Anyone rebel against our beloved and august Monarch!' cried the courtiers; 'anyone resist *him*? Pooh! He is invincible, irresistible. He will bring home Padella a prisoner, and tie him to a donkey's tail, and drive him round the town, saying, "This is the way the great Cavolfiore treats rebels."'

The King went forth to vanquish Padella; and the poor Queen, who was a very timid, anxious creature, grew so frightened and ill, that I am sorry to say she died; leaving injunctions with her ladies to take care of the dear little Rosalba. – Of course they said they would. Of course they vowed they would die rather than any harm should happen to the Princess. At first the 'Crim Tartar Court Journal' stated that the King was obtaining great victories over the audacious rebel: then it was announced that the troops of the infamous Padella were in flight: then it was said that the royal army would soon come up with the enemy, and then – then the news came that King Cavolfiore was vanquished and slain by his Majesty, King Padella the First!

At this news, half the courtiers ran off to pay their duty to the conquering chief, and the other half ran away, laying hands on all the best articles in the palace; and poor little Rosalba was left there quite alone – quite alone; and she toddled from one room to another, crying, 'Countess! Duchess! (only she said "Tountess, Duttess," not being able to speak plain) bring me my mutton sop; my Royal Highness hungy! Tountess! Duttess!' And she went from the private apartments into the ball-room and nobody was there; and thence into the pages' room and nobody was there; and she toddled down the great staircase into the hall and nobody was there; and the door was open, and she went into the court, and into the garden, and thence into the wilderness, and thence into the forest where the wild beasts live, and was never heard of any more!

A piece of her torn mantle and one of her shoes were found in the wood in the mouths of two lioness's cubs, whom KING PADELLA and a royal hunting party shot – for he was King now, and reigned over Crim Tartary. 'So the poor little Princess is done for,' said he; 'well, what's done can't be helped. Gentlemen, let us go to luncheon!' And one of the courtiers took up the shoe and put it in his pocket. And there was an end of Rosalba!

# 4

## How BLACKSTICK WAS NOT ASKED TO THE PRINCESS ANGELICA'S
### CHRISTENING

When the Princess Angelica was born, her parents not only did not ask the Fairy Blackstick to the christening party, but gave orders to their porter, absolutely to refuse her if she called. This porter's name was Gruffanuff, and he had been selected for the post by their Royal Highnesses because he was a very tall fierce man, who could say 'Not at home' to a tradesman or an unwelcome visitor with a rudeness which frightened most such persons away. He was the husband of that Countess whose picture we have just seen, and as long as they were together they quarrelled from morning till night. Now this fellow tried his rudeness once too often, as you shall hear. For the Fairy Blackstick coming to call upon the Prince and Princess, who were actually sitting at the open drawing-room window, Gruffanuff not only denied them, but made the most *odious vulgar sign* as he was going to slam the door in the Fairy's face! 'Git away, hold Blackstick!' said he. 'I tell you, Master and Missis ain't at home to you': and he was, as we have said, *going* to slam the door.

But the Fairy, with her wand, prevented the door being shut; and Gruffanuff came out again in a fury, swearing in the most abominable way, and asking the Fairy 'whether she thought he was a going to stay at that there door hall day?'

'You *are* going to stay at that door all day and all night, and for many a long year,' the Fairy said, very majestically; and Gruffanuff, coming out of the door, straddling before it with his great calves, burst out laughing, and cried 'Ha, ha, ha! this *is* a good un! Ha – ah – what's this? Let me down – O – o – H'm!' and then he was dumb!

For, as the Fairy waved her wand over him, he felt himself rising off the ground, and fluttering up against the door, and then, as if a screw ran into his stomach, he felt a dreadful pain there, and was pinned to the door; and then his arms flew up over his head; and his legs, after writhing about wildly, twisted under his body; and he felt cold, cold, growing over him, as if he was turning into metal; and he said, 'O – o – H'm!' and could say no more, because he was dumb.

He *was* turned into metal! He was from being *brazen*, *brass!* He was neither more nor less than a knocker! And there he was, nailed to the door in the blazing summer day till he burned almost red hot; and there he was, nailed to the door all the bitter winter nights, till his brass nose was dropping with icicles. And the postman came and rapped at him, and the vulgarest boy with a letter came and hit him up against the door. And the King and Queen (Princess and Prince they were then), coming home from a walk that evening, the King said, 'Hullo, my dear! you have had a new knocker put on the door. Why, it's rather like our Porter in the face! What has become of that boozy vagabond?' And the housemaid came and scrubbed his nose with sandpaper; and once, when the Princess Angelica's little sister was born, he was tied up in an old kid glove; and another night, some *larking* young men tried to wrench him off, and put him to the most excruciating agony with a turnscrew. And then the Queen had a fancy to have the colour of the door altered, and the painters dabbed him over the mouth and eyes, and nearly choked him, as they painted him pea-green. I warrant he had leisure to repent of having been rude to the Fairy Blackstick!

As for his wife, she did not miss him; and as he was always guzzling beer at the public-house, and notoriously quarrelling with his wife, and in debt to the tradesmen, it was supposed he had run away from all these evils, and emigrated to Australia or America. And when the Prince and Princess chose to become King and Queen, they left their old house, and nobody thought of the Porter any more.

# Christopher Pearse Cranch (1813–1892)

Despite the strong strain of realism in American nine-teenth-century children's books, there was also some ori-ginal fantasy writing, much of it emanating from the New England 'romantic' writers. Richard Henry Stoddard, for example, produced *Adventures in Fairy-Land* (1853); Louisa Alcott's first book was *Flower Fables* (1855).

Cranch consciously borrowed from the European tradi-tion: when his hero, Jacky Cable – 'Little Jacket' – is ship-wrecked, he 'had read *Robinson Crusoe* and *Gulliver's Travels*, and had half believed the wonderful stories of Brobdignag; but he never thought that he should ever be actually wrecked on a giant's island'. He is obviously linked to Jack (of the beanstalk), but is also a presager of the 'bad boy' figure that was to have a major effect on American boys' stories: 'though small in size he was big in wit, being an uncommonly smart lad, though he did play truant sometimes, and seldom knew well his school-lessons'.

However, this is fantasy with one foot on the ground. Like the hero of Mark Twain's sour Arthurian fantasy–satire *A Connecticut Yankee in King Arthur's Court* (1889), Jacky 'was a smart Yankee lad', and like *The Wizard of Oz* the story is driven by a commercially minded showman. The Huggermuggers – much like the Brobdignagians – turn out to be a benevolent couple, but, betrayed to one of Barnum's curiosity collectors by the jealous dwarf Kob-boltozo, they both die.

This extract describes Little Jacket's first visit to the island. After his escape, he is picked up by a ship carrying Zebedee Nabbum, the curiosity-hunter, and returns to the island to be greeted in a friendly way by the Huggermuggers.

Cranch was a Unitarian minister and Transcendentalist, who later became an artist. He wrote a sequel to *The Last of the Huggermuggers, Kobboltozo* (1857) which concerns the fate of the jealous dwarves.

## from *The Last of the Huggermuggers, a Giant Story* (1855) [dated 1856]

### CHAPTER FOUR

### HOW HUGGERMUGGER CAME ALONG

Now it happened that Little Jacket was not altogether wrong in his fancies about giants, for there *was* a giant living in this island where the poor sailors were wrecked. His name was Huggermugger, and he and his giantess wife lived at the foot of the great cliffs they had seen in the distance. Hug-germugger was something of a farmer, something of a hunter, and something of a fisherman. Now, it being a warm, clear, moonlight night, and Huggermugger being disposed to roam about, thought he would take a walk down to the beach to see if the late storm had washed up any clams* or oysters, or other shell-fish, of which he was very fond. Having gathered a good basket full, he was about returning, when his eye fell upon the group of great shells in which Little Jacket and his friends were reposing, all sound asleep.

'Now,' thought Huggermugger, 'my wife has often asked me to fetch home one of these big shells. She thinks it would look pretty on her mantel-piece, with sunflowers sticking in it. Now I may as well gratify her, though I can't exactly see the use of a shell without a fish in it. Mrs. Hug-germugger must see something in these shells that I don't.'

So he didn't stop to choose, but picked up the first one that came to his hand, and put it in his basket. It was the very one in which Little Jacket was asleep. The little sailor slept too soundly to know that he was travelling, free of expense, across the country at a railroad speed, in a carriage made of a giant's fish-basket. Huggermugger reached his house, mounted his huge stairs, set down his basket, and placed the big shell on the mantel-piece.

---

* The 'clam' is an American bivalve shell-fish, so called from hiding itself in the sand. A 'clam chowder' is a very savory kind of thick soup, of which the clam is a chief ingredient. I put in this note for the benefit of little English boys and girls, if it should chance that this story should find its way to their country. (Author's Note)

'Wife,' says he, 'here's one of those good-for-nothing big shells you have often asked me to bring home.'

'Oh, what a beauty,' says she, as she stuck a sunflower in it, and stood gazing at it in mute admiration. But, Huggermugger being hungry, would not allow her to stand idle.

'Come,' says he, 'let's have some of these beautiful clams cooked for supper – they are worth all your fine shells with nothing in them.'

So they sat down, and cooked and ate their supper, and then went to bed.

Little Jacket, all this time, heard nothing of their great rumbling voices, being in as sound a sleep as he ever enjoyed in his life. He awoke early in the morning, and crept out of his shell – but he could hardly believe his eyes, and thought himself still dreaming, when he found himself and his shell on a very high, broad shelf, in a room bigger than any church he ever saw. He fairly shook and trembled in his shoes, when the truth came upon him that he had been trapped by a giant, and was here a prisoner in his castle. He had time enough, however, to become cool and collected, for there was not a sound to be heard, except now and then something resembling a thunder-like snoring, as from some distant room. 'Aha,' thought Little Jacket to himself, 'it is yet very early, and the giant is asleep, and there may be time yet to get myself out of his clutches.'

He was a brave little fellow, as well as a true Yankee in his smartness and ingenuity. So he took a careful observation of the room, and its contents. The first thing to be done was to let himself down from the mantel-piece. This was not an easy matter, as it was very high. If he jumped, he would certainly break his legs. He was not long in discovering one of Huggermugger's fishing-lines tied up and lying not far from him. This he unrolled, and having fastened one end of it to a nail which he managed just to reach, he let the other end drop (it was as large as a small rope) and easily let himself down to the floor. He then made for the door, but that was fastened. Jacky, however, was determined to see what could be done, so he pulled out his jackknife, and commenced cutting into the corner of the door at the bottom, where it was a good deal worn, as if it had been gnawed by the rats. He thought that by cutting a little now and then, and hiding himself when the giant should make his appearance, in time he might make an opening large enough for him to squeeze himself through. Now Huggermugger was by this time awake, and heard the noise which Jacky made with his knife.

'Wife,' says he, waking her up – she was dreaming about her beautiful shell – 'wife, there are those eternal rats again, gnawing, gnawing at that door; we must set the trap for them to-night.'

Little Jacket heard the giant's great voice, and was very much astonished that he spoke English. He thought that giants spoke nothing but 'chow-chow-whangalorum-hallaballoo with a-ruffle-bull-bagger!' This made him hope that Huggermugger would not eat him. So he grew very hopeful, and determined to persevere. He kept at his work, but as softly as he could. But Huggermugger heard the noise again, or fancied he heard it, and this time came to see if he could not kill the rat that gnawed so steadily and so fearlessly. Little Jacket heard him coming, and rushed to hide himself. The nearest place of retreat was one of the giant's great boots, which lay on the floor, opening like a cave before him. Into this he rushed. He had hardly got into it before Huggermugger entered.

## CHAPTER FIVE

### WHAT HAPPENED TO LITTLE JACKET IN THE GIANT'S BOOT

Huggermugger made a great noise in entering, and ran up immediately to the door at which Little Jacket had been cutting, and threshed about him with a great stick, right and left. He then went about the room, grumbling and swearing, and poking into all the corners and holes in search of the rat; for he saw that the hole under the door had been enlarged, and he was sure that the rats had done it. So he went peeping and poking about, making Little Jacket not a little troubled, for he expected every moment that he would pick up the boot in which he was concealed, and shake him out of his hiding-place. Singularly enough, however, the giant never thought of looking into his own boots, and very soon he went back to his chamber to dress himself. Little Jacket now ventured to peep out of the boot, and stood considering what was next to be done. He hardly dared to go again to the door, for Huggermugger was now dressed, and his wife too, for he heard their voices in the next room, where they seemed to be preparing their breakfast. Little Jacket now was puzzling his wits to think what he should do, if the giant should take a fancy to put his boots on before he could discover another hiding-place. He noticed, however, that there were other boots and shoes near by, and so there was a chance that Huggermugger might choose to put on some other pair. If this should be the case, he might lie concealed where he was during the day, and at night work away again at the hole in the door, which he hoped to enlarge enough soon, to enable him to escape. He had not much time, however, for thought; for the giant and his wife soon came in. By peeping out a little, he could just see their great feet shuffling over the wide floor.

'And now, wife,' says Huggermugger, 'bring me my boots.' He was a lazy giant, and his wife spoiled him, by waiting on him too much.

'Which boots, my dear,' says she.

'Why, the long ones,' says he; 'I am going a hunting to-day, and shall have to cross the marshes.'

Little Jacket hoped the long boots were not those in one of which he was concealed, but unfortunately they were the very ones. So he felt a great hand clutch up the boots, and him with them, and put them down in another place. Huggermugger then took up one of the boots and drew it on, with a great grunt. He now proceeded to take up the other. Little Jacket's first impulse was to run out and throw himself on the giant's mercy, but he feared lest he should be taken for a rat. Besides he now thought of a way to defend himself, at least for a while. So he drew from his belt one of the long thorns he had cut from the bush by the seaside, and held it ready to thrust it into his adversary's foot, if he could. But he forgot that though it was as a sword in *his* hand, it was but a thorn to a giant. Huggermugger had drawn the boot nearly on, and Little Jacket's daylight was all gone, and the giant's great toes were pressing down on him, when he gave them as fierce a thrust as he could with his thorn.

'Ugh!' roared out the giant, in a voice like fifty mad bulls; 'wife, wife, I say!'

'What's the matter, dear?' says wife.

'Here's one of your confounded needles in my boot. I wish to gracious you'd be more careful how you leave them about!'

'A needle in your boot?' said the giantess, 'how can that be? I haven't been near your boots with my needles.'

'Well, you feel there yourself, careless woman, and you'll see.'

Whereupon the giantess took the boot, and put her great hand down into the toe of it, when Little Jacket gave another thrust with his weapon.

'O-o-o-o!!' screams the wife. 'There's something here, for it ran into my finger; we must try to get it out.' She then put her hand in again, but very cautiously, and Little Jacket gave it another stab, which made her cry out more loudly than before. Then Huggermugger put his hand in, and again he roared out as he felt the sharp prick of the thorn.

'It's no use,' says he, flinging down the boot in a passion, almost breaking Little Jacket's bones, as it fell. 'Wife, take that boot to the cobbler, and tell him to take that sharp thing out, whatever it is, and send it back to me in an hour, for I must go a hunting to-day.'

So off the obedient wife trotted to the shoemaker's, with the boot under her arm. Little Jacket was curious to see whether the shoemaker was a giant too. So when the boot was left in his workshop, he contrived to peep out a little, and saw, instead of another Huggermugger, only a crooked little dwarf, not more than two or three times bigger than himself. He went by the name of Kobboltozo.

'Tell your husband,' says he, 'that I will look into his boot presently – I am busy just at this moment – and will bring it myself to his house.'

Little Jacket was quite relieved to feel that he was safe out of the giant's house, and that the giantess had gone. 'Now,' thought he, 'I think I know what to do.'

After a while, Kobboltozo took up the boot and put his hand down into it slowly and cautiously. But Little Jacket resolved to keep quiet this time. The dwarf felt around so carefully, for fear of having his finger pricked, and his hand was so small in comparison with that of the giant's, that

Little Jacket had time to dodge around his fingers and down into the toe of the boot, so that Kobboltozo could feel nothing there. He concluded, therefore, that whatever it was that hurt the giant and his wife, whether needle, or pin, or tack, or thorn, it must have dropped out on the way to his shop. So he laid the boot down, and went for his coat and hat. Little Jacket knew that now was his only chance of escape – he dreaded being carried back to Huggermugger – so he resolved to make a bold move. No sooner was the dwarf's back turned, as he went to reach down his coat, than Little Jacket rushed out of the boot, made a spring from the table on which it lay, reached the floor, and made his way as fast as he could to a great pile of old boots and shoes that lay in a corner of the room, where he was soon hidden safe from any present chance of detection.

# Charlotte Mary Yonge (1823–1901)

One of the major genres of children's literature has been the family story. *The Daisy Chain* is one of the landmarks in that genre (as befits a 'chronicle', it had a sequel, *The Trial*, or, *More Links of the Daisy Chain* in 1864).

Charlotte Yonge was a prolific novelist whose work was enjoyed by both adults and children. Her most famous adult novel is *The Heir of Redclyffe* (1853) – which Jo March cries over in some British editions of *Little Women* – and she described *The Daisy Chain* in its preface as 'an overgrown book of a nondescript class, neither the "tale" for the young, nor the novel for their elders, but a mixture of both'. The book was serialized in *The Monthly Packet* which Yonge edited between 1851 and 1894.

'The Daisy Chain' is Dr May's description of his family, and the book begins with a crowded portrait of happy family life: as Mrs May says, 'Affection is round us like sunshine'. One morning, however, tragedy strikes. Some of the eleven children are having 'a shipwreck in the field'; another group have been for a walk, and having seen the state of the poor people at Cocksmoor, resolve, one day, to build a church there. The extract reprinted below describes what they found as they came home. The rest of the book follows the family's progress and recovery – and the eventual building of the church.

Yonge's biographer, Georgina Battiscombe (1943), remarked that her 'particular gift is to make ordinary, everyday goodness appear the most exciting thing in the world'; equally, although her books have unswerving religious (and specifically Church of England) faith behind them, it is not obtrusive. Virtue is encouraged by character and example, rather than by exhortation; imagination is constrained by worldly responsibilities, and childhood firmly bounded by adult values. A comparison of this book with *Little Women*, *Seven Little Australians* and *The Treasure Seekers* demonstrates its pivotal position.

So well known was the book that Edith Nesbit was able to gently satirize it in *The Wouldbegoods* (1901): '"It's by Miss Charlotte M. Yonge," Daisy interrupted, "and it's about a family of poor motherless children who tried so hard to be good, and they were confirmed, and had a bazaar, and went to church at the Minster, and one of them got married and wore black watered silk and ornaments. So her baby died, and then she was sorry, she had not been a good mother to it. And –" Here Dickie got up and said he'd got some snares to attend to.'

## from *The Daisy Chain; or, Aspirations. A Family Chronicle* (1856)

## from CHAPTER 3

They were almost at home, when the sight of a crowd in the main street checked them. Norman and Mr. Ernescliffe went forward to discover the cause, and spoke to some one on the outskirts – then Mr. Ernescliffe hurried back to the ladies. 'There's been an accident,' he said, hastily – 'you had better go down the lane, and in by the garden.'

He was gone in an instant, and they obeyed in silence. Whence came Ethel's certainty that the accident concerned themselves? In an agony of apprehension, though without one outward sign of it, she walked home. They were in the garden – all was apparently as usual, but no one was in sight. Ethel had been first, but she held back, and let Miss Winter go forward into the house. The front door was open – servants were standing about in confusion and one of the maids, looking dreadfully frightened, gave a cry, 'Oh! Miss – Miss – have you heard?'

'No – what? What has happened? Not Mrs. May –' exclaimed Miss Winter.

'Oh! ma'am! it's all of them. The carriage is overturned, and –'

'Who's hurt? Mamma! papa! Oh! tell me!' cried Flora.

'There's nurse,' and Ethel flew up to her. 'What is it? Oh! nurse!'

'My poor, poor children,' said old nurse, passionately kissing Ethel. Harry and Mary were on the stairs behind her, clinging together.

A stranger looked into the house, followed by Adams, the stableman. 'They are going to bring Miss May in,' some one said.

Ethel could bear it no longer. As if she could escape, she fled up-stairs, into her room, and, falling on her knees, hid her face on her bed.

There were heavy steps in the house, then a sound of heavy feet coming up to her. Norman dashed into the room, and threw himself on a chair. He was ghastly pale, and shuddered all over.

'Oh! Norman, Norman, speak. What is it?'

He groaned, but could not speak; he rested his head against her, and gasped. She was terribly frightened. 'I'll call –' and she would have gone, but he held her. 'No – no – they can't!' He was prevented from saying more, by chattering teeth and deadly faintness. She tried to support him, but could only guide him as he sank, till he lay at full length on the floor, where she put a pillow under his head, and gave him some water. 'Is it – oh! tell me. Are they much hurt? Oh, try to say.'

'They say Margaret is alive,' said Norman, in gasps; 'but – And papa – he stood up – sat – walked – was better –'

'Is he hurt – much hurt?'

'His arm –' and the tremor and fainting stopped him again.

'Mamma?' whispered Ethel; but Norman only pressed his face into the pillow.

She was so bewildered as to be more alive to the present distress of his condition, than to the vague horrors down-stairs. Some minutes passed in silence, Norman lying still, excepting a nervous trembling that agitated his whole frame. Again was heard the strange tread, doors opening and shutting, and suppressed voices, and he turned his face upwards, and listened, with his hand pressed to his forehead, as if to keep himself still enough to listen.

'Oh, what is the matter? What is it?' cried Ethel, startled and recalled to the sense of what was passing. 'Oh! Norman!' then springing up, with a sudden thought, 'Mr. Ward! Oh! is he there?'

'Yes,' said Norman, in a low, hopeless tone, 'he was at the place. He said it –'

'What?'

Again Norman's face was out of sight.

'Mamma?' Ethel's understanding perceived, but her mind refused to grasp the extent of the calamity. There was no answer, save a convulsive squeezing of her hand.

Fresh sounds below recalled her to speech and action. 'Where is she? What are they doing for her? What –'

'There's nothing to be done. She – when they lifted her up, she was –'

'Dead?'

'Dead.'

The boy lay with his face hidden, the girl sat by him on the floor, too much crushed for even the sensations belonging to grief, neither moving nor looking. After an interval Norman spoke again: 'The carriage turned right over – her head struck on the kerb-stone –'

'Did you see?' said Ethel, presently.

'I saw them lift her up.' He spoke at intervals, as he could get breath, and bear to utter the words. 'And papa – he was stunned – but soon he sat up, said he would go to her – he looked at her – felt her pulse, and then – sank down over her!'

'And did you say, I can't remember – was he hurt?'

The shuddering came again: 'His arm – all twisted – broken,' and his voice sank into a faint whisper; Ethel was obliged to sprinkle him again with water. 'But he won't die?' said she, in a tone calm from its bewilderment.

'Oh! no, no, no –'

'And Margaret?'

'They were bringing her home. I'll go and see. O! what's the meaning of this?' exclaimed he, scolding himself, as, sitting up, he was forced to rest his head on his shaking hand.

'You are still faint, dear Norman; you had better lie still, and I'll go and see.'

'Faint – stuff – how horridly stupid!' but he was obliged to lay his head down again; and Ethel, scarcely less trembling, crept carefully towards the stairs, but a dread of what she might meet came over her, and she turned towards the nursery.

The younger ones sat there in a frightened huddle. Mary was on a low chair by the infant's cot, Blanche in her lap, Tom and Harry leaning against her, and Aubrey almost asleep. Mary held up her finger as Ethel entered, and whispered, 'Hush! don't wake baby for anything!'

The first true pang of grief shot through Ethel like a dart, stabbing and taking away her breath. 'Where are they?' she said; 'how is papa? who is with him?'

'Mr. Ward and Alan Ernescliffe,' said Harry. 'Nurse came up just now, and said they were setting his arm.'

'Where is he?'

'On the bed in his dressing-room,' said Harry.

'Has he come to himself – is he better?'

They did not seem to know, and Ethel asked where to find Flora. 'With Margaret,' she was told, and she was thinking whether she could venture to seek her, when she herself came fast up the stairs. Ethel and Harry both darted out. 'Don't stop me,' said Flora – 'they want some hand-kerchiefs.'

'What, is not she in her own room?'

'No,' said Harry, 'in mamma's;' and then his face quivered all over, and he turned away. Ethel ran after her sister, and pulling out drawers without knowing what she sought, begged to hear how papa and Margaret were.

'We can't judge of Margaret – she has moved, and made a little moaning – there are no limbs broken, but we are afraid for her head. Oh! if papa could but –'

'And papa?'

'Mr. Ward is with him now – his arm is terribly hurt.'

'But oh! Flora – one moment – is he sensible?'

'Hardly; he does not take any notice – but don't keep me.'

'Can I do anything?' following her to the head of the stairs.

'No; I don't see what you can do. Miss Winter and I are with Margaret; there's nothing to do for her.'

It was a relief. Etheldred shrank from what she might have to behold, and Flora hastened down, too busy and too useful to have time to think. Harry had gone back to his refuge in the nursery, and Ethel returned to Norman. There they remained for a long time, both unwilling to speak or stir, or even to observe to each other on the noises that came in to them, as their door was left ajar, though in those sounds they were so absorbed, that they did not notice the cold of a frosty October evening, or the darkness that closed in on them.

They heard the poor babe crying, one of the children going down to call nurse, and nurse coming up; then Harry, at the door of the room where the boys slept, calling Norman in a low voice. Norman, now nearly recovered, went and brought him into his sister's room, and his tidings were, that their father's arm had been broken in two places, and the elbow frightfully injured, having been crushed and twisted by the wheel. He was also a good deal bruised, and though Mr. Ward trusted there was no positive harm to the head, he was in an unconscious state, from which the severe pain of the operation had only roused him, so far as to evince a few signs of suffering. Margaret was still insensible.

The piteous sound of the baby's wailing almost broke their hearts. Norman walked about the room in the dark, and said he should go down, he could not bear it; but he could not make up his mind to go; and after about a quarter of an hour, to their great relief, it ceased.

Next Mary opened the door, saying, 'Norman, here's Mr. Wilmot come to ask if he can do anything – Miss Winter sent word that you had better go to him.'

'How is baby?' asked Harry.

'Nurse has fed her, and is putting her to bed; she is quiet now,' said Mary; 'will you go down, Norman?'

'Where is he?'

'In the drawing-room.'

Norman paused to ask what he was to say. 'Nothing,' said Mary, 'nobody can do anything. Make haste. Don't you want a candle?'

'No, thank you, I had rather be in the dark. Come up as soon as you have seen him,' said Etheldred.

Norman went slowly down, with failing knees hardly able to conquer the shudder that came over him, as he passed those rooms. There were voices in the drawing-room, and he found a sort of council there, Alan Ernescliffe, the surgeon, and Mr. Wilmot. They turned as he came in, and Mr. Wilmot held out his hand, with a look of affection and kindness that went to his heart, making room for him on the sofa, while going on with what he was saying. 'Then you think it would be better for me not to sit up with him.'

'I should decidedly say so,' replied Mr. Ward. 'He has recognized Mr. Ernescliffe, and any change might excite him, and lead him to ask questions. The moment of his full consciousness is especially to be dreaded.'

'But you do not call him insensible?'

'No, but he seems stunned – stupefied by the shock, and by pain. He spoke to Miss Flora when she brought him some tea.'

'And admirably she managed,' said Alan Ernescliffe. 'I was much afraid of some answer that would rouse him, but she kept her self-possession beautifully, and seemed to compose him in a moment.'

'She is valuable indeed – so much judgment and activity,' said Mr. Ward, 'I don't know what we should have done without her. But we ought to have Mr. Richard – has no one sent to him?'

Alan Ernescliffe and Norman looked at each other.

'Is he at Oxford, or at his tutor's?' asked Mr. Wilmot.

'At Oxford; he was to be there to-day, was he not, Norman?'

'What o'clock is it? Is the post gone? – seven – no; it is all safe,' said Mr. Ward.

Poor Norman! he knew he was the one who ought to write, but his icy trembling hand seemed to shake more helplessly than ever, and a piteous glance fell upon Mr. Wilmot.

'The best plan would be,' said Mr. Wilmot, 'for me to go to him at once, and bring him home. If I go by the mail-train, I shall get to him sooner than a letter could.'

'And it will be better for him,' said Mr. Ward. 'He will feel it dreadfully, poor boy. But we shall all do better when we have him. You can get back to-morrow evening.'

'Sunday,' said Mr. Wilmot, 'I believe there is a train at four.'

'Oh! thank you, sir,' said Norman.

'Since that is settled, perhaps I had better go up to the Doctor,' said Alan; 'I don't like leaving Flora alone with him,' and he was gone.

'How fortunate that that youth is here,' said Mr. Wilmot; 'he seems to be quite taking Richard's place.'

'And to feel it as much,' said Mr. Ward. 'He has been invaluable with his sailor's resources and handiness.'

'Well, what shall I tell poor Richard?' asked Mr. Wilmot.

'Tell him there is no reason his father should not do very well, if we can keep him from agitation – but there's the point. He is of so excitable a constitution, that his faculties being so far confused, is the best thing, perhaps, that could be. Mr. Ernescliffe manages him very well – used to illness on that African coast, and the Doctor is very fond of him. As to Miss May, one can't tell what to say about her yet – there's no fracture, at least – it must be a work of time to judge.'

Flora at that moment half-opened the door, and called Mr. Ward, stopping for a moment to say it was nothing of any consequence. Mr. Wilmot and Norman were left together. Norman put his hands over his face and groaned – his master looked at him with kind anxiety, but did not feel as if it were yet time to speak of consolation.

'God bless and support you, and turn this to your good, my dear boy,' said he, affectionately, as he pressed his hand; 'I hope to bring your brother to-morrow.'

'Thank you, sir,' was all Norman could say; and as Mr. Wilmot went out by the front door, he slowly went up again, and lingering on the landing-place, was met by Mr. Ward, who told him, to his relief – for the mere thinking of it renewed the faint sensation – that he had better not go to his father's room.

There was nothing to be done but to return to Ethel and Harry, and tell them all; with some humiliation at being helpless, where Flora was doing so much, and to leave their father to be watched by a stranger. If he had been wanted, Norman might have made the effort, but being told that he would be worse than useless, there was nothing for him but to give way.

They sat together in Ethel's room till somewhere between eight and nine o'clock, when good old nurse, having put her younger ones to bed, came in search of them. 'Dear, dear! poor darlings,' said she, as she found them sitting in the dark; she felt their cold hands, and made them all come into the nursery, where Mary was already, and, fondling them one by one, as they passively obeyed her, she set them down on their little old stools round the fire, took away the high fender, and gave them each a cup of tea. Harry and Mary ate enough to satisfy her from a weary craving feeling, and for want of employment; Norman sat with his elbow on his knee, and a very aching head resting on his hand, glad of drink, but unable to eat; Ethel could be persuaded to do neither, till she found old nurse would let her have no peace.

The nurse sent them all to bed, taking the two girls to their own room, undressing them, and never leaving them until Mary was in a fair way of crying herself to sleep – for saying her prayers had brought the tears; while Ethel lay so wide awake that it was of no use to wait for her; and then she went to the boys, tucked them each in, as when they were little children, and saying, 'Bless your dear hearts!' bestowed on each of them a kiss which came gratefully to Norman's burning brow, and which even Harry's boyish manliness could not resist.

Flora was in Margaret's room, too useful to be spared.

So ended that dreadful Saturday.

# A. L. O. E. [A Lady of England]
# (Charlotte Maria Tucker) (1821–1893)

Middle-class benevolence and the plight of the poor became a major theme of children's books in the second half of the century, both in Britain and the USA. Charlotte Maria Tucker was something of a throwback to uncompromising evangelism, and the messages she gives are very clear. In her preface to *The Rambles of a Rat* she is nothing if not direct: 'Let not my readers suppose that in writing *The Rambles of a Rat* I have simply been blowing bubbles of fancy for their amusement, to divert them during an idle hour. Like the hollow glass balls which children delight in, my bubbles of fancy have something solid within them – facts are enclosed in my fiction.'

Ratto, our narrator, begins his story in the London docks, introducing his piebald youngest brother, Oddity. Almost immediately (as in this extract) we come across two small boys, Bob and his little brother Billy, who are starving and homeless. Fortunately, Bob is caught trying to pick the pocket of a passing philanthropist, who puts him into the Ragged School, where he makes a living as a bootblack. Meanwhile, Ratto goes on an educational visit to the zoo and an informative voyage to St Petersburg, but by spectacular coincidence he and his companions meet Oddity on their return to England. He is now a pet rat living on a farm where Billy and Bob are working and is prepared to defend his master's property to the death. The whole performance is unsubtle in the extreme, but it has a zest and commitment that make it very entertaining reading.

A. L. O. E. was a highly successful writer who spent the last eighteen years of her life as a missionary in India.

## from *The Rambles of a Rat* (1857)

## from CHAPTER I

There had been a great deal of moving about in the warehouse during the day, running of trucks, and rolling of casks. Brisk, the liveliest of my brothers, had sat watching in a hole from noon until dusk, and now hurried through our little passage into the shed, where we were all nestling behind some old canvas. He brought us news of a coming feast.

'A ship has arrived from India,' said he, 'and we'll have a glance at the cargo. They've been busy stowing it away next door. There's rice –'

The brotherhood of rats whisked their tails for joy.

'Sugar–'

There was a universal squeak of approbation.

'Indigo–'

'That's nothing but a blue dye obtained from a plant,' observed Furry, an old, blind rat, who in his days had travelled far, and seen much of the world, and had reflected upon what he had viewed far more than is common with a rat. Indeed, he passed amongst us for a philosopher, and I had learned not a little from his experience; for he delighted in talking over his travels, and, but for a little testiness of temper, would have been a very agreeable companion. He very frequently joined our party; indeed, his infirmities obliged him to do so, as he could not have lived without assistance. But I must now return to Brisk, and his catalogue of the cargo.

'Opium –'

'The juice of the white poppy,' said our aged friend, who had a taste for general information. 'I've seen it produce strange effects when eaten in large quantities by men.'

'What effects?' said I. I was a very inquisitive rat, and especially curious about all that related to the large creatures upon two legs, called Man, whom I believed to be as much wiser as they are stronger than the race of Mus, to which I belong.

'Why, opium makes men first wild and bold, so that they will rush into danger or run into folly, quarrel with their friends and fight their foes, laugh and dance, and be merry they know not why. Then they grow sleepy, and though their lives might depend on it, not a step would they stir. Then, when they awake from their unnatural sleep, their bodies are cold, their heads heavy; they feel sick, and faint, and sad. And if this should happen day after day, at last the strong grows weak and the healthy ill, the flesh goes from the bones and the life from the eyes, and the whole man becomes like some old, empty hulk, whose timbers will hardly hold together. And all this from eating opium!'

'Ugh!' exclaimed Brisk; 'leave opium to man; it is a great deal too bad for rats.'

## CHAPTER II

## A CLAP-TRAP DISCOVERY

With eager haste we scrambled into the warehouse, Furry, as usual, remaining behind on account of his infirmities. We were almost too impatient to wait till the men within should have finished their work, till the doors should be shut and locked, and the place left in quiet for us.

I soon found out what was to me a singular curiosity – a tooth; I felt certain that it was a tooth; but it was twice as long as any rat, counting from the tip of his nose to the end of his tail. I could not help wondering in my mind to what huge animal it could ever have belonged.

'Isn't that called ivory?' said Oddity, as he waddled past me.

I felt inexpressible pleasure in gnawing and nibbling at the huge tusk, and polishing my sharp teeth upon it. 'How I should like to see the enormous rat that could have carried such a tusk!' I exclaimed. 'Oh, how I should delight in travelling and seeing the world!'

'You've something to see worth the seeing, without travelling far!' cried Brisk. 'Such a fragrance of cheese as there is yonder. Why, Ratto, its delicious scent reaches us even here.'

I was so busy with my tusk, and my reflections, that I scarcely looked up; but Oddity turned his eyes eagerly towards the spot.

'Now, I propose that we have a race to the place,' cried Brisk; 'and he who gets first shall have his pick of the feast. Leave Ratto to his old bone. Here are seven of us: now for it; – once, twice, thrice, and away!'

Off they scampered helter-skelter, all my seven brothers, awkward heavy Oddity, as usual, in the rear. He had often been laughed at for his slowness, but this time it was well for him that he was slow. On rushed the six foremost, almost together, scrambling one over another in their haste; they disappeared into what looked like a dark hole, and then – alas! alas! what a terrible squeaking.

Poor unhappy brothers! all caught in a trap! All at the mercy of their cruel enemy, Man! I ran to the spot in a terrible fright. Nothing of my six companions could I see; but Oddity, with a very disconsolate look, was staring at the drop of the trap. His had been a very narrow escape – it had grazed his ugly nose as it fell.

This is a very melancholy part of my story, and I will hasten over it as fast as I can. In vain the poor captive rats tried to gnaw their way to freedom from within, while Oddity and I nibbled from without. There was something which defied even our sharp little teeth, and all our efforts were in vain. My poor brothers could not touch the fatal feast which had lured them to their ruin. They passed a miserable night, and were every one carried off in a bag to be worried by dogs in the morning.

'Cruel, wicked man!' I exclaimed, as with my piebald companion I sought my old shelter behind the canvas in our shed. My exclamation was overheard by old Furry.

'Cruel, wicked man!' he repeated, but in a different tone from mine; 'well, I think that even when setting a trap to catch inexperienced rats, man may have something to say for himself. I have often noticed the big creatures at work, and much they labour, and hard they toil, and we can't expect them to be willing to take so much trouble to collect dainties just to feed us. Those who live on the property of others, like rats, have no right to expect civil treatment.'

'Are there any creatures that lay traps for man?' said I, in the bitterness of my spirit almost hoping that there might be.

'As well as I can understand,' replied Furry, 'man himself lays traps for man. I have seen several of these traps. They are large, and generally built of brick, with a board and gilt letters in front. They are baited with a certain drink, which has effects something like opium, which destroys slowly but surely those who give themselves up recklessly to its enjoyment.'

'Well,' cried Oddity, 'having once seen what comes of running into a trap, I, for one, shall be always on my guard against them, and am never likely to be caught in that way. I suppose that it is the same with man. When he sees that one or two of his companions are lost by the big man-trap, he takes good care never to go near it himself.'

'Not a whit!' exclaimed Furry, with a scornful whisk of his tail. 'They like the bait, though they know its effects quite well. They walk with open eyes into the great man-trap, they hasten merrily into the great man-trap, when the gas-lights are flaring, and the spirits flowing, and the sound of laughter and jesting is heard within. They know that they are going the straight, direct way to be worried by sickness, poverty, and shame – (what these are I never heard clearly explained, but I have gathered that they are great enemies of man, who are always waiting at the door of the great man-trap) – and yet they go gaily to their ruin!'

'So this is your account of the wise creature man!' I exclaimed; – 'he is a great deal more foolish than any rat.'

## Chapter III

### Poorer than Rats

We had not our shed always to ourselves. One cold evening in autumn, when there was a sharp east wind, and a drizzling rain, two human creatures came into the place and cowered down in a corner of our shed. I call them human creatures, for they certainly were not men; they were so different from the tall powerful fellows whom I had occasionally seen at their work in the warehouse. These were much smaller, and so thin that their bones seemed almost ready to break through the skin. Their hair hung in long loose masses about their ears. They had nothing on their feet to protect them from the stones, and one of them had a hurt upon his heel, which looked red and inflamed.

I found that these were young human beings neglected and uncared for, as young rats would not have been. We were at first afraid of them, and only peered out curiously upon them from our holes and hiding-places; but when, gathering courage, we ventured to come forward, we seemed to frighten them as much as they had frightened us.

'Look there – there, Bob!' screamed the younger child, clinging more closely to his brother.

'Them bees rats,' said the other one, more quietly. His poor thin little face looked as if the life and spirit had been so starved out of it, that he could not be much astonished at anything.

'I don't like staying here, Bob, amongst the rats!' cried the terrified little one, attempting to pull his brother towards the entrance by the sleeve of his jacket. The wretched rag gave way even under his weak pull, and another rent was added to the many by which the cold crept in through the poor boy's tattered dress. 'I won't stay here; let us go, let us go!'

'We've nowheres to go to,' replied Bob, in the same dull, lifeless tone. 'Never you mind the rats, Billy, them won't hurt you,' he added.

Hurt him! not we! If ever I felt pity, it was for those ragged little urchins. We were well-fed, but they were hungry; Nature had given us sleek warm coats, but they trembled with cold. It was very clear that it was much harder to them to support life than if they had been rats. I wondered if in this great city there were many such helpless children, and if there were none to care for them.

'I say, Ratto,' observed Oddity, licking his soft coat till the beautiful polish upon it made one almost forget its ugly colour, ''tis a pity that these children are so dirty; but may be they are not so particular about such matters as we rats.'

In time a sort of acquaintance grew up between me and the ragged boys. We ceased to fear each other, and I would venture almost close to Billy's thin little hand when he had a crust of bread to eat, for he always broke off a little bit for me. The poor little fellow was crippled and lame, so he rarely left the shed. Bob often went out in the morning, and returned when it was growing dark, sometimes with food, and sometimes without it; but whenever he had anything to eat, he always shared it with his little lame brother. I see them now, crouched close up together for the sake of warmth. Sometimes Billy cried from hunger and cold, and his tears made long lines down his grimy face. Bob never cried, he suffered quite quietly; he patted his little brother's shaggy head, and spoke kindly to him, in his dull, cheerless way. I felt more sorry for him than for Billy.

The little one was the more talkative of the two. Perhaps he was more lively in his nature; or, perhaps, from having been a shorter time in a world of sorrow, he had not learned its sad lessons so well. I certainly never heard him laugh but once, and then it was when Oddity, who was more shy than I, ventured for the first time since Billy's coming to cross the shed.

'Oh! look – look, Bob! what a funny rat! what a beauty rat!' he cried, clapping his bony hands together with childish glee.

It was comical to see the expression on Oddity's blunt face on hearing this unexpected compliment, perhaps the first that he had ever received in his life. It was enough to have turned the head of a less sober rat; but he, honest fellow, only lifted up his snub nose with a sort of bull-dog look, which seemed to say, 'Well, there's no accounting for taste.'

'Bob,' said little Billy one evening, with more animation than usual, 'I'se been a watching the rats, and I saw – only think what I saw!'

'Eh, what did ye see?' replied Bob, drowsily, rubbing his eyes with the back of his hand. He looked very hungry and tired.

'I was a-watching for the fat spotted one which ran across yesterday, when out came creeping, creeping, two others' – the child with his fingers on the floor suited his action to his words – 'and one had some white on its back; it looked old and weak; and Bob, I saw as how it was blind.'

'A blind rat!' cried Bob; ''twould soon starve, I take it.'

'But there was the other rat at its side, with such shining eyes, and such a sharp little nose!' I plead guilty to vanity; I could not hear such a description of myself with Oddity's sober composure. 'And the old blind rat had a little bit of stick in its mouth, just as the blind man in the lane has a stick in his hand, and the pretty black rat took the other end in his teeth, and so pulled the old un on his way.'

'I'se never heard of rats doing that afore,' said Bob.

'That's not all that I saw about 'em,' continued Billy. 'Out comes the funny spotted rat from its hole; so I keeps very quiet, not to frighten it away. And it pattered up to the place where I put the little crumbs; and what do you think as it did?'

'Ate them,' was Bob's quiet reply.

'No, but it didn't, though!' cried Billy triumphantly; 'it pushed them towards the old blind rat. Neither the black un nor the spotted un ate up one crumb; they left 'em all for the poor blind rat. Now wasn't them famous little fellows!'

'So rats help one another,' said Bob. He did not speak more; but as he leaned back his head, and looked straight up at the roof of the shed (there was a great hole in it which the stars shone through, and now and then a big drop of water from the top came plash, plash, on the muddy floor below), – he looked up, I say, and I wonder whether he was thinking the same thing as I was at that moment: 'Rats help one another; do none but human beings leave their fellow-creatures to perish!'

# Thomas Hughes (1822–1896)

*Tom Brown's Schooldays* set the agenda for a huge genre of children's books that lasted well into the twentieth century before petering out into occasional examples. There had been earlier books about schools, the most notable being Harriet Martineau's *The Crofton Boys* (1841). Thomas Hughes, reacting to the unrealistic didacticism that he saw in children's books, set out to write a book for his eight-year-old son, who was about to go to boarding school, that was neither unrealistic nor didactic: 'I want to give you a true picture of what everyday school life was in my time, and not a kid-glove and go-to-meeting-coat picture.'

In doing so, he hit upon what became a formula: the overall themes – initiation into a new community, learning to cope with life, the idiosyncrasies of society (and especially restricted society); the character types – the upright hero, the best friend, the decent head of house or dormitory, the small, frightened (but often highly religious) child, the bully, the God-like headmaster; and conventional plot devices – bullying and the defeat of the bully, the hero who is nearly led astray but who is saved by a good friend, the dramatic rescue (commonly from drowning) and encounters with the local people. Most of all, the (largely) enclosed world of school allowed codes of conduct to be stressed which had great implications for life *after* school, especially in the contexts of a class-conscious society that was building an empire.

Our eponymous hero, a strong country lad, goes to Rugby School in the 1830s not, as his father says, to become a scholar, but to 'turn out a brave, helpful, truth-telling Englishman, and a gentleman, and a Christian'. Tom goes through initiation ceremonies, is bullied by the archetypal bully, Flashman, and learns the often arcane rules and traditions of Rugby. Being a 'real' rather than idealized boy, he breaks rules, is caught poaching, and at one point is flogged by the headmaster for attending a local fair. He is, however, redeemed by befriending a younger boy, George Arthur, and ends as captain of the cricket team. The book also contains a sympathetic portrait of Thomas Arnold who, as headmaster of Rugby, was highly influential in the development of the English public school system.

The narrative style of *Tom Brown's Schooldays* is very personal and oral, rather in the manner of Charles Kingsley, and the story is continually interrupted by asides on political and social issues. Hughes was not only a politician (he was a Liberal Member of Parliament from 1865 to 1871) but also a Christian Socialist, and the fashion for 'muscular Christianity' appears throughout the book. Tom has to stand up for himself and behave in what was rapidly becoming the 'correct' British way. Hughes's narrative persona is blunt and hearty, and addresses the readers directly: 'Boys will quarrel, and when they quarrel will sometimes fight. Fighting with fists is the natural and English way for English boys to settle their quarrels. What substitute for it is there, amongst any nation under the sun?' Similarly, bullying has to be dealt with by the bullied. As Brooke, the 'head of the eleven, the head of big-side football' says: 'there's a deal of bullying going on. . . . It's very little kindness for the sixth [form] to meddle generally – you youngsters, mind that. You'll be all the better football players for learning to stand it, and to take your own parts, and fight it through.' (This might be compared to the attitude to bullying expressed in Kipling's *Stalky and Co*, 42 years later.)

Hughes, then, spoke for a generation that saw school as a practical testing ground for the principles of a nation. In this famous sequence, beginning in chapter 8, Tom and his friend East encounter the archetypal bully (and coward) Flashman, as the boys hold a lottery to draw horses for the major British horse-race, the Derby. One boy, 'the opener', is distributing the tickets, and Tom draws a favourite.

## from *Tom Brown's Schooldays* (1857)

### from Chapter 8

### The War of Independence

'Give me the ticket,' says Flashman with an oath, leaning across the table with open hand and his face black with rage.

'Wouldn't you like it?' replies the opener, not a bad fellow at the bottom, and no admirer of Flashman's. 'Here, Brown, catch hold,' and he hands the ticket to Tom, who pockets it; whereupon Flashman makes for the door at once, that Tom and the ticket may not escape, and there keeps watch until the drawing is over and all the boys are gone except the sporting set of five or six, who stay to compare books, make bets, and so on, Tom, who doesn't choose to move while Flashman is at the door, and East, who stays by his friend, anticipating trouble.

The sporting set now gathered round Tom. Public opinion wouldn't allow them actually to rob him of his ticket, but any humbug or intimidation by which he could be driven to sell the whole or part at an under-value was lawful.

'Now, young Brown, come, what'll you sell me Harkaway for? I hear he isn't going to start. I'll give you five shillings for him,' begins the boy who had opened the ticket. Tom, remembering his good deed, and moreover in his forlorn state wishing to make a friend, is about to accept the offer, when another cries out, 'I'll give you seven shillings.' Tom hesitated, and looked from one to the other.

'No, no!' said Flashman, pushing in, 'leave me to deal with him; we'll draw lots for it afterwards. Now, sir, you know me – you'll sell Harkaway to us for five shillings, or you'll repent it.'

'I won't sell a bit of him,' answered Tom shortly.

'You hear that now!' said Flashman, turning to the others. 'He's the coxiest young blackguard in the house – I always told you so. We're to have all the trouble and risk of getting up the lotteries for the benefit of such fellows as he.'

Flashman forgets to explain what risk they ran, but he speaks to willing ears. Gambling makes boys selfish and cruel as well as men.

'That's true – we always draw blanks,' cries one. 'Now, sir, you shall sell half at any rate.'

'I won't,' said Tom, flushing up to his hair, and lumping them all in his mind with his sworn enemy.

'Very well then, let's roast him,' cried Flashman, and catches hold of Tom by the collar: one or two boys hesitate, but the rest join in. East seizes Tom's arm and tries to pull him away, but is knocked back by one of the boys, and Tom is dragged along struggling. His shoulders are pushed against the mantelpiece, and he is held by main force before the fire, Flashman drawing his trousers tight by way of extra torture. Poor East, in more pain even than Tom, suddenly thinks of Diggs, and darts off to find him. 'Will you sell now for ten shillings?' says one boy who is relenting.

Tom only answers by groans and struggles.

'I say, Flashey, he has had enough,' says the same boy, dropping the arm he holds.

'No, no, another turn'll do it,' answers Flashman. But poor Tom is done already, turns deadly pale, and his head falls forward on his breast, just as Diggs in frantic excitement rushes into the hall with East at his heels.

'You cowardly brutes!' is all he can say, as he catches Tom from them and supports him to the Hall table. 'Good God! he's dying. Here, get some cold water – run for the housekeeper.'

Flashman and one or two others slink away; the rest, ashamed and sorry, bend over Tom or run for water, while East darts off for the housekeeper. Water comes, and they throw it on his hands and face, and he begins to come to. 'Mother!' – the words came feebly and slowly – 'it's very cold tonight.' Poor old Diggs is blubbering like a child. 'Where am I?' goes on Tom, opening his eyes. 'Ah! I remember now,' and he shut his eyes again and groaned.

'I say,' is whispered, 'we can't do any good, and the housekeeper will be here in a minute,' and all but one steal away; he stays with Diggs, silent and sorrowful, and fans Tom's face.

The housekeeper comes in with strong salts, and Tom soon recovers enough to sit up. There is a smell of burning; she examines his clothes, and looks up inquiringly. The boys are all silent.

'How did he come so?' No answer.

'There's been some bad work here,' she adds, looking very serious, 'and I shall speak to the Doctor about it.' Still no answer.

'Hadn't we better carry him to the sick-room?' suggests Diggs.

'Oh, I can walk now,' says Tom; and supported by East and the housekeeper, goes to the sick-room. The boy who held his ground is soon amongst the rest, who are all in fear of their lives. 'Did he peach?' 'Does she know about it?'

'Not a word – he's a staunch little fellow.' And pausing a moment he adds, 'I'm sick of this work: what brutes we've been.'

Meantime Tom is stretched on the sofa in the housekeeper's room, with East by his side, while she gets wine and water and other restoratives.

'Are you much hurt, dear old boy?' whispers East.

'Only the back of my legs,' answers Tom. They are indeed badly scorched, and part of his trousers burnt through. But soon he is in bed with cold bandages. At first he feels broken, and thinks of writing home and getting taken away; and the verse of a hymn he had learned years ago sings through his head, and he goes to sleep, murmuring –

> Where the wicked cease from troubling,
> and the weary are at rest.

But after a sound night's rest, the old boy-spirit comes back again. East comes in reporting that the whole house is with him, and he forgets everything except their old resolve, never to be beaten by that bully Flashman.

Not a word could the housekeeper extract from either of them, and though the Doctor knew all that she knew that morning, he never knew any more.

I trust and believe that such scenes are not possible now at school, and that lotteries and betting-books have gone out; but I am writing of schools as they were in our time, and must give the evil with the good.

## Chapter 9

## A Chapter of Accidents

*'Wherein I [speak] of most disastrous chances.*
*Of moving accidents by flood and field,*
*Of hair-breadth 'scapes.'*

Shakespeare

When Tom came back into school after a couple of days in the sick-room, he found matters much changed for the better, as East had led him to expect. Flashman's brutality had disgusted most even of his intimate friends, and his cowardice had once more been made plain to the House; for Diggs had encountered him on the morning after the lottery, and after high words on both sides had struck him, and the blow was not returned. However, Flashey was not unused to this sort of thing, and had lived through as awkward affairs before, and, as Diggs had said, fed and toadied himself back into favour again. Two or three of the boys who had helped to roast Tom came up and begged his pardon, and thanked him for not telling anything. Morgan sent for him, and was inclined to take the matter up warmly, but Tom begged him not to do it; to which he agreed, on Tom's promising to come to him at once in future – a promise which I regret to say he didn't keep. Tom kept Harkaway all to himself, and won the second prize in the lottery, some thirty shillings, which he and East contrived to spend in about three days, in the purchase of pictures for their study, two new bats and a cricket-ball, all the best that could be got, and a supper of sausages, kidneys, and beef-steak pies to all the rebels. Light come, light go; they wouldn't have been comfortable with money in their pockets in the middle of the half.

The embers of Flashman's wrath, however, were still smouldering, and burst out every now and then in sly blows and taunts, and they both felt that they hadn't quite done with him yet. It wasn't long, however, before the last act of that drama came, and with it, the end of bullying for Tom and East at Rugby. They now often stole out into the Hall at nights, incited thereto, partly by the hope of finding Diggs there and having a talk with him, partly by the excitement of doing something which was against rules; for, sad to say, both of our youngsters, since their loss of character for steadiness in their form, had got into the habit of doing things which were forbidden, as a matter of adventure; just in the same way, I should fancy, as men fall into smuggling, and for the same sort of reasons. Thoughtlessness in the first place. It never occurred to them to consider why such and such rules were laid down, the reason was nothing to them, and they only looked upon rules as a sort of challenge from the rule-makers, which it would be rather bad pluck in them not to accept; and then again, in the lower parts of the school they hadn't enough to do. The work of the form they could manage to get through pretty easily, keeping a good enough place to get their regular yearly remove; and not having much ambition beyond this, their whole superfluous steam was available for games and scrapes. Now one rule of the House which it was a daily pleasure of all such boys to break, was that after supper all fags, except the three on duty in the passages, should remain in their own studies until nine o'clock; and if caught about the passages or hall, or in one another's studies, they were liable to punishments or caning. The rule was stricter than its observance, for most of the sixth spent their evenings in the fifth-form room, where the library was, and the lessons were learnt in common. Every now and then, however, a praepostor would be seized with a fit of district visiting, and would make a tour of the passages and hall, and the fags' studies. Then, if the owner were entertaining a friend or two, the first kick at the door and ominous 'open here', had the effect of the shadow of a hawk over a chicken-yard; every one cut to cover – one small boy diving under the sofa, another under the table, while the owner would hastily pull down a book or two and open them, and cry out in a meek voice, 'Hullo, who's there?' casting an anxious eye round, to see that no protruding leg or elbow could betray the hidden boys. 'Open, sir, directly, it's Snooks.' 'Oh, I'm very sorry, I didn't know it was you, Snooks;' and then, with well-feigned zeal, the door would be opened, young hopeful praying that that beast Snooks mightn't have heard the scuffle caused by his coming. If a study was empty, Snooks proceeded to draw the passage and hall to find the truants.

Well, one evening, in forbidden hours, Tom and East were in the Hall. They occupied the seats before the fire nearest the door, while Diggs sprawled as usual before the further fire. He was busy with a copy of verses, and East and Tom were chatting together in whispers by the light of the fire, and splicing a favourite old fives' bat which had sprung. Presently a step came down the bottom passage; they listened a moment, assured themselves that it wasn't a praepostor, and then went on with their work, and the door swung open, and in walked Flashman. He didn't see Diggs, and thought it a good chance to keep his hand in; and as the boys didn't move for him, struck one of them, to make them get out of his way.

'What's that for?' growled the assaulted one.

'Because I choose. You've no business here – go to your study.'

'You can't send us.'

'Can't I? Then I'll thrash you if you stay,' said Flashman, savagely.

'I say, you two,' said Diggs from the end of the Hall, rousing up and resting himself on his elbow, 'you'll never get rid of that fellow till you lick him. Go in at him, both of you – I'll see fair play.'

Flashman was taken aback, and retreated two steps. East looked at Tom, 'Shall we try?' said he. 'Yes,' said Tom, desperately. So the two advanced on Flashman with clenched fists and beating hearts. They were about up to his shoulder, but tough boys of their age and in perfect training; while he, though strong and big, was in poor condition from his monstrous habits of stuffing and want of exercise. Coward as he was, however, Flashman couldn't swallow such an insult as this; besides, he was confident of having easy work, and so faced the boys, saying, 'You impudent young blackguards!' – Before he could finish his abuse they rushed in on him, and began pummelling at all of him which they could reach. He hit out wildly and savagely, but the full force of his blows didn't tell, they were too near him. It was long odds though in point of strength, and in another minute Tom went spinning backwards over a form, and Flashman turned to demolish East with a savage grin. But now Diggs jumped down from the table on which he had seated himself. 'Stop there,' shouted he, 'the round's over – half-minute time allowed.'

'What the – is it to you?' faltered Flashman, who began to lose heart.

'I'm going to see fair, I tell you,' said Diggs with a grin, and snapping his great red fingers; ''tain't fair for you to be fighting one of them at a time. Are you ready, Brown? Time's up.'

The small boys rushed in again. Closing they saw was their best chance, and Flashman was wilder and more flurried than ever: he caught East by the throat and tried to force him back on the iron-bound table; Tom grasped his waist, and remembering the old throw he had learned in the Vale from Harry Winburn, crooked his leg inside Flashman's, and threw his whole weight forward. The three tottered for a moment, and then over they went on to the floor, Flashman striking his head against a form in the fall.

The two youngsters sprang to their legs, but he lay there still. They began to be frightened. Tom stooped down, and then cried out, scared out of his wits, 'He's bleeding awfully; come here, East, Diggs – he's dying!'

'Not he,' said Diggs, getting leisurely off the table; 'it's all sham, he's only afraid to fight it out.' East was as frightened as Tom. Diggs lifted Flashman's head, and he groaned.

'What's the matter?' shouted Diggs.

'My skull's fractured,' sobbed Flashman.

'Oh, let me run for the housekeeper,' cried Tom. 'What shall we do?'

'Fiddlesticks! it's nothing but the skin broken,' said the relentless Diggs, feeling his head. 'Cold water and a bit of rag's all he'll want.'

'Let me go,' said Flashman, surlily, sitting up; 'I don't want your help.'

'We're really very sorry,' began East.

'Hang your sorrow,' answered Flashman, holding his handkerchief to the place; 'you shall pay for this, I can tell you, both of you.' And he walked out of the Hall.

'He can't be very bad,' said Tom with a deep sigh, much relieved to see his enemy march so well.

'Not he,' said Diggs, 'and you'll see you won't be troubled with him any more. But, I say, your head's broken too – your collar is covered with blood.'

'Is it though?' said Tom, putting up his hand, 'I didn't know it.'

'Well, mop it up, or you'll have your jacket spoilt. And you have got a nasty eye, Scud; you'd better go and bathe it well in cold water.'

'Cheap enough too, if we've done with our old friend Flashy,' said East, as they made off upstairs to bathe their wounds.

They had done with Flashman in one sense, for he never laid finger on either of them again; but whatever harm a spiteful heart and venomous tongue could do them, he took care should be done. Only throw dirt enough, and some of it is sure to stick; and so it was with the fifth form and the bigger boys in general, with whom he associated more or less, and they not at all, Flashman managed to get Tom and East into disfavour, which did not wear off for some time after the author of it had disappeared from the School world. This event, much prayed for by the small fry in general, took place a few months after the above encounter. One fine summer evening Flashman had been regaling himself on gin-punch, at Brownsover; and having exceeded his usual limits, started home uproarious. He fell in with a friend or two coming back from bathing, proposed a glass of beer, to which they assented, the weather being hot, and they thirsty souls, and unaware of the quantity of drink which Flashman had already on board. The short result was, that Flashy became beastly drunk; they tried to get him along, but couldn't, so they chartered a hurdle and two men to carry him. One of the masters came upon them, and they naturally enough fled. The flight of the rest raised the master's suspicions, and the good angel of the fags incited him to examine the freight, and after examination, to convoy the hurdle himself up to the School-house; and the Doctor, who had long had his eye on Flashman, arranged for his withdrawal next morning.

The evil that men, and boys too, do, lives after them: Flashman was gone, but our boys, as hinted above, still felt the effects of his hate. Besides, they had been the movers of the strike against unlawful fagging. The cause was righteous, the result had been triumphant to a great extent; but the best of the fifth, even those who had never fagged the small boys, or had given up the practice cheerfully, couldn't help feeling a small grudge against the first rebels. After all, their form had been defied; on just grounds, no doubt, so just indeed, that they had at once acknowledged the wrong, and remained passive in the strife: had they sided with Flashman and his set, the rebels must have given way at once. They couldn't help, on the whole, being glad that they had so acted, and that the resistance had been successful against such of their own form as had shewn fight; they felt that law and order had gained thereby, but the ringleaders they couldn't quite pardon at once. 'Confoundedly coxy those young rascals will get if we don't mind,' was the general feeling.

So it is, and must be always, my dear boys. If the Angel Gabriel were to come down from Heaven, and head a successful rise against the most abominable and unrighteous vested interest which this poor old world groans under, he would most certainly lose his character for many years, probably for centuries, not only with upholders of said vested interest, but with the respectable mass of the people whom he had delivered. They wouldn't ask him to dinner, or let their names appear with his in the papers; they would be very careful how they spoke of him in the Palaver or at their clubs. What can we expect then, when we have only poor gallant blundering men like Kossuth, Garibaldi, Mazzini, and righteous causes which do not triumph in their hands; men who have holes enough in their armour, God knows, easy to be hit by respectabilities sitting in their lounging chairs, and having large balances at their bankers? But you are brave gallant boys, who hate easy-chairs, and have no balances or bankers. You only want to have your heads set straight to take the right side: so bear in mind that majorities, especially respectable ones, are nine times out of ten in the wrong; and that if you see man or boy striving earnestly on the weak side, however wrong-headed or blundering he may be, you are not to go and join the cry against him. If you can't join him and help him, and make him wiser, at any rate remember that he has found something in the world which he will fight and suffer for, which is just what you have got to do for yourselves, and so think and speak of him tenderly.

# Frances Browne (1816–1897)

At the end of *Granny's Wonderful Chair* Frances Browne laments the absence of fairies and magic in the present day, 'for the fairies dance no more. Some say it was the hum of schools – some think it was the din of factories that frightened them; but nobody has been known to have seen them for many a year' (with the exception, she adds, of Hans Christian Andersen).

But the folk-tale and the fairy-tale were making a steady advance in children's literature, as the seven stories of *Granny's Wonderful Chair*, which owe something to the folk-tales collected by the Grimm brothers, demonstrate. The tales are set in a 'frame' story to which they contribute:

Snowflower is left her granny's chair that can take her anywhere, and tell a story every day. The stories it tells at the court of King Winwealth (and Queen Wantall and Princess Greedalind) are moralistic rather than moral tales. As with *The King of the Golden River* (see p. 98) and many popular folk-tales, goodness and virtue win through without overt teaching (although the names of the characters belong to a less subtle tradition).

Frances Browne was born in Ireland and made her living by writing, despite having been blinded by smallpox as a child.

## from *Granny's Wonderful Chair and its Tales of Fairy Times* (1857)

### CHAPTER 8

### THE STORY OF MERRYMIND

Once upon a time there lived in the north country a certain poor man and his wife, who had two cornfields, three cows, five sheep and thirteen children. Twelve of these children were called by names common in the north country – Hardhead, Stiffneck, Tightfingers and the like; but when the thirteenth came to be named, either the poor man and his wife could remember no other name, or something in the child's look made them think it proper, for they called him Merrymind, which the neighbours thought a strange name and very much above their station: however, as they showed no other signs of pride, the neighbours let that pass. Their thirteen children grew taller and stronger every year, and they had hard work to keep them in bread. But when the youngest was old enough to look after his father's sheep, there happened the great fair, to which everybody in the north country went, because it came only once in seven years, and was held on Midsummer Day – not in any town or village, but on a green plain, lying between a broad river and a high hill, where it was said the fairies used to dance in old and merry times.

Merchants and dealers of all sorts crowded to that fair from far and near. There was nothing known in the north country that could not be bought or sold in it, and neither old nor young were willing to go home without a fairing. The poor man who owned this large family could afford them little to spend in such ways; but as the fair happened only once in seven years, he would not show a poor spirit. Therefore, calling them about him, he opened the leathern bag in which his savings were stored and gave every one of the thirteen a silver penny.

The boys and girls had never before owned so much pocket-money; and, wondering what they should buy, they dressed themselves in their holiday clothes, and set out with their father and mother to the fair. When they came near the ground that midsummer morning, the stalls, heaped up with all manner of merchandise, from gingerbread upwards, the tents for fun and feasting, the puppet shows, the rope-dancers and the crowd of neighbours and strangers, all in their best attire, made those simple people think their north country fair the finest sight in the world. The day wore away in seeing wonders and in chatting with old friends. It was surprising how far silver pennies went in those days; but before evening twelve of the thirteen had got fairly rid of their money. One bought a pair of brass buckles, another a crimson riband, a third green garters; the father bought a tobacco-pipe, the mother a horn snuffbox – in short, all had provided themselves with fairings except Merrymind.

The cause of the silver penny remaining in his pocket was that he had set his heart upon a fiddle; and fiddles enough there were in the fair – small and large, plain and painted. He looked at and priced the most of them, but there was not one that came within the compass of a silver penny. His father and mother warned him to make haste with his purchase, for they must all go home at sunset, because the way was long.

The sun was getting low and red upon the hill; the fair was growing thin, for many dealers had packed up their stalls and departed; but there was a mossy hollow in the great hillside, to which the outskirts of the fair had reached, and Merrymind thought he would see what might be there. The first thing was a stall of fiddles, kept by a young merchant from a far country, who had many customers, his goods being fine and new; but hard by sat a little grey-haired man, at whom everybody had laughed that day, because he had nothing on his stall but one old dingy fiddle, and all its strings were broken. Nevertheless the little man sat as stately, and cried 'Fiddles to sell!' as if he had the best stall in the fair.

'Buy a fiddle, my young master?' he said as Merrymind came forward. 'You shall have it cheap: I ask but a silver penny for it; and if the strings were mended, its like would not be in the north country.'

Merrymind thought this a great bargain. He was a handy boy and could mend the strings while watching his father's sheep. So down went the silver penny on the little man's stall and up went the fiddle under Merrymind's arm.

'Now, my young master,' said the little man, 'you see that we merchants have a deal to look after, and if you help me to bundle up my stall, I will tell you a wonderful piece of news about that fiddle.'

Merrymind was good-natured and fond of news, so he helped him to tie up with an old rope the loose boards and stocks that composed his stall, and when they were hoisted on his back like a faggot, the little man said:

'About that fiddle, my young master: it is certain the strings can never be mended nor made new, except by threads from the night-spinners, which, if you get, it will be a good pennyworth'; and up the hill he ran like a greyhound.

Merrymind thought that was queer news, but being given to hope the best, he believed the little man was only jesting, and made haste to join the rest of the family, who were soon on their way home. When they got there everyone showed his bargain, and Merrymind showed his fiddle; but his brothers and sisters laughed at him for buying such a thing when he had never learned to play. His sisters asked him what music he could bring out of broken strings; and his father said:

'Thou hast shown little prudence in laying out thy first penny, from which token I fear thou wilt never have many to lay out.'

In short, everybody threw scorn on Merrymind's bargain except his mother. She, good woman, said if he laid out one penny ill, he might lay out the next better; and who knew but his fiddle would be of use some day? To make her words good, Merrymind fell to repairing the strings – he spent all his time, both night and day, upon them; but, true to the little man's parting words, no mending would stand, and no string would hold on that fiddle. Merrymind tried everything and wearied himself to no purpose. At last he thought of inquiring after people who spun at night; and this seemed such a good joke to the north country people that they wanted no other till the next fair.

In the meantime Merrymind lost credit at home and abroad. Everybody believed in his father's prophecy; his brothers and sisters valued him no more than a herd boy; the neighbours thought he must turn out a scapegrace. Still the boy would not part with his fiddle. It was his silver pennyworth, and he had a strong hope of mending the strings for all that had come and gone; but since nobody at home cared for him except his mother, and as she had twelve other children, he resolved to leave the scorn behind him, and go to seek his fortune.

The family were not very sorry to hear of that intention, being in a manner ashamed of him; besides, they could spare one out of thirteen. His father gave him a barley cake, and his mother her blessing. All his brothers and sisters wished him well. Most of the neighbours hoped that no harm would happen to him; and Merrymind set out one summer morning with the broken-stringed fiddle under his arm.

There were no highways then in the north country – people took whatever path pleased them best; so Merrymind went over the fairground and up the hill, hoping to meet the little man and learn something of the night-spinners. The hill was covered with heather to the top, and he went up without meeting anyone. On the other side it was steep and rocky, and after a hard scramble down he came to a narrow glen all overgrown with wild furze and brambles. Merrymind had never met with briars so sharp, but he was not the boy to turn back readily, and pressed on in spite of torn clothes and scratched hands, till he came to the end of the glen, where two paths met: one of them wound through a pine wood, he knew not how far, but it seemed green and pleasant. The other was a rough, stony way leading to a wide valley surrounded by high hills and overhung by a dull thick mist, though it was yet early in the summer evening.

Merrymind was weary with his long journey, and stood thinking of what path to choose, when by the way of the valley there came an old man as tall and large as any three men of the north country. His white hair and beard hung like tangled flax about him; his clothes were made of sackcloth; and on his back he carried a heavy burden of dust heaped high in a great pannier.

'Listen to me, you lazy vagabond!' he said, coming near to Merrymind. 'If you take the way through the wood I know not what will happen to you; but if you choose this path you must help me with my pannier, and I can tell you it's no trifle.'

'Well, father,' said Merrymind, 'you seem tired, and I am younger than you, though not quite so tall; so, if you please, I will choose this way and help you along with the pannier.'

Scarce had he spoken when the huge man caught hold of him, firmly bound one side of the pannier to his shoulders with the same strong rope that fastened it on his own back, and never ceased scolding and calling him names as they marched over the stony ground together. It was a rough way and a heavy burden, and Merrymind wished himself a thousand times out of the old man's company, but there was no getting off; and at length, in hopes of beguiling the way and putting him in better humour, he began to sing an old rhyme which his mother had taught him. By this time they had entered the valley, and the night had fallen very dark and cold. The old man ceased scolding, and by a feeble glimmer of the moonlight, which now began to shine, Merrymind saw that they were close by a deserted cottage, for its door stood open to the night winds. Here the old man paused, and loosed the rope from his own and Merrymind's shoulders.

'For seven times seven years,' he said, 'have I carried this pannier, and no one ever sang while helping me before. Night releases all men, so I release you. Where will you sleep – by my kitchen fire, or in that cold cottage?'

Merrymind thought he had got quite enough of the old man's society, and therefore answered: 'The cottage, good father, if you please.'

'A sound sleep to you then!' said the old man, and he went off with his pannier.

Merrymind stepped into the deserted cottage. The moon was shining through door and window, for the mist was gone, and the night looked clear as day; but in all the valley he could hear no sound, nor was there any trace of inhabitants in the cottage. The hearth looked as if there had not been a fire there for years. A single article of furniture was not to be seen; but Merrymind was sore weary, and laying himself down in a corner, with his fiddle close by, he fell fast asleep.

The floor was hard and his clothes were thin, but all through his sleep there came a sweet sound of singing voices and spinning-wheels, and Merrymind thought he must have been dreaming when he opened his eyes next morning on the bare and solitary house. The beautiful night was gone, and the heavy mist had come back. There was no blue sky nor bright sun to be seen. The light was cold and grey, like that of mid-winter; but Merrymind ate the half of his barley cake, drank from a stream hard by and went out to see the valley.

It was full of inhabitants, and they were all busy in houses, in fields, in mills and in forges. The men hammered and delved; the women scrubbed and scoured; the very children were hard at work: but Merrymind could hear neither talk nor laughter among them. Every face looked careworn and cheerless, and every word was something about work or gain.

Merrymind thought this unreasonable, for everybody there appeared rich. The women scrubbed in silk, the men delved in scarlet. Crimson curtains, marble floors and shelves of silver tankards were to be seen in every house; but their owners took neither ease nor pleasure in them, and everyone laboured as it were for life.

The birds of that valley did not sing – they were too busy pecking and building. The cats did not lie by the fire – they were all on the watch for mice. The dogs went out after hares on their own account. The cattle and sheep grazed as if they were never to get another mouthful; and the herdsmen were all splitting wood or making baskets.

In the midst of the valley there stood a stately castle, but instead of park and gardens, brewhouses and washing-greens lay round it. The gates stood open and Merrymind ventured in. The courtyard was full of coopers. They were churning in the banquet hall. They were making cheese on the dais, and spinning and weaving in all its principal chambers. In the highest tower of that busy castle, at a window from which she could see the whole valley, there sat a noble lady. Her dress was rich, but of a dingy drab colour. Her hair was iron-grey; her look was sour and gloomy. Round her sat twelve maidens of the same aspect, spinning on ancient distaffs, and the lady spun as hard as they, but all the yarn they made was jet black.

No one in or out of the castle would reply to Merrymind's salutations, nor answer him any questions. The rich men pulled out their purses, saying: 'Come and work for wages!' The poor men said: 'We have no time to talk!' A cripple by the wayside wouldn't answer him, he was so busy begging; and a child by a cottage door said it must go to work. All day Merrymind wandered about with his broken-stringed fiddle, and all day he saw the great old man marching round and round the valley with his heavy burden of dust.

'It is the dreariest valley that ever I beheld!' he said to himself. 'And no place to mend my fiddle in; but one would not like to go away without knowing what has come over the people, or if they have always worked so hard and heavily.'

By this time the night again came on: he knew it by the clearing mist and the rising moon. The people began to hurry home in all directions. Silence came over house and field; and near the deserted cottage Merrymind met the old man.

'Good father,' he said, 'I pray you tell me what sport or pastime have the people of this valley?'

'Sport and pastime!' cried the old man in great wrath. 'Where did you hear of the like? We work by day and sleep by night. There is no sport in Dame Dreary's land!' And, with a hearty scolding for his idleness and levity, he left Merrymind to sleep once more in the cottage.

That night the boy did not sleep so soundly; though too drowsy to open his eyes, he was sure there had been singing and spinning near him all night; and resolving to find out what this meant before he left the valley, Merrymind ate the other half of his barley cake, drank again from the stream and went out to see the country.

The same heavy mist shut out sun and sky; the same hard work went forward wherever he turned his eyes; and the great old man with the dust pannier strode on his accustomed round. Merrymind could find no one to answer a single question; rich and poor wanted him to work still more earnestly than the day before; and fearing that some of them might press him into service, he wandered away to the farthest end of the valley.

There, there was no work, for the land lay bare and lonely, and was bounded by grey crags, as high and steep as any castle wall. There was no passage or outlet, but through a great iron gate secured with a heavy padlock: close by it stood a white tent, and in the door a tall soldier, with one arm, stood smoking a long pipe. He was the first idle man Merrymind had seen in the valley, and his face looked to him like that of a friend; so coming up with his best bow, the boy said:

'Honourable master soldier, please to tell me what country is this and why do the people work so hard?'

'Are you a stranger in this place, that you ask such questions?' answered the soldier.

'Yes,' said Merrymind; 'I came but the evening before yesterday.'

'Then I am sorry for you, for here you must remain. My orders are to let everybody in and nobody out; and the giant with the dust pannier guards the other entrance night and day,' said the soldier.

'That is bad news,' said Merrymind; 'but since I am here, please to tell me why were such laws made, and what is the story of this valley?'

'Hold my pipe, and I will tell you,' said the soldier, 'for nobody else will take the time. This valley belongs to the lady of yonder castle, whom, for seven times seven years, men have called Dame Dreary. She had another name in her youth – they called her Lady Littlecare; and then the valley was the fairest spot in all the north country. The sun shone brightest there; the summers lingered longest. Fairies danced on the hill tops; singing-birds sat on all the trees. Strongarm, the last of the giants, kept the pine forest and hewed yule logs out of it, when he was not sleeping in the sun. Two fair maidens, clothed in white, with silver wheels on their shoulders, came by night and spun golden threads by the hearth of every cottage. The people wore homespun and drank out of horn; but they had merry times. There were May games, harvest homes and Christmas cheer among them. Shepherds piped on the hillsides, reapers sang in the fields, and laughter came with the red firelight out of every house in the evening. All that was changed, nobody knows how, for the old folks who remembered it are dead. Some say it was because of a magic ring which fell from the lady's finger; some because of a spring in the castle court which went dry. However it was, the lady became Dame Dreary. Hard work and hard times over-spread the valley. The mist came down; the fairies departed; the giant Strongarm grew old and took up a burden of dust; and the night-spinners were seen no more in any man's dwelling. They say it will be so till Dame Dreary lays down her distaff and dances; but all the fiddlers of the north country have tried their merriest tunes to no purpose. The king is a wise prince and a great warrior. He has filled two treasure-houses, and conquered all his enemies; but he cannot change the order of Dame Dreary's land. I cannot tell you what great rewards he offered to any who could do it; but when no good came of his offers, the king feared that similar fashions might spread among his people, and therefore made a law that whomsoever entered should not leave it. His majesty took me captive in war, and placed me here to keep the gate and save his subjects trouble. If I had not brought my pipe with me, I should have been working as hard as any of them by this time, with my one arm. Young master, if you take my advice you will learn to smoke.'

'If my fiddle were mended it would be better,' said Merrymind; and he sat talking with the soldier till the mist began to clear and the moon to rise, and then went home to sleep in the deserted cottage.

It was late when he came near it, and the moonlight night looked lovely beside the misty day. Merrymind thought it was a good time for trying to get out of the valley. There was no foot abroad and no appearance of the giant; but as Merrymind drew near to where the two paths met, there was he fast asleep beside a fire of pine-cones, with his pannier at his head and a heap of stones close by him. 'Is that your kitchen fire?' thought the boy to himself, and he tried to steal past; but Strongarm started up, and pursued him with stones, calling him bad names, half-way back to the cottage.

Merrymind was glad to run the whole way for fear of him. The door was still open, and the moon was shining in; but by the fireless hearth there sat two fair maidens, all in white, spinning on silver wheels, and singing together a blithe and pleasant tune like the larks on May morning. Merrymind could have listened all night, but suddenly he bethought him that these must be the night-spinners, whose threads would mend his fiddle; so, stepping with reverence and good courage, he said:

'Honourable ladies, I pray you give a poor boy a thread to mend his fiddle strings.'

'For seven times seven years,' said the fair maidens, 'have we spun by night in this deserted cottage, and no mortal has seen or spoken to us. Go and gather sticks through all the valley to make a fire for us on this cold hearth, and each of us will give you a thread for your pains.'

Merrymind took his broken fiddle with him, and went through all the valley gathering sticks by the moonlight; but so careful were the people of Dame Dreary's land, that scarce a stick could be found, and the moon was gone, and the misty day had come before he was able to come back with a small faggot. The cottage door was still open; the fair maidens and their silver wheels were gone; but on the floor where they sat lay two long threads of gold.

Merrymind first heaped up his faggot on the hearth, to be ready against their coming at night, and next took up the golden threads to mend his fiddle. Then he learned the truth of the little man's saying at the fair, for no sooner were the strings fastened with those golden threads than they became firm. The old dingy fiddle too began to shine and glisten, and at length it was golden also. This sight made Merrymind so joyful, that, unlearned as he was in music, he tried to play. Scarce had his bow touched the strings when they began to play of themselves the same blithe and pleasant tune which the night-spinners sang together.

'Some of the workers will stop for the sake of this tune,' said Merrymind, and he went out along the valley with his fiddle. The music filled the air; the busy people heard it; and never was such a day seen in Dame Dreary's land. The men paused in their delving; the women stopped their scrubbing; the little children dropped their work; and everyone stood still in their places while Merrymind and his fiddle passed on. When he came to the castle, the coopers cast down their tools in the court; the churning and cheesemaking ceased in the banquet hall; the looms and spinning-wheels stopped in the principal chambers; and Dame Dreary's distaff stood still in her hand.

Merrymind played through the halls and up the tower stairs. As he came near the dame cast down her distaff and danced with all her might. All her maidens did the like; and as they danced she grew young again – the sourness passed from her looks and the greyness from her hair. They brought her the dress of white and cherry colour she used to wear in her youth, and she was no longer Dame Dreary, but the Lady Littlecare, with golden hair and laughing eyes and cheeks like summer roses.

Then a sound of merrymaking came up from the whole valley. The heavy mist rolled away over the hills; the sun shone out; a blue sky was seen; a clear spring gushed up in the castle court; a white falcon came from the east with a golden ring, and put it on the lady's finger. After that Strongarm broke the rope, tossed the pannier of dust from his shoulder and lay down to sleep in the sun. That night the fairies danced on the hill tops; and the night-spinners, with their silver wheels, were seen by every hearth, and no more in the deserted cottage. Everybody praised Merrymind and his fiddle; and when news of his wonderful playing came to the king's ears, he commanded the iron gate to be taken away; he made the captive soldier a free man; and promoted Merrymind to be his first fiddler, which under that wise monarch was the highest post in his kingdom.

As soon as Merrymind's family and neighbours heard of the high preferment his fiddle had gained for him, they thought music must be a good thing; and man, woman and child took to fiddling. It is said that none of them ever learned to play a single tune except Merrymind's mother, on whom her son bestowed great presents.

# Robert Michael Ballantyne (1825–1894)

While the folk-tale and fairy-tale and moral stories of street urchins and ministering children were occupying girl readers, the adventure story, often with empire-building overtones, was occupying their brothers. The most enduring of these is *The Coral Island*, which was very influential, its most notable successors perhaps being *Treasure Island* and *Peter Pan*. Its conventions were so well known in the twentieth century that they were ironically parodied in William Golding's adult novel about childhood, *The Lord of the Flies* (1954).

*The Coral Island* was Ballantyne's third novel, after two which had described his own adventures in Canada. Ralph, the narrator, Jack and Peterkin are shipwrecked in the Pacific on an island 'about ten miles in circumference', which Ballantyne draws as an earthly paradise. They explore and have several adventures (one of which is described below) before the book develops into a more fantastic (and brutal) tale of natives and pirates and missionaries. Like other Robinsonnades, the details of daily life can be as interesting as specific excitements, although the implied superiority of the British over other races may have accounted for some of the book's contemporary appeal.

Ballantyne releases his adolescents from any adult influence, and not only is the book virtually free from any reli-gious moralizing, at one point there is an ironic comment on such attitudes. When the dying Bloody Bill, the murderous pirate, confesses his deeds, Ralph, desperately trying to remember anything helpful from the Bible, quotes at him: '"Though your sins be red like crimson, they shall be white as snow." Only believe', to which Bill replies, with a logic which shows a subtle step away from the entrenched didacticism of the children's book: '"Only believe!"... I've heard men talk o' believing as if it was easy. Ha! 'tis easy enough for a man to point to a rope and say, "I believe that would bear my weight"; but 'tis another thing for a man to catch hold o' that rope and swing himself by it over the edge of a precipice.'

Ballantyne produced a sequel to *The Coral Island*, *The Gorilla Hunters* (1861) which leaned even more heavily towards imperialism. He then embarked on a long series of adventure stories, all of which he researched personally – driving trains, diving, mining, living with lighthouse keepers, and so on. Whatever his defects as a craftsman (particularly in plotting) Ballantyne had an infectious boyish enthusiasm and simplicity of outlook which, through his wide popularity, played an important part in the development of Victorian society.

## from *The Coral Island: A Tale of the Pacific Ocean* (1858)

### CHAPTER VII

*Jack's ingenuity – We get into difficulties about fishing, and get out of them by a method which gives us a cold bath – Horrible encounter with a shark.*

For several days after the excursion related in the last chapter we did not wander far from our encampment, but gave ourselves up to forming plans for the future and making our present abode comfortable.

There were various causes that induced this state of comparative inaction. In the first place, although everything around us was so delightful, and we could without difficulty obtain all that we required for our bodily comfort, we did not quite like the idea of settling down here for the rest of our lives, far away from our friends and our native land. To set energetically about preparations for a permanent residence seemed so like making up our minds to saying adieu to home and friends for ever, that we tacitly shrank from it, and put off our preparations, for one reason and another, as long as we could. Then there was a little uncertainty still as to there being natives on the island, and we entertained a kind of faint hope that a ship might come and take us off. But as day after day passed, and neither savages nor ships appeared, we gave up all hope of an early deliverance, and set diligently to work at our homestead.

During this time, however, we had not been altogether idle. We made several experiments in cooking the cocoa-nut, most of which did not improve it. Then we removed our goods, and took up our abode in the cave, but found the change so bad that we returned gladly to the bower. Besides this, we bathed very frequently, and talked a great deal: at least Jack and Peterkin did – I listened. Among other useful things, Jack, who was ever the most active and diligent, converted about three inches of the hoop-iron into an excellent knife. First he beat it quite flat with the axe. Then he made a rude handle, and tied the hoop-iron to it with our piece of whipcord, and ground it to an edge on a piece of sandstone. When it was finished, he used it to shape a better handle, to which he fixed it with a strip of his cotton handkerchief – in which operation he had, as Peterkin pointed out, torn off one of Lord Nelson's noses. However, the whip-cord, thus set free, was used by Peterkin as a fishing-line. He merely tied a piece of oyster to the end of it. This the fish were allowed to swallow, and then they were pulled quickly ashore. But as the line was very short and we had no boat, the fish we caught were exceedingly small.

One day Peterkin came up from the beach, where he had been angling, and said in a very cross tone, 'I'll tell you what, Jack, I'm not going to be humbugged with catching such contemptible things any longer. I want you to swim out with me on your back, and let me fish in deep water!'

'Dear me, Peterkin!' replied Jack, 'I had no idea you were taking the thing so much to heart, else I would have got you out of that difficulty long ago. Let me see' – and Jack looked down at a piece of timber on which he had been labouring, with a peculiar gaze of abstraction, which he always assumed when trying to invent or discover anything.

'What say you to building a boat?' he inquired, looking up hastily.

'Take far too long,' was the reply; 'can't be bothered waiting. I want to begin at once!'

Again Jack considered. 'I have it!' he cried. 'We'll fell a large tree and launch the trunk of it in the water, so that when you want to fish you've nothing to do but to swim out to it.'

'Would not a small raft do better?' said I.

'Much better; but we have no ropes to bind it together with. Perhaps we may find something hereafter that will do as well, but in the meantime let us try the tree.'

This was agreed on, so we started off to a spot not far distant, where we knew of a tree that would suit us, which grew near the water's edge. As soon as we reached it Jack threw off his coat, and, wielding the axe with his sturdy arms, hacked and hewed at it for a quarter of an hour without stopping. Then he paused, and while he sat down to rest I continued the work. Then Peterkin made a vigorous attack on it, so that when Jack renewed his powerful blows, a few minutes' cutting brought it down with a terrible crash.

'Hurrah! now for it,' cried Jack; 'let us off with its head.'

So saying he began to cut through the stem again, at about six yards from the thick end. This done, he cut three strong, short poles or levers from the stout branches, with which to roll the log down the beach into the sea; for, as it was nearly two feet thick at the large end, we could not move it without such helps. With the levers, however, we rolled it slowly into the sea.

Having been thus successful in launching our vessel, we next shaped the levers into rude oars or paddles, and then attempted to embark. This was easy enough to do; but after seating ourselves astride the log, it was with the utmost difficulty we kept it from rolling round and plunging us into the water. Not that we minded that much; but we preferred, if possible, to fish in dry clothes. To be sure, our trousers were necessarily wet, as our legs were dangling in the water on each side of the log; but as they could be easily dried, we did not care. After half-an-hour's practice, we became expert enough to keep our balance pretty steadily. Then Peterkin laid down his paddle, and having baited his line with a whole oyster, dropped it into deep water.

'Now then, Jack,' said he, 'be cautious; steer clear o' that seaweed. There! that's it; gently now, gently. I see a fellow at least a foot long down there, coming to – ha! that's it! Oh bother! he's off.'

'Did he bite?' said Jack, urging the log onwards a little with his paddle.

'Bite? ay! He took it into his mouth, but the moment I began to haul he opened his jaws and let it out again.'

'Let him swallow it next time,' said Jack, laughing at the melancholy expression of Peterkin's visage.

'There he's again,' cried Peterkin, his eyes flashing with excitement. 'Look out! Now then! No! Yes! No! Why the brute *won't* swallow it!'

'Try to haul him up by the mouth, then,' cried Jack. 'Do it gently.'

A heavy sigh and a look of blank despair showed that poor Peterkin had tried and failed again.

'Never mind, lad,' said Jack, in a voice of sympathy, 'we'll move on, and offer it to some other fish.' So saying, Jack plied his paddle; but scarcely had he moved from the spot, when a fish with an enormous head and a little body darted from under a rock and swallowed the bait at once.

'Got him this time – that's a fact!' cried Peterkin, hauling in the line. 'He's swallowed the bait right down to his tail, I declare. Oh, what a thumper!'

As the fish came struggling to the surface, we leaned forward to see it, and overbalanced the log. Peterkin threw his arms round the fish's neck, and in another instant we were all floundering in the water.

A shout of laughter burst from us as we rose to the surface like three drowned rats, and seized hold of the log. We soon recovered our position, and sat more warily, while Peterkin secured the fish, which had well-nigh escaped in the midst of our struggles. It was little worth having, however; but, as Peterkin remarked, it was better than the smouts he had been catching for the last two or three days; so we laid it on the log before us, and having re-baited the line, dropped it in again for another.

Now, while we were thus intent upon our sport, our attention was suddenly attracted by a ripple on the sea, just a few yards away from us. Peterkin shouted to us to paddle in that direction, as he thought it was a big fish, and we might have a chance of catching it. But Jack, instead of complying, said, in a deep, earnest tone of voice, which I never before heard him use–

'Haul up your line, Peterkin; seize your paddle; quick – it's a shark!'

The horror with which we heard this may well be imagined, for it must be remembered that our legs were hanging down in the water, and we could not venture to pull them up without upsetting the log. Peterkin instantly hauled up the line, and grasping his paddle, exerted himself to the utmost, while we also did our best to make for shore. But we were a good way off, and the log being, as I have before said, very heavy, moved but slowly through the water. We now saw the shark quite distinctly swimming round and round us, its sharp fin every now and then protruding above the water. From its active and unsteady motions, Jack knew it was making up its mind to attack us, so he urged us vehemently to paddle for our lives, while he himself set us the example. Suddenly he shouted, 'Look out! there he comes!' and in a second we saw the monstrous fish dive close under us, and turn half over on his side. But we all made a great commotion with our paddles, which no doubt frightened it away for that time, as we saw it immediately after circling round us as before.

'Throw the fish to him,' cried Jack, in a quick, suppressed voice; 'we'll make the shore in time yet if we can keep him off for a few minutes.'

Peterkin stopped one instant to obey the command, and then plied his paddle again with all his might. No sooner had the fish fallen on the water than we observed the shark to sink. In another second we saw its white breast rising; for sharks always turn over on their sides when about to seize their prey, their mouths being not at the point of their heads like those of other fish, but, as it were, under their chins. In another moment his snout rose above the water; his wide jaws, armed with a terrific double row of teeth, appeared. The dead fish was engulfed, and the shark sank out of sight. But Jack was mistaken in supposing that it would be satisfied. In a very few minutes it returned to us, and its quick motions led us to fear that it would attack us at once.

'Stop paddling,' cried Jack suddenly. 'I see it coming up behind us. Now, obey my orders *quickly*. Our lives may depend on it. Ralph, Peterkin, do your best to *balance the log*. Don't look out for the shark. Don't glance behind you. Do nothing but balance the log.'

Peterkin and I instantly did as we were ordered, being only too glad to do anything that afforded us a chance or a hope of escape, for we had implicit confidence in Jack's courage and wisdom. For a few seconds, that seemed long minutes to my mind, we sat thus silently; but I could not resist glancing backward, despite the orders to the contrary. On doing so, I saw Jack sitting rigid like a statue, with his paddle raised, his lips compressed, and his eyebrows bent over his eyes, which glared savagely from beneath them down into the water. I also saw the shark, to my horror, quite close under the log, in the act of darting towards Jack's foot. I could scarce suppress a cry on beholding this. In another moment the shark rose. Jack drew his leg suddenly from the water, and threw it over the log. The monster's snout rubbed against the log as it passed, and revealed its hideous jaws, into which Jack instantly plunged the paddle, and thrust it down its throat. So violent was this act that Jack rose to his feet in performing it; the log was thereby rolled completely over, and we were once more plunged into the water. We all rose, spluttering and gasping, in a moment.

'Now, then, strike out for shore,' cried Jack. 'Here, Peterkin, catch hold of my collar, and kick out with a will.'

Peterkin did as he was desired, and Jack struck out with such force that he cut through the water like a boat; while I, being free from all encumbrance, succeeded in keeping up with him. As we had by this time drawn pretty near to the shore, a few minutes more sufficed to carry us into shallow water; and, finally, we landed in safety, though very much exhausted, and not a little frightened by our terrible adventure.

# Frederick William Farrar (1831–1903)

A century and a half after its publication, *Eric*, another famous school story, written by a man who knew about British 'public' schools – he was a master at Harrow and headmaster of Marlborough – reads almost like a parody of *Tom Brown's Schooldays*. It has, however, been frequently parodied itself, and the wry comments on the book's sanctimoniousness by the characters in Kipling's *Stalky and Co* led to Kipling apologizing to Farrar.

Nonetheless, as *Tom Brown* with a heavy moral and excessive sentimentality, it was very popular in its day, although Charlotte Yonge disapproved of its extremism – it seemed to her that virtue was rewarded by death – and thought it unsuitable for girls to read. The book uses all the devices explored in *Tom Brown*, but everything is more highly coloured. Eric's drinking and dissolution is far more severe than Tom's: whereas Tom's pious friend George Arthur *nearly* dies, Eric's friend Edwin Russell is swept away to sea, rescued, and then dies a protracted death. Eric's adventures outside school lead not to a caning and reform, but to eventual expulsion, after which he is shanghaied on a boat, and savagely beaten, which leads to his eventual pious death.

It is easy to see disturbing elements here. On the occasion when Eric hears 'indecent words' in the dormitory, Farrar interrupts the narrative for two pages of rousing sermonizing: 'Now Eric, now or never! Life and death, ruin and salvation, corruption and purity, are perhaps in the balance together, and the scale of your destiny may hang on a single word of yours. Speak out, boy!...Ah, Eric, Eric! how little we know the moments which decide the destinies of life!'

Equally, one might wonder whether there is an element of religious pornography in Farrar's apparent relish at describing punishment: 'Again the rope whistled in the air, again it grided across the boy's naked back, and once more the crimson furrow bore witness to the violent laceration.... Once more, and again, the rope rose and fell, and under its marks the blood first dribbled, and then streamed from the white and tender skin.' This, then, was puritanism with a vengeance; the book has been described as 'a moral jellyfish left behind by the tide', and John Rowe Townsend remarked that it is a preposterous book, but it is 'the projection of a view of life in which everything matters'.

Eric's erratic progress downwards is arrested partly by the death of Russell, and partly by the presence of his younger brother, Vernon. Nevertheless, he is tempted by the 'anti-muffs' (a 'muff' being a weak, virtuous child) into a drinking bout at 'The Jolly Herring'. The headmaster, Dr Rowlands, is persuaded by Eric's contrition not to punish him, but Eric is soon tempted again.

## from *Eric; or, Little by Little. A Tale of Roslyn School* (1858)

### CHAPTER THE EIGHTH

### SOWING THE WIND

Next evening when preparation began, Pietrie and Graham got everything ready for the carouse in their classroom. Wildney, relying on the chance of names not being called over (which was only done in case any one's absence was observed), had absented himself altogether from the boarders' room, and helped busily to spread the table for the banquet. The cook had roasted for them the fowls and pigeons, and Billy had brought an ample supply of beer and some brandy for the occasion. A little before eight o'clock everything was ready, and Eric, Attlay, and Llewellyn were summoned to join the rest.

The fowls, pigeons, and beer had soon vanished, and the boys were in the highest spirits. Eric's reckless gaiety was kindled by Wildney's frolicsome vivacity and Graham's sparkling wit; they were all six in a roar of perpetual laughter at some fresh sally of fun elicited by the more phlegmatic natures of Attlay or Llewellyn, and the dainties of Wildney's parcel were accompanied by draughts of brandy and water, which were sometimes exchanged for potations of the raw liquor. It was not the first time, be it remembered, that the members of that young party had been present at similar scenes, and even the scoundrel Billy was astonished, and occasionally alarmed, at the quantities of spirits and other inebriating drinks that of late had found their way to the studies. The disgraceful and deadly habit of tippling had already told physically on both Eric and Wildney. The former felt painfully that he was losing his clear-headedness, and that his intellectual tastes were getting not only blunted but destroyed; and while he perceived in himself the terrible effects of his sinful indulgence, he saw them still more indisputably in the gradual coarseness which seemed to be spreading, like a gray lichen, over the countenance, the mind, and the manners of his younger companion. Sometimes the vision of a Nemesis breaking in fire out of his darkened future, terrified his guilty conscience in the watches of the night; and the conviction of some fearful Erinnys, some discovery dawning out of the night of his undetected sins, made his heart beat fast with agony and fear. But he fancied it too late to repent. He strangled the half-formed resolutions as they rose, and trusted to the time when, by leaving school, he should escape, as he idly supposed, the temptations to which he had yielded. Meanwhile, the friends who would have rescued him had been alienated by his follies, and the principles which might have preserved him had been eradicated by his guilt. He had long flung away the shield of prayer and the helmet of holiness, and the sword of the Spirit, which is the word of God; and now, unarmed and helpless, Eric stood alone, a mark for the fiery arrows of his enemies, while, through the weakened inlet of every corrupted sense, temptation rushed in upon him perpetually and unawares.

As the classroom they had selected was in a remote part of the building, there was little immediate chance of detection. So the laughter of the party grew louder and sillier; the talk more foolish and random; the merriment more noisy and meaningless. But still most of them mingled some sense of caution with their enjoyment, and warned Eric and Wildney more than once that they must look out, and not take too much that night for fear of being caught. But it was Wildney's birthday, and Eric's boyish mirth, suppressed by his recent troubles, was blazing out unrestrained. In the riot of their feasting the caution had been utterly neglected, and the two boys were far from being sober when the sound of the prayer-bell ringing through the great hall startled them into momentary consciousness.

'Good heavens!' shouted Graham, springing up; 'there's the prayer-bell; I'd no notion it was so late. Here, let's shove these brandy bottles and things into the cupboards and drawers, and then we must run down.'

There was no time to lose. The least muddled of the party had cleared the room in a moment, and then addressed themselves to the more difficult task of trying to quiet Eric and Wildney, and conduct them steadily into the prayer-room.

Wildney's seat was near the door, so there was little difficulty in getting him to his place comparatively unobserved. Llewellyn took him by the arm, and after a little stumbling helped him safely to his seat, where he assumed a look of preternatural gravity. But Eric sat near the head of the first table, not far from Dr. Rowlands's desk, and none of the others had to go to that part of the room. Graham grasped his arm tight, led him carefully down stairs, and, as they were reaching the door, said to him, in a most earnest and imploring tone –

'Do try and walk sensibly to your place, Eric, or we shall all be caught.'

It was rather late when they got down. Everybody was quietly seated, and most of the Bibles were already open, although the Doctor had not yet come in. Consequently, the room was still, and the entrance of Graham and Eric after the rest attracted general notice. Eric had just sense enough to try and assume his ordinary manner; but he was too giddy with the fumes of drink to walk straight or act naturally.

Vernon was sitting next to Wright, and stared at his brother with great eyes and open lips. He was not the only observer.

'Wright,' whispered he in a timid voice; 'just see how Eric walks. What can be the matter with him? Good gracious, he must be ill!' he said, starting up, as Eric suddenly made a great stagger to one side, and nearly fell in the attempt to recover himself.

Wright pulled the little boy down with a firm hand.

'Hush!' he whispered; 'take no notice; he's been drinking, Verny, and I fear he'll be caught.'

Vernon instantly sat down, and turned deadly pale. He thought, and he had hoped, that since the day at 'The Jolly Herring' his brother had abandoned all such practices, for Eric had been most careful to conceal from him the worst of his failings. And now he trembled violently with fear for his discovery, and horror at his disgraceful condition.

The sound of Eric's unsteady footsteps had made Mr. Rose quickly raise his head; but at the same moment Duncan hastily made room for the boy on the seat beside him, and held out his hand to assist him. It was not Eric's proper place; but Mr. Rose, after one long glance of astonishment, looked down at his book again, and said nothing.

It made other hearts besides Vernon's ache to see the unhappy boy roll to his place in that helpless way.

Dr. Rowlands came in and prayers commenced.

When they were finished, the names were called, and Eric, instead of quietly answering his 'adsum,' as he should have done, stood up, with a foolish look, and said, 'Yes, sir.' The head-master looked at him for a minute; the boy's glassy eyes and jocosely stupid appearance told an unmistakable tale; but Dr. Rowlands only remarked, 'Williams, you don't look well. You had better go at once to bed.'

It was hopeless for Eric to attempt getting along without help so Duncan at once got up, took him by the arm, and with much difficulty (for Eric staggered at every step) conducted him to his bedroom, where he left him without a word.

Wildney's condition was also too evident; and Mr. Rose, while walking up and down the dormitories, had no doubt left on his mind that both Eric and Wildney had been drinking. But he made no remarks to them, and merely went to the Doctor, to talk over the steps which were to be taken.

'I shall summon the school,' said Dr. Rowlands, 'on Monday, and by that time we will decide on the punishment. Expulsion, I fear, is the only course open to us.'

'Is not that a *very* severe line to take?'

'Perhaps; but the offence is of the worst character. I must consider the matter.'

'Poor Williams!' sighed Mr. Rose, as he left the room.

The whole of the miserable Sunday that followed was spent by Eric and his companions in vain inquiries and futile restlessness. It seemed clear that two of them at least were detected, and they were inexpressibly wretched with anxiety and suspense. Wildney, who had to stay in bed, was even more depressed; his head ached violently, and he was alone with his own terrified thoughts. He longed for the morrow, that at least he might have the poor consolation of knowing his fate. No one came near him all day. Eric wished to do so, but as he could not have visited the room without express leave, the rest dissuaded him from asking, lest he should excite further suspicion. His apparent neglect made poor Wildney even more unhappy, for Wildney loved Eric as much as it was possible for his volatile mind to love any one; and it seemed hard to be deserted in the moment of disgrace and sorrow by so close a friend.

At school the next morning the various masters read out to their forms a notice from Dr. Rowlands, that the whole school were to meet at ten in the great schoolroom. The object of the summons was pretty clearly understood; and few boys had any doubt that it had reference to the drinking on Saturday night. Still nothing had been *said* on the subject as yet; and every guilty heart among those 250 boys beat fast lest *his* sin too should have been discovered, and he should be called out for some public and heavy punishment.

The hour arrived. The boys, thronging into the great schoolroom, took their places according to their respective forms. The masters in their caps and gowns were all seated on a small semicircular bench at the upper end of the room, and in the centre of them, before a small table, sate Dr. Rowlands.

The sound of whispering voices sank to a dead and painful hush. The blood was tingling consciously in many cheeks, and not even a breath could be heard in the deep expectation of that anxious and solemn moment.

Dr. Rowlands spread before him the list of the school, and said, 'I shall first read out the names of the boys in the first-fifth and upper-fourth forms.'

This was done to ascertain formally whether the boys were present on whose account the meeting was convened; and it at once told Eric and Wildney that *they* were the boys to be punished, and that the others had escaped.

The names were called over, and an attentive observer might have told, from the sound of the boys' voices as they answered, which of them were afflicted with a troubled conscience.

Another slight pause and breathless hush.

'Eric Williams and Charles Wildney, stand forward.'

The boys obeyed. From his place in the fifth, where he was sitting with his head propped on his hand, Eric rose and advanced: and Wildney, from the other end of the room, where the younger boys sat, getting up, came and stood by his side.

Both of them fixed their eyes on the ground, whence they never once raised them: and in the deadly pallor of their haggard faces you could scarcely have recognised the joyous high-spirited friends, whose laugh and shout had often rung so merrily through the playground, and woke the echoes of the rocks along the shore. Every eye was on them, and they were conscious of it, though they could not see it – painfully conscious of it, so that they wished the very ground to yawn beneath their feet for the moment and swallow up their shame. Companionship in disgrace increased the suffering; had either of them been alone, he would have been less acutely sensible to the trying nature of his position; but that they, so different in their ages and position in the school, should thus have their friendship and the results of it blazoned, or rather branded, before their friends and enemies, added keenly to the misery they felt. So with eyes bent on the floor, Eric and Charlie awaited their sentence.

'Williams and Wildney,' said Dr. Rowlands in a solemn voice, of which every articulation thrilled to the heart of every hearer, 'you have been detected in a sin most disgraceful and most dangerous. On Saturday night you were both drinking, and you were guilty of such gross excess, that you were neither of you in a fit state to appear among your companions – least of all to appear among them at the hour of prayer. I shall not waste many words on an occasion like this; only I trust that those of your school-fellows who saw you staggering and rolling into the room on Saturday evening in a manner so unspeakably shameful and degrading, will learn from that melancholy sight the lesson which the Spartans taught their children by exhibiting a drunkard before them – the lesson of the brutalising and fearful character of this most ruinous vice. Eric Williams and Charles Wildney, your punishment will be public expulsion, for which you will prepare this very evening. I am unwilling that for a single day, either of you – especially the elder of you – should linger, so as possibly to contaminate others with the danger of so pernicious an example.'

Such a sentence was wholly unexpected; it took boys and masters equally by surprise. The announcement of it caused an uneasy sensation, which was evident to all present, though no one spoke a word; but Dr. Rowlands took no notice of it, and only said to the culprits –

'You may return to your seats.'

The two boys found their way back instinctively, they hardly knew how. They seemed confounded and thunderstruck by their sentence, and the painful accessories of its publicity. Eric leaned over the desk with his head resting on a book, too stunned even to think; and Wildney looked straight before him, with his eyes fixed in a stupid and unobservant stare.

Form by form the school dispersed, and the moment he was liberated Eric sprang away from the boys, who would have spoken to him, and rushed wildly to his study, where he locked the door. In a moment, however, he re-opened it, for he heard Wildney's step, and, after admitting him, locked it once more.

Without a word Wildney, who looked very pale, flung his arms round Eric's neck, and, unable to bear up any longer, burst into a flood of tears. Both of them felt relief in giving the reins to their sorrow, and silently satiating the anguish of their hearts.

'Oh, my father! my father!' sobbed Wildney at length, 'what will he say? He will disown me, I know; he is so stern always with me when he thinks I bring disgrace on him.'

Eric thought of Fairholm, and of his own far-distant parents, and of the pang which *his* disgrace would cause their loving hearts; but he could say nothing, and only stroked Wildney's dark hair again and again with a soothing hand.

They sat there long, hardly knowing how the time passed; Eric could not help thinking how very very different their relative positions might have been; how, while he might have been aiding and ennobling the young boy beside him, he had alternately led and followed him into wickedness and disgrace. His heart was full of misery and bitterness, and he felt almost indifferent to all the future, and weary of his life.

A loud knocking at the door disturbed them. It was Carter, the school servant.

'You must pack up to go this evening, young gentlemen.'

'Oh no! no! no!' exclaimed Wildney; 'I *cannot* be sent away like this. It would break my father's heart. Eric, *do* come and entreat Dr. Rowlands to forgive us only this once.'

'Yes,' said Eric, starting up with sudden energy; 'he *shall* forgive us – *you* at any rate. I will not leave him till he does. Cheer up, Charlie, cheer up, and come along.'

Filled with an irresistible impulse, he pushed Carter aside, and sprang down stairs three steps at a time, with Wildney following him. They went straight for the Doctor's study, and without waiting for the answer to their knock at the door, Eric walked up to Dr. Rowlands, who sate thinking in his arm-chair by the fire, and burst out passionately, 'Oh, sir, forgive us, forgive us this once.'

The Doctor was completely taken by surprise, so sudden was the intrusion, and so intense was the boy's manner. He remained silent a moment from astonishment, and then said with asperity –

'Your offence is one of the most dangerous possible. There could be no more perilous example for the school, than the one you have been setting, Williams. Leave the room,' he added with an authoritative gesture; 'my mind is made up.'

But Eric was too excited to be overawed by the master's manner; an imperious passion blinded him to all ordinary considerations, and, heedless of the command, he broke out again –

'Oh, sir, try me but once, *only* try me. I promise you most faithfully that I will never again commit the sin. Oh, sir, do, do trust me, and I will be responsible for Wildney too.'

Dr. Rowlands, seeing that in Eric's present mood he must and would be heard, unless he were ejected by actual force, began to pace silently up and down the room in perplexed and anxious thought; at last he stopped and turned over the pages of a thick school register, and found Eric's name.

'It is not your first offence, Williams, even of this very kind. That most seriously aggravates your fault.'

'Oh, sir! give us one more chance to mend. Oh, I feel that I *could* do such great things, if you will but be merciful, and give me time to change. Oh, I entreat you, sir, to forgive us only this once, and I will never ask again. Let us bear *any* other punishment but this. Oh, sir,' he said, approaching the Doctor in an imploring attitude, 'spare us this one time for the sake of our friends.'

The head-master made no reply for a time, but again paced the room in silence. He was touched, and seemed hardly able to restrain his emotion.

'It was my deliberate conclusion to expel you, Williams. I must not weakly yield to entreaty. You must go.'

Eric wrung his hands in agony. 'Oh, sir, then if you must do so, expel me only, and not Charlie. *I* can bear it, but do not let me ruin him also. Oh, I implore you, sir, for the love of God, do, do forgive him! It is I who have misled him;' and he flung himself on his knees, and lifted his hands entreatingly towards the Doctor.

Dr. Rowlands looked at him – at his blue eyes drowned with tears, his agitated gesture, his pale, expressive face, full of passionate supplication. He looked at Wildney too, who stood trembling with a look of painful and miserable suspense, and occasionally added his wild word of entreaty, or uttered sobs more powerful still, that seemed to come from the depth of his heart. He was shaken in his resolve, wavered for a moment, and then once more looked at the register.

'Yes,' he said, after a long pause, 'here is an entry which shall save you this time. I find written here against your name, "April 3. Risked his life in the endeavour to save Edwin Russell at the Stack." That one good and noble deed shall be the proof that you are capable of better things. It may be weak perhaps – I know that it will be called weak – and I do not feel certain that I am doing right; but if I err it shall be on the side of mercy. I shall change expulsion into some other punishment. You may go.'

Wildney's face lighted up as suddenly and joyously as when a ray of sunlight gleams for an instant out of a dark cloud.

'Oh, thank you, thank you, sir,' he exclaimed, drying his eyes, and pouring into the words a world of expression, which it was no light pleasure to have heard. But Eric spoke less impulsively, and while the two boys were stammering out their deep gratitude, a timid hand knocked at the door, and Vernon entered.

'I have come, sir, to speak for poor Eric,' he said in a voice low and trembling with emotion, as, with downcast eyes, he modestly approached towards Dr. Rowlands, not even observing the presence of the others in the complete absorption of his feelings. He stood in a sorrowful attitude, not venturing to look up, and his hand played nervously with the ribbon of his straw hat.

'I have just forgiven him, my little boy,' said the Doctor kindly, patting his stooping head; 'there he is, and he has been speaking for himself.'

'O Eric, I am so, so glad, I don't know what to say for joy. O Eric, thank God that you are not to be expelled;' and Vernon went to his brother and embraced him with the deepest affection.

Dr. Rowlands watched the scene with moist eyes. He was generally a man of prompt decision, and he well knew that he would incur by this act the charge of vacillation. It was a noble self-denial in him to be willing to do so, but it would have required an iron heart to resist such earnest supplications, and he was more than repaid when he saw how much anguish he had removed by yielding to their entreaties.

Once more humbly expressing their gratitude, the boys retired.

They did not know that other influences had been also exerted in their favour, which, although ineffectual at the time, had tended to alter the Doctor's intention. Immediately after school Mr. Rose had been strongly endeavouring to change the Doctor's mind, and had dwelt forcibly on all the good points in Eric's character, and the promise of his earlier career. And Montague had gone with Owen and Duncan to beg that the expulsion might be commuted into some other punishment. They had failed to convince him; but perhaps, had they not thus exerted themselves, Dr. Rowlands might have been unshaken, though he could not be unmoved, by Vernon's gentle intercession and Eric's passionate prayers.

Wildney, full of joy, and excited by the sudden revulsion of feeling, only shook Eric's hands with all his might, and then darted out into the playground to announce the happy news. The boys all flocked round him, and received the intelligence with unmitigated pleasure. Among them all there was not one who did not rejoice that Eric and Wildney were yet to continue of their number.

But the two brothers returned to the study, and there, sorrowful in his penitence, with his heart still aching with remorse, Eric sat down on a chair facing the window, and drew Vernon to his side. The sun was setting behind the purple hills, flooding the green fields and silver sea with the crimson of his parting rays. The air was full of peace and coolness, and the merry sounds of the cricket-field blended joyously with the whisper of the evening breeze. Eric was fond of beauty in every shape, and his father had early taught him a keen appreciation of the glories of nature. He had often gazed before on that splendid scene, as he was now gazing on it thoughtfully with his brother by his side. He looked long and wistfully at the gorgeous pageantry of quiet clouds, and passed his arm more fondly round Vernon's shoulder.

'What are you thinking of, Eric? Why, I declare you are crying still,' said Vernon playfully, as he wiped away a tear which had overflowed on his brother's cheek; 'aren't you glad that the Doctor has forgiven you?'

'Gladder, far gladder than I can say, Verny, O Verny, Verny, I hope your school-life may be happier than mine has been. I would give up all I have, Verny, to have kept free from the sins I have learnt. God grant that I may yet have time and space to do better.'

'Let us pray together, Eric,' whispered his brother reverently, and they knelt down and prayed; they prayed for their distant parents and friends; they prayed for their schoolfellows and for each other, and for Wildney, and they thanked God for all His goodness to them; and then Eric poured out his heart in a fervent prayer that a holier and happier future might atone for his desecrated past, and that his sins might be forgiven for his Saviour's sake.

The brothers rose from their knees calmer and more light-hearted in the beauty of holiness, and gave each other a solemn affectionate kiss, before they went down again to the playground. But they avoided the rest of the boys, and took a stroll together along the sands, talking quietly and happily, and hoping bright hopes for future days.

# Samuel Griswold Goodrich (1793–1860)

Samuel Goodrich was one of the most successful writers of educational non-fiction and semi-fiction. His series of 'Peter Parley' books, beginning with *The Tales of Peter Parley About America* (1827), ran to over 100 volumes, sold millions of copies and were widely imitated. The formula was straightforward (and is still being followed in current educational publishing): simple facts in readable language, told in the first person, sometimes with numbered paragraphs and with 'comprehension questions' at the foot of the page.

An interesting side-effect of the series was to greatly encourage the growth and respectability of the fairy-tale in Britain. Sir Henry Cole took exception to 'Parleyism', which he saw as driving out the imaginative, and as 'Felix Summerley' published the 'Home Treasury' (from 1843), a long series of fairy-tales, nursery rhymes and other imaginative works, including primers and toys.

Goodrich was an effective, if plain storyteller, as this extract shows. *Peter Parley's Tales of the Sea* was prefaced by this 'NOTICE: This is the last of Peter Parley's Series of Tales, designed to instruct children in Geography and History. The other volumes are, America, Europe, Africa, Asia, and islands in the Pacific.'

## from *Peter Parley's Tales of the Sea* (1860)

### CHAPTER VII

### STORY OF A CABIN BOY

I am now going to tell you the story of a cabin boy. His name was George Gordon. His mother was a widow, who lived at Marblehead in Massachusetts. George was her only child. His father, who was a sailor, had not been heard of for several years. He sailed from Boston for South America, and that was the last that was ever known of him.

Mrs. Gordon was a poor woman, but she was very industrious, and, with a little help from some kind neighbors, she got along pretty well. She lived in a little brown house, but she kept it very neat and clean, so that it was quite comfortable.

She contrived to send George to school; and, although he was more fond of play than books, yet he learned to read and write. At length, he was fifteen years old; and then he was very anxious to go to sea. His mother was opposed to this, for she thought the life of a sailor to be a hard one; and, besides, she was afraid that he would fall into bad company, and become thoughtless and wicked, like many other sailors. The fate of his father, too, had impressed her mind with such a dread of the sea, that she shrank from the thought of intrusting her only child to the treacherous waves.

But George had been familiar with the water from childhood. He could manage a boat with the greatest dexterity. In catching fish with a hook and line, he was more expert than any other boy in the town. He loved the very dangers of the water; and, when an easterly storm heaved the surf upon the rocks, he delighted to be out in a little skiff, and hover like a sea-gull on the tops of the breaking billows.

His love for the sea became at length his ruling passion; and, as his mother withheld her consent, he resolved to leave her by stealth, and go abroad in a ship. Accordingly, one night, after his mother was gone to bed, he packed up his clothes, passed silently out of the door, and set off on foot for Boston.

It was sunrise when he arrived at the city. He immediately went down to one of the wharves, and offered himself as cabin boy to the captain of a whale ship, that was just about to sail. The captain received him on board the vessel, and in a few hours they set off on their voyage.

They had a fair wind, and in a short time they were out to sea. George's plans had all succeeded to his mind; he had escaped from his mother, he had found a birth on board a ship, and he was now actually out upon the broad ocean, going in search of adventures.

For two days, he was quite happy. His business was to take care of the cabin, to keep it in good order, and attend to the personal wants of the captain. He found his situation an easy one, and he saw many things to please him. He was delighted with the sparkling of the sea at night; he would often sit upon the bow-sprit, and look at the waters that were heaped up before the bows of the vessel. These seemed sometimes to be a liquid mass of fire, so brilliant as to make it quite light for a considerable space around.

The second day after they left Boston, George saw a multitude of strange looking creatures all around the ship. They were quite black, and they looked like a parcel of hogs rolling along in the waves. George knew them to be porpoises; he had occasionally seen them before, but never in such numbers. There were more than a thousand of them, and they seemed to be all engaged in a frolic.

George was delighted with these creatures, and seemed to consider it all a very pleasant affair. But an old sailor, who was looking at the porpoises, shook his head, and said they should have foul weather to-morrow. George took little notice of this, for the weather was now extremely pleasant.

In a few hours, however, the prospects began to change. The sky became cloudy, and the sea began to roll in long, heavy waves. The captain had put on a thick over-coat, called a pea-jacket, and was very busy in ordering the men to put every part of the ship in complete trim. He wore a look of some anxiety, and this seemed gradually to communicate itself to all on board the vessel.

The wind began now to blow in heavy gusts, and, as they fell upon the sails of the ship, she leaned over as if she would upset. Night was now approaching, and it was already beginning to be dark. At this moment, a little bird flew on board the ship, and, overcome by fatigue, fell upon the deck. George ran, picked it up, and carried it down into the cabin; but the little creature soon died.

This little bird was one of what the sailors call Mother Carey's chickens. These birds are never seen but out to sea; and, as they most frequently appear in stormy weather, the sailors consider them as forerunners of evil. In the present instance, they looked upon the little bird's coming on board the ship, as the sign of some melancholy event that was speedily to happen.

The sun went down, and, as the darkness settled upon the waters, the howling tempest swept over the ocean with resistless fury. The rattling of the cordage, the creaking of the masts, the roar of the waters, the flapping of the sails, the groaning of the ship as she struggled with the waves, the cries of the captain and the mate to the sailors, – all these sounds came upon the ear of the cabin boy with a new and frightful meaning. He had never imagined a scene like this.

Afraid to be on deck, he went down into the cabin; but there he was uneasy, and again he went upon deck. All was darkness around, except that, here and there, the breaking of the waves gave a momentary view of their white and sparkling tops. Occasionally, too, a broad flash of lightning disclosed the tumbling waters to the sight. Then the thunder broke in, and, for an instant, the peal seemed to silence the uproar of the ship, and the clamor of the waves.

Overawed by the scene, George retired to his cabin, and crept into his birth. He wrapped the clothes about his head to keep out the lightning, and he held his ears to exclude the thunder. But there was a feeling at his heart that he could not shut out. It whispered of his poor mother, and the folly and wickedness of her son, that had stolen from her roof, and left her to weep in solitude and sorrow. This feeling was far more bitter than fear, and, for a short time, the poor boy forgot the dangers of the storm, in his distress at the thoughts of his mother, and his own misconduct.

But at length he was roused from his reflections by a loud noise, and a sudden cry of the men on deck. He sprang from his birth, ran up the companion-way, and, as he came upon the deck, he discovered the occasion of what he had heard. The lightning had struck the vessel, and set it on fire. The flame had already extended itself nearly over the main sail, which, at the time, was the only sail spread.

The destruction of the ship seemed inevitable; and, for the moment, all on board gave themselves up for lost. But, the next instant, a tremendous wave struck the side of the ship, and, passing over it, fell upon the main sail, and in an instant extinguished the flame.

The remainder of the night was spent in fear and anxiety. The waves repeatedly broke over the vessel, and several times it seemed that she would inevitably be overwhelmed. But Providence watched over its inmates, and, as the morning came, the tempest began to abate.

When the sun rose, the wind had quite subsided; the water, however, continued to roll, with a heavy swell, for several hours. But this ceased at length, and it gradually settled into a state of perfect rest. All around, the ocean seemed like a vast lake, whose surface was not disturbed by a breath of wind. The vessel sat on the water as motionless as a stone upon the land.

The sailors took advantage of the calm to repair the ship. At length the night came, and the moon shed its beautiful light upon the waves. The cabin boy, who now had, in some measure, forgotten his sorrow, looked upon the scene with pleasing wonder. The whole ocean beneath the moon appeared like a broad bay of silver. The sailors seemed to forget the peril they had passed. One of them had a violin, on which he played some lively tunes; some of them danced, some of them sang songs, and they all seemed to be thoughtless and happy.

The next morning, a breeze sprang up, and the vessel proceeded on its voyage.

# Charles Kingsley (1819–1875)

*The Water Babies* is often regarded as a landmark text in British children's literature, the first book of the first 'golden age' of children's literature, when children's imaginations were liberated. However, for all that it has attained a status somewhere between the classic and folklore, it remains a somewhat curious item in the children's literature canon. The tone of voice is erratic – sometimes playful, but more often that of a lecturer condescending to an inexperienced audience, while indulging itself with political and social asides and jokes. Similarly, the force of the story – which has, certainly, something elemental and mythic about it – is continually undercut by the proliferation (not to say conflicts) of religious and social ideas.

It is perhaps best seen as a quintessential product of its age. Kingsley was a dissenting clergyman, whose life demonstrates the gap between personal and public service and repressed personal sexuality, and it has been argued that the book is the product of Kingsley's loss of faith and his search for a substitute. He explores many areas which would later become staples of children's literature, but also repeats the devices of the evangelists and moralists and educators, while attacking them. He singles out 'Peter Parley': 'Some people think there are no fairies. Cousin Cramchild tells little folks so in his Conversations. Well, perhaps there are none – in Boston, U.S., where he was raised.'

The book begins with a sardonic and harshly realistic portrait of Tom, the poor chimney-sweep. However, when Tom (being pursued from the great house, where he has been assumed to be a thief) is drowned (Kingsley believed in the curative and transformative powers of water) he enters an allegorical world where the two faces of the fairy (who also appears as a mysterious Irishwoman) Mrs Doasyouwouldbedoneby/Mrs Bedonebyasyoudid make moral points, and exact a crude revenge on those whom Kingsley disliked. For all Kingsley's imaginative originality, much of this part of the book seems to be highly expedient, not to say, in narrative terms, a shambles: for example, Tom discovers both Grimes, his evil master, and Ellie, the little girl in white, in the land of the dead, and at the end Tom seems to have grown up and might marry (or might have married) Ellie. There is even a (mock) 'moral' attached to the book, which ends: 'Meanwhile, do you learn your lessons, and thank God that you have plenty of cold water to wash in; and wash in it too, like a true Englishman. And then, if my story is not true, something better is.... But remember always...that this is a fairy tale...and therefore you are not to believe a word of it, even if it is true.'

Kingsley was a notable public figure – a novelist, for a time a prominent Christian Socialist, Regius Professor of History at Cambridge, and a Canon of Westminster – and, partly as a result of his reputation, *The Water Babies* was widely read. It has survived, very often in abridged versions which remove its more obvious eccentricities.

The opening, reprinted here, is in many ways the most impressive part of the book, as Kingsley moves, apparently effortlessly, between the realistic and the allegoric, with some wry asides. The social comment and the sexual–religious symbolism is, however, quite evident.

## from *The Water-Babies. A Fairy Tale for a Land-Baby* (1863)

### CHAPTER I

Once upon a time there was a little chimney-sweep, and his name was Tom. That is a short name, and you have heard it before, so you will not have much trouble in remembering it. He lived in a great town in the North country, where there were plenty of chimneys to sweep, and plenty of money for Tom to earn and his master to spend. He could not read nor write, and did not care to do either; and he never washed himself, for there was no water up the court where he lived. He had never been taught to say his prayers. He never had heard of God, or of Christ, except in words which you never have heard, and which it would have been well if he had never heard. He cried half his time, and laughed the other half. He cried when he had to climb the dark flues, rubbing his poor knees and elbows raw; and when the soot got into his eyes, which it did every day in the week; and when his master beat him, which he did every day in the week; and when he had not enough to eat, which happened every day in the week likewise. And he laughed the other half of the day, when he was tossing halfpennies with the other boys, or playing leap-frog over the posts, or bowling stones at the horses' legs as they trotted by, which last was excellent fun, when there was a wall at hand behind which to hide. As for chimney-sweeping, and being hungry, and being beaten, he took all that for the way of the world, like the rain and snow and thunder, and stood manfully with his back to it till it was over, as his old donkey did to a hail-storm; and then shook his ears and was as jolly as ever; and thought of the fine times coming, when he would be a man, and a master sweep, and sit in the public-house with a quart of beer and a long pipe, and play cards for silver money, and wear velveteens and ankle-jacks, and keep a white bull-dog with one gray ear, and carry her puppies in his pocket, just like a man. And he would have apprentices, one, two, three, if he could. How he would bully them, and knock them about, just as his master did to him; and make them carry home the soot sacks, while he rode before them on his donkey, with a pipe in his mouth and a flower in his button-hole, like a king at the head of his army. Yes, there were good times coming; and, when his master let him have a pull at the leavings of his beer, Tom was the jolliest boy in the whole town.

One day a smart little groom rode into the court where Tom lived. Tom was just hiding behind a wall, to heave half a brick at his horse's legs, as is the custom of that country when they welcome strangers; but the groom saw him, and hallooed to him to know where Mr. Grimes, the chimney-sweep, lived. Now, Mr. Grimes was Tom's own master, and Tom was a good man of business, and always civil to customers, so he put the half-brick down quietly behind the wall, and proceeded to take orders.

Mr. Grimes was to come up next morning to Sir John Harthover's, at the Place, for his old chimney-sweep was gone to prison, and the chimneys wanted sweeping. And so he rode away, not giving Tom time to ask what the sweep had gone to prison for, which was a matter of interest to Tom, as he had been in prison once or twice himself. Moreover, the groom looked so very neat and clean, with his drab gaiters, drab breeches, drab jacket, snow-white tie with a smart pin in it, and clean round ruddy face, that Tom was offended and disgusted at his appearance, and considered him a stuck-up fellow, who gave himself airs because he wore smart clothes, and other people paid for them; and went behind the wall to fetch the half-brick after all; but did not, remembering that he had come in the way of business, and was, as it were, under a flag of truce.

His master was so delighted at his new customer that he knocked Tom down out of hand, and drank more beer that night than he usually did in two, in order to be sure of getting up in time next morning; for the more a man's head aches when he wakes, the more glad he is to turn out, and have a breath of fresh air. And, when he did get up at four the next morning, he knocked Tom down again, in order to teach him (as young gentlemen used to be taught at public schools) that he must be an extra good boy that day, as they were going to a very great house, and might make a very good thing of it, if they could but give satisfaction.

And Tom thought so likewise, and, indeed, would have done and behaved his best, even without being knocked down. For, of all places upon earth, Harthover Place (which he had never seen) was the most wonderful, and, of all men on earth, Sir John (whom he had seen, having been sent to gaol by him twice) was the most awful.

Harthover Place was really a grand place, even for the rich North country; with a house so large that in the frame-breaking riots, which Tom could just remember, the Duke of Wellington, and ten thousand soldiers to match, were easily housed therein; at least, so Tom believed; with a park full of deer, which Tom believed to be monsters who were in the habit of eating children; with miles of game-preserves, in which Mr. Grimes and the collier lads poached at times, on which occasions Tom saw pheasants, and wondered what they tasted like; with a noble salmon-river, in which Mr. Grimes and his friends would have liked to poach; but then they must have got into cold water, and that they did not like at all. In short, Harthover was a grand place, and Sir John a grand old man, whom even Mr. Grimes respected; for not only could he send Mr. Grimes to prison when he deserved it, as he did once or twice a week; not only did he own all the land about for miles; not only was he a jolly, honest, sensible squire, as ever kept a pack of hounds, who would do what he thought right by his neighbours, as well as get what he thought right for himself; but, what was more, he weighed full fifteen stone, was nobody knew how many inches round the chest, and could have thrashed Mr. Grimes himself in fair fight, which very few folk round there could do, and which, my dear little boy, would not have been right for him to do, as a great many things are not which one both can do, and would like very much to do. So Mr. Grimes touched his hat to him when he rode through the town, and called him a 'buirdly awd chap,' and his young ladies 'gradely lasses,' which are two high compliments in the North country; and thought that that made up for his poaching Sir John's pheasants; whereby you may perceive that Mr. Grimes had not been to a properly-inspected Government National School.

Now, I dare say, you never got up at three o'clock on a midsummer morning. Some people get up then because they want to catch salmon; and some because they want to climb Alps; and a great many more because they must, like Tom. But, I assure you, that three o'clock on a midsummer morning is the pleasantest time of all the twenty-four hours, and all the three hundred and sixty-five days; and why every one does not get up then, I never could tell, save that they are all determined to spoil their nerves and their complexions by doing all night what they might just as well do all day. But Tom, instead of going out to dinner at half-past eight at night, and to a ball at ten, and finishing off somewhere between twelve and four, went to bed at seven, when his master went to the public-house, and slept like a dead pig; for which reason he was as piert as a game-cock (who always gets up early to wake the maids), and just ready to get up when the fine gentlemen and ladies were just ready to go to bed.

So he and his master set out; Grimes rode the donkey in front, and Tom and the brushes walked behind; out of the court, and up the street, past the closed window-shutters, and the winking weary policemen, and the roofs all shining gray in the gray dawn.

They passed through the pitmen's village, all shut up and silent now, and through the turnpike; and then they were out in the real country, and plodding along the black dusty road, between black slag walls, with no sound but the groaning and thumping of the pit-engine in the next field. But soon the road grew white, and the walls likewise; and at the wall's foot grew long grass and gay flowers, all drenched with dew; and instead of the groaning of the pit-engine, they heard the skylark saying his matins high up in the air, and the pit-bird warbling in the sedges, as he had warbled all night long.

All else was silent. For old Mrs. Earth was still fast asleep; and, like many pretty people, she looked still prettier asleep than awake. The great elm-trees in the gold-green meadows were fast asleep above, and the cows fast asleep beneath them; nay, the few clouds which were about were fast asleep likewise, and so tired that they had lain down on the earth to rest, in long white flakes and bars, among the stems of the elm-trees, and along the tops of the alders by the stream, waiting for the sun to bid them rise and go about their day's business in the clear blue overhead.

On they went; and Tom looked, and looked, for he never had been so far into the country before; and longed to get over a gate, and pick buttercups, and look for birds' nests in the hedge; but Mr. Grimes was a man of business, and would not have heard of that.

Soon they came up with a poor Irishwoman, trudging along with a bundle at her back. She had a gray shawl over her head, and a crimson madder petticoat; so you may be sure she came from Galway. She had neither shoes nor stockings, and limped along as if she were tired and footsore; but she was a very tall handsome woman, with bright gray eyes, and heavy black hair hanging about her cheeks. And she took Mr. Grimes' fancy so much, that when he came alongside he called out to her:

'This is a hard road for a gradely foot like that. Will ye up, lass, and ride behind me?'

But, perhaps, she did not admire Mr. Grimes' look and voice; for she answered quietly:

'No, thank you: I'd sooner walk with your little lad here.'

'You may please yourself,' growled Grimes, and went on smoking.

So she walked beside Tom, and talked to him, and asked him where he lived, and what he knew, and all about himself, till Tom thought he had never met such a pleasant-spoken woman. And she asked him, at last, whether he said his prayers! and seemed sad when he told her that he knew no prayers to say.

Then he asked her where she lived, and she said far away by the sea. And Tom asked her about the sea; and she told him how it rolled and roared over the rocks in winter nights, and lay still in the bright summer days, for the children to bathe and play in it; and many a story more, till Tom longed to go and see the sea, and bathe in it likewise.

At last, at the bottom of a hill, they came to a spring; not such a spring as you see here, which soaks up out of a white gravel in the bog, among red fly-catchers, and pink bottle-heath, and sweet white orchis; nor such a one as you may see, too, here, which bubbles up under the warm sand-bank in the hollow lane, by the great tuft of lady ferns, and makes the sand dance reels at the bottom, day and night, all the year round; not such a spring as either of those; but a real North country limestone fountain, like one of those in Sicily or Greece, where the old heathen fancied the nymphs sat cooling themselves the hot summer's day, while the shepherds peeped at them from behind the bushes. Out of a low cave of rock, at the foot of a limestone crag, the great fountain rose, quelling, and bubbling, and gurgling, so clear that you could not tell where the water ended and the air began; and ran away under the road, a stream large enough to turn a mill; among blue geranium, and golden globe-flower, and wild raspberry, and the bird-cherry with its tassels of snow.

And there Grimes stopped, and looked; and Tom looked too. Tom was wondering whether anything lived in that dark cave, and came out at night to fly in the meadows. But Grimes was not wondering at all. Without a word, he got off his donkey, and clambered over the low road wall, and knelt down, and began dipping his ugly head into the spring – and very dirty he made it.

Tom was picking the flowers as fast as he could. The Irishwoman helped him, and showed him how to tie them up; and a very pretty nosegay they had made between them. But when he saw Grimes actually wash, he stopped, quite astonished; and when Grimes had finished, and began shaking his ears to dry them, he said:

'Why, master, I never saw you do that before.'

'Nor will again, most likely. 'Twasn't for cleanliness I did it, but for coolness. I'd be ashamed to want washing every week or so, like any smutty collier lad.'

'I wish I might go and dip my head in,' said poor little Tom. 'It must be as good as putting it under the town-pump; and there is no beadle here to drive a chap away.'

'Thou come along,' said Grimes; 'what dost want with washing thyself? Thou did not drink half a gallon of beer last night, like me.'

'I don't care for you,' said naughty Tom, and ran down to the stream, and began washing his face.

Grimes was very sulky, because the woman preferred Tom's company to his; so he dashed at him with horrid words, and tore him up from his knees, and began beating him. But Tom was accustomed to that, and got his head safe between Mr. Grimes' legs, and kicked his shins with all his might.

'Are you not ashamed of yourself, Thomas Grimes?' cried the Irishwoman over the wall.

Grimes looked up, startled at her knowing his name; but all he answered was, 'No, nor never was yet;' and went on beating Tom.

'True for you. If you ever had been ashamed of yourself, you would have gone over into Vendale long ago.'

'What do you know about Vendale?' shouted Grimes; but he left off beating Tom.

'I know about Vendale, and about you, too. I know, for instance, what happened in Aldermire Copse, by night, two years ago come Martinmas.'

'You do?' shouted Grimes; and leaving Tom, he climbed up over the wall, and faced the woman. Tom thought he was going to strike her; but she looked him too full and fierce in the face for that.

'Yes; I was there,' said the Irishwoman quietly.

'You are no Irishwoman, by your speech,' said Grimes, after many bad words.

'Never mind who I am. I saw what I saw; and if you strike that boy again, I can tell what I know.'

Grimes seemed quite cowed, and got on his donkey without another word.

'Stop!' said the Irishwoman. 'I have one more word for you both; for you will both see me again before all is over. Those that wish to be clean, clean they will be; and those that wish to be foul, foul they will be. Remember.'

And she turned away, and through a gate into the meadow. Grimes stood still a moment, like a man who had been stunned. Then he rushed after her, shouting, 'You come back.' But when he got into the meadow, the woman was not there.

Had she hidden away? There was no place to hide in. But Grimes looked about, and Tom also, for he was as puzzled as Grimes himself at her disappearing so suddenly; but look where they would, she was not there.

Grimes came back again, as silent as a post, for he was a little frightened; and, getting on his donkey, filled a fresh pipe, and smoked away, leaving Tom in peace.

And now they had gone three miles and more, and came to Sir John's lodge-gates.

Very grand lodges they were, with very grand iron gates and stone gate-posts, and on the top of each a most dreadful bogy, all teeth, horns, and tail, which was the crest which Sir John's ancestors wore in the Wars of the Roses; and very prudent men they were to wear it, for all their enemies must have run for their lives at the very first sight of them.

Grimes rang at the gate, and out came a keeper on the spot, and opened.

'I was told to expect thee,' he said. 'Now thou'lt be so good as to keep to the main avenue, and not let me find a hare or a rabbit on thee when thou comest back. I shall look sharp for one, I tell thee.'

'Not if it's in the bottom of the soot-bag,' quoth Grimes, and at that he laughed; and the keeper laughed and said:

'If that's thy sort, I may as well walk up with thee to the hall.'

'I think thou best had. It's thy business to see after thy game, man, and not mine.'

So the keeper went with them; and, to Tom's surprise, he and Grimes chatted together all the way quite pleasantly. He did not know that a keeper is only a poacher turned outside in, and a poacher a keeper turned inside out.

They walked up a great lime avenue, a full mile long, and between their stems Tom peeped trembling at the horns of the sleeping deer, which stood up among the ferns. Tom had never seen such enormous trees, and as he looked up he fancied that the blue sky rested on their heads. But he was puzzled very much by a strange murmuring noise, which followed them all the way. So much puzzled, that at last he took courage to ask the keeper what it was.

He spoke very civilly, and called him Sir, for he was horribly afraid of him, which pleased the keeper, and he told him that they were the bees about the lime flowers.

'What are bees?' asked Tom.

'What make honey.'

'What is honey?' asked Tom.

'Thou hold thy noise,' said Grimes.

'Let the boy be,' said the keeper. 'He's a civil young chap now, and that's more than he'll be long if he bides with thee.'

Grimes laughed, for he took that for a compliment.

'I wish I were a keeper,' said Tom, 'to live in such a beautiful place, and wear green velveteens, and have a real dog-whistle at my button, like you.'

The keeper laughed; he was a kind-hearted fellow enough.

'Let well alone, lad, and ill too at times. Thy life's safer than mine at all events, eh, Mr. Grimes?'

And Grimes laughed again, and then the two men began talking quite low. Tom could hear, though, that it was about some poaching fight; and at last Grimes said surlily, 'Hast thou anything against me?'

'Not now.'

'Then don't ask me any questions till thou hast, for I am a man of honour.'

And at that they both laughed again, and thought it a very good joke.

And by this time they were come up to the great iron gates in front of the house; and Tom stared through them at the rhododendrons and azaleas, which were all in flower; and then at the house itself, and wondered how many chimneys there were in it, and how long ago it was built, and what was the man's name that built it, and whether he got much money for his job?

These last were very difficult questions to answer. For Harthover had been built at ninety different times, and in nineteen different styles, and looked as if somebody had built a whole street of houses of every imaginable shape, and then stirred them together with a spoon.

*For the attics were Anglo-Saxon.*

*The third floor Norman.*

*The second Cinque-cento.*

*The first-floor Elizabethan.*

*The right wing Pure Doric.*

*The centre Early English, with a huge portico copied from the Parthenon.*

*The left wing pure Bœotian, which the country folk admired most of all, because it was just like the new barracks in the town, only three times as big.*

*The grand staircase was copied from the Catacombs at Rome.*

*The back staircase from the Tajmahal at Agra. This was built by Sir John's great-great-great-uncle, who won, in Lord Clive's Indian Wars, plenty of money, plenty of wounds, and no more taste than his betters.*

*The cellars were copied from the caves of Elephanta.*

*The offices from the Pavilion at Brighton.*

And the rest from nothing in heaven, or earth, or under the earth.

So that Harthover House was a great puzzle to antiquarians, and a thorough Naboth's vineyard to critics, and architects, and all persons who like meddling with other men's business, and spending other men's money. So they were all setting upon poor Sir John, year after year, and trying to talk him into spending a hundred thousand pounds or so, in building, to please them and not himself. But he always put them off, like a canny North-countryman as he was. One wanted him to build a Gothic house, but he said he was no Goth; and another to build an Elizabethan, but he said he lived under good Queen Victoria, and not good Queen Bess; and another was bold enough to tell him that his house was ugly, but he said he lived inside it, and not outside; and another, that there was no unity in it, but he said that that was just why he liked the old place. For he liked to see how each Sir John, and Sir Hugh, and Sir Ralph, and Sir Randal, had left his mark upon the place, each after his own taste; and he had no more notion of disturbing his ancestors' work than of disturbing their graves. For now the house looked like a real live house, that had a history, and had grown and grown as the world grew; and that it was only an upstart fellow who did not know who his own grandfather was, who would change it for some spick and span new Gothic or Elizabethan thing, which looked as if it had been all spawned in a night, as mushrooms are. From which you may collect (if you have wit enough) that Sir John was a very sound-headed, sound-hearted squire, and just the man to keep the country side in order, and show good sport with his hounds.

But Tom and his master did not go in through the great iron gates, as if they had been Dukes or Bishops, but round the back way, and a very long way round it was; and into a little back-door, where the ash-boy let them in, yawning horribly; and then in a passage the housekeeper met them, in such a flowered chintz dressing-gown, that Tom mistook her for My Lady herself, and she gave Grimes solemn orders about 'You will take care of this, and take care of that,' as if he was going up the chimneys, and not Tom. And Grimes listened, and said every now and then, under his voice, 'You'll mind that, you little beggar?' and Tom did mind, all at least that he could. And then the housekeeper turned them into a grand room, all covered up in sheets of brown paper, and bade them begin, in a lofty and tremendous voice; and so after a whimper or two, and a kick from his master, into the grate Tom went, and up the chimney, while a housemaid stayed in the room to watch the furniture; to whom Mr. Grimes paid many playful and chivalrous compliments, but met with very slight encouragement in return.

How many chimneys Tom swept I cannot say; but he swept so many that he got quite tired, and puzzled too, for they were not like the town flues to which he was accustomed, but such as you would find – if you would only get up them and look, which perhaps you would not like to do – in old country-houses, large and crooked chimneys, which had been altered again and again, till they ran one into another, anastomosing (as Professor Owen would say) considerably. So Tom fairly lost his way in them; not that he cared much for that, though he was in pitchy darkness, for he was as much at home in a chimney as a mole is underground; but at last, coming down as he thought the right chimney, he came down the wrong one, and found himself standing on the hearthrug in a room the like of which he had never seen before.

Tom had never seen the like. He had never been in gentlefolks' rooms but when the carpets were all up, and the curtains down, and the furniture huddled together under a cloth, and the pictures covered with aprons and dusters; and he had often enough wondered what the rooms were like when they were all ready for the quality to sit in. And now he saw, and he thought the sight very pretty.

The room was all dressed in white, – white window-curtains, white bed-curtains, white furniture, and white walls, with just a few lines of pink here and there. The carpet was all over gay little flowers; and the walls were hung with pictures in gilt frames, which amused Tom very much. There were pictures of ladies and gentlemen, and pictures of horses and dogs. The horses he liked; but the dogs he did not care for much, for there were no bull-dogs among them, not even a terrier. But the two pictures which took his fancy most were, one a man in long garments, with little children and their mothers round him, who was laying his hand upon the children's heads. That was a very pretty picture, Tom thought, to hang in a lady's room. For he could see that it was a lady's room by the dresses which lay about.

The other picture was that of a man nailed to a cross, which surprised Tom much. He fancied that he had seen something like it in a shop-window. But why was it there? 'Poor man,' thought Tom, 'and he looks so kind and quiet. But why should the lady have such a sad picture as that in her room? Perhaps it was some kinsman of hers, who had been murdered by the savages in foreign parts, and she kept it there for a remembrance.' And Tom felt sad, and awed, and turned to look at something else.

The next thing he saw, and that too puzzled him, was a washing-stand, with ewers and basins, and soap and brushes, and towels, and a large bath full of clean water – what a heap of things all for washing! 'She must be a very dirty lady,' thought Tom, 'by my master's rule, to want as much scrubbing as all that. But she must be very cunning to put the dirt out of the way so well afterwards, for I don't see a speck about the room, not even on the very towels.'

And then, looking toward the bed, he saw that dirty lady, and held his breath with astonishment.

Under the snow-white coverlet, upon the snow-white pillow, lay the most beautiful little girl that Tom had ever seen. Her cheeks were almost as white as the pillow, and her hair was like threads of gold spread all about over the bed. She might have been as old as Tom, or maybe a year or two older; but Tom did not think of that. He thought only of her delicate skin and golden hair, and wondered whether she was a real live person, or one of the wax dolls he had seen in the shops. But when he saw her breathe, he made up his mind that she was alive, and stood staring at her, as if she had been an angel out of heaven.

No. She cannot be dirty. She never could have been dirty, thought Tom to himself. And then he thought, 'And are all people like that when they are washed?' And he looked at his own wrist, and tried to rub the soot off, and wondered whether it ever would come off. 'Certainly I should look much prettier then, if I grew at all like her.'

And looking round, he suddenly saw, standing close to him, a little ugly, black, ragged figure, with bleared eyes and grinning white teeth. He turned on it angrily. What did such a little black ape want in that sweet young lady's room? And behold, it was himself, reflected in a great mirror, the like of which Tom had never seen before.

And Tom, for the first time in his life, found out that he was dirty; and burst into tears with shame and anger; and turned to sneak up the chimney again and hide; and upset the fender and threw the fire-irons down, with a noise as of ten thousand tin kettles tied to ten thousand mad dogs' tails.

Up jumped the little white lady in her bed, and, seeing Tom, screamed as shrill as any peacock. In rushed a stout old nurse from the next room, and seeing Tom likewise, made up her mind that he had come to rob, plunder, destroy, and burn; and dashed at him, as he lay over the fender, so fast that she caught him by the jacket.

But she did not hold him. Tom had been in a policeman's hands many a time, and out of them too, what is more; and he would have been ashamed to face his friends for ever if he had been stupid enough to be caught by an old woman; so he doubled under the good lady's arm, across the room, and out of the window in a moment.

He did not need to drop out, though he would have done so bravely enough. Nor even to let himself down a spout, which would have been an old game to him; for once he got up by a spout to the church roof, he said to take jackdaws' eggs, but the policeman said to steal lead; and, when he was seen on high, sat there till the sun got too hot, and came down by another spout, leaving the policemen to go back to the stationhouse and eat their dinners.

But all under the window spread a tree, with great leaves and sweet white flowers, almost as big as his head. It was magnolia, I suppose; but Tom knew nothing about that, and cared less; for down the tree he went, like a cat, and across the garden lawn, and over the iron railings, and up the park towards the wood, leaving the old nurse to scream murder and fire at the window.

The under gardener, mowing, saw Tom, and threw down his scythe; caught his leg in it, and cut his shin open, whereby he kept his bed for a week; but in his hurry he never knew it, and gave chase to poor Tom. The dairymaid heard the noise, got the churn between her knees, and tumbled over it, spilling all the cream; and yet she jumped up, and gave chase to Tom. A groom cleaning Sir John's hack at the stables let him go loose, whereby he kicked himself lame in five minutes; but he ran out and gave chase to Tom. Grimes upset the soot-sack in the new-gravelled yard, and spoilt it all utterly; but he ran out and gave chase to Tom. The old steward opened the park-gate in such a hurry, that he hung up his pony's chin upon the spikes, and, for aught I know, it hangs there still; but he jumped off, and gave chase to Tom. The ploughman left his horses at the headland, and one jumped over the fence, and pulled the other into the ditch, plough and all; but he ran on, and gave chase to Tom. The keeper, who was taking a stoat out of a trap, let the stoat go, and caught his own finger; but he jumped up, and ran after Tom; and considering what he said, and how he looked, I should have been sorry for Tom if he had caught him. Sir John looked out of his study window (for he was an early old gentleman) and up at the nurse, and a marten dropped mud in his eye, so that he had at last to send for the doctor; and yet he ran out, and gave chase to Tom. The Irish-woman, too, was walking up to the house to beg, – she must have got round by some byway, – but she threw away her bundle, and gave chase to Tom likewise. Only my Lady did not give chase; for when she had put her head out of the window, her night-wig fell into the garden, and she had to ring up her lady's-maid, and send her down for it privately, which quite put her out of the running, so that she came in nowhere, and is consequently not placed.

In a word, never was there heard at Hall Place – not even when the fox was killed in the con-servatory, among acres of broken glass, and tons of smashed flower-pots – such a noise, row, hub-bub, babel, shindy, hullabaloo, stramash, charivari, and total contempt of dignity, repose, and order, as that day, when Grimes, gardener, the groom, the dairymaid, Sir John, the steward, the ploughman, the keeper, and the Irishwoman, all ran up the park, shouting 'Stop thief,' in the belief that Tom had at least a thousand pounds' worth of jewels in his empty pockets; and the very mag-pies and jays followed Tom up, screaking and screaming, as if he were a hunted fox, beginning to droop his brush.

And all the while poor Tom paddled up the park with his little bare feet, like a small black gorilla fleeing to the forest. Alas for him! there was no big father gorilla therein to take his part – to scratch out the gardener's inside with one paw, toss the dairymaid into a tree with another, and wrench off Sir John's head with a third, while he cracked the keeper's skull with his teeth as easily as if it had been a cocoa-nut or a paving-stone.

However, Tom did not remember ever having had a father; so he did not look for one, and expected to have to take care of himself; while as for running, he could keep up for a couple of miles with any stage-coach, if there was the chance of a copper or a cigar-end, and turn coach-wheels on his hands and feet ten times following, which is more than you can do. Wherefore his pursuers found it very difficult to catch him; and we will hope that they did not catch him at all.

Tom, of course, made for the woods. He had never been in a wood in his life; but he was sharp enough to know that he might hide in a bush, or swarm up a tree, and, altogether, had more chance there than in the open. If he had not known that, he would have been foolisher than a mouse or a minnow.

But when he got into the wood, he found it a very different sort of place from what he had fan-cied. He pushed into a thick cover of rhododendrons, and found himself at once caught in a trap.

The boughs laid hold of his legs and arms, poked him in his face and his stomach, made him shut his eyes tight (though that was no great loss, for he could not see at best a yard before his nose); and when he got through the rhododendrons, the hassock-grass and sedges tumbled him over, and cut his poor little fingers afterwards most spitefully; the birches birched him as soundly as if he had been a nobleman at Eton, and over the face too (which is not fair swishing, as all brave boys will agree); and the lawyers tripped him up, and tore his shins as if they had sharks' teeth – which lawyers are likely enough to have.

'I must get out of this,' thought Tom, 'or I shall stay here till somebody comes to help me – which is just what I don't want.'

But how to get out was the difficult matter. And indeed I don't think he would ever have got out at all, but have stayed there till the cock-robins covered him with leaves, if he had not suddenly run his head against a wall.

Now running your head against a wall is not pleasant, especially if it is a loose wall, with the stones all set on edge, and a sharp cornered one hits you between the eyes and makes you see all manner of beautiful stars. The stars are very beautiful, certainly; but unfortunately they go in the twenty-thousandth part of a split second, and the pain which comes after them does not. And so Tom hurt his head; but he was a brave boy, and did not mind that a penny. He guessed that over the wall the cover would end; and up it he went, and over like a squirrel.

And there he was, out on the great grouse-moors, which the country folk called Harthover Fell – heather and bog and rock, stretching away and up, up to the very sky.

Now, Tom was a cunning little fellow – as cunning as an old Exmoor stag. Why not? Though he was but ten years old, he had lived longer than most stags, and had more wits to start with into the bargain.

He knew as well as a stag that if he backed he might throw the hounds out. So the first thing he did when he was over the wall was to make the neatest double sharp to his right, and run along under the wall for nearly half a mile.

Whereby Sir John, and the keeper, and the steward, and the gardener, and the ploughman, and the dairymaid, and all the hue-and-cry together, went on ahead half a mile in the very opposite direction, and inside the wall, leaving him a mile off on the outside; while Tom heard their shouts die away in the woods and chuckled to himself merrily.

At last he came to a dip in the land, and went to the bottom of it, and then he turned bravely away from the wall and up the moor; for he knew that he had put a hill between him and his enemies, and could go on without their seeing him.

But the Irishwoman, alone of them all, had seen which way Tom went. She had kept ahead of every one the whole time; and yet she neither walked nor ran. She went along quite smoothly and gracefully, while her feet twinkled past each other so fast that you could not see which was foremost; till every one asked the other who the strange woman was; and all agreed, for want of anything better to say, that she must be in league with Tom.

But when she came to the plantation, they lost sight of her; and they could do no less. For she went quietly over the wall after Tom, and followed him wherever he went. Sir John and the rest saw no more of her; and out of sight was out of mind.

Plate 4    Frontispiece from *The Water Babies*, illustration by J. Noel Paton. Courtesy of the Victoria and Albert Museum, London

# William [Still] Stitt Jenkins (?–?)

As with prose fiction, Australian verse for children took some time to break away from the traditions of Britain. A good example is William Anderson Cawthorne (1824–97), who emigrated to Australia in 1841 and was a schoolteacher and businessman. His 'Who Killed Cockatoo?' (*c.* 1865) is a valiant attempt to naturalize a famous nursery rhyme: 'Who saw him die? | I, said the Opossum, | From the gum-blossom: | I saw him die.'

With Jenkins's *The Lost Children* we come to a genuinely Australian theme, even if the diction of the verse harks back to earlier generations. The fear of children being lost in the Australian outback was a very real one and has inspired many writers: the most famous examples are probably Ethel Pedley's *Dot and the Kangaroo* (1899; see p. 449, this volume), James Vance Marshall's *Walkabout* (1961) and, in modified form, Ivan Southall's *To the Wild Sky* (1967). *The Lost Children*, subtitled 'In Perpetual Remembrance of Jane Duff' was a true story: the three Duff children, Isaac (9), Jane (7) and Frank (3) were lost for nine days; there were several other versions of the same story. The title page of Jenkins's poem also says: 'The proceeds of sale will be added to the fund for the benefit of the children'. A similar motif can be found in Canadian children's literature, and in a romanticized form in Catherine Parr Traill's *Canadian Crusoes* (p. 104).

## The Lost Children (1864)

### I

Come, let us sing a truthful mournful ditty,
    Of little children who went forth to play,
Within the forests of our fair Victoria,
    And from their parents wandered far away.
Come, let us sing how on and on they rambled,
    And plucked each fragrant flower in joyous glee,
And gathered broom to cheer the humble dwelling –
    A home, alas, they never more may see.

### II

And brightly beamed the sun upon the children;
    The trees majestic, decked in glorious green,
A flood of glory rushed o'er hill and valley,
    And glanced upon the water's crystal sheen.
While hand in hand go on the little darlings,
    And round and round the insects flutter by;
And birds, melodious chant the hallelujah
    Within the vaulted azure of the sky.

### III

Anon the hoary woods looked grim and solemn,
    The owl is peeping from her drear abode,
The blessed light of day is slowly fading,
    And lone and silent now appears the road –
If road it be – wherein the children wander
    Amid the mighty trees that tower on high;
Ah, here and there, poor souls, they rush affrighted,
    And for their home and parents wildly cry.

IV

While from his lair comes forth the savage dingo,
    The cat-a-mountain hurries from his den,
The bats their doleful wings are flapping o'er them,
    And distant are the homes of busy men.
Pale lightnings glare, and roars the dismal thunder,
    And peal on peal succeeds each vivid flash;
No help is nigh, the winds of Heaven are rising,
    And foaming torrents down their waters dash.

V

And forest monarchs bend their stubborn branches,
    And feel their Maker's power in every limb;
Aye, bow their lofty heads to Great Jehovah,
    And in the storm and whirlwind worship Him.
And He is with the wanderers – He, The Master,
    Who had of yore no place to lay His head;
His is the hand that smooths their leafy pillow,
    And bids His angels guard their lonely bed.

VI

And so the days go on, and still they wander,
    And nine sad dreary nights go rolling on;
The brambles tear their flesh and scanty clothing,
    And even hope, alas! at length is gone.
For they have borne the bitter storms wild pelting,
    And felt the drenching of the blinding rain;
Have, famished, hailed each sun, and then distracted,
    And broken-hearted *slept in peace* again.

VII

(As in the olden time, in our loved Britain,
    Babes in the Wood laid down to wail and cry,
While Robin Redbreasts gathered bright leaves o'er them
    And left them with their God in peace to die.)
The moon resplendent, 'mid a sea of glory,
    Gazed down in pity on the woeful sight –
And so the little children of our story
    Were lowly lying in the silent night.

VIII

They rise, and, hunger-driven, totter onward,
    And gaze, with tear fraught eyes, o'er hill and plain,
And wail, poor souls, for their lamenting mother,
    Whose face, alas! they ne'er may see again,
So they go on, *and now attend, good people,*
    *For tale more piteous never yet was told:*
*Jane Duff, the elder darling, stripped her clothing*
    *To shield her brother from the bitter cold.*

IX

Come, let us sing of this fair child heroic,
    And let her name in Austral history glow!
Aye, be a household word in every dwelling,

And to a thousand generations go.
And men shall tell the tale unto their children,
    And bid them emulate her saintlike fame;
Nor shall her memory ever be forgotten,
        But all shall know and bless her honored name.


### X

Meanwhile the father and heart-riven mother
    Their neighbours raised, in truth, a gallant band
Of horse and foot, who soon in each direction
    The country scoured around on every hand,
Each gorge and glen, each rock and mountain,
    Re-echoed with their anxious tearful cries.
Ah! must the children in the forest perish,
    And gladden never more their parents' eyes?


### XI

This way and that, aye, every way they wander,
    And peer in every cave and desert place;
No hope, alas! appears – they faint and weary,
    And blank despair is seen in every face,
When, lo! slight indications of the long lost children
    Are found. Hurrah! at last behold the tracks;
*And now, with eager eyes rush on the natives –*
    *The long-neglected and down-trodden blacks.*


### XII

And now they find a little tattered garment,
    And, here again, behold the leafy beds
Wherein, some wretched night, had lain the children,
    And found a pillow for their wearied heads.
On, on, ye sable heroes, right before you,
    See where their bleeding feet have stained the track;
Hurrah! hurrah! *here Jane, the little darling,*
    *Hath borne her trembling brother on her back.*


### XIII

Ah, here they tottered on, and here they tumbled,
    And here to bear the boy she strove in vain.
See, see, ye gallant blacks, how here she stumbled,
    And fainting, bleeding, sank upon the plain.
What, are ye weary? On, O sable brothers –
    Think of the father's grief, the mother's woe;
Restore the children to their longing bosoms,
    And God shall bless you wheresoe'er you go.


### XIV

Away they dash, and now the stricken father
    Beholds on yon wild waste a speck of white –
What! shall he once again behold his darlings,
    And shall they *living* greet his longing sight?
Hurrah! they onward rush. Oh, joy for ever!
    Ha, ha, the frenzied father, weeping sees

His three poor little wanderers, calmly sleeping
   Within each others' arms amid the trees.

### XV

And little Jane, poor soul! was worn and speechless,
   The elder brother could but 'Father' cry,
And 'Ah, why came you not before, dear father,'
   The wail bewildered of the youngest boy.
And oh, so tenderly they homeward bear them,
   Mid wild huzzahs and hats triumphant waved,
And soon the weeping mother hears the tidings,
   And praises God her children all are saved.

### XVI

And noble, generous, hearts have heard the story
   Of these poor brothers, and of dear *Jane Duff*,
And, ah, for her throughout our fair Victoria
   The people give, and none cry, 'hold, enough.'
My child, farewell! a Rhymer's blessing guard thee,
   Although thy face on earth I ne'er may see:
Ah, in thy prayers to thine Almighty Father,
   When lowly bending, darling, think of me.

# Mary Elizabeth Mapes Dodge (1831–1905)

*Hans Brinker* is a highly readable curiosity. Deeply appreciative of the Netherlands, it has extensive descriptions of that country (part of the book is in effect a travelogue), although Mary Elizabeth Mapes Dodge never went there. It contains the 'legend' of the boy who put his finger in the hole in the dike ('The Hero of Haarlem'), the popularity of which – in an interesting example of art affecting life – led the Dutch to erect a statue.

*Hans Brinker* has two interwoven plots. In the first, which has an air of authenticity if a certain amount of conventional pathos, Hans and Gretel, poor children whose father has been brain damaged, make friends with local children and join the annual races for the prize of the silver skates. In the second, Hans persuades an eminent brain surgeon to operate on his father; this plot ends in a good deal of melodramatic revelation.

The mixture of conventional characters – Hans is the archetypal poor-but-honest lad who is rewarded (eventually becoming a great surgeon); Gretel is the poor-but-talented girl who becomes a winner; Peter is the noble leader of the gang; Carl the villain – and the narrator's enthusiasm for details of the setting, combine to make *Hans Brinker* compulsive reading. As the climactic scene, reprinted below, demonstrates, the characters are satisfying (if satisfyingly simple), the background intrinsically interesting, and the narrative voice (especially in its use of shifts of tense) engaging. As Jerry Griswold (1992) has suggested, there is a tension in the book between the self-control that the narrator constantly recommends and the tricks of the sentimental novelist which are designed to promote self-indulgence. This tension enabled Dodge to create 'the juvenile version of the romance novel'.

Its preface belies the vitality of the text itself, with its pious hope that 'this simple narrative [shall] serve to give my young readers a just idea of Holland and its resources ... [and] free them from certain current prejudices', and 'to cause even one heart to feel a deeper trust in God's goodness and love'. Even Hans outgrows his simple characterization, and may well have been the archetype for the series of unquenchably cheerful children in American children's books through to Little Orphan Annie and Pollyanna. The book was a great international success and won the French Academy's Montyon Prize.

Dodge, yet another widow supporting her family by the pen, assisted Harriet Beecher Stowe in editing *Hearth and Home*, and later edited the leading American children's magazine, *St. Nicholas* (1873–1905). In this latter capacity, she had an immense influence on American children's literature, publishing many of the leading children's authors.

## from *Hans Brinker; or, The Silver Skates* (1865)

### Chapter XLIV

### The Race

The Twentieth of December came at last, bringing with it the perfection of winter weather. All over the level landscape lay the warm sunlight. It tried its power on lake, canal, and river; but the ice flashed defiance and showed no sign of melting. The very weather-cocks stood still to enjoy the sight. This gave the windmills a holiday. Nearly all the past week they had been whirling briskly; now, being rather out of breath, they rocked lazily in the clear, still air. Catch a windmill working when the weather-cocks have nothing to do!

There was an end to grinding, crushing, and sawing for that day. It was a good thing for the millers near Broek. Long before noon they concluded to take in their sails, and go to the race. Everybody would be there – already the north side of the frozen Y was bordered with eager spectators; the news of the great skating match had travelled far and wide. Men, women, and children in holiday attire were flocking toward the spot. Some wore furs, and wintry cloaks or shawls; but many, consulting their feelings rather than the almanac, were dressed as for an October day.

The site selected for the race was a faultless plain of ice near Amsterdam, on that great *arm* of the Zuider Zee which Dutchmen of course must call – the Eye. The townspeople turned out in large numbers. Strangers in the city deemed it a fine chance to see what was to be seen. Many a peasant from the northward had wisely chosen the Twentieth as the day for the next city-trading. It seemed that everybody, young and old, who had wheels, skates, or feet at command, had hastened to the scene.

There were the gentry in their coaches, dressed like Parisians, fresh from the Boulevards; Amsterdam children in charity uniforms; girls from the Roman Catholic orphan house, in sable gowns and white headbands; boys from the Burgher Asylum, with their black tights and short-skirted, harlequin coats.[1] There were old-fashioned gentlemen in cocked hats and velvet knee breeches; old-fashioned ladies, too, in stiff, quilted skirts and bodies of dazzling brocade. These were accompanied by servants bearing foot-stoves and cloaks. There were the peasant folk arrayed in every possible Dutch costume. Shy young rustics in brazen buckles; simple village maidens con-cealing their flaxen hair under fillets of gold; women whose long, narrow aprons were stiff with embroidery; women with short, corkscrew curls hanging over their foreheads; women with shaved heads and close-fitting caps, and women in striped skirts and windmill bonnets. Men in leather, in homespun, in velvet and broadcloth; burghers in model European attire, and burghers in short jackets, wide trousers, and steeple-crowned hats.

There were beautiful Friesland girls in wooden shoes and coarse petticoats, with solid gold cres-cents encircling their heads, finished at each temple with a golden rosette, and hung with lace a century old. Some wore necklaces, pendants, and ear-rings of the purest gold. Many were content with gilt or even with brass, but it is not an uncommon thing for a Friesland woman to have all the family treasure in her head-gear. More than one rustic lass displayed the value of two thousand guilders upon her head that day.

Scattered throughout the crowd were peasants from the Island of Marken, with sabots, black stockings, and the widest of breeches; also women from Marken with short blue petticoats, and black jackets, gaily figured in front. They wore red sleeves, white aprons, and a cap like a bishop's mitre over their golden hair.

The children often were as quaint and odd-looking as their elders. In short, one-third of the crowd seemed to have stepped bodily from a collection of Dutch paintings.

Everywhere could be seen tall women, and stumpy men, lively-faced girls, and youths whose expression never changed from sunrise to sunset.

There seemed to be at least one specimen from every known town in Holland. There were Utrecht water-bearers, Gouda cheese-makers, Delft pottery-men, Schiedam distillers, Amsterdam diamond-cutters, Rotterdam merchants, dried-up herring-packers, and two sleepy-eyed shepherds from Texel. Every man of them had his pipe and tobacco-pouch. Some carried what might be called the smoker's complete outfit – a pipe, tobacco, a pricker with which to clean the tube, a silver net for protecting the bowl, and a box of the strongest of brimstone matches.

A true Dutchman, you must remember, is rarely without his pipe on any possible occasion. He may for a moment neglect to breathe, but when the pipe is forgotten, he must be dying indeed. There were no such sad cases here. Wreaths of smoke were rising from every possible quarter. The more fantastic the smoke wreath, the more placid and solemn the smoker.

Look at those boys and girls on stilts! That is a good idea. They can see over the heads of the tallest. It is strange to see those little bodies high in the air, carried about on mysterious legs. They have such a resolute look on their round faces, what wonder that nervous old gentlemen, with ten-der feet, wince and tremble while the long-legged little monsters stride past them.

You will read in certain books that the Dutch are a quiet people – so they are generally – but listen; did ever you hear such a din? All made up of human voices – no, the horses are helping somewhat, and the fiddles are squeaking pitifully (how it must pain fiddles to be tuned!), but the mass of the sound comes from the great *vox humana* that belongs to a crowd.

---

1   This is not said in derision. Both the girls and boys of this institu-tion wear garments quartered in red and black alternately. By making the dress thus conspicuous, the children are, in a measure, deterred from wrong-doing while going about the city. The Burgher Orphan Asylum affords a comfortable home to several hundred boys and girls. Holland is famous for its charitable institutions. (Author's note)

That queer little dwarf going about with a heavy basket, winding in and out among the people, helps not a little. You can hear his shrill cry above all the other sounds, 'Pypen en tabac! Pypen en tabac!'

Another, his big brother, though evidently some years younger, is selling doughnuts and bonbons. He is calling on all pretty children far and near to come quickly or the cakes will be gone.

You know quite a number among the spectators. High up in yonder pavilion, erected upon the border of the ice, are some persons whom you have seen very lately. In the centre is Madame van Gleck. It is her birthday, you remember; she has the post of honour. There is Mynheer van Gleck, whose meerschaum has not really grown fast to his lips – it only appears so. There are grandfather and grandmother whom you met at the St. Nicholas *fête*. All the children are with them. It is so mild they have brought even the baby. The poor little creature is swaddled very much after the manner of an Egyptian mummy, but it can crow with delight, and when the band is playing, open and shut its animated mittens in perfect time to the music.

Grandfather, with his pipe and spectacles and fur cap, makes quite a picture as he holds baby upon his knee. Perched high upon their canopied platforms, the party can see all that is going on. No wonder the ladies look complacently at the glassy ice; with a stove for a footstool one might sit cozily beside the North Pole.

There is a gentleman with them who somewhat resembles St. Nicholas as he appeared to the young Van Glecks on the fifth of December. But the saint had a flowing white beard; and this face is as smooth as a pippin. His saintship was larger around the body, too, and (between ourselves) he had a pair of thimbles in his mouth, which this gentleman certainly has not. It cannot be Saint Nicholas after all.

Near by, in the next pavilion, sit the Van Holps with their son and daughter (the Van Gends) from the Hague. Peter's sister is not one to forget her promises. She has brought bouquets of exquisite hot-house flowers for the winners.

These pavilions, and there are others beside, have all been erected since daylight. That semicircular one, containing Mynheer Korbes' family, is very pretty, and proves that the Hollanders are quite skilled at tent-making, but I like the Van Glecks' best – the centre one – striped red and white, and hung with evergreens.

The one with the blue flags contains the musicians. Those pagoda-like affairs, decked with seashells and streamers of every possible hue, are the judges' stands, and those columns and flag-staffs upon the ice mark the limit of the race-course. The two white columns twined with green, connected at the top by that long, floating strip of drapery, form the starting-point. Those flag-staffs, half a mile off, stand at each end of the boundary line, cut sufficiently deep to be distinct to the skaters, though not enough so to trip them when they turn to come back to the starting-point.

The air is so clear it seems scarcely possible that the columns and flag-staffs are so far apart. Of course the judges' stands are but little nearer together.

Half a mile on the ice, when the atmosphere is like this, is but a short distance after all, especially when fenced with a living chain of spectators.

The music has commenced. How melody seems to enjoy itself in the open air! The fiddles have forgotten their agony, and everything is harmonious. Until you look at the blue tent it seems that the music springs from the sunshine, it is so boundless, so joyous. Only when you see the staid-faced musicians you realise the truth.

Where are the racers? All assembled together near the white columns. It is a beautiful sight. Forty boys and girls in picturesque attire darting with electric swiftness in and out among each other, or sailing in pairs and triplets, beckoning, chatting, whispering in the fullness of youthful glee.

A few careful ones are soberly tightening their straps; others halting on one leg, with flushed, eager faces, suddenly cross the suspected skate over their knee, give it an examining shake, and dart off again. One and all are possessed with the spirit of motion. They cannot stand still. Their skates are a part of them, and every runner seems bewitched.

Holland is the place for skaters after all. Where else can nearly every boy and girl perform feats on the ice that would attract a crowd if seen in any park? Look at Ben! I did not see him before. He is really astonishing the natives; no easy thing to do in the Netherlands. Save your strength, Ben, you will need it soon. Now other boys are trying! Ben is surpassed already. Such jumping, such poising, such spinning, such indiarubber exploits generally! That boy with a red cap is the lion now; his back is a watch-spring, his body is cork – no, it is iron, or it would snap at that! He's a bird, a top, a rabbit, a corkscrew, a sprite, a flesh-ball, all in an instant. When you think he's erect he is down; and when you think he is down he is up. He drops his glove on the ice and turns a somersault as he picks it up. Without stopping, he snatches the cap from Jacob Poot's astonished head and claps it back again 'hind side before.' Lookers-on hurrah and laugh. Foolish boy! It is Arctic weather under your feet, but more than temperate overhead. Big drops already are rolling down your forehead. Superb skater as you are, you may lose the race.

A French traveller standing with a note-book in his hand, sees our English friend, Ben, buy a doughnut of the dwarf's brother, and eat it. Thereupon he writes in his note-book that the Dutch take enormous mouthfuls, and universally are fond of potatoes boiled in molasses.

There are some familiar faces near the white columns. Lambert, Ludwig, Peter, and Carl are all there, cool and in good skating order. Hans is not far off. Evidently he is going to join in the race, for his skates are on – the very pair that he sold for seven guilders! He had soon suspected that his fairy godmother was the mysterious 'friend' who bought them. This settled, he had boldly charged her with the deed, and she, knowing well that all her little savings had been spent in the purchase, had not had the face to deny it. Through the fairy godmother, too, he had been rendered amply able to buy them back again. Therefore Hans is to be in the race. Carl is more indignant than ever about it, but as three other peasant boys have entered, Hans is not alone.

Twenty boys and twenty girls. The latter by this time are standing in front, braced for the start, for they are to have the first 'run.' Hilda, Rychie, and Katrinka are among them – two or three bend hastily to give a last pull at their skate-straps. It is pretty to see them stamp, to be sure that all is firm. Hilda is speaking pleasantly to a graceful little creature in a red jacket and a new brown petticoat. Why, it is Gretel! What a difference those pretty shoes make, and the skirt, and the new cap. Annie Bouman is there too. Even Janzoon Kolp's sister has been admitted – but Janzoon himself has been voted out by the directors, because he killed the stork, and only last summer was caught in the act of robbing a bird's nest, a legal offence in Holland.

This Janzoon Kolp, you see, was — There, I cannot tell the story just now. The race is about to commence.

Twenty girls are formed in a line. The music has ceased.

A man, whom we shall call the Crier, stands between the columns and the first judges' stand. He reads the rules in a loud voice:

'THE GIRLS AND BOYS ARE TO RACE IN TURN, UNTIL ONE GIRL AND ONE BOY HAS BEATEN TWICE. THEY ARE TO START IN A LINE FROM THE UNITED COLUMNS – SKATE TO THE FLAG-STAFF LINE, TURN, AND THEN COME BACK TO THE STARTING-POINT; THUS MAKING A MILE AT EACH RUN.'

A flag is waved from the judges' stand. Madame van Gleck rises in her pavilion. She leans forward with a white handkerchief in her hand. When she drops it, a bugler is to give the signal for them to start.

The handkerchief is fluttering to the ground. Hark!

They are off!

No. Back again. Their line was not true in passing the judges' stand.

The signal is repeated.

Off again. No mistake this time. Whew! how fast they go!

The multitude is quiet for an instant, absorbed in eager, breathless watching.

Cheers spring up along the line of spectators. Huzza! five girls are ahead. Who comes flying back from the boundary mark? We cannot tell. Something red, that is all. There is a blue spot flitting near it, and a dash of yellow nearer still. Spectators at this end of the line strain their eyes and wish they had taken their post nearer the flag-staff.

The wave of cheers is coming back again. Now we can see! Katrinka is ahead!

She passes the Van Holp pavilion. The next is Madame van Gleck's. That leaning figure gazing from it is a magnet. Hilda shoots past Katrinka, waving her hand to her mother as she passes. Two others are close now, whizzing on like arrows. What is that flash of red and grey? Hurrah, it is Gretel! She too waves her hand, but toward no gay pavilion. The crowd is cheering, but she hears only her father's voice, 'Well done, little Gretel!' Soon Katrinka, with a quick merry laugh, shoots past Hilda. The girl in yellow is gaining now. She passes them all, all except Gretel. The judges lean forward without seeming to lift their eyes from their watches. Cheer after cheer fills the air; the very columns seem rocking. Gretel has passed them. She has won.

'Gretel Brinker – one mile!' shouts the crier.

The judges nod. They write something upon a tablet which each holds in his hand.

While the girls are resting – some crowding eagerly around our frightened little Gretel, some standing aside in high disdain – the boys form in a line.

Mynheer van Gleck drops the handkerchief this time. The buglers give a vigorous blast!

The boys have started.

Half-way already! Did ever you see the like!

Three hundred legs flashing by in an instant. But there are only twenty boys. No matter, there were hundreds of legs I am sure! Where are they now? There is such a noise one gets bewildered. What are the people laughing at? Oh, at that fat boy in the rear. See him go! See him! He'll be down in an instant – no, he won't. I wonder if he knows he is all alone; the other boys are nearly at the boundary line. Yes, he knows it. He stops! He wipes his hot face. He takes off his cap and looks about him. Better to give up with a good grace. He has made a hundred friends by that hearty, astonished laugh. Good Jacob Poot!

The fine fellow is already among the spectators gazing as eagerly as the rest.

A cloud of feathery ice flies from the heels of the skaters as they 'bring to' and turn at the flag-staffs.

Something black is coming now, one of the boys – it is all we know. He has touched the *vox humana* stop of the crowd, it fairly roars. Now they come nearer – we can see the red cap. There's Ben – there's Peter – there's Hans!

Hans is ahead! Young Madame van Gend almost crushes the flowers in her hand; she had been quite sure that Peter would be first. Carl Schummel is next, then Ben, and the youth with the red cap. The others are pressing close. A tall figure darts from among them. He passes the red cap, he passes Ben, then Carl. Now it is an even race between him and Hans. Madame van Gend catches her breath.

It is Peter! He is ahead! Hans shoots past him. Hilda's eyes fill with tears, Peter *must* beat. Annie's eyes flash proudly. Gretel gazes with clasped hands – four strokes more will take her brother to the columns.

He is there! Yes, but so was young Schummel just a second before. At the last instant, Carl, gathering his powers, had whizzed between them and passed the goal.

'Carl Schummel! one mile!' shouts the crier.

Soon Madame van Gleck rises again. The falling handkerchief starts the bugle; and the bugle, using its voice as a bow-string, shoots off twenty girls like so many arrows.

It is a beautiful sight, but one has not long to look; before we can fairly distinguish them they are far in the distance. This time they are close upon one another; it is hard to say as they come speeding back from the flag-staff which will reach the columns first. There are new faces among the foremost – eager, glowing faces, unnoticed before. Katrinka is there, and Hilda, but Gretel and Rychie are in the rear. Gretel is wavering, but when Rychie passes her, she starts forward afresh. Now they are nearly beside Katrinka. Hilda is still in advance, she is almost 'home.' She has not faltered since that bugle note sent her flying; like an arrow still she is speeding toward the goal. Cheer after cheer rises in the air. Peter is silent but his eyes shine like stars. 'Huzza! Huzza!'

The crier's voice is heard again.

'Hilda van Gleck, one mile!'

A loud murmur of approval runs through the crowd, catching the music in its course, till all seems one sound, with a glad rhythmic throbbing in its depths. When the flag waves all is still.

Once more the bugle blows a terrific blast. It sends off the boys like chaff before the wind – dark chaff I admit, and in big pieces.

It is whisked around at the flag-staff, driven faster yet by the cheers and shouts along the line. We begin to see what is coming. There are three boys in advance this time, and all abreast. Hans, Peter, and Lambert. Carl soon breaks the ranks, rushing through with a whiff! Fly Hans, fly Peter, don't let Carl beat again. Carl the bitter, Carl the insolent. Van Mounen is flagging, but you are strong as ever. Hans and Peter, Peter and Hans; which is foremost? We love them both. We scarcely care which is the fleeter.

Hilda, Annie, and Gretel, seated upon the long crimson bench, can remain quiet no longer. They spring to their feet – so different, and yet one in eagerness. Hilda instantly reseats herself; none shall know how interested she is, none shall know how anxious, how filled with one hope. Shut your eyes then, Hilda – hide your face rippling with joy. Peter has beaten.

'PETER VAN HOLP, ONE MILE!' calls the crier.

The same buzz of excitement as before, while the judges take notes, the same throbbing of music through the din – but something is different. A little crowd presses close about some object near the column. Carl has fallen. He is not hurt, though somewhat stunned. If he were less sullen he would find more sympathy in these warm young hearts. As it is they forget him as soon as he is fairly on his feet again.

The girls are to skate their third mile.

How resolute the little maidens look as they stand in a line! Some are solemn with a sense of responsibility, some wear a smile half bashful, half provoked, but one air of determination pervades them all.

This third mile may decide the race. Still if neither Gretel nor Hilda win, there is yet a chance among the rest for the Silver Skates.

Each girl feels sure that this time she will accomplish the distance in one half the time. How they stamp to try their runners, how nervously they examine each strap – how erect they stand at last, every eye upon Madame van Gleck!

The bugle thrills through them again. With quivering eagerness they spring forward, bending, but in perfect balance. Each flashing stroke seems longer than the last.

Now they are skimming off in the distance. .

Again the eager straining of eyes – again the shouts and cheering, again the thrill of excitement as, after a few moments, four or five, in advance of the rest, come speeding back, nearer, nearer to the white columns.

Who is first? Not Rychie, Katrinka, Annie, nor Hilda, nor the girl in yellow – but Gretel – Gretel, the fleetest sprite of a girl that ever skated. She was but playing in the earlier race, *now* she is in earnest, or rather something within her has determined to win. That lithe little form makes no effort; but it cannot stop – not until the goal is passed!

In vain the crier lifts his voice – he cannot be heard. He has no news to tell – it is already ringing through the crowd. *Gretel has won the Silver Skates!*

Like a bird she has flown over the ice, like a bird she looks about her in a timid, startled way. She longs to dart to the sheltered nook where her father and mother stand. But Hans is beside her – the girls are crowding round. Hilda's kind, joyous voice breathes in her ear. From that hour, none will despise her. Goose-girl or not, Gretel stands acknowledged Queen of the Skaters!

With natural pride Hans turns to see if Peter van Holp is witnessing his sister's triumph. Peter is not looking toward them at all. He is kneeling, bending his troubled face low, and working hastily at his skate-strap. Hans is beside him at once.

'Are you in trouble, mynheer?'

'Ah, Hans! that you? Yes, my fun is over. I tried to tighten my strap – to make a new hole – and this botheration of a knife has cut it nearly in two.'

'Mynheer,' said Hans, at the same time pulling off a skate – 'you must use my strap!'

'Not I, indeed, Hans Brinker,' cried Peter, looking up, 'though I thank you warmly. Go to your post, my friend, the bugle will sound in a minute.'

'Mynheer,' pleaded Hans in a husky voice. 'You have called me your friend. Take this strap – quick! There is not an instant to lose. I shall not skate this time – indeed I am out of practice. Mynheer, you *must* take it,' – and Hans, blind and deaf to any remonstrance, slipped his strap into Peter's skate and implored him to put it on.

'Come, Peter!' cried Lambert, from the line, 'we are waiting for you.'

'For madame's sake,' pleaded Hans, 'be quick. She is motioning to you to join the racers. There, the skate is almost on; quick, mynheer, fasten it. I could not possibly win. The race lies between Master Schummel and yourself.'

'You are a noble fellow, Hans!' cried Peter, yielding at last. He sprang to his post just as the white handkerchief fell to the ground. The bugle sends forth its blast, loud, clear, and ringing.

Off go the boys!

'See them!' cries a tough old fellow from Delft. 'They beat everything, these Amsterdam youngsters.'

See them, indeed! They are winged Mercuries every one of them. What mad errand are they on? Ah, I know; they are hunting Peter van Holp. He is some fleet-footed runaway from Olympus. Mercury and his troop of winged cousins are in full chase. They will catch him! Now Carl is the runaway – the pursuit grows furious – Ben is foremost!

The chase turns in a cloud of mist. It is coming this way. Who is hunted now? Mercury himself. It is Peter, Peter van Holp; fly, Peter – Hans is watching you. He is sending all his fleetness, all his strength into your feet. Your mother and sister are pale with eagerness. Hilda is trembling and dare not look up. Fly, Peter! the crowd has not gone deranged, it is only cheering. The pursuers are close upon you! Touch the white column! It beckons – it is reeling before you – it –

Huzza! Huzza! Peter has won the Silver Skates!

'PETER VAN HOLP!' shouted the crier. But who heard him? 'Peter van Holp!' shouted a hundred voices, for he was the favourite boy of the place. Huzza! Huzza!

Now the music was resolved to be heard. It struck up a lively air, then a tremendous march. The spectators, thinking something new was about to happen, deigned to listen and to look.

The racers formed in single file. Peter, being tallest, stood first. Gretel, the smallest of all, took her place at the end. Hans, who had borrowed a strap from the cake-boy, was near the head.

Three gaily twined arches were placed at intervals upon the river facing the Van Gleck pavilion.

Skating slowly, and in perfect time to the music, the boys and girls moved forward, led on by Peter. It was beautiful to see the bright procession glide along like a living creature. It curved and doubled, and drew its graceful length in and out among the arches – whichever way Peter the head went, the body was sure to follow. Sometimes it steered direct for the centre arch, then, as if seized with a new impulse, turned away and curled itself about the first one; then unwound slowly and bending low, with quick, snakelike curvings, crossed the river, passing at length through the furthest arch.

When the music was slow, the procession seemed to crawl like a thing afraid; it grew livelier, and the creature darted forward with a spring, gliding rapidly among the arches, in and out, curling, twisting, turning, never losing form until, at the shrill call of the bugle rising above the music, it suddenly resolved itself into boys and girls standing in double semicircle before Madame van Gleck's pavilion.

Peter and Gretel stand in the centre in advance of the others. Madame van Gleck rises majestically. Gretel trembles, but feels that she must look at the beautiful lady. She cannot hear what is said, there is such a buzzing all around her. She is thinking that she ought to try and make a courtesy, such as her mother makes to the meester, when suddenly something so dazzling is placed in her hand that she gives a cry of joy.

Then she ventures to look about her. Peter, too, has something in his hands – 'Oh! oh! how splendid!' she cries, and 'Oh! how splendid!' is echoed as far as people can see.

Meantime the silver skates flash in the sunshine, throwing dashes of light upon those two happy faces.

Mevrouw van Gend sends a little messenger with her bouquets. One for Hilda, one for Carl, and others for Peter and Gretel.

At sight of the flowers the Queen of the Skaters becomes uncontrollable. With a bright stare of gratitude she gathers skates and bouquet in her apron – hugs them to her bosom, and darts off to search for her father and mother in the scattering crowd.

# 'Hesba Stretton' (Sarah Smith) (1832–1911)

Sarah Smith was a moderately successful writer of experimental novels with evangelical roots, such as the now forgotten *The Clives of Burcot* (1867) published by the Religious Tract Society (she had also written for Dickens's *All the Year Round*). When *Jessica's First Prayer* was first published in 1866 in *Sunday at Home* (an RTS publication) it was an immediate bestseller (the figure of over 1,500,000 copies being cited in Darton) and virtually founded a genre. Children had ministered to the poor for some years, but Smith placed the emphasis upon the plight of the poor, not on middle-class philanthropy.

Sarah Smith's work, although increasingly formulaic, was driven by a genuine and practical commitment to improving child poverty, and Jessica is drawn with something of the force of the crossing-sweeper, Tom, in Dickens's *Bleak House*. The descent (if it can be so described) of the genre to the sentimental and ersatz (although not necessarily less affecting), exemplified by the starving child in the baker's-shop doorway in Frances Hodgson Burnett's *Sara Crewe*, was driven by the increasingly corrupting forces (in terms of authenticity of realism or feeling) of piety, sentimentality and commercialism. Thus some of the books of this type, such as Mrs. O. F. Walton's *Christie's Old Organ* (1874) – quite apart from the tides of language – have not worn well, because their pious children and holy deaths seem to be a long way from any form of realism, and hark back fifty years to a world of harsher sensitivities. In others, notably *Froggy's Little Brother* (1875) by 'Brenda' (Mrs Castle Smith), pathos has been worn by the years into bathos.

Nevertheless, the genre was very popular, and many books were produced by the Religious Tract Society (1799–) and the New York (later American) Tract Society (1812–) with this theme. In the USA, however, the genre often embraced a more optimistic, classless and dynamic approach, as in the books of Horatio Alger.

The real force of *Jessica's First Prayer* is that it is a critique of the very religious system that produced it. Jessica, whose mother is a drunken actress, is befriended by Daniel Standring, who runs a coffee-stall and is a chapel caretaker. The dilemma presented to Daniel, the minister and his children is faced squarely, and if both Jessica and Daniel eventually find true religion, they find it not through pious exhortations but by a recognition of their human responsibilities.

## from *Jessica's First Prayer* (1867)

### CHAPTER III

### AN OLD FRIEND IN A NEW DRESS

Week after week, through the three last months of the year, Jessica appeared every Wednesday at the coffee-stall, and after waiting patiently till the close of the breakfasting business, received her pittance from the charity of her new friend. After a while Daniel allowed her to carry some of his load to the coffee-house, but he never suffered her to follow him farther, and he was always particular to watch her out of sight before he turned off through the intricate mazes of the streets in the direction of his own home. Neither did he encourage her to ask him any more questions: and often but very few words passed between them during Jessica's breakfast time.

As to Jessica's home, she made no secret of it, and Daniel might have followed her any time he pleased. It was a single room, which had once been a hayloft over the stable of an old inn, now in use for two or three donkeys, the property of costermongers dwelling in the court about it. The mode of entrance was by a wooden ladder, whose rungs were crazy and broken, and which led up through a trap-door in the floor of the loft. The interior of the home was as desolate and comfortless as that of the stable below, with only a litter of straw for the bedding, and a few bricks and boards for the furniture. Everything that could be pawned had disappeared long ago, and Jessica's mother often lamented that she could not thus dispose of her child. Yet Jessica was hardly a burden to her. It was a long time since she had taken any care to provide her with food or clothing, and the girl had to earn or beg for herself the meat which kept a scanty life within her. Jess was the drudge and errand-girl of the court; and what with being cuffed and beaten by her mother, and over-worked and ill-used by her numerous employers, her life was a hard one. But now there was always Wednesday morning to count upon and look forward to; and by and by a second scene of amazed delight opened upon her.

Jessica had wandered far away from home in the early darkness of a winter's evening, after a violent outbreak of her drunken mother, and she was still sobbing now and then with long-drawn sobs of pain and weariness, when she saw, a little way before her, the tall, well-known figure of her friend Mr. Daniel. He was dressed in a suit of black, with a white neckcloth, and he was pacing with brisk yet measured steps along the lighted streets. Jessica felt afraid of speaking to him, but she followed at a little distance, until presently he stopped before the iron gates of a large building, and, unlocking them, passed on to the arched doorway, and with a heavy key opened the folding-doors and entered in. The child stole after him, but paused for a few minutes, trembling upon the threshold, until the gleam of a light lit up within tempted her to venture a few steps forward, and to push a little way open an inner door, covered with crimson baize, only so far as to enable her to peep through at the inside. Then, growing bolder by degrees, she crept through herself, drawing the door to noiselessly behind her. The place was in partial gloom, but Daniel was kindling every gaslight, and each minute lit it up in more striking grandeur. She stood in a carpeted aisle, with high oaken pews on each side, almost as black as ebony. A gallery of the same dark old oak ran round the walls, resting upon massive pillars, behind one of which she was partly concealed, gazing with eager eyes at Daniel, as he mounted the pulpit steps and kindled the lights there, disclosing to her curious delight the glittering pipes of an organ behind it. Before long the slow and soft-footed chapel-keeper disappeared for a minute or two into a vestry; and Jessica, availing herself of his short absence, stole silently up under the shelter of the dark pews until she reached the steps of the organ loft, with its golden show. But at this moment Mr. Daniel appeared again, arrayed in a long gown of black serge; and as she stood spell-bound gazing at the strange appearance of her patron, his eyes fell upon her, and he also was struck speechless for a minute, with an air of amazement and dismay upon his grave face.

'Come, now,' he exclaimed, harshly, as soon as he could recover his presence of mind, 'you must take yourself out of this. This isn't any place for such as you. It's for ladies and gentlemen; so you must run away sharp before anybody comes. How ever did you find your way here?'

He had come very close to her, and bent down to whisper in her ear, looking nervously round to the entrance all the time. Jessica's eager tongue was loosened.

'Mother beat me,' she said, 'and turned me into the streets, and I see you there, so I followed you up. I'll run away this minute, Mr. Daniel; but it's a nice place. What do the ladies and gentlemen do when they come here? Tell me, and I'll be off sharp.'

'They come here to pray,' whispered Daniel.

'What is pray?' asked Jessica.

'Bless the child!' cried Daniel, in perplexity. 'Why, they kneel down in those pews; most of them sit, though; and the minister up in the pulpit tells God what they want.'

Jessica gazed into his face with such an air of bewilderment that a faint smile crept over the sedate features of the pew-opener.

'What is a minister and God?' she said; 'and do ladies and gentlemen want anything? I thought they'd everything they wanted, Mr. Daniel.'

'Oh!' cried Daniel, 'you must be off, you know. They'll be coming in a minute, and they'd be shocked to see a ragged little heathen like you. This is the pulpit where the minister stands and preaches to 'em; and there are the pews, where they sit to listen to him, or to go to sleep, may be; and that's the organ to play music to their singing. There, I've told you everything, and you must never come again, never.'

'Mr. Daniel,' said Jessica, 'I don't know nothing about it. Isn't there a dark little corner somewhere that I could hide in?'

'No, no,' interrupted Daniel, impatiently; 'we couldn't do with such a little heathen, with no shoes or bonnet on. Come now, it's only a quarter to the time, and somebody will be here in a minute. Run away, do!'

Jessica retraced her steps slowly to the crimson door, casting many a longing look backwards; but Mr. Daniel stood at the end of the aisle, frowning upon her whenever she glanced behind. She gained the lobby at last, but already some one was approaching the chapel door, and beneath the lamp at the gate stood one of her natural enemies, a policeman. Her heart beat fast, but she was quickwitted, and in another instant she spied a place of concealment behind one of the doors, into which she crept for safety until the path should be clear, and the policeman passed on upon his beat.

The congregation began to arrive quickly. She heard the rustling of silk dresses, and she could see the gentlemen and ladies pass by the niche between the door and the post. Once she ventured to stretch out a thin little finger and touch a velvet mantle as the wearer of it swept by, but no one caught her in the act, or suspected her presence behind the door. Mr. Daniel, she could see, was very busy ushering the people to their seats; but there was a startled look lingering upon his face, and every now and then he peered anxiously into the outer gloom and darkness, and even once called to the policeman to ask if he had seen a ragged child hanging about. After a while the organ began to sound, and Jessica, crouching down in her hiding-place, listened entranced to the sweet music. She could not tell what made her cry, but the tears came so rapidly that it was of no use to rub the corners of her eyes with her hard knuckles; so she lay down upon the ground, and buried her face in her hands, and wept without restraint. When the singing was over, she could only catch a confused sound of a voice speaking. The lobby was empty now, and the crimson doors closed. The policeman, also, had walked on. This was the moment to escape. She raised herself from the ground with a feeling of weariness and sorrow; and thinking sadly of the light, and warmth, and music that were within the closed doors, she stepped out into the cold and darkness of the streets, and loitered homewards with a heavy heart.

## Chapter IV

### Peeps into Fairy Land

It was not the last time that Jessica concealed herself behind the baize-covered door. She could not overcome the urgent desire to enjoy again and again the secret and perilous pleasure; and Sunday after Sunday she watched in the dark streets for the moment when she could slip in unseen. She soon learned the exact time when Daniel would be occupied in lighting up, before the policeman would take up his station at the entrance, and again, the very minute at which it would be wise and safe to take her departure. Sometimes the child laughed noiselessly to herself, until she shook with suppressed merriment, as she saw Daniel standing unconsciously in the lobby, with his solemn face and grave air, to receive the congregation, much as he faced his customers at the coffee-stall. She learned to know the minister by sight, the tall, thin, pale gentleman, who passed through a side door, with his head bent as if in deep thought, while two little girls, about her own age, followed him with sedate yet pleasant faces. Jessica took a great interest in the minister's children. The younger one was fair, and the elder was about as tall as herself, and had eyes and hair as dark; but oh, how cared for, how plainly waited on by tender hands! Sometimes, when they were gone by, she would close her eyes, and wonder what they would do in one of the high black pews inside, where there was no place for a ragged, barefooted girl like her; and now and then her wonderings almost ended in a sob, which she was compelled to stifle.

It was an untold relief to Daniel that Jessica did not ply him with questions, as he feared when she came for breakfast every Wednesday morning; but she was too shrewd and cunning for that. She wished him to forget that she had ever been there, and by and by her wish was accomplished, and Daniel was no longer uneasy, while he was lighting the lamps, with the dread of seeing the child's wild face starting up before him.

But the light evenings of summer-time were drawing near apace, and Jessica foresaw with dismay that her Sunday treats would soon be over. The risk of discovery increased every week, for the sun was later and later in setting and there would be no chance of creeping in and out unseen in the broad daylight. Already it needed both watchfulness and alertness to dart in at the right moment in the grey twilight; but still she could not give it up; and if it had not been for the fear of offending Mr. Daniel, she would have resolved upon going until she was found out. They could not punish her very much for standing in the lobby of a chapel.

Jessica was found out, however, before the dusky evenings were quite gone. It happened one night that the minister's children, coming early to the chapel, saw a small tattered figure, bare-headed and barefooted, dart swiftly up the steps before them and disappear within the lobby. They paused and looked at one another, and then, hand in hand, their hearts beating quickly, and the colour coming and going on their faces, they followed this strange new member of their father's congregation. The pew-opener was nowhere to be seen, but their quick eyes detected the prints of the wet little feet which had trodden the clean pavement before them, and in an instant they discovered Jessica crouching behind the door.

'Let us call Daniel Standring,' said Winny, the younger child, clinging to her sister; but she had spoken aloud, and Jessica overheard her, and before they could stir a step she stood before them with an earnest and imploring face.

'Oh, don't have me drove away,' she cried; 'I'm a very poor little girl, and it's all the pleasure I've got. I've seen you lots of times, with that tall gentleman as stoops, and I didn't think you'd have me drove away. I don't do any harm behind the door, and if Mr. Daniel finds me out, he won't give me any more coffee.'

'Little girl,' said the elder child, in a composed and demure voice, 'we don't mean to be unkind to you; but what do you come here for, and why do you hide yourself behind the door?'

'I like to hear the music,' answered Jessica, 'and I want to find out what pray is, and the minister, and God. I know it's only for ladies and gentlemen, and fine children like you; but I'd like to go inside just for once, and see what you do.'

'You shall come with us into our pew,' cried Winny, in an eager and impulsive tone; but Jane laid her hand upon her outstretched arm, with a glance at Jessica's ragged clothes and matted hair. It was a question difficult enough to perplex them. The little outcast was plainly too dirty and neglected for them to invite her to sit side by side with them in their crimson-lined pew, and no poor people attended the chapel with whom she could have a seat. But Winny, with flushed cheeks and indignant eyes, looked reproachfully at her elder sister.

'Jane,' she said, opening her Testament, and turning over the leaves hurriedly, 'this was papa's text a little while ago: – "For if there come into your assembly a man with a gold ring, in goodly apparel, and there come in also a poor man in vile raiment; and ye have respect to him that weareth the gay clothing, and say unto him, Sit thou here in a good place; and say to the poor, Stand thou there, or sit here under my footstool; are ye not then partial in yourselves, and are become judges of evil thoughts?" If we don't take this little girl into our pew, [do] we "have the faith of our Lord Jesus Christ, the Lord of glory, with respect of persons."'

'I don't know what to do,' answered Jane, sighing; 'the Bible seems plain; but I'm sure papa would not like it. Let us ask the chapel-keeper.'

'Oh, no, no!' cried Jessica; 'don't let Mr. Daniel catch me here. I won't come again, indeed; and I'll promise not to try to find out about God and the minister, if you'll only let me go.'

'But, little girl,' said Jane, in a sweet but grave manner, 'we ought to teach you about God, if you don't know him. Our papa is the minister, and if you'll come with us, we'll ask him what we must do.'

'Will Mr. Daniel see me?' asked Jessica.

'Nobody but papa is in the vestry,' answered Jane, 'and he'll tell us all, you and us, what we ought to do. You'll not be afraid of him, will you?'

'No,' said Jessica, cheerfully, following the minister's children as they led her along the side of the chapel towards the vestry.

'He is not such a terrible personage,' said Winny, looking round encouragingly, as Jane tapped softly at the door, and they heard a voice saying 'Come in.'

## CHAPTER V

## A NEW WORLD OPENS

The minister was sitting in an easy chair before a comfortable fire, with a hymn-book in his hand, which he closed as the three children appeared in the open doorway. Jessica had seen his pale and thoughtful face many a time from her hiding-place, but she had never met the keen, earnest, searching gaze of his eyes, which seemed to pierce through all her wretchedness and misery, and to read at once the whole history of her desolate life. But before her eyelids could droop, or she could drop a reverential curtsey, the minister's face kindled with such a glow of pitying tenderness and compassion, as fastened her eyes upon him, and gave her new heart and courage. His children ran to him, leaving Jessica upon the mat at the door, and with eager voices and gestures told him the difficulty they were in.

'Come here, little girl,' he said; and Jessica walked across the carpeted floor till she stood right before him, with folded hands, and eyes that looked frankly into his.

'What is your name, my child?' he asked.

'Jessica,' she answered.

'Jessica,' he repeated, with a smile; 'that is a strange name.'

'Mother used to play "Jessica" at the theatre, sir,' she said, 'and I used to be a fairy in the pantomime, till I grew too tall and ugly. If I'm pretty when I grow up, mother says I shall play too; but I've a long time to wait. Are you the minister, sir?'

'Yes,' he answered, smiling again.

'What is a minister?' she enquired.

'A servant!' he replied, looking away thoughtfully into the red embers of the fire.

'Papa!' cried Jane and Winny, in tones of astonishment; but Jessica gazed steadily at the minister, who was now looking back again into her bright eyes.

'Please, sir, whose servant are you?' she asked.

'The servant of God and of man,' he answered, solemnly. 'Jessica, I am your servant.'

The child shook her head, and laughed shrilly as she gazed round the room, and at the handsome clothing of the minister's daughters, while she drew her rags closer about her, and shivered a little, as if she felt a sting of the east wind, which was blowing keenly through the streets. The sound of her shrill, childish laugh made the minister's heart ache, and the tears burn under his eyelids.

'Who is God?' asked the child. 'When mother's in a good temper, sometimes she says "God bless me!" Do you know him, please, minister?'

But before there was time to answer, the door into the chapel was opened, and Daniel stood upon the threshold. At first he stared blandly forwards, but then his grave face grew ghastly pale, and he laid his hand upon the door to support himself until he could recover his speech and senses. Jessica also looked about her, scared and irresolute, as if anxious to run away or to hide herself. The minister was the first to speak.

'Jessica,' he said, 'there is a place close under my pulpit where you shall sit, and where I can see you all the time. Be a good girl and listen, and you will hear something about God. Standring, put this little one in front of the pews by the pulpit steps.'

But before she could believe it for very gladness, Jessica found herself inside the chapel, facing the glittering organ, from which a sweet strain of music was sounding. Not far from her Jane and Winny were peeping over the front of their pew, with friendly smiles and glances. It was evident that the minister's elder daughter was anxious about her behaviour, and she made energetic signs to her when to stand up and when to kneel; but Winny was content with smiling at her, whenever her head rose above the top of the pew. Jessica was happy, but not in the least abashed. The ladies and gentlemen were not at all unlike those whom she had often seen when she was a fairy at the theatre;

and very soon her attention was engrossed by the minister, whose eyes often fell upon her, as she gazed eagerly, with uplifted face, upon him. She could scarcely understand a word of what he said, but she liked the tones of his voice, and the tender pity of his face as he looked down upon her. Daniel hovered about a good deal, with an air of uneasiness and displeasure, but she was unconscious of his presence. Jessica was intent upon finding out what a minister and God were.

## Chapter VI

## The First Prayer

When the service was ended, the minister descended the pulpit steps, just as Daniel was about to hurry Jessica away, and taking her by the hand in the face of all the congregation, he led her into the vestry, whither Jane and Winny quickly followed them. He was fatigued with the services of the day, and his pale face was paler than ever, as he placed Jessica before his chair, into which he threw himself with an air of exhaustion: but bowing his head upon his hands, he said in a low but clear tone, 'Lord, these are the lambs of Thy flock. Help me to feed Thy lambs!'

'Children,' he said, with a smile upon his weary face, 'it is no easy thing to know God. But this one thing we know, that he is our Father – my Father and your Father, Jessica. He loves you, and cares for you more than I do for my little girls here.'

He smiled at them and they at him, with an expression which Jessica felt and understood, though it made her sad. She trembled a little, and the minister's ear caught the sound of a faint though bitter sob.

'I never had any father,' she said, sorrowfully.

'God is your Father,' he answered, very gently; 'he knows all about you, because he is present everywhere. We cannot see him, but we have only to speak, and he hears us, and we may ask him for whatever we want.'

'Will he let me speak to him as well as these fine children that are clean and have got nice clothes?' asked Jessica, glancing anxiously at her muddy feet and her soiled and tattered frock.

'Yes,' said the minister, smiling, yet sighing at the same time; 'you may ask him this moment for what you want.'

Jessica gazed round the room with large, wide-open eyes, as if she were seeking to see God: but then she shut her eyelids tightly, and bending her head upon her hands, as she had seen the minister do, she said. 'O God: I want to know about you. And please pay Mr. Daniel for all the warm coffee he's give me.'

Jane and Winny listened with faces of unutterable amazement: but the tears stood in the minister's eyes, and he added 'Amen' to Jessica's first prayer.

# Martha Farquharson Finley (1828–1909)

*Elsie Dinsmore* was a phenomenon, and demonstrates (along with other books such as Elizabeth Wetherell's *The Wide, Wide World*, 1850) how closely allied adults' and children's books were until the end of the nineteenth century, particularly the 'family' romance for female readers.

Famous, or perhaps infamous, for the amount of tearfulness and piety it contains, the book, with its energetic but otherwise suitably conventional heroine, clearly struck a chord. It had 27 sequels, ending with *Grandmother Elsie* (1905) and with variations of the author's name on the title pages: 'Martha Farquharson' and 'Martha Finley (Farquharson)'.

Yet another child whose mother is dead, and whose father is away in Europe, Elsie suffers from the coolness of her relations (although she is much loved by the black servants). On her father's return, however, she wins him over and he becomes (as in this extract) a devotee. We can see here something both of the priggishness of which later readers have accused Elsie, and the shift in the attitudes between different generations. Rather more

disturbing for the modern reader is the perhaps over-intimate attitude of Elsie's father (she eventually marries a man of her father's age). What Gillian Avery (1994) called the 'chaste eroticism' of these books suggests links between religious repression and sexuality, and ironically for religious novelists, it suggests that in them adolescent readers could see a gateway to a forbidden world. Just as Mary Mapes Dodge's books preach self-control while undermining it with her narrative, so Martha Finley exploits (consciously or not) all the features of the romance while roundly condemning it. The 'adolescent' novel is born, with all those ambiguities that have not yet been resolved (if they are resolvable).

Elsie Dinsmore was also popular in Britain, and Martha Finley produced over one hundred children's books. Not everyone regarded them with approval; Robert F. Richards's *Dictionary of American Literature* (1956) dismisses her work as 'incredibly sentimental propaganda pieces to inculcate smugness and piety in the innocent child reader'.

## from *Elsie Dinsmore* (1867)

### CHAPTER IX

*'Keep the Sabbath day to sanctify it, as the Lord thy God hath commanded thee.'* Deut, v. 19.

> *'She is mine own;*
> *And I as rich in having such a jewel*
> *As twenty seas, if all their sand were pearl,*
> *The water nectar, and the rocks pure gold.'*
> SHAKSPEARE, *Two Gentlemen of Verona*

And now happy days had come to the little Elsie. Her father treated her with the tenderest affection, and kept her with him almost constantly, seeming scarcely willing to have her out of his sight for an hour. He took her with him wherever he went in his rides and walks and visits to the neighboring planters.

She was much admired for her beauty and sweetness of disposition, much caressed and flattered, but, through it all, lost none of her native modesty, but was ever the same meek, gentle little girl. She felt grateful for all the kindness she received, and liked to visit with her papa; but her happiest days were spent at home on those rare occasions when they were free from visitors, and she could sit for hours on his knee, or by his side, talking or reading to him, or working at her embroidery, or knitting and listening while he read. He helped her with all her studies, taught her something of botany and geology in their walks, helped her to see and correct the faults of her drawings, sang with her when she played, bought her quantities of new music, and engaged the best masters to instruct her – in short, took a lively interest in all her pursuits and pleasures, gave her every indulgence, and lavished upon her the tenderest caresses. He was very proud of her beauty, her sweetness, her intelligence, and talent; and nothing pleased him better than to hear them spoken of by others in terms of praise.

And Elsie was very happy; the soft eyes grew bright with happiness, and the little face lost its pensive expression, and became as round and rosy and merry as Enna's.

Miss Day went North, expecting to be absent several months, and Elsie's papa took her travelling, spending some time at different watering-places. It was her first journey since she had been old enough to care for such things, and she enjoyed it exceedingly. They left home in July, and did not return until September, so that the little girl had time to rest and recruit, both mentally and physically, and was ready to begin her studies again with zeal and energy; yet it was so pleasant to be her papa's constant companion, and she had so enjoyed her freedom from the restraints of the school-room, that she was not at all sorry to learn, on their arrival at Roselands, that the governess would still be absent for some weeks.

'How bright and happy the child looks!' was Adelaide's remark on the day of their return, as, from the opposite side of the room, she watched the speaking countenance of the little girl, who was giving Enna and the boys an animated description of her journey.

'Yes' said Lora, 'and how entirely she seems to have overcome her fear of her father!' for at that instant Elsie suddenly left the little group, and running to him, leaned confidingly on his knee, while apparently urging some request, which he answered with a smile and a nod of acquiescence; when she left the room, and presently returned carrying a richly bound book of engravings.

Yes, Elsie had lost her fear of her father, and could now talk to him, and tell him her feelings and wishes, as freely as ever Enna did; and no wonder, for in all these weeks he had never given her one harsh word or look; but indeed he had had no occasion to do so, for she was always docile and obedient.

It was Sabbath afternoon – the first Sabbath after their return – and Elsie was in her own room alone with the books she loved best – her Bible, hymnbook, and 'Pilgrim's Progress.'

She had spent a very happy hour in self-examination, reading, and prayer, and was singing to herself in a low tone her favorite hymn,

'I lay my sins on Jesus,'

while turning over the leaves of her Bible to find the story of Elijah, which she had promised to read to Chloe that afternoon – when a child's footsteps were heard coming down the hall, the handle of the door was turned hastily, and then, as it refused to yield, Enna's voice called out in a fretful, imperious tone, 'Open this door, Elsie Dinsmore. I want in, I say.'

Elsie sighed, as she thought, 'There is an end to my nice afternoon,' but she rose at once, and quick crossing the room, opened the door, asking pleasantly 'What do you want, Enna?'

'I *told* you I wanted to come *in*,' replied Enna, saucily, 'and now you've got to tell me a story to amuse me; mamma says so, because you know I've got a cold, and she won't let me go out.'

'Well, Enna,' said Elsie, patiently, 'I am going to read a very beautiful story to mammy, and you are quite welcome to sit here and listen.'

'I sha'n't have it read! I said you were to *tell* it. I don't like to hear reading,' replied Enna in her imperious way, at the same time taking quiet possession of Elsie's little rosewood rocking-chair – a late present from her papa, and highly prized by the little girl on that account – and beginning to scratch with her thumb nail upon the arm.

'Oh! don't scratch my pretty new chair, Enna!' Elsie entreated; 'it is papa's present, and I wouldn't have it spoiled for a great deal.'

'I will: who cares for your old chair?' was the reply in a scornful tone, as she gave another and harder dig with her nail. 'You're a little old maid – so particular with all your things – that's what mamma says you are. Now tell me that story.'

'I will tell you a story if you will stop scratching my chair, Enna,' said Elsie, almost with tears in her eyes. 'I will tell you about Elijah on Mount Carmel, or Belshazzar's feast, or the children in the fiery furnace, or –'

'I sha'n't hear any of those! I don't want any of your old Bible stories,' interrupted Enna, insolently. 'You must tell me that pretty fairy tale Herber Carrington is so fond of.'

'No, Enna; I cannot tell you that *to-day*,' replied Elsie, speaking gently, but very firmly.

'I say you *shall!*' screamed Enna, springing to her feet. 'I'll just go and tell mamma, and she'll *make* you do it.'

'Stay, Enna,' said Elsie, catching her hand to detain her; 'I will tell you any story I know that is suitable for the Sabbath; but I cannot tell the fairy tale to-day, because you know it would be wrong. I will tell it to you to-morrow, though, if you will wait.'

'You're a *bad* girl, and I'll just tell mamma of you,' exclaimed Enna, passionately, jerking her hand away and darting from the room.

'Oh! if papa was only at home,' sighed Elsie, sinking into her rocking-chair, pale and trembling; but she knew that he had gone out riding, and would probably not return for some time; he had invited her to accompany him, but she had begged to be allowed to stay at home, and he had let her have her wish.

As she feared, she was immediately summoned to Mrs. Dinsmore's presence.

'Elsie,' said that lady, severely, 'are you not ashamed of yourself, to refuse Enna such a small favor! especially when the poor child is not well. I must say you are the most selfish, disobliging child I ever saw.'

'I offered to tell her a Bible story, or anything suitable for the Sabbath day,' replied Elsie, meekly, 'but I cannot tell the fairy tale, because it would be wrong.'

'Nonsense! there's no harm at all in telling fairy tales to-day, any more than any other day; that is just an excuse, Elsie,' said Mrs. Dinsmore angrily.

'I don't want her old Bible stories. I won't have them. I want that pretty fairy tale,' sobbed Enna passionately; '*make* her tell it, mamma.'

'Come, come, what is all this fuss about!' asked the elder Mr. Dinsmore, coming in from an adjoining room.

'Nothing,' said his wife, 'except that Enna is not well enough to go out, and wants a fairy story to pass away the time, which Elsie alone is acquainted with, but is too lazy or too self-willed to relate.'

He turned angrily to his little granddaughter.

'Ah! indeed, is that it! Well, there is an old saying, "A bird that *can* sing, and *won't* sing, must be *made* to sing." '

Elsie was opening her lips to speak, but Mrs. Dinsmore bade her be silent, and then went on. 'She pretends it is all on account of conscientious scruples. "It isn't fit for the Sabbath," she says. Now *I* say it is a great piece of impertinence for a child of her years to set up her opinion against yours and mine; and I know very well it is nothing but an excuse, because she doesn't choose to be obliging.'

'Of *course* it is; nothing in the *world* but an excuse,' responded Mr. Dinsmore, hotly.

Elsie's face flushed, and she answered a little indignantly,

'No, grandpa, indeed it is *not* merely an excuse, but –'

'Do you *dare* to contradict me, you impertinent little hussy!' cried the old gentleman, interrupting her in the middle of her sentence; and catching her by the arm, he shook her violently; then picking her up and setting her down hard upon a chair, he said, 'Now, miss, sit you there until your father comes home, then we will see what *he* thinks of such impertinence; and if he doesn't give you the complete whipping you deserve, I miss my guess.'

'Please, grandpa, I –'

'Hold your tongue! don't dare to speak another word until your father comes home,' said he, threateningly. 'If you don't choose to say what you're wanted to, you shall not talk at all.'

Then going to the door, he called a servant and bade him tell 'Mr. Horace,' as soon as he returned, that he wished to see him.

For the next half-hour – and a very long one it seemed to her – Elsie sat there wishing for, and yet dreading her father's coming. Would he inflict upon her the punishment which her grandfather evidently wished her to receive, without pausing to inquire into the merits of the case! or would he listen patiently to *her* story! And even if he did, might he not still think her deserving of punishment! She could not answer these questions to her own satisfaction. A few months ago she would have been certain of a very severe chastisement, and even now she trembled with fear; for though she knew beyond a doubt that he loved her dearly, she knew also that he was a strict and severe disciplinarian, and never excused her faults.

At last her ear caught the sound of his step in the hall, and her heart beat fast and faster as it drew nearer, until he entered, and addressing his father, asked, 'Did you wish to see me, sir?'

'Yes, Horace, I want you to attend to this girl,' replied the old gentleman, with a motion of the head toward Elsie. 'She has been very impertinent to me.'

'What! *Elsie* impertinent! is it possible? I certainly expected better things of her.'

His tone expressed great surprise, and turning to his little daughter, he regarded her with a grave, sad look that brought the tears to her eyes: dearly as she loved him, it seemed almost harder to bear than the old expression of stern severity.

'It is hard to believe,' he said, 'that my little Elsie would be guilty of such conduct; but if she has been, of course she must be punished, for I cannot allow anything of the kind. Go, Elsie, to my dressing-room and remain there until I come to you.'

'Papa —' she began, bursting into tears.

'Hush!' he said, with something of the old sternness; 'not a word; but obey me instantly.'

Then as Elsie went sobbing from the room, he seated himself, and turning to his father, said, 'Now, sir, if you please, I should like to hear the whole story; precisely what Elsie has done and said, and what was the provocation; for *that* must also be taken into the account, in order that I may be able to do her justice.'

'If you do her *justice*, you will whip her well,' remarked his father in a tone of asperity.

Horace colored violently, for nothing aroused his ire sooner than any interference between him and his child; but controlling himself, he replied quite calmly, 'If I find her deserving of punishment, I will not spare her; but I should be sorry indeed to punish her unjustly. Will you be so good as to tell me what she has done?'

Mr. Dinsmore referred him to his wife for the commencement of the trouble, and she made out as bad a case against Elsie as possible: but even then there seemed to her father to be very little to condemn: and when Mrs. Dinsmore was obliged to acknowledge that it was Elsie's refusal to humor Enna in her desire for a particular story which Elsie thought it not best to relate on the Sabbath, he bit his lip with vexation, and told her in a haughty tone, that though he did not approve of Elsie's strict notions regarding such matters, yet he wished her to understand that *his* daughter was not to be made a slave to Enna's whims. If she *chose* to tell her a story, or to do anything else for her amusement, he had no objection, but she was never to be *forced* to do it against her inclinations, and Enna must understand that it was done as a favor, and not at all as her right.

'You are right enough there, Horace,' remarked his father, 'but that does not excuse Elsie for her impertinence to me. In the first place, I must say I agree with my wife in thinking it quite a piece of impertinence for a child of her years to set up her opinion against mine; and besides, she contradicted me flatly.'

He then went on to repeat what he had said, and Elsie's denial of the charge, using her exact words, but quite a different tone, and suppressing the fact that he had interrupted her before she had finished her sentence.

Elsie's tone, though slightly indignant, had still been respectful, but from her grandfather's rehearsal of the scene her father received the impression that she had been exceedingly saucy, and he left the room with the intention of giving her almost as severe a punishment as her grandfather would have prescribed.

On the way up to his room, however, his anger had a little time to cool, and it occurred to him that it would be no more than just to hear *her* side of the story ere he condemned her.

Elsie was seated on a couch at the far side of the room, and as he entered she turned on him a tearful, pleading look, that went straight to his heart.

His face was grave and sad, but there was very little sternness in it, as he sat down and took her in his arms.

For a moment he held her without speaking, while she lifted her eyes timidly to his face. Then he said, as he gently stroked the hair back from her forehead, 'I am very sorry, *very sorry indeed*, to hear so bad an account of my little daughter. I am afraid I shall have to punish her, and I don't like to do it.'

She answered not a word, but burst into tears, and hiding her face on his breast, sobbed aloud.

'I will not condemn you unheard, Elsie,' he said after a moment's pause; 'tell me how you came to be so impertinent to your grandfather.'

'I did not mean to be saucy, papa, indeed I did not,' she sobbed.

'Stop crying then, daughter,' he said kindly, 'and tell me all about it. I know there was some trouble between you and Enna, and I want you to tell me all that occurred, and every word spoken by either of you, as well as all that passed between Mrs. Dinsmore, your grandfather, and yourself. I am very glad that I can trust my little girl to speak the truth. I am quite sure she would not tell a falsehood even to save herself from punishment,' he added tenderly.

'Thank you, dear papa, for saying that,' said Elsie, raising her head and almost smiling through her tears. 'I will *try* to tell it just as it happened.'

She then told her story simply and truthfully, repeating, as he bade her, every word that had passed between Enna and herself, and between her and her grandparents. Her words to her grandfather sounded very different, repeated in her quiet, respectful tones; and when she added that if he would have allowed her, she was going on to explain that it was not any unwillingness to oblige Enna, but the fear of doing wrong, that led her to refuse her request, her father thought that after all she deserved very little blame.

'Do you think I was very saucy, papa?' she asked anxiously, when she had finished her story.

'So much depends upon the tone, Elsie,' he said, 'that I can hardly tell: if you used the same tone in speaking to your grandpa that you did in repeating your words to me just now, I don't think it was *very* impertinent; though the words themselves were not as respectful as they ought to have been. You must always treat my father quite as respectfully as you do me; and I think with him, too, that there is something quite impertinent in a little girl like you setting up her opinion against that of her elders. You must never try it with me, my daughter.'

Elsie hung down her head in silence for a moment, then asked in a tremulous tone, 'Are you going to punish me, papa?'

'Yes,' he said, 'but first I am going to take you down-stairs and make you beg your grandfather's pardon. I see you don't want to do it,' he added, looking keenly into her face, 'but you *must*, and I hope I shall not be obliged to *enforce* obedience to my commands.'

'I will do whatever you bid me, papa,' she sobbed, 'but I did not mean to be saucy. Please, papa, tell me what to say.'

'You must say, Grandpa, I did not intend to be impertinent to you, and I am very sorry for whatever may have seemed saucy in my words or tones: will you please to forgive me, and I will try always to be perfectly respectful in future. You can say all that with truth, I think!'

'Yes, papa, I *am* sorry, and I *do* intend to be respectful to grandpa always,' she answered, brushing away her tears, and putting her hand in his.

He then led her into her grandfather's presence saying, 'Elsie has come to beg your pardon, sir.'

'That is as it should be,' replied the old gentleman, glancing triumphantly at his wife; 'I told her you would not uphold her in any such impertinence.'

'No,' said his son, with some displeasure in his tone; 'I will neither uphold her in wrong doing, nor suffer her to be imposed upon. Speak, my daughter, and say what I bade you.'

Elsie sobbed out the required words.

'Yes, I must forgive you, of course,' replied her grandfather, coldly, 'but I hope your father is not going to let you off without proper punishment.'

'I will attend to that; I certainly intend to punish her *as she deserves*,' said his son, laying a marked emphasis upon the concluding words of his sentence.

Elsie wholly misunderstood him, and so trembled with fear as he led her from the room, that she could scarcely walk; seeing which, he took her in his arms and carried her up-stairs, she sobbing on his shoulder.

He did not speak until he had locked the door, carried her across the room, and seated himself upon the couch again, with her upon his knee.

Then he said, in a soothing tone, as he wiped away her tears and kissed her kindly, 'You need not tremble so, my daughter; I am not going to be severe with you.'

She looked up in glad surprise.

'I said I would punish you as you *deserve*,' he said, with a smile, 'and I intend to keep you shut up here with me until bed-time. I shall not allow you to go down-stairs to tea, and besides, I am going to give you a long lesson to learn, which I shall require you to recite to me quite perfectly before you can go to bed.'

Elsie grew frightened again at the mention of the lesson, for she feared it might be something which she could not conscientiously study on the Sabbath; but all her fear and trouble vanished as she saw her father take up a Bible that lay on the table, and turn over the leaves as though selecting a passage.

Presently he put it into her hands, and pointing to the thirteenth and fourteenth chapters of John's Gospel, bade her carry the book to a low seat by the window, and sit there until she had learned them perfectly.

'O papa! what a nice lesson!' she exclaimed, looking up delightedly into his face; 'but it won't be any punishment, because I love these chapters dearly, and have read them so often that I almost know every word already.'

'Hush, hush!' he said, pretending to be very stern; 'don't tell me that my punishments are *no* punishment, I don't allow you to talk so; just take the book and learn what I bid you; and if you know those two already, you may learn the next.'

Elsie laughed, kissed his hand, and tripped away to her window, while he threw himself down on the couch and took up a newspaper, more as a screen to his face, however, than for the purpose of reading; for he lay there closely watching his little daughter, as she sat in the rich glow of the sunset, with her sweet, grave little face bending over the holy book.

'The darling!' he murmured to himself; 'she is lovely as an angel, and she is *mine*, mine only, mine own precious one; and loves me with her whole soul. Ah! how can I ever find it in my heart to be stern to her! Ah! if *I* were but *half* as good and pure as she is, I should be a better man than I am.' And he heaved a deep sigh.

Half an hour had passed, and still Elsie bent over her book. The tea-bell rang, and Mr. Dinsmore started up, and crossing the room, bent down and stroked her hair.

'Do you know it, darling?' he asked.

'Almost, papa,' and she looked up into his face with a bright, sweet smile, full of affection.

With a sudden impulse he caught her in his arms, and kissing her again and again, said with emotion, 'Elsie, my darling, I love you *too* well; I could never bear to lose you.'

'You must love Jesus better, my own precious papa,' she replied, clasping her little arms around his neck, and returning his caresses.

He held her a moment, and then putting her down, said, 'I shall send you up some supper, and I want you to eat it; don't behave as you did about the bread and water once, a good while ago.'

'Will it be bread and water this time, papa?' she asked, with a smile.

'You will see,' he said laughingly, and quitted the room.

Elsie turned to her book again, but in a few moments was interrupted by the entrance of a servant carrying on a silver waiter a plate of hot, buttered muffins, a cup of jelly, another of hot coffee, and a piece of broiled chicken. Elsie was all astonishment.

'Why, Pomp,' she asked, 'did papa send it?'

'Yes, Miss Elsie, 'deed he did,' replied the servant, with a grin of satisfaction, as he set down his burden. 'I reckon you been berry nice gal dis day or else Marster Horace tink you little bit sick.'

'Papa is very good; and I am much obliged to you too, Pomp,' said the little girl, laying aside her book, and seating herself before the waiter.

'Jes ring de bell, Miss Elsie, ef you want more; and dis chile fotch 'em up; Marster Horace say so hisself.' And the grinning negro bowed himself out, chuckling with delight, for Elsie had always been a great favorite with him.

'Dear papa,' Elsie said, when he came in again and smilingly asked if she had eaten her prison fare, 'what a good supper you sent me! But I thought you didn't allow me such things!'

'Don't you know,' said he playfully, laying his hand upon her head, 'that I am absolute monarch of this small kingdom, and you are not to question my doings or decrees?'

Then in a more serious tone, 'No daughter, I do not allow it as a regular thing, because I do not think it for your good; but for once, I thought it would not hurt you. I know you are not one to presume upon favors, and I wanted to indulge you a little, because I fear my little girl has been made to suffer perhaps more than she quite deserved this afternoon.'

His voice had a very tender tone as he uttered the concluding words, and stooping, he pressed his lips to her forehead.

# John Townsend Trowbridge (1827–1916)

Trowbridge was joint editor of the leading American magazine for children, *Our Young Folks* (from 1865) and worked on *St Nicholas*, which absorbed *Our Young Folks* in 1873. He was the author of the popular 'Jack Hazard' books (1871–). This poem was published in *Our Young Folks* and was often reprinted in illustrated editions. There are, perhaps, echoes here of 'The Pied Piper' (see p. 67) in the energetic verse forms and the ironic non-moral at the end, but this is firmly in the home-grown tradition of the tall tale.

## 'DARIUS GREEN AND HIS FLYING MACHINE' (1867)

If ever there lived a Yankee lad,
Wise or otherwise, good or bad,
Who, seeing the birds fly, didn't jump
With flapping arms from stake or stump,
  Or, spreading the tail
  Of his coat for a sail,
Take a soaring leap from post or rail,
  And wonder why
  *He* couldn't fly,
And flap and flutter and wish and try –
If ever you knew a country dunce
Who didn't try that as often as once,
All I can say is, that's a sign
He never would do for a hero of mine.

An aspiring genius was D. Green:
The son of a farmer, age fourteen;
His body was long and lank and lean,
Just right for flying, as will be seen;
He had two eyes each bright as a bean,
And a freckled nose that grew between,
A little awry – for I must mention
That he had riveted his attention
Upon his wonderful invention,
Twisting his tongue as he twisted the strings,
And working his face as he worked the wings,
And with every turn of gimlet and screw
Turning and screwing his mouth round too,
  Till his nose seemed bent
  To catch the scent,
Around some corner, of new-baked pies,
And his wrinkled cheeks and his squinting eyes
Grew puckered into a queer grimace,
That made him look very droll in the face,
  And also very wise.

And wise he must have been, to do more
Than ever a genius did before,

Excepting Daedalus of yore
And his son Icarus, who wore
    Upon their backs
    Those wings of wax
He had read of in the old almanacs.
Darius was clearly of the opinion
That the air is also man's dominion,
And that, with paddle or fin or pinion,
    We soon or late
    Shall navigate
The azure as now we sail the sea.
The thing looks simple enough to me;
    And if you doubt it,
Hear how Darius reasoned about it.

    'Birds can fly,
    An' why can't I?
    Must we give in,'
    Says he with a grin,
    'That the bluebird an' phoebe
    Are smarter 'n we be?
Jest fold our hands an' see the swaller
An' blackbird an' catbird beat us holler?
Doos the little chatterin', sassy wren,
No bigger 'n my thumb, know more than men?
    Jest show me that!
    Er prove 't the bat
Hez got more brains than's in my hat,
An' I'll back down, an' not till then!'

He argued further: 'Ner I can't see
What's th' use o' wings to a bumble-bee,
Fer to git a livin' with, more 'n to me:
    Ain't my business
    Important's his'n is?

    'That Icarus
    Made a perty muss,
Him an' his daddy Daedalus.
They might a knowed wings made o' wax
Wouldn't stand sun-heat an' hard whacks.
    I'll make mine o' luther,
    Er suthin' er other.'

And he said to himself, as he tinkered and planned:
'But I ain't goin' to show my hand
To nummies that never can understand
The fust idee that's big an' grand.
They'd a laft an' made fun
O' Creation itself afore't was done!'
So he kept his secret from all the rest,
Safely buttoned within his vest;
And in the loft above the shed

Himself he locks, with thimble and thread
And wax and hammer and buckles and screws,
And all such things as geniuses use;
Two bats for patterns, curious fellows!
A charcoal-pot and a pair of bellows;
An old hoop-skirt or two, as well as
Some wire, and several old umbrellas;
A carriage-cover, for tail and wings;
A piece of harness; and straps and strings;
    And a big strong box,
    In which he locks
These and a hundred other things.

His grinning brothers, Reuben and Burke
And Nathan and Jotham and Solomon, lurk
Around the corner to see him work,
Sitting cross-legged, like a Turk,
Drawing the waxed end through with a jerk,
And boring the holes with a comical quirk
Of his wise old head, and a knowing smirk.
But vainly they mounted each other's backs,
And poked through knot-holes and pried through cracks;
With wood from the pile and straw from the stacks
He plugged the knot-holes and caulked the cracks;
And a bucket of water, which one would think
He had brought up into the loft to drink
    When he chanced to be dry,
    Stood always nigh,
    For Darius was sly!
And whenever at work he happened to spy
At chink or crevice a blinking eye,
He let a dipper of water fly.
'Take that! an' ef ever ye git a peep,
Guess ye'll ketch a weasel asleep!'
    And he sings as he locks
    His big strong box:

'The weasel's head is small an' trim,
An' he is little an' long an' slim,
An' quick of motion an' nimble of limb,
    An' ef you'll be
    Advised by me,
Keep wide awake when ye're ketchin' him!'

    So day after day
He stitched and tinkered and hammered away,
    Till at last 'twas done –
The greatest invention under the sun!
'An' now,' says Darius, 'hooray fer some fun!'

    'Twas the Fourth of July,
    And the weather was dry,
And not a cloud was on all the sky,

Save a few light fleeces, which here and there,
        Half mist, half air,
Like foam on the ocean went floating by:
Just as lovely a morning as ever was seen
For a nice little trip in a flying-machine.

Thought cunning Darius: 'Now I shan't go
Along with the fellers to see the show.
I'll say I've got sich a terrible cough!
An' then, when the folks 'ave all gone off,
        I'll hev full swing
        Fer to try the thing,
An' practise a little on the wing.'

'Ain't goin' to see the celebration?'
Says brother Nate. 'No, botheration!
I've got sich a cold – a toothache – I –
My gracious! – feel's though I should fly!'
        Said Jotham, ''Sho!
        Guess ye better go.'
        But Darius said, 'No!
Shouldn't wonder ef you might see me, though,
'Long 'bout noon, ef I git red
O' this jumpin', thumpin' pain in my head.'
For all the while to himself he said:

        'I tell ye what!
I'll fly a few times around the lot,
To see how't seems, then soon's I've got
The hang o' the thing, ez likely's not,
        I'll astonish the nation,
        An' all creation,
By flyin' over the celebration!
Over their heads I'll sail like an eagle;
I'll balance myself on my wings like a seagull;
I'll dance on the chimbleys; I'll stand on the steeple;
I'll flop up to winders an' scare the people!
I'll light on the liberty-pole, an' crow;
An' I'll say to the gawpin' fools below,
        "What world's this 'ere
        That I've come near?"
Fer I'll make 'em believe I'm a chap from the moon;
An' I'll try a race with their ol' balloon!'

        He crept from his bed;
And, seeing the others were gone, he said,
'I'm a gittin' over the cold in my head.'
        And away he sped,
To open the wonderful box in the shed.

His brothers had walked but a little way
When Jotham to Nathan chanced to say,
'What is the feller up to, hey?'

'Don'no – there's suthin' er other to pay,
Er he wouldn't a stayed to hum today.'
Says Burke, 'His toothache's all in his eye!
*He* never'd miss a Fo'th-o'-July,
Ef he hedn't got some machine to try.'
Then Sol, the Little one spoke: 'By darn!
Let's hurry back an' hide in the barn,
An' pay him fer tellin' us that yarn!'
'Agreed!' Through the orchard they creep back,
Along by the fences, behind the stack,
And one by one, through a hole in the wall,
In under the dusty barn they crawl,
Dressed in their Sunday garments all;
And a very astonishing sight was that,
When each in his cobwebbed coat and hat
Came up through the floor like an ancient rat.
   And there they hid;
   And Reuben slid
The fastenings back, and the door undid.
   'Keep dark!' said he,
'While I squint an' see what there is to see.'

As knights of old put on their mail –
   From head to foot
   An iron suit,
Iron jacket and iron boot,
Iron breeches, and on the head
No hat, but an iron pot instead,
   And under the chin the bail
(I believe they called the thing a helm),
Then sallied forth to overwhelm
The dragons and pagans that plagued the realm –
   So this modern knight
   Prepared for flight,
Put on his wings and strapped them tight,
Jointed and jaunty, strong and light;
Buckled them fast to shoulder and hip –
Ten feet they measured from tip to tip!
And a helm had he, but that he wore,
Not on his head like those of yore,
   But more like the helm of a ship.

   'Hush!' Reuben said,
   'He's up in the shed!
He's opened the winder – I see his head!
   He stretches it out,
   An' pokes it about,
Lookin' to see ef the coast is clear,
   An' nobody near –
Guess he don'no who's hid in here! –
He's riggin' a spring-board over the sill!
Stop laffin', Solomon! Burke, keep still!
He's a climbin' out now – Of all the things!

What's he got on? I van, it's wings!
An' that t'other thing? I vum, it's a tail!
An' there he sets like a hawk on a rail!
Steppin' careful, he travels the length
Of his spring-board, and teeters to try its strength.
Now he stretches his wings, like a monstrous bat;
Peeks over his shoulder, this way an' that,
Fer to see ef there's anyone passin' by;
But there's on'y a calf an' a goslin' nigh.
*They* turn up at him a wonderin' eye,
To see – The dragon! he's goin' to fly!
Away he goes! Jimminy! what a jump!
      Flop – flop – an' plump
       To the ground with a thump!
Flutt'rin' an' flound'rin', all in a lump!'

As a demon is hurled by an angel's spear,
Heels over head, to his proper sphere –
Heels over head, and head over heels,
Dizzily down the abyss he wheels –
So fell Darius. Upon his crown,
In the midst of the barnyard, he came down,
In a wonderful whirl of tangled strings,
Broken braces and broken springs,
Broken tail and broken wings,
Shooting-stars, and various things!
Away with a bellow fled the calf,
And what was that? Did the gosling laugh?
      'Tis a merry roar
       From the old barn-door,
And he hears the voice of Jotham crying,
'Say, D'rius! how de you like flyin'?'

Slowly, ruefully, where he lay,
Darius just turned and looked that way,
As he staunched his sorrowful nose with his cuff.
'Wal, I like flyin' well enough,'
He said, 'but there ain't sich a thunderin' sight
O' fun in it when ye come to light.'

*Moral*

I just have room for the moral here,
And this is the moral: Stick to your sphere.
Or if you insist, as you have the right,
On spreading your wings for a loftier flight,
The moral is – Take care how you light.

# Louisa May Alcott (1832–1888)

*Little Women* and *Tom Sawyer* are probably the two most famous American children's books and they have at least one thing in common: they took powerful narrative traditions and transformed them by introducing a plausible illusion of realism.

Louisa May Alcott's *Little Women* revolutionized the domestic tale by bringing together the traditions of religion, sentiment, benevolence and something approaching a deathbed scene (although Beth actually escapes death until the sequel) and grafting them on to believable characters and lifelike situations. While it has, for a century, been read as an anthem to the American domestic way and to the stability of the family, with the father in the traditional place of God (see *The Fairchild Family*, p. 17), it also holds a central conflict between freedom (especially female freedom) and subservience to the male.

The four March sisters, Meg (eldest and most attached to fashionable femininity), Jo (the tomboy individualist writer), Beth (the frail embodiment of virtue) and Amy (the impulsive youngest child), spend a year with their mother, 'Marmee', in the absence (at the civil war) of their father. They work, play, socialize (notably with the rich boy next door) and nurse Beth through a serious illness, and morals are frequently drawn about their behaviour. All of these elements – the domesticity, the relations between the children, and the moral basis of the book – are contained in the chapter reprinted here: 'Experiments'.

There has sprung up, over the last twenty years, something of an academic industry in Alcott studies, concentrating on the often bitter undercurrents of what might appear to be a quite sunny book. *Little Women*, for all the vibrancy of its characterization (especially of Jo March), remains close to the evangelical tradition: it is consciously based on *The Pilgrim's Progress* and almost every episode provides a form of humiliation for the girls. On the other hand, it is an example of an all-female household where men, although important, are essentially peripheral.

Louisa Alcott supported her family, including her liberal and intellectual – but improvident – father, by relentless hack writing (she taught herself to be ambidextrous in order to maintain her output). She moved in respectable American intellectual circles, and knew Thoreau and the Emersons. *Little Women*, a book she undertook reluctantly, and did not much like in the writing, brought financial stability to family life. *Good Wives* (which had various titles), *Little Men* and *Jo's Boys* followed by popular demand, although Alcott was ambivalent about the pressure put upon her by her readership to provide conventional resolutions.

## from *Little Women* (1868)

### CHAPTER 11

### EXPERIMENTS

'The first of June! The Kings are off to the seashore tomorrow, and I'm free, Three months' vacation – how I shall enjoy it!' exclaimed Meg, coming home one warm day to find Jo laid upon the sofa in an unusual state of exhaustion, while Beth took off her dusty boots, and Amy made lemonade for the refreshment of the whole party.

'Aunt March went today, for which, oh, be joyful!' said Jo. 'I was mortally afraid she'd ask me to go with her; if she had, I should have felt as if I ought to do it; but Plumfield is about as gay as a churchyard, you know, and I'd rather be excused. We had a flurry getting the old lady off, and I had a fright every time she spoke to me, for I was in such a hurry to be through that I was uncommonly helpful and sweet, and feared she'd find it impossible to part from me. I quaked till she was fairly in the carriage, and had a final fright, for, as it drove off, she popped out her head, saying, "Josyphine, won't you –?" I didn't hear any more, for I basely turned and fled; I did actually run, and whisked round the corner, where I felt safe.'

'Poor old Jo! she came in looking as if bears were after her,' said Beth, as she cuddled her sister's feet with a motherly air.

'Aunt March is a regular samphire, is she not?' observed Amy, tasting her mixture critically.

'She means *vampire*, not seaweed; but it doesn't matter; it's too warm to be particular about one's parts of speech,' murmured Jo.

'What shall you do all your vacation?' asked Amy, changing the subject, with tact.

'I shall lie abed late and do nothing,' replied Meg, from the depths of the rocking-chair. 'I've been routed up early all winter, and had to spend my days working for other people; so now I'm going to rest and revel to my heart's content.'

'No,' said Jo; 'that dozy way wouldn't suit me. I've laid in a heap of books, and I'm going to improve my shining hours reading on my perch in the old apple-tree, when I'm not having L —'

'Don't say "larks"!' implored Amy, as a return snub for the 'samphire' correction.

'I'll say "nightingales", then, with Laurie; that's proper and appropriate, since he's a warbler.'

'Don't let us do any lessons, Beth, for a while, but play all the time, and rest, as the girls mean to,' proposed Amy.

'Well, I will, if Mother doesn't mind. I want to learn some new songs, and my children need fitting up for the summer; they are dreadfully out of order, and really suffering for clothes.'

'May we, Mother?' asked Meg, turning to Mrs March, who sat sewing in what they called 'Marmee's corner'.

'You may try your experiment for a week, and see how you like it. I think by Saturday night you will find that all play and no work is as bad as all work and no play.'

'Oh, dear, no! it will be delicious, I'm sure,' said Meg, complacently.

'I now propose a toast, as my "friend and pardner, Sairy Gamp", says. Fun for ever, and no grubbing!' cried Jo, rising, glass in hand, as the lemonade went round.

They all drank it merrily, and began the experiment by lounging for the rest of the day. Next morning Meg did not appear till ten o'clock; her solitary breakfast did not taste nice and the room seemed lonely and untidy; for Jo had not filled the vases, Beth had not dusted, and Amy's books lay scattered about. Nothing was neat and pleasant but 'Marmee's corner', which looked as usual; and there Meg sat, to 'rest and read', which meant yawn, and imagine what pretty summer dresses she would get with her salary. Jo spent the morning on the river with Laurie, and the afternoon reading and crying over *The Wide, Wide World*, up in the apple-tree. Beth began by rummaging everything out of the big closet where her family resided; but, getting tired before half done, she left her establishment topsy-turvy, and went to her music, rejoicing that she had no dishes to wash. Amy arranged her bower, put on her best white frock, smoothed her curls, and sat down to draw, under the honeysuckles, hoping someone would see and inquire who the young artist was. As no one appeared but an inquisitive daddy long-legs, who examined her work with interest, she went for a walk, got caught in a shower, and came home dripping.

At tea-time they compared notes, and all agreed that it had been a delightful, though unusually long day. Meg, who went shopping in the afternoon, and got a 'sweet blue muslin', had discovered, after she had cut the breadths off, that it wouldn't wash, which mishap made her slightly cross. Jo had burnt the skin off her nose boating, and got a raging headache by reading too long. Beth was worried by the confusion of her closet, and the difficulty of learning three or four songs at once; and Amy deeply regretted the damage done her frock, for Katy Brown's party was to be the next day, and now, like Flora M'Flimsey, she had 'nothing to wear'. But these were mere trifles; and they assured their mother that the experiment was working finely. She smiled, said nothing, and, with Hannah's help, did their neglected work, keeping home pleasant, and the domestic machinery running smoothly. It was astonishing what a peculiar and uncomfortable state of things was produced by the 'resting and revelling' process. The days kept getting longer and longer; the weather was unusually variable, and so were tempers; an unsettled feeling possessed everyone, and Satan found plenty of mischief for the idle hands to do. As the height of luxury, Meg put out some of her sewing, and then found time hang so heavily that she fell to snipping and spoiling her clothes, in her attempts to furbish them up *à la* Moffat. Jo read till her eyes gave out, and she was sick of books; got so fidgety that even good-natured Laurie had a quarrel with her, and so reduced in spirits that she desperately wished she had gone out with Aunt March. Beth got on pretty well, for she was constantly forgetting that it was to be *all play, and no work*, and fell back into her old ways now and then; but something in the air affected her, and more than once her tranquillity was much disturbed; so much so, that, on one occasion, she actually shook poor dear Joanna, and told her she was a 'fright'. Amy fared worst of all, for her resources were small; and when her sisters left her to amuse and care for herself, she soon found that accomplished and important little self a great burden. She didn't like dolls, fairy tales were childish, and one couldn't draw all the time; tea parties didn't amount to much, neither did picnics, unless very well conducted. 'If one could have a fine house, full of nice girls, or go travelling, the summer would be delightful; but to stay at home with three selfish sisters and a grown-up boy was enough to try the patience of a "Boaz",' complained Miss Malaprop, after several days devoted to pleasure, fretting, and *ennui*.

No one would own that they were tired of the experiment; but, by Friday night, each acknowledged to herself that she was glad the week was nearly done. Hoping to impress the lesson more deeply, Mrs March, who had a good deal of humour, resolved to finish off the trial in an appropriate manner; so she gave Hannah a holiday, and let the girls enjoy the full effect of the play system.

When they got up on Saturday morning, there was no fire in the kitchen, no breakfast in the dining room, and no mother anywhere to be seen.

'Mercy on us! what *has* happened?' cried Jo, staring about her in dismay.

Meg ran upstairs, and soon came back again, looking relieved, but rather bewildered, and a little ashamed.

'Mother isn't sick, only very tired, and she says she is going to stay quietly in her room all day, and let us do the best we can. It's a very queer thing for her to do, she doesn't act a bit like herself; but she says it has been a hard week for her, so we mustn't grumble, but take care of ourselves.'

'That's easy enough, and I like the idea; I'm aching for something to do – that is, some new amusement, you know,' added Jo, quickly.

In fact it *was* an immense relief to them all to have a little work, and they took hold with a will, but soon realized the truth of Hannah's saying, 'Housekeeping ain't no joke.' There was plenty of food in the larder, and, while Beth and Amy set the table, Meg and Jo got breakfast, wondering, as they did so, why servants ever talked about hard work.

'I shall take some up to Mother, though she said we were not to think of her, for she'd take care of herself,' said Meg, who presided, and felt quite matronly behind the teapot.

So a tray was fitted out before anyone began, and taken up with the cook's compliments. The boiled tea was very bitter, the omelette scorched, and the biscuits speckled with saleratus; but Mrs March received her repast with thanks, and laughed heartily over it after Jo was gone.

'Poor little souls, they will have a hard time, I'm afraid; but they won't suffer, and it will do them good,' she said, producing the more palatable viands with which she had provided herself, and disposing of the bad breakfast, so that their feelings might not be hurt – a motherly little deception for which they were grateful.

Many were the complaints below, and great the chagrin of the head cook at her failures. 'Never mind, I'll get the dinner and be servant; you be mistress, keep your hands nice, see company, and give orders,' said Jo, who knew still less than Meg about culinary affairs.

This obliging offer was gladly accepted; and Margaret retired to the parlour, which she hastily put in order by whisking the litter under the sofa, and shutting the blinds, to save the trouble of dusting. Jo, with perfect faith in her own powers, and a friendly desire to make up the quarrel, immediately put a note in the office, inviting Laurie to dinner.

'You'd better see what you have got before you think about having company,' said Meg, when informed of the hospitable but rash act.

'Oh, there's corned beef and plenty of potatoes; and I shall get some asparagus, and a lobster, "for a relish", as Hannah says. We'll have lettuce, and make a salad. I don't know how, but the book tells. I'll have blancmange and strawberries for dessert; and coffee, too, if you want to be elegant.'

'Don't try too many messes, Jo, for you can't make anything but gingerbread and molasses candy fit to eat. I wash my hands of the dinner-party; and since you have asked Laurie on your own responsibility, you may just take care of him.'

'I don't want you to do anything but be civil to him, and help with the pudding. You'll give me your advice if I get in a muddle, won't you?' asked Jo, rather hurt.

'Yes; but I don't know much, except about bread, and a few trifles. You had better ask Mother's leave before you order anything,' returned Meg, prudently.

'Of course I shall; I'm not a fool,' and Jo went off in a huff at the doubts expressed of her powers.

'Get what you like, and don't disturb me; I'm going out to dinner, and can't worry about things at home,' said Mrs March, when Jo spoke to her. 'I never enjoyed housekeeping, and I'm going to take a vacation today, and read, and write, go visiting, and amuse myself.'

The unusual spectacle of her busy mother rocking comfortably and reading, early in the morning, made Jo feel as if some natural phenomenon had occurred; for an eclipse, an earthquake, or a volcanic eruption would hardly have seemed stranger.

'Everything is out of sorts somehow,' she said to herself, going downstairs. 'There's Beth crying; that's a sure sign that something is wrong with this family. If Amy is bothering, I'll shake her.'

Feeling very much out of sorts herself, Jo hurried into the parlour to find Beth sobbing over Pip, the canary, who lay dead in the cage, with his little claws pathetically extended, as if imploring the food for want of which he had died.

'It's all my fault – I forgot him – there isn't a seed or a drop left. O Pip! O Pip! how could I be so cruel to you?' cried Beth, taking the poor thing in her hands, and trying to restore him.

Jo peeped into his half-open eye, felt his little heart, and finding him stiff and cold shook her head, and offered her domino box for a coffin.

'Put him in the oven, and maybe he will get warm and revive,' said Amy, hopefully.

'He's been starved, and he shan't be baked, now he's dead. I'll make him a shroud, and he shall be buried in the garden; and I'll never have another bird, never, my Pip! for I'm too bad to own one,' murmured Beth, sitting on the floor with her pet folded in her hands.

'The funeral shall be this afternoon, and we will all go. Now, don't cry, Betty; it's a pity, but nothing goes right this week, and Pip has had the worst of the experiment. Make the shroud, and lay him in my box; and, after the dinner party, we'll have a nice little funeral,' said Jo, beginning to feel as if she had undertaken a good deal.

Leaving the others to console Beth, she departed to the kitchen, which was in a most discouraging state of confusion. Putting on a big apron she fell to work, and got the dishes piled up ready for washing, when she discovered that the fire was out. 'Here's a sweet prospect!' muttered Jo, slamming the stove-door open, and poking vigorously among the cinders.

Having rekindled the fire, she thought she would go to market while the water heated. The walk revived her spirits; and flattering herself that she had made good bargains, she trudged home again, after buying a very young lobster, some very old asparagus, and two boxes of acid strawberries. By the time she got cleared up the dinner arrived, and the stove was red-hot. Hannah had left a pan of bread to rise, Meg had worked it up early, set it on the hearth for a second rising, and forgotten it. Meg was entertaining Sallie Gardiner in the parlour, when the door flew open, and a floury, crocky, flushed, and dishevelled figure appeared, demanding tartly:

'I say, isn't bread "riz" enough when it runs over the pans?'

Sallie began to laugh; but Meg nodded, and lifted her eyebrows as high as they would go, which caused the apparition to vanish, and put the sour bread into the oven without further delay. Mrs March went out, after peeping here and there to see how matters went, also saying a word of comfort to Beth, who sat making a winding sheet, while the dear departed lay in state in the domino box. A strange sense of helplessness fell upon the girls as the grey bonnet vanished round the corner; and despair seized them when, a few minutes later, Miss Crocker appeared, and said she'd come to dinner. Now, this lady was a thin, yellow spinster, with a sharp nose and inquisitive eyes, who saw everything, and gossiped about all she saw. They disliked her, but had been taught to be kind to her, simply because she was old and poor, and had few friends. So Meg gave her the easy-chair, and tried to entertain her, while she asked questions, criticized everything, and told stories of the people who she knew.

Language cannot describe the anxieties, experiences, and exertions which Jo underwent that morning; and the dinner she served up became a standing joke. Fearing to ask any more advice, she did her best alone, and discovered that something more than energy and goodwill is necessary to make a cook. She boiled the asparagus for an hour, and was grieved to find the heads cooked off and the stalks harder than ever. The bread burnt black, for the salad-dressing so aggravated her that she let everything else go till she had convinced herself that she could not make it fit to eat. The lobster was a scarlet mystery to her, but she hammered and poked till it was unshelled, and its meagre proportions concealed in a grove of lettuce leaves. The potatoes had to be hurried, not to keep the asparagus waiting, and were not done at last. The blancmange was lumpy, and the strawberries not as ripe as they looked, having been skilfully 'deaconed'.

'Well, they can eat beef, and bread and butter, if they are hungry; only it's mortifying to have to spend your whole morning for nothing,' thought Jo, as she rang the bell half an hour later than usual, and stood, hot, tired, and dispirited, surveying the feast spread for Laurie, accustomed to all sorts of elegance, and Miss Crocker, whose curious eyes would mark all failures, and whose tattling tongue would report them far and wide.

Poor Jo would gladly have gone under the table, as one thing after another was tasted and left; while Amy giggled, Meg looked distressed, Miss Crocker pursed up her lips, and Laurie talked and laughed with all his might, to give a cheerful tone to the festive scene. Jo's one strong point was the fruit, for she had sugared it well, and had a pitcher of rich cream to eat with it. Her hot cheeks cooled a trifle, and she drew a long breath, as the pretty glass plates went round, and everyone looked graciously at the little rosy islands floating in a sea of cream. Miss Crocker tasted first, made a wry face, and drank some water hastily. Jo, who had refused, thinking there might not be enough, for they dwindled sadly after the picking over, glanced at Laurie, but he was eating away manfully, though there was a slight pucker about his mouth, and he kept his eye fixed on his plate. Amy, who was fond of delicate fare, took a heaping spoonful, choked, hid her face in her napkin, and left the table precipitately.

'Oh, what is it?' exclaimed Jo, trembling.

'Salt instead of sugar, and the cream is sour,' replied Meg, with a tragic gesture.

Jo uttered a groan, and fell back in her chair; remembering that she had given a last hasty powdering to the berries out of one of the two boxes on the kitchen table, and had neglected to put the milk in the refrigerator. She turned scarlet, and was on the verge of crying, when she met Laurie's eyes, which *would* look merry in spite of his heroic efforts; the comical side of the affair suddenly struck her, and she laughed till the tears ran down her cheeks. So did everyone else, even 'Croaker', as the girls called the old lady; and the unfortunate dinner ended gaily, with bread and butter, olives, and fun.

'I haven't strength of mind enough to clear up now, so we will sober ourselves with a funeral,' said Jo, as they rose; and Miss Crocker made ready to go, being eager to tell the new story at another friend's dinner-table.

They did sober themselves for Beth's sake; Laurie dug a grave under the ferns in the grove, little Pip was laid in, with many tears, by his tender-hearted mistress, and covered with moss, while a wreath of violets and chickweed was hung on the stone which bore his epitaph, composed by Jo while she struggled with the dinner:

> Here lies Pip March,
> Who died the 7th of June;
> Loved and lamented sore,
> And not forgotten soon.

At the conclusion of the ceremonies, Beth retired to her room, overcome with emotion and lobster; but there was no place of repose, for the beds were not made, and she found her grief much assuaged by beating up pillows and putting things in order. Meg helped Jo clear away the remains of the feast, which took half the afternoon, and left them so tired that they agreed to be contented with tea and toast for supper. Laurie took Amy for a drive, which was a deed of charity, for the sour cream seemed to have had a bad effect upon her temper. Mrs March came home to find the three older girls hard at work in the middle of the afternoon, and a glance at the closet gave her an idea of the success of one part of the experiment.

Before the housewives could rest several people called, and there was a scramble to get ready to see them; then tea must be got, errands done; and one or two necessary bits of sewing neglected till the last minute. As twilight fell, dewy and still, one by one they gathered in the porch where the June roses were budding beautifully, and each groaned or sighed as she sat down as if tired or troubled.

'What a dreadful day this has been!' began Jo, usually the first to speak.

'It has seemed shorter than usual, but *so* uncomfortable,' said Meg.

'Not a bit like home,' added Amy.

'It can't seem so without Marmee and little Pip,' sighed Beth, glancing with full eyes at the empty cage above her head.

'Here's Mother, dear; and you shall have another bird tomorrow, if you want it.'

As she spoke, Mrs March came and took her place among them, looking as if her holiday had not been much pleasanter than theirs.

'Are you satisfied with your experiment, girls, or do you want another week of it?' she asked, as Beth nestled up to her, and the rest turned towards her with brightening faces, as flowers turn towards the sun.

'I don't,' cried Jo, decidedly.

'Nor I,' echoed the others.

'You think, then, that it is better to have a few duties, and live a little for others, do you?'

'Lounging and larking doesn't pay,' observed Jo, shaking her head. 'I'm tired of it, and mean to go to work at something right off.'

'Suppose you learn plain cooking; that's a useful accomplishment which no woman should be without,' said Mrs March, laughing inaudibly at the recollection of Jo's dinner-party; for she had met Miss Crocker, and heard her account of it.

'Mother, did you go away and let everything be, just to see how we'd get on?' cried Meg, who had had suspicions all day.

'Yes; I wanted you to see how the comfort of all depends on each doing her share faithfully. While Hannah and I did your work you got on pretty well, though I don't think you were very happy or amiable; so I thought, as a little lesson, I would show you what happens when everyone thinks only of herself. Don't you feel that it is pleasanter to help one another, to have daily duties which make leisure sweet when it comes, and to bear and forbear, that home may be comfortable and lovely to us all?'

'We do, Mother, we do!' cried the girls.

'Then let me advise you to take up your little burdens again; for though they seem heavy sometimes, they are good for us, and lighten as we learn to carry them. Work is wholesome, and there is plenty for everyone; it keeps us from *ennui* and mischief, is good for health and spirits, and gives us a sense of power and independence better than money or fashion.'

'We'll work like bees, and love it too; see if we don't!' said Jo. 'I'll learn plain cooking for my holiday task; and the next dinner-party I have shall be a success.'

'I'll make the set of shirts for Father, instead of letting you do it, Marmee. I can and I will, though I'm not fond of sewing; that will be better than fussing over my own things, which are plenty nice enough as they are,' said Meg.

'I'll do my lessons every day, and not spend so much time with my music and dolls. I am a stupid thing, and ought to be studying, not playing,' was Beth's resolution; while Amy followed their example by heroically declaring, 'I shall learn to make buttonholes, and attend to my parts of speech.'

'Very good! then I am quite satisfied with the experiment, and fancy that we shall not have to repeat it; only don't go to the other extreme, and delve like slaves. Have regular hours for work and play; make each day both useful and pleasant, and prove that you understand the worth of time by employing it well. Then youth will be delightful, old age will bring few regrets, and life become a beautiful success, in spite of poverty.'

'We'll remember, Mother!' and they did.

# Charles Dickens (1812–1870)

Although some of Charles Dickens's books have been solidly popular with children, a good case could be made that apart from *A Child's History of England* (1851–3) Dickens never really wrote *for* children. His most famous Christmas story, *A Christmas Carol*, belongs to that category of the 'family' story so common in films today, which is to say that it has a double audience, and primarily an adult one.

*A Holiday Romance* should best be classified with Kenneth Grahame's *The Golden Age*: it is not so much a transcription of child-writing, but a sentimental version of childhood, directed at adults (for their own ends). In the 'Introductory Romance from the Pen of William Tinkling, esq', the (perhaps somewhat precious) situation is set up: children writing stories with childish mistakes and pretensions. The tone was clearly highly influential, resting somewhere between Grahame's sophisticated (but arguably demeaning) use of it, and Edith Nesbit's 'Bastable' novels where the viewpoint is that of the children. As William writes: 'This beginning-part is not made out of anybody's head, you know. It's real. You must believe this beginning-part more than what comes after, else you won't understand how what comes after came to be written.' How successful Dickens was in capturing children's writing styles might be judged by comparing this with that literary oddity, the nine-year-old Daisy Ashford's *The Young Visitors* (1919).

Part 2 of *A Holiday Romance*, the story of the magic fishbone, has proved to be the most popular of the stories. It is probably best read not merely as a pastiche of the Grimms, but also a reflection on how children perceive (or were thought to perceive) the tales.

## from *A Holiday Romance* (1868)

## PART II

## ROMANCE. FROM THE PEN OF MISS ALICE RAINBIRD[1]

There was once a king, and he had a queen; and he was the manliest of his sex, and she was the loveliest of hers. The king was, in his private profession, under government. The queen's father had been a medical man out of town.

They had nineteen children, and were always having more. Seventeen of these children took care of the baby; and Alicia, the eldest, took care of them all. Their ages varied from seven years to seven months.

Let us now resume our story.

One day the king was going to the office, when he stopped at the fishmonger's to buy a pound and a half of salmon not too near the tail, which the queen (who was a careful housekeeper) had requested him to send home. Mr. Pickles, the fishmonger, said, 'Certainly, Sir; is there any other article? Good morning.'

The king went on towards the office in a melancholy mood; for quarter-day was such a long way off, and several of the dear children were growing out of their clothes. He had not proceeded far, when Mr. Pickles's errand-boy came running after him, and said, 'Sir, you didn't notice the old lady in our shop.'

'What old lady?' inquired the king. 'I saw none.'

Now the king had not seen any old lady, because this old lady had been invisible to him, though visible to Mr. Pickles's boy. Probably because he messed and splashed the water about to that degree, and flopped the pairs of soles down in that violent manner, that, if she had not been visible to him, he would have spoilt her clothes.

---

1 Aged seven.

Just then the old lady came trotting up. She was dressed in shot-silk of the richest quality, smelling of dried lavender.

'King Watkins the First, I believe?' said the old lady.

'Watkins,' replied the king, 'is my name.'

'Papa, if I am not mistaken, of the beautiful Princess Alicia?' said the old lady.

'And of eighteen other darlings,' replied the king.

'Listen. You are going to the office,' said the old lady.

It instantly flashed upon the king that she must be a fairy, or how could she know that?

'You are right,' said the old lady, answering his thoughts. 'I am the good Fairy Grandmarina. Attend! When you return home to dinner, politely invite the Princess Alicia to have some of the salmon you bought just now.'

'It may disagree with her,' said the king.

The old lady became so very angry at this absurd idea, that the king was quite alarmed, and humbly begged her pardon.

'We hear a great deal too much about this thing disagreeing, and that thing disagreeing,' said the old lady, with the greatest contempt it was possible to express. 'Don't be greedy. I think you want it all yourself.'

The king hung his head under this reproof, and said he wouldn't talk about things disagreeing any more.

'Be good, then,' said the Fairy Grandmarina, 'and don't. When the beautiful Princess Alicia consents to partake of the salmon, – as I think she will, – you will find she will leave a fish-bone on her plate. Tell her to dry it, and to rub it, and to polish it till it shines like mother-of-pearl, and to take care of it as a present from me.'

'Is that all?' asked the king.

'Don't be impatient, Sir,' returned the Fairy Grandmarina, scolding him severely. 'Don't catch people short, before they have done speaking. Just the way with you grown-up persons. You are always doing it.'

The king again hung his head, and said he wouldn't do so any more.

'Be good, then,' said the Fairy Grandmarina, 'and don't! Tell the Princess Alicia, with my love, that the fish-bone is a magic present which can only be used once; but that it will bring her, that once, whatever she wishes for, PROVIDED SHE WISHES FOR IT AT THE RIGHT TIME. That is the message. Take care of it.'

The king was beginning, 'Might I ask the reason?' when the fairy became absolutely furious.

'*Will* you be good, Sir?' she exclaimed, stamping her foot on the ground. 'The reason for this, and the reason for that, indeed! You are always wanting the reason. No reason. There! Hoity toity me! I am sick of your grown-up reasons.'

The king was extremely frightened by the old lady's flying into such a passion, and said he was very sorry to have offended her, and he wouldn't ask for reasons any more.

'Be good, then,' said the old lady, 'and don't!'

With those words, Grandmarina vanished, and the king went on and on and on, till he came to the office. There he wrote and wrote and wrote, till it was time to go home again. Then he politely invited the Princess Alicia, as the fairy had directed him, to partake of the salmon. And when she had enjoyed it very much, he saw the fish-bone on her plate, as the fairy had told him he would, and he delivered the fairy's message, and the Princess Alicia took care to dry the bone, and to rub it, and to polish it, till it shone like mother-of-pearl.

And so, when the queen was going to get up in the morning, she said, 'O, dear me, dear me; my head, my head!' and then she fainted away.

The Princess Alicia, who happened to be looking in at the chamber-door, asking about breakfast, was very much alarmed when she saw her royal mamma in this state, and she rang the bell for Peggy, which was the name of the lord chamberlain. But remembering where the smelling-bottle was, she climbed on a chair and got it; and after that she climbed on another chair by the bedside, and held the smelling-bottle to the queen's nose; and after that she jumped down and got some water; and after that she jumped up again and wetted the queen's forehead; and, in short, when the lord chamberlain came in, that dear old woman said to the little princess, 'What a trot you are! I couldn't have done it better myself!'

But that was not the worst of the good queen's illness. O, no! She was very ill indeed, for a long time. The Princess Alicia kept the seventeen young princes and princesses quiet, and dressed and undressed and danced the baby, and made the kettle boil, and heated the soup, and swept the hearth, and poured out the medicine, and nursed the queen, and did all that ever she could, and was as busy, busy, busy as busy could be; for there were not many servants at that palace for three reasons: because the king was short of money, because a rise in his office never seemed to come, and because quarter-day was so far off that it looked almost as far off and as little as one of the stars.

But on the morning when the queen fainted away, where was the magic fish-bone? Why, there it was in the Princess Alicia's pocket! She had almost taken it out to bring the queen to life again, when she put it back, and looked for the smelling-bottle.

After the queen had come out of her swoon that morning, and was dozing, the Princess Alicia hurried upstairs to tell a most particular secret to a most particularly confidential friend of hers, who was a duchess. People did suppose her to be a doll; but she was really a duchess, though nobody knew it except the princess.

This most particular secret was the secret about the magic fish-bone, the history of which was well known to the duchess, because the princess told her everything. The princess kneeled down by the bed on which the duchess was lying, full-dressed and wide awake, and whispered the secret to her. The duchess smiled and nodded. People might have supposed that she never smiled and nodded; but she often did, though nobody knew it except the princess.

Then the Princess Alicia hurried downstairs again, to keep watch in the queen's room. She often kept watch by herself in the queen's room; but every evening, while the illness lasted, she sat there watching with the king. And every evening the king sat looking at her with a cross look, wondering why she never brought out the magic fish-bone. As often as she noticed this, she ran upstairs, whispered the secret to the duchess over again, and said to the duchess besides, 'They think we children never have a reason or a meaning!' And the duchess, though the most fashionable duchess that ever was heard of, winked her eye.

'Alicia,' said the king, one evening, when she wished him good night.

'Yes, papa.'

'What is become of the magic fish-bone?'

'In my pocket, papa!'

'I thought you had lost it?'

'O, no, papa!'

'Or forgotten it?'

'No, indeed, papa.'

And so another time the dreadful little snapping pug-dog, next door, made a rush at one of the young princes as he stood on the steps coming home from school, and terrified him out of his wits; and he put his hand through a pane of glass, and bled, bled, bled. When the seventeen other young princes and princesses saw him bleed, bleed, bleed, they were terrified out of their wits too, and screamed themselves black in their seventeen faces all at once. But the Princess Alicia put her hands over all their seventeen mouths, one after another, and persuaded them to be quiet because of the sick queen. And then she put the wounded prince's hand in a basin of fresh cold water, while they stared with their twice seventeen are thirty-four, put down four and carry three, eyes, and then she looked in the hand for bits of glass, and there were fortunately no bits of glass there. And then she said to two chubby-legged princes, who were sturdy though small, 'Bring me in the royal rag-bag: I must snip and stitch and cut and contrive.' So these two young princes tugged at the royal rag-bag, and lugged it in; and the Princess Alicia sat down on the floor, with a large pair of scissors and a needle and thread, and snipped and stitched and cut and contrived, and made a bandage, and put it on, and it fitted beautifully; and so when it was all done, she saw the king her papa looking on by the door.

'Alicia.'

'Yes, papa.'

'What have you been doing?'

'Snipping, stitching, cutting, and contriving, papa.'

'Where is the magic fish-bone?'

'In my pocket, papa.'

'I thought you had lost it?'

'O, no, papa.'

'Or forgotten it?'

'No, indeed, papa.'

After that, she ran upstairs to the duchess, and told her what had passed, and told her the secret over again; and the duchess shook her flaxen curls, and laughed with her rosy lips.

Well! and so another time the baby fell under the grate. The seventeen young princes and princesses were used to it; for they were almost always falling under the grate or down the stairs; but the baby was not used to it yet, and it gave him a swelled face and a black eye. The way the poor little darling came to tumble was, that he was out of the Princess Alicia's lap just as she was sitting, in a great coarse apron that quite smothered her, in front of the kitchen-fire, beginning to peel the turnips for the broth for dinner; and the way she came to be doing that was, that the king's cook had run away that morning with her own true love, who was a very tall but very tipsy soldier. Then the seventeen young princes and princesses, who cried at everything that happened, cried and roared. But the Princess Alicia (who couldn't help crying a little herself) quietly called to them to be still, on account of not throwing back the queen upstairs, who was fast getting well, and said, 'Hold your tongues, you wicked little monkeys, every one of you, while I examine baby!' Then she examined baby, and found that he hadn't broken anything; and she held cold iron to his poor dear eye, and smoothed his poor dear face, and he presently fell asleep in her arms. Then she said to the seventeen princes and princesses, 'I am afraid to let him down yet, lest he should wake and feel pain; be good, and you shall all be cooks.' They jumped for joy when they heard that, and began making themselves cooks' caps out of old newspapers. So to one she gave the salt-box, and to one she gave the barley, and to one she gave the herbs, and to one she gave the turnips, and to one she gave the carrots, and to one she gave the onions, and to one she gave the spice-box, till they were all cooks, and all running about at work, she sitting in the middle, smothered in the great coarse apron, nursing baby. By-and-by the broth was done; and the baby woke up, smiling like an angel, and was trusted to the sedatest princess to hold, while the other princes and princesses were squeezed into a far-off corner to look at the Princess Alicia turning out the saucepanful of broth, for fear (as they were always getting into trouble) they should get splashed and scalded. When the broth came tumbling out, steaming beautifully, and smelling like a nosegay good to eat, they clapped their hands. That made the baby clap his hands; and that, and his looking as if he had a comic toothache, made all the princes and princesses laugh. So the Princess Alicia said, 'Laugh and be good; and after dinner we will make him a nest on the floor in a corner, and he shall sit in his nest and see a dance of eighteen cooks.' That delighted the young princes and princesses, and they ate up all the broth, and washed up all the plates and dishes, and cleared away, and pushed the table into a corner; and then they in their cooks' caps, and the Princess Alicia in the smothering coarse apron that belonged to the cook that had run away with her own true love that was the very tall but very tipsy soldier, danced a dance of eighteen cooks before the angelic baby, who forgot his swelled face and his black eye, and crowed with joy.

And so then, once more the Princess Alicia saw King Watkins the First, her father, standing in the doorway looking on, and he said, 'What have you been doing, Alicia?'

'Cooking and contriving, papa.'

'What else have you been doing, Alicia?'

'Keeping the children light-hearted, papa.'

'Where is the magic fish-bone, Alicia?'

'In my pocket, papa.'

'I thought you had lost it?'

'O, no, papa!'

'Or forgotten it?'

'No, indeed, papa.'

The king then sighed so heavily, and seemed so low-spirited, and sat down so miserably, leaning his head upon his hand, and his elbow upon the kitchen-table pushed away in the corner, that the seventeen princes and princesses crept softly out of the kitchen, and left him alone with the Princess Alicia and the angelic baby.

'What is the matter, papa?'

'I am dreadfully poor, my child.'

'Have you no money at all, papa?'

'None, my child.'

'Is there no way of getting any, papa?'

'No way,' said the king. 'I have tried very hard, and I have tried all ways.'

When she heard those last words, the Princess Alicia began to put her hand into the pocket where she kept the magic fish-bone.

'Papa,' said she, 'when we have tried very hard, and tried all ways, we must have done our very, very best?'

'No doubt, Alicia.'

'When we have done our very, very best, papa, and that is not enough, then I think the right time must have come for asking help of others.' This was the very secret connected with the magic fish-bone, which she had found out for herself from the good Fairy Grandmarina's words, and which she had so often whispered to her beautiful and fashionable friend, the duchess.

So she took out of her pocket the magic fish-bone, that had been dried and rubbed and polished till it shone like mother-of-pearl; and she gave it one little kiss, and wished it was quarter-day. And immediately it *was* quarter-day; and the king's quarter's salary came rattling down the chimney, and bounced into the middle of the floor.

But this was not half of what happened, – no, not a quarter; for immediately afterwards the good Fairy Grandmarina came riding in, in a carriage and four (peacocks), with Mr. Pickles's boy up behind, dressed in silver and gold, with a cocked-hat, powdered-hair, pink silk stockings, a jewelled cane, and a nosegay. Down jumped Mr. Pickles's boy, with his cocked-hat in his hand, and wonderfully polite (being entirely changed by enchantment), and handed Grandmarina out; and there she stood, in her rich shot-silk smelling of dried lavender, fanning herself with a sparkling fan.

'Alicia, my dear,' said this charming old fairy, 'how do you do? I hope I see you pretty well? Give me a kiss.'

The Princess Alicia embraced her; and then Grandmarina turned to the king, and said rather sharply, 'Are you good?'

The king said he hoped so.

'I suppose you know the reason *now*, why my god-daughter here,' kissing the princess again, 'did not apply to the fish-bone sooner?' said the fairy.

The king made a shy bow.

'Ah! but you didn't *then*?' said the fairy.

The king made a shyer bow.

'Any more reasons to ask for?' said the fairy.

The king said, No, and he was very sorry.

'Be good, then,' said the fairy, 'and live happy ever afterwards.'

Then Grandmarina waved her fan, and the queen came in most splendidly dressed; and the seventeen young princes and princesses, no longer grown out of their clothes, came in, newly fitted out from top to toe, with tucks in everything to admit of its being let out. After that, the fairy tapped the Princess Alicia with her fan; and the smothering coarse apron flew away, and she appeared exquisitely dressed, like a little bride, with a wreath of orange-flowers and a silver veil. After that, the kitchen dresser changed of itself into a wardrobe, made of beautiful woods and gold and looking-glass, which was full of dresses of all sorts, all for her and all exactly fitting her. After that, the angelic baby came in, running alone, with his face and eye not a bit the worse, but much the better. Then Grandmarina begged to be introduced to the duchess; and, when the duchess was brought down, many compliments passed between them.

A little whispering took place between the fairy and the duchess; and then the fairy said out loud, 'Yes, I thought she would have told you.' Grandmarina then turned to the king and queen, and said, 'We are going in search of Prince Certainpersonio. The pleasure of your company is requested at church in half an hour precisely.' So she and the Princess Alicia got into the carriage; and Mr. Pickles's boy handed in the duchess, who sat by herself on the opposite seat; and then Mr. Pickles's boy put up the steps and got up behind, and the peacocks flew away with their tails behind.

Prince Certainpersonio was sitting by himself, eating barley-sugar, and waiting to be ninety. When he saw the peacocks, followed by the carriage, coming in at the window, it immediately occurred to him that something uncommon was going to happen.

'Prince,' said Grandmarina, 'I bring you your bride.'

The moment the fairy said those words, Prince Certainpersonio's face left off being sticky, and his jacket and corduroys changed to peach-bloom velvet, and his hair curled, and a cap and feather flew in like a bird and settled on his head. He got into the carriage by the fairy's invitation; and there he renewed his acquaintance with the duchess, whom he had seen before.

In the church were the prince's relations and friends, and the Princess Alicia's relations and friends, and the seventeen princes and princesses, and the baby, and a crowd of the neighbours. The marriage was beautiful beyond expression. The duchess was bridesmaid, and beheld the ceremony from the pulpit, where she was supported by the cushion of the desk.

Grandmarina gave a magnificent wedding-feast afterwards, in which there was everything and more to eat, and everything and more to drink. The wedding-cake was delicately ornamented with white satin ribbons, frosted silver, and white lilies, and was forty-two yards round.

When Grandmarina had drunk her love to the young couple, and Prince Certainpersonio had made a speech, and everybody had cried, Hip, hip, hip, hurrah! Grandmarina announced to the king and queen that in future there would be eight quarter-days in every year, except in leap-year, when there would be ten. She then turned to Certainpersonio and Alicia, and said, 'My dears, you will have thirty-five children, and they will all be good and beautiful. Seventeen of your children will be boys, and eighteen will be girls. The hair of the whole of your children will curl naturally. They will never have the measles, and will have recovered from the whooping-cough before being born.'

On hearing such good news, everybody cried out 'Hip, hip, hip, hurrah!' again.

'It only remains,' said Grandmarina in conclusion, 'to make an end of the fish-bone.'

So she took it from the hand of the Princess Alicia, and it instantly flew down the throat of the dreadful little snapping pug-dog, next door, and choked him, and he expired in convulsions.

# Horatio Alger Jr (1832–1899)

It has been said that 'Oliver Optic's' major achievement was to publish Alger's first serial in the magazine *The Student and Schoolmate* (it was rewritten for publication in book form). The genre of the 'rags to riches' story has never been better exemplified than by Alger's books. The potent mixture of the American ethic of social optimism and the highly popular street-urchin story, repeated almost endlessly, made Alger's name. Whereas in the 1840s there was serious concern by writers such as Sara Parton ('Fanny Fern') for the many thousands of destitute children on the streets of American cities, by the 1850s, this had been replaced by the kind of middle-class and fundamentally sentimentalized concern common in Britain.

However, Alger had a genuine commitment to reform (he was chaplain of the Newsboys' Lodging House in New York). He wrote:

The author hopes that, while the volumes in this series may prove interesting as stories, they may also have the effect of enlisting the sympathies of his readers in [*sic*] behalf of the unfortunate children whose life is described, and of leading them to co-operate with the praiseworthy efforts now making by the Children's Aid Society and other organizations to ameliorate their condition.

The key point about Alger's work is that he was aiming not (as that preface might suggest) at the middle classes, but at the working classes; in fact at the very boys whom he took as his heroes. The ethics of giving the fantasy of improbable good fortune to such boys is debatable, but there is no doubt that Alger epitomized one aspect of the American Dream.

Dick, working his way (he hopes) upwards as a shoe-shine boy, has been showing a rich boy, Frank Whitney, around New York, and is rewarded with a 'half worn' suit of clothes. At this point (in the extract reprinted below) he encounters the bully, Micky Maguire; Dick's behaviour is a complex blend of the approved motivations of the deserving poor and the upright young hero of fiction; and there is no doubt about the author's approving attitude to capitalism.

*Ragged Dick* was serialized in 1867 and appeared in book form in 1868. Despite his success, producing over 130 boys' books, Alger regarded himself as a literary failure.

## from *Ragged Dick; or, Street Life in New York with the Boot Blacks* (1868)

### CHAPTER XIV

### A BATTLE AND A VICTORY

'What's that for?' demanded Dick, turning round to see who had struck him.

'You're gettin' mighty fine!' said Micky Maguire, surveying Dick's new clothes with a scornful air.

There was something in his words and tone, which Dick, who was disposed to stand up for his dignity, did not at all relish.

'Well, what's the odds if I am?' he retorted. 'Does it hurt you any?'

'See him put on airs, Jim,' said Micky, turning to his companion. 'Where'd you get them clo'es?'

'Never mind where I got 'em. Maybe the Prince of Wales gave 'em to me.'

'Hear him, now, Jim,' said Micky. 'Most likely he stole 'em.'

'Stealin' ain't in *my* line.'

It might have been unconscious the emphasis which Dick placed on the word 'my.' At any rate Micky chose to take offence.

'Do you mean to say *I* steal?' he demanded, doubling up his fist, and advancing towards Dick in a threatening manner.

'I don't say anything about it,' answered Dick, by no means alarmed at this hostile demonstration. 'I know you've been to the Island twice. P'r'aps 'twas to make a visit along of the Mayor and Aldermen. Maybe you was a innocent victim of oppression. I ain't a goin' to say.'

Micky's freckled face grew red with wrath, for Dick had only stated the truth.

'Do you mean to insult me?' he demanded shaking the fist already doubled up in Dick's face. 'Maybe you want a lickin'?'

'I ain't partic'larly anxious to get one,' said Dick, coolly. 'They don't agree with my constitution which is nat'rally delicate. I'd rather have a good dinner than a lickin' any time.'

'You're afraid,' sneered Micky. 'Isn't he, Jim?'

'In course he is.'

'P'r'aps I am,' said Dick, composedly, 'but it don't trouble me much.'

'Do you want to fight?' demanded Micky, encouraged by Dick's quietness, fancying he was afraid to encounter him.

'No, I don't,' said Dick. 'I ain't fond of fightin'. It's a very poor amusement, and very bad for the complexion, 'specially for the eyes and nose, which is apt to turn red, white, and blue.'

Micky misunderstood Dick, and judged from the tenor of his speech that he would be an easy victim. As he knew, Dick very seldom was concerned in any street fight, – not from cowardice, as he imagined, but because he had too much good sense to do so. Being quarrelsome, like all bullies, and supposing that he was more than a match for our hero, being about two inches taller, he could no longer resist an inclination to assault him, and tried to plant a blow in Dick's face which would have hurt him considerably if he had not drawn back just in time.

Now, though Dick was far from quarrelsome, he was ready to defend himself on all occasions, and it was too much to expect that he would stand quiet and allow himself to be beaten.

He dropped his blacking-box on the instant, and returned Micky's blow with such good effect that the young bully staggered back, and would have fallen, if he had not been propped up by his confederate, Limpy Jim.

'Go in, Micky!' shouted the latter, who was rather a coward on his own account, but liked to see others fight. 'Polish him off, that's a good feller.'

Micky was now boiling over with rage and fury, and required no urging. He was fully determined to make a terrible example of poor Dick. He threw himself upon him, and strove to bear him to the ground; but Dick, avoiding a close hug, in which he might possibly have got the worst of it, by an adroit movement, tripped up his antagonist, and stretched him on the side-walk.

'Hit him, Jim!' exclaimed Micky, furiously.

Limpy Jim did not seem inclined to obey orders. There was a quiet strength and coolness about Dick, which alarmed him. He preferred that Micky should incur all the risks of battle, and accordingly set himself to raising his fallen comrade.

'Come, Micky,' said Dick, quietly, 'you'd better give it up. I wouldn't have touched you if you hadn't hit me first. I don't want to fight. It's low business.'

'You're afraid of hurtin' your clo'es,' said Micky, with a sneer.

'Maybe I am,' said Dick. 'I hope I haven't hurt yours.'

Micky's answer to this was another attack, as violent and impetuous as the first. But his fury was in the way. He struck wildly, not measuring his blows, and Dick had no difficulty in turning aside, so that his antagonist's blow fell upon the empty air, and his momentum was such that he nearly fell forward headlong. Dick might readily have taken advantage of his unsteadiness, and knocked him down; but he was not vindictive, and chose to act on the defensive, except when he could not avoid it.

Recovering himself, Micky saw that Dick was a more formidable antagonist than he had supposed, and was meditating another assault, better planned, which by its impetuosity might beat our hero to the ground. But there was an unlooked-for interference.

'Look out for the "copp,"' said Jim, in a low voice.

Micky turned round and saw a tall policeman heading towards him, and thought it might be prudent to suspend hostilities. He accordingly picked up his black-box, and, hitching up his pants, walked off, attended by Limpy Jim.

'What's that chap been doing?' asked the policeman of Dick.

'He was amoosin' himself by pitchin' into me,' replied Dick.

'What for?'

'He didn't like it 'cause I patronized a different tailor from him.'

'Well, it seems to me you *are* dressed pretty smart for a boot-black,' said the policeman.

'I wish I wasn't a boot-black,' said Dick.

'Never mind, my lad. It's an honest business,' said the policeman, who was a sensible man and a worthy citizen. 'It's an honest business. Stick to it till you get something better.'

'I mean to,' said Dick. 'It ain't easy to get out of it, as the prisoner remarked, when he was asked how he liked his residence.'

'I hope you don't speak from experience.'

'No,' said Dick; 'I don't mean to get into prison if I can help it.'

'Do you see that gentleman over there?' asked the officer, pointing to a well-dressed man who was walking on the other side of the street.

'Yes.'

'Well, he was once a newsboy.'

'And what is he now?'

'He keeps a bookstore, and is quite prosperous.'

Dick looked at the gentleman with interest, wondering if he should look as respectable when he was a grown man.

It will be seen that Dick was getting ambitious. Hitherto he had thought very little of the future, but was content to get along as he could, dining as well as his means would allow, and spending the evenings in the pit of the Old Bowery, eating peanuts between the acts if he was prosperous, and if unlucky supping on dry bread or an apple, and sleeping in an old box or a wagon. Now, for the first time, he began to reflect that he could not black boots all his life. In seven years he would be a man, and, since his meeting with Frank, he felt that he would like to be a respectable man. He could see and appreciate the difference between Frank and such a boy as Micky Maguire, and it was not strange that he preferred the society of the former.

In the course of the next morning, in pursuance of his new resolutions for the future, he called at a savings bank, and held out four dollars in bills besides another dollar in change. There was a high railing, and a number of clerks busily writing at desks behind it. Dick, never having been in a bank before, did not know where to go. He went, by mistake, to the desk where money was paid out.

'Where's your book?' asked the clerk.

'I haven't got any.'

'Have you any money deposited here?'

'No, sir, I want to leave some here.'

'Then go to the next desk.'

Dick followed directions, and presented himself before an elderly man with gray hair, who looked at him over the rims of his spectacles.

'I want you to keep that for me,' said Dick, awkwardly emptying his money out on the desk.

'How much is there?'

'Five dollars.'

'Have you got an account here?'

'No, sir.'

'Of course you can write?'

The 'of course' was said on account of Dick's neat dress.

'Have I got to do any writing?' asked our hero, a little embarrassed.

'We want you to sign your name in this book,' and the old gentleman shoved round a large folio volume containing the names of depositors.

Dick surveyed the book with some awe.

'I ain't much on writin',' he said.

'Very well; write as well as you can.'

The pen was put into Dick's hand, and, after dipping it in the inkstand, he succeeded after a hard effort, accompanied by many contortions of the face, in inscribing upon the book of the bank the name

DICK HUNTER.

'Dick! – that means Richard, I suppose,' said the bank officer, who had some difficulty in making out the signature.

'No; Ragged Dick is what folks call me.'

'You don't look very ragged.'

'No, I've left my rags to home. They might get wore out if I used 'em too common.'

'Well, my lad, I'll make out a book in the name of Dick Hunter, since you seem to prefer Dick to Richard. I hope you will save up your money and deposit more with us.'

Our hero took his bank-book, and gazed on the entry 'Five Dollars' with a new sense of importance. He had been accustomed to joke about Erie shares, but now, for the first time, he felt himself a capitalist; on a small scale, to be sure, but still it was no small thing for Dick to have five dollars which he could call his own. He firmly determined that he would lay by every cent he could spare from his earnings towards the fund he hoped to accumulate.

But Dick was too sensible not to know that there was something more than money needed to win a respectable position in the world. He felt that he was very ignorant. Of reading and writing he only knew the rudiments, and that, with a slight acquaintance with arithmetic, was all he did know of books. Dick knew he must study hard, and he dreaded it. He looked upon learning as attended with greater difficulties than it really possesses. But Dick had good pluck. He meant to learn, nevertheless, and resolved to buy a book with his first spare earnings.

When Dick went home at night he locked up his bank-book in one of the drawers of the bureau. It was wonderful how much more independent he felt whenever he reflected upon the contents of that drawer, and with what an important air of joint ownership he regarded the bank building in which his small savings were deposited.

# Thomas Bailey Aldrich (1836–1907)

Like the 'tall story' the 'bad boy' genre seems to be an essentially American phenomenon. It can be traced back to this autobiographical novel that led directly through *Tom Sawyer* and *Peck's Bad Boy* to a whole genre, including Booth Tarkington's *Penrod* (1914). The most lasting British example is Richmal Crompton's 'William' series (1922–70).

However, despite its reputation, this seminal story is a cheerful and straightforward biographical piece. As Aldrich states in the first chapter, it may have been written in response to the evangelical–puritan literary tradition, but that did not make it revolutionary *per se*. 'I call my story the story of a bad boy, partly to distinguish myself from those faultless young gentlemen who generally figure in narratives of this kind, and partly because I really was *not* a cherub. I may truthfully say I was an amiable, impulsive lad, blessed with fine digestive powers, and no hypocrite.' He consciously contrasts his self-portrait with 'the impossible boy in a story-book' and the moralizing (if any) is restricted to the implication that the boys are essentially good, even if, in society's terms, badly behaved. Whether this marks a genuine realism in American children's books, or the decay of moral standards, is debatable.

Aldrich's slightly ironic tone – and adult viewpoint – pervades the novel. The adventures of the 'Centipede' club at the school at 'Rivermouth' (Portsmouth, NH) may be hair-raising, as when the boys blow up the battery, and rooted in literary tradition (when they confront a bully, there is a reference to Tom Brown), but they are generally boy-sized, such as the spectacular snowball-fight. Overall, one can only assume that Aldrich was right when he said that 'There is a special Providence that watches over idiots, drunken men, and boys'. That adult-oriented grouping betrays the double audience intended by the text.

*The Story of a Bad Boy* was serialized in *St. Nicholas* in 1869.

## from *The Story of a Bad Boy* (1870)

### CHAPTER VII

### ONE MEMORABLE NIGHT

Two months had elapsed since my arrival at Rivermouth, when the approach of an important celebration produced the greatest excitement among the juvenile population of the town.

There was very little hard study done in the Temple Grammar School the week preceding the Fourth of July. For my part, my heart and brain were so full of fire-crackers, Roman-candles, rockets, pin-wheels, squibs, and gunpowder in various seductive forms, that I wonder I didn't explode under Mr. Grimshaw's very nose. I couldn't do a sum to save me; I couldn't tell, for love or money, whether Tallahassee was the capital of Tennessee or of Florida; the present and the pluperfect tenses were inextricably mixed in my memory, and I didn't know a verb from an adjective when I met one. This was not alone my condition, but that of every boy in the school.

Mr. Grimshaw considerately made allowances for our temporary distraction, and sought to fix our interest on the lessons by connecting them directly or indirectly with the coming Event. The class in arithmetic, for instance, was requested to state how many boxes of fire-crackers, each box measuring sixteen inches square, could be stored in a room of such and such dimensions. He gave us the Declaration of Independence for a parsing exercise, and in geography confined his questions almost exclusively to localities rendered famous in the Revolutionary War.

'What did the people of Boston do with the tea on board the English vessels?' asked our wily instructor.

'Threw it into the river!' shrieked the smaller boys, with an impetuosity that made Mr. Grimshaw smile in spite of himself. One luckless urchin said, 'Chucked it,' for which happy expression he was kept in at recess.

Notwithstanding these clever stratagems, there was not much solid work done by anybody. The trail of the serpent (an inexpensive but dangerous fire-toy) was over us all. We went round deformed by quantities of Chinese crackers artlessly concealed in our trousers-pockets; and if a boy whipped out his handkerchief without proper precaution, he was sure to let off two or three torpedoes.

Even Mr. Grimshaw was made a sort of accessory to the universal demoralization. In calling the school to order, he always rapped on the table with a heavy ruler. Under the green baize tablecloth, on the exact spot where he usually struck, a certain boy, whose name I withhold, placed a fat torpedo. The result was a loud explosion, which caused Mr. Grimshaw to look queer. Charley Marden was at the water-pail, at the time, and directed general attention to himself by strangling for several seconds and then squirting a slender thread of water over the blackboard.

Mr. Grimshaw fixed his eyes reproachfully on Charley, but said nothing. The real culprit (it was n't Charley Marden, but the boy whose name I withhold) instantly regretted his badness, and after school confessed the whole thing to Mr. Grimshaw, who heaped coals of fire upon the nameless boy's head by giving him five cents for the Fourth of July. If Mr. Grimshaw had caned this unknown youth, the punishment would not have been half so severe.

On the last day of June the Captain received a letter from my father, enclosing five dollars 'for my son Tom,' which enabled that young gentleman to make regal preparations for the celebration of our national independence. A portion of this money, two dollars, I hastened to invest in fireworks; the balance I put by for contingencies. In placing the fund in my possession, the Captain imposed one condition that dampened my ardor considerably, – I was to buy no gunpowder. I might have all the snapping-crackers and torpedoes I wanted; but gunpowder was out of the question.

I thought this rather hard, for all my young friends were provided with pistols of various sizes. Pepper Whitcomb had a horse-pistol nearly as large as himself, and Jack Harris, though he to be sure was a big boy, was going to have a real old-fashioned flint-lock musket. However, I did n't mean to let this drawback destroy my happiness. I had one charge of powder stowed away in the little brass pistol which I brought from New Orleans, and was bound to make a noise in the world once, if I never did again.

It was a custom observed from time immemorial for the towns-boys to have a bonfire on the Square on the midnight before the Fourth. I did n't ask the Captain's leave to attend this ceremony, for I had a general idea that he would n't give it. If the Captain, I reasoned, does n't forbid me, I break no orders by going. Now this was a specious line of argument, and the mishaps that befell me in consequence of adopting it were richly deserved.

On the evening of the 3d I retired to bed very early, in order to disarm suspicion. I did n't sleep a wink, waiting for eleven o'clock to come round; and I thought it never would come round, as I lay counting from time to time the slow strokes of the ponderous bell in the steeple of the Old North Church. At length the laggard hour arrived. While the clock was striking I jumped out of bed and began dressing.

My grandfather and Miss Abigail were heavy sleepers, and I might have stolen down stairs and out at the front door undetected; but such a commonplace proceeding did not suit my adventurous disposition. I fastened one end of a rope (it was a few yards cut from Kitty Collins's clothes-line) to the bedpost nearest the window, and cautiously climbed out on the wide pediment over the hall door. I had neglected to knot the rope; the result was, that, the moment I swung clear of the pediment, I descended like a flash of lightning, and warmed both my hands smartly. The rope, moreover, was four or five feet too short; so I got a fall that would have proved serious had I not tumbled into the middle of one of the big rose-bushes growing on either side of the steps.

I scrambled out of that without delay, and was congratulating myself on my good luck, when I saw by the light of the setting moon the form of a man leaning over the garden gate. It was one of the town watch, who had probably been observing my operations with curiosity. Seeing no chance of escape, I put a bold face on the matter and walked directly up to him.

'What on airth air you a doin'?' asked the man, grasping the collar of my jacket.

'I live here, sir, if you please,' I replied, 'and am going to the bonfire. I did n't want to wake up the old folks, that's all.'

The man cocked his eye at me in the most amiable manner, and released his hold.

'Boys is boys,' he muttered. He did n't attempt to stop me as I slipped through the gate.

Once beyond his clutches, I took to my heels and soon reached the Square, where I found forty or fifty fellows assembled, engaged in building a pyramid of tar-barrels. The palms of my hands still tingled so that I could n't join in the sport. I stood in the doorway of the Nautilus Bank, watching the workers, among whom I recognized lots of my schoolmates. They looked like a legion of imps, coming and going in the twilight, busy in raising some infernal edifice. What a Babel of voices it was, everybody directing everybody else, and everybody doing everything wrong!

When all was prepared, some one applied a match to the sombre pile. A fiery tongue thrust itself out here and there, then suddenly the whole fabric burst into flames, blazing and crackling beautifully. This was a signal for the boys to join hands and dance around the burning barrels, which they did shouting like mad creatures. When the fire had burnt down a little, fresh staves were brought and heaped on the pyre. In the excitement of the moment I forgot my tingling palms, and found myself in the thick of the carousal.

Before we were half ready, our combustible material was expended, and a disheartening kind of darkness settled down upon us. The boys collected together here and there in knots, consulting as to what should be done. It yet lacked four or five hours of daybreak, and none of us were in the humor to return to bed. I approached one of the groups standing near the town-pump, and discovered in the uncertain light of the dying brands the figures of Jack Harris, Phil Adams, Harry Blake, and Pepper Whitcomb, their faces streaked with perspiration and tar, and their whole appearance suggestive of New Zealand chiefs.

'Hullo! here's Tom Bailey!' shouted Pepper Whitcomb; 'he'll join in!'

Of course he would. The sting had gone out of my hands, and I was ripe for anything, – none the less ripe for not knowing what was on the *tapis*. After whispering together for a moment, the boys motioned me to follow them.

We glided out from the crowd and silently wended our way through a neighboring alley, at the head of which stood a tumble-down old barn, owned by one Ezra Wingate. In former days this was the stable of the mail-coach that ran between Rivermouth and Boston. When the railroad superseded that primitive mode of travel, the lumbering vehicle was rolled into the barn, and there it stayed. The stage-driver, after prophesying the immediate downfall of the nation, died of grief and apoplexy, and the old coach followed in his wake as fast as it could by quietly dropping to pieces. The barn had the reputation of being haunted, and I think we all kept very close together when we found ourselves standing in the black shadow cast by the tall gable. Here, in a low voice, Jack Harris laid bare his plan, which was to burn the ancient stage-coach.

'The old trundle-cart is n't worth twenty-five cents,' said Jack Harris, 'and Ezra Wingate ought to thank us for getting the rubbish out of the way. But if any fellow here does n't want to have a hand in it, let him cut and run, and keep a quiet tongue in his head ever after.'

With this he pulled out the staples that held the rusty padlock, and the big barn door swung slowly open. The interior of the stable was pitch-dark, of course. As we made a movement to enter, a sudden scrambling, and the sound of heavy bodies leaping in all directions, caused us to start back in terror.

'Rats!' cried Phil Adams.

'Bats!' exclaimed Harry Blake.

'Cats!' suggested Jack Harris. 'Who's afraid?'

Well, the truth is, we were all afraid; and if the pole of the stage had not been lying close to the threshold, I don't believe anything on earth would have induced us to cross it. We seized hold of the pole-straps and succeeded with great trouble in dragging the coach out. The two fore wheels had rusted to the axle-tree, and refused to revolve. It was the merest skeleton of a coach. The cushions had long since been removed, and the leather hangings, where they had not crumbled away, dangled in shreds from the worm-eaten frame. A load of ghosts and a span of phantom horses to drag them would have made the ghastly thing complete.

Luckily for our undertaking, the stable stood at the top of a very steep hill. With three boys to push behind, and two in front to steer, we started the old coach on its last trip with little or no difficulty. Our speed increased every moment, and, the fore wheels becoming unlocked as we arrived at the foot of the declivity, we charged upon the crowd like a regiment of cavalry, scattering the people right and left. Before reaching the bonfire, to which some one had added several bushels of shavings, Jack Harris and Phil Adams, who were steering, dropped on the ground, and allowed the vehicle to pass over them, which it did without injuring them; but the boys who were clinging for dear life to the trunk-rack behind fell over the prostrate steersmen, and there we all lay in a heap, two or three of us quite picturesque with the nose-bleed.

The coach, with an intuitive perception of what was expected of it, plunged into the centre of the kindling shavings, and stopped. The flames sprung up and clung to the rotten woodwork, which burned like tinder. At this moment a figure was seen leaping wildly from the inside of the blazing coach. The figure made three bounds towards us, and tripped over Harry Blake. It was Pepper Whitcomb, with his hair somewhat singed, and his eyebrows completely scorched off!

Pepper had slyly ensconced himself on the back seat before we started, intending to have a neat little ride down hill, and a laugh at us afterwards. But the laugh, as it happened, was on our side, or would have been, if half a dozen watchmen had not suddenly pounced down upon us, as we lay scrambling on the ground, weak with mirth over Pepper's misfortune. We were collared and marched off before we well knew what had happened.

The abrupt transition from the noise and light of the Square to the silent, gloomy brick room in the rear of the Meat Market seemed like the work of enchantment. We stared at each other aghast.

'Well,' remarked Jack Harris, with a sickly smile, 'this *is* a go!'

'No go, I should say,' whimpered Harry Blake, glancing at the bare brick walls and the heavy iron-plated door.

'Never say die,' muttered Phil Adams, dolefully.

The Bridewell was a small low-studded chamber built up against the rear end of the Meat Market, and approached from the Square by a narrow passage-way. A portion of the room was partitioned off into eight cells, numbered, each capable of holding two persons. The cells were full at the time, as we presently discovered by seeing several hideous faces leering out at us through the gratings of the doors.

A smoky oil-lamp in a lantern suspended from the ceiling threw a flickering light over the apartment, which contained no furniture excepting a couple of stout wooden benches. It was a dismal place by night, and only little less dismal by day, for the tall houses surrounding 'the lock-up' prevented the faintest ray of sunshine from penetrating the ventilator over the door, – a long narrow window opening inward and propped up by a piece of lath.

As we seated ourselves in a row on one of the benches, I imagine that our aspect was anything but cheerful. Adams and Harris looked very anxious, and Harry Blake, whose nose had just stopped bleeding, was mournfully carving his name, by sheer force of habit, on the prison bench. I don't think I ever saw a more 'wrecked' expression on any human countenance than Pepper Whitcomb's presented. His look of natural astonishment at finding himself incarcerated in a jail was considerably heightened by his lack of eyebrows.

As for me, it was only by thinking how the late Baron Trenck would have conducted himself under similar circumstances that I was able to restrain my tears.

None of us were inclined to conversation. A deep silence, broken now and then by a startling snore from the cells, reigned throughout the chamber. By and by Pepper Whitcomb glanced nervously towards Phil Adams and said, 'Phil, do you think they will – *hang us?*'

'Hang your grandmother!' returned Adams, impatiently; 'what I'm afraid of is that they'll keep us locked up until the Fourth is over.'

'You ain't smart ef they do!' cried a voice from one of the cells. It was a deep bass voice that sent a chill through me.

'Who are you?' said Jack Harris, addressing the cells in general; for the echoing qualities of the room made it difficult to locate the voice.

'That don't matter,' replied the speaker, putting his face close up to the gratings of No. 3, 'but ef I was a youngster like you, free an' easy outside there, this spot would n't hold *me* long.'

'That's so!' chimed several of the prison-birds, wagging their heads behind the iron lattices.

'Hush!' whispered Jack Harris, rising from his seat and walking on tip-toe to the door of cell No. 3. 'What would you do?'

'Do? Why, I'd pile them 'ere benches up agin that 'ere door, an' crawl out of that 'ere winder in no time. That's my advice.'

'And werry good adwice it is, Jim,' said the occupant of No. 5, approvingly.

Jack Harris seemed to be of the same opinion, for he hastily placed the benches one on the top of another under the ventilator, and, climbing up on the highest bench, peeped out into the passage-way.

'If any gent happens to have a ninepence about him,' said the man in cell No. 3, 'there's a sufferin' family here as could make use of it. Smallest favors gratefully received, an' no questions axed.'

This appeal touched a new silver quarter of a dollar in my trousers-pocket; I fished out the coin from a mass of fireworks, and gave it to the prisoner. He appeared to be so good-natured a fellow that I ventured to ask what he had done to get into jail.

'Intirely innocent. I was clapped in here by a rascally nevew as wishes to enjoy my wealth afore I'm dead.'

'Your name, sir?' I inquired, with a view of reporting the outrage to my grandfather and having the injured person reinstated in society.

'Git out, you insolent young reptyle!' shouted the man, in a passion.

I retreated precipitately, amid a roar of laughter from the other cells.

'Can't you keep still?' exclaimed Harris, withdrawing his head from the window.

A portly watchman usually sat on a stool outside the door day and night; but on this particular occasion, his services being required elsewhere, the bridewell had been left to guard itself.

'All clear,' whispered Jack Harris, as he vanished through the aperture and dropped softly on the ground outside. We all followed him expeditiously, – Pepper Whitcomb and myself getting stuck in the window for a moment in our frantic efforts not to be last.

'Now, boys, everybody for himself!'

# Jean Ingelow (1820–1897)

*Mopsa the Fairy* is the Victorian original fairy-tale at its peak: rambling and portentiously symbolic, with incidental more-or-less-moral points, and seeming to the modern reader to be ultimately inconsequential. In this respect it contrasts strikingly with the work of Lewis Carroll, by which it is often said to have been influenced: a much more obvious antecedent is Kingsley's *The Water Babies*, with its incessant insistence on secondary meanings (Carroll was at some pains to disguise his).

Jack finds a nest of fairies and travels through Fairyland. He becomes very attached to Mopsa, who is initially a young fairy, but because fairies grow so quickly, she is Queen of the Fairies by the end of the book. On their way to Fairyland, Jack and Mopsa even pass through 'one of the border countries, where things are set right again that people have caused to go wrong in the world'

– such as a racehorse, shot when she was injured taking a jump.

The book is inventive rather than ingenious, and in its episodic (not to say expedient) structure, it looks forward to many other fantasies, notably *The Wizard of Oz*. John Goldthwaite in (1996) saw it as 'a wonderfully lucid tale scene by scene but so brooding and intellectually detached overall as to be even more baffling than *Alice* in the end'.

Certainly, children's books in the nineteenth century reflected the intellectual trends of the novel in general, and *Mopsa* partakes of the slightly enervated later Victorian atmosphere of English literature. Jean Ingelow was a poet of some reputation, her most famous work being probably 'The High Tide on the Coast of Lincolnshire 1571'.

This episode sees Jack and Mopsa in mid-career.

## from *Mopsa the Fairy* (1869)

### CHAPTER XIV

### REEDS AND RUSHES

*"'Tis merry, 'tis merry in Fairyland,*
*When Fairy birds are singing;*
*When the court doth ride by their monarch's side,*
*With bit and bridle ringing.'*
Walter Scott

There were many fruit-trees on that slope of the mountain, and Jack and Mopsa, as they came down, gathered some fruit for breakfast, and did not feel very tired, for the long ride on the wing had rested them.

They could not see the plain, for a slight blue mist hung over it; but the sun was hot already, and as they came down they saw a beautiful bed of high reeds, and thought they would sit awhile and rest in it. A rill of clear water ran beside the bed, so when they had reached it they sat down, and began to consider what they should do next.

'Jack,' said Mopsa, 'did you see anything particular as you came down with the shooting stars?'

'No, I saw nothing so interesting as they were,' answered Jack. 'I was looking at them and watching how they squeaked to one another, and how they had little hooks in their wings, with which they held the large wing that we sat on.'

'But I saw something,' said Mopsa. 'Just as the sun rose I looked down, and in the loveliest garden I ever saw, and all among trees and woods, I saw a most beautiful castle. O Jack! I am sure that castle is the place I am to live in, and now we have nothing to do but to find it. I shall soon be a queen, and there I shall reign.'

'Then I shall be king there,' said Jack; 'shall I?'

'Yes, if you can,' answered Mopsa. 'Of course, whatever you can do you may do. And, Jack, this is a much better fairy country than either the stony land or the other that we first came to, for this castle is a real place! It will not melt away. There the people can work, they know how to love each other: common fairies cannot do that, I know. They can laugh and cry, and I shall teach them several things that they do not know yet. Oh! do let us make haste and find the castle.'

So they arose; but they turned the wrong way, and by mistake walked farther and farther in among the reeds, whose feathery heads puffed into Mopsa's face, and Jack's coat was all covered with the fluffy seed.

'This is very odd,' said Jack. 'I thought this was only a small bed of reeds when we stepped into it; but really we must have walked a mile already.'

But they walked on and on, till Mopsa grew quite faint, and her sweet face became very pale, for she knew that the beds of reeds were spreading faster than they walked, and then they shot up so high that it was impossible to see over their heads; so at last Jack and Mopsa were so tired, that they sat down, and Mopsa began to cry.

However, Jack was the braver of the two this time, and he comforted Mopsa, and told her that she was nearly a queen, and would never reach her castle by sitting still. So she got up and took his hand, and he went on before, parting the reeds and pulling her after him, till all on a sudden they heard the sweetest sound in the world: it was like a bell, and it sounded again and again.

It was the castle clock, and it was striking twelve at noon.

As it finished striking they came out at the farther edge of the great bed of reeds, and there was the castle straight before them – a beautiful castle, standing on the slope of a hill. The grass all about it was covered with beautiful flowers; two of the taller turrets were over-grown with ivy, and a flag was flying on a staff; but everything was so silent and lonely that it made one sad to look on. As Jack and Mopsa drew near they trod as gently as they could, and did not say a word.

All the windows were shut, but there was a great door in the centre of the building, and they went towards it, hand in hand.

What a beautiful hall! The great door stood wide open, and they could see what a delightful place this must be to live in: it was paved with squares of blue and white marble, and here and there carpets were spread, with chairs and tables upon them. They looked and saw a great dome overhead, filled with windows of coloured glass, and they cast down blue and golden and rosy reflections.

'There is my home that I shall live in,' said Mopsa; and she came close to the door, and they both looked in, till at last she let go of Jack's hand, and stepped over the threshold.

The bell in the tower sounded again more sweetly than ever, and the instant Mopsa was inside there came from behind the fluted columns, which rose up on every side, the brown doe, followed by troops of deer and fawns!

'Mopsa! Mopsa!' cried Jack, 'come away! come back!' But Mopsa was too much astonished to stir, and something seemed to hold Jack from following; but he looked and looked, till, as the brown doe advanced, the door of the castle closed – Mopsa was shut in, and Jack was left outside.

So Mopsa had come straight to the place she thought she had run away from.

'But I am determined to get her away from those creatures,' thought Jack; 'she does not want to reign over deer.' And he began to look about him, hoping to get in. It was of no use: all the windows in that front of the castle were high, and when he tried to go round, he came to a high wall with battlements. Against some parts of this wall the ivy grew, and looked as if it might have grown there for ages; its stems were thicker than his waist, and its branches were spread over the surface like network; so by means of them he hoped to climb to the top.

He immediately began to try. Oh, how high the wall was! First he came to several sparrows' nests, and very much frightened the sparrows were; then he reached starlings' nests, and very angry the starlings were; but at last, just under the coping, he came to jackdaws' nests, and these birds were very friendly, and pointed out to him the best little holes for him to put his feet into. At last he reached the top, and found to his delight that the wall was three feet thick, and he could walk upon it quite comfortably, and look down into a lovely garden, where all the trees were in blossom, and creepers tossed their long tendrils from tree to tree, covered with puffs of yellow, or bells of white, or bunches and knots of blue or rosy bloom.

He could look down into the beautiful empty rooms of the castle, and he walked cautiously on the wall till he came to the west front, and reached a little casement window that had latticed panes.

Jack peeped in; nobody was there. He took his knife, and cut away a little bit of lead to let out the pane, and it fell with such a crash on the pavement below that he wondered it did not bring the deer over to look at what he was about. Nobody came.

He put in his hand and opened the latchet, and with very little trouble got down into the room. Still nobody was to be seen. He thought that the room, years ago, might have been a fairies' school-room, for it was strewn with books, slates, and all sorts of copybooks. A fine soft dust had settled down over everything – pens, papers, and all. Jack opened a copybook: its pages were headed with maxims, just as ours are, which proved that these fairies must have been superior to such as he had hitherto come among. Jack read some of them:

> 'Turn your back on the light, and you'll follow a shadow.'
> 'The deaf queen Fate has dumb courtiers.'
> 'If the hound is your foe, don't sleep in his kennel.'
> 'That that is, is.'

And so on; but nobody came, and no sound was heard, so he opened the door, and found himself in a long and most splendid gallery, all hung with pictures, and spread with a most beautiful carpet, which was as soft and white as a piece of wool, and wrought with a beautiful device. This was the letter M, with a crown and sceptre, and underneath a beautiful little boat, exactly like the one in which he had come up the river. Jack felt sure that this carpet had been made for Mopsa, and he went along the gallery upon it till he reached a grand staircase of oak that was almost black with age, and he stole gently down it, for he began to feel rather shy, more especially as he could now see the great hall under the dome and that it had a beautiful lady in it, and many other people, but no deer at all.

These fairy people were something like the one-foot-one fairies, but much larger and more like children, and they had very gentle, happy faces, and seemed to be extremely glad and gay. But seated on a couch, where lovely painted windows threw down all sorts of rainbow colours on her, was a beautiful fairy lady, as large as a woman. She had Mopsa in her arms, and was looking down upon her with eyes full of love, while at her side stood a boy, who was exactly and precisely like Jack himself. He had rather long light hair and grey eyes, and a velvet jacket. That was all Jack could see at first, but as he drew nearer the boy turned, and then Jack felt as if he was looking at himself in the glass.

Mopsa had been very tired, and now she was fast asleep, with her head on that lady's shoulder. The boy kept looking at her, and he seemed very happy indeed; so did the lady, and she presently told him to bring Jack something to eat.

It was rather a curious speech that she made to him; it was this:

'Jack, bring Jack some breakfast.'

'What!' thought Jack to himself, 'has he got a face like mine, and a name like mine too?'

So that other Jack went away, and presently came back with a golden plate full of nice things to eat.

'I know you don't like me,' he said, as he came up to Jack with the plate.

'Not like him?' repeated the lady; 'and pray what reason have you for not liking my royal nephew?'

'O dame!' exclaimed the boy, and laughed.

The lady, on hearing this, turned pale, for she perceived that she herself had mistaken the one for the other.

'I see you know how to laugh,' said the real Jack. 'You are wiser people than those whom I went to first; but the reason I don't like you is, that you are so exactly like me.'

'I am not!' exclaimed the boy. 'Only hear him, dame! You mean, I suppose, that you are so exactly like me. I am sure I don't know what you mean by it.'

'Nor I either,' replied Jack, almost in a passion.

'It couldn't be helped, of course,' said the other Jack.

'Hush! hush!' said the fairy woman; 'don't wake our dear little Queen. Was it you, my royal nephew, who spoke last?'

'Yes, dame,' answered the boy, and again he offered the plate; but Jack was swelling with indignation, and he gave the plate a push with his elbow, which scattered the fruit and bread on the ground.

'I won't eat it,' he said; but when the other Jack went and picked it up again, and said, 'Oh, yes, do, old fellow; it's not my fault, you know,' he began to consider that it was no use being cross in Fairyland; so he forgave his double, and had just finished his breakfast when Mopsa woke.

# Mary Anne, Lady Barker (1831–1911)

The life of Lady Barker is an object lesson not merely in Victorian enterprise and fortitude, but of personal (and possibly feminist) enterprise. She was born in Jamaica, educated in England, travelled across India with her first husband (a soldier), and settled in New Zealand with her second husband, where they ran a sheep farm. Subsequently they moved to London and then around the world; her husband was for a time Governor of Western Australia. Lady Barker produced eighteen books, including the classic *Station Life in New Zealand* (1870) and what is arguably the first English novel for teenage girls, *Sybil's Book* (1872). All this is quite apart from reviewing for the London *Times*, becoming Principal of the First School of Cookery, and writing what is arguably the only genuinely original and lasting children's book to come out of New Zealand in the nineteenth century.

As with Australia, much of that country's early children's books were either written in Britain, or were pale imitations of British books. Lady Barker's writings were straightforward and robust, and included the autobiographical *Stories About–* (1870), the title of which is a respectful nod towards the work of Samuel Goodrich (she was not anti-fairy tale, only anti the florid style of much contemporary writing for children). The *Times* reviewer observed: 'If ladies who write books for children would but write them as they speak to them there would be more books like this.'

Another success was *Boys* (1874), a companion piece to *Sybil's Book*, which gave realistic accounts of twelve boys (including 'An Invalid Boy' and 'My Missionary Boy'). In 'My Emigrant Boy', part of which is reprinted here, she paints a picture of colonial life which manages to be interesting and exciting without recourse to the clichés of the adventure story. Louis Roden eventually succeeds in becoming a 'runholder', but there is nothing greatly heroic about his progress; nor is there any false romanticism. Lady Barker makes it clear that his success is exceptional, and even less likely 'now' than when the story was set, twenty years before. The reader should be under no illusions: the New Zealand climate is 'the most detestable climate in the world! There! and I'll tell you why. 'Tis always blowing half a gale of wind and when it does not blow half a gale, it blows a whole one.... It's the healthiest climate on the face of the globe. Of course it is; why, an infectious disorder ... would be whisked right off the patient if his window was opened. ... When it does not blow, or rain, or snow, or do all three together, *then*, I grant you, New Zealand has the most exquisite climate under the sun, but such days are not so common as could be wished.'

This engagingly clear-eyed approach extends to her ideas on the didactic. She describes the effect of simple, healthy living on her hero, but observes, 'I don't want to set him up as a model, or to talk at boys who smoke and drink beer', for 'if they had been within reach there is no doubt Master Louis would have had his pipe and his glass of beer every day'. The story plays with literary conventions of the day and has its share of prejudices, but Lady Barker was not only a remarkable person, she was an outstandingly original writer for children: very few writers for the next fifty years matched either her style or her respect for her audience.

In this episode, from 'Louis Roden, My Emigrant Boy', Louis has just arrived in New Zealand as a sponsored emigrant.

## from *Boys* (1874)

### CHAPTER II

One of the ship's cabin passengers, a Mr. Gale, had taken a great fancy to Louis Roden. He both liked and respected the quiet, gentlemanly boy, who showed so plainly in every word and look, that, although he was no milksop, he could discern between coarse vulgarity and frank independence. As soon, therefore, as the ship dropped her anchor in Auckland harbour, on the 1st of August, 1855, Mr. Gale proposed that Louis and he should go for a run ashore. The first thing they did after having eaten that most delicious of meals after five months at sea – a breakfast on land, with its dainties of fresh bread and butter, eggs and milk – was to go and inquire about the best means of getting across Cook's Strait to the middle island of New Zealand. They learned that a ship was to sail in a week, and arranged with the agent for the transfer of their luggage, and paid their passage money. All this was very quickly settled, and an hour's walking having tired their cramped sea-legs, and exhausted the sight of the Auckland of those days, Mr. Gale said, 'What would you like to do now, Louis?'

'Have something more to eat, and then go shooting,' answered Louis, promptly.

Now you must know that among Louis's outfit was a single-barrel gun, which, between our-selves, kicked so frightfully after it had been fired two or three times, that its owner let him have it as a bargain for five pounds. It is true that it had only cost three pounds originally, but that is the way with bargains. Louis had originally fired a few shots at sparrows or blackbirds out of a neighbour's gun, and looked forward to much sport in New Zealand. When this gun there-fore was bought for him (out of Colonel Townshend's present), he felt himself at once the richest and the happiest boy 'that e'er the sun shone on;' and during his first dreadful days of sea-sickness on board *The Good Intent*, the only thing which saved him from despair, was the recollection of his gun stowed away in a leathern gun-case beneath his berth.

Mr. Gale had been in those parts before, and therefore knew right well how little there was to shoot at in either of the New Zealand islands, except in the great bushes or native forests. Towns are not usually built in the heart of a 'bush,' and in the neighbourhood of Auckland no feathered creature could be found at which to fire at that bright spring morning, nor any four-footed game larger than a rat. What was to be done? Louis had brought his gun ashore, and could not be per-suaded that there was no food for the powder and shot which he carried in such sportsmanlike fashion.

The two friends were sauntering near the Wynyard pier, when a wily boatman hailed them. He had observed Louis's gun over his shoulder and his disconsolate face, and said, 'Have a boat, gen-tlemen? Fine day for a sail; plenty of pigeons on that island,' pointing with his finger to a few little dots rising out of the foggy sea. This worthy owned a heavy tub of a boat, for which he demanded twenty-five shillings a day's hire, but eventually took fifteen shillings. Just as Louis, full of glee, was stepping into her, a lad came running up, the son of the harbour-master, whom Mr. Gale knew, and cried, 'Father says you must wait a minute till he can send you down a blanket and some grub, if you're going to sail in that thing, for it may come on to blow and you might be out all night. Here he is.' As he spoke, his father came down; and after trying to dissuade Mr. Gale from going, put a few necessaries into the boat. I think the elder passenger would have been glad enough to stay on shore, but Louis's entreaties carried the day, and they both set out – the boatman remaining behind. At first they tried to sail, but the wind being contrary, miles of tacking had to be accomplished before the nearest island could be reached, where no living creature, how-ever, was to be found except an old man, who told them *he* had come there to get some shooting, and that there were plenty of pigeons on the next island. Accordingly they made a fresh start, and reached the promised land of game about 4.30. By this time they were very cold and tired, for they had been obliged to pull a great deal, and tremendously hungry. After beaching the boat, as it was plain they could not get back that evening – August answering to our February, and the night clos-ing in with both wind and rain – they made, under the old man's directions, a sort of tent out of the blanket, and collected some firewood. He dissuaded them from going to look for pigeons, and pro-posed a search for oysters instead. These they found in large quantities on the rocks, and made a good meal off them, with the help of some bread which was in the sack, and a little whisky. Then they all lay down inside the tent, made up the fire, and went to sleep.

I cannot truthfully say any of the party passed a good night, except, perhaps, the old man, who had been used to that sort of thing all his life. But uncomfortable as were the dark hours, they must have been luxurious compared to the wretchedness of the morning. A thick fog had settled like a curtain over the sea. On no side could they perceive a ray of light or the least break in its grey dens-ity, and a fine mizzling rain began to come steadily down. The fire had been out for many hours, and they found it impossible to relight it. Everything got thoroughly damp; Louis's gun took a fine coating of rust, and would not go off, his powder was a black paste, the matches would not strike, and the bread was a mass of doughy pulp; as for the whisky, there was none. Their new acquaint-ance had arisen many times stealthily in the night, under pretence of attending to the fire, which he let out, letting some whisky *in* every time he got up. He said it was sure to spoil too, so he took care of it. At midnight they were crouching inside the heavy, sodden blanket-tent, when crack went their roof-tree, and down came the tent on them, driving them out to seek for fresh props. As they were obliged to turn out and get wet to the skin in two minutes, they thought they would bring in some more oysters for breakfast, and so they did; but raw oysters are somewhat cold and sickening on an empty stomach, and they found them very unsatisfying. All that day it was impossible to leave their island; not a pigeon was to be seen or heard, but towards the afternoon a wretched parrot unwarily ventured within reach of Louis's stick, and was brought down by a clever fling. But poor Polly's neck was twisted in vain, for when they came to pluck her, the skin had very unpleasant tints of black and green about it, insomuch that in spite of their hunger they could not be tempted to eat the bird.

Another night spent under shelter of the boat, with no softer bed than the shingle, reduced our wanderers to such a pitch of desperation, that they vowed they would get off their island next morning if they had to feel every step of their way. So after bolting a few more clammy oysters, they embarked, and rowed at random towards the land, still through a dense fog, until the sound of breakers warned them to lie on their oars a bit. It must have been about midday, when the fog lifting a little, showed them a line of surf. Through this they made the best of their way, the old man steering and Mr. Gale and Louis pulling, until a wave lifted the boat high up on the beach, when they all jumped out of her, and allowed her to be washed back again by the retreating water. They were now in a desperate plight, not knowing where they had got to; but with wonderful traveller's-luck, after walking straight inland for some hundred yards or so, they came upon a cottage. A poor desolate little hovel it was, but it seemed a very palace of luxury and comfort after the two nights spent out of doors. The shepherd who lived in it was away walking his boundary, but his kind Scotch wife came to the door and made them heartily welcome. They dreaded to ask her how far they were from Auckland; but after drinking nearly a quart of hot coffee, Mr. Gale took courage to put the question.

'Twenty miles as the crow would fly,' she answered, 'and ten more round by the shore; and there's a big bush between you and it from here.'

To Louis's English ears, a bush, be it ever so large, did not sound a formidable obstacle; he had yet to learn that 'a bush' meant not only many acres, or even miles of bushes, but many thousand tall forest-trees as well.

'It's a bad job, that bush,' said Mr. Gale, thoughtfully; 'however, we'll rest here a bit, if you'll let us, good mother, and then we'll tackle it in the morning.'

'Rest and welcome,' she said.

So they rested and dried themselves, and ate up nearly everything in the cottage, in payment for which, however, Mr. Gale left a handsome present of one-pound notes. The old man had quite fastened himself on to them, and came in for all this good cheer, which he took as a matter of course, for you see he was an 'old colonist,' and that term means, or used to mean, a person who knows right well how to take care of himself, and thinks first of his own comfort on all occasions. If that be a true definition of the words, their new acquaintance must have been a very old colonist indeed. He offered to buy Louis's gun 'off him,' as he phrased it, 'for ten bob;' a bid which Louis indignantly rejected.

Early next morning they set out, but in spite of walking at their best pace, it was nightfall before the bush was reached, and Louis, who still clung to the idea of a good-sized clump of holly or laurel, saw, for the first time, the great dark mass of timber, which is called by the name of bush, stretching for miles and miles away. Luckily, a track had been cut through it; but this could only be safely followed by daylight, so they camped that night, and went on in the morning, the old man always taking good care to get the warmest place by the fire, and the largest share of the food. It was the afternoon of the next day before they reached Auckland; and when the travellers were about to separate, the old man coolly demanded payment for his services, alleging that they never would have found their way home without him, whereas, all he had done was to loiter behind and require frequent nips from Mr. Gale's replenished whisky flask to get him on. However, he was not quite enough of an old colonist to induce them to pay him for having been a great trouble to them, so they shook him off, and went on board their new ship. But first they had to pay for the lost boat, which the owner called a 'derelict,' and valued at the price of a small ironclad.

A week's tossing in the chopping seas of Cook's Straights brought them to Port Lyttleton, and there they landed. The next thing to be done was to collect Louis's goods and chattels, especially the precious gun, which had been cleaned until it shone again, hire a dray, and start across the Port Hills to Christchurch, the youthful capital lying in a flax swamp on the other side of the range. Louis trudged manfully along by the dray, and tried to enter into conversation with its driver, but that worthy possessed only one set of ideas. His whole life was spent in going across these hills between the few wooden shanties and public-houses, which formed the Christchurch of those days, and the still more crazy, wooden buildings, then called Lyttleton; consequently, he had no interest in life beyond that road and its history. He listened in stolid silence to Louis's remarks, and did not vouchsafe any reply to his questions. Every now and then he pointed with his whip down some steep precipice, took his pipe out of his mouth, spat, and remarked, 'Billy the Buster's team went down there last wool-season; wheeler got killed.' Louis would fain have learned the particulars of this mishap, but not a word more could be got out of the drayman until a particularly dangerous pitch called forth another reminiscence. 'Jim Goggle's black mare run away with him jest here. Jim was a-stoopin' to put on the drag, and he kinder tickled her up with his whip, it's s'posed, for she ups with her hind legs and knocks Jim down. Over him she goes, and down the hill as hard as she can split, and I'm blessed if she ever drawed breath till she got to Sumner – that's down there, foot of the hill – with a bit o' one shaft hanging to her, and she kicked *that* clean off before she'd let him catch her. Bad job that was for Jim, werry bad.'

After Sumner was passed the road became a dead level, but it was none the easier to travel for that. Instead of up and down hill they floundered in and out of holes, so the dray did not get on much faster.

'Best come to the "Mitre" to-night,' said the drayman, 'and you'll hear all about the colonel in the morning.'

So to the 'Mitre' they went, and Louis had a good supper and a hard bed at a price which made him open his eyes pretty wide. If he had only known it, that drayman was a kind-hearted fellow after all, for although he was perfectly well aware of what there was to hear about the colonel, he thought it better for Louis to have a good night's sleep before he learned bad news.

Bad, indeed, the news was, but I cannot stop to dwell on how and where our poor little friend heard it. All that I need tell you is the sum-total, which was that Louis found himself in a perfectly strange country without a friend or acquaintance on its shores, and – after he had paid the drayman – a ten-pound note in his pocket. No one knew where the colonel had gone. Mrs. Townshend had died when her baby was born, three months before *The Good Intent* reached Auckland; the poor little creature only survived its mother a week, and after its death the unhappy father and husband threw up his farm, sold his effects, and went on board the first coasting steamer which touched at Port Lyttleton. It is supposed that his grief had driven Louis's expected arrival (for he had heard from Doctor Roden of the lad's departure from England) out of his head, as he left no instructions with his agent about him. I may as well tell you here that the colonel was never heard of again.

All the talking and the questions in the world could not alter the fact of Louis's position – friendless and alone in a new country; and the only point to be decided speedily was, what could be done? His money would only keep him for a week at the 'Mitre,' so high were prices in those days, but he did not like to spend his last shilling in that way.

'Now that you have come to the colony, you'd better stay,' was the advice of Colonel Townshend's solicitor. 'Food is dear, but then wages are good, and hands are scarce, so you'll easy get a billet. Here's Mr. Gale, we'll ask him what he thinks.'

Great was Mr. Gale's surprise to hear of his young friend and fellow-passenger's predicament, but he pooh-poohed the idea of his returning to England, or being at all down-hearted. 'It was very careless of the colonel to leave no instructions about you,' he said, 'but you'll get on right enough, no fear. Why, there's Tom Day, of Mellatoto who wants some one to help him at his place, and he'll give you a pound a week and your grub; come along, we'll go and find him.'

Mr. Day was soon found, a good-natured, easy-going sort of man. He had once been a gentle-man and had not fallen, but deliberately stepped down from his position, preferring a half-drunken state to any other. He soon tired out the patience of his friends and relations in England, and they persuaded him to collect the wreck of his property, and go out to the new settlement; just as if change of air could cure a man of so frightful a habit. Luckily he was not always tipsy, and Mr. Gale seeing him pretty sober that morning, hoped he was improving and that he would make a good master for poor desolate Louis. Mr. Day had been vainly trying to find some one to come and live with him, so he closed with Tom's modest demand at once, and walked back with him to the 'Mitre' to get his luggage. I think I have told you it was early spring, but the wind and sun had not yet dried the road out of Christchurch to Mellatoto, three miles up the Avon, the river on which the young town was being built; consequently the track was almost impassable for wheels. There are wild legends afloat to this day of certain miry 'bottoms' on that road which have engulphed bullock-drays, teams, drivers, stock-whips, and all.

'I'm only living in a wharre* at present, Roden,' said Mr. Day, 'but the frame of a four-roomed wooden house has come out from England in the same ship which brought you, and we'll take it up to the run in no time. I've taken up ten thousand acres of first-class sheep country beyond those low ranges there, towards the gorge of the Selwyn, and I mean to go and live there this summer. Can you cook at all, young sir?'

'Well, not much, sir,' answered Louis, modestly. This speech meant that he had never tried to cook at all in his life; unless stuffing some baby carp and tench, unscraped and uncleaned, into the oven at home, when the cook's back was turned, could be called cookery.

'Because I ain't *on* cooking myself, not much,' said Mr. Day thoughtfully, lighting his short, black pipe; 'but we must have our victuals somehow. I dare say you could learn how to make damper, now, couldn't you?'

'Oh yes, sir,' cried Louis, as a bright thought struck him; 'but I'll tell you what I *could* do. I'd shoot you lots of small birds, you know, and you could make them into a pie.'

'I dare say,' said Mr. Gale; 'first catch your hare, young man. There ain't no small birds here, and precious few big ones, barring wild duck. Why, I saw a canary sold last week for £18, and a black-bird is worth a five-pound note if it's worth a farthing. As for sparrows, there has never been one near the place. There are a few little willow wrens, but it would be a shame to kill them.'

'Then what's the good of my gun?' asked Louis, almost crying with disappointment.

'Not any good at all, and that's the truth. I can't think why, but every young man that comes out to the colony brings a lot of firearms. First he has his revolvers; those are for the bushrangers and Maories. There's never been a bushranger in the whole of New Zealand, not nearer than Australia, and that is a thousand miles away. There are only a few very peaceable Maories in this island, and the fighting natives in the North island would take very good care to keep out of pistol shot. Then there are their rifles and double-barrel Purdy's. I suppose they think they'll have to shoot the sheep! Never mind, Roden,' he concluded, seeing Louis's face of misery, 'we'll manage for you to have a shot sometimes, and we'll go wild cattle hunting in the Black Country down North as soon as you can ride. You've got to learn how to stick on a horse's back first you know.'

So they trudged along the muddy streets – now so well paved and lighted, with their drinking-fountains and pillar-posts at every corner – till they arrived at the 'Mitre,' where Mr. Day went in and *shouted* champagne in honour of his having secured Louis's valuable services. *Shouting*, in colo-nial phraseology, means 'standing treat;' and Tom Day shouted himself off his legs, and had to carried to the wooden steps leading down to the Avon.

Most of the traffic was done by water in those days on account of the badness of the roads, and as Mr. Day's farm, Mellatoto, was on the bank of the river, it was easier to take baggage up by boat. I cannot say there was very much gained however, for the Avon used, until a very late date when an Act of the local Parliament came into force, to be so chocked up with watercress, that it resembled a strip of a particularly green meadow more than a good-sized river. But the boatman poled and

---

* A sort of Maori wigwam made out of flax-leaves. (Author's note)

Louis pulled, until they came to the wharre, or rather a couple of wharres which Mr. Day had put upon his farm. The ground was in very good order, and the young crops were coming up nicely.

'Where are the sheep?' asked Louis.

'This is only a bit of a freehold farm,' explained the boatman, Mr. Day being fast asleep at the bottom of the boat; 'the sheep is all up at the run, fifty miles off. There ain't no sheep, not hereabouts, only grain crops.'

He helped Louis to get his things ashore, and shook Mr. Day so vigorously that at last he jumped up, took off his coat and offered to fight the boatman and Louis first separately, and then both together. This proposal being declined, he walked majestically as far as the wharre, and tried to stalk in at the door in a stately way, but as the entrance was only about four feet high, and Mr. Tom stood six feet in his stockings, he could not manage it, much to his surprise. He kept saying, 'Why, the door's grown smaller,' until at last he sank on his knees and crept in. Louis thought the hut was a dismal hole, and felt glad enough to be told to go and light a fire outside, to fry some chops and boil some rice. There was nothing to cook the chops with, and Louis mentioned this fact.

'There's the spade; what better can you want, you young aristocrat?' shouted Mr. Day, who was always quarrelsome in his cups.

So Louis put the chops on the spade, and held the spade over the fire, but he soon got tired of that, and picking up a couple of stones, propped his extempore frying-pan nicely up in the middle of a good blaze. He found a pot, and, fetching some water from the river, put on several handfuls of rice to boil.

'Aren't the chops ready?' roared Mr. Day from the dark recesses of the wharre.

'I'll see, sir,' answered Louis, and he went to look. Alas, what a sight met his eyes! The flame had burnt through the handle of the spade – and spades were precious things in those days – leaving the iron part glowing, a beautiful red-hot plate, in the midst of the fire. A few little black frizzling lumps on the spade he took to be the chops, but he wasn't sure. Louis was too frightened to proclaim his failure, so as Mr. Day had gone off to sleep he said nothing about it, thinking it a pity to awaken him to hear bad news. He gave all his attention to the rice, though he was much amazed to see how it swelled in process of boiling, and was half inclined to think it must have been bewitched. However he tasted it frequently, and when it was soft he carried the pot bodily into the wharre, and ate some himself, feeding Mr. Day, who made very wry faces over the dinner, but did not ask about the chops, so Louis carefully held his tongue. By this time it was dark, and Louis rolled himself up in his blankets and laid down. In spite of his strange surroundings he slept well until daylight, when he was roused by Mr. Day groaning and saying,

'Oh, Roden, I ate too many chops last night, I've got such a splitting headache.'

Louis thought that could hardly be the reason of his illness, but he said nothing, and got up to see what the weather was like. A sou'-wester had set in with a deluge of steadily-descending cold rain, so there was nothing for it but to go to bed again, and for three days Mr. Day and young Roden lived on that huge pot of rice. It was impossible to light a fire or to cook anything, and it was a lucky accident which led Louis to put so much rice into the iron pot, or 'billy,' as it is called. They slept and ate rice alternately, and Mr. Day smoked. It was a very wretched beginning of colonial life for our poor young friend, but when the fourth day dawned bright and sunny, with a delicious soft air, and he got up early to take a dip in the Avon, he soon forgot all his troubles, and only thought what a beautiful place it was and how hungry he felt.

# Thomas March Clark (1812–1903)

*John Whopper the Newsboy* is the apotheosis of the American 'tall tale', but from 1854 its author was Bishop of Rhode Island for 49 years: on the face of it, a splendid paradox. The book comprises real 'whoppers' (the word has been used in the sense of 'fantastic lie' since the eighteenth century). The fantasy is distinctive: it combines the modern world of travel, newspapers, commerce and science with the dry exaggeration of the oral tale. In a way, this is the new mythology, the new fairy-tales of a new continent, owing little or nothing to the European tradition. In his *Reminiscences* (1895) Clark contrasted the relative pleasantness for children of the Sundays of his old age with the grim Calvinistic attitudes of his boyhood. The genial *John Whopper* may have contributed to this change.

## from *John Whopper the Newsboy* (1870)

### CHAPTER I

#### HOW JOHN WHOPPER DISCOVERED THE AIR-LINE TO CHINA

Two years ago last February, I think it was on a Tuesday morning, I started as usual very early to distribute my papers. I had a large bundle to dispose of that day, and thought that if I took a short cut across the fields, instead of following the road from Roxbury to Jamaica Plain, I could go my rounds in much less time. I do not care to tell precisely where it was that I jumped over the fence; but it is a rough, barren kind of spot, which nobody has ever done any thing to improve.

After walking about a third of a mile, I began to think that I had better have kept to the turnpike; for I found that I was obliged to clamber over an uneven, rocky place, among trees and bushes and shrubs, that grew just thick enough to bother me, so that I hardly knew where to put my feet. All at once I lost my balance, and felt that I was sliding down the side of a smooth, steep rock; while underneath, to my horror, I saw what looked like a circular cave, or well, some five or six feet in diameter. I tried to grasp the rock with my hands, and ground my heels as hard as I could against the surface, but it was of no use; down I slipped, faster and faster, until at last I plunged, feet foremost, into the dark hole below. For a moment I held my breath, expecting to be dashed to pieces; and oh, how many things I thought of in that short minute! It seemed as if every thing that I had ever done came back to me, especially all the *bad* things; and how I wished then that I had lived a better life! I thought, too, of my poor mother and my little brother and sister at home, and how they would wait breakfast for me that morning; and how they would keep on waiting and waiting, hour after hour and day after day; and how the neighbors would all turn out and search for me; and how I should never be found, and nobody would ever know what had become of me. And then I wondered whether Mr. Simpson, who employed me to distribute the papers, would suppose that I had run away somewhere, to sell them on my own account; and so I went on thinking and wondering, until it seemed as if there was no end to the time. And yet I didn't strike the bottom of the cave, but just went on falling and falling, faster and faster, in the darkness, and sometimes just grazing the sides, and still not so as to hurt me much. My great trouble was to breathe; when it occurred to me to lay the sleeve of my coat across my mouth: and then I found that I could breathe through the cloth with tolerable ease. After a while, I recovered my senses; and though I continued to fall on still faster and faster, I experienced no great inconvenience. How long this continued, I cannot tell; it appeared to be an age; and I must have been falling for several hours, when I began to feel as though I was not sinking as fast as I had been; and after a while, it seemed as if I were rising up, rather than tumbling down. As I was now able to breathe much more freely than I had done, I began to think calmly about my condition; and then the thought flashed across my mind, that perhaps I had passed the centre of the earth, and was gradually rising to the surface on the other side.

This gave me hope; and when I found that I continued to move slower and slower, I tried to collect my faculties, so that I might know just what it would be best to do, if I should be so fortunate as to reach the other end of the hole into which I had tumbled. At last, looking down, I saw a little speck of light, like a very faint star; and then, I tell you, my heart bounded with joy. At this moment it suddenly occurred to me that it would not do to come out of the hole *feet foremost*; and, by a tremendous effort, I managed to turn a complete summersault – what the boys always called a *somerset*, – which, of course, brought me into the right position. How thankful I felt that I had been taught to practise gymnastic exercises at the school in Roxbury! In my present attitude I couldn't see the bright spot any longer: but, before long, I perceived that it was growing lighter around me; and I was confident that the time of my release drew near. I had determined exactly what I would do when I reached the surface of the earth again; and, accordingly, on the instant that my head came out of the hole, I grasped the edge with all my might, and, by another terrible effort, swung myself up into the air, and leaped upon the ground.

It is impossible to describe the strange thrill that passed over me when I thus found myself standing on what I knew must be the eastern side of the globe. As soon as I had fairly recovered the use of my reason, I began to speculate as to the region of the country into which I emerged. If I had come directly through the centre of the earth, I knew, of course, just where I ought to be; but this hardly seemed possible, considering how short a time it had required for my journey. It then occurred to me that I was really unable to form any accurate idea of the number of hours that had elapsed since I left the soil of Massachusetts; for, before I had fallen a hundred feet, a whole age appeared to have passed. I knew that it was about six o'clock in the morning when I started; and, on looking at my watch, I found that it had stopped at 6.45, owing, as I afterwards ascertained, to the influence of magnetic currents upon the hair-spring.

The country around was in a high state of cultivation, except in the immediate vicinity of the spot where I stood. This was rough and barren, and so situated that the small cavity in the earth from which I had just been released, would be very likely to escape observation. Thinking that it might be important for me to be able hereafter to identify the locality, I took a careful observation of its general bearings, and twisted together a few of the twigs that grew near the hole, but in such a manner as would not be likely to arrest attention.

Striking off now at random, I soon found myself in a low, marshy region, covered with a species of grain unlike any thing I had ever seen before, but which I concluded must be rice; and then the thought came to me, that very probably I was in China. After walking for an hour or two, I reached a rising ground, and saw in the distance an immense city on the water's edge; which from its position, and resemblance to certain pictures that I had once seen in Boston, I believed to be Canton. Refreshing myself with some fruit that grew by the wayside, I started off in haste, in order, if possible, to reach the city before nightfall. Just as the sun was setting, I entered what appeared to be one of the main streets; when, tired and hungry and footsore, I began to think seriously what I should do to procure food and lodging. Here I was, – a poor boy in a strange land, unable to address a word to the people around me, and with only a few cents and two or three bits of paper currency in my pocket, that could be of no value in that country. *What was I to do?* Just then I came to a large and respectable-looking building; and over the door there was this sign, in good plain characters: –

'ENGLISH AND AMERICAN COFFEE-HOUSE.'

Tears of joy filled my eyes. In an instant, I said to myself, 'Your fortune is made, old fellow! Here you have thirty or forty Boston newspapers, not twenty-four hours old, strapped around your neck; and I rather think they will be in some demand in Canton.'

With a light heart I now entered the office of the hotel, and threw down my bundle, with a good, black-leather covering around the papers, so that it looked like an ordinary piece of luggage, which gave me the appearance of a regular traveller; then called for a room, and ordered supper. It was true that I had very little money in my possession, – not enough, certainly, to pay my bill at the hotel; but no questions were asked, and I gave myself little concern as to the future. I had a first-rate appetite, and ate voraciously.

After supper was over, I took my bundle in my hand, and strolled leisurely into a pleasant and spacious room, where a number of gentlemen – English and American – were sitting around in groups, some chatting together, and others reading the London and New York and Boston papers. Among them I recognized the face of a merchant whom I had seen several times in State Street; and slinging the strap over my shoulder in a careless, every-day sort of tone, just as any newsboy would have done at home, I went up to him and said, 'Have the morning papers, Mister? – "morning papers?" – "Advertiser," "Journal," "Post," "Herald," last edition, – published this morning, *only five dollars!*' Everybody in the room looked up, for I managed, as newsboys generally do, to speak loud enough to drown every other sound; but no one uttered a word. It was evident that they thought I was crazy, or something worse; and so I just cried out again, 'Have the morning paper, sir?' at the same time thrusting a copy of 'The Advertiser' into his hand. He looked like an 'Advertiser' kind of man, – well dressed and highly respectable.

Involuntarily his eye glanced at the date, – 'Tuesday, Feb. 16, 1867'; and then, in an excited, quivering tone, he said, 'Let me look at your other papers.' There was a long table in the centre of the room, which I approached; and, slowly unfolding my bundle, I laid a few of the papers wide open in front of the gentlemen, who crowded around in the highest state of excitement. Still there was dead silence; when one of them suddenly burst out with the exclamation, 'Good heavens! Here is the notice of the arrival of "The Golconda" at New York, with a full account of the cargo, and every thing else correct. Why, this must be genuine!'

One after another followed with a cry of surprise at some news which they had found; until, in a few minutes, every gentleman in the room was absorbed in reading the papers, appearing to have entirely forgotten all about me, and not caring to ask how it was that I had brought them to China in less than twenty-four hours. After I had stood there whistling carelessly as long as I thought worth while, I spoke up in a loud voice, and said, 'Well, gentlemen, you seem to be enjoying the news pretty well. I hope you don't mean to forget to pay for the papers, – *only five dollars a copy!*'

At this speech every one of them looked at me with a strange expression, as if they hardly knew whether I was a real human boy or something else; when the Boston gentleman said, 'How on earth did you get these papers here?' To which I answered very carelessly, 'I didn't get them here *on* earth.'

'What do you mean?'

'I will tell you what I mean, and answer your questions, after you have paid me *five dollars each; and cheap at that, considering.*'

'Indeed it is, for me at least,' said one of the gentlemen. 'What I have learned from this paper is worth to me, in a business way, thousands of dollars'; and with that he came forward and put a hundred into my hand, in the good, solid form of gold-pieces. His example had its effect upon the others. Instead of the two hundred which I had hoped to receive for my forty newspapers, I was actually in possession of not less than – well, I don't care to tell exactly how much, on account of the income-tax.

'Come, now,' said the gentlemen, almost in one breath, 'tell us how these papers came to China.'

'I brought them myself.'

'When did you leave America?'

'The morning when these papers were printed: but how long ago that was, I really don't know, as my watch stopped while I was on my voyage; only I thought it was just as well to call out, as I always used to do at home, "Morning paper!" although, perhaps, for all I can tell, they may be two or perhaps three days old; anyhow, I guess you find them a good deal fresher than the rest you have got on hand.'

Having delivered myself of this somewhat protracted speech, I began moving towards the door with the air of one who had said every thing that could reasonably be expected, in reply to the curious inquiries of my liberal patrons, when the Boston merchant motioned for me to stop, saying with some severity, 'Did you not promise that you would inform the company how these papers came from America to China in such an incredibly short period of time, whenever you should have received your pay for the same?'

'Yes, sir; and I just told you that I brought them over – not exactly *over* – but – in short, I brought them here.'

'You say "not exactly *over*"; do you mean by that phrase to be understood to say that you did not come over land?'

'Your honor has hit my meaning precisely.'

'You don't pretend to say that you came by water?'

'Far from it, sir.'

'How then, *under the heavens*, did you come?'

'I didn't come under the heavens at all.'

'I don't believe,' said the irritated gentleman, turning to his companions, 'that the fellow came at all; he must be lying.'

All the answer that he received was the rustling of forty newspapers, bearing the imprint, 'February 16, 1867, Boston.' There was no getting over this.

After a pause of several minutes, during which a bright idea entered my mind, I came forward into the circle, and said, 'Well, gentlemen, I want to see if I can make a good bargain with you; and when that is settled, I will tell you how I came over – I mean, I will tell you how I got here; that is, I will tell you *the route* that I took. If I can arrange for the delivery in Canton of the New York and Boston daily papers, within thirty-six hours of the time when they are issued in those cities, will you all promise to give me your generous patronage?'

'Of course we will,' they cried all together.

'Very well; then I pledge myself to appear again in this place one week from this day, ready to carry out my part of the bargain. And now, in bidding you good-night, allow me to inform you that I came from America to China by the *air-line*.'

With this I retired at once to my room, and was soon sleeping soundly.

# 'Lewis Carroll' (Charles Lutwidge Dodgson) (1832–1898)

*Alice's Adventures in Wonderland* (1865) is generally regarded as the greatest turning point in nineteenth-century children's fiction, a book where children's imaginations were first given absolutely free rein, with no moral messages. Indeed, it might well have been anti-moral, for, in the first chapter, there is a satirical aside attacking the book's predecessors. Alice has found a bottle labelled 'DRINK ME'.

It was all very well to say 'Drink Me', but wise little Alice was not going to do *that* in a hurry. 'No, I'll look first,' she said, 'and see whether it's marked "*poison*" or not': for she had read several nice little stories about children who had got burnt, and eaten up by wild beasts, and other unpleasant things, all because they *would* not remember the simple rules their friends had taught them: such as, that a red-hot poker will burn you if you hold it too long; and that, if you cut your finger *very* deeply with a knife, it usually bleeds; and she had never forgotten that, if you drink much from a bottle marked 'poison', it is almost certain to disagree with you, sooner or later.

Of course, as this anthology has demonstrated, this grandly pivotal position of *Alice* is something of an exaggeration. It is more accurate to say *Alice's Adventures* and *Through the Looking-glass* are outstanding examples of a trend that is visible in British children's literature from the mid-century, towards apparently light-hearted and un-didactic fantasy. They are also characteristic of the growing tendency for authors to exploit the inevitable: consciously or subconsciously, authors must incorporate into their books for children their attitudes to childhood – their own, as well as generalized or specific childhood. And although it is not immediately obvious, Carroll seems to have followed writers like Kingsley in using his books as vehicles for intricate social and political comment. As a result, the Alice books can lay some claim to being the most deliberately if not obviously complex texts ever designed for children.

The fact that they are among the very few children's books to have achieved *adult* canonical status naturally reinforces this: books which are not taken seriously are not given the attention that yields complex meanings. But the cumulative evidence of thousands of academic articles, and a substantial shelf of books on Carroll and his work, do suggest that Carroll made some very ingenious (not to say devious) uses of his books.

*Alice's Adventures in Wonderland* was developed from *Alice's Adventures Underground*, a present from the Oxford mathematics don, the Revd Charles Dodgson, to one of his child-friends, Alice Liddell, in 1864. The story had been originally told extempore on a Thames boat trip, although the circumstances (and the weather conditions) have been romanticized. A good deal of biographical ink has been spilt on Carroll, either focusing on or evading his predilection for the company (and the photographing of) pre-pubescent girls, on his manic personality, on his association with celebrities, on his involvement with college politics and his views on national politics. Among the most recent publications on his work have been Martin Gardner's *The Annotated Alice: The Definitive Edition* (2000) and Jo Elwyn Jones's and J. Francis Gladstone's *The Alice Companion* (1998), the select bibliography to which runs to ten pages.

Some critics have found in the Alice books a network of personal references, sublimations and declarations. But there is a great deal more. The books not only tell surreal tales, but are layered with linguistic, philosophical and mathematical games and jokes, local and national political satire, and parodies. In *Alice's Adventures in Wonderland*, for example, the pool of tears is populated by Alice's sisters and local Oxford characters; Alice's changes in size have been given sexual interpretations; the (beagle) puppy that Alice meets is a caricature of Charles Darwin (and Alice dodges behind 'a great thistle' who may well be the non-Darwinian William Turner Thistleton Dyer, another Oxford don); and so on (perhaps endlessly). It becomes clear that Carroll's choice of a major political cartoonist, Sir John Tenniel, to illustrate his books, was not made at random.

Whatever political, philosophical or religious interpretations are placed on the books, and in among the death jokes and the mathematical ingenuity, many readers have seen, on the most obvious narrative level, a portrait of repressive Victorian society and the place of the child within it. The insouciant Alice is more puzzled than disturbed by the mad adults who surround her and who seem intent on playing arbitrary linguistic games and imposing irrational rules on life.

The books were an immense success and Carroll produced one other major book, the highly surreal and symbolic *The Hunting of the Snark* (1876), which few commentators regard as being for children. At the other extreme, he rewrote *Alice's Adventures in Wonderland* as *The Nursery Alice* (1890), a sickly-sentimental piece ('So it really *was* a *little* Puppy, you see. And isn't it a little *pet?*) which demonstrated a quite different side of Carroll's character – and a quite different side of the Victorian temper. The sentimentalization of childhood was to continue well into the twentieth century (A. A. Milne was a late exponent), but it sits in particularly curious contrast to the often savage intellectualism of the Alice books.

Virtually all of the elements discussed above are to be found in the eighth chapter of *Through The Looking-glass*,

'It's My Own Invention'. The book is constructed as a chess game, and Alice has been playing the part of a pawn, unable to see the moves of the other characters. Just before she reaches the last rank, where she will become a queen (a metaphor for puberty), she is captured by the White Knight. This character seems to be an ironic self-portrait of Carroll, with all his eccentricities of manner, his inventions, his logic, his interest in language and his symbolic falls in front of Alice – attempts, perhaps, to stop her growing up and away from him (he also catches her hair). It is important to recognize that there is not a superfluous word in this passage: there is a (flawed) lesson in the logic of names; a demonstration of the art of parody (the White Knight's song is a merciless treatment of Wordsworth's 'Resolution and Independence') and a sad reflection on the Knight's relationship with Alice (the tune of the White Knight's song is a lachrymose Victorian romantic ballad). In this scene, Carroll seems to be taking leave of his association with childhood, and with Alice in particular.

Carroll's books are among the most widely translated and widely read works of fiction in the world; they have been illustrated by well over a hundred artists, filmed, endlessly adapted, and have become a byword for nonsense. Their influence has, however, been indirect; he gave licence for cleverness rather than simplicity, and for independence of thought in children's literature, but independence of thought both for the adults and children involved. Direct imitations such as *The Wallypug of Why* (see p. 422) were relative failures, while writers who accorded childhood the same *respect* as Carroll, such as Kipling and Nesbit, succeeded.

## from *Through the Looking-glass and What Alice Found There* (1871)

### CHAPTER VIII

### 'IT'S MY OWN INVENTION'

After a while the noise seemed gradually to die away, till all was dead silence, and Alice lifted up her head in some alarm. There was no one to be seen, and her first thought was that she must have been dreaming about the Lion and the Unicorn and those queer Anglo-Saxon Messengers. However, there was the great dish still lying at her feet, on which she had tried to cut the plum-cake, 'So I wasn't dreaming, after all,' she said to herself, 'unless – unless we're all part of the same dream. Only I do hope it's *my* dream, and not the Red King's! I don't like belonging to another person's dream,' she went on in a rather complaining tone: 'I've a great mind to go and wake him, and see what happens!'

At this moment her thoughts were interrupted by a loud shouting of 'Ahoy! Ahoy! Check!' and a Knight, dressed in crimson armour, came galloping down upon her, brandishing a great club. Just as he reached her, the horse stopped suddenly: 'You're my prisoner!' the Knight cried, as he tumbled off his horse.

Startled as she was, Alice was more frightened for him than for herself at the moment, and watched him with some anxiety as he mounted again. As soon as he was comfortably in the saddle, he began once more. 'You're my –' but here another voice broke in 'Ahoy! Ahoy! Check!' and Alice looked round in some surprise for the new enemy.

This time it was a White Knight. He drew up at Alice's side, and tumbled off his horse just as the Red Knight had done: then he got on again, and the two Knights sat and looked at each other for some time without speaking. Alice looked from one to the other in some bewilderment.

'She's *my* prisoner, you know!' the Red Knight said at last.

'Yes, but then *I* came and rescued her!' the White Knight replied.

'Well, we must fight for her, then,' said the Red Knight, as he took up his helmet (which hung from the saddle, and was something the shape of a horse's head) and put it on.

'You will observe the Rules of Battle, of course?' the White Knight remarked, putting on his helmet too.

'I always do,' said the Red Knight, and they began banging away at each other with such fury that Alice got behind a tree to be out of the way of the blows.

'I wonder, now, what the Rules of Battle are,' she said to herself, as she watched the fight, timidly peeping out from her hiding-place. 'One Rule seems to be, that if one Knight hits the other, he knocks him off his horse; and, if he misses, he tumbles off himself – and another Rule seems to be that they hold their clubs with their arms, as if they were Punch and Judy – What a noise they make when they tumble! Just like a whole set of fire-irons falling into the fender! And how quiet the horses are! They let them get on and off them just as if they were tables!'

Another Rule of Battle, that Alice had not noticed, seemed to be that they always fell on their heads; and the battle ended with their both falling off in this way, side by side. When they got up again, they shook hands, and then the Red Knight mounted and galloped off.

'It was a glorious victory, wasn't it?' said the White Knight, as he came up panting.

'I don't know,' Alice said doubtfully. 'I don't want to be anybody's prisoner. I want to be a Queen.'

'So you will, when you've crossed the next brook,' said the White Knight. 'I'll see you safe to the end of the wood – and then I must go back, you know. That's the end of my move.'

'Thank you very much,' said Alice. 'May I help you off with your helmet?' It was evidently more than he could manage by himself: however she managed to shake him out of it at last.

'Now one can breathe more easily,' said the Knight, putting back his shaggy hair with both hands, and turning his gentle face and large mild eyes to Alice. She thought she had never seen such a strange-looking soldier in all her life.

He was dressed in tin armour, which seemed to fit him very badly, and he had a queer-shaped little deal box fastened across his shoulders, upside-down, and with the lid hanging open. Alice looked at it with great curiosity.

'I see you're admiring my little box,' the Knight said in a friendly tone. 'It's my own invention – to keep clothes and sandwiches in. You see I carry it upside-down, so that the rain can't get in.'

'But the things can get *out*,' Alice gently remarked. 'Do you know the lid's open?'

'I didn't know it,' the Knight said, a shade of vexation passing over his face. 'Then all the things must have fallen out! And the box is no use without them.' He unfastened it as he spoke, and was just going to throw it into the bushes, when a sudden thought seemed to strike him, and he hung it carefully on a tree. 'Can you guess why I did that?' he said to Alice.

Alice shook her head.

'In hopes some bees may make a nest in it – then I should get the honey.'

'But you've got a bee-hive – or something like one – fastened to the saddle,' said Alice.

'Yes, it's a very good bee-hive,' the Knight said in a discontented tone, 'one of the best kind. But not a single bee has come near it yet. And the other thing is a mouse-trap. I suppose the mice keep the bees out – or the bees keep the mice out, I don't know which.'

'I was wondering what the mouse-trap was for,' said Alice. 'It isn't very likely there would be any mice on the horse's back.'

'Not very likely, perhaps,' said the Knight; 'but, if they *do* come, I don't choose to have them running all about.'

'You see,' he went on after a pause, 'it's as well to be provided for *everything*. That's the reason the horse has all those anklets round his feet.'

'But what are they for?' Alice asked in a tone of great curiosity.

'To guard against the bites of sharks,' the Knight replied. 'It's an invention of my own. And now help me on. I'll go with you to the end of the wood – What's that dish for?'

'It's meant for plum-cake,' said Alice.

'We'd better take it with us,' the Knight said. 'It'll come in handy if we find any plum-cake. Help me to get it into this bag.'

This took a long time to manage, though Alice held the bag open very carefully, because the Knight was so *very* awkward in putting in the dish: the first two or three times that he tried he fell in himself instead. 'It's rather a tight fit, you see,' he said, as they got it in at last; 'there are so many candlesticks in the bag.' And he hung it to the saddle, which was already loaded with bunches of carrots, and fire-irons, and many other things.

'I hope you've got your hair well fastened on?' he continued, as they set off.

'Only in the usual way,' Alice said, smiling.

'That's hardly enough,' he said, anxiously. 'You see the wind is so *very* strong here. It's as strong as soup.'

Plate 5    The White Knight from *Through the Looking-glass*, illustrated by Sir John Tenniel, By permission of the British Library

'Have you invented a plan for keeping the hair from being blown off?' Alice enquired.

'Not yet,' said the Knight. 'But I've got a plan for keeping it from *falling* off.'

'I should like to hear it, very much.'

'First you take an upright stick,' said the Knight. 'Then you make your hair creep up it, like a fruit-tree. Now the reason hair falls off is because it hangs *down* – things never fall *upwards*, you know. It's a plan of my own invention. You may try it if you like.'

It didn't sound a comfortable plan, Alice thought, and for a few minutes she walked on in silence, puzzling over the idea, and every now and then stopping to help the poor Knight, who certainly was *not* a good rider.

Whenever the horse stopped (which it did very often), he fell off in front; and, whenever it went on again (which it generally did rather suddenly), he fell off behind. Otherwise he kept on pretty well, except that he had a habit of now and then falling off sideways; and, as he generally did this on the side on which Alice was walking, she soon found that it was the best plan not to walk *quite* close to the horse.

'I'm afraid you've not had much practice in riding,' she ventured to say, as she was helping him up from his fifth tumble.

The Knight looked very much surprised, and a little offended at the remark. 'What makes you say that?' he asked, as he scrambled back into the saddle, keeping hold of Alice's hair with one hand, to save himself from falling over on the other side.

'Because people don't fall off quite so often, when they've had much practice.'

'I've had plenty of practice,' the Knight said very gravely: 'plenty of practice!'

Alice could think of nothing better to say than 'Indeed?' but she said it as heartily as she could. They went on a little way in silence after this, the Knight with his eyes shut, muttering to himself, and Alice watching anxiously for the next tumble.

'The great art of riding,' the Knight suddenly began in a loud voice, waving his right arm as he spoke, 'is to keep –' Here the sentence ended as suddenly as it had begun, as the Knight fell heavily on the top of his head exactly in the path where Alice was walking. She was quite frightened this time, and said in an anxious tone, as she picked him up, 'I hope no bones are broken?'

'None to speak of,' the Knight said, as if he didn't mind breaking two or three of them. 'The great art of riding, as I was saying, is – to keep your balance properly. Like this, you know –'

He let go the bridle, and stretched out both his arms to show Alice what he meant, and this time he fell flat on his back, right under the horse's feet.

'Plenty of practice!' he went on repeating, all the time that Alice was getting him on his feet again. 'Plenty of practice!'

'It's too ridiculous!' cried Alice, losing all her patience this time. 'You ought to have a wooden horse on wheels, that you ought!'

'Does that kind go smoothly?' the Knight asked in a tone of great interest, clasping his arms round the horse's neck as he spoke, just in time to save himself from tumbling off again.

'Much more smoothly than a live horse,' Alice said, with a little scream of laughter, in spite of all she could do to prevent it.

'I'll get one,' the Knight said thoughtfully to himself. 'One or two – several.'

There was a short silence after this, and then the Knight went on again. 'I'm a great hand at inventing things. Now, I daresay you noticed, the last time you picked me up, that I was looking rather thoughtful?'

'You *were* a little grave,' said Alice.

'Well, just then I was inventing a new way of getting over a gate – would you like to hear it?'

'Very much indeed,' Alice said politely.

'I'll tell you how I came to think of it,' said the Knight. 'You see, I said to myself "The only difficulty is with the feet: the *head* is high enough already." Now, first I put my head on the top of the gate – then the head's high enough – then I stand on my head – then the feet are high enough, you see – then I'm over, you see.'

'Yes, I suppose you'd be over when that was done,' Alice said thoughtfully: 'but don't you think it would be rather hard?'

'I haven't tried it yet,' the Knight said, gravely; 'so I can't tell for certain – but I'm afraid it *would* be a little hard.'

He looked so vexed at the idea, that Alice changed the subject hastily. 'What a curious helmet you've got!' she said cheerfully. 'Is that your invention too?'

The Knight looked down proudly at his helmet, which hung from the saddle. 'Yes,' he said; 'but I've invented a better one than that – like a sugar-loaf. When I used to wear it, if I fell off the horse, it always touched the ground directly. So I had a *very* little way to fall, you see – But there *was* the danger of falling *into* it, to be sure. That happened to me once – and the worst of it was, before I could get out again, the other White Knight came and put it on. He thought it was his own helmet.'

The Knight looked so solemn about it that Alice did not dare to laugh. 'I'm afraid you must have hurt him,' she said in a trembling voice, 'being on the top of his head.'

'I had to kick him, of course,' the Knight said, very seriously. 'And then he took the helmet off again – but it took hours and hours to get me out. I was as fast as – as lightning, you know.'

'But that's a different kind of fastness,' Alice objected.

The Knight shook his head. 'It was all kinds of fastness with me, I can assure you!' he said. He raised his hands in some excitement as he said this, and instantly rolled out of the saddle, and fell headlong into a deep ditch.

Alice ran to the side of the ditch to look for him. She was rather startled by the fall, as for some time he had kept on very well, and she was afraid that he really *was* hurt this time. However, though she could see nothing but the soles of his feet, she was much relieved to hear that he was talking on in his usual tone. 'All kinds of fastness,' he repeated: 'but it was careless of him to put another man's helmet on – with the man in it, too.'

'How *can* you go on talking so quietly, head downwards?' Alice asked, as she dragged him out by the feet, and laid him in a heap on the bank.

The Knight looked surprised at the question. 'What does it matter where my body happens to be?' he said. 'My mind goes on working all the same. In fact, the more head downwards I am, the more I keep inventing new things.

'Now the cleverest thing of the sort that I ever did,' he went on after a pause, 'was inventing a new pudding during the meat-course.'

'In time to have it cooked for the next course?' said Alice. 'Well, that *was* quick work, certainly!'

'Well, not the *next* course,' the Knight said in a slow thoughtful tone: 'no, certainly not the next *course.*'

'Then it would have to be the next day. I suppose you wouldn't have two pudding-courses in one dinner?'

'Well, not the *next* day,' the Knight repeated as before: 'not the next *day.* In fact,' he went on, holding his head down, and his voice getting lower and lower, 'I don't believe that pudding ever *was* cooked! In fact, I don't believe that pudding ever *will* be cooked! And yet it was a very clever pudding to invent.'

'What did you mean it to be made of?' Alice asked, hoping to cheer him up, for the poor Knight seemed quite low-spirited about it.

'It began with blotting-paper,' the Knight answered with a groan.

'That wouldn't be very nice, I'm afraid –'

'Not very nice *alone*,' he interrupted, quite eagerly: 'but you've no idea what a difference it makes, mixing it with other things – such as gunpowder and sealing wax. And here I must leave you.' They had just come to the end of the wood.

Alice could only look puzzled: she was thinking of the pudding.

'You are sad,' the Knight said in an anxious tone: 'let me sing you a song to comfort you.'

'Is it very long?' Alice asked, for she had heard a good deal of poetry that day.

'It's long,' said the Knight, 'but it's very, *very* beautiful. Everybody that hears me sing it – either it brings the *tears* into their eyes, or else –'

'Or else what?' said Alice, for the Knight had made a sudden pause.

'Or else it doesn't, you know. The name of the song is called "*Haddocks' Eyes.*"'

'Oh, that's the name of the song, is it?' Alice said, trying to feel interested.

'No, you don't understand,' the Knight said, looking a little vexed. 'That's what the name is *called*. The name really *is* "*The Aged Aged Man.*"'

'Then I ought to have said "That's what the *song* is called"?' Alice corrected herself.

'No, you oughtn't: that's quite another thing! The *song* is called "*Ways And Means*": but that's only what it's *called*, you know!'

'Well, what *is* the song, then?' said Alice, who was by this time completely bewildered.

'I was coming to that,' the Knight said. 'The song really *is* "*A-sitting On A Gate*": and the tune's my own invention.'

So saying, he stopped his horse and let the reins fall on its neck: then, slowly beating time with one hand, and with a faint smile lighting up his gentle foolish face, as if he enjoyed the music of his song, he began.

Of all the strange things that Alice saw in her journey Through The Looking-Glass, this was the one that she always remembered most clearly. Years afterwards she could bring the whole scene back again, as if it had been only yesterday – the mild blue eyes and kindly smile of the Knight – the setting sun gleaming through his hair, and shining on his armour in a blaze of light that quite dazzled her – the horse quietly moving about, with the reins hanging loose on his neck, cropping the grass at her feet – and the black shadows of the forest behind – all this she took in like a picture, as, with one hand shading her eyes, she leant against a tree, watching the strange pair, and listening, in a half-dream, to the melancholy music of the song.

'But the tune *isn't* his own invention,' she said to herself: 'it's "*I give thee all, I can no more.*"' She stood and listened very attentively, but no tears came into her eyes.

I'll tell thee everything I can:
There's little to relate.

I saw an aged aged man,
   A sitting on a gate.
"Who are you, aged man?" I said.
   "And how is it you live?"
And his answer trickled through my head,
   Like water through a sieve.

He said "I look for butterflies
   That sleep among the wheat:
I make them into mutton-pies,
   And sell them in the street.
I sell them unto men," he said,
   "Who sail on stormy seas;
And that's the way I get my bread –
   A trifle, if you please."

But I was thinking of a plan
   To dye one's whiskers green,
And always use so large a fan
   That they could not be seen.
So, having no reply to give
   To what the old man said,
I cried "Come, tell me how you live!"
   And thumped him on the head.

His accents mild took up the tale:
   He said "I go my ways,
And when I find a mountain-rill,
   I set it in a blaze;
And thence they make a stuff they call
   Rowland's Macassar-Oil –
Yet twopence-halfpenny is all
   They give me for my toil."

But I was thinking of a way
   To feed oneself on batter,
And so go on from day to day
   Getting a little fatter.
I shook him well from side to side,
   Until his face was blue:
"Come, tell me how you live," I cried,
   "And what it is you do!"

He said "I hunt for haddocks' eyes
   Among the heather bright,
And work them into waistcoat-buttons
   In the silent night.
And these I do not sell for gold
   Or coin of silvery shine,
But for a copper halfpenny,
   And that will purchase nine.

"I sometimes dig for buttered rolls,
   Or set limed twigs for crabs:
I sometimes search the grassy knolls
   For wheels of Hansom-cabs.
And that's the way" (he gave a wink)
   "By which I get my wealth –

And very gladly will I drink
    Your Honour's noble health."

I heard him then, for I had just
    Completed my design
To keep the Menai bridge from rust
    By boiling it in wine.
I thanked him much for telling me
    The way he got his wealth,
But chiefly for his wish that he
    Might drink my noble health.

And now, if e'er by chance I put
    My fingers into glue,
Or madly squeeze a right-hand foot
    Into a left-hand shoe,
Or if I drop upon my toe
    A very heavy weight,
I weep, for it reminds me so
Of that old man I used to know −
Whose look was mild, whose speech was slow,
Whose hair was whiter than the snow,
Whose face was very like a crow,
With eyes, like cinders, all aglow,
Who seemed distracted with his woe,
Who rocked his body to and fro,
And muttered mumblingly and low,
As if his mouth were full of dough,
Who snorted like a buffalo −
That summer evening long ago,
    A-sitting on a gate.'

As the Knight sang the last words of the ballad, he gathered up the reins, and turned his horse's head along the road by which they had come. 'You've only a few yards to go,' he said, 'down the hill and over that little brook, and then you'll be a Queen − But you'll stay and see me off first?' he added as Alice turned with an eager look in the direction to which he pointed. 'I shan't be long. You'll wait and wave your handkerchief when I get to that turn in the road! I think it'll encourage me, you see.'

'Of course I'll wait,' said Alice: 'and thank you very much for coming so far − and for the song − I liked it very much.'

'I hope so,' the Knight said doubtfully: 'but you didn't cry so much as I thought you would.'

So they shook hands, and then the Knight rode slowly away into the forest. 'It won't take long to see him *off*, I expect,' Alice said to herself, as she stood watching him. 'There he goes! Right on his head as usual! However, he gets on again pretty easily − that comes of having so many things hung round the horse −' So she went on talking to herself, as she watched the horse walking leisurely along the road, and the Knight tumbling off, first on one side and then on the other. After the fourth or fifth tumble he reached the turn, and then she waved her handkerchief to him, and waited till he was out of sight.

'I hope it encouraged him,' she said, as she turned to run down the hill: 'and now for the last brook, and to be a Queen! How grand it sounds!' A very few steps brought her to the edge of the brook. 'The Eighth Square at last!' she cried as she bounded across, and threw herself down to rest on a lawn as soft as moss, with little flower-beds dotted about it here and there. 'Oh, how glad I am to get here! And what *is* this on my head?' she exclaimed in a tone of dismay, as she put her hands up to something very heavy, that fitted tight all round her head.

'But how *can* it have got there without my knowing it?' she said to herself, as she lifted it off, and set it on her lap to make out what it could possibly be.

It was a golden crown.

# 'Susan Coolidge' (Sarah Chauncey Woolsey) (1845–1905)

The longevity of *What Katy Did* is good evidence of the untidiness of history, for the book is an American classic much better known in Britain; given that, it is, at least on the surface, a throwback to more evangelical days. Admittedly, the happy family of the widowed Dr Carr is a broadly liberal one, and Katy's sufferings after her accident are not borne quite in the religiously stoic manner of her forebears. But the fact of her suffering at all, the fact that it is punishment for disobedience, and the fact that her recovery is presided over by Cousin Helen, who is presumably intended to be a model of self-control and saintliness (but who appears to many modern readers as unconvincing and sanctimonious), are unmistakable marks of puritanical thinking. On the other hand, modern feminist critics such as Shirley Foster and Judy Simons have seen in Katy's severe punishment a reaction not merely to her disobedience but to her pushing back the boundaries of acceptable female behaviour. The continuing success of the book suggests that the combination of the moral tale and the ultimate success of individual perseverance still retains its appeal (back injuries became epidemic in children's books for a time).

The sequel *What Katy Did at School* (1873) is an interesting early example of the school story genre and even the pale *What Katy Did Next* (1886), an essay in the teenage-to-marriage sub-genre, is still read.

The central dramatic incident of *What Katy Did*, with its attendant moralizing, is reprinted here.

## from *What Katy Did* (1872)

### CHAPTER VIII

### TO-MORROW

'To-morrow I will begin,' thought Katy, as she dropped asleep that night. How often we all do so! And what a pity it is that when morning comes and to-morrow is to-day, we so frequently wake up feeling quite differently; careless or impatient, and not a bit inclined to do the fine things we planned over-night.

Sometimes it seems as if there must be wicked little imps in the world, who are kept tied up so long as the sun shines, but who creep into our bedrooms when we are asleep to tease us and ruffle our tempers. Else, why, when we go to rest good-natured and pleasant, should we wake up so cross? Now, there was Katy. Her last sleepy thought was an intention to be an angel from that time on, and as much like Cousin Helen as she could; and when she opened her eyes she was all out of sorts, and as fractious as a bear! Old Mary said that she got out of bed on the wrong side. I wonder, by the way, if anybody will ever be wise enough to tell us which side that is, so that we may always choose the other? How comfortable it would be if they could!

You know how, if we begin the day in a cross mood, all sorts of unfortunate accidents seem to occur to add to our vexations. The very first thing Katy did this morning was to break her precious vase – the one Cousin Helen had given her.

It was standing on the bureau with a little cluster of blush-roses in it. The bureau had a swing-glass. While Katy was brushing her hair, the glass tipped a little so that she could not see. At a good-humoured moment, this accident wouldn't have troubled her much. But being out of temper to begin with, it made her angry. She gave the glass a violent push. The lower part swung forward, there was a smash, and the first thing Katy knew the blush-roses lay scattered all over the floor, and Cousin Helen's pretty present was ruined.

Katy just sat down on the carpet and cried as hard as if she had been Phil himself. Aunt Izzie heard her lamenting, and came in.

'I'm very sorry,' she said, picking up the broken glass, 'but it's no more than I expected, you're so careless, Katy. Now don't sit there in that foolish way! Get up and dress yourself. You'll be late for breakfast.'

'What's the matter?' asked papa, noticing Katy's red eyes as she took her seat at the table.

'I've broken my vase,' said Katy, dolefully.

'It was extremely careless of you to put it in such a dangerous place,' said her aunt. 'You might have known that the glass would swing and knock it off.' Then, seeing a big tear fall in the middle of Katy's plate, she added: 'Really, Katy, you're too big to behave like a baby. Why, Dorry would be ashamed to do so. Pray control yourself!'

This snub did not improve Katy's temper. She went on with her breakfast in sulky silence.

'What are you all going to do to-day?' asked Dr. Carr, hoping to give things a more cheerful turn.

'Swing!' cried John and Dorry both together.

'Alexander's put us up a splendid one in the wood-shed.'

'No, you're not,' said Aunt Izzie, in a positive tone; 'the swing is not to be used till to-morrow. Remember that, children. Not till to-morrow. And not then, unless I give you leave.'

This was unwise of Aunt Izzie. She would have done better to have explained further. The truth was, that Alexander, in putting up the swing, had cracked one of the staples which fastened it to the roof. He meant to get a new one in the course of the day, and, meantime, he had cautioned Miss Carr to let no one use the swing, because it really was not safe. If she had told this to the children, all would have been right; but Aunt Izzie's theory was, that young people must obey their elders without explanation.

John, and Elsie, and Dorry, all pouted when they heard this order. Elsie recovered her good-humour first.

'I don't care,' she said, 'because I'm going to be very busy; I've got to write a letter to Cousin Helen about somefing.' (Elsie never could quite pronounce the *th*.)

'What?' asked Clover.

'Oh, somefing!' answered Elsie, wagging her head mysteriously. 'None of the rest of you must know, Cousin Helen said so; it's a secret she and me has got.'

'I don't believe Cousin Helen said so at all,' said Katy, crossly. 'She wouldn't tell secrets to a silly little girl like you.'

'Yes, she would too,' retorted Elsie, angrily. 'She said I was just as good to trust as if I was ever so big. And she said I was her pet. So there, Katy Carr!'

'Stop disputing,' said Aunt Izzie. 'Katy, your top drawer is all out of order. I never saw anything look so badly. Go upstairs at once and straighten it, before you do anything else. Children, you must keep in the shade this morning. It's too hot for you to be running about in the sun. Elsie, go into the kitchen and tell Debby I want to speak to her.'

'Yes,' said Elsie, in an important tone. 'And afterwards I am coming back to write my letter to Cousin Helen.'

Katy went slowly upstairs, dragging one foot after the other. It was a warm, languid day. Her head ached a little, and her eyes smarted and felt heavy from crying so much. Everything seemed dull and hateful. She said to herself, that Aunt Izzie was very unkind to make her work in vacation, and she pulled the top-drawer open with a disgusted groan.

It must be confessed that Miss Izzie was right. A bureau-drawer could hardly look worse than this one did. It reminded one of the White Knight's recipe for a pudding, which began with blotting-paper, and ended with sealing-wax and gunpowder. All sorts of things were mixed together, as if somebody had put in a long stick, and stirred them well up. There were books and paint-boxes and bits of scribbled paper, and lead pencils and brushes. Stocking-legs had come unrolled, and twisted themselves about pocket-handkerchiefs, and ends of ribbon, and linen collars. Ruffles, all crushed out of shape, stuck up from under the heavier things, and sundry little paper boxes lay empty on top, the treasures they once held having sifted down to the bottom of the drawer, and disappeared beneath the general mass.

It took much time and patience to bring order out of this confusion. But Katy knew that Aunt Izzie would be up by and by, and she dared not stop till all was done. By the time it was finished, she was very tired. Going downstairs, she met Elsie coming up with a slate in her hand, which, as soon as she saw Katy, she put behind her.

'You mustn't look,' she said, 'it's my letter to Cousin Helen. Nobody but me knows the secret. It's all written, and I'm going to send it to the office. See – there's a stamp on it;' and she exhibited a corner of the slate. Sure enough, there was a stamp stuck on the frame.

'You little goose!' said Katy, impatiently; 'you can't send *that* to the post-office. Here, give me the slate. I'll copy what you've written on paper, and papa'll give you an envelope.'

'No, no,' cried Elsie, struggling, 'you mustn't! You'll see what I have said, and Cousin Helen said I wasn't to tell. It's a secret. Let go of my slate, I say! I'll tell Cousin Helen what a mean girl you are, and then she won't love you a bit.'

'There, then, take your old slate!' said Katy, giving her a vindictive push. Elsie slipped, screamed, caught at the banisters, missed them, and rolling over and over, fell with a thump on the hall floor.

It wasn't much of a fall, only half a dozen steps, but the bump was a hard one, and Elsie roared as if she had been half-killed. Aunt Izzie and Mary came rushing to the spot.

'Katy – pushed – me,' sobbed Elsie. 'She wanted me to tell her my secret, and I wouldn't. She's a bad, naughty girl!'

'Well, Katy Carr, I *should* think you'd be ashamed of yourself,' said Aunt Izzie, 'wreaking your temper on your poor little sister! I think your Cousin Helen will be surprised when she hears this. There, there, Elsie! Don't cry any more, dear. Come upstairs with me. I'll put on some arnica, and Katy shan't hurt you again.'

So they went upstairs. Katy, left below, felt very miserable: repentant, defiant, discontented, and sulky all at once. She knew in her heart that she had not meant to hurt Elsie, and was thoroughly ashamed of that push; but Aunt Izzie's hint about telling Cousin Helen had made her too angry to allow of her confessing this to herself or anybody else.

'I don't care!' she murmured, choking back her tears. 'Elsie is a real cry-baby, anyway. And Aunt Izzie always takes her part. Just because I told the little silly not to go and send a great heavy slate to the post-office!'

She went out by the side-door into the yard. As she passed the shed, the new swing caught her eye.

'How exactly like Aunt Izzie,' she thought, 'ordering the children not to swing till she gives them leave! I suppose she thinks it's too hot, or something. *I* shan't mind her, anyhow.'

She seated herself in the swing. It was a first-rate one, with a broad comfortable seat, and thick new ropes. The seat hung just the right distance from the floor. Alexander was a capital hand at putting up swings, and the wood-shed the nicest possible spot in which to have one.

It was a big place, with a very high roof. There was not much wood left in it just now, and the little there was, was piled neatly about the sides of the shed, so as to leave plenty of room. The place felt cool and dark, and the motion of the swing seemed to set the breeze blowing. It waved Katy's hair like a great fan, and made her dreamy and quiet. All sorts of sleepy ideas began to flit through her brain. Swinging to and fro like the pendulum of a great clock, she gradually rose higher and higher, driving herself along by the motion of her body, and striking the floor smartly with her foot, at every sweep. Now she was at the top of the high arched door. Then she could almost touch the cross-beam above it, and through the small square window could see pigeons sitting and pluming themselves on the eaves of the barn, and white clouds blowing over the blue sky. She had never swung so high before. It was like flying, she thought, and she bent and curved more strongly in the seat, trying to send herself yet higher, and graze the roof with her toes.

Suddenly, at the very highest point of the sweep, there was a sharp noise of cracking. The swing gave a violent twist, spun half round, and tossed Katy into the air. She clutched the rope – felt it dragged from her grasp – then, down – down – down – she fell. All grew dark, and she knew no more.

When she opened her eyes she was lying on the sofa in the dining-room. Clover was kneeling beside her with a pale, scared face, and Aunt Izzie was dropping something cold and wet on her forehead.

'What's the matter?' asked Katy, faintly.

'Oh, she's alive – she's alive!' and Clover put her arms round Katy's neck and sobbed.

'Hush, dear!' Aunt Izzie's voice sounded unusually gentle. 'You've had a bad tumble, Katy. Don't you recollect?'

'A tumble? Oh, yes – out of the swing!' said Katy, as it all came slowly back to her. 'Did the rope break, Aunt Izzie? I can't remember about it.'

'No, Katy, not the rope. The staple drew out of the roof. It was a cracked one, and not safe. Don't you recollect my telling you not to swing to-day. Did you forget?'

'No, Aunt Izzie – I didn't forget. I –' but here Katy broke down. She closed her eyes, and big tears rolled from under the lids.

'Don't cry,' whispered Clover, crying herself, 'please don't. Aunt Izzie isn't going to scold you.' But Katy was too weak and shaken not to cry.

'I think I'd like to go upstairs and lie on the bed,' she said. But when she tried to get off the sofa, everything swam before her, and she fell back again on the pillow.

'Why, I can't stand up!' she gasped, looking very much frightened.

'I'm afraid you've given yourself a sprain somewhere,' said Aunt Izzie, who looked rather frightened herself. 'You'd better lie still a while, dear, before you try to move. Ah, here's the doctor! well, I *am* glad.' And she went forward to meet him. It wasn't papa, but Dr. Alsop, who lived quite near them.

'I am so relieved that you could come,' Aunt Izzie said. 'My brother is gone out of town not to return till to-morrow, and one of the little girls has had a bad fall.'

Dr. Alsop sat down beside the sofa and counted Katy's pulse. Then he began feeling all over her. 'Can you move this leg?' he asked.

Katy gave a feeble kick.

'And this?'

The kick was a good deal more feeble.

'Did that hurt you?' asked Dr. Alsop, seeing a look of pain on her face.

'Yes, a little,' replied Katy, trying hard not to cry.

'In your back, eh? Was the pain high up or low down?' And the doctor punched Katy's spine for some minutes, making her squirm uneasily.

'I'm afraid she's done some mischief,' he said at last, 'but it's impossible to tell yet exactly what. It may be only a twist, or a slight sprain,' he added, seeing a look of terror on Katy's face. 'You'd better get her upstairs and undress her as soon as you can, Miss Carr. I'll leave a prescription to rub her with.' And Dr. Alsop took out a bit of paper and began to write.

'Oh, must I go to bed?' said Katy. 'How long will I have to stay there, doctor?'

'That depends on how fast you get well,' replied the doctor; 'not long, I hope. Perhaps only a few days.'

'A few days!' repeated Katy, in a despairing tone.

After the doctor was gone, Aunt Izzie and Debby lifted Katy, and carried her slowly upstairs. It was not easy, for every motion hurt her, and the sense of being helpless hurt most of all. She couldn't help crying after she was undressed and put into bed. It all seemed so dreadful and strange. If only papa was here, she thought. But Dr. Carr had gone into the country to see somebody who was very sick, and couldn't possibly be back till to-morrow.

Such a long, long afternoon as that was! Aunt Izzie sent up some dinner, but Katy couldn't eat. Her lips were parched and her head ached violently. The sun began to pour in, the room grew warm. Flies buzzed in the window, and tormented her by lighting on her face. Little prickles of pain ran up and down her back. She lay with her eyes shut, because it hurt to keep them open, and all sorts of uneasy thoughts went rushing through her mind.

'Perhaps, if my back is really sprained, I shall have to lie here as much as a week,' she said to herself. 'Oh, dear, dear! I *can't*. The vacation is only eight weeks and I was going to do such lovely things! How can people be so patient as Cousin Helen when they have to lie still? Won't she be sorry when she hears! Was it really yesterday that she went away? It seems a year. If only I hadn't got into that nasty old swing!' And then Katy began to imagine how it would have been if she *hadn't*, and how she and Clover had meant to go to Paradise that afternoon. They might have been there under the cool trees now. As these thoughts ran through her mind, her head grew hotter and her position in the bed more uncomfortable.

Suddenly she became conscious that the glaring light from the window was shaded, and that the wind seemed to be blowing freshly over her. She opened her heavy eyes. The blinds were shut, and there beside the bed sat little Elsie, fanning her with a palm-leaf fan.

'Did I wake you up, Katy?' she asked, in a timid voice.

Katy looked at her with startled, amazed eyes.

'Don't be frightened,' said Elsie, 'I won't disturb you. Johnny and me are *so* sorry you're ill;' and her little lips trembled. 'But we mean to keep quiet, and never bang the nursery door, or make noises on the stairs, till you're all well again. And I've brought you somefing real nice. Some of it's from John, and some from me. It's because you got tumbled out of the swing. See!' And Elsie pointed triumphantly to a chair, which she had pulled up close to the bed, and on which were solemnly set forth: 1st, A pewter tea-set; 2nd, A box with a glass lid, on which flowers were painted; 3rd, A jointed doll; 4th, A transparent slate; and lastly, two new lead pencils!

'They're all yours – yours to keep,' said generous little Elsie. 'You can have Pikery, too, if you want. Only he's pretty big, and I'm afraid he'd be lonely without me. Don't you like the fings, Katy? They're real pretty!'

It seemed to Katy as if the hottest sort of a coal of fire was burning into the top of her head as she looked at the treasures on the chair, and then at Elsie's face all lighted up with affectionate self-sacrifice. She tried to speak, but began to cry instead, which frightened Elsie very much.

'Does it hurt you so bad?' she asked, crying too, from sympathy.

'Oh, no! it isn't *that*,' sobbed Katy; 'but I was so cross to you this morning, Elsie, and pushed you. Oh, please forgive me, please do!'

'Why, it's got well!' said Elsie, surprised. 'Aunt Izzie put a fing out of a bottle on it, and the bump all went away. Shall I go and ask her to put some on you too – I will.' And she ran toward the door.

'Oh, no!' cried Katy; 'don't go away, Elsie. Come here and kiss me, instead.'

Elsie turned, as if doubtful whether this invitation could be meant for her. Katy held out her arms. Elsie ran right into them, and the big sister and the little exchanged an embrace which seemed to bring their hearts closer together than they had ever been before.

'You're the most *precious* little darling!' murmured Katy, clasping Elsie tight. 'I've been just horrid to you, Elsie. But I'll never be again. You shall play with me and Clover, and Cecy, just as much as you like, and write notes in all the post-offices, and everything else.'

'Oh, goody! goody!' cried Elsie, executing little skips of transport. 'How sweet you are, Katy! I mean to love you next best to Cousin Helen and papa! And' – racking her brains for some way of repaying this wonderful kindness – 'I'll tell you the secret, if you want me to *very* much. I am sure Cousin Helen would let me.'

'No,' said Katy; 'never mind about the secret. I don't want you to tell it to me. Sit down by the bed, and fan me some more instead.'

'No!' persisted Elsie, who, now that she had made up her mind to part with the treasured secret, could not bear to be stopped. 'Cousin Helen gave me a half-dollar, and told me to give it to Debby, and tell her she was much obliged to her for making her such nice things to eat. And I did. And Debby was very pleased. And I wrote Cousin Helen a letter, and told her that Debby liked the half-dollar. That's the secret! Isn't it a nice one? Only you mustn't tell anybody about it, ever – just as long as you live.'

'No!' said Katy, smiling faintly, 'I won't.'

All the rest of the afternoon Elsie sat beside the bed with her palm-leaf fan, keeping off the flies, and 'shoo'-ing away the other children when they peeped in at the door. 'Do you really like to have me here?' she asked, more than once, and smiled, oh, *so* triumphantly! when Katy said 'Yes!' But though Katy said yes, I am afraid it was only half the truth, for the sight of the dear little forgiving girl, whom she had treated unkindly, gave her more pain than pleasure.

'I'll be *so* good to her when I get well,' she thought to herself, tossing uneasily to and fro.

Aunt Izzie slept in her room that night. Katy was feverish. When morning came, and Dr. Carr returned, he found her in a good deal of pain, hot and restless, with wide-open, anxious eyes.

'Papa!' she cried the first thing, 'must I lie here as much as a week?'

'My darling, I'm afraid you must,' replied her father, who looked worried, and very grave.

'Dear, dear!' sobbed Katy, 'how can I bear it?'

## CHAPTER IX

## DISMAL DAYS

If anybody had told Katy, that first afternoon, that at the end of a week she would still be in bed, and in pain, and with no time fixed for getting up, I think it would have almost killed her. She was so restless and eager, that to lie still seemed one of the hardest things in the world. But to lie still, and have her back ache all the time, was worse yet. Day after day she asked papa with quivering lips: 'May not I get up and go downstairs this morning?' And when he shook his head, the lip would quiver more, and tears would come. But if she tried to get up, it hurt her so much, that in spite of herself she was glad to sink back again on the soft pillows and mattress, which felt so comfortable to her poor bones.

Then there came a time when Katy didn't ever ask to be allowed to get up. A time when sharp, dreadful pain, such as she never imagined before, took hold of her. When days and nights got all confused and tangled up together, and Aunt Izzie never seemed to go to bed. A time when papa was constantly in her room. When other doctors came and stood over her, and punched and felt her back, and talked to each other in low whispers. It was all like a long, bad dream, from which she couldn't wake up, though she tried ever so hard. Now and then she would rouse a little, and catch the sound of voices, or be aware that Clover or Elsie stood at the door, crying softly; or that Aunt Izzie, in creaking slippers, was going about the room on tiptoe. Then all these things would slip away again, and she would drop off into a dark place where there was nothing but pain, and sleep, which made her forget pain, and so seemed the best thing in the world.

We will hurry over this time, for it is hard to think of our bright Katy in such a sad plight. By and by the pain grew less, and the sleep quieter. Then, as the pain became easier still, Katy woke up as it were – began to take notice of what was going on about her; to put questions.

'How long have I been ill?' she asked one morning.

'It is four weeks yesterday,' replied papa.

'Four weeks!' said Katy. 'Why, I didn't know it was so long as that. Was I very ill, Papa?'

'Very, dear. But you are a great deal better now.'

'How did I hurt myself when I tumbled out of the swing?' asked Katy, who was in an unusually wakeful mood.

'I don't believe I could make you understand, dear.'

'But try, Papa.'

'Well, did you know that you had a long bone down your back called a spine?'

'I thought that was a disease,' said Katy. 'Clover said that Cousin Helen had the spine!'

'No, the spine is a bone. It is made up of a row of smaller bones – or knobs – and in the middle of it is a sort of rope of nerves called the spinal cord. Nerves, you know, are the things we feel with. Well, this spinal cord is rolled up for safe-keeping in a soft wrapping, called membrane. When you fell out of the swing, you struck against one of these knobs, and bruised the membrane inside, and the nerve inflamed, and gave you a fever in the back. Do you see?'

'A little,' said Katy, not quite understanding, but too tired to question further. After she had rested a while, she said: 'Is the fever well now, Papa? Can I get up again and go downstairs yet?'

'Not yet, I'm afraid,' said Dr. Carr, trying to speak cheerfully.

Katy didn't ask any more questions then. Another week passed, and another. The pain was almost gone. It only came back now and then for a few minutes. She could sleep now, and eat, and be raised in bed without feeling giddy. But still the once active limbs hung heavy and lifeless, and she was not able to walk, or even stand alone.

'My legs feel so queer,' she said one morning; 'they are just like the Prince's legs which were turned to black marble in the *Arabian Nights*. What do you suppose is the reason, Papa? Won't they feel natural soon?'

'Not soon,' answered Dr. Carr. Then he said to himself, 'Poor child! she had better know the truth.' So he went on aloud, 'I am afraid, my darling, that you must make up your mind to stay in bed a long time.'

'How long?' said Katy, looking frightened; 'a month more?'

'I can't tell exactly how long,' answered her father. 'The doctors think, as I do, that the injury to your spine is one which you will outgrow by and by, because you are so young and strong. But it may take a good while to do it. It may be that you will have to lie here for months, or it may be more. The only cure for such a hurt is time and patience. It is hard, darling' – for Katy began to sob wildly, – 'but you have hope to help you along. Think of poor Cousin Helen, bearing all these years without hope!'

'Oh, Papa!' gasped Katy between her sobs, 'doesn't it seem dreadful, that just getting into the swing for a few minutes should do so much harm? Such a little thing as that!'

'Yes, such a little thing!' repeated Dr. Carr, sadly. 'And it was only a little thing, too, forgetting Aunt Izzie's order about the swing. Just for the want of the small "horse-shoe nail" of Obedience, Katy.'

# George MacDonald (1824–1905)

George MacDonald successfully harnessed the traditional fairy-tale to the purposes of religion and philosophy (rather than to the moral tale) and has a reputation as one of the first British writers to produce original fairy stories. His two most lasting books are *The Princess and the Goblin*, first serialized (1870–1) in *Good Words for the Young*, a major children's magazine which ran from 1868 to 1877, and *The Princess and Curdie* (1882), both of which have survived into the twenty-first century in print, audio and cartoon form.

Although the plotting seems to be very loose, the tone somewhat winsome, and in the manner of many Victorian fairy-tales there is a good deal of portentous suggesting of symbolic significance, the tales retain a strong, almost claustrophobic power. They seem to have influenced writers as apparently disparate as Frances Hodgson Burnett, J. R. R. Tolkien (notably in *The Hobbit*) and Maurice Sendak.

In the first book, Curdie the shepherd boy and Irene the young princess are at the centre of a battle between good and evil. On one side are the goblins, representing greed and corruption, who (literally) undermine Irene's (absent) father's castle; on the other is Irene's great-great-grandmother in her tower, who can be seen only by the pure and initiated. In this extract, Curdie has been captured and Irene saves him, guided by an invisible thread provided by her grandmother. The often uneasy relationship between the mystic, the adventure tale and MacDonald's idea of the humorous–grotesque emerges clearly.

*The Princess and Curdie* is a much darker book, dealing with human corruption in general. Although the reign of the eponymous couple as king and queen briefly restores purity, after their deaths the book ends in an apocalyptic destruction of the city.

MacDonald was a prolific writer whose adult fantasies, such as *Lilith* (1895), were also very influential (notably on C. S. Lewis). He was a friend of Lewis Carroll and Mark Twain, and through his life moved from Calvinism to the 'freethinking' Christian Socialism. Among his other notable books for children is *At The Back of the North Wind* (1871), an allegory based in social realism – somewhat in the manner of a more focused *The Water Babies* – marred for some readers by his weakness for page-filling doggerel.

## from *The Princess and the Goblin* (1871) [dated 1872]

## XXI

### THE ESCAPE

As the princess lay and sobbed, she kept feeling the thread mechanically, following it with her finger many times up to the stones in which it disappeared. By and by she began, still mechanically, to poke her finger in after it between the stones as far as she could. All at once it came into her head that she might remove some of the stones and see where the thread went next. Almost laughing at herself for never having thought of this before, she jumped to her feet. Her fear vanished; once more she was certain her grandmother's thread could not have brought her there just to leave her there; and she began to throw away the stones from the top as fast as she could, sometimes two or three at a handful, sometimes taking both hands to lift one. After clearing them away a little, she found that the thread turned and went straight downwards. Hence, as the heap sloped a good deal, growing of course wider towards its base, she had to throw away a multitude of stones to follow the thread. But this was not all, for she soon found that the thread, after going straight down for a little way, turned first sideways in one direction, then sideways in another, and then shot, at various angles, hither and thither inside the heap, so that she began to be afraid that to clear the thread, she must remove the whole huge gathering. She was dismayed at the very idea, but, losing no time, set to work with a will; and with aching back, and bleeding fingers and hands, she worked on, sustained by the pleasure of seeing the heap slowly diminish, and begin to show itself on the opposite side of the fire. Another thing which helped to keep up her courage was, that as often as she uncovered a turn of the thread, instead of lying loose upon the stones, it tightened up: this made her sure that her grandmother was at the end of it some-where.

She had got about half-way down when she started, and nearly fell with fright. Close to her ear as it seemed, a voice broke out singing –

'Jabber, bother, smash!
You'll have it all in a crash.
Jabber, smash, bother!
You'll have the worst of the pother
Smash, bother, jabber! – '

Here Curdie stopped, either because he could not find a rhyme to *jabber*, or because he remem-bered what he had forgotten when he woke up at the sound of Irene's labours, that his plan was to make the goblins think he was getting weak. But he had uttered enough to let Irene know who he was.

'It's Curdie!' she cried joyfully.

'Hush! hush!' came Curdie's voice again from somewhere. 'Speak softly.'

'Why, you were singing loud!' said Irene.

'Yes. But they know I am here, and they don't know you are. Who are you?'

'I'm Irene,' answered the princess. 'I know who you are quite well. You're Curdie.'

'Why, however did you come here, Irene?'

'My great-great-grandmother sent me; and I think I've found out why. You can't get out, I sup-pose?'

'No, I can't. What are you doing?'

'Clearing away a huge heap of stones.'

'There's a princess!' exclaimed Curdie, in a tone of delight, but still speaking in little more than a whisper. 'I can't think how you got here though.'

'My grandmother sent me after her thread.'

'I don't know what you mean,' said Curdie; 'but so you're there, it doesn't much matter.'

'Oh, yes it does!' returned Irene. 'I should never have been here but for her.'

'You can tell me all about it when we get out, then. There's no time to lose now,' said Curdie. And Irene went to work, as fresh as when she began.

'There's such a lot of stones!' she said. 'It will take me a long time to get them all away.'

'How far on have you got?' asked Curdie.

'I've got about the half away, but the other half is ever so much bigger.'

'I don't think you will have to move the lower half. Do you see a slab laid up against the wall?'

Irene looked, and felt about with her hands, and soon perceived the outlines of the slab.

'Yes,' she answered, 'I do.'

'Then, I think,' rejoined Curdie, 'when you have cleared the slab about half-way down, or a little more, I shall be able to push it over.'

'I must follow my thread,' returned Irene, 'whatever I do.'

'What *do* you mean?' exclaimed Curdie.

'You will see when you get out,' answered the princess, and went on harder than ever.

But she was soon satisfied that what Curdie wanted done, and what the thread wanted done, were one and the same thing. For she not only saw that by following the turns of the thread she had been clearing the face of the slab, but that, a little more than half-way down, the thread went through the clink between the slab and the wall into the place where Curdie was confined, so that she could not follow it any farther until the slab was out of her way. As soon as she found this, she said in a right joyous whisper –

'Now, Curdie! I think if you were to give a great push, the slab would tumble over.'

'Stand quite clear of it then,' said Curdie, 'and let me know when you are ready.'

Irene got off the heap, and stood on one side of it.

'Now, Curdie!' she cried.

Curdie gave a great rush with his shoulder against it. Out tumbled the slab on the heap, and out crept Curdie over the top of it.

'You've saved my life, Irene!' he whispered.

'Oh, Curdie! I'm so glad! Let's get out of this horrid place as fast as we can.'

'That's easier said than done,' returned he.

'Oh, no! it's quite easy,' said Irene. 'We have only to follow my thread. I am sure that it's going to take us out now.'

She had already begun to follow it over the fallen slab into the hole, while Curdie was searching the floor of the cavern for his pickaxe.

'Here it is!' he cried. 'No, it is not!' he added, in a disappointed tone. 'What can it be then? – I declare it's a torch. That *is* jolly! It's better almost than my pickaxe. Much better if it weren't for those stone shoes!' he went on, as he lighted the torch by blowing the last embers of the expiring fire.

When he looked up, with the lighted torch casting a glare into the great darkness of the huge cavern, he caught sight of Irene disappearing in the hole out of which he had himself just come.

'Where are you going there?' he cried. 'That's not the way out. That's where I couldn't get out.'

'I know that,' whispered Irene. 'But this is the way my thread goes, and I must follow it.'

'What nonsense the child talks!' said Curdie to himself. 'I must follow her, though, and see that she comes to no harm. She will soon find she can't get out that way, and then she will come with me.'

So he crept over the slab once more into the hole with his torch in his hand. But when he looked about in it, he could see her nowhere. And now he discovered that although the hole was narrow, it was much longer than he had supposed; for in one direction the roof came down very low, and the hole went off in a narrow passage, of which he could not see the end. The princess must have crept in there. He got on his knees and one hand, holding the torch with the other, and crept after her. The hole twisted about, in some parts so low that he could hardly get through, in others so high that he could not see the roof, but everywhere it was narrow – far too narrow for a goblin to get through, and so I presume they never thought that Curdie might. He was beginning to feel very uncomfortable lest something should have befallen the princess, when he heard her voice almost close to his ear, whispering –

'Aren't you coming, Curdie?'

And when he turned the next corner, there she stood waiting for him.

'I knew you couldn't go wrong in that narrow hole, but now you must keep by me, for here is a great wide place,' she said.

'I can't understand it,' said Curdie, half to himself, half to Irene.

'Never mind,' she returned. 'Wait till we get out.'

Curdie, utterly astonished that she had already got so far, and by a path he had known nothing of, thought it better to let her do as she pleased.

'At all events,' he said again to himself, 'I know nothing about the way, miner as I am; and she seems to think she does know something about it, though how she should, passes my comprehension. So she's just as likely to find her way as I am, and as she insists on taking the lead, I must follow. We can't be much worse off than we are, anyhow.'

Reasoning thus, he followed her a few steps, and came out in another great cavern, across which Irene walked in a straight line, as confidently as if she knew every step of the way. Curdie went on after her, flashing his torch about, and trying to see something of what lay around them. Suddenly he started back a pace as the light fell upon something close by which Irene was passing. It was a platform of rock raised a few feet from the floor and covered with sheep skins, upon which lay two horrible figures asleep, at once recognized by Curdie as the king and queen of the goblins. He lowered his torch instantly lest the light should awake them. As he did so, it flashed upon his pickaxe, lying by the side of the queen, whose hand lay close by the handle of it.

'Stop one moment,' he whispered. 'Hold my torch, and don't let the light on their faces.'

Irene shuddered when she saw the frightful creatures, whom she had passed without observing them, but she did as he requested, and turning her back, held the torch low in front of her. Curdie drew his pickaxe carefully away, and as he did so, spied one of her feet, projecting from under the skins. The great clumsy granite shoe, exposed thus to his hand, was a temptation not to be resisted.

He laid hold of it, and, with cautious efforts, drew it off. The moment he succeeded, he saw to his astonishment that what he had sung in ignorance, to annoy the queen, was actually true: she had six horrible toes. Overjoyed at his success, and seeing by the huge bump in the sheep skins where the other foot was, he proceeded to lift them gently, for, if he could only succeed in carrying away the other shoe as well, he would be no more afraid of the goblins than of so many flies. But as he pulled at the second shoe, the queen gave a growl and sat up in bed. The same instant the king awoke also, and sat up beside her.

'Run, Irene!' cried Curdie, for though he was not now in the least afraid for himself, he was for the princess.

Irene looked once round, saw the fearful creatures awake, and like the wise princess she was, dashed the torch on the ground and extinguished it, crying out –

'Here, Curdie, take my hand.'

He darted to her side, forgetting neither the queen's shoe nor his pickaxe, and caught hold of her hand, as she sped fearlessly where her thread guided her. They heard the queen give a great bellow; but they had a good start, for it would be some time before they could get torches lighted to pursue them. Just as they thought they saw a gleam behind them, the thread brought them to a very narrow opening, through which Irene crept easily, and Curdie with difficulty.

'Now,' said Curdie; 'I think we shall be safe.'

'Of course we shall,' returned Irene.

'Why do you think so?' asked Curdie.

'Because my grandmother is taking care of us.'

'That's all nonsense,' said Curdie. 'I don't know what you mean.'

'Then if you don't know what I mean, what right have you to call it nonsense?' asked the princess, a little offended.

'I beg your pardon, Irene,' said Curdie; 'I did not mean to vex you.'

'Of course not,' returned the princess. 'But why do *you* think we shall be safe?'

'Because the king and queen are far too stout to get through that hole.'

'There might be ways round,' said the princess.

'To be sure there might: we are not out of it yet,' acknowledged Curdie.

'But what do you mean by the king and queen?' asked the princess. 'I should never call such creatures as those a king and a queen.'

'Their own people do, though,' answered Curdie.

The princess asked more questions, and Curdie, as they walked leisurely along, gave her a full account, not only of the character and habits of the goblins, so far as he knew them, but of his own adventures with them, beginning from the very night after that in which he had met her and Lootie upon the mountain. When he had finished, he begged Irene to tell him how it was that she had come to his rescue. So Irene too had to tell a long story, which she did in rather a roundabout manner, interrupted by many questions concerning things she had not explained. But her tale, as he did not believe more than half of it, left everything as unaccountable to him as before, and he was nearly as much perplexed as to what he must think of the princess. He could not believe that she was deliberately telling stories, and the only conclusion he could come to was that Lootie had been playing the child tricks, inventing no end of lies to frighten her for her own purposes.

'But how ever did Lootie come to let you go into the mountain alone?' he asked.

'Lootie knows nothing about it. I left her fast asleep – at least I think so. I hope my grandmother won't let her get into trouble, for it wasn't her fault at all, as my grandmother very well knows.'

'But how *did* you find your way to me?' persisted Curdie.

'I told you already,' answered Irene; – 'by keeping my finger upon my grandmother's thread, as I am doing now.'

'You don't mean you've got the thread there?'

'Of course I do. I have told you so ten times already. I have hardly – except when I was removing the stones – taken my finger off it. There!' she added, guiding Curdie's hand to the thread; 'you feel it yourself – don't you?'

'I feel nothing at all,' replied Curdie,

'Then what *can* be the matter with your finger? *I* feel it perfectly. To be sure it is very thin, and in the sunlight looks just like the thread of a spider, though there are many of them twisted together to make it – but for all that I can't think why you shouldn't feel it as well as I do.'

Curdie was too polite to say he did not believe there was any thread there at all. What he did say was –

'Well, I can make nothing of it.'

'I can though, and you must be glad of that, for it will do for both of us.'

'We're not out yet,' said Curdie.

'We soon shall be,' returned Irene confidently.

And now the thread went downwards, and led Irene's hand to a hole in the floor of the cavern, whence came a sound of running water which they had been hearing for some time.

'It goes into ground now, Curdie,' she said, stopping.

He had been listening to another sound, which his practised ear had caught long ago, and which also had been growing louder. It was the noise the goblin miners made at their work, and they seemed to be at no great distance now. Irene heard it the moment she stopped.

'What is that noise?' she asked. 'Do you know, Curdie?'

'Yes. It is the goblins digging and burrowing,' he answered.

'And you don't know what they do it for?'

'No; I haven't the least idea. Would you like to see them?' he asked, wishing to have another try after their secret.

'If my thread took me there, I shouldn't much mind; but I don't want to see them, and I can't leave my thread. It leads me down into the hole, and we had better go at once.'

'Very well. Shall I go in first?' said Curdie.

'No; better not. You can't feel the thread,' she answered, stepping down through a narrow break in the floor of the cavern. 'Oh!' she cried, 'I am in the water. It is running strong – but it is not deep, and there is just room to walk. Make haste, Curdie.'

He tried, but the hole was too small for him to get in.

'Go on a little bit,' he said, shouldering his pickaxe.

In a few moments he had cleared a larger opening and followed her. They went on, down and down with the running water, Curdie getting more and more afraid it was leading them to some terrible gulf in the heart of the mountain. In one or two places he had to break away the rock to make room before even Irene could get through – at least without hurting herself. But at length they spied a glimmer of light, and in a minute more, they were almost blinded by the full sunlight into which they emerged. It was some little time before the princess could see well enough to discover that they stood in her own garden, close by the seat on which she and her king-papa had sat that afternoon. They had come out by the channel of the little stream. She danced and clapped her hands with delight.

'Now, Curdie!' she cried, 'won't you believe what I told you about my grandmother and her thread?'

For she had felt all the time that Curdie was not believing what she told him.

'There! – don't you see it shining on before us?' she added.

'I don't see anything,' persisted Curdie.

'Then you must believe without seeing,' said the princess; 'for you can't deny it has brought us out of the mountain.'

'I can't deny we *are* out of the mountain, and I should be very ungrateful indeed to deny that *you* had brought *me* out of it.'

'I couldn't have done it but for the thread,' persisted Irene.

'That's the part I don't understand.'

'Well, come along, and Lootie will get you something to eat. I am sure you must want it very much.'

'Indeed I do. But my father and mother will be so anxious about me, I must make haste – first up the mountain to tell my mother, and then down into the mine again to let my father know.'

'Very well, Curdie; but you can't get out without coming this way, and I will take you through the house, for that is nearest.'

They met no one by the way, for indeed, as before, the people were here and there and everywhere searching for the princess. When they got in, Irene found that the thread, as she had half expected, went up the old staircase, and a new thought struck her. She turned to Curdie and said –

'My grandmother wants me. Do come up with me, and see her. Then you will know that I have been telling you the truth. Do come – to please me, Curdie. I can't bear you should think I say what is not true.'

'I never doubted you believed what you said,' returned Curdie. 'I only thought you had some fancy in your head that was not correct.'

'But do come, dear Curdie.'

The little miner could not withstand this appeal, and though he felt shy in what seemed to him such a huge grand house, he yielded, and followed her up the stair.

# XXII

## The Old Lady and Curdie

Up the stair then they went, and the next and the next, and through the long rows of empty rooms, and up the little tower stair, Irene growing happier and happier as she ascended. There was no answer when she knocked at length at the door of the work-room, nor could she hear any sound of the spinning-wheel, and once more her heart sank within her – but only for one moment, as she turned and knocked at the other door.

'Come in,' answered the sweet voice of her grandmother, and Irene opened the door and entered, followed by Curdie.

'You darling!' cried the lady, who was seated by a fire of red roses mingled with white – 'I've been waiting for you, and indeed getting a little anxious about you, and beginning to think whether I had not better go and fetch you myself.'

As she spoke she took the little princess in her arms and placed her upon her lap. She was dressed in white now, and looking if possible more lovely than ever.

'I've brought Curdie, grandmother. He wouldn't believe what I told him, and so I've brought him.'

'Yes – I see him. He is a good boy, Curdie, and a brave boy. Aren't you glad you've got him out?'

'Yes, grandmother. But it wasn't very good of him not to believe me when I was telling him the truth.'

'People must believe what they can, and those who believe more must not be hard upon those who believe less. I doubt if you would have believed it all yourself if you hadn't seen some of it.'

'Ah! yes, grandmother, I dare say. I'm sure you are right. But he'll believe now.'

'I don't know that,' replied her grandmother.

'Won't you, Curdie?' said Irene, looking round at him as she asked the question.

He was standing in the middle of the floor, staring, and looking strangely bewildered. This she thought came of his astonishment at the beauty of the lady.

'Make a bow to my grandmother, Curdie,' she said.

'I don't see any grandmother,' answered Curdie rather gruffly.

'Don't see my grandmother, when I'm sitting in her lap!' exclaimed the princess.

'No, I don't,' reiterated Curdie, in an offended tone.

'Don't you see the lovely fire of roses – white ones amongst them this time?' asked Irene, almost as bewildered as he.

'No, I don't,' answered Curdie, almost sulkily.

'Nor the blue bed? Nor the rose-coloured counterpane? Nor the beautiful light, like the moon, hanging from the roof?'

'You're making game of me, your royal highness; and after what we have come through together this day, I don't think it is kind of you,' said Curdie, feeling very much hurt.

'Then what *do* you see?' asked Irene, who perceived at once that for her not to believe him was at least as bad as for him not to believe her.

'I see a big, bare, garret-room – like the one in mother's cottage, only big enough to take the cottage itself in, and leave a good margin all round,' answered Curdie.

'And what more do you see?'

'I see a tub, and a heap of musty straw, and a withered apple, and a ray of sunlight coming through a hole in the middle of the roof, and shining on your head, and making all the place look a curious dusky brown. I think you had better drop it, princess, and go down to the nursery, like a good girl.'

'But don't you hear my grandmother talking to me?' asked Irene, almost crying.

'No. I hear the cooing of a lot of pigeons. If you won't come down, I will go without you. I think that will be better anyhow, for I'm sure nobody who met us would believe a word we said to them. They would think we made it all up. I don't expect anybody but my own father and mother to believe me. They *know* I wouldn't tell a story.'

'And yet *you* won't believe *me*, Curdie?' expostulated the princess, now fairly crying with vexation, and sorrow at the gulf between her and Curdie.

'No. I *can't*, and I can't help it,' said Curdie, turning to leave the room.

'What *shall* I do, grandmother?' sobbed the princess, turning her face round upon the lady's bosom, and shaking with suppressed sobs.

'You must give him time,' said her grandmother; 'and you must be content not to be believed for a while. It is very hard to bear; but I have had to bear it, and shall have to bear it many a time yet. I will take care of what Curdie thinks of you in the end. You must let him go now.'

'You're not coming, are you?' asked Curdie.

'No, Curdie; my grandmother says I must let you go. Turn to the right when you get to the bottom of all the stairs, and that will take you to the hall where the great door is.'

'Oh! I don't doubt I can find my way – without you, princess, or your old grannie's thread either,' said Curdie quite rudely.

'Oh! Curdie! Curdie!'

'I wish I had gone home at once. I'm very much obliged to you, Irene, for getting me out of that hole, but I wish you hadn't made a fool of me afterwards.'

He said this as he opened the door, which he left open, and, without another word, went down the stair. Irene listened with dismay to his departing footsteps. Then turning again to the lady –

'What does it all mean, grandmother?' she sobbed, and burst into fresh tears.

'It means, my love, that I did not mean to show myself. Curdie is not yet able to believe some things. Seeing is not believing – it is only seeing. You remember I told you that if Lootie were to see me, she would rub her eyes, forget the half she saw, and call the other half nonsense.'

'Yes; but I should have thought Curdie –'

'You are right. Curdie is much farther on than Lootie, and you will see what will come of it. But in the mean time, you must be content, I say, to be misunderstood for a while. We are all very anxious to be understood, and it is very hard not to be. But there is one thing much more necessary.'

'What is that, grandmother?'

'To understand other people.'

'Yes, grandmother. I must be fair – for if I'm not fair to other people, I'm not worth being understood myself. I see. So as Curdie can't help it, I will not be vexed with him, but just wait.'

'There's my own dear child,' said her grandmother, and pressed her close to her bosom.

'Why weren't you in your work-room, when we came up, grandmother?' asked Irene, after a few moments' silence.

'If I had been there, Curdie would have seen me well enough. But why should I be there rather than in this beautiful room?'

'I thought you would be spinning.'

'I've nobody to spin for just at present. I never spin without knowing for whom I am spinning.'

'That reminds me – there is one thing that puzzles me,' said the princess: 'how are you to get the thread out of the mountain again? Surely you won't have to make another for *me*! That would be such a trouble!'

The lady set her down, and rose, and went to the fire. Putting in her hand, she drew it out again, and held up the shining ball between her finger and thumb.

'I've got it now, you see,' she said, coming back to the princess, 'all ready for you when you want it.' Going to her cabinet, she laid it in the same drawer as before.

'And here is your ring,' she added, taking it from the little finger of her left hand, and putting it on the forefinger of Irene's right hand.

'Oh! thank you, grandmother. I feel so safe now!'

'You are very tired, my child,' the lady went on. 'Your hands are hurt with the stones, and I have counted nine bruises on you. Just look what you are like.'

And she held up to her a little mirror which she had brought from the cabinet. The princess burst into a merry laugh at the sight. She was so draggled with the stream, and dirty with creeping through narrow places, that if she had seen the reflection without knowing it was a reflection, she would have taken herself for some gypsy-child whose face was washed and hair combed about once in a month. The lady laughed too, and lifting her again upon her knee, took off her cloak and night-gown. Then she carried her to the side of the room. Irene wondered what she was going to do with her, but asked no questions – only starting a little when she found that she was going to lay her in the large silver bath; for as she looked into it, again she saw no bottom, but the stars shining miles away, as it seemed, in a great blue gulf. Her hands closed involuntarily on the beautiful arms that held her, and that was all.

The lady pressed her once more to her bosom, saying –

'Do not be afraid, my child.'

'No, grandmother,' answered the princess, with a little gasp; and the next instant she sank in the clear cool water.

When she opened her eyes, she saw nothing but a strange lovely blue over and beneath and all about her. The lady and the beautiful room had vanished from her sight, and she seemed utterly alone. But instead of being afraid, she felt more than happy – perfectly blissful. And from somewhere came the voice of the lady, singing a strange sweet song, of which she could distinguish every word; but of the sense she had only a feeling – no understanding. Nor could she remember a single line after it was gone. It vanished, like the poetry in a dream, as fast as it came. In after years, however, she would sometimes fancy that snatches of melody suddenly rising in her brain, must be little phrases and fragments of the air of that song; and the very fancy would make her happier, and abler to do her duty.

How long she lay in the water, she did not know. It seemed a long time – not from weariness, but from pleasure. But at last she felt the beautiful hands lay hold of her, and through the gurgling water she was lifted out into the lovely room. The lady carried her to the fire, and sat down with her in her lap, and dried her tenderly with the softest towel. It was so different from Lootie's drying! When the lady had done, she stooped to the fire, and drew from it her night-gown, as white as snow.

'How delicious!' exclaimed the princess. 'It smells of all the roses in the world, I think.'

When she stood up on the floor, she felt as if she had been made over again. Every bruise and all weariness were gone, and her hands were soft and whole as ever.

'Now I am going to put you to bed for a good sleep,' said her grandmother.

'But what will Lootie be thinking? And what am I to say to her when she asks me where I have been?'

'Don't trouble yourself about it. You will find it all come right,' said her grandmother, and laid her into the blue bed, under the rosy counterpane.

'There is just one thing more,' said Irene. 'I am a little anxious about Curdie. As I brought him into the house, I ought to have seen him safe on his way home.'

'I took care of all that,' answered the lady. 'I told you to let him go, and therefore I was bound to look after him. Nobody saw him, and he is now eating a good dinner in his mother's cottage, far up the mountain.'

'Then I will go to sleep,' said Irene, and in a few minutes, she was fast asleep.

# Christina Georgina Rossetti (1830–1894)

Christina Rossetti's reputation in the history of children's literature is a curious one; it rests on three things. The first is a collection of highly sentimental, not to say maudlin poems, *Sing-Song* (1872), which may have struck the temper of the times – but it is hard now to imagine that it speaks to *any* childhood. The poems are largely from an adult point of view: 'Love me, – I love you, | Love me, my baby', and several pieces would have no doubt drawn tears from parents: 'A baby's cradle with no baby in it, | A baby's grave where autumn leaves drop sere'.

The second is 'Goblin Market' (1862) and here it is hard to fathom why any but consenting adults should be exposed to it. The fact that it is constantly reprinted in anthologies for children says something about the attitudes of adults to what they give to their children, or the gap between canonical and critical reading: 'She cried, "Laura" up the garden, | "Did you miss me? | Come and kiss me. | Never mind my bruises, | Hug me, kiss me, suck my juices | Squeezed from Goblin fruits for you, | Goblin pulp and goblin dew. | Eat me, drink me, love me; | Laura make much of me"'.

*Speaking Likenesses*, Rossetti's third claim to fame, is a foray into the fairy-tale, much in the manner of Jean Ingelow (they were friends), although it is less imaginative, and more inclined to draw a moral. The format is an old one used, for example, by Charlotte Barton in *A Mother's Offering* (see p. 55); a group of children are sitting around the narrator, sewing (and interrupting). It begins: 'Come sit round me, my dear little girls, and I will tell you a story. Each of you bring your sewing.... What Maude! pouting over that nice clean white stocking because it wants a darn? Put away your pout and pull out your needle, my dear; for pouts make a sad beginning to my story.' The interruptions invite snippets of information, but their general bent seems to be to stress that 'this is all make-believe'.

The first story centres on Flora's eighth birthday: her siblings and cousins fight and Flora wanders down the yew alley (as in this extract). Her experiences turn out to have been a dream ('you have been fast asleep ever so long in the yew walk'). The other two stories in the book are equally inconsequential. The extract reprinted here demonstrates that while Rossetti's work 'for children' was out-of-date both in technique and attitude as far as children's books were concerned, it carried great potential for psychological, rather than allegorical symbolism. (It also gives a sample of the kind of material that has been privileged by past critics.) The book was first published with rather nightmarish pictures by Arthur Hughes which accurately reflect the sinister undertones of the text.

## from *Speaking Likenesses* (1874)

Would you like, any of you, a game at hide-and-seek in a garden, where there are plenty of capital hiding-places and all sorts of gay flowers to glance at while one goes seeking? I should have liked such a game, I assure you, forty years ago. But these children on this particular day could not find it in their hearts to like it. Oh dear no. Serena affected to be afraid of searching along the dusky yew alley unless Alfred went with her; and at the very same moment Flora was bent on having him lift her up to look down into a hollow tree in which it was quite obvious Susan could not possibly have hidden. 'It's my birthday,' cried Flora; 'it's my birthday.' George and Richard pushed each other roughly about till one slipped on the gravel walk and grazed his hands, when both turned cross and left off playing. At last in sheer despair Susan stepped out of her hiding-place behind the summer-house: but even then she did her best to please everybody, for she brought in her hand a basket full of ripe mulberries which she had picked up off the grass as she stood in hiding.

Then they all set to running races across the smooth sloping lawn: till Anne tumbled down and cried, though she was not a bit hurt; and Flora, who was winning the race against Anne, thought herself ill-used and so sat and sulked. Then Emily smiled, but not good-naturedly, George and Richard thrust each a finger into one eye and made faces at the two cross girls. Serena fanned herself, and Alfred looked at Susan, and Susan at Alfred, fairly at their wits' end.

An hour yet before tea-time: would another hour ever be over? Two little girls looking sullen, two boys looking provoking: the sight was not at all an encouraging one. At last Susan took pouting Flora and tearful Anne by the hand, and set off with them for a walk perforce about the grounds; whilst Alfred fairly dragged Richard and George after the girls, and Emily arm-in-arm with Serena strolled beside them.

The afternoon was sunny, shady, breezy, warm, all at once. Bees were humming and harvesting as any bee of sense must have done amongst so many blossoms: leafy boughs danced with their dancing shadows; bell flowers rang without clappers: –

[Could they, Aunt? – Well, not exactly, Maude: but you're coming to much more wonderful matters!]

Now and then a pigeon cooed its soft water-bottle note; and a long way off sheep stood bleating.

Susan let go the little hot hands she held, and began as she walked telling a story to which all her companions soon paid attention – all except Flora.

Poor little Flora: was this the end of her birthday? was she eight years old at last only for this? Her sugar-plums almost all gone and not cared for, her chosen tart not a nice one, herself so cross and miserable: is it really worth while to be eight years old and have a birthday, if this is what comes of it?

' – So the frog did not know how to boil the kettle; but he only replied: I can't bear hot water,' went on Susan telling her story. But Flora had no heart to listen, or to care about the frog. She lagged and dropped behind not noticed by any one, but creeping along slowly and sadly by herself.

Down the yew alley she turned, and it looked dark and very gloomy as she passed out of the sunshine into the shadow. There were twenty yew trees on each side of the path, as she had counted over and over again a great many years ago when she was learning to count; but now at her right hand there stood twenty-one: and if the last tree was really a yew tree at all, it was at least a very odd one, for a lamp grew on its topmost branch. Never before either had the yew walk led to a door: but now at its further end stood a door with bell and knocker, and 'Ring also' printed in black letters on a brass plate; all as plain as possible in the lamplight.

Flora stretched up her hand, and knocked and rang also.

She was surprised to feel the knocker shake hands with her, and to see the bell handle twist round and open the door. 'Dear me,' thought she, 'why could not the door open itself instead of troubling the bell?' But she only said, 'Thank you,' and walked in.

The door opened into a large and lofty apartment, very handsomely furnished. All the chairs were stuffed arm-chairs, and moved their arms and shifted their shoulders to accommodate sitters. All the sofas arranged and rearranged their pillows as convenience dictated. Footstools glided about, and rose or sank to meet every length of leg. Tables were no less obliging, but ran on noiseless castors here or there when wanted. Tea-trays ready set out, saucers of strawberries, jugs of cream, and plates of cake, floated in, settled down, and floated out again empty, with considerable tact and good taste: they came and went through a square hole high up in one wall, beyond which I presume lay the kitchen. Two harmoniums, an accordion, a pair of kettledrums and a peal of bells played concerted pieces behind a screen, but kept silence during conversation. Photographs and pictures made the tour of the apartment, standing still when glanced at and going on when done with. In case of need the furniture flattened itself against the wall, and cleared the floor for a game, or I dare say for a dance. Of these remarkable details some struck Flora in the first few minutes after her arrival, some came to light as time went on. The only uncomfortable point in the room, that is, as to furniture, was that both ceiling and walls were lined throughout with looking-glasses: but at first this did not strike Flora as any disadvantage; indeed she thought it quite delightful, and took a long look at her little self full length.

[Jane and Laura, don't *quite* forget the pocket-handkerchiefs you sat down to hem. See how hard Ella works at her fern leaves, and what pains she is taking to paint them nicely. Yes, Maude, that darn will do: now your task is ended, but if I were you I would help Clara with hers.]

The room was full of boys and girls, older and younger, big and little. They all sat drinking tea at a great number of different tables; here half a dozen children sitting together, here more or fewer; here one child would preside all alone at a table just the size for one comfortably. I should tell you that the tables were like telescope tables; only they expanded and contracted of themselves without extra pieces, and seemed to study everybody's convenience.

Every single boy and every single girl stared hard at Flora and went on staring: but not one of them offered her a chair, or a cup of tea, or anything else whatever. She grew very red and uncomfortable under so many staring pairs of eyes: when a chair did what it could to relieve her embarrassment by pressing gently against her till she sat down. It then bulged out its own back comfortably into hers, and drew in its arms to suit her small size. A footstool grew somewhat taller beneath her feet. A table ran up with tea for one; a cream-jug toppled over upon a saucerful of strawberries, and then righted itself again; the due quantity of sifted sugar sprinkled itself over the whole.

[How could it sprinkle itself? – Well, Jane, let us suppose it sprang up in its china basin like a fountain; and overflowed on one side only, but that of course the right side, whether it was right or left.]

Flora could not help thinking everyone very rude and ill-natured to go on staring without speaking, and she felt shy at having to eat with so many eyes upon her: still she was hot and thirsty, and the feast looked most tempting. She took up in a spoon one large, very large strawberry with plenty of cream; and was just putting it into her mouth when a voice called out crossly: 'You shan't, they're mine.' The spoon dropped from her startled hand, but without any clatter: and Flora looked round to see the speaker.

[Who was it? Was it a boy or a girl? – Listen, and you shall hear, Laura.]

The speaker was a girl enthroned in an extra high armchair; with a stool as high as an ottoman under her feet, and a table as high as a chest of drawers in front of her. I suppose as she had it so she liked it so, for I am sure all the furniture laid itself out to be obliging. Perched upon her hair she wore a coronet made of tinsel; her face was a red face with a scowl: sometimes perhaps she looked nice and pretty, this time she looked ugly. 'You shan't, they're mine,' she repeated in a cross grumbling voice: 'it's my birthday, and everything is mine.'

Flora was too honest a little girl to eat strawberries that were not given her: nor could she, after this, take even a cup of tea without leave. Not to tantalize her, I suppose, the table glided away with its delicious untasted load; whilst the armchair gave her a very gentle hug as if to console her.

If she could only have discovered the door Flora would have fled through it back into the gloomy yew-tree walk, and there have moped in solitude, rather than remain where she was not made welcome: but either the door was gone, or else it was shut to and lost amongst the multitude of mirrors. The birthday Queen, reflected over and over again in five hundred mirrors, looked frightful, I do assure you: and for one minute I am sorry to say that Flora's fifty million-fold face appeared flushed and angry too; but she soon tried to smile good-humouredly and succeeded, though she could not manage to feel very merry.

[But, Aunt, how came she to have fifty million faces? I don't understand. – Because in such a number of mirrors there were not merely simple reflections, but reflections of reflections, and reflections of reflections of reflections, and so on and on and on, over and over again, Maude: don't you see?]

The meal was ended at last: most of the children had eaten and stuffed quite greedily; poor Flora alone had not tasted a morsel. Then with a word and I think a kick from the Queen, her high footstool scudded away into a corner: and all the furniture taking the hint arranged itself as flat as possible round the room, close up against the walls.

[And across the door? – Why, yes, I suppose it may have done so, Jane: such active and willing furniture could never be in the way anywhere. – And was there a chimney corner? – No, I think not: that afternoon was warm we know, and there may have been a different apartment for winter. At any rate, as this is all make-believe, I say No. Attention!]

All the children now clustered together in the middle of the empty floor; elbowing and jostling each other, and disputing about what game should first be played at. Flora, elbowed and jostled in their midst, noticed points of appearance that quite surprised her. Was it themselves, or was it their clothes? (only who indeed would wear such clothes, so long as there was another suit in the world to put on?) One boy bristled with prickly quills like a porcupine, and raised or depressed them at pleasure; but he usually kept them pointed outwards. Another instead of being rounded like most people was facetted at very sharp angles. A third caught in everything he came near, for he was hung round with hooks like fishhooks. One girl exuded a sticky fluid and came off on the fingers; another, rather smaller, was slimy and slipped through the hands. Such exceptional features could not but prove inconvenient, yet patience and forbearance might still have done something towards keeping matters smooth: but these unhappy children seemed not to know what forbearance was; and as to patience, they might have answered me nearly in the words of a celebrated man – 'Madam, I never saw patience.'

[Who was the celebrated man, Aunt? – Oh, Clara, you an English girl and not know Lord Nelson! But I go on.]

'Tell us some new game,' growled Hooks threateningly, catching in Flora's hair and tugging to get loose.

Flora did not at all like being spoken to in such a tone, and the hook hurt her very much. Still, though she could not think of anything new, she tried to do her best, and in a timid voice suggested 'Les Grâces.'

'That's a girl's game,' said Hooks contemptuously.

'It's as good any day as a boy's game,' retorted Sticky.

'I wouldn't give *that* for your girl's games,' snarled Hooks, endeavouring to snap his fingers, but entangling two hooks and stamping.

'Poor dear fellow!' drawled Slime, affecting sympathy.

'It's quite as good,' harped on Sticky: 'It's as good or better.'

Angles caught and would have shaken Slime, but she slipped through his fingers demurely.

'Think of something else, and let it be new,' yawned Quills, with quills laid for a wonder.

'I really don't know anything new,' answered Flora half crying: and she was going to add, 'But I will play you at any game you like, if you will teach me;' when they all burst forth into a yell of 'Cry, baby, cry! – Cry, baby, cry!' – They shouted it, screamed it, sang it: they pointed fingers, made grimaces, nodded heads at her. The wonder was she did not cry outright.

At length the Queen interfered: 'Let her alone; – who's she? It's *my* birthday, and we'll play at Hunt the Pincushion.'

So Hunt the Pincushion it was. This game is simple and demands only a moderate amount of skill. Select the smallest and weakest player (if possible let her be fat: a hump is best of all), chase her round and round the room, overtaking her at short intervals, and sticking pins into her here or there as it happens: repeat, till you choose to catch and swing her; which concludes the game. Short cuts, yells, and sudden leaps give spirit to the hunt.

[Oh, Aunt, what a horrid game! surely there cannot be such a game? – Certainly not, Ella: yet I have seen before now very rough cruel play, if it can be termed play. – And did they get a poor little girl with a hump? – No, Laura, not this time: for]

The Pincushion was poor little Flora. How she strained and ducked and swerved to this side or that, in the vain effort to escape her tormentors! Quills with every quill erect tilted against her, and needed not a pin: but Angles whose corners almost cut her, Hooks who caught and slit her frock, Slime who slid against and passed her, Sticky who rubbed off on her neck and plump bare arms, the scowling Queen, and the whole laughing scolding pushing troop, all wielded longest sharpest pins, and all by turns overtook her. Finally the Queen caught her, swung her violently round, let go suddenly, – and Flora losing her balance dropped upon the floor. But at least that game was over.

Do you fancy the fall jarred her? Not at all: for the carpet grew to such a depth of velvet pile below her, that she fell quite lightly.

Indeed I am inclined to believe that even in that dreadful sport of Hunt the Pincushion, Flora was still better off than her stickers: who in the thick of the throng exasperated each other and fairly maddened themselves by a free use of cutting corners, pricking quills, catching hooks, glue, slime, and I know not what else. Slime, perhaps, would seem not so much amiss for its owner: but then if a slimy person cannot be held, neither can she hold fast. As to Hooks and Sticky they often in wrenching themselves loose got worse damage than they inflicted: Angles many times cut his own fingers with his edges: and I don't envy the individual whose sharp quills are flexible enough to be bent point inwards in a crush or a scuffle. The Queen must perhaps be reckoned exempt from particular personal pangs: but then, you see, it was her birthday! And she must still have suffered a good deal from the eccentricities of her subjects.

The next game called for was Self Help. In this no adventitious aids were tolerated, but each boy depended exclusively on his own resources. Thus pins were forbidden: but every natural advantage, as a quill or fishhook, might be utilized to the utmost.

[Don't look shocked, dear Ella, at my choice of words; but remember that my birthday party is being held in the Land of Nowhere. Yet who knows whether something not altogether unlike it has not ere now taken place in the Land of Somewhere? Look at home, children.]

The boys were players, the girls were played (if I may be allowed such a phrase): all except the Queen who, being Queen, looked on, and merely administered a slap or box on the ear now and then to some one coming handy. Hooks, as a Heavy Porter, shone in this sport; and dragged about with him a load of attached captives, all vainly struggling to unhook themselves. Angles, as an Ironer, goffered or fluted several children by sustained pressure. Quills, an Engraver, could do little more than prick and scratch with some permanence of result. Flora falling to the share of Angles had her torn frock pressed and plaited after quite a novel fashion: but this was at any rate preferable to her experience as Pincushion, and she bore it like a philosopher.

Yet not to speak of the girls, even the boys did not as a body extract unmixed pleasure from Self Help; but much wrangling and some blows allayed their exuberant enjoyment. The Queen as befitted her lofty lot did, perhaps, taste of mirth unalloyed; but if so, she stood alone in satisfaction as in dignity. In any case, pleasure palls in the long run.

The Queen yawned a very wide loud yawn: and as everyone yawned in sympathy the game died out.

# John Howard Clark (1830–1878)

*Bertie and the Bullfrogs* begins with 'The Author's Apology to Lewis Carroll Esq.': 'Pardon a humble follower whose hand | Plucks this poor twig from out thy crown of laurel | To plant it in the far Australian land, | And grow, inspired by thee, a Christmas Carroll.' What follows owes much to Carroll and like *A Mother's offering* (see p. 55) it demonstrates the continuing debt that Australian writers owed to Britain. However, it can be regarded as a key text because of the thorough way in which it domesticates Carroll's logical nonsense.

The story was first published 'in the Christmas number of the *Adelaide Observer*' in 1873 and reprinted anonymously 'for private circulation' the following year. Clark was born in Birmingham, England and was editor of the *South Australian Register* from 1870–8. The complete text is reprinted here.

## *Bertie and the Bullfrogs: an Australian Story for Big and Little Children* (1874)

### CHAPTER I

Bertie did not care to go to bed that hot summer evening, so he sat half undressed on the verandah-sill kicking his bare feet in the gravel, and watching the bright red clouds where the sun had just set. He thought it would be time enough to go in when his mamma came to his room to see if he was all right, but just now it was much cooler and pleasanter outside. He listened to the cows, who were being driven up to the yard to be milked, and lazily wondered whether Strawberry would kick over the milk pail on such a quiet evening. Then he looked along the path running down to the creek at the bottom of the garden, and saw the bright crimson of the sky shining in the still water-hole, and thought how nice it would be to have a bathe and come out that beautiful colour all over. But his mamma would not let him bathe there, for it was too deep for such a little fellow, so he sat still and wondered whether the opossums who lived in the old hollow gum tree in the creek enjoyed being able to go right down to the water without being seen by any one outside. Presently the frogs in the creek began their chorus, and he tried to make out what they said; but they went on so fast, without ever stopping, that they gave him no time to think. Then the bullfrogs began to make their strange noise, and he said to himself –

'I wish I knew what they say. It sounds like "Pump! pump!" only they have plenty of water without pumping. Sometimes I think they say "Soup! soup!" but then you don't have soup at tea-time, so it can't be that either.'

He puzzled over it for a long time, and at last he thought he would try to get close to one of the bullfrogs, and perhaps then he should make out what they meant. So he went down the path very quietly, for he knew if they saw or heard him they would stop directly, and when he got to the bank he took hold of a wattle branch, and leaned over to listen. Just then he heard his mamma calling from the verandah, 'Oh, Bertie, Bertie, my dear, come back!' – and at the same moment the wattle branch broke, and he fell splash into the deep water.

### CHAPTER II

Bertie shut his eyes as he fell, and went down, down, down, till he wondered when he should get to the bottom. At last he caught hold of something that felt like a little cold wet hand which pulled him along very fast till suddenly he opened his eyes and found himself in a snug room with a sanded floor, and a ceiling just the colour of the bright clouds he had been looking at. The walls seemed strangely wavy, sometimes close to him and sometimes a long way off, except one dark corner that never changed at all. The room was very smoky, and he was putting up his hand to cough when he found he had got hold of a large bullfrog's leg.

'Come,' said the bullfrog, 'you just let go, will you?'

'I'm very sorry, Sir,' said Bertie, 'I didn't know —'

'Oh yes,' said the bullfrog; 'I daresay! You catch a fellow by the leg, and then pretend you didn't know it. You're as bad as the larrikins who put stones on the railway. Hallo! stop; it's my turn next.'

All this was said in a shrill rough little voice, like a baby with a bad cold, but just then Bertie once more heard the regular loud 'poof' the bullfrog makes, and looking round he saw his friend jump up on to a comfortable toadstool among a row of great bullfrogs, and take from the one on his right hand something that looked like a pipe. He put it to his mouth and drew in the smoke till he had swelled up to double his proper size, and his eyes seemed nearly starting out of his head. Then he passed the pipe on to the bullfrog on his left, and suddenly opened his mouth and let the smoke out with a loud 'poof!'

Bertie sat watching the bullfrogs a long time as each took his turn with the pipe, and then blew out the smoke with a 'poof!' and at last he said to the one who had brought him there —

'If you please, Sir, do bullfrogs smoke every night?'

'Suppose I don't please!' said the bullfrog; 'how then? Don't you?'

'Don't I what?' said Bertie.

'Don't you smoke every night?' said the bullfrog.

'No!' said Bertie; 'but papa does.'

'Very well then!' said the bullfrog triumphantly.

Just then his turn came again for the pipe, and he swelled himself up with it so much that Bertie was really afraid be might burst in the wrong place. He didn't though; and as soon as he had puffed out the smoke he said —

'Why don't you smoke?'

'Because I'm not big enough,' said Bertie.

'Pooh' said the bullfrog; 'you're a deal bigger than you're bonny. You aren't like our little uns.'

He nodded as he spoke to one side of the room, where for the first time Bertie noticed a great crowd of little frogs, all jumping about and coughing – 'Ke-heck, ke-heck, ke-heck' – and looking very uncomfortable.

'Poor little frogs!' he said; 'what makes them cough so?'

'Smoke' said the bullfrog. 'They've got to get used to it, and they won't, so they have to keep on coughing all night. Serve the little plagues right!'

Bertie thought the bullfrog was very ill-natured, but he did not like to say so. So to change the subject he asked: —

'Do you smoke tobacco, Sir?'

'No,' said the bullfrog, 'tea leaves.'

'Tea leaves!' said Bertie.

'Of course!' said the bullfrog. 'What else do you suppose we grow all the teatree in the swamp for, stupid?'

This was a difficult question, so Bertie thought he had better change the subject again.

'That is a very funny pipe,' he said; 'what is it made of, please?'

'Horn,' said the bullfrog.

'Horn?' said Bertie, wondering.

'I shan't say it again!' said the bullfrog; 'but you must be silly if you never heard of a frog's horn-pipe.'

'I thought that was a dance,' said Bertie.

'So it is,' said the bullfrog; 'they dance and we pipe.'

This was very puzzling too, so Bertie asked —

'What sort of horn is the pipe made of?'

'I told you,' said the bullfrog; 'frog's horn. Bulls have horns, so why not bullfrogs? Don't you know the song?' And he sang in a very cracked voice —

'Little bullfrog, come blow me your horn! I'll sleep in the shadow, and croak in the morn.'

'That's not right,' said Bertie. 'I always say –

'Little boy Blue, come blow me your horn –'

'Stuff!' said the bullfrog. 'That can't be right. If the little boy blew, why should you tell him to blow any more?'

Bertie began to feel very cross at being asked so many questions he could not answer, but he did not like to let the bullfrog see it, so he only said –

'How is a frog's hornpipe made?'

'Well,' said the bullfrog; 'you see we first cut our best capers – some call them hops, but I call them capers. I suppose you know what capers are?' he asked, looking as if he were quite sure Bertie didn't.

Bertie remembered the sauce they had with the boiled leg of mutton last Sunday, and said 'Yes.'

'Very well then!' said the bullfrog.

'But,' said Bertie, after waiting a long time for the bullfrog to go on – 'I want to know how the pipes are made?'

'They aren't made,' said the bullfrog; 'we toss for them.'

'Toss for them?' said Bertie, wondering what he meant.

'Of course!' said the bullfrog; 'bulls toss, so why not bullfrogs?'

'Bulls toss people,' said Bertie, 'but bullfrogs can't.'

'That's because the bulls are angry,' said the bullfrog; 'and we are only in play.'

Bertie was glad to hear that, and ventured to ask –

'But what do you toss to get pipes?'

'Tadpoles,' said the bullfrog. 'Heads and tails, you know.'

He said this as if it settled the question, and before Bertie had time to puzzle over the answer he heard a voice behind him saying, 'Let me go, mother!' Turning round, he saw a young bullfrog dressed in his best clothes, with a shiny hat on one side of his head, a new pair of gloves in one hand, and a little walking-cane in the other; and holding on to his coat-tail was an ugly old frog in a yellow gown and a very dirty cap.

'Let me go, mother,' said the young frog. 'I'm only going for a stroll across the creek.'

'You shan't go, Jem,' said she, 'You're going after that little Polly Wog. She's too young and giddy for you; and you'll get into trouble, I know you will.' And here she took up one corner of her gown and began crying dreadfully. Jem seemed inclined to stay when his mother cried so much, but the bullfrog Bertie had been talking to cried out – 'Off you go, Jem; never mind what the old woman says!' and then Jem ran out, and his mother hobbled after him trying in vain to stop him, till at last she fell down, and lay there crying and scolding and calling Jem all sorts of bad names.

'Why,' said Bertie, 'I know a song something like that.'

Here a very large bullfrog, who sat on the tallest toadstool, gave the table a loud knock, and said very solemnly – 'Gentlemen, our young friend, Mr. Bertie, will oblige.' All the little frogs left off coughing 'Ke-heck, ke-heck, ke-heck,' and came crowding round, crying 'Hear, hear, hear,' until the Chairman gave another knock, and then there was a dead silence. Bertie felt rather frightened when he saw so many staring eyes all fixed upon him, but he took courage, and began to sing –

> 'A frog he would a wooing go,
>   Heigho, says Rowley!
> A frog he would a wooing go,
> Whether his mother would let him or no –
>   With his roley-poley, gam —'

Here he was stopped by a voice crying out – 'How dare you sing that way about my Jem?' and the old frog in the yellow gown came hobbling towards him and looking so fierce that he was quite frightened. Then the Chairman gave another knock and cried out – 'Go on; nobody may stop singing till he has done.' Bertie tried to explain, but the bullfrogs came crowding round him angrily; and the little ones set up their noisy chorus of 'Ke-heck, ke-heck, ke-heck, ke-heck;' and the sides of the room seemed to close in upon him; and the bright light of the ceiling faded away; and he made one jump into the dark corner he had noticed at first, and then the water seemed to rush in and sweep away all the frogs together, and he found himself climbing a curious little flight of stairs, at the top of which stood a motherly old opossum with a candle in her hand to light him up.

## Chapter III

'Well!' said the opossum, after Bertie had had some tea and told his story; 'it was lucky you got hold of our stairs or them frogs might have drownded you. Nasty slimy things! I never could abide 'em.'

'Thank you, Ma'am,' said Bertie; 'but now I should like to go home, please.'

'Home, child!' cried the opossum. 'What do you mean?'

'Why,' said Bertie, 'isn't this the old gum tree that stands in the creek at the bottom of the garden?'

'Gum tree, indeed' said the opossum, looking quite vexed. 'This is my house, child, and a very nice one it is. And it's time for little folks to be off to bed, for it's nearly daylight.'

Here five little opossums came in gaping, and one cried out –

'Oh, mother, I'm so sleepy. All the little stars have run into their holes already, and now the big ones are getting sleepy too.'

'Have the stars got holes?' asked Bertie, opening his eyes, though he felt quite as sleepy as the stars.

'Bless the child!' said the opossum. 'I shall think as you've never been sent to school, if you don't know no better nor that. The stars come out every night, don't they? And if they didn't go into their holes again in the morning they'd soon get lost. If I was to venture out in broad daylight I should be that dazed I'd never find my way back again.'

'And then, you know,' said the smallest opossum, with his eyes wide open; 'if the little stars got lost, they couldn't grow into big moons, and then we should have no more moons when the old ones died.'

'Ay, child,' said his mother proudly; 'and without the fresh moons to give us light opossums couldn't live, and so the world would soon come to an end.'

'Then, perhaps, you can tell me,' said Bertie, seized with a bright idea, 'where the old moons go to.'

'Well,' said the opossum, doubtfully, 'I can't say for certain as I can. I did hear an old wombat as comes from a long way south tell of a place they call Biscuit Flat, where, he says, the old moons lie all about, as round and flat as can be, and just as hard and cold as a stone. But I don't set much store by what them wombats say. They're a poor sort of creature as grubs in the dirt, and can scarce make shift to get a decent living. But there! They've not had the same chances of a good bringing up as me and mine has had, so we shouldn't be hard on 'em, should we?'

Bertie had listened as long as he could, but he was so tired that he could not even remember the difference between a wombat and a cricket bat, so he only said – 'Mayn't I go to bed, please?'

'There!' said the opossum: 'that's just what it is that's a worriting me. You're so much bigger than my children that I don't believe I've a bed big enough to put you in, and whatever I'm to do I know no more than the mantis in the moonshine.'

Just then a great owl put his head in at the door and said in a very gruff voice – 'Aren't you all gone to bed yet? Don't you know –

> "Moonshine at night
> Is the 'possum's delight;
> Sunshine at morning
> Is the 'possum's warning." '

'Well, to be sure!' said the opossum; 'you'd never think it, neighbour, but you was that very minute in my head, for I thought as you'd tell me what to do with this poor foolish child.'

The owl came slowly in staring at Bertie all the time. Then he took out a very large pair of spectacles and put them on. They were not common spectacles, but stood out a long way from his nose, and looked just like the field-glass Bertie's papa kept in a leather case, only instead of looking through the small ends the owl had the big ends turned next to his eyes. Then he spread his legs very wide apart, turned up the tips of his wings behind him just as though he were putting his hands under his coat-tails, and stared at Bertie so hard that he quite woke up again. All this time the opossum was telling Bertie's story, and when she had finished the owl shook his head very solemnly and said to Bertie –

'Where are your shoes and stockings?'

'Please, Sir!' said Bertie, 'I took them off in the evening when I was undressing to go to bed.'

'Going to bed in the evening!' said the owl. 'What do you mean by that?'

'Why,' said Bertie, 'isn't evening the proper time to go to bed?'

'Bless the child!' cried the opossum, holding up both hands in astonishment; 'whoever heard of such ways?'

'Ugh!' said the owl. 'That's what makes you boys so silly. Don't you know –

"Mornings to bed and evenings to rise
Make the owls healthy and stealthy and wise?"

Next to owls the wisest folks in the world are newspaper editors, and they follow just the same rule.'

Bertie knew what a newspaper editor was, for he had heard his papa speak of a friend of his in town who had the complaint very badly, and could never get up in the morning because of it, so he began to wonder whether the owl was right after all. But before he had done thinking about it the owl said –

'Come, now, if sleeping at night has not made you silly, let us see if you can pass an examination! First class, stand up!'

Here all the little opossums jumped up and stood in a row beside Bertie; and the owl asked –

'What is the first letter?'

'A,' said Bertie, thinking that if all the questions were as easy as that the owl would make a very nice examiner.

'Wrong!' said the owl; 'next boy!'

'O,' cried the first opossum.

'Right!' said the owl. 'Take him down.'

'But, please Sir,' said Bertie, 'A *is* the first letter.'

'That shows what *you* know about it,' said the owl. 'Only vulgar people say "a possum;" we say "o-possum;" and I should like to know how you'd spell "owl" if O isn't the first letter of that too! Now, what does the clock say?'

Bertie looked all round the room, and said – 'Please, Sir, I can't see the clock.'

'Next boy!' said the owl.

'Tick!' cried the second opossum.

'Right!' said the owl. 'Take him down. Now for arithmetic! What do two peaches for each of these five little opossums come to?'

'Ten,' said Bertie, thinking he must be right this time.

'Wrong!' said the owl. 'If they came to ten opossums that would be only one a piece. Next boy!'

'Please, Sir,' said the third opossum, 'they've got no legs, so they can't come without being fetched.'

'That's much better,' said the owl. 'Take him down. Next boy, what do *you* say?'

'The peaches come to be eaten,' said the fourth opossum.

'Right!' said the owl. 'Take them both down. Now try another question. If you cut off a frog's fore legs how many would he have left?'

Bertie determined he would not be caught this time, so he said –

'Do you mean all his *four* legs, or only both his *fore* legs?'

'Both!' said the owl.

This was more puzzling than ever, but Bertie thought he would manage not to make any mistake, so he said –

'If you cut off all his four legs he would have none left, but if you only cut off his two fore legs he would have two left.'

'Wrong!' said the owl. 'Next boy!'

'Please, Sir,' said the fifth opossum, 'a frog has only got two fore legs, and so if they were both cut off he wouldn't have any left.'

'Right!' said the owl. 'Take him down.'

Bertie felt ready to cry when he found himself at the bottom of the class, but he didn't like to let them see it, so he said –

'It isn't fair to ask such questions. I can read and write, and I know that's more than the others can do.'

'Read and write, indeed!' said the owl. 'As if any one cared about that! Don't you know –

> "Let geese delight to read and write,
>     While spiders sit and sew;
> Let owls and possums play all night,
>     Nor home till morning go.
> Young cockatoos should never let
>     Their angry topknots rise;
> Their little beaks aren't half so sharp
>     As bright opossum's eyes."'

'That's not right,' said Bertie. 'I always say –

> "Let dogs delight to bark and bite –"'

'For shame, child,' said the old opossum. 'You ought to know better than let them do anything so wicked. Why, my old man had like to have got his death with one of them dogs a barking and a biting at him. But there! whatever am I to do about getting you to bed?'

'That's easy enough,' said the owl. 'Here's my spare bedroom.' And he opened the door of a little room with a bed in it about nine inches long.

'I can't sleep there,' said Bertie; 'it's too small for me.'

'Nonsense!' said the owl. 'I suppose you don't know what a looking-glass is, do you?'

'Of course I do,' said Bertie. 'I use one to brush my hair every morning.'

'Brush your hair with the looking-glass, do you?' said the owl. 'No wonder it's in such a mess, then! You might as well fasten your shoes with the fire shovel.'

'Well, I mean I look in the glass when I'm brushing my hair,' said Bertie, vexed to see all the little opossums laughing at him.

'Ah!' said the owl. 'Then you just put on my spectacles and look at yourself in that looking-glass.'

Bertie did not much like doing this, but he was a brave boy and thought he would not let them laugh at him again. So he took the spectacles, and was going to look through them just as he would with his papa's field-glass.

'Stop!' said the owl, 'that's the wrong way; you must look through the big ends as I do.'

Bertie did as he was told, and looked at himself in the looking glass, when to his astonishment he saw he was so little that the spare bed was much too long for him. Then he remembered that he had once looked through the wrong end of his papa's glass, and that it had made everything very small; and as he thought that if he was really so little as the owl's spectacles had made him he might never find his way home again, he threw them down and burst out crying. Then the owl began to scold and flap his wings, which frightened Bertie all the more; but the old opossum snatched Bertie up and put him straight into bed, and before she had tucked him up, somehow or other he went fast asleep as comfortably as if he had been in his own little bed at home.

## CHAPTER IV

Bertie was at last awakened by a shrill whistle just like that of a steam-engine. It sounded so loud and long in his ears that he jumped up wide awake and found himself on a railway-platform with a train just ready to start, and a crowd of passengers getting into the carriages. Among them he saw Jem the bullfrog, whose clothes looked finer than ever. Jem first handed in a pretty young mouse, who wore a silk dress, and had a crimson parasol and a chignon and bonnet that made her nearly as tall as the carriage, and then he got in himself, and choosing the most comfortable corner, sat down, and put the nob of his walking-cane into his mouth. Bertie was puzzled at first to notice that the bullfrog looked a great deal taller than he did the day before, but then he remembered the owl's spectacles, and saw that it was he himself that was so much smaller. Seeing the bullfrog and the mouse together put him in mind of another verse of his song, but now that he was so little he did not venture to sing it. Just then a magpie who seemed to be the guard came up and said –

'Where to, Sir?'

'I want to get down out of the gum-tree,' said Bertie, thinking of the owl and the opossums and where he had slept.

'All right!' said the guard. 'This is the down train on the branch line; jump in, Sir.'

All this time the shrill whistle kept on sounding till Bertie could hardly hear himself speak.

'Why don't you stop that whistle?' he asked.

'Well!' said the guard, 'You see it's one of them yang-yangs – cicadas, some folks call 'em – on the engine, and when you've once set 'em off, they haven't the sense to know when to stop.'

Bertie had no time to ask any more questions for the bell was ringing, so he jumped in and sat down thinking it was well he was so small, or he could never have got through the door. As it was, a laughing-jackass, who followed him, had a great squeeze to get in. He thought it a good joke, however, and as soon as he was seated he threw himself back and gave a loud 'Ha, ha! ha! whoo! whoo! huggle-uggle!' finishing off with a sort of choke as if the fun were altogether too much for him. Bertie saw the mouse look at the bullfrog and smile scornfully, and Jem, though he seemed rather frightened, whispered to her, 'Awful snob, isn't he?' The last passenger to get in was a lizard, and as he was standing in the doorway while they made room for him the guard slammed the door and nipped his tail right off. Bertie cried out, but the lizard took no notice of it and sat down looking quite cheerful and happy. Presently the guard put his head in at the window with the tail in his hand, and said –

'Has any of you gents dropped this here?'

'Why!' said the lizard, looking down at himself, 'I do believe it's mine. Never mind, Guard, it's of no consequence, thank you. There's a handkerchief in one of the pockets that I should like to have, but you may keep the tail for your trouble.'

The guard looked rather puzzled to know what to do with it, but he touched his hat and said, 'Thank ye, Sir!' and then went away as the train started.

'Awkward accident, losing your tail, Sir!' said the laughing-jackass, 'You'll have to set a *tailor* to work, I think. Ha! ha! ha! whoo! whoo! huggle-uggle!'

An old crayfish that was sitting opposite with a little one on his lap laughed at this joke, and some of the others smiled, but on looking at the bullfrog Bertie saw that he was fast asleep and snoring in a very rude way with his mouth wide open, while the mouse looked quite cross and tried to waken him by poking at his sides with her parasol. He snored so loud that soon all the passengers noticed it.

'Vulgar fellow!' said the crayfish.

'Only a railway sleeper,' said the laughing-jackass; 'ha! ha! ha! whoo! whoo! huggle-uggle!'

'What a dreadful sluggard!' said the lizard.

'Ah!' said the crayfish. 'My little boy can speak a piece about that. Come, Billy, stand up like a good boy, and speak your piece for the company.'

Every one looked as if he didn't want to hear it, but as nobody objected the little crayfish stood up on the seat, and made an awkward bow, and then recited these lines, at the same time waving about his claws and his long feelers in a very ungraceful and absurd way: –

'Tis the voice of the bullfrog, I heard him complain,
You have waked me too soon, I shall wait for next train;
As a swell on his travels, so he for a swag
Bears his rug, and his hatbox, and his carpet-bag.
A little more scent, and a newer belltopper;
Thus he wastes all his cash till he hasn't a copper;
And when he's dressed up he sits stiff as a stock,
Or saunters down Rundle street doing the block
I passed by the Corner and saw the Town Crier,
The cads and the cabmen crowd round to admire,
For the clothes that he wore were as glossy and tight
As if he'd been kept in a bandbox all night.'

Bertie did not wonder that the little crayfish said these lines all wrong, for his father had to help him at almost every word, and by the end of the third verse he could wait no longer, but cried out, 'That's not right. I always say' – and he was getting up to speak the lines correctly, when the laughing-jackass said, 'What, another piece! If we go on like this we shall all come to pieces very soon. Ha! ha! ha! whoo! whoo! huggle-uggle!' and he gave such a laugh that Bertie sat down again, feeling quite ashamed of himself. When he looked up again he saw that the mouse had taken a spinning-wheel out of her little hand-bag, and was getting the bullfrog, who had wakened up, to help her with it. 'Ah!' he thought, 'now something is sure to happen, for you know –

'Just as they were sitting to spin,
    Heigho, says Rowley!
Just as they were sitting to spin,
The cat and her kit —'

Before Bertie could finish singing the verse to himself there came a jolt and a crash, and the roof and sides of the carriage disappeared, and they were all sitting on the grass, and right in amongst them came bouncing his pet cat, Mrs. Macstinger, and her two kittens, Max and Minx. Before the poor little mouse could get away Mrs. Macstinger had seized upon her, and was carrying her off in her mouth. Bertie ran after her and shouted, but he was so little that she did not know him, and showed her teeth in a very unpleasant way. Max attacked the laughing-jackass, who gave him two or three pecks with his great bill, and then flew up into a gum-tree, whence he looked down with a loud 'ha! ha! ha! whoo! whoo! huggle-uggle!' The lizard ran under a stone, and Minx sprang after the bullfrog and the crayfish, who seemed to be making off to the creek. Bertie was just think-ing that now he would try to find his way home, when he saw Max rushing at him, and looking so fierce that he turned and ran away as fast as he could. He ran till he was out of breath, and then looking round he saw to his delight that Max was off in another direction after a grasshopper. He stopped to take breath and found that he was by the creek, and that Jem the bullfrog and the two crayfish were sitting comfortably on a stone in the water making faces and laughing at Minx, who tried in vain to get at them without wetting her feet. Bertie sat down very quietly for fear Minx should see him and take it into her head to make a rush at him, and picked up the biggest stick he could lift to defend himself with if she attacked him. Presently he saw his own ducks come swimming round the corner, and just as the bullfrog was hopping away on his hind legs and at the same time putting his thumb to his nose and making a very rude sign to the kitten, the large white duck made a dash at him, and fairly gobbled him up before he knew what had happened.

'There,' said Bertie, 'that's just what I could have told him if they'd let me finish my song:' and he sang –

'Just as froggy was crossing the brook,
   Heigho, says Rowley!
Just as froggy was crossing the brook,
A lily white duck she gobbled him up,
   With his roley, poley, gammon and spin' –

But once more Bertie could not finish the verse, for he was suddenly seized by the shoulders, and a voice cried in his ears, 'What have you done with my Jem?' Looking up he found the old bullfrog in the yellow gown had got hold of him. He tried to get away, but she was now larger and stronger than he was, and dragged him along, struggling and crying out till, with a jerk and a jump, they plunged into the creek together. Bertie felt the water rush into his nose and mouth, and half choking he gave one more struggle to get his arm loose from the old bullfrog, when —

All at once he found himself sitting on his mother's lap on the bank of the creek, with his clothes all dripping with wet and the broken wattle branch still in his hand.


## CHAPTER THE LAST

When Bertie's mamma, after talking to him very seriously about his disobedience in going down to the water, was tucking him up in bed that night, he asked her –

'Was I very long in the water, mamma?'

'No, my dear,' she said, 'not more than half a minute, for I ran down and caught hold first of the wattle branch and then of your arm and pulled you out as quickly as I could. But if I had not seen you fall in you would most likely have been drowned.'

Bertie lay awake a long time that night, but the more he thought about it the more puzzled he was to make out how so many strange things could have happened in so short a time, and I am afraid I can't tell you how it was any more than Bertie could.

# 'Mark Twain' (Samuel Langhorne Clemens) (1835–1910)

*Tom Sawyer* began life as a memoir of childhood, rather than a book for children, an obvious distinction not much regarded by publishers and some critics. It was also a reinvention of Twain's childhood, and in a letter to William Dean Howells he observed: 'It is *not* a boy's book, at all. It will only be read for adults. It is only written for adults', although under the influence of his wife, Livy, and of Howells, he changed his mind. This situation produced a book of characteristic ambivalence, moving between the romantic and the ironic, the light and the dark.

The book also has a strong vein of parody of evangelical writing: Twain had written unsuccessful essays mocking the tradition, and, combining the spirit of these with a deadpan adoption of Aldrich's 'bad boy' memoirs, he produced what has been read as a commentary on American society as a whole.

The book has been claimed for the children's-book canon largely because Twain retains a certain elemental gleefulness which places him in opposition to adults, if not exactly on the child's side. Consequently, I make no apology for reprinting the most famous (opening) episode, which epitomizes this spirit. Like the opening of the greatest Brit-

ish book *about* boyhood, Richard Jefferies' *Bevis*, the fence-painting sequence of *Tom Sawyer* captures both an idyllic, Arcadian vision of the world of childhood (in this case, small-town, mid-west, sunshine) and the unapologetic image of a cheerfully anarchic, amoral child. In both cases, the question might be: who enjoys the implications of this image most? (And in both books, the authors encapsulate whole childhoods in a single summer.) In Twain's case, the idyll is overlaid, or perhaps undercut, by the commercial urge, but despite this (or because of it) the episode remains, as it were, a direct line to real childhood, before the book darkens with the introduction of Injun Joe, or perhaps leaves the male Eden of boyhood with the introduction of Becky Thatcher.

*Tom Sawyer* is sometimes regarded as a transitional work in Twain's career, between his humorous pieces and his major works, such as *Huckleberry Finn*. This latter book is often assumed to be a children's book, and it would be nice to think that one of the strongest candidates for the title of 'the Great American Novel' was actually for children. The Huck Finn of this 'sequel', however, is not a hero of boyhood, nor for children; rather, he is a lens through which an acerbic writer can view the corruptions of society.

## from *The Adventures of Tom Sawyer* (1876)

### CHAPTER II

### STRONG TEMPTATIONS – STRATEGIC MOVEMENTS – THE INNOCENTS BEGUILED

Saturday morning was come, and all the summer world was bright and fresh, and brimming with life. There was a song in every heart; and if the heart was young the music issued at the lips. There was cheer in every face, and a spring in every step. The locust trees were in bloom, and the fragrance of the blossoms filled the air. Cardiff Hill, beyond the village and above it, was green with vegetation, and it lay just far enough away to seem a Delectable Land, dreamy, reposeful, and inviting.

Tom appeared on the side-walk with a bucket of whitewash and a long-handled brush. He surveyed the fence, and all gladness left him, and a deep melancholy settled down upon his spirits Thirty yards of board-fence nine feet high! Life to him seemed hollow, and existence but a burden. Sighing he dipped his brush and passed it along the topmost plank; repeated the operation; did it again; compared the insignificant whitewashed streak with the far-reaching continent of unwhitewashed fence, and sat down on a tree-box discouraged. Jim came skipping out at the gate with a tin pail, and singing 'Buffalo Gals'. Bringing water from the town pump had always been hateful work in Tom's eyes before, but now it did not strike him so. He remembered that there was company at the pump. White, mulatto, and negro boys and girls were always there waiting their turns, resting, trading play-things, quarrelling, fighting, skylarking. And he remembered that although the pump was only a hundred and fifty yards off, Jim never got back with a bucket of water under an hour; and even then somebody generally had to go after him: Tom said:

'Say, Jim; I'll fetch the water if you'll whitewash some.'

Jim shook his head and said:

'Can't, Mars Tom. Ole missis, she tole me I got to go an git dis water an' not stop foolin' roun' wid anybody. She say she spec' Mars Tom gwine to ax me to whitewash, an' so she tole me go 'long an' 'tend to my own business – she 'lowed *she'd* 'tend to de whitewashin'.'

'Oh, never you mind what she said, Jim. That's the way she always talks. Gimme the bucket – I won't be gone only a minute. *She* won't ever know.'

'Oh, I dasn't Mars Tom. Ole missis she'd take an' tar de head off'n me. 'Deed she would.'

'*She!* She never licks anybody – whacks 'em over the head with her thimble, and who cares for that, I'd like to know? She talks awful, but talk don't hurt – anyways, it don't if she don't cry. Jim, I'll give you a marvel. I'll give you a white alley!'

Jim began to waver.

'White alley, Jim! And it's a bully taw.'

'My! Dat's a mighty gay marvel, *I* tell you! But, Mars Tom, I's powerful 'fraid ole missis —'

'And besides, if you will I'll show you my sore toe.'

Jim was only human – this attraction was too much for him. He put down his pail, took the white alley, and bent over the toe with absorbing interest while the bandage was being unwound. In another moment he was flying down the street with his pail and a tingling rear, Tom was white-washing with vigour, and Aunt Polly was retiring from the field with a slipper in her hand and tri-umph in her eye.

But Tom's energy did not last. He began to think of the fun he had planned for this day, and his sorrows multiplied. Soon the free boys would come tripping along on all sorts of delicious expedi-tions, and they would make a world of fun of him for having to work – the very thought of it burnt him like fire. He got out his worldly wealth and examined it – bits of toys, marbles and trash; enough to buy an exchange of *work*, maybe, but not half enough to buy so much as half an hour of pure freedom. So he returned his straitened means to his pocket, and gave up the idea of trying to buy the boys. At this dark and hopeless moment an inspiration burst upon him! Noth-ing less than a great, magnificent inspiration.

He took up his brush and went tranquilly to work. Ben Rogers hove in sight presently – the very boy, of all boys, whose ridicule he had been dreading. Ben's gait was the hop-skip-and-jump – proof enough that his heart was light and his anticipations high. He was eating an apple, and giving a long, melodious whoop at intervals, followed by a deep-toned ding-dong-dong, ding-dong-dong, for he was personating a steamboat. As he drew near he slackened speed, took the middle of the street, leaned far over to starboard, and rounded-to ponderously and with laborious pomp and cir-cumstance – for he was personating the 'Big Missouri,' and considered himself to be drawing nine feet of water. He was boat, and captain, and engine-bells combined, so he had to imagine himself standing on his own hurricane deck giving the orders and executing them:

'Stop her, sir! Ting-a-ling-ling.' The headway ran almost out, and he drew up slowly toward the sidewalk.

'Ship up to back! Ting-a-ling-ling!' His arms straightened and stiffened down his sides.

'Set her back on the stabboard! Ting-a-ling-ling! Chow! ch-chow-wow! Chow!' His right hand meantime describing stately circles, for it was representing a forty-foot wheel.

'Let her go back on the labboard! Ting-a-ling-ling! Chow-ch-chow-chow!' The left hand began to describe circles.

'Stop the stabboard! Ting-a-ling-ling! Stop the labboard! Come ahead on the stabboard! Stop her! Let your outside turn over slow! Ting-a-ling-ling! Chow-ow-ow! Get out that head-line! *Lively*, now! Come – out with your spring-line – what're you about there? Take a turn round that stump with the bight of it! Stand by that stage now – let her go! Done with the engines, sir! Ting-a-ling-ling! *Sh't! s'h'tl sh'tl'* (trying the gauge-cocks).

Tom went on whitewashing – paid no attention to the steamboat. Ben stared a moment, and then said:

'Hi-yi! *You're* up a stump, ain't you?'

No answer. Tom surveyed his last touch with the eye of an artist; then he gave his brush another gentle sweep, and surveyed the result, as before. Ben ranged up alongside him. Tom's mouth watered for the apple, but he stuck to his work. Ben said:

'Hello, old chap; you got to work, hey?'

Tom wheeled suddenly and said:

'Why, it's you. Ben! I warn't noticing.'

'Say – *I'm* going in a-swimming, *I* am. Don't you wish you could? But of course you'd druther *work* – wouldn't you? Course you would!'

Tom contemplated the boy a bit, and said:

'What do you call work?'

'Why, ain't *that* work?'

Tom resumed his whitewashing, and answered carelessly:

'Well, maybe it is, and maybe it ain't. All I know is, it suits Tom Sawyer.'

'Oh, come now, you don't mean to let on that you *like* it?'

The brush continued to move.

'Like it? Well, I don't see why I oughtn't to like it. Does a boy get a chance to whitewash a fence every day?'

That put the thing in a new light. Ben stopped nibbling his apple. Tom swept his brush daintily back and forth – stepped back to note the effect – added a touch here and there – criticized the effect again – Ben watching every move, and getting more and more interested, more and more absorbed.

Presently he said: 'Say, Tom, let *me* whitewash a little.'

Tom considered – was about to consent; but he altered his mind:

'No, no; I reckon it wouldn't hardly do, Ben. You see, Aunt Polly's awful particular about this fence – right here on the street, you know – but if it was the back fence I wouldn't mind, and *she* wouldn't. Yes, she's awful particular about this fence; it's got to be done very careful; I reckon there ain't one boy in a thousand, maybe two thousand, that can do it the way it's got to be done.'

'No – is that so? Oh, come now; lemme just try, only just a little. I'd let *you*, if you was me, Tom.'

'Ben, I'd like to, honest Injun; but Aunt Polly – well, Jim wanted to do it, but she wouldn't let him. Sid wanted to do it, and she wouldn't let Sid. Now, don't you see how I'm fixed? If you was to tackle this fence, and anything was to happen to it –'

'Oh, shucks; I'll be just as careful. Now lemme try. Say – I'll give you the core of my apple.'

'Well, here – No, Ben; now don't; I'm afeard –'

'I'll give you *all* of it!'

Tom gave up the brush with reluctance in his face but alacrity in his heart. And while the late steamer 'Big Missouri' worked and sweated in the sun, the retired artist sat on a barrel in the shade close by, dangled his legs, munched his apple, and planned the slaughter of more innocents. There was no lack of material; boys happened along every little while; they came to jeer, but remained to whitewash. By the time Ben was fagged out, Tom had traded the next chance to Billy Fisher for a kite, in good repair; and when *he* played out, Johnny Miller bought in for a dead rat and a string to swing it with; and so on, and so on, hour after hour. And when the middle of the afternoon came, from being a poor poverty-stricken boy in the morning, Tom was literally rolling in wealth. He had, beside the things before mentioned, twelve marbles, part of a jew's-harp, a piece of blue bottle-glass to look through, a spool-cannon, a key that wouldn't unlock anything, a fragment of chalk, a glass stopper of a decanter, a tin soldier, a couple of tadpoles, six fire-crackers, a kitten with only one eye, a brass door-knob, a dog-collar – but no dog – the handle of a knife, four pieces of orange-peel, and a dilapidated old window-sash. He had had a nice, good, idle time all the while – plenty of company – and the fence had three coats of whitewash on it! If he hadn't run out of whitewash, he would have bankrupted every boy in the village.

Tom said to himself that it was not such a hollow world, after all. He had discovered a great law of human action, without knowing it – namely, that in order to make a man or a boy covet a thing, it is only necessary to make the thing difficult to attain. If he had been a great and wise philosopher, like the writer of this book, he would now have comprehended that Work consists of whatever a body is *obliged* to do, and that Play consists of whatever a body is not obliged to do. And this would help him to understand why constructing artificial flowers or performing on a treadmill is work, while rolling ten-pins or climbing Mont Blanc is only amusement. There are wealthy gentlemen in England who drive four-horse passenger-coaches twenty or thirty miles on a daily line in the summer, because the privilege costs them considerable money; but if they were offered wages for the service, that would turn it into work, and then they would resign.

The boy mused a while over the substantial change which had taken place in his worldly circum-stances, and then wended toward head-quarters to report.

## from CHAPTER III

### TOM AS A GENERAL – TRIUMPH AND REWARD – DISMAL FELICITY – COMMISSION AND OMISSION

Tom presented himself before Aunt Polly, who was sitting by an open window in a pleasant rear-ward apartment, which was bedroom, breakfast-room, dining-room, and library combined. The balmy summer air, the restful quiet, the odour of the flowers, and the drowsing murmur of the bees, had had their effect, and she was nodding over her knitting – for she had no company but the cat, and it was asleep in her lap. Her spectacles were propped up on her grey head for safety. She had thought that of course Tom had deserted long ago, and she wondered at seeing him place himself in her power again in this intrepid way. He said:

'Mayn't I go and play now, aunt?'

'What, a'ready? How much have you done?'

'It's all done, aunt.'

'Tom, don't lie to me – I can't bear it.'

'I ain't, aunt; it *is* all done.'

Aunt Polly placed small trust in such evidence. She went out to see for herself; and she would have been content to find twenty per cent. of Tom's statement true. When she found the entire fence whitewashed, and not only whitewashed but elaborately coated and re-coated, and even a streak added to the ground, her astonishment was almost unspeakable. She said:

'Well, I never! There's no getting round it: you *can* work when you're a mind to, Tom.' And then she diluted the compliment by adding, 'But it's powerful seldom you're a mind to, I'm bound to say. Well, go 'long and play; but mind you get back sometime in a week, or I'll tan you.'

She was so overcome by the splendour of his achievement that she took him into the closet and selected a choice apple, and delivered it to him, along with an improving lecture upon the added value and flavour a treat took to itself when it came without sin through virtuous effort. And while she closed with a happy Scriptural flourish, he 'hooked' a doughnut.

Then he skipped out, and saw Sid just starting up the outside stairway that led to the back rooms on the second floor. Clods were handy, and the air was full of them in a twinkling. They raged around Sid like a hailstorm; and before Aunt Polly could collect her surprised faculties and sally to the rescue, six or seven clods had taken personal effect, and Tom was over the fence and gone. There was a gate, but as a general thing he was too crowded for time to make use of it. His soul was at peace, now that he had settled with Sid for calling attention to his black thread and getting him into trouble . . .

# Anna Sewell (1820–1878)

There is a satisfying sense of 'something attempted, something done' about *Black Beauty*. The author's only book, designed to 'induce kindness, sympathy, and an understanding treatment of horses' (and specifically to combat the cruel and fashionable bearing-rein), it is the equine equivalent of the human riches-to rags-to riches fairy-tale. As Black Beauty passes through the hands of various owners, we are given a wide-ranging picture of Victorian society, as well as plenty of drama. Black Beauty saves his master from disaster at a flooded bridge and has a dramatic night-ride to fetch the doctor to save his mistress; he survives a fire in a stable; he is ill-treated by the use of the bearing-rein; his knees are ruined by a drunken rider, and he descends to being a cab-horse, with a kind owner and an evil owner.

The book is infused with Sewell's Quaker thinking, notably against violence and drunkenness, and her values are shown not by direct comment but by the approving portrayal of characters such as Jerry the cab-man and his poor but honest family.

Black Beauty's only half-comprehending view of human society is not only a sharp comment on it, but also empowers child-readers by letting them understand more than the narrator – and to identify with him. Although *Black Beauty* has antecedents in first-person animal narratives, and although its separate elements are very much of its time, the deft combination of melodrama, social realism and social criticism makes for a book which seems to be more like folklore than literature.

The three chapters printed here show part of the range of the book: 'A Stormy Day' is an adventure, 'The Devil's Trade Mark' makes a point about cruelty, and, from later in the book, when Black Beauty and his friend Ginger have been sold to a fashionable family, 'A Strike for Liberty' is an explicit attack on the bearing-rein.

From the point of view of this anthologist, *Black Beauty* presented the greatest problem of selection: almost every episode is of the appropriate length, almost every one makes a relevant point, and almost every one is equally vivid.

## from *Black Beauty, his Grooms and Companions; the Autobiography of a Horse. Translated from the Original Equine* (1877)

### CHAPTER 12

### A STORMY DAY

One day late in the autumn, my master had a long journey to go on business. I was put into the dog-cart, and John went with his master. I always liked to go in the dog-cart, it was so light, and the high wheels ran along so pleasantly. There had been a great deal of rain, and now the wind was very high, and blew the dry leaves across the road in a shower. We went along merrily till we came to the toll-bar, and the low wooden bridge. The river banks were rather high, and the bridge, instead of rising, went across just level, so that in the middle, if the river was full the water would be nearly up to the woodwork and planks; but as there were good substantial rails on each side, people did not mind it.

The man at the gate said the river was rising fast, and he feared it would be a bad night. Many of the meadows were under water, and in one low part of the road the water was half-way up to my knees; the bottom was good, and master drove gently, so it was no matter.

When we got to the town, of course, I had a good bait, but as the master's business engaged him a long time, we did not start for home till rather late in the afternoon. The wind was then much higher, and I heard the master say to John, he had never been out in such a storm; and so I thought, as we went along the skirts of the wood, where the great branches were swaying about like twigs, and the rushing sound was terrible.

'I wish we were well out of this wood,' said my master.

'Yes, sir,' said John, 'it would be rather awkward if one of these branches came down upon us.'

The words were scarcely out of his mouth, when there was a groan, and a crack, and a splitting sound, and tearing, crashing down amongst the other trees, came an oak, torn up by the roots, and it fell right across the road just before us. I will never say I was not frightened, for I was. I stopped still, and I believe I trembled; of course I did not turn round or run away; I was not brought up to that. John jumped out and was in a moment at my head.

'That was a very near touch,' said my master. 'What's to be done now?'

'Well, sir, we can't drive over that tree nor yet get round it; there will be nothing for it, but to go back to the four crossways, and that will be a good six miles before we get round to the wooden bridge again; it will make us late, but the horse is fresh.'

So back we went, and round by the crossroads; but by the time we got the bridge, it was very nearly dark, we could just see that the water was over the middle of it; but as that happened sometimes when the floods were out, master did not stop. We were going along at a good pace, but the moment my feet touched the first part of the bridge, I felt sure there was something wrong. I dare not go forward, and I made a dead stop. 'Go on, Beauty,' said my master, and he gave me a touch with the whip, but I dare not stir; he gave me a sharp cut, I jumped, but I dare not go forward.

'There's something wrong, sir,' said John, and he sprang out of the dog-cart and came to my head and looked all about. He tried to lead me forward, 'Come on, Beauty, what's the matter?' Of course I could not tell him, but I knew very well that the bridge was not safe.

Just then, the man at the toll-gate on the other side ran out of the house, tossing a torch about like one mad.

'Hoy, hoy, hoy, halloo, stop!' he cried.

'What's the matter?' shouted my master.

'The bridge is broken in the middle and part of it is carried away; if you come on you'll be into the river.'

'Thank God!' said my master. 'You Beauty!' said John, and took the bridle and gently turned me round to the right-hand road by the riverside. The sun had set some time, the wind seemed to have lulled off after that furious blast which tore up the tree. It grew darker and darker, stiller and stiller. I trotted quietly along, the wheels hardly making a sound on the soft road. For a good while neither master nor John spoke, and then master began in a serious voice. I could not understand much of what they said, but I found they thought, if I had gone on as the master wanted me, most likely the bridge would have given way under us, and horse, chaise, master, and man would have fallen into the river; and as the current was flowing very strongly, and there was no light and no help at hand, it was more than likely we should all have been drowned. Master said, God had given men reason, by which they could find out things for themselves, but He had given animals knowledge which did not depend on reason, and which was much more prompt and perfect in its way, and by which they had often saved the lives of men. John had many stories to tell of dogs and horses, and the wonderful things they had done; he thought people did not value their animals half enough, nor make friends of them as they ought to do. I am sure he makes friends of them if ever a man did.

At last we came to the Park gates, and found the gardener looking out for us. He said that mistress had been in a dreadful way ever since dark, fearing some accident had happened, and that she had sent James off on Justice, the roan cob, towards the wooden bridge to make inquiry after us.

We saw a light at the hall door and at the upper windows, and as we came up, mistress ran out, saying, 'Are you really safe, my dear? Oh! I have been so anxious, fancying all sorts of things. Have you had no accident?'

'No, my dear; but if your Black Beauty had not been wiser than we were, we should all have been carried down the river at the wooden bridge.' I heard no more, as they went into the house, and John took me to the stable. Oh! what a good supper he gave me that night, a good bran mash and some crushed beans with my oats, and such a thick bed of straw, and I was glad of it, for I was tired.

## CHAPTER 13

## THE DEVIL'S TRADE MARK

One day when John and I had been out on some business of our master's, and were returning gently on a long straight road, at some distance we saw a boy trying to leap a pony over a gate; the pony would not take the leap, and the boy cut him with the whip, but he only turned off on one side; he whipped him again, but the pony turned off on the other side. Then the boy got off and gave him a hard thrashing, and knocked him about the head; then he got up again and tried to make him leap the gate, kicking him all the time shamefully, but still the pony refused. When we were nearly at the spot, the pony put down his head and threw up his heels and sent the boy neatly over into a broad quickset hedge, and with the rein dangling from his head, he set off home at a full gallop. John laughed out quite loud. 'Served him right,' he said.

'Oh! oh! oh!' cried the boy, as he struggled about amongst the thorns; 'I say, come and help me out.'

'Thank ye,' said John, 'I think you are quite in the right place, and maybe a little scratching will teach you not to leap a pony over a gate that is too high for him,' and so with that John rode off. 'It may be,' said he to himself, 'that young fellow is a liar as well as a cruel one; we'll just go home by Farmer Bushby's, Beauty, and then if anybody wants to know, you and I can tell 'em, ye see'; so we turned off to the right, and soon came up to the stack yard and within sight of the house. The farmer was hurrying out into the road, and his wife was standing at the gate, looking very frightened.

'Have you seen my boy?' said Mr. Bushby, as we came up, 'he went out an hour ago on my black pony, and the creature is just come back without a rider.'

'I should think, sir,' said John, 'he had better be without a rider, unless he can be ridden properly.'

'What do you mean?' said the farmer.

'Well, sir, I saw your son whipping, and kicking, and knocking that good little pony about shamefully because he would not leap a gate that was too high for him. The pony behaved well, sir, and showed no vice; but at last he just threw up his heels, and tipped the young gentleman into a thorn hedge: he wanted me to help him out; but I hope you will excuse me, sir, I did not feel inclined to do so. There's no bones broken, sir, he'll only get a few scratches. I love horses, and it roiles me to see them badly used; it is a bad plan to aggravate an animal till he uses his heels; the first time is not always the last.'

During this time the mother began to cry, 'Oh! my poor Bill, I must go and meet him, he must be hurt.'

'You had better go into the house, wife,' said the farmer; 'Bill wants a lesson about this, and I must see that he gets it; this is not the first time nor the second that he has ill-used that pony, and I shall stop it. I am much obliged to you, Manly. Good evening.'

So we went on, John chuckling all the way home, then he told James about it, who laughed and said, 'Serve him right. I knew that boy at school; he took great airs on himself because he was a farmer's son; he used to swagger about and bully the little boys; of course we elder ones would not have any of that nonsense, and let him know that in the school and the playground, farmers' sons and labourers' sons were all alike. I well remember one day, just before afternoon school, I found him at the large window catching flies and pulling off their wings. He did not see me, and I gave him a box on the ears that laid him sprawling on the floor. Well, angry as I was, I was almost frightened, he roared and bellowed in such a style. The boys rushed in from the playground, and the master ran in from the road to see who was being murdered. Of course I said fair and square at once what I had done, and why; then I showed the master the poor flies, some crushed and some crawling about helpless, and I showed him the wings on the window sill. I never saw him so angry before; but as Bill was still howling and whining, like the coward that he was, he did not give him any more punishment of that kind, but set him up on a stool for the rest of the afternoon, and said that he should not go out to play for that week. Then he talked to all the boys very seriously about cruelty, and said how hard-hearted and cowardly it was to hurt the weak and the helpless; but what stuck in my mind was this, he said that cruelty was the devil's own trade mark, and if we saw any-one who took pleasure in cruelty, we might know who he belonged to, for the devil was a murderer from the beginning, and a tormentor to the end. On the other hand, where we saw people who loved their neighbours, and were kind to man and beast, we might know that was God's mark, for "God is Love."'

'Your master never taught you a truer thing,' said John; 'there is no religion without love, and people may talk as much as they like about their religion, but if it does not teach them to be good and kind to man and beast, it is all a sham – all a sham, James, and it won't stand when things come to be turned inside out and put down for what they are.'

# Chapter 23

## A Strike for Liberty

One day my lady came down later than usual, and the silk rustled more than ever.

'Drive to the Duchess of B —'s,' she said, and then after a pause – 'Are you never going to get those horses' heads up, York? Raise them up at once, and let us have no more of this humouring and nonsense.'

York came to me first, whilst the groom stood at Ginger's head. He drew my head back and fixed the rein so tight that it was almost intolerable; then he went to Ginger, who was impatiently jerking her head up and down against the bit, as was her way now. She had a good idea of what was coming, and the moment York took the rein off the terret in order to shorten it, she took her opportunity, and reared up so suddenly that York had his nose roughly hit, and his hat knocked off; the groom was nearly thrown off his legs. At once they both flew to her head, but she was a match for them, and went on plunging, rearing, and kicking in a most desperate manner; at last she kicked right over the carriage pole and fell down, after giving me a severe blow on my near quarter. There is no knowing what further mischief she might have done, had not York promptly sat him-self down flat on her head, to prevent her struggling, at the same time calling out, 'Unbuckle the black horse! run for the winch and unscrew the carriage pole; cut the trace here, somebody, if you can't unhitch it.' One of the footmen ran for the winch, and another brought a knife from the house. The groom soon set me free from Ginger and the carriage, and led me to my box. He just turned me in as I was, and ran back to York. I was much excited by what had happened, and if I had ever been used to kick or rear, I am sure I should have done it then; but I never had, and there I stood angry, sore in my leg, my head still strained up to the terret on the saddle, and no power to get it down. I was very miserable, and felt much inclined to kick the first person who came near me.

Before long, however, Ginger was led in by two grooms, a good deal knocked about and bruised. York came with her and gave his orders, and then came to look at me. In a moment he let down my head.

'Confound these bearing-reins!' he said to himself; 'I thought we should have some mischief soon – master will be sorely vexed; but there – if a woman's husband can't rule her, of course a servant can't; so I wash my hands of it, and if she can't get to the Duchess's garden party, I can't help it.'

York did not say this before the men; he always spoke respectfully when they were by. Now, he felt me all over, and soon found the place above my hock where I had been kicked. It was swelled and painful; he ordered it to be sponged with hot water, and then some lotion was put on.

Lord W —— was much put out when he learned what had happened; he blamed York for giving way to his mistress, to which he replied, that in future he would much prefer to receive his orders only from his lordship; but I think nothing came of it, for things went on the same as before. I thought York might have stood up better for his horses, but perhaps I am no judge.

Ginger was never put into the carriage again, but when she was well of her bruises, one of Lord W —— 's younger sons said he should like to have her; he was sure she would make a good hunter. As for me, I was obliged still to go in the carriage, and had a fresh partner called Max; he had always been used to the tight rein. I asked him how it was he bore it.

'Well,' he said, 'I bear it because I must, but it is shortening my life, and it will shorten yours too, if you have to stick to it.'

'Do you think,' I said, 'that our masters know how bad it is for us?'

'I can't say,' he replied, 'but the dealers and the horse doctors know it very well. I was at a dealer's once, who was training me and another horse to go as a pair; he was getting our heads up, as he said, a little higher and a little higher every day. A gentleman who was there asked him why he did so. "Because," said he, "people won't buy them unless we do. The London people always want their horses to carry their heads high, and to step high; of course it is very bad for the horses, but then it is good for trade. The horses soon wear up, or get diseased, and they come for another pair." That, said Max, 'is what he said in my hearing and you can judge for yourself.'

What I suffered with that rein for four long months in my lady's carriage, it would be hard to describe; but I am quite sure that, had it lasted much longer, either my health or my temper would have given way. Before that, I never knew what it was to foam at the mouth, but now the action of the sharp bit on my tongue and jaw, and the constrained position of my head, and throat, always caused me to froth at the mouth more or less. Some people think it very fine to see this, and say, 'What fine, spirited creatures!' But it is just as unnatural for horses as for men, to foam at the mouth: it is a sure sign of something wrong, and generally proceeds from suffering. Besides this, there was a pressure on my windpipe, which often made my breathing very uncomfortable; when I returned from my work, my neck and chest were strained and painful, my mouth and tongue tender, and I felt worn and depressed.

In my old home, I always knew that John and my master were my friends; but here, although in many ways I was well treated, I had no friend. York might have known, and very likely did know, how that rein harassed me; but I suppose he took it as a matter of course that could not be helped; at any rate, nothing was done to relieve me.

# Mary Louisa [Stewart] Molesworth (1839–1921)

Mrs Molesworth represents Victorian children's book authors (female) at their formidable height, when the shift towards the child's point of view and the child's understanding was becoming clearer. Her work is solidly moralistic and she was at home with domestic realism (*Carrots,* 1876) and fantasy, notably *The Tapestry Room* (1878) and *The Cuckoo Clock* (both originally published as 'by Ennis Graham'), and in common with many of her contemporaries, was prolific, producing over a hundred books.

Griselda, the hero of *The Cuckoo Clock*, is enough of an individualist to rebel against her staid aunts (' "Improve these golden hours of youth, Griselda; they will never return." "I hope not," muttered Griselda, "if it means doing sums." ') and to throw a book at the cuckoo clock when the cuckoo seems to be repeating Aunt Grizzel's admonitions. The cuckoo, a rather sanctimonious creature, and direct ancestor of E. Nesbit's Phoenix and Psammead, eventually takes her on some rather disappointingly unde-

manding excursions, but not before, as in this chapter, she has learnt some self-discipline.

Mrs Molesworth's literary reputation has suffered from two things. The first is that the most invisible class of writing to modern critics has been (at least until very recently) the mainstream, the female and the children's author: Molesworth was all three. More specifically, she was given to making her small children speak in a lisping (not to say nauseatingly 'cute') language that has not been fashionable since the 1920s; and her texts are spotted with phrases like 'the prettiest, the loveliest little boat', 'oh, how pretty it was!', 'the loveliest, loveliest garden that ever or never a little girl's eyes saw' (all from *The Cuckoo Clock*). Despite (or because of) what the modern eye might regard as a flaw, she was immensely popular, and is often bracketed with Juliana Horatia Ewing as one who provided the characteristic materials which writers such as Frances Hodgson Burnett and Edith Nesbit refined into classics.

## from *The Cuckoo Clock* (1877)

### CHAPTER 3

### OBEYING ORDERS

There was moonlight, though not so much, in the saloon and the ante-room, too; for though the windows, like those in Griselda's bedroom, had the shutters closed, there was a round part at the top, high up, which the shutters did not reach to, and in crept, through these clear uncovered panes, quite as many moonbeams, you may be sure, as could find their way.

Griselda, eager though she was, could not help standing still a moment to admire the effect.

'It looks prettier with the light coming in at those holes at the top than even if the shutters were open,' she said to herself. 'How goldy-silvery the cabinet looks, and, yes, I do declare, the mandarins are nodding! I wonder if it is out of politeness to me, or does Aunt Grizzel come in last thing at night and touch them to make them keep nodding till morning? I *suppose* they're a sort of policemen to the palace and I dare say there are all sorts of beautiful things inside. How I should like to see all through it!'

But at this moment the faint tick-tick of the cuckoo clock in the next room, reaching her ear, reminded her of the object of this midnight expedition of hers. She hurried into the ante-room.

It looked darker than the great saloon, for it had but one window. But through the uncovered space at the top of this window there penetrated some brilliant moonbeams, one of which lighted up brightly the face of the clock with its queer overhanging eaves.

Griselda approached it and stood below, looking up.

'Cuckoo,' she said softly – very softly.

But there was no reply.

'Cuckoo,' she repeated rather more loudly. 'Why won't you speak to me? I know you are there, and you're not asleep, for I heard your voice in my own room. Why won't you come out, cuckoo?'

'Tick-tick,' said the clock, but there was no other reply.

Griselda felt ready to cry.

'Cuckoo,' she said reproachfully, 'I didn't think you were so hard-hearted. I have been *so* unhappy about you, and I was so pleased to hear your voice again, for I thought I had killed you, or hurt you very badly; and I didn't *mean* to hurt you, cuckoo. I was sorry the moment I had done it, *dreadfully* sorry. Dear cuckoo, won't you forgive me?'

There was a little sound at last – a faint *coming* sound, and by the moonlight Griselda saw the doors open, and out flew the cuckoo. He stood still for a moment, looked round him as it were, then gently flapped his wings, and uttered his usual note – 'Cuckoo'.

Griselda stood in breathless expectation, but in her delight she could not help very softly clapping her hands.

The cuckoo cleared his throat. You never heard such a funny little noise as he made; and then, in a very clear, distinct, but yet 'cuckoo-y' voice, he spoke.

'Griselda,' he said, 'are you truly sorry?'

'I told you I was,' she replied. 'But I didn't *feel* so very naughty, cuckoo. I didn't really. I was only vexed for one minute, and when I threw the book I seemed to be a very little in fun, too. And it made me so unhappy when you went away, and my poor aunts have been dreadfully unhappy too. If you hadn't come back I should have told them tomorrow what I had done. I would have told them before, but I was afraid it would have made them more unhappy. I thought I had hurt you dreadfully.'

'So you did,' said the cuckoo.

'But you *look* quite well,' said Griselda.

'It was my *feelings*', replied the cuckoo, 'and I couldn't help going away. I have to obey orders like other people.'

Griselda stared. 'How do you mean?' she asked.

'Never mind. You *can't* understand at present,' said the cuckoo. 'You can understand about obeying *your* orders, and you see, when you don't, things go wrong.'

'Yes,' said Griselda humbly, 'they certainly do. But, cuckoo,' she continued, 'I never used to get into tempers at home – *hardly* never, at least; and I liked my lessons then, and I never was scolded about them.'

'What's wrong here, then?' said the cuckoo. 'It isn't often that things go wrong in this house.'

'That's what Dorcas says,' said Griselda. 'It must be with my being a child – my aunts and the house and everything have got out of children's ways.'

'About time they did,' remarked the cuckoo drily.

'And so,' continued Griselda, 'it is really very dull. I have lots of lessons, but it isn't so much that I mind. It is that I've no one to play with.'

'There's something in that,' said the cuckoo. He flapped his wings and was silent for a minute or two. 'I'll consider about it,' he observed at last.

'Thank you,' said Griselda, not exactly knowing what else to say.

'And in the meantime,' continued the cuckoo, 'you'd better obey present orders and go back to bed.'

'Shall I say good-night to you, then?' asked Griselda somewhat timidly.

'You're quite welcome to do so,' replied the cuckoo. 'Why shouldn't you?'

'You see I wasn't sure if you would like it,' returned Griselda, 'for of course you're not like a person, and – and – I've been told all sorts of queer things about what fairies like and don't like.'

'Who said I was a fairy?' inquired the cuckoo.

'Dorcas did, and, *of course*, my own common sense did too,' replied Griselda. 'You must be a fairy – you couldn't be anything else.'

'I might be a fairyfied cuckoo,' suggested the bird.

Griselda looked puzzled.

'I don't understand,' she said, 'and I don't think it could make much difference. But whatever you are, I wish you would tell me one thing.'

'What?' said the cuckoo.

'I want to know, now that you've forgiven me for throwing the book at you, have you come back for good?'

'Certainly not for evil,' replied the cuckoo.

Griselda gave a little wriggle. 'Cuckoo, you're laughing at me,' she said. 'I mean, have you come back to stay and cuckoo as usual and make my aunts happy again?'

'You'll see in the morning,' said the cuckoo. 'Now go off to bed.'

'Good-night,' said Griselda, 'and thank you, and please don't forget to let me know when you've considered.'

'Cuckoo, cuckoo,' was her little friend's reply. Griselda thought it was meant for good-night, but the fact of the matter was that at that exact second of time it was two o'clock in the morning.

She made her way back to bed. She had been standing some time talking to the cuckoo, but, though it was now well on in November, she did not feel the least cold, nor sleepy! She felt as happy and light-hearted as possible, and she wished it was morning, that she might get up. Yet the moment she laid her little brown curly head on the pillow, she fell asleep, and it seemed to her that just as she dropped off a soft feathery wing brushed her cheek gently and a tiny 'Cuckoo' sounded in her ear.

When she woke it was bright morning, really bright morning, for the wintry sun was already sending some clear yellow rays out into the pale grey-blue sky.

'It must be late,' thought Griselda, when she had opened the shutters and seen how light it was. 'I must have slept a long time. I feel so beautifully unsleepy now. I must dress quickly – how nice it will be to see my aunts look happy again! I don't even care if they scold me for being late.'

But, after all, it was not so much later than usual; it was only a much brighter morning than they had had for some time. Griselda did dress herself very quickly, however. As she went downstairs two or three of the clocks in the house, for there were several, were striking eight. These clocks must have been a little before the right time, for it was not till they had again relapsed into silence that there rang out from the ante-room the clear sweet tones, eight times repeated, of 'Cuckoo'.

Miss Grizzel and Miss Tabitha were already at the breakfast-table, but they received their little niece most graciously. Nothing was said about the clock, however, till about half-way through the meal, when Griselda, full of eagerness to know if her aunts were aware of the cuckoo's return, could restrain herself no longer.

'Aunt Grizzel,' she said, 'isn't the cuckoo all right again?'

'Yes, my dear. I am delighted to say it is,' replied Miss Grizzel.

'Did you get it put right, Aunt Grizzel?' inquired Griselda, slyly.

'Little girls should not ask so many questions,' replied Miss Grizzel mysteriously. 'It *is* all right again, and that is enough. During fifty years that cuckoo has never, till yesterday, missed an hour. If you, in your sphere, my dear, do as well during fifty years, you won't have done badly.'

'No, indeed, you won't have done badly,' repeated Miss Tabitha.

But though the two old ladies thus tried to improve the occasion by a little lecturing, Griselda could see that at the bottom of their hearts they were both so happy that, even if she had been very naughty indeed, they could hardly have made up their minds to scold her.

She was not at all inclined to be naughty this day. She had something to think about and look forward to, which made her quite a different little girl, and made her take heart in doing her lessons as well as she possibly could.

'I wonder when the cuckoo will have considered enough about my having no one to play with?' she said to herself, as she was walking up and down the terrace at the back of the house.

'Caw, caw!' screamed a rook just over her head, as if in answer to her thought.

Griselda looked up at him.

'Your voice isn't half so pretty as the cuckoo's, Mr Rook,' she said. 'All the same, I dare say I should make friends with you, if I understood what you meant. How funny it would be to know all the languages of the birds and the beasts, like the prince in the fairy-tale! I wonder if I should wish for that, if a fairy gave me a wish? No, I don't think I would. I'd *far* rather have the fairy carpet that would take you anywhere you liked in a minute. I'd go to China to see if all the people there look like Aunt Grizzel's mandarins, and I'd first of all, of course, go to fairyland.'

'You must come in now, little missie,' said Dorcas's voice. 'Miss Grizzel says you have had play enough, and there's a nice fire in the ante-room for you to do your lessons by.'

'Play!' repeated Griselda indignantly, as she turned to follow the old servant. 'Do you call walking up and down the terrace "play", Dorcas? I mustn't loiter even to pick a flower, if there were any, for fear of catching cold, and I mustn't run for fear of overheating myself. I declare, Dorcas, if I don't have some play soon, or something to amuse me, I think I'll run away.'

'Nay, nay, missie, don't talk like that. You'd never do anything so naughty, and you so like Miss Sybilla, who was so good.'

'Dorcas, I'm tired of being told I'm like Miss Sybilla,' said Griselda, impatiently. 'She was my grandmother; no one would like to be told they were like their grandmother. It makes me feel as if my face must be all screwy up and wrinkly, and as if I should have spectacles on and a wig.'

'*That* is not like what Miss Sybilla was when I first saw her,' said Dorcas. 'She was younger than you, missie, and as pretty as a fairy.'

'*Was* she?' exclaimed Griselda, stopping short.

'Yes, indeed she was. She might have been a fairy, so sweet she was and gentle – and yet so merry. Every creature loved her; even the animals about seemed to know her, as if she was one of themselves. She brought good luck to the house, and it was a sad day when she left it.'

'I thought you said it was the cuckoo that brought good luck?' said Griselda.

'Well, so it was. The cuckoo and Miss Sybilla came here the same day. It was left to her by her mother's father, with whom she had lived since she was a baby, and when he died she came here to her sisters. She wasn't *own* sister to my ladies, you see, missie. Her mother had come from Germany, and it was in some strange place there, where her grandfather lived, that the cuckoo clock was made. They make wonderful clocks there, I've been told, but none more wonderful than our cuckoo, I'm sure.'

'No, I'm *sure* not,' said Griselda, softly. 'Why didn't Miss Sybilla take it with her when she was married and went away?'

'She knew her sisters were so fond of it. It was like a memory of her left behind for them. It was like a part of her. And do you know, missie, the night she died – she died soon after your father was born, a year after she was married – for a whole hour, from twelve to one, that cuckoo went on cuckooing in a soft, sad way, like some living creature in trouble. Of course, we did not know anything was wrong with her, and folks said something had caught some of the springs of the works; but *I* didn't think so, and never shall. And –'

But here Dorcas's reminiscences were abruptly brought to a close by Miss Grizzel's appearance at the other end of the terrace.

'Griselda, what are you loitering so for? Dorcas, you should have hastened, not delayed Miss Griselda.'

So Griselda was hurried off to her lessons, and Dorcas to her kitchen. But Griselda did not much mind. She had plenty to think of and wonder about, and she liked to do her lessons in the ante-room, with the tick-tick of the clock in her ears, and the feeling that *perhaps* the cuckoo was watching her through some invisible peep-hole in his closed doors.

'And if he sees,' thought Griselda, 'if he sees how hard I am trying to do my lessons well, it will perhaps make him be quick about "considering".'

So she did try very hard. And she didn't speak to the cuckoo when he came out to say it was four o'clock. She was busy, and he was busy. She felt it was better to wait till he gave her some sign of being ready to talk to her again.

For fairies, you know, children, however charming, are sometimes *rather* queer to have to do with. They don't like to be interfered with, or treated except with very great respect, and they have their own ideas about what is proper and what isn't, I can assure you.

I suppose it was with working so hard at her lessons – most people would say it was with having been up the night before, running about the house in the moonlight, but as she had never felt so 'fresh' in her life as when she got up that morning, it could hardly have been that – that Griselda felt so tired and sleepy that evening, she could hardly keep her eyes open. She begged to go to bed quite half an hour earlier than usual, which made Miss Tabitha afraid again that she was going to be ill. But as there is nothing better for children than to go to bed early, even if they *are* going to be ill, Miss Grizzel told her to say good-night, and to ask Dorcas to give her a wineglassful of elderberry wine, nice and hot, after she was in bed.

Griselda had no objection to the elderberry wine, though she felt she was having it on false pretences. She certainly did not need it to send her to sleep, for almost before her head touched the pillow she was as sound as a top. She had slept a good long while, when again she wakened suddenly – just as she had done the night before, and again with the feeling that something had wakened her. And the queer thing was that the moment she was awake she felt so *very* awake – she had no inclination to stretch and yawn and hope it wasn't quite time to get up, and think how nice and warm bed was, and how cold it was outside! She sat straight up, and peered out into the darkness, feeling quite ready for an adventure.

'Is it you, cuckoo?' she said softly.

There was no answer, but listening intently, the child fancied she heard a faint rustling or fluttering in the corner of the room by the door. She got up and, feeling her way, opened it, and the instant she had done so she heard, a few steps only in front of her it seemed, the familiar notes, very, *very* soft and whispered, 'Cuckoo, cuckoo.'

It went on and on, down the passage, Griselda trotting after. There was no moon tonight, heavy clouds had quite hidden it, and outside the rain was falling heavily. Griselda could hear it on the window-panes, through the closed shutters and all. But dark as it was, she made her way along without any difficulty, down the passage, across the great saloon, in through the ante-room door, guided only by the little voice now and then to be heard in front of her. She came to a standstill right before the clock, and stood there for a minute or two patiently waiting.

She had not very long to wait. There came the usual murmuring sound, then the doors above the clock face opened – she heard them open, it was far too dark to see – and in his ordinary voice, clear and distinct (it was just two o'clock, so the cuckoo was killing two birds with one stone, telling the hour and greeting Griselda at once), the bird sang out, 'Cuckoo, cuckoo.'

'Good-evening, cuckoo,' said Griselda, when he had finished.

'Good-morning, you mean,' said the cuckoo.

'Good-morning, then, cuckoo,' said Griselda. 'Have you considered about me, cuckoo?'

The cuckoo cleared his throat.

'Have you learnt to obey orders yet, Griselda?' he inquired.

'I'm trying,' replied Griselda. 'But you see, cuckoo, I've not had very long to learn in – it was only last night you told me, you know.'

The cuckoo sighed.

'You've a great deal to learn, Griselda.'

'I dare say I have,' she said. 'But I can tell you one thing, cuckoo – whatever lessons I have, I *couldn't* ever have any worse than those addition sums of Mr Knee-breeches'. I have made up my mind about that, for today, do you know, cuckoo –'

'Yesterday,' corrected the cuckoo. 'Always be exact in your statements, Griselda.'

'Well, yesterday, then,' said Griselda, rather tartly, 'though when you know quite well what I mean, I don't see that you need be so *very* particular. Well, as I was saying, I tried and *tried*, but still they were fearful. They were, indeed.'

'You've a great deal to learn, Griselda,' repeated the cuckoo.

'I wish you wouldn't say that so often,' said Griselda. 'I thought you were going to *play* with me.'

'There's something in that,' said the cuckoo, 'there's something in that. I should like to talk about it. But we could talk more comfortably if you would come up here and sit beside me.'

Griselda thought her friend must be going out of his mind.

'Sit beside you up there!' she exclaimed. 'Cuckoo, how *could* I? I'm far, far too big.'

'Big!' returned the cuckoo. 'What do you mean by big? It's all a matter of fancy. Don't you know that if the world and everything in it, counting yourself of course, was all made little enough to go into a walnut, you'd never find out the difference?'

'*Wouldn't* I?' said Griselda, feeling rather muddled, 'but, *not* counting myself, cuckoo, I would then, wouldn't I?'

'Nonsense,' said the cuckoo hastily. 'You've a great deal to learn, and one thing is, not to *argue*. Nobody should argue; it's a shocking bad habit, and ruins the digestion. Come up here and sit beside me comfortably. Catch hold of the chain; you'll find you can manage if you try.'

'But it'll stop the clock,' said Griselda. 'Aunt Grizzel said I was never to touch the weights or the chains.'

'Stuff,' said the cuckoo, 'it won't stop the clock. Catch hold of the chains and swing yourself up. There now – I told you you could manage it.'

# Talbot Baines Reed (1852–1893)

The Boy's Own Paper (BOP) was published in Britain by the Religious Tract Society from 1879 to 1967, initially to counteract what was seen as the pernicious effects of the 'Penny Dreadfuls' – cheap, sensationalized magazines for children. It was not alone in this: moral superiority was the stock-in-trade of other magazines such as Good Words for the Young (1868–77) and Harmsworth's Marvel (1893–1922) and its companions. Even the perhaps notorious Edwin Brett, a publisher of several series of 'dreadfuls', produced Boys of England in 1866 with an emphasis on 'healthy fiction'. (A similar aim was expressed in the USA in Demorest's Young America (1866–75) although the tradition of 'respectable' magazines was far stronger in that country.)

The BOP was intended to be 'pure and entertaining reading', and printed an extraordinary range of fiction and non-fiction, designed for both the working and middle classes. The emphasis was on sport, healthy living, self-improvement and 'pure' entertainment, all of which was a great improvement on the gruesome materials purveyed in the 'dreadfuls'. Of course, how far the content of even the most respectable of the British magazines of the late nineteenth century would now be regarded as desirable for young readers might be questioned, as the fiction, at least, was resolutely imperialist, racist and sexist. The BOP was not excessively militaristic, taking in general a realistic attitude to fighting and fear. However, it did preach a straightforward, manly code of behaviour of the cold bath and stiff-upper-lip variety, reflecting and forming the behaviour of the British empire-builders.

Among the major writers who contributed to the paper, such as R. M. Ballantyne, W. H. G. Kingston and G. A. Henty, Talbot Baines Reed's preoccupation was with school stories. 'My First Football Match' has all the ingredients that were to make this type of story a major British genre. Reed's own work for the BOP was instrumental in this: he felt that the work of Frederick Farrar, for example, was too didactic, and in several novels, all serialized in the BOP, notably The Fifth Form at St Dominic's (1881–2, 1887), did much to popularize the stories. (Reed himself had never attended a public school).

The Religious Tract Society also published The Girl's Own Paper (1880–1965).

## from The Boy's Own Paper, Volume 1, Number 1
### (Saturday 18 January 1879)

### 'My First Football Match, by an Old Boy'

It was a proud moment in my existence when Wright, captain of our football club, came up to me in school one Friday and said, 'Adams, your name is down to play in the match against Craven tomorrow.'

I could have knighted him on the spot. To be one of the picked 'fifteen,' whose glory it was to fight the battles of their school in the Great Close, had been the leading ambition of my life – I suppose I ought to be ashamed to confess it – ever since, as a little chap of ten, I entered Parkhurst six years ago. Not a winter Saturday but had seen me either looking on at some big match, or oftener still scrimmaging about with a score or so of other juniors in a scratch game. But for a long time, do what I would, I always seemed as far as ever from the coveted goal, and was half despairing of ever rising to win my 'first fifteen cap.' Latterly, however, I had noticed Wright and a few others of our best players more than once lounging about in the Little Close where we juniors used to play, evidently taking observations with an eye to business. Under the awful gaze of these heroes, need I say I exerted myself as I had never done before? What cared I for hacks or bruises, so only that I could distinguish myself in their eyes? And never was music sweeter than the occasional 'Bravo, young 'un!' with which some of them would applaud any special feat of skill or daring.

So I knew my time was coming at last, and only hoped it would arrive before the day of the Craven match, the great match of our season, – always looked forward to as the event of the Christmas term, when victory was regarded by us boys as the summit of all human glory, and defeat as an overwhelming disgrace.

It will therefore be understood why I was almost beside myself with delight when, the very day before the match, Wright made the announcement I have referred to.

I scarcely slept a wink that night for dreaming of the wonderful exploits which were to signalise my first appearance in the Great Close – how I was to run the ball from one end of the field to the other, overturning, dodging, and distancing every one of the enemy, finishing up with a brilliant and mighty kick over the goal. After which I was to have my broken limbs set by a doctor on the spot, to receive a perfect ovation from friend and foe, to be chaired round the field, to be the 'lion' at the supper afterwards, and finally to have a whole column of the 'Times' devoted to my exploits! What glorious creatures we are in our dreams!

Well, the eventful day dawned at last. It was a holiday at Parkhurst, and as fine a day as any one could wish.

As I made my appearance, wearing the blue-and-red jersey of a 'first fifteen-man' under my jacket, I found myself quite an object of veneration among the juniors who had lately been my compeers, and I accepted their homage with a vast amount of condescension. Nothing was talked of during the forenoon but the coming match. Would the Craven fellows turn up a strong team? Would that fellow Slider, who made the tremendous run last year, play for them again this? Would Wright select the chapel end or the other if we won the choice? How were we off behind the scrimmage?

'Is Adams to be trusted?' I hear one voice ask.

Two or three small boys promptly replied 'Yes;' but the seniors said nothing, except Wright, who took the opportunity of giving me a little good advice in private.

'Look here, Adams; you are to play "half-back," you know. All you've got to take care of is to keep cool, and never let your eyes go off the ball. You know all the rest.'

A lecture half an hour long could not have made more impression. I remembered those two hints, 'Keep cool and watch the ball,' as long as I played football, and I would advise every 'half-back' to take them to heart in like manner.

At noon the Craven team came down in an omnibus and had lunch in Hall with us, and half an hour later found us all in a straggling procession, making for the scene of conflict in the Great Close. There stood the goals and the boundary-posts, and there was Granger, the ground-keeper, with a bran-new lemon-shaped ball under his arm.

'Look sharp and peel!' cried our captain.

So we hurried to the tent and promptly divested ourselves of our outer garments, turned up the sleeves of our jerseys, and tied an extra knot in our bootlaces. As we emerged, the Craven men were making their appearance on the ground in battle array. I felt so nervous myself that I could not, for the life of me, imagine how some of them could look so unconcerned, whistling, and actually playing leapfrog to keep themselves warm!

An officer in the Crimean War once described his sensation in some of the battles there as precisely similar to those he had experienced when a boy on the football field at Rugby. I can appreciate the comparison, for one. Certainly never soldier went into action with a more solemn do-or-die feeling than that with which I took my place on the field that afternoon.

'They've won the choice of sides,' said somebody, 'and are going to play with the wind.'

'Take your places, Parkhurst!' shouted our captain.

The ball lies in the centre of the ground, and Wright stands ten yards or so behind it, ready for the kick off. Of our fifteen, the ten 'forwards' are extended in a line with the ball across the field, ready to charge after it the moment it goes flying. The two best runners of our team are stationed 'quarter back,' where they can skirmish on the outskirts of the scrimmage. I am posted a little in rear of them at 'half back,' – an unusual post for so young a player, but one which was accorded to me by virtue of my light weight and not inconsiderable running powers. Behind me are the two 'backs,' on whom, when all else fails, the issue of the conflict depends. The Craven players are similarly disposed, and waiting impatiently for our captain's kick.

'Are you ready?' he shouts.

Silence gives consent.

He gives a quick glance round at us, then springs forward, and in an instant the ball is soaring high in the direction of the Cravens' goal amid the shouts of onlooking friend and foe.

Our forwards were after it like lightning, but not before a Craven back had got hold of it and run some distance in the direction of our goal. He did not wait to be attacked, but by a clever drop kick, a knack peculiar to all good 'backs,' sent it spinning right over the forwards' heads into the hands of one of our quarter-backs. He, tucking it under his arm and crushing his cap on to his head, started to run. Going slowly at first, he steered straight for the forwards of the enemy till within a pace or two of them, when he doubled suddenly, and amid the shouts of our partisans slipped past them and was seen heading straight for the Craven goal. But although he had escaped their forwards, he had yet their rearguard to escape, which was far harder work, for was not one of that rearguard the celebrated Slider himself, who by his prowess had last year carried defeat to our school; and the other, was it not the stalwart Naylor, who only a month ago had played gloriously for his county against Gravelshire?

Yet our man was not to be daunted by the prestige of these distinguished adversaries, but held on his way pluckily, and without a swerve. It was a sight to see those two cunningly lay wait for him, like two spiders for a fly. There was nothing for it but to plunge headlong into their web in a desperate effort to break through. Alas! brave man! Naylor has him in his clutches, the Craven forwards come like a deluge on the spot, our forwards pour over the Craven, and in an instant our hero and the ball have vanished from sight under a heap of writhing humanity.

The next thing I was conscious of was that about twenty people had fallen to the ground all of a heap, and that I and the ball were at the bottom.

At last the ball got well away from the scrimmage, and who should secure it but the redoubtable Slider! I felt a passing tremor of deep despair as I saw that hero spring like the wind towards our goal.

'Look out, Adams!' shouted Wright.

Sure enough he was coming in my direction! With the desperation of a doomed man I strode out to meet him. He rushed furiously on, – swerving slightly to avoid my reach, and stretching out his arm to ward off my grasp. I flung myself wildly in his path. There was a heavy thud, and the earth seemed to jump up and strike me. The next moment I was sprawling on my back on the grass. I don't pretend to know how it all happened, but somehow or other I had succeeded in checking the onward career of the victorious Slider; for though I had fallen half stunned before the force of his charge, he had recoiled for an instant from the same shock, and that instant gave time for Wright to get hold of him, and so put an end for the time to his progress.

'Well played!' said some one, as I picked myself up. So I was comforted, and began to think that, after all, football was rather a fine game.

Time would fail me to tell of all the events of that afternoon – how Wright carried the ball within a dozen yards of our opponents' goal; how their forwards passed the ball one to another, and got a 'touch-down' behind our line, but missed the kick; how Naylor ran twenty yards with one of our men hanging on his back; how our quarter-back sent the ball nearly over their goal with as neat a drop-kick as ever it has been my lot to witness.

The afternoon was wearing. I heard the timekeeper call out, 'Five minutes more!' The partisans of either side were getting frantic with excitement. Unless we could secure an advantage now we should be as good as defeated, for the Craven had scored a 'touch-down' to our nothing. Was this desperate fight to end so? Was victory, after all, to escape us? But I had no time for reflection then.

'Now Parkhurst,' sang out Wright, 'pull yourselves together for once!'

A Craven man is standing to throw the ball out of 'touch,' and either side stands in confronting rows, impatient for the fray. Wright is at the end of the line, face to face with Naylor, and I am a little behind Wright.

'Keep close!' exclaims the latter to me, as the ball flies towards us.

Wright has it, but in an instant Naylor's long arms are round him, bearing him down.

'Adams!' ejaculates our captain, and in a trice he passes the ball into my hands, and I am off like the wind. So suddenly has it all been done that I have already a yard or two start before my flight is discovered. There is a yelling and a rush behind me; there is a roar from the crowds on either side; there is a clear 'Follow up, Parkhurst!' from Wright in the rear; there is a loud 'Collar him!' from the Craven captain ahead. I am steering straight for their goal; three men only are between me and it – one, their captain, right back, and Slider and another man in front of him.

I see at a glance that my only hope is to keep as I am going and waste no time in dodging, or assuredly the pursuing host will be upon me. Slider and his companion are closing in right across my path, almost close together. With a bound I dashed between them. Have they got me, or have I escaped them? A shout louder than ever, and a 'Bravo!' from Wright tells me I am clear of that danger and have now but their last defence to pass. He is a tall, broad fellow, and a formidable foe to encounter, and waits for me close under their goal. The pace, I feel, is telling on me, the shouting behind sounds nearer, only a few yards divides us now. Shall I double, shall I venture a kick, or shall I charge straight at him?

'Charge at him!' sounds Wright's voice, as if in answer to my thought. I gather up all my remaining force, and charge. There is a flash across my eyes, and a dull shock against my chest. I reel and stagger, and forget where I am. I am being swept along in a torrent; the waters with a roar rush past me and over me. Every moment I get nearer and nearer the fatal edge – I am at it – I hang a moment on the brink, and then –

'Down!' shouts a voice close at my ear, and there is such a noise of cheering and rejoicing that I sit up and rub my eyes like one waking bewildered from a strange dream.

Then I find out what has happened. When I charged at the Craven captain the shock sent me back staggering into the very arms of Wright and our forwards, who were close at my heels, and who then, in a splendid and irresistible rush, carried me and the ball and half of the other side along with them right behind the enemy's goal line, where we fall *en masse* to the earth – I, with the ball under me, being at the bottom.

Even if I had been hurt – which I was not – there was no time to be wasted on condolences or congratulations. The time-keeper held his watch in his hand, and our goal must be kicked at once, if it was to be kicked at all. So the fifteen paces out were measured, the 'nick' for the ball was carefully made, the enemy stood along their goal-line ready to spring the moment the ball should touch the earth. Wright, cool and self-possessed, placed himself in readiness a yard or two behind the ball, which one of our side held an inch off the ground. An anxious moment of expectation followed; then came a sharp 'Now!' from our captain. The ball was placed cunningly in the nick, the Craven forwards rushed out on it in a body, but long before they could reach it, Wright's practised foot had sent it flying straight as an arrow over the bar, and my first football match had ended in a glorious victory for the Old School.

# William Makepeace Thayer (1820–1898)

A very few book titles have become proverbial, but no anthology of nineteenth-century children's literature would be complete without a sample of this quintessential statement of the American Dream of upward mobility. Thayer, a Congregationalist minister, began his biographical excursions with Abraham Lincoln: *The Pioneer Boy, and How He Became President* (1864). In the preface to *From Log Cabin to White House* he is at pains to point out the similarities between his two subjects: both born in log cabins, both losing a parent, both improving themselves by self-help, both teaching in the backwoods, studying the law, and both the 'youngest member of the legislature, and the youngest officer in the army, when he served' (although, despite what might have been the temptation of symmetry, he does not mention the similarity of their deaths).

As a piece of myth-making that taps into the key elements of the American psyche, *From Log Cabin to White House* is hard to fault. This extract is reprinted from the British edition of 1882.

## from *From Log Cabin to White House: The Story of President Garfield's Life* (1880)

### V

### BOY FARMER

At eight years of age, James had his daily labour to perform as steadily as Thomas. The latter went out to work among the neighbours, often imposing thereby quite a responsibility upon James, who looked after the stock and farm at home. He could chop wood, milk cows, shell corn, cultivate vegetables, and do many other things that farmers must do.

It was very great assistance to the family when Thomas could earn a little money by his labour. That money procured some indispensable articles, the absence of which was a real privation both to mother and children. They needed more money now than ever, because all must have shoes, and all must have books; and there were the teachers to pay, and occasional meetings at the school-house now were some expense. So that the earnings of Thomas just met a demand of the time, in which every member of the household shared.

'You are eight years old, my son, and Thomas is seventeen,' said Mrs. Garfield to James. 'Thomas was not eleven years old when your father died, and he had to take your father's place on the farm. You must be getting ready to take Thomas's place, for he will soon be of age, and then he will have to go out into the world to seek his fortune, and you will have to take care of the farm.'

'I can do that,' James answered.

'Not without learning how to do it,' said his mother. '"Practice makes perfect," is an old and true proverb.'

'I know that I can take care of the farm if Tom could,' interrupted James, with some assurance.

'Yes, when you are as old as he,' suggested his mother.

'That is what I mean, – when I get to be as old as he was.'

'I hope that some day you will do something better than farming,' continued Mrs. Garfield.

'What is there better than farming?' James asked.

'It is better for some men to teach and preach. Wouldn't you like to teach school?'

'When I am old enough, I should.'

'Well, it won't be long before you are old enough. If you are qualified, you can teach school when you are as old as Thomas is now.'

'When I am seventeen?' James responded with some surprise. All of his teachers had been older than that, and he could scarcely see how he could do the same at seventeen.

'Yes, at seventeen or eighteen. Many young men teach school as early as that. But farming comes first in order, as we are situated.'

'And it is time to get the cows now,' remarked James hurrying off for them, and terminating the conversation.

James was a self-reliant boy, just the one to take hold of farm work with tact and vigour. He scarcely knew what '*I can't*' meant. It was an expression that he never used. The phrase that he had just employed in reply to his mother, '*I can do that*,' was a common one with him. Once it put him into a laughable position. He was after hens' eggs in the barn, with his playmate Edwin Mapes. It was just about the time he was eight years old, perhaps a little older. Edwin found a pullet's egg, rather smaller than they usually discovered.

'Isn't that cunning?' said Edwin, holding up the egg.

'I can swaller that,' was James' prompt answer.

'Whole?'

'Yes, whole.'

'You can't do it.'

'I *can* do it.'

'I dare you to swaller it,' continued Edwin, eager to see the experiment tried.

'Not much to dare me to,' responded James. 'Here it goes;' and into his mouth the egg went, proving larger than he anticipated, or else his throat was smaller, for it would not go down at his bidding.

'No use, Jim,' exclaimed Edwin, laughing outright over his failure. 'The egg is small, but it won't fit your throat.'

'It's going down, yet,' said James, resolutely, and the second time the egg was thrust into his mouth.

'Shell and all, I s'pose,' remarked Edwin. 'S'pose it should stick in your crop, you'd be in a pretty fix.'

'But it won't stick in my crop,' replied James; 'it's going' down. I undertook to swaller it, and I'm goin' to.'

The egg broke in his mouth when he almost unconsciously brought his teeth together, making a very disagreeable mush of shell and meat. It was altogether too much of a good thing, and proved rather a nauseating dose. His stomach heaved, his face scowled, and Edwin roared; still James held to the egg, and made for the house as fast as his nimble limbs could take him, Edwin following after, to learn what next. Rushing into the house, James seized a piece of bread, thrust it into his mouth, chewed it up with the dilapidated egg, and swallowed the whole together.

'There!' he exclaimed, 'it's done.'

He did what he said he would, excepting only that the egg did not find its way down the throat whole; and he felt like a conqueror. Edwin swayed to and fro with laughter; and, although forty years have elapsed since that day, it is not impossible for him to get up a laugh over it still. Mrs. Garfield looked on with curious interest, not comprehending the meaning of the affair until an explanation followed. Then she only smiled, and said, 'Foolish boy!'

It was true, what she said. He was a 'foolish boy' to undertake such a feat; 'foolish,' just as many promising boys are 'foolish' at times. But the spirit of the lad appeared through the 'foolish' act. Nevertheless, the '*I can*' element of his character rather dignified the performance. The more we think of it the more we are inclined to take back our endorsement of that word 'foolish,' because the act was an outcome of his self-reliance. When William Carey, the renowned missionary to India, was a boy, he possessed a daring, adventurous spirit, that expressed itself in climbing trees and buildings, and in going where, and doing what, few boys would do because of the peril. One day he fell from the top of a tree, on which he perched like an owl, and broke one of his legs. He was confined to the house and bed several weeks; but the first thing he did on his recovery was to climb that identical tree to its very top, and seat himself on the bough from which he had fallen, to show that the feat was not impossible. There is no doubt that his mother called him 'a foolish boy,' to risk his limbs and life again on the tree; but his admirers have ever loved to rehearse the deed, as proof of the boy's invincible, reliant spirit. No one who reads of Carey's immense labours for the heathen, his fearlessness in great danger, his hair-breadth escapes from death, his tact and coolness in every emergency, can fail to see that his 'foolish' act of climbing the tree was a good illustration of the maxim, that 'The boy is father of the man.'

James was not egotistical or self-confident; these are no part of self-reliance. Nor was he proud; pride is no part of self-reliance. He was not conscious of having anything to be proud of. No boy was ever more simple-hearted and confiding in others than was he. He did not tell his mother that he could run the farm because he overrated his abilities; it was the honest expression of what he was willing to do, and what he thought he could do. It was the opposite of that inefficient, irresolute boyhood that exclaims, 'I can't,' when it ought to be ashamed to say it; and when a decided, hearty, 'I can,' would prove a trumpet-call to duty, rallying all the powers to instant action. This was one thing that encouraged his mother to expect so much of him when he should become a man. On one occasion, after he began to labour on the farm, and quite a task was before him, she said to him:

'James, half the battle is in thinking you can do a thing. My father used to say, "Where there's a will, there's a way;" repeating a proverb that is as old as the hills.'

'What does that mean?' interrupted James, referring to the proverb.

'It means, that he who *wills* to do anything *will* do it. That is, the boy who relies upon himself, and determines to perform a task in spite of difficulties, will accomplish his purpose. You can do that?' And his mother waited for a reply.

'I can,' James answered, with emphasis.

'Depend upon yourself. Feel that you are equal to the work in hand, and it will be easily done. "God helps those who help themselves," it is said, and I believe it. He has helped me wonderfully since your father died. I scarcely knew which way to turn when he died; I scarcely saw how I could live here in the woods; and yet I could find no way to get out of them and live. But just as soon as I fell back upon God and myself, I took up the cross, and bore it easily. We have fared much better than I expected; and it is because I was made to feel that "Where there's a will, there's a way." God will bless all our efforts to do the best we can.'

'What'll He do when we don't do the best we can?' inquired James.

'He will withhold His blessing; and that is the greatest calamity that could possibly happen to us. We can do nothing well without His blessing.'

'I thought God only helped people be *good*,' remarked James, who was beginning to inquire within himself whether He helped farmers.

'God helps folks to be good in everything – good boys, good men, good workers, good thinkers, good farmers, good teachers, good everything. And without His help we can be good in nothing.'

James drank in every word, and looked very much as if he believed that he and God could run the farm successfully. His mother continued:

'If you do one thing well you will do another well, and so on to the end. You will soon learn that your own efforts are necessary to accomplish anything, and so you will form the habit of depending upon yourself – the only way to make the most of yourself.'

Such was the instruction that James received from the wisest of mothers, just when such lessons respecting self-reliance would do him the most good. It was on this line that he was started off in his boyhood, and he followed that line thereafter. He had no one to help him upward, and he had no desire to have anybody help him. Unlike boys who depend upon some rich father or uncle to give them 'a good start,' or upon superior advantages, he settled down upon the stubborn fact, that if anything was ever made out of him he must do it himself. Hard work was before him, and hard fare, and he expected nothing less. A statesman who rose from obscurity to eminence once said, 'Whatever may be thought of my attainments, it must be conceded that I made as much out of the stuff put into my hands as was possible.' That the germ of such an impulse must have taken root in James' heart early, is quite evident from some remarks of his to young men after he was forty years old.

'Occasion cannot make spurs, young men. If you expect to wear spurs, you must win them. If you wish to use them, you must buckle them to your own heels before you go into the fight. Any success you may achieve is not worth having unless you fight for it. Whatever you win in life you must conquer by your own efforts, and then it is yours – a part of yourself. . . . Let not poverty stand as an obstacle in your way. Poverty is uncomfortable, as I can testify; but nine times out of ten the best thing that can happen to a young man is to be tossed overboard, and compelled to sink or swim for himself. In all my acquaintance I have never known one to be drowned who was worth saving. . . . To a young man who has in himself the magnificent possibilities of life it is not fitting that he should be permanently commanded; he should be a commander. You must not continue to be *employed*; you must be an *employer*. You must be promoted from the ranks to a command. There is something, young men, that you can command; go and find it, and command it. You can at least command a horse and dray, can be generalissimo of them, and may carve out a fortune with them.'

Another incident of James' early life illustrates the phase of his character in question, and, at the same time, shows his aptitude in unexpected emergencies. He was eight or ten years of age when it occurred, a pupil in school with his cousin, Henry Boynton. Sitting side by side, one day they became more roguish than usual, without intending to violate the rules of school. Sly looks and an occasional laugh satisfied the teacher, who was a sharp disciplinarian, that something unusual was going on, and he concluded that the wisest treatment would be to stop it at once.

'James and Henry!' he called out, loudly, 'lay aside your books and go home, both of you.'

A clap of thunder would not have startled them more. They looked at each other seriously, as if the result was entirely unexpected, and delayed for a moment.

'Don't dilly-dally,' exclaimed the teacher; 'both of you go home immediately.'

'I will go,' answered James. Henry said nothing; and both passed out. James made an express of his dexterous legs, shortening the distance from the school-house to home to about three or four minutes, and an equal time to return. Returning to school, he entered the room, puffing like an engine, and resumed his seat.

'James! did I not tell you to go home?' shouted the teacher, never dreaming that the boy had had time to obey the mandate.

'I have been home,' answered James, not in the least disconcerted. He had obeyed his teacher promptly, though he took very good care that his mother did not see him when he reached the cabin.

'Been home?' responded the teacher, inquiringly, surprised that the boy had been home in so short a time.

'Yes, sir, I have been home,' replied James; 'you didn't tell me to *stay*.'

'Well, you can *stay* here now,' answered the teacher with a smile, thinking that was the best way to dispose of so good a joke. James remained, and was very careful not to be sent home again, lest the affair might not terminate so pleasantly. Henry sulked about the school-house for a while, and then went home and stayed the remainder of the day. That was the difference between the two boys. James saw the way out of the trouble at once, through the most literal obedience, and, believing that he was equal to the emergency, he started promptly to fulfil the command. He was neither sulky nor rebellious, but happy as a lark, lively as a cricket, and smiling as a morning in May. Such a little episode rather tightened the bond existing between the teacher and James. The former discovered more of that sharp discrimination and practical wit in the affair, for which he had already learned that James was distinguished.

James was now eleven years old, and Thomas was twenty. The district concluded to erect a frame school-house, and sold the old one to Thomas for a trifle. Thomas and James, assisted by their cousins, the Boynton boys, took it down, and put it up again directly in the rear of their mother's cabin, thus providing her with an additional room, which was a great convenience. Thomas did it in anticipation of leaving home when he should attain his majority.

# Joel Chandler Harris (1848–1908)

The presence of 'Brer Rabbit' in this collection is questionable on three grounds: the first, that the stories are retellings; the second is that they were not (all) intended for children, and the third is that they are now politically unacceptable. It has been strongly argued that in writing down and editing the tales, Harris was indulging in cultural theft: stultifying an oral tradition by imposing upon it an inappropriate written form, quite apart from using a dialect which in itself is demeaning to the black narrator (see Moore and MacCann, 1986). As John Goldthwaite (1996) puts it: 'An Uncle Remus may have been the right, the necessary choice of character for the telling of these tales, but he was, everyone agreed, the wrong one for the preserving of them'.

These reasons seem to me to be indisputable; but equally indisputable is the phenomenal impact that the tales had on American children's literature, and, indeed, on literature in general (and Beatrix Potter, Rudyard Kipling, Thornton Burgess and many others in particular). The stories, for roughly 100 years, became part of American folklore in general, adapted and modified much as any other folklore, including, of course, versions by Walt Disney. There have been modern retellings, notably by Julius Lester in *The Tales of Uncle Remus*, which have attempted to act as correctives to Harris's version.

Reprinting one tale here, then, is an acknowledgement of the political incorrectness of children's literature at the extreme. It is very hard to find a children's book in the nineteenth century that does not insult someone: for example, a large proportion of this anthology should alienate ex-colonial citizens, and especially women. The arguments that the Uncle Remus stories, complete with their dialect, were acts of good faith; that they preserve important tales; that they relate directly to an important area of myth; that they – perhaps ironically – articulate the subversive strength of the quintessential trickster – all of these can be demolished by straightforward disapproval.

Joel Chandler Harris was a journalist on the *Atlanta Constitution*. As with the folk-tales collected by the brothers Grimm, it is not clear where his sources end and his work begins. In the introduction to the first volume, he wrote: 'my purpose has been to preserve the legends in their original simplicity, and to wed them permanently to the quaint dialect – if, indeed, it can be called a dialect – through the medium of which they have become a part of the domestic history of every southern family'. How far that can be seen, in its historical context, as patronizing or well-meaning is a matter for debate, as is Harris's comment that Uncle Remus 'has nothing but pleasant memories of the discipline of slavery'.

This extract is reprinted from the new and revised edition of 1896.

## from *Uncle Remus, his Songs and Sayings. The Folk-Lore of the Old Plantation* (1880) [dated 1881]

### Mr. Rabbit Grossly Deceives Mr. Fox

One evening when the little boy, whose nights with Uncle Remus were as entertaining as those Arabian ones of blessed memory, had finished supper and hurried out to sit with his venerable patron, he found the old man in great glee. Indeed, Uncle Remus was talking and laughing to himself at such a rate that the little boy was afraid he had company. The truth is, Uncle Remus had heard the child coming, and when the rosy-cheeked chap put his head in at the door, was engaged in a monologue, the burden of which seemed to be –

> 'Ole Molly Har',
> W'at you doin' dar,
> Settin' in de cornder
> Smokin' yo' seegyar?'

As a matter of course this vague allusion reminded the little boy of the fact that the wicked Fox was still in pursuit of the Rabbit, and he immediately put his curiosity in the shape of a question. 'Uncle Remus, did the Rabbit have to go clean away when he got loose from the Tar-Baby?'

'Bless gracious, honey, dat he didn't. Who? Him? You dunno nothin' 'tall 'bout Brer Rabbit ef dat's de way you puttin' 'im down. W'at he gwine 'way fer? He moughter stayed sorter close twel de pitch rub off'n his ha'r, but twern't menny days 'fo' he wuz lopin' up en down de neighborhood same ez ever, en I dunno ef he weren't mo' sassier dan befo.

'Seem like dat de tale 'bout how he got mixt up wid de Tar-Baby got "roun" 'mongst de neighbors. Leas'ways, Miss Meadows en de gals got win' un it, en de nex' time Brer Rabbit paid um a visit Miss Meadows tackled 'im 'bout it, en de gals sot up a monstus gigglement. Brer Rabbit, he sot up des ez cool ez a cowcumber, he did, en let 'em run on.'

'Who was Miss Meadows, Uncle Remus?' inquired the little boy.

'Don't ax me, honey. She wuz in de tale, Miss Meadows en de gals wuz, en de tale I give you like hit wer' gun ter me. Brer Rabbit, he sot dar, he did, sorter lam' like, en den bimeby he cross his legs, he did, and wink his eye slow, en up and say, sezee:

' "Ladies, Brer Fox wuz my daddy's ridin'-hoss fer thirty year; maybe mo', but thirty year dat I knows un," sezee; en den he paid um his 'specks, en tip his beaver, en march off, he did, des ez stiff en ez stuck up ez a fier-stick.

'Nex' day, Brer Fox cum a callin', and w'en he 'gun fer ter laugh 'bout Brer Rabbit, Miss Meadows en de gals, dey ups en tells 'im 'bout w'at Brer Rabbit say. Den Brer Fox grit his tushes sho nuff, he did, en he look mighty dumpy, but w'en he riz fer ter go he up en say, sezee:

' "Ladies, I ain't 'sputin' w'at you say, but I'll make Brer Rabbit chaw up his words en spit um out right yer whar you kin see 'im," sezee, en wid dat off Brer Fox put.

'En w'en he got in de big road, he shuck de dew off'n his tail, en made a straight shoot fer Brer Rabbit's house. W'en he got dar, Brer Rabbit wuz spectin' un 'im, en de do' wuz shet fas'. Brer Fox knock. Nobody ain't ans'er. Brer Fox knock. Nobody ans'er. Den he knock agin – blam! blam! Den Brer Rabbit holler out mighty weak:

' "Is dat you, Brer Fox? I want you ter run en fetch de doctor. Dat bait er pusly w'at I e't dis mawnin' is gittin' 'way wid me. Do, please, Brer Fox, run quick," sez Brer Rabbit, sezee.

' "I come atter you, Brer Rabbit," sez Brer Fox, sezee. "Dar's gwine ter be a party up at Miss Meadows's," sezee. "All de gals 'll be dere, en I promus' dat I'd fetch you. De gals, dey 'lowed dat hit wouldn't be no party ceppin' I fotch you," sez Brer Fox, sezee.

'Den Brer Rabbit say he wuz too sick, en Brer Fox say he wuzzent, en dar dey had it up and down, 'sputin' en contendin'. Brer Rabbit say he can't walk. Brer Fox say he tote 'im. Brer Rabbit say how? Brer Fox say in his arms. Brer Rabbit say he drap 'im. Brer Fox 'low he won't. Bimeby Brer Rabbit say he go ef Brer Fox tote 'im on his back. Brer Fox say he would. Brer Rabbit say he can't ride widout a saddle. Brer Fox say he git de saddle. Brer Rabbit say he can't set in saddles less he have bridle fer ter hol' by. Brer Fox say he git de bridle. Brer Rabbit say he can't ride widout blin' bridle, kaze Brer Fox be shyin' at stumps 'long de road, en fling 'im off. Brer Fox say he git blin' bridle. Den Brer Rabbit say he go. Den Brer Fox say he ride Brer Rabbit mos' up ter Miss Meadows's, en den he could git down en walk de balance er de way. Brer Rabbit 'greed, en den Brer Fox lipt out atter de saddle en de bridle.

'Co'se Brer Rabbit know de game dat Brer Fox wuz fixin' fer ter play, en he 'termin' fer ter outdo 'im, en by de time he koam his ha'r en twis' his mustash, en sorter rig up, yer come Brer Fox, saddle en bridle on, en lookin' ez peart ez a circus pony. He trot up ter de do' en stan' dar pawin' de ground en chompin' de bit same like sho nuff hoss, en Brer Rabbit he mount, he did, en dey amble off. Brer Fox can't see behime wid de blin' bridle on, but bimeby he feel Brer Rabbit raise one er his foots.

' "W'at you doin' now, Brer Rabbit?" sezee.

' "Short'nin' de lef' stir'p, Brer Fox," sezee.

'Bimeby Brer Rabbit raise up de udder foot.

' "W'at you doin' now, Brer Rabbit?" sezee.

' "Pullin' down my pants, Brer Fox," sezee.

'All de time, bless gracious, honey, Brer Rabbit wer' puttin' on his spurrers, en w'en dey got close to Miss Meadows's, whar Brer Rabbit wuz to git off, en Brer Fox made a motion fer ter stan' still, Brer Rabbit slap de spurrers into Brer Fox flanks, en you better b'lieve he got over groun'. W'en dey got ter de house, Miss Meadows en all de gals wuz settin' on de peazzer, en stidder stoppin' at de gate, Brer Rabbit rid on by, he did, en den come gallopin' down de road en up ter de hoss-rack, w'ich he hitch Brer Fox at, en den he sa'nter inter de house, he did, en shake han's wid de gals, en set dar, smokin' his seegyar same ez a town man. Bimeby he draw in a long puff, en den let hit out in a cloud, en squar hisse'f back en holler out, he did:

'"Ladies, ain't I done tell you Brer Fox wuz de ridin'-hoss fer our fambly? He sorter losin' his gait now, but I speck I kin fetch 'im all right in a mont' er so," sezee.

'En den Brer Rabbit sorter grin, he did, en de gals giggle, en Miss Meadows, she praise up de pony, en dar wuz Brer Fox hitch fas' ter de rack, en couldn't he'p hisse'f.'

'Is that all, Uncle Remus?' asked the little boy as the old man paused.

'Dat ain't all, honey, but 'twon't do fer ter give out too much cloff fer ter cut one pa'r pants,' replied the old man sententiously.

# James Otis [Kaler] (1848–1912)

*Toby Tyler* features the good boy out of luck, rather than the bad boy in luck. In some ways it is an antidote to the cheerful Horatio Alger school of self-help novel: Toby, a foundling, tries hard, but his best efforts are not always rewarded. Despite the strangeness and excitement of circus life, emphasis is placed on the cruelty of the circus-man Job Lord towards Toby, and Toby's incessant hunger. Even when Toby tries to atone for his original mistake of running away from Uncle Daniel, by running away from the circus, his only reward is that his pet monkey, Mr Stubbs, is shot. The happy ending, such as it is, is a reaffirmation of family values, an act of authorial faith, rather than any reward for Toby's virtue.

It is as if the grimmer side of the spirit of *The Pilgrim's Progress* hangs over the book (just as the benign side did over *Little Women*). Toby's journey to maturity is marked by moments of tragic carelessness (as when the monkey throws his money away), and his recovery from these setbacks is quite unrelated to the recoveries of earlier heroes who were fired by the evangelical tradition.

For all that this has the trappings of an adventure story, and for all its sentimental tendencies, *Toby Tyler* has considerable psychological depth as a story of a maturing child, and the death of Mr Stubbs marks the key point of Toby's maturing progress. The final chapter, reprinted here, picks up the story at Mr Stubbs's death.

It is interesting to note that Otis wrote another book which implicitly criticized the Alger tradition: *The Boys' Revolt* (1894) about a corrupted boot-blacks' union. He was a prolific author, but *Toby Tyler* was by far his most successful book.

## from *Toby Tyler, or Ten Weeks with a Circus* (1881)

### CHAPTER XX

### HOME AND UNCLE DANIEL

Meanwhile the author of all this misery had come upon the scene. He was a young man, whose rifle and well-filled game-bag showed that he had been hunting, and his face expressed the liveliest sorrow for what he had so unwittingly done.

'I didn't know I was firing at your pet,' he said to Toby as he laid his hand on his shoulder and endeavored to make him look up. 'I only saw a little patch of fur through the trees, and, thinking it was some wild animal, I fired. Forgive me, won't you, and let me put the poor brute out of his misery?'

Toby looked up fiercely at the murderer of his pet and asked, savagely, 'Why don't you go away? Don't you see that you have killed Mr. Stubbs, an' you'll be hung for murder?'

'I wouldn't have done it under any circumstances,' said the young man, pitying Toby's grief most sincerely. 'Come away, and let me put the poor thing out of its agony.'

'How can you do it?' asked Toby, bitterly. 'He's dying already.'

'I know it, and it will be a kindness to put a bullet through his head.'

If Toby had been big enough perhaps there might really have been a murder committed, for he looked up at the man who so coolly proposed to kill the poor monkey after he had already received his death-wound that the young man stepped back quickly, as if really afraid that in his desperation the boy might do him some injury.

'Go 'way off,' said Toby, passionately, 'an' don't ever come here again. You've killed all I ever had in this world of my own to love me, an' I hate you – I hate you!'

Then, turning again to the monkey, he put his hands on each side of his head, and, leaning down, kissed the little brown lips as tenderly as a mother would kiss her child.

The monkey was growing more and more feeble, and when Toby had shown this act of affection he reached up his tiny paws, grasped Toby's finger, half-raised himself from the ground, and then with a convulsive struggle fell back dead, while the tiny fingers slowly relaxed their hold of the boy's hand.

Toby feared that it was death, and yet hoped that he was mistaken; he looked into the half-open, fast-glazing eyes, put his hand over his heart, to learn if it were still beating; and getting no responsive look from the dead eyes, feeling no heart-throbs from under that gory breast, he knew that his pet was really dead, and flung himself by his side in all the childish abandonment of grief.

He called the monkey by name, implored him to look at him, and finally bewailed that he had ever left the circus, where at least his pet's life was safe, even if his own back received its daily flogging.

The young man, who stood a silent spectator of this painful scene, understood everything from Toby's mourning. He knew that a boy had run away from the circus, for Messrs. Lord and Castle had stayed behind one day, in the hope of capturing the fugitive, and they had told their own version of Toby's flight.

For nearly an hour Toby lay by the dead monkey's side, crying as if his heart would break, and the young man waited until his grief should have somewhat exhausted itself, and then approached the boy again.

'Won't you believe that I didn't mean to do this cruel thing?' he asked, in a kindly voice. 'And won't you believe that I would do anything in my power to bring your pet back to life?'

Toby looked at him a moment earnestly, and then said, slowly, 'Yes, I'll try to.'

'Now will you come with me, and let me talk to you? for I know who you are, and why you are here.'

'How do you know that?'

'Two men stayed behind after the circus had left, and they hunted everywhere for you.'

'I wish they had caught me,' moaned Toby; 'I wish they had caught me, for then Mr. Stubbs wouldn't be here dead.'

And Toby's grief broke out afresh as he again looked at the poor little stiff form that had been a source of so much comfort and joy to him.

'Try not to think of that now, but think of yourself, and of what you will do,' said the man, soothingly, anxious to divert Toby's mind from the monkey's death as much as possible.

'I don't want to think of myself, and I don't care what I'll do,' sobbed the boy, passionately.

'But you must; you can't stay here always, and I will try to help you to get home, or wherever it is you want to go, if you will tell me all about it.'

It was some time before Toby could be persuaded to speak or think of anything but the death of his pet; but the young man finally succeeded in drawing his story from him, and then tried to induce him to leave that place and accompany him to the town.

'I can't leave Mr. Stubbs,' said the boy, firmly; 'he never left me the night I got thrown out of the wagon an' he thought I was hurt.'

Then came another struggle to induce him to bury his pet; and finally Toby, after realizing the fact that he could not carry a dead monkey anywhere with him, agreed to it; but he would not allow the young man to help him in any way, or even to touch the monkey's body.

He dug a grave under a little fir-tree near by, and lined it with wild flowers and leaves, and even then hesitated to cover the body with the earth. At last he bethought himself of the fanciful costume which the skeleton and his wife had given him, and in this he carefully wrapped his dead pet. He had not one regret at leaving the bespangled suit, for it was the best he could command, and surely nothing could be too good for Mr. Stubbs.

Tenderly he laid him in the little grave, and, covering the body with flowers, said, pausing a moment before he covered it over with earth, and while his voice was choked with emotion, 'Good-bye, Mr. Stubbs, good-bye! I wish it had been me instead of you that died, for I'm an awful sorry little boy now that you're dead!'

Even after the grave had been filled, and a little mound made over it, the young man had the greatest difficulty to persuade Toby to go with him; and when the boy did consent to go at last he walked very slowly away, and kept turning his head to look back just so long as the little grave could be seen.

Then, when the trees shut it completely out from sight, the tears commenced again to roll down Toby's cheeks, and he sobbed out, 'I wish I hadn't left him. Oh, why didn't I make him lie down by me? an' then he'd be alive now; an' how glad he'd be to know that we was getting out of the woods at last!'

But the man who had caused Toby this sorrow talked to him about other matters, thus taking his mind from the monkey's death as much as possible, and by the time the boy reached the village he had told his story exactly as it was, without casting any reproaches on Mr. Lord, and giving himself the full share of censure for leaving his home as he did.

Mr. Lord and Mr. Castle had remained in the town but one day, for they were told that a boy had taken the night train that passed through the town about two hours after Toby had escaped, and they had set off at once to act on that information.

Therefore Toby need have no fears of meeting either of them just then, and he could start on his homeward journey in peace.

The young man who had caused the monkey's death tried first to persuade Toby to remain a day or two with him, and, failing in that, he did all he could toward getting the boy home as quickly and safely as possible. He insisted on paying for his ticket on the steamboat, although Toby did all he could to prevent him, and he even accompanied Toby to the next town, where he was to take the steamer.

He had not only paid for Toby's ticket, but he had paid for a state-room for him; and when the boy said that he could sleep anywhere, and that there was no need of such expense, the man replied, 'Those men who were hunting for you have gone down the river, and will be very likely to search the boat, when they discover that they started on the wrong scent. They will never suspect that you have got a state-room; and if you are careful to remain in it during the trip, you will get through safely.'

Then, when the time came for the steamer to start, the young man said to Toby, 'Now, my boy, you won't feel hard at me for shooting the monkey, will you? I would have done anything to have brought him to life; but, as I could not do that, helping you to get home was the next best thing I could do.'

'I know you didn't mean to shoot Mr. Stubbs,' said Toby, with moistening eyes as he spoke of his pet, 'an' I'm sorry I said what I did to you in the woods.'

Before there was time to say any more the warning whistle was sounded, the plank pulled in, the great wheels commenced to revolve, and Toby was really on his way to Uncle Daniel and Guilford.

It was then but five o'clock in the afternoon, and he could not expect to reach home until two or three o'clock in the afternoon of the next day; but he was in a tremor of excitement as he thought that he should walk through the streets of Guilford once more, see all the boys, and go home to Uncle Daniel.

And yet, whenever he thought of that home, of meeting those boys, of going once more to all those old familiar places, the memory of all that he had planned when he should take the monkey with him would come into his mind and damp even his joy, great as it was.

That night he had considerable difficulty in falling asleep, but did finally succeed in doing so; and when he awoke the steamer was going up the river, whose waters seemed like an old friend, because they had flowed right down past Guilford on their way to the sea.

At each town where a landing was made Toby looked eagerly out on the pier, thinking that by chance some one from his home might be there and he would see a familiar face again. But all this time he heeded the advice given him and remained in his room, where he could see and not be seen; and it was well for him that he did so, for at one of the landings he saw both Mr. Lord and Mr. Castle come on board the boat.

Toby's heart beat fast and furious, and he expected every moment to hear them at the door demanding admittance, for it seemed to him that they must know exactly where he was secreted.

But no such misfortune occurred. The men had evidently only boarded the boat to search for the boy, for they landed again before the steamer started, and Toby had the satisfaction of seeing their backs as they walked away from the pier. It was some time before he recovered from the fright which the sight of them gave him; but when he did his thoughts and hopes far outstripped the steamer which, it seemed, was going so slowly, and he longed to see Guilford with an impatience that could hardly be restrained.

At last he could see the spire of the little church on the hill, and when the steamer rounded the point, affording a full view of the town, and sounded her whistle as a signal for those on the shore to come to the pier, Toby could hardly restrain himself from jumping up and down and shouting in his delight.

He was at the gang-plank ready to land fully five minutes before the steamer was anywhere near the wharf, and when he recognized the first face on the pier what a happy boy he was!

He was at home! The dream of the past ten weeks was at length realized, and neither Mr. Lord nor Mr. Castle had any terrors for him now.

He ran down the gang-plank before it was ready and clasped every boy he saw there round the neck, and would have kissed them, if they had shown an inclination to let him do so.

Of course he was overwhelmed with questions, but before he would answer any he asked for Uncle Daniel and the others at home.

Some of the boys ventured to predict that Toby would get a jolly good whipping for running away, and the only reply which the happy Toby made to that was,

'I hope I will, an' then I'll feel as if I had kinder paid for runnin' away. If Uncle Dan'l will only let me stay with him again he may whip me every mornin', an' I won't open my mouth to holler.'

The boys were impatient to hear the story of Toby's travels, but he refused to tell it them, saying,

'I'll go home; an' if Uncle Dan'l forgives me for bein' so wicked I'll sit down this afternoon an' tell you all you want to know about the circus.'

Then, far more rapidly than he had run away from it, Toby ran toward the home which he had called his ever since he could remember, and his heart was full almost to bursting as he thought that perhaps he would be told that he had forfeited all claim to it, and that he could never more call it 'home' again.

When he entered the old familiar sitting-room Uncle Daniel was seated near the window, alone, looking out wistfully – as Toby thought – across the fields of yellow waving grain.

Toby crept softly in, and, going up to the old man, knelt down and said, very humbly, and with his whole soul in the words, 'Oh, Uncle Dan'l! if you'll only forgive me for bein' so wicked an' runnin' away, an' let me stay here again – for it's all the home I ever had – I'll do everything you tell me to, an' never whisper in meetin' or do anything bad.'

And then he waited for the words which would seal his fate. They were not long in coming.

'My poor boy,' said Uncle Daniel, softly, as he stroked Toby's refractory red hair, 'my love for you was greater than I knew, and when you left me I cried aloud to the Lord as if it had been my own flesh and blood that had gone afar from me. Stay here, Toby, my son, and help to support this poor old body as it goes down into the dark valley of the shadow of death; and then, in the bright light of that glorious future, Uncle Daniel will wait to go with you into the presence of Him who is ever a father to the fatherless.'

And in Uncle Daniel's kindly care we may safely leave Toby Tyler.

# 'Margaret Sidney' (Harriett Mulford [Stone] Lothrop) (1844–1924)

The 1909 edition of *Five Little Peppers*, from which these extracts are reprinted, has two interesting items on the verso of the title page, both of which demonstrate what a phenomenon the book was: '*Four Hundredth Thousand*' and '"Pepper" Trade Mark, Registered in U.S. Patent Office'. The Peppers had become an industry, with five sequels to the original book, such as *Five Little Peppers Grown Up* (*c.* 1892).

An episodic, amiable (not to say unrealistic) story of a poor, but almost permanently cheerful family, the Pepper's fairly lightweight adventures culminate in their moving in with the rich King family. The whole story contrasts strongly with the image of the poor in British children's books especially, and is unmarked by British class-consciousness.

Indeed, so sunny is the book, that it often reads like a gentle satire on the evangelical tale. The exhortations of the upright Miss Jerushy Henderson have no perceptible effect on the family (in fact, they seem to be slightly puzzled by them). When Joel falls ill with measles, the whole affair parodies the long-drawn-out illnesses of a thousand books, including *What Katy Did* and *Little Women*. The dramatic announcement: 'How he fell sick, they scarcely knew, it all came so suddenly. The poor, bewildered family had hardly time to think, before delirium and, perhaps, death, stared them in the face', and the relief: '"Joel's goin' to get well"' are separated by exactly two pages. Restoring Polly's sight takes a mere ten more – and the family members are then overwhelmed with gifts from their rich admirers. Here is an optimism to match Horatio Alger's, softened (at last, one might say) by comedy. It was not the last of its kind.

'Margaret Sidney' was married to the publisher Daniel Lothrop; *Five Little Peppers* was serialized in the Lothrop magazine *Wide Awake* (1875–93) in 1878. In order to give a flavour of the book, I have reprinted two extracts: in the first we are introduced to the chaotic 'little brown house'; in the second, the family's fortune is finally made.

## from *Five Little Peppers and How they Grew* (1881)

### CHAPTER 1

### A HOME VIEW

The little old kitchen had quieted down from the bustle and confusion of midday; and now, with its afternoon manners on, presented a holiday aspect, that as the principal room in the brown house, it was eminently proper it should have. It was just on the edge of the twilight; and the little Peppers, all except Ben, the oldest of the flock, were taking a 'breathing spell' as their mother called it, which meant some quiet work suitable for the hour. All the 'breathing spell' they could remember, however, poor things; for times were always hard with them now-a-days; and since the father died, when Phronsie was a baby, Mrs. Pepper had had hard work to scrape together money enough to put bread into her children's mouths, and to pay the rent of the little brown house.

But she had met life too bravely to be beaten down now. So with a stout heart and a cheery face, she had worked away day after day at making coats, and tailoring and mending of all descriptions; and she had seen with pride that couldn't be concealed, her noisy, happy brood growing up around her, and filling her heart with comfort, and making the little brown house fairly ring with jollity and fun.

'Poor things!' she would say to herself, 'they haven't had any bringing up; they've just scrambled up!' And then she would set her lips together tightly, and fly at her work faster than ever. 'I must get learning for 'em someway, but I don't see *how!*'

Once or twice she had thought, 'Now the time's coming!' but it never did: for winter shut in very cold, and it took so much more to feed and warm them, that the money went faster than ever. And then, when the way seemed clear again, the store changed hands, so that for a long time she failed to get her usual supply of sacks and coats to make; and that made sad havoc in the quarters and half dollars laid up as her nest egg. But – 'Well, it'll come *some* time,' she would say to herself; 'because it *must!*' And so at it again she would fly, brisker than ever.

'To help mother,' was the great ambition of all the children, older and younger; but in Polly's and Ben's souls, the desire grew so overwhelmingly great as to absorb all lesser things. Many and vast were their secret plans, by which they were to astonish her at some future day, which they would only confide – as they did everything else – to one another. For this brother and sister were everything to each other, and stood loyally together through thick and thin.

Polly was ten, and Ben one year older; and the younger three of the 'Five Little Peppers,' as they were always called, looked up to them with the intensest admiration and love. What *they* failed to do, *couldn't* very well be done by *any* one!

'Oh, dear!' exclaimed Polly, as she sat over in the corner by the window, helping her mother pull out basting threads from a coat she had just finished, and giving an impatient twitch to the sleeve, 'I do wish we could ever have any light – just as much as we want!'

'You don't need any light to see these threads,' said Mrs. Pepper, winding up hers carefully, as she spoke, on an old spool. 'Take care, Polly, you broke that; thread's dear now.'

'I couldn't help it,' said Polly, vexedly; 'it snapped; everything's dear now, seems to me! I wish we could have – oh! ever an' ever so many candles; as many as we wanted! I'd light 'em all, so there! and have it light here *one* night, anyway!'

'Yes, and go dark all the rest of the year, like as anyway,' observed Mrs. Pepper, stopping to untie a knot. 'Folks who do so never have any candles,' she added, sententiously.

'How many'd you have, Polly?' asked Joel, curiously, laying down his hammer, and regarding her with the utmost anxiety.

'Oh, two hundred!' said Polly, decidedly. 'I'd have two hundred, all in a row!'

'*Two hundred candles!*' echoed Joel, in amazement. 'My whockety! what a lot!'

'Don't say such dreadful words, Joel,' put in Polly, nervously, stooping to pick up her spool of basting thread that was racing away all by itself; ''tisn't nice.'

''Tisn't worse 'n to wish you'd got things you haven't,' retorted Joel. 'I don't believe you'd light 'em all at once,' he added, incredulously.

'Yes, I would too!' replied Polly, recklessly; 'two hundred of 'em, if I had a chance; all at once, so there, Joey Pepper!'

'Oh!' said little Davie, drawing a long sigh. 'Why, 'twould be just like heaven, Polly! but wouldn't it cost money, though!'

'I don't care,' said Polly, giving a flounce in her chair, which snapped another thread; 'oh dear me! I didn't mean to, mammy; well, I wouldn't care how much money it cost, we'd have as much light as we wanted for once; so!'

'Goodness!' said Mrs. Pepper, 'you'd have the house afire! Two hundred candles! who ever heard of such a thing!'

'Would they burn?' asked Phronsie, anxiously, getting up from the floor where she was crouching with David, overseeing Joel nail on the cover of an old box; and going to Polly's side she awaited her answer patiently.

'Burn?' said Polly. 'There, that's done now, mamsie dear!' And she put the coat, with a last little pat, into her mother's lap. 'I guess they *would*, Phronsie pet.' And Polly caught up the little girl, and spun round and round the old kitchen till they were both glad to stop.

'Then,' said Phronsie, as Polly put her down and stood breathless after her last glorious spin, 'I do so wish we might, Polly; oh, just this very one minute!' And Phronsie clasped her fat little hands in rapture at the thought.

'Well,' said Polly, giving a look up at the old clock in the corner; 'goodness me! it's half-past five; and most time for Ben to come home!'

Away she flew to get supper. So for the next few moments nothing was heard but the pulling out of the old table into the middle of the floor, the laying of the cloth, and all the other bustle attendant upon the getting ready for Ben. Polly went skipping around, cutting the bread, and bringing dishes; only stopping long enough to fling some scraps of reassuring nonsense to the two boys, who were thoroughly dismayed at being obliged to remove their traps into a corner.

Phronsie still stood just where Polly left her. *Two hundred candles!* oh! what *could* it mean! She gazed up to the old beams overhead, and around the dingy walls, and to the old black stove, with the fire nearly out, and then over everything the kitchen contained, trying to think how it would seem. To have it bright and winsome and warm! to suit Polly – '*oh!*' she screamed.

'Goodness!' cried Polly, taking her head out of the old cupboard in the corner, 'how you scared me, Phronsie!'

'Would they *never* go out?' asked the child, gravely, still standing where Polly left her.

'What?' asked Polly, stopping with a dish of cold potatoes in her hand. 'What, Phronsie?'

'Why, the candles,' said the child, 'the ever-an'-ever so many pretty lights!'

'Oh, my senses!' cried Polly, with a little laugh, 'haven't you forgotten that! Yes – no, that is, Phronsie, if we could have 'em at all, we wouldn't *ever* let 'em go out!'

'Not once?' asked Phronsie, coming up to Polly with a little skip, and nearly upsetting her, potatoes and all – 'not once, Polly, truly?'

'No, not forever-an'-ever,' said Polly; 'take care, Phronsie! there goes a potato; no, we'd keep 'em always!'

'No, you don't want to,' said Mrs. Pepper, coming out of the bedroom in time to catch the last words; 'they won't be good to-morrow; better have 'em to-night, Polly.'

'Ma'am!' said Polly, setting down her potato-dish on the table, and staring at her mother with all her might – 'have *what*, mother?'

'Why, the potatoes, to be sure,' replied Mrs. Pepper; 'didn't you say you better keep 'em, child?'

''Twasn't potatoes – at all,' said Polly, with a little gasp; ''twas – oh, dear me! here's Ben!' for the door opened, and Phronsie, with a scream of delight, bounded into Ben's arms.

'It's just jolly,' said Ben, coming in, his chubby face all aglow, and his big blue eyes shining so honest and true; 'it's just jolly to get home! supper ready, Polly?'

'Yes,' said Polly; 'that is – all but – ' and she dashed off for Phronsie's eating apron.

'Sometime,' said Phronsie, with her mouth half-full, when the meal was nearly over, 'we're going to be *awful* rich; we are, Ben truly!'

'No?' said Ben, affecting the most hearty astonishment; 'you don't say so, Chick!'

'Yes,' said Phronsie, shaking her yellow head very wisely at him, and diving down into her cup of very weak milk and water to see if Polly *had* put any sugar in by mistake – a custom always expectantly observed. 'Yes, we are really, Bensie, very dreadful rich!'

'I wish we could be rich now then,' said Ben, taking another generous slice of the brown bread; 'in time for mamsie's birthday,' and he cast a sorrowful glance at Polly.

'I know,' said Polly; 'oh dear! if we only *could* celebrate it!'

'I don't want any other celebration,' said Mrs. Pepper, beaming on them so that a little flash of sunshine seemed to hop right down on the table, 'than to look round on you all; I'm rich now, and that's a fact!'

'Mamsie doesn't mind her five bothers,' cried Polly, jumping up and running to hug her mother, thereby producing a like desire in all the others, who immediately left their seats and followed her example.

'Mother's rich enough,' ejaculated Mrs. Pepper, her bright, black eyes glistening with delight, as the noisy troop filed back to their bread and potatoes; 'if we can only keep together, dears, and grow up good, so that the little brown house won't be ashamed of us, that's all I ask.'

'Well,' said Polly, in a burst of confidence to Ben, after the table had been pushed back against the wall, the dishes nicely washed, wiped, and set up neatly in the cupboard, and all traces of the meal cleared away; 'I don't care; let's *try* and get a celebration, somehow, for mamsie!'

'How are you going to do it?' asked Ben, who was of a decidedly practical turn of mind, and thus couldn't always follow Polly in her flights of imagination.

'I don't know,' said Polly; 'but we *must* some way.'

'Phoh! that's no good,' said Ben, disdainfully; then seeing Polly's face, he added, kindly, 'let's think, though; and p'raps there'll be some way.'

'Oh, I know,' cried Polly, in delight; 'I know the very thing, Ben! let's make her a cake; a big one, you know, and – '

'She'll see you bake it,' said Ben; 'or else she'll smell it, and that'd be just as bad.'

'No, she won't either,' replied Polly. 'Don't you know she's going to help Mrs. Henderson to-morrow; so there!'

'So she is,' said Ben; 'good for you, Polly, you always think of everything!'

'And then,' said Polly, with a comfortable little feeling at her heart at Ben's praise, 'why, we can have it all out of the way perfectly splendid when she comes home – and besides, Grandma Bascom'll tell me how. You know we've only got brown flour, Ben; I mean to go right over and ask her now.'

'Oh, no, you mustn't,' cried Ben, catching hold of her arm as she was preparing to fly off. 'Mammy'll find it out; better wait till to-morrow; and besides, Polly – ' and Ben stopped, unwilling to dampen this propitious beginning. 'The stove'll act like everything, to-morrow! I know 'twill; then what'll you do!'

'It *sha'n't!*' said Polly, running up to look it in the face; 'if it does, I'll shake it; the mean old thing!'

The idea of Polly's shaking the lumbering old black affair, sent Ben into such a peal of laughter that it brought all the other children running to the spot; and nothing would do, but they must one and all be told the reason. So Polly and Ben took them into confidence, which so elated them that half an hour after, when long past her bedtime, Phronsie declared, 'I'm not going to bed! I want to sit up like Polly!'

'Don't tease her,' whispered Polly to Ben. who thought she ought to go; so she sat straight up on her little stool, winking like everything to keep awake.

At last, as Polly was in the midst of one of her liveliest sallies, over tumbled Phronsie, a sleepy little heap, right on to the floor.

'I want – to go – to bed!' she said; 'take me – Polly!'

'I thought so,' laughed Polly, and bundled her off into the bedroom.


## from CHAPTER XXII

### GETTING READY FOR MAMSIE AND THE BOYS

'Mrs. Pepper!'

'Sir?' said Mrs. Pepper, trying to answer, which she couldn't do very well surrounded as she was by the crowd of little chatterers. 'Yes, sir; excuse me, what is it, sir?'

'We've got to come to an understanding about this thing,' said the old gentleman, 'and I can't talk much to-day, because my headache won't allow it.'

Here the worried look came into Phronsie's face again, and she began to try to smooth his head with both little hands.

'And so I must say it all in as few words as possible,' he continued.

'What is it, sir?' again asked Mrs. Pepper, wonderingly.

'Well, the fact is, I must have somebody who will keep this house. Now, Marian, not a word!' as he saw symptoms of Mrs. Whitney's joining in the conversation. 'You've been good; just as good as can be under the circumstances; but Mason will be home in the fall, and then I suppose you'll have to go with him. Now *I,*' said the old gentleman, forgetting all about his head, and straightening himself up suddenly in the chair, 'am going to get things into shape, so that the house will be kept for all of us; so that we can come or go. And how can I do it better than to have the Peppers – you, Mrs. Pepper, and all your children – come here and live, and – '

'*Oh, father!*' cried Jasper, rushing up to him; and flinging his arms around his neck, he gave him such a hug as he hadn't received for many a day.

'Goodness me, Jasper!' cried his father, feeling of his throat. 'How can you express your feelings so violently! And, besides, you interrupt.'

'Beg pardon, sir,' said Jasper, swallowing his excitement, and trying to control his eagerness.

'Do you say yes, Mrs. Pepper?' queried the old gentleman, impatiently. 'I must get this thing fixed up to-day. I'm really too ill to be worried, ma'am.'

'Why, sir,' stammered Mrs. Pepper, 'I don't know what to say. I couldn't think of imposing all my children on you, and – '

'*Imposing!* Who's talking of *imposing!*' said Mr. King, in a loud key. 'I want my house kept; will you live here and keep it? That is the question.'

'But, sir,' began Mrs. Pepper again, 'you don't think – '

'I do think; I tell you, ma'am, I *do* think,' snapped the old gentleman. 'It's just because I *have* thought that I've made up my mind. Will you do it, Mrs. Pepper?'

'What are you going to do, mamsie?' asked Joel, quickly.

'I don't know as I'm going to do anything yet,' said poor Mrs. Pepper, who was almost stunned.

'To come here and live!' cried Jasper, unable to keep still any longer – and springing to the children. 'Don't you want to, Joe?'

'To live!' screamed Joel. 'Oh, whickety, *yes!* Do, ma, do come here and live – do'

'To live?' echoed Phronsie, over in the old gentleman's lap. 'In this be-*you*-ti-ful place? Oh, *oh!*'

'Oh, *mamsie!*' that was all Polly could say. And even Ben had his arms around his mother's neck, whispering 'Do' into her ear, while little Davie got into her lap and teased her with all his might.

'What shall I do!' cried the poor woman. 'Did ever anybody see the like?'

'It's the very best thing you could possibly do,' cried the old gentleman. 'Don't you see it's for the children's advantage? They'll get such educations, Mrs. Pepper, as you want for them. And it accommodates me immensely. What obstacle can there be to it?'

'If I was only sure 'twould be for the best?' said Mrs. Pepper, doubtfully.

'Oh, dear Mrs. Pepper,' said Mrs. Whitney, laying her hand on hers. 'Can you doubt it?'

'Then,' said Mr. King, getting up, but still holding on to Phronsie, 'we'll consider it settled. This is your home, children,' he said, waving his hand at the five little Peppers in a bunch. And having thus summarily disposed of the whole business, he marched out with Phronsie on his shoulder.

# [John] Richard Jefferies (1848–1887)

There are many books that have had an influence disproportionate to their intrinsic value, and *Wood Magic* is a good example. It was the only book written for children by Richard Jefferies, British naturalist and mystic, who is best known for his *Bevis, The Story of a Boy* (1882) a 'tripledecker' novel *about* boyhood which has been adopted by (and adapted for) children.

Bevis, who appears in both these books, is wilful and independent, but not in the same way as the 'bad boys' of American literature. Jefferies was aiming to portray the amorality of boyhood and to imbue it with a romantic and mystical innocence. Both books are set at Jefferies' childhood home, Coate Farm in Wiltshire, which (rather like Mark Twain and Hannibal, Missouri) he reinvented in a slightly modified form.

Whereas *Bevis* is a 'realistic' novel, *Wood Magic* is a fantasy, in which Bevis leads a dual life as a boy on a farm, and also as an observer of a complex power struggle between the birds, whose language he understands. Jefferies was at his best when writing about nature, and all the elements of animal and bird life in *Wood Magic* are described accurately. He was less sure of himself as a novelist, and *Wood Magic* develops, or descends, into a farrago of melodrama, fable and snippets of social realism, from which little 'Sir' Bevis emerges more as a spoiled brat than trailing clouds of glory. (Some idea of the tenor of Jefferies' mind might be deduced from the observation by the Toad to Bevis: 'Although a man very soon gets tired of swimming, the water never gets tired of waiting, but is always ready to drown him'.)

It has been said that the opening chapters of *Bevis* supply the best description *of* childhood in literature; the opening chapter of *Wood Magic* shows Jefferies trying to adapt the same material *for* childhood. It shows many of the characteristics of children's writing of the time – sentimentality and whimsicality – but also has an inherent toughness that looks forward to the next century.

## from *Wood Magic, a Fable* (1881)

### CHAPTER I

### SIR BEVIS

One morning as little 'Sir' Bevis [such was his pet name] was digging in the farmhouse garden, he saw a daisy, and throwing aside his spade, he sat down on the grass to pick the flower to pieces. He pulled the pink-tipped petals off one by one, and as they dropped they were lost. Next he gathered a bright dandelion, and squeezed the white juice from the hollow stem, which drying presently, left his fingers stained with brown spots. Then he drew forth a bennet from its sheath, and bit and sucked it till his teeth were green from the sap. Lying at full length, he drummed the earth with his toes, while the tall grass blades tickled his cheeks.

Presently, rolling on his back, he drummed again with his heels. He looked up at the blue sky, but only for a moment, because the glare of light was too strong in his eyes. After a minute, he turned on his side, thrust out one arm, placed his head on it, and drew up one knee, as if going to sleep. His little brown wrist, bared by the sleeve shortening as he extended his arm, bent down the grass, and his still browner fingers played with the blades, and every now and then tore one off.

A flutter of wings sounded among the blossom on an apple-tree close by, and instantly Bevis sat up, knowing it must be a goldfinch thinking of building a nest in the branches. If the trunk of the tree had not been so big, he would have tried to climb it at once, but he knew he could not do it, nor could he see the bird for the leaves and bloom. A puff of wind came and showered the petals down upon him; they fell like snowflakes on his face and dotted the grass.

Buzz! A great humble-bee, with a band of red gold across his back, flew up, and hovered near, wavering to and fro in the air as he stayed to look at a flower.

Buzz! Bevis listened, and knew very well what he was saying. It was, 'This is a sweet little garden, my darling; a very pleasant garden; all grass and daisies, and apple-trees, and narrow patches with flowers and fruit-trees one side, and a wall and currant-bushes another side, and a low box-hedge and a haha, where you can see the high mowing grass quite underneath you; and a round summer-house in the corner, painted as blue inside as a hedge-sparrow's egg is outside; and then another haha with iron railings, which you are always climbing up, Bevis, on the fourth side, with stone steps leading down to a meadow, where the cows are feeding, and where they have left all the buttercups standing as tall as your waist, sir. The gate in the iron railings is not fastened, and besides, there is a gap in the box-hedge, and it is easy to drop down the haha wall, but that is mowing grass there. You know very well you could not come to any harm in the meadow: they said you were not to go outside the garden, but that's all nonsense, and very stupid. *I* am going outside the garden, Bevis. Good morning, dear.' Buzz! And the great humble-bee flew slowly between the iron railings, out among the buttercups, and away up the field.

Bevis went to the railings, and stood on the lowest bar; then he opened the gate a little way, but it squeaked so loud upon its rusty hinges that he let it shut again. He walked round the garden along beside the box-hedge to the patch by the lilac trees; they were single lilacs, which are much more beautiful than the double, and all bowed down with a mass of bloom. Some rhubarb grew there, and to bring it up the faster, they had put a round wooden box on it, hollowed out from the sawn butt of an elm, which was rotten within and easily scooped. The top was covered with an old board, and every time that Bevis passed he lifted up the corner of the board and peeped in, to see if the large red, swelling knobs were yet bursting.

One of these round wooden boxes had been split and spoilt, and half of it was left lying with the hollow part downwards. Under this shelter a Toad had his house. Bevis peered in at him, and touched him with a twig to make him move an inch or two, for he was so lazy, and sat there all day long, except when it rained. Sometimes the Toad told him a story, but not very often, for he was a silent old philosopher, and not very fond of anybody. He had a nephew, quite a lively young fellow, in the cucumber frame on the other side of the lilac bushes, at whom Bevis also peered nearly every day after they had lifted the frame and propped it up with wedges.

The gooseberries were no bigger than beads, but he tasted two, and then a thrush began to sing on an ash-tree in the hedge of the meadow. 'Bevis! Bevis!' said the thrush, and he turned round to listen: 'My dearest Bevis, have you forgotten the meadow, and the buttercups, and the sorrel? You know the sorrel, don't you, that tastes so pleasant if you nibble the leaf? And I have a nest in the bushes, not very far up the hedge, and you may take just one egg; there are only two yet. But don't tell any more boys about it, or we shall not have one left. That is a very sweet garden, but it is very small. I like all these fields to fly about in, and the swallows fly ever so much farther than I can; so far away and so high, that I cannot tell you how they find their way home to the chimney. But they will tell you, if you ask them. Good morning! *I* am going over the brook.'

Bevis went to the iron railings and got up two bars, and looked over; but he could not yet make up his mind, so he went inside the summer-house, which had one small round window. All the lower part of the blue walls was scribbled and marked with pencil, where he had written and drawn, and put down his ideas and notes. The lines were somewhat intermingled, and crossed each other, and some stretched out long distances, and came back in sharp angles. But Bevis knew very well what he meant when he wrote it all. Taking a stump of cedar pencil from his pocket, one end of it much gnawn, he added a few scrawls to the inscriptions, and then stood on the seat to look out of the round window, which was darkened by an old cob-web.

Once upon a time there was a very cunning spider – a very cunning spider indeed. The old Toad by the rhubarb told Bevis there had not been such a cunning spider for many summers; he knew almost as much about flies as the old Toad, and caught such a great number, that the Toad began to think there would be none left for him. Now the Toad was extremely fond of flies, and he watched the spider with envy, and grew more angry about it every day.

As he sat blinking and winking by the rhubarb in his house all day long, the Toad never left off thinking, thinking, thinking about this spider. And as he kept thinking, thinking, thinking, so he told Bevis, he recollected that he knew a great deal about a good many other things besides flies. So one day, after several weeks of thinking, he crawled out of his house in the sunshine, which he did not like at all, and went across the grass to the iron railings, where the spider had then got his web. The spider saw him coming, and being very proud of his cleverness, began to taunt and tease him.

'Your back is all over warts, and you are an old toad,' he said. 'You are so old, that I heard the swallows saying their great, great, great grandmothers, when they built in the chimney, did not know when you were born. And you have got foolish, and past doing anything, and so stupid that you hardly know when it is going to rain. Why, the sun is shining bright, you stupid old toad, and there isn't a chance of a single drop falling. You look very ugly down there in the grass. Now, don't you wish that you were me, and could catch more flies than you could eat? Why, I can catch wasps and bees, and tie them up so tight with my threads that they cannot sting nor even move their wings, nor so much as wriggle their bodies. I am the very cleverest and most cunning spider that ever lived.'

'Indeed, you are,' replied the Toad. 'I have been thinking so all the summer; and so much do I admire you, that I have come all this way, across in the hot sun, to tell you something.'

'Tell *me* something!' said the spider, much offended. '*I* know everything.'

'Oh, yes, honoured sir,' said the Toad; 'you have such wonderful eyes, and such a sharp mind, it is true that you know everything about the sun, and the moon, and the earth, and flies. But, as you have studied all these great and important things, you could hardly see all the very little trifles like a poor old toad.'

'Oh yes, I can. I know everything – everything!'

'But, sir,' went on the Toad so humbly, 'this is such a little – such a very little – thing, and a spider like you in such a high position of life, could not mind me telling you such a mere nothing.'

'Well, I don't mind,' said the spider – 'you may go on, and tell me, if you like.'

'The fact is,' said the Toad, 'while I have been sitting in my hole, I have noticed that such a lot of the flies that come into this garden presently go into the summer-house there, and when they are in the summer-house, they always go to that little round window, which is sometimes quite black with them; for it is the nature of flies to buzz over glass.'

'I do not know so much about that,' said the spider; 'for I have never lived in houses, being an independent insect; but it is possible you may be right. At any rate, it is not of much consequence. You had better go up into the window, old toad.' Now this was a sneer on the part of the spider.

'But I can't climb up into the window,' said the Toad; 'all I can do is to crawl about the ground, but you can run up a wall quickly. How I do wish I was a spider, like you. Oh, dear!' And then the Toad turned round, after bowing to the clever spider, and went back to his hole.

Now the spider was secretly very much mortified and angry with himself, because he had not noticed this about the flies going to the window in the summer-house. At first he said to himself that it was not true; but he could not help looking that way now and then, and every time he looked, there was the window crowded with flies. They had all the garden to buzz about in, and all the fields, but instead of wandering under the trees, and over the flowers, they preferred to go into the summer-house and crawl over the glass of the little window, though it was very dirty from so many feet. For a long time, the spider was too proud to go there too; but one day such a splendid blue-bottle fly got in the window and made such a tremendous buzzing, that he could not resist it any more.

So he left his web by the railings, and climbed up the blue-painted wall, over Bevis's writings and marks, and spun such a web in the window as had never before been seen. It was the largest and the finest, and the most beautifully-arranged web that had ever been made, and it caught such a number of flies that the spider grew fatter every day. In a week's time he was so big that he could no longer hide in the crack he had chosen, he was quite a giant; and the Toad came across the grass one night and looked at him, but the spider was now so bloated he would not recognise the Toad.

But one morning a robin came to the iron railings, and perched on the top, and put his head a little on one side, to show his black eye the better. Then he flew inside the summer-house, alighted in the window, and gobbled up the spider in an instant. The old Toad shut his eye and opened it again, and went on thinking, for that was just what he knew would happen. Ever so many times in his very long life he had seen spiders go up there, but no sooner had they got fat than a robin or a wren came in and ate them. Some of the clever spider's web was there still when Bevis looked out of the window, all dusty and draggled, with the skins and wings of some gnats and a dead leaf entangled in it.

As he looked, a white butterfly came along the meadow, and instantly he ran out, flung open the gate, rushed down the steps, and taking no heed of the squeak the gate made as it shut behind him, raced after the butterfly.

The tall buttercups brushed his knees, and bent on either side as if a wind was rushing through them. A bennet slipped up his knickerbockers and tickled his leg. His toes only touched the ground, neither his heels nor the hollow of his foot; and from so light a pressure the grass, bowed but not crushed, rose up, leaving no more mark of his passage than if a grasshopper had gone by.

Daintily fanning himself with his wings, the butterfly went before Bevis, not yet knowing that he was chased, but sauntering along just above the buttercups. He peeped as he flew under the lids of the flowers' eyes, to see if any of them loved him. There was a glossy green leaf which he thought he should like to feel, it looked so soft and satin-like. So he alighted on it, and then saw Bevis coming, his hat on the very back of his head, and his hand stretched out to catch him. The butterfly wheeled himself round on the leaf, shut up his wings, and seemed so innocent, till Bevis fell on his knee, and then under his fingers there was nothing but the leaf. His cheek flushed, his eye lit up, and away he darted again after the butterfly, which had got several yards ahead before he could recover himself. He ran now faster than ever.

'Race on,' said the buttercups; 'race on, Bevis; that butterfly disdains us because we are so many, and all alike.'

'Be quick,' said a great moon-daisy to him; 'catch him, dear. I asked him to stay and tell me a story, but he would not.'

'Never mind me,' said the clover; 'you may step on me if you like, love.'

'But just look at me for a moment, pet, as you go by,' cried the purple vetch by the hedge.

A colt in the field seeing Bevis running so fast, thought he too must join the fun, so he whisked his tail, stretched his long floundering legs, and galloped away. Then the mare whinnied and galloped too, and the ground shook under her heavy hoofs. The cows lifted their heads from gathering the grass close round the slender bennets, and wondered why any one could be so foolish as to rush about, when there was plenty to eat and no hurry.

The cunning deceitful butterfly, so soon as Bevis came near, turned aside and went along a furrow. Bevis running in the furrow, caught his foot in the long creepers of the crowfoot, and fell down bump, and pricked his hand with a thistle. Up he jumped again, red as a peony, and shouting in his rage, ran on so quickly that he nearly overtook the butterfly. But they were now nearer the other hedge. The butterfly, frightened at the shouting and Bevis's resolution, rose over the brambles, and Bevis stopping short flung his hat at him. The hat did not hit the butterfly, but the wind it made puffed him round, and so frightened him, that he flew up half as high as the elms, and went into the next field.

When Bevis looked down, there was his hat, hung on a branch of ash, far beyond his reach. He could not touch the lowest leaf, jump as much as he would. His next thought was a stone to throw, but there were none in the meadow. Then he put his hand in his jacket pocket for his knife, to cut a long stick. It was not in that pocket, nor in the one on the other side, nor in his knickers. Now the knife was Bevis's greatest treasure – his very greatest. He looked all round bewildered, and the tears rose in his eyes.

Just then Pan, the spaniel, who had worked his head loose from the collar and followed him, ran out of the hedge between Bevis's legs with such joyful force, that Bevis was almost overthrown, and burst into a fit of laughter. Pan ran back into the hedge to hunt, and Bevis, with tears rolling down his cheeks into the dimples made by his smiles, dropped on hands and knees and crept in after the dog under the briars. On the bank there was a dead grey stick, a branch that had fallen from the elms. It was heavy, but Bevis heaved it up, and pushed it through the boughs and thrust his hat off.

Creeping out again, he put it on, and remembering his knife, walked out into the field to search for it. When Pan missed him, he followed, and presently catching scent of a rabbit, the spaniel rushed down a furrow, which happened to be the very furrow where Bevis had tumbled. Going after Pan, Bevis found his knife in the grass, where it had dropped when shaken from his pocket by the jerk of his fall. He opened the single blade it contained at once, and went back to the hedge to cut a stick. As he walked along the hedge, he thought the briar was too prickly to cut, and the thorn was too hard, and the ash was too big, and the willow had no knob, and the elder smelt so strong, and the sapling oak was across the ditch, and out of reach, and the maple had such rough bark. So he wandered along a great way through that field and the next, and presently saw a nut-tree stick that promised well, for the sticks grew straight, and not too big.

He jumped into the ditch, climbed half up the mound, and began to cut away at one of the rods, leaning his left arm on the moss-grown stole. The bark was easily cut through, and he soon made a notch, but then the wood seemed to grow harder, and the chips he got out were very small. The harder the wood, the more determined Bevis became, and he cut and worked away with such force that his chest heaved, his brow was set and frowning, and his jacket all green from rubbing against the hazel. Suddenly something passed between him and the light. He looked up, and there was Pan, whom he had forgotten, in the hedge looking down at him. 'Pan! Pan!' cried Bevis. Pan wagged his tail, but ran back, and Bevis, forsaking his stick, scrambled up into the stole, then into the mound, and through a gap into the next field. Pan was nowhere to be seen.

There was a large mossy root under a great oak, and, hot with his cutting, Bevis sat down upon it. Along came a house martin, the kind of swallow that has a white band across his back, flying very low, and only just above the grass. The swallow flew to and fro not far from Bevis, who watched it, and presently asked him to come closer. But the swallow said, 'I shall not come any nearer, Bevis. Don't you remember what you did last year, sir? Don't you remember Bill, the carters' boy, put a ladder against the wall, and you climbed up the ladder, and put your paw, all brown and dirty, into my nest and took my eggs? And you tried to string them on a bennet, but the bennet was too big, so you went indoors for some thread. And you made my wife and me dreadfully unhappy, and we said we would never come back any more to your house, Bevis.'

'But you have come back, swallow.'

'Yes, we have come back – just once more; but if you do it again we shall go away for ever.'

'But I won't do it again; no, that I won't! Do come near.'

So the swallow came a little nearer, only two yards away, and flew backwards and forwards, and Bevis could hear the snap of his beak as he caught the flies.

'Just a little bit nearer still,' said he. 'Let me stroke your lovely white back.'

'Oh, no, I can't do that. I don't think you are quite safe, Bevis. Why don't you gather the cowslips?'

Bevis looked up and saw that the field was full of cowslips – yellow with cowslips. 'I will pick every one,' said he, 'and carry them all back to my mother.'

'You cannot do that,' said the swallow, laughing, 'you will not try long enough.'

'I hate you!' cried Bevis in a passion, and flung his knife, which was in his hand, at the bird. The swallow rose up, and the knife whizzed by and struck the ground.

'I told you you were not safe,' said the swallow over his head; 'and I am sure you won't pick half the cowslips.'

Bevis picked up his knife and put it in his pocket; then he began to gather the cowslips, and kept on for a quarter of an hour as fast as ever he could, till both hands were full. There was a rustle in the hedge, and looking up he saw Pan come out, all brown with sand sticking to his coat. He shook himself, and sent the sand flying from him in a cloud, just like he did with the water when he came up out of the pond. Then he looked at Bevis, wagged his tail, cried 'yowp!' and ran back into the hedge again.

Bevis rushed to the spot, and saw that there was a large rabbits' hole. Into this hole Pan had worked his way so far that there was nothing of him visible but his hind legs and tail. Bevis could hear him panting in the hole, he was working so hard to get at the rabbit, and tearing with his teeth at the roots to make the hole bigger. Bevis clapped his hands, dropping his cowslips, and called 'Loo! Loo!' urging the dog on. The sand came flying out behind Pan, and he worked harder and harder, as if he would tear the mound to pieces.

Bevis sat down on the grass under the shadow of the oak, by a maple bush, and taking a cowslip, began to count the spots inside it. It was always five in all the cowslips – five brown little spots – that he was sure of, because he knew he had five fingers on each hand. He lay down at full length on his back, and looked up at the sky through the boughs of the oak. It was very very blue, and very near down. With a long ladder he knew he could have got up there easily, and it looked so sweet. 'Sky,' said Bevis, 'I love you like I love my mother.' He pouted his lips, and kissed at it. Then turning a little on one side to watch Pan, in an instant he fell firm asleep.

Pan put his head out of the hole to breathe two or three times, and looked aside at Bevis, and seeing that he was still, went back to work again. Two butterflies came fluttering along together. The swallow returned, and flew low down along the grass near Bevis. The wind came now and then, and shook down a shower of white and pink petals from a crab-tree in the hedge. By and by a squirrel climbing from tree to tree reached the oak, and stayed to look at Bevis beneath in the shadow. He knew exactly how Bevis felt – just like he did himself when he went to sleep.

# George Alfred Henty (1832–1902)

G. A. Henty represents the height of Victorian imperialism in children's books. His formula was straightforward: he placed a young man into a real historical situation (*With Clive in India, or The Beginnings of Empire* (1884), *With Buller in Natal, or, A Born Leader* (1901)) and mixed slabs of scarcely edited history with extravagant adventure. His heroes embodied simple, manly, Christian values of hardiness, chivalry and honesty, and won through, as one title had it *By Sheer Pluck*. Henty's historical and geographical range was wide, but a good deal of time was spent in implicit or explicit praise of the builders of empire. His estimated 14 million words in around 90 volumes were produced, often by dictation, at the rate of up to 6,000 words a day.

Henty was hugely popular and inspired an industry of boys' adventure stories. His influence on the nation has been seen by some historians to have been pernicious, encouraging the idea of the innate British superiority over the 'natives' and virtually everyone else. In 1885, he wrote: 'the courage of our forefathers has created the greatest empire in the world around a small and in itself insignificant island; if this empire is ever lost, it will be by the cowardice of their descendants.'

But whatever might be said of Henty's style or attitudes, he gave his readers value for money. To say that *Winning His Spurs* is a 'tale of the crusades' is a masterpiece of understatement. The young landless Cuthbert begins by helping to capture the castle of the evil Baron of Wortham. He then joins King Richard's crusade, which takes him across Europe (encountering, for example, pirates); he is involved in the capture of Cyprus (two pages), moves on to Jerusalem where he is captured by the Saracens, and escapes; he returns via Switzerland (storms in the Alps) and Germany. Back in England he rescues Lady Margaret of Evesham from the villainous Sir Rudolph (capturing another castle in the process), with the help of Saxon outlaws. Finally, he accompanies the minstrel Blondel on his mission back to France and Austria to find King Richard, comes into his rightful estates and on the last page is married.

*Winning His Spurs* was also issued as *The Boy Knight; Fighting the Saracens*. In this characteristic chapter, set in France on the way to Jerusalem, Cuthbert rescues the Princess Berengaria, King Richard's betrothed, from a dastardly plot.

## from *Winning His Spurs. A Tale of the Crusades* (1882)

### CHAPTER IX

### THE PRINCESS BERENGARIA

One night it chanced that Cuthbert was late in his return to camp, and his road took him through a portion of the French encampment; the night was dark, and Cuthbert presently completely lost all idea as to his bearings. Presently he nearly ran against a tent; he made his way to the entrance in order to crave directions as to his way – for it was a wet night; the rain was pouring in torrents, and few were about of whom he could demand the way – and, as he was about to draw aside the hangings, he heard words said in a passionate voice which caused him to withdraw his hand suddenly.

'I tell you,' said a voice, 'I would rather drive a dagger myself into her heart, than allow our own princess to be insulted by this hot-headed island dog.'

'It is said indeed,' said another, but in a calmer and smoother tone, 'that the success of a great expedition like this, which has for its object the recovery of the holy sepulchre from the infidels, should be wrecked by the headstrong fancies of one man. It is even, as is told by the old Grecian poet, as when Helen caused a great war between peoples of that nation.'

'I know nothing,' another voice said, 'either of Helen or the Greeks, or of their poets. They are a shifty race, and I can believe aught that is bad of them. But touching this princess of Navarre, I agree with our friend, it would be a righteous deed to poniard her, and so to remove the cause of dispute between the two kings, and, indeed, the two nations. This insult laid upon our princess is more than we, as French knights and gentlemen, can brook; and if the king says the word, there is not a gentleman in the army but will be ready to turn his sword against the islanders.'

Then the smooth voice spoke again.

'It would, my brethren, be wrong and useless to shed blood; but methinks, that if this apple of discord could be removed, a good work would be done; not, as our friend the count has suggested, by a stab of the dagger; that indeed would be worse than useless. But surely there are scores of religious houses, where this bird might be placed in a cage without a soul knowing where she was, and where she might pass her life in prayer that she may be pardoned for having caused grave hazards of the failure of an enterprise in which all the Christian world is concerned.'

The voices of the speakers now fell, and Cuthbert was straining his ear to listen, when he heard footsteps approaching the tent, and he glided away into the darkness.

With great difficulty he recovered the road to the camp, and when he reached his tent he confided to the Earl of Evesham what he had heard.

'This is serious indeed,' the earl said, 'and bodes no little trouble and danger. It is true that the passion which King Richard has conceived for Berengaria bids fair to wreck the Crusade, by the anger which it has excited in the French king and his nobles; but the disappearance of the princess would no less fatally interfere with it, for the king would be like a raging lion deprived of his whelps, and would certainly move no foot eastward until he had exhausted all the means in his power of tracing his lost lady love. You could not, I suppose, Cuthbert, point out the tent where this conversation took place?'

'I could not,' Cuthbert answered; 'in the darkness one tent is like another. I think I should recognize the voices of the speakers did I hear them again; indeed, one voice I did recognize, it was that of the Count of Brabant, with whom we had trouble before.'

'That is good,' the earl said, 'because we have at least an object to watch. It would never do to tell the king what you have heard. In the first place, his anger would be so great that it would burst all bounds, and would cause, likely enough, a battle at once between the two armies: nor would it have any good effect, for he of Brabant would of course deny the truth of your assertions, and would declare it was merely a got-up story to discredit him with the king, and so to wipe out the old score now standing between us. No, if we are to succeed, alike in preventing harm happening to the princess, and an open break between the two monarchs, it must be done by keeping a guard over the princess, unsuspected by all, and ourselves frustrating any attempt which may be made.'

Cuthbert expressed his willingness to carry out the instructions which the earl might give him; and, much disturbed by the events of the day, both earl and page retired to rest, to think over what plan had best be adopted.

The princess was staying at the palace of the bishop of the town; this he, having another residence a short distance outside the walls, had placed at the disposal of the Queen of Navarre and her suite; and the first step of Cuthbert in the morning was to go into the town, to reconnoitre the position and appearance of the building. It was a large and irregular pile, and communicated with the two monasteries lying alongside of it. It would therefore clearly be a most difficult thing to keep up a complete watch on the exterior of so large a building. There were so many ways in which the princess might be captured and carried off by unscrupulous men, that Cuthbert in vain thought over every plan by which it could be possible to safeguard her. She might be seized upon returning from a tournament or entertainment; but this was improbable, as the queen would always have an escort of knights with her, and no attempt could be successful except at the cost of a public fraças and much loss of blood. Cuthbert regarded as out of the question that an outrage of this kind would be attempted.

The fact that one of the speakers in the tent had used the words 'my sons,' showed that one priest or monk, at least, was connected with the plot. It was possible that this man might have power in one of the monasteries, or he might be an agent of the bishop himself; and Cuthbert saw that it would be easy enough in the night for a party from one or other of the monasteries to enter by the door of communication with the palace, and carry off the princess without the slightest alarm being given. Once within the walls of the convent, she could be either hidden in the dungeons or secret places, which buildings of that kind were sure to possess, or could be at once carried out by some quiet entrance, and taken into the country, or transferred to some other building in the town.

When Cuthbert joined the earl he told him the observations that he had made, and Sir Walter praised the judgment which he had shown in his conclusions. The earl was of opinion that it would be absolutely necessary to get some clue as to the course which the abductors purposed to take; indeed it was possible that on after-consideration they might drop their plan altogether, for the words which Cuthbert had overheard scarcely betokened a plan completely formed and finally decided upon.

The great point he considered, therefore, was that the tent of his old enemy should be carefully watched, and that an endeavour should be made to hear something of what passed within, which might give a clue to the plan fixed upon. They did not, of course, know whether the tent in which the conversation had been heard by Cuthbert was that of Sir de Jacquelin Barras, or of one of the other persons who had spoken; and Cuthbert suggested that the first thing would be to find out whether the count, after nightfall, was in the habit of going to some other tent, or whether, on the other hand, he remained within, and was visited by others.

It was easy, of course, to discover which was his tent; and Cuthbert soon got its position, and then took Cnut into his counsels.

'The matter is difficult,' Cnut said, 'and I see no way by which a watch can be kept up by day; but after dark – I have several men in my band who can track a deer, and surely could manage to follow the steps of this baron without being observed. There is little Jack, who is no bigger than a boy of twelve, although he can shoot, and run, and play with the quarter-staff, or, if need be, with the bill, against the best man in the troop. I warrant me that if you show him the tent, he will keep such sharp watch that no one shall enter or depart without his knowing where they go to. On a dark night he will be able to slip among the tents, and to move here and there without being seen. He can creep on his stomach without moving a leaf, and trust me the eyes of these French men-at-arms will look in vain for a glimpse of him.'

'You understand, Cnut, all that I want to know is whether the other conspiritors in this matter visit his tent, or whether he goes to theirs.'

'I understand,' Cnut said. 'That is the first point to be arrived at.'

Three days later Cnut brought news that each night after dark a party of five men met in the tent that was watched; that one of the five always came out when all had assembled, and took his station before the entrance of the tent, so as to be sure that no eavesdropper was near.

Cuthbert smiled –

'It is a case of locking the door after the horse has gone'

'What is to be done now?' Cnut asked.

'I will talk with the earl before I tell you, Cnut. This matter is too serious for me to take a step without consulting Sir Walter.'

That night there was a long talk between the earl and his page as to the best course to be pursued. It was clear that their old enemy was the leading person in the plot, and that their only plan to baffle it with any fair chances of success was to keep a constant eye upon his movements, and also to have three or four of the sturdiest men of the band told off to watch, without being perceived, each time that the princess was in her palace.

The Earl of Evesham left the arrangements entirely in the hands of his page, of whose good sense and sagacity he had a very high opinion.

His own first impulse had been to go before the king and denounce the Count of Brabant. But the ill-will between them was already well known; for not only was there the original dispute at the banquet, but when the two armies had joined at Sicily, King Richard, who had heard from the earl of the attempt at the assassination of Cuthbert, had laid a complaint before King Phillip of the conduct of his subject.

Sir de Jacquelin Barras, however, had denied that he had any finger in the matter.

'He had,' he said, 'discharged his page after the encounter with Cuthbert, and knew nothing further whatever of his movements.'

Although it was morally certain that the page could not have purchased the services of the men who assisted him, from his own purse, or gain them by any means of persuasion, but that they were either the followers of the Count of Brabant, or ruffians hired with his money, as no proof could be obtained, the matter was allowed to drop.

The earl felt, however, that an accusation against the count by him of an intention to commit a high crime, and this merely on the evidence of his page, would appear like an attempt to injure the fair fame of his rival.

Feeling, therefore, that nothing could be done save to watch, he left the matter entirely in the hands of his page, telling him that he could take as many men-at-arms or archers as he might choose and use them in his name.

Cnut entered warmly into Cuthbert's plans; and finally it was arranged between them that six of the archers should nightly keep watch opposite the various entrances of the bishop's palace and of the two monasteries joining. Of course they could not patrol up and down without attracting attention, but they were to take up posts where they could closely observe the entrances, and were either to lie down and feign drunken sleep, or to conceal themselves within the shadow of an arch or other hiding-place.

Down on the sea-shore, Cuthbert made an arrangement with one of the owners of small craft lying there that ten of his men should sleep on board every night, together with some fishermen accustomed to the use of the oar.

Cuthbert himself determined to be always with this party.

Night after night passed, and so long a time went by that Cuthbert began to think the design must have been given up.

However, he resolved to relax none of his watchfulness during the remaining time that the expedition might stop in Sicily.

It was in January, three weeks after the first watch had been set, when one of the men who had been placed to watch the entrance to one of the monasteries, leapt on board the craft and shook Cuthbert by the shoulder.

'A party of some five men,' he said, 'have just issued out from the monastery. They are bearing a burden – what I cannot see. They are making in the direction of the water. I whistled to Dick, who was next to me in the lane. He is following them, and I came on to tell you to prepare.'

The night was pitch dark, and it was difficult in the extreme to see any one moving at a short distance off.

There were two or three streets that led from the monastery, which stood at the top of the town, towards the sea; and a party coming down might take any of these, according to the position in which the boat they were seeking was placed.

Cuthbert now instantly sent five or six of his men, with instructions to avoid all noise, along the line of the port, with orders to bring in word should any one come down and take boat, or should they hear any noise in the town.

He himself with the sailors loosed the ropes which fastened the boat to shore, got out the oars, and prepared to put off at a moment's notice.

He was of course ignorant whether the abductors would try to carry the princess off by water, or would hide her in one of the convents in the town; but he was inclined to think that the former would be the course adopted; for the king in his wrath would be ready to lay the town in flames, and to search every convent from top to bottom for the princess. Besides, there would be too many aware of the secret.

Cuthbert was not wrong in his supposition.

Soon the man he had sent to the extreme right came running up with the news that a boat had embarked at the farther end, with a party of some ten men on board. As he came along he had warned the others, and in five minutes the whole party were collected in the craft, numbering in all twelve of Cuthbert's men and six sailors. They instantly put out, and rowed in the direction in which the boat would have gone, the boatmen expressing their opinion that probably the party would make for a vessel which was lying anchored at some little distance from the shore. The bearings of the position of this ship was known to the boatmen, but the night was so dark that they were quite unable to find it. Orders had been given that no sound or whisper was to be heard on board the boat; and after rowing as far as they could the boatmen said they were in the direction of the ship.

The boatmen all lay on their oars, and all listened intently. Presently the creaking of a pulley was heard in the still night, at a distance of a few hundred yards. This was enough. It was clear that the vessel was getting up sail. The boat's head was turned in that direction; the crew rowed steadily but noiselessly, and in a few minutes the tall mast of a vessel could be seen faintly against the sky. Just as they perceived the situation, a hail from on board showed that their approach was now observed.

'Stretch to your oars,' Cuthbert said, 'we must make a dash for it now.'

The rowers bent to their work and in a minute the boat ran alongside the craft.

As Cuthbert and his followers scrambled upon deck, they were attacked by those of the crew and passengers who were standing near; but it was evident at once that the chiefs of the expedition had not heard the hail, and that there was no general plan of defence against them.

It was not until the last of them had gained a footing, and were beginning to fight their way along the vessel, that from below three or four men-at-arms ran up, and one in a tone of authority demanded what was the matter. When he heard the clash of swords and the shouts of the combatants, he put himself at once at the head of the party, and a fierce and obstinate fight now took place.

The assailants had, however, the advantage.

Cuthbert and his men were all lightly clad, and this on the deck of a ship lumbered with ropes and gear, and in the dark, was a great advantage, for the mailed men-at-arms frequently stumbled and fell. The fight lasted for several minutes. Cnut, who was armed with a heavy mace, did great service, for with each of his sweeping blows he broke down the guard of an opponent, and generally levelled him to the deck.

The numbers at the beginning of the fight were not unequal, but the men to whom the vessel belonged made but a faint resistance when they perceived that the day was going against them. The men-at-arms, however, consisting of three, who appeared to be the leaders, and of eight pikemen, fought stubbornly and well.

Cuthbert was not long in detecting in the tones of the man who was clearly at the head of affairs the voice of Sir de Jacquelin Barras. To do him justice he fought with extreme bravery, and when almost all his followers were cut down or beaten overboard he resisted staunchly and well. With a heavy two-handed sword he cleaved a space at the end of the boat, and kept the whole of Cuthbert's party at bay.

At last Cnut, who had been engaged elsewhere, came to the front, and a tough fight ensued between them.

It might have ended badly for the brave forester, for his lack of armour gave an enormous advantage to his opponent. Soon, however, the count's foot slipped on the boards of the deck, and before he could recover himself the mace of Cnut descended with tremendous force upon his head, which was unprotected, as he had taken off his casque on arriving at the ship. Without a word or a cry the count fell forward on the deck, killed as a bullock by a blow of a pole-axe.

While this conflict had been going on, occasionally the loud screams of a woman had been heard below.

Cuthbert, attended by Cnut and two of his followers, now descended.

At the bottom of the steps they found a man-at-arms placed at the door of a cabin. He challenged them as they approached, but being speedily convinced that the vessel was in their hands, and that his employer and party were all conquered, he made a virtue of necessity, and laid down his arms.

'You had better go in alone,' Cnut said, 'Master Cuthbert. The lady is less likely to be frightened by your appearance than by us, for she must wonder indeed what is going on.'

On entering the cabin, which had evidently been fitted up for the use of a lady, Cuthbert saw standing at the other end the princess, whom of course he knew well by sight. A lamp was burning in the cabin, and by its light he could see that her face was deadly pale. Her robes were torn and disarranged, and she wore a look at once of grave alarm and surprise upon seeing a handsomely dressed page enter with a deep reverence.

'What means this outrage, young sir? Whoever you be, I warn you that the King of England will revenge this indignity.'

'Your Highness,' Cuthbert said, 'you have no further reason for alarm; the knaves who carried you off from the bishop's palace and conveyed you to this ship are all either killed or in our power. I am the page of the Earl of Evesham, a devoted follower of King Richard. Some of the designs of the bold men came to the ears of my lord, and he ordered me and a band of his followers to keep good guard over the palace and buildings adjoining. We were unable to gather our strength in time to prevent your being taken on board, but we lost no time in putting forth when he found that your abductors had taken boat, and by good fortune arrived here in time; a few minutes later, and the knaves would have succeeded in their object, for the sails were already being hoisted, and the vessel making way, when we arrived. Your abductors are all either killed or thrown overboard, and the vessel's head is now turned towards the shore, and I hope in a few minutes to have the honour of escorting you to the palace.'

The princess, with a sigh of much satisfaction and relief, sank on to a couch.

'I am indeed indebted to you, young sir,' she said. 'Believe me, the Princess Berengaria is not ungrateful, and should it be ever in her power to do aught for your lord, or for yourself, or for those who have accompanied you to rescue her, believe me that she will do it.'

'May I be so bold as to ask a boon?' Cuthbert said, dropping on one knee before her.

'It is granted at once, whatever it be, if in my power.'

'My boon is, lady,' he said, 'that you will do your best to assuage the natural anger which the King of England will feel at this bold and most violent attempt. That he should be told, is of course necessary; but, lady, much depends upon the telling, and I am sure that at your request the king would restrain his anger. Were it not for that, I fear that such quarrels and disputes might arise as would bring the two armies to blows, and destroy for ever all hope of the successful termination of our joint enterprise.'

'You are a wise and good youth,' the princess said, holding out her hand to Cuthbert, which, as in duty bound, he placed to his lips. 'Your request is wise and most thoughtful. I will use any poor influence which I may possess' – and Cuthbert could see that the blood came back now to the white face – 'to induce King Richard to allow this matter to pass over. There is no reason why he should take up the case. I am no more under his protection than under that of the King of France, and it is to the latter I should appeal, for as I believe the men who abducted me were his subjects.'

'The leader of them, madam, was a certain Sir de Jacquelin Barras, a Count of Brabant, with whom my master has had an old feud, and who has been just killed by the leader of our men-at-arms. The others, who have had the most active hand in the matter, have also perished; and it would, I think, be doubtful whether any clue could be obtained to those who were in league with them. The only man in the party who is alive, was placed as a sentry at your door, and as he is but a man-at-arms, we may be sure that he knows nought of the enterprise, but has merely carried out the orders of his master.'

The vessel had by this time brought up close to the port. The princess determined to wait on board until the first dawn was seen in the skies, and then under the escort of her deliverers to go back to the palace, before the town was moving. This plan was carried out, and soon after dawn the princess was safe in the palace from which she had been carried a few hours previously.

# Robert Louis Stevenson (1850–1894)

*Treasure Island* was the work of one of the most popular story-tellers of his time, a highly talented writer of romances, who found writing for children a natural form. Stories of pirates, exploration, desert islands and seafaring (in any combination) were firmly established, both in 'respectable' novels for adults and (especially) boys, and in the 'penny dreadfuls'. Stevenson drew heavily on this tradition, even to the extent, as he later discovered and admitted, of unconsciously plagiarizing some of the key elements of *Treasure Island* from Washington Irving's *Tales of a Traveller*. In an article, 'My First Book', he wrote

> No doubt the parrot once belonged to Robinson Crusoe. No doubt the skeleton is conveyed from Poe.... The stockade, I am told is from *Masterman Ready*.... It is my debt to Washington Irving that exercises my conscience, and justly so, for I believe plagiarism was rarely carried farther. I chanced to pick up the *Tales of a Traveller* some years ago... and the book flew up and struck me; Billy Bones, his chest, the company in the parlour, the whole inner spirit, and a good deal of the material detail of my first chapters – all were there.

Stevenson manages to combine a fast-paced and elegantly contrived plot with rather more subtle and ambiguous character-drawing than was the norm. His major creation is the smooth villain, Long John Silver, who, despite being a devious and brutal murderer, seems to have had immense appeal – and not only to the readers. At the end of the book, Stevenson allows Silver to escape

– and he escaped into at least three sequels by other hands written in the twentieth century. Stevenson's interest in the often conflicting sides of human characters and motivations is explored throughout the book: thus the narrator, Jim Hawkins, is far from being the brave and upstanding lad of empire-building stories. This subtlety is achieved despite a full-blooded enthusiasm for the conventions of the genre, although Stevenson has been criticized for his use of the deformed and the grotesque as shorthand indicators of character.

Stevenson was well aware of the difficulties, and wrote to Henry James: 'the characters need to be presented with but one class of qualities.... To add more traits, to be too clever, to start the hare of moral or intellectual interest while we are running the fox of material interest, is not to enrich but to stultify your tale.'

In this extract, the narrator Jim Hawkins is alone on board the *Hispaniola* with the wounded coxswain, Israel Hands. Both the treasure seekers, and the piratical crew (led by Silver) are on the island, and Jim is sailing the ship to a favourable place so that the treasure seekers can escape. Jim's self-righteousness and lack of self-awareness provide a neat parody of the Christian manly boy figure in less subtle adventure stories.

*Treasure Island* was serialized in *Young Folks* in 1881. Among Stevenson's other works are *Kidnapped* (1886) and *The Strange Case of Dr Jekyll and Mr Hyde* (1886), which explore the paradoxical aspects of human nature, and *A Child's Garden of Verses* (1885) (see p. 348).

## from *Treasure Island* (1883)

### CHAPTER 26

### ISRAEL HANDS

The wind, serving us to a desire, now hauled into the west. We could run so much the easier from the north-east corner of the island to the mouth of the North Inlet. Only, as we had no power to anchor, and dared not beach her till the tide had flowed a good deal farther, time hung on our hands. The coxswain told me how to lay the ship to; after a good many trials I succeeded, and we both sat in silence, over another meal.

'Cap'n,' said he, at length, with that same uncomfortable smile, 'here's my old shipmate, O'Brien; s'pose you was to heave him overboard. I ain't partic'lar as a rule, and I don't take no blame for settling his hash; but I don't reckon him ornamental, now, do you?'

'I'm not strong enough, and I don't like the job; and there he lies, for me,' said I.

'This here's an unlucky ship – this *Hispaniola*, Jim,' he went on, blinking. 'There's a power of men been killed in this *Hispaniola* – a sight o' poor seamen dead and gone since you and me took ship to Bristol. I never seen sich dirty luck, not I. There was this here O'Brien, now – he's dead, ain't he? Well, now, I'm no scholar, and you're a lad as can read and figure; and to put it straight, do you take it as a dead man is dead for good, or do he come alive again?'

'You can kill the body, Mr Hands, but not the spirit; you must know that already,' I replied, 'O'Brien there is in another world, and maybe watching us.'

'Ah!' says he. 'Well, that's unfort'nate – appears as if killing parties was a waste of time. Howsomever, sperrits don't reckon for much, by what I've seen. I'll chance it with the sperrits, Jim. And now, you've spoke up free, and I'll take it kind if you'd step down into that there cabin and get me a – well, a – shiver my timbers! I can't hit the name on't; well, you get me a bottle of wine, Jim – this here brandy's too strong for my head.'

Now, the coxswain's hesitation seemed to be unnatural; and as for the notion of his preferring wine to brandy, I entirely disbelieved it. The whole story was a pretext. He wanted me to leave the deck – so much was plain; but with what purpose I could in no way imagine. His eyes never met mine; they kept wandering to and fro, up and down, now with a look to the sky, now with a flitting glance upon the dead O'Brien. All the time he kept smiling, and putting his tongue out in the most guilty, embarrassed manner, so that a child could have told that he was bent on some deception. I was prompt with my answer, however, for I saw where my advantage lay; and that with a fellow so densely stupid I could easily conceal my suspicions to the end.

'Some wine?' I said. 'Far better. Will you have white or red?'

'Well, I reckon it's about the blessed same to me, shipmate,' he replied; 'so it's strong, and plenty of it, what's the odds?'

'All right,' I answered. 'I'll bring you port, Mr Hands. But I'll have to dig for it.'

With that I scuttled down the companion with all the noise I could, slipped off my shoes, ran quietly along the sparred gallery, mounted the forecastle ladder, and popped my head out of the fore companion. I knew he would not expect to see me there; yet I took every precaution possible; and certainly the worst of my suspicions proved too true.

He had risen from his position to his hands and knees; and, though his leg obviously hurt him pretty sharply when he moved – for I could hear him stifle a groan – yet it was at a good, rattling rate that he trailed himself across the deck. In half a minute he had reached the port scuppers, and picked, out of a coil of rope, a long knife, or rather a short dirk, discoloured to the hilt with blood. He looked upon it for a moment, thrusting forth his under jaw, tried the point upon his hand, and then, hastily concealing it in the bosom of his jacket, trundled back again into his old place against the bulwark.

This was all that I required to know. Israel could move about; he was now armed; and if he had been at so much trouble to get rid of me, it was plain that I was meant to be the victim. What he would do afterwards – whether he would try to crawl right across the island from North Inlet to the camp among the swamps, or whether he would fire Long Tom, trusting that his own comrades might come first to help him, was, of course, more than I could say.

Yet I felt sure that I could trust him in one point, since in that our interests jumped together, and that was in the disposition of the schooner. We both desired to have her stranded safe enough, in a sheltered place, and so that, when the time came, she could be got off again with as little labour and danger as might be; and until that was done I considered that my life would certainly be spared.

While I was thus turning the business over in my mind, I had not been idle with my body. I had stolen back to the cabin, slipped once more into my shoes, and laid my hand at random on a bottle of wine, and now, with this for an excuse, I made my reappearance on the deck.

Hands lay as I had left him, all fallen together in a bundle, and with his eyelids lowered, as though he were too weak to bear the light. He looked up, however, at my coming, knocked the neck off the bottle, like a man who had done the same thing often, and took a good swig, with his favourite toast of 'Here's luck!' Then he lay quiet for a little, and then, pulling out a stick of tobacco, begged me to cut him a quid.

'Cut me a junk o' that,' says he, 'for I haven't no knife, and hardly strength enough, so be as I had. Ah, Jim, Jim, I reckon I've missed stays! Cut me a quid, as'll likely be the last, lad; for I'm for my long home, and no mistake.'

'Well,' said I, 'I'll cut you some tobacco; but if I was you and thought myself so badly, I would go to my prayers, like a Christian man.'

'Why?' said he. 'Now, you tell me why.'

'Why?' I cried. 'You were asking me just now about the dead. You've broken your trust; you've lived in sin and lies and blood; there's a man you killed lying at your feet this moment; and you ask me why! For God's mercy, Mr Hands, that's why.'

I spoke with a little heat, thinking of the bloody dirk he had hidden in his pocket, and designed, in his ill thoughts, to end me with. He, for his part, took a great draught of the wine, and spoke with the most unusual solemnity.

'For thirty years,' he said, 'I've sailed the seas, and seen good and bad, better and worse, fair weather and foul, provisions running out, knives going, and what not. Well, now I tell you, I never seen good come o' goodness yet. Him as strikes first is my fancy; dead men don't bite; them's my views – amen, so be it. And now, you look here,' he added, suddenly changing his tone, 'we've had about enough of this foolery. The tide's made good enough by now. You just take my orders, Cap'n Hawkins, and we'll sail slap in and be done with it.'

All told, we had scarce two miles to run; but the navigation was delicate, the entrance to this northern anchorage was not only narrow and shoal, but lay east and west, so that the schooner must be nicely handled to be got in. I think I was a good, prompt subaltern, and I am very sure that Hands was an excellent pilot; for we went about and about, and dodged in, shaving the banks, with a certainty and a neatness that were a pleasure to behold.

Scarcely had we passed the heads before the land closed around us. The shores of North Inlet were as thickly wooded as those of the southern anchorage; but the space was longer and narrower, and more like, what in truth it was, the estuary of a river. Right before us, at the southern end, we saw the wreck of a ship in the last stages of dilapidation. It had been a great vessel of three masts, but had lain so long exposed to the injuries of the weather, that it was hung about with great webs of dripping seaweed, and on the deck of it shore bushes had taken root, and now flourished thick with flowers. It was a sad sight, but it showed us that the anchorage was calm.

'Now,' said Hands, 'look there; there's a pet bit to beach a ship in. Fine flat sand, never a cat-spaw, trees all around of it, and flowers a-blowing like a garding on that old ship'.

'And once beached,' I inquired, 'how shall we get her off again?'

'Why, so,' he replied; 'you take a line ashore there on the other side at low water: take a turn about one o' them big pines; bring it back, take a turn round the capstan, and lie-to for the tide. Come high water, all hands take a pull upon the line, and off she comes as sweet as natur'. And now, boy, you stand by. We're near the bit now, and she's too much way on her. Starboard a little – so – steady – starboard – larboard a little – steady – steady!'

So he issued his commands, while I breathlessly obeyed; till, all of a sudden, he cried, 'Now, my hearty, luff!' And I put the helm hard up, and the *Hispaniola* swung round rapidly, and ran stem on for the low wooded shore.

The excitement of these last manoeuvres had somewhat interfered with the watch I had kept hitherto, sharply enough, upon the coxswain. Even then I was still so much interested, waiting for the ship to touch, that I had quite forgot the peril that hung over my head, and stood craning over the starboard bulwarks and watching the ripples spreading wide before the bows. I might have fallen without a struggle for my life, had not a sudden disquietude seized upon me, and made me turn my head. Perhaps I had heard a creak, or seen his shadow moving with the tail of my eye; perhaps it was an instinct like a cat's; but, sure enough, when I looked around, there was Hands, already half-way towards me, with the dirk in his right hand.

We must both have cried out aloud when our eyes met; but while mine was the shrill cry of terror, his was a roar of fury like a charging bull's. At the same instant he threw himself forward, and I leapt sideways towards the bows. As I did so, I left hold of the tiller, which sprang sharp to leeward; and I think this saved my life, for it struck Hands across the chest, and stopped him, for the moment, dead.

Before he could recover, I was safe out of the corner where he had me trapped, with all the deck to dodge about. Just forward of the mainmast I stopped, drew a pistol from my pocket, took a cool aim, though he had already turned and was once more coming directly after me, and drew the trigger. The hammer fell, but there followed neither flash nor sound; the priming was useless with sea water. I cursed myself for my neglect. Why had not I, long before, reprimed and reloaded my only weapons? Then I should not have been, as now, a mere fleeing sheep before this butcher.

Wounded as he was, it was wonderful how fast he could move, his grizzled hair tumbling over his face, and his face itself as red as a red ensign with his haste and fury. I had no time to try my other pistol, nor, indeed, much inclination, for I was sure it would be useless. One thing I saw plainly: I must not simply retreat before him, or he would speedily hold me boxed into the bows, as a moment since he had so nearly boxed me in the stern. Once so caught, and nine or ten inches of the blood-stained dirk would be my last experience on this side of eternity. I placed my palms against the mainmast, which was of a goodish bigness, and waited, every nerve upon the stretch.

Seeing that I meant to dodge, he also paused; and a moment or two passed in feints on his part, and corresponding movements upon mine. It was such a game as I had often played at home about the rocks of Black Hill Cove; but never before, you may be sure, with such a wildly beating heart as now. Still, as I say, it was a boy's game, and I thought I could hold my own at it, against an elderly seaman with a wounded thigh. Indeed, my courage had begun to rise so high, that I allowed myself a few darting thoughts on what would be the end of the affair; and while I saw certainly that I could spin it out for long, I saw no hope of any ultimate escape.

Well, while things stood thus, suddenly the *Hispaniola* struck, staggered, ground for an instant in the sand, and then, swift as a blow, canted over to the port side, till the deck stood at an angle of forty-five degrees, and about a puncheon of water splashed into the scupper-holes, and lay, in a pool, between the deck and bulwark.

We were both of us capsized in a second, and both of us rolled, almost together, into the scuppers; the dead red-cap, with his arms still spread out, tumbling stiffly after us. So near were we, indeed, that my head came against the coxswain's foot with a crack that made my teeth rattle. Blow and all, I was the first afoot again; for Hands had got involved with the dead body. The sudden canting of the ship had made the deck no place for running on; I had to find some new way of escape, and that upon the instant, for my foe was almost touching me. Quick as thought I sprang into the mizzen shrouds, rattled up hand over hand, and did not draw a breath till I was seated on the cross-trees.

I had been saved by being prompt; the dirk had struck not half a foot below me, as I pursued my upward flight; and there stood Israel Hands with his mouth open and his face upturned to mine, a perfect statue of surprise and disappointment.

Now that I had a moment to myself, I lost no time in changing the priming of my pistol, and then, having one ready for service, and to make assurance doubly sure, I proceeded to draw the load of the other, and recharge it afresh from the beginning.

My new employment struck Hands all of a heap; he began to see the dice going against him; and after an obvious hesitation, he also hauled himself heavily into the shrouds, and, with the dirk in his teeth, began slowly and painfully to mount. It cost him no end of time and groans to haul his wounded leg behind him; and I had quietly finished my arrangements before he was much more than a third of the way up. Then, with a pistol in either hand, I addressed him.

'One more step, Mr Hands,' said I, 'and I'll blow your brains out! Dead men don't bite, you know,' I added, with a chuckle.

He stopped instantly. I could see by the working of his face that he was trying to think, and the process was so slow and laborious that, in my new-found security, I laughed aloud. At last, with a swallow or two, he spoke, his face still wearing the same expression of extreme perplexity. In order to speak he had to take the dagger from his mouth, but, in all else, he remained unmoved.

'Jim,' says he, 'I reckon we're fouled, you and me, and we'll have to sign articles. I'd have had you but for that there lurch; but I don't have no luck, not I; and I reckon I'll have to strike, which comes hard, you see, for a master mariner to a ship's younker like you, Jim.'

I was drinking in his words and smiling away, as conceited as a cock upon a wall, when, all in a breath, back went his right hand over his shoulder. Something sang like an arrow through the air; I felt a blow and then a sharp pang, and there I was pinned by the shoulder to the mast. In the horrid pain and surprise of the moment – I scarce can say it was by my own volition, and I am sure it was without a conscious aim – both my pistols went off, and both escaped out of my hands. They did not fall alone; with a choked cry, the coxswain loosed his grasp upon the shrouds, and plunged head first into the water.

# Juliana Horatia [Gatty] Ewing (1841–1885)

Mrs Ewing was the daughter of Margaret Gatty, who founded and edited *Aunt Judy's Magazine* (1866–85), which was instrumental in shifting the tone of British children's writing away from the evangelical to the 'purely' entertaining. Marghanita Laski (1950) dates the dawn of 'the golden age of children's literature' from 1866, when Mrs Ewing's *Mrs Overtheway's Remembrances* appeared in its pages. Certainly, her work, although very much of its time in terms of plot devices (there are a lot of orphans in her books), does not moralize, and in some stories, such as *Mary's Meadow*, the last serial that she wrote (1833–4), the children are both independent and outspoken: 'Lady Catherine is Mother's aunt by marriage, and Mother is one of the few people she is not rude to. She is very rude, and yet she is very kind, especially to the poor. But she does kind things so rudely, that people now and then wish that she would mind her own business'. Here is the honest tone that was to mark the books of the beginning of the twentieth century, although Ewing could indulge in great sentimentality – as in *The Story of A Short Life* (1882, 1885) whose hero is a velvet-suited precursor of Cedric Erroll in Hodgson Burnett's *Little Lord Fauntleroy*.

Many of Ewing's books, such as the rural *Jan of the Windmill* (1876) or *Daddy Darwin's Dovecote* (1884), lie on the boundary between children's and adult books. *The Brownies and Other Stories* (1870) inspired Lord Baden-Powell to adopt the name for the junior branch of his Girl Guide movement from 1918.

In Henry James's opinion, *Jackanapes* 'is a genuine masterpiece, a wonderful little mixture of nature and art, and touching beyond anything I have read in a long time. I defy anyone to read it without an access of the melting mood. The subject is lovely and the lightness and grace of touch, without effort or mannerism, place the thing quite apart.'

Inspired by the death of the son of Napoleon III, who was an observer with the British army in the Zulu wars in 1879, *Jackanapes* is a carefully constructed story. The orphan Jackanapes is brought up in the rural idyll of Goose Green with his pony Lollo, his friend Tony and his Aunt Jessamine, until he goes to war.

## from *Jackanapes* (1883)

## from CHAPTER IV

Tony Johnson had no more natural taste for fighting than for riding, but he was as devoted as ever to Jackanapes, and that was how it come about that Mr. Johnson bought him a commission in the same cavalry regiment that the General's grandson (whose commission had been given him by the Iron Duke) was in, and that he was quite content to be the butt of the mess where Jackanapes was the hero; and that when Jackanapes wrote home to Miss Jessamine, Tony wrote with the same purpose to his mother; namely, to demand her congratulations that they were on active service at last, and were ordered to the front. And he added a postscript to the effect that she could have no idea how popular Jackanapes was, nor how splendidly he rode the wonderful red charger, whom he had named after his old friend Lollo.

'Sound Retire!'

A Boy Trumpeter, grave with the weight of responsibilities and accoutrements beyond his years, and stained, so that his own mother would not have known him, with the sweat and dust of battle, did as he was bid; and then pushing his trumpet pettishly aside, adjusted his weary legs for the hundredth time to the horse which was a world too big for him, and muttering, ''Taint a pretty tune,' tried to see something of this, his first engagement, before it came to an end.

Being literally in the thick of it, he could hardly have seen less or known less of what happened in that particular skirmish if he had been at home in England. For many good reasons; including dust and smoke, and that what attention he dared distract from his commanding officer was pretty well absorbed by keeping his hard-mouthed troop-horse in hand, under pain of execration by his neighbours in the melée. By-and-by, when the newspapers came out, if he could get a look at one before it was thumbed to bits, he would learn that the enemy had appeared from ambush in over-whelming numbers, and that orders had been given to fall back, which was done slowly and in good order, the men fighting as they retired.

Born and bred on the Goose Green, the youngest of Mr. Johnson's gardener's numerous offspring, the boy had given his family 'no peace' till they let him 'go for a soldier' with Master Tony and Master Jackanapes. They consented at last, with more tears than they shed when an elder son was sent to gaol for poaching, and the boy was perfectly happy in his life, and full of *esprit de corps*. It was this which had been wounded by having to sound retreat for 'the young gentleman's regiment,' the first time he served with it before the enemy, and he was also harassed by having completely lost sight of Master Tony. There had been some hard fighting before the backward movement began, and he had caught sight of him once, but not since. On the other hand, all the pulses of his village pride had been stirred by one or two visions of Master Jackanapes whirling about on his wonderful horse. He had been easy to distinguish, since an eccentric blow had bared his head without hurting it, for his close golden mop of hair gleamed in the hot sunshine as brightly as the steel of the sword flashing round it.

Of the missiles that fell pretty thickly, the Boy Trumpeter did not take much notice. First, one can't attend to everything, and his hands were full. Secondly, one gets used to anything. Thirdly, experience soon teaches one, in spite of proverbs, how very few bullets find their billet. Far more unnerving is the mere suspicion of fear or even of anxiety in the human mass around you. The Boy was beginning to wonder if there were any dark reason for the increasing pressure, and whether they would be allowed to move back more quickly, when the smoke in front lifted for a moment, and he could see the plain, and the enemy's line some two hundred yards away.

And across the plain between them, he saw Master Jackanapes galloping alone at the top of Lollo's speed, their faces to the enemy, his golden head at Lollo's ear.

But at this moment noise and smoke seemed to burst out on every side, the officer shouted to him to sound retire, and between trumpeting and bumping about on his horse, he saw and heard no more of the incidents of his first battle.

Tony Johnson was always unlucky with horses, from the days of the giddy-go-round onwards. On this day – of all days in the year – his own horse was on the sick list, and he had to ride an inferior, ill-conditioned beast, and fell off that, at the very moment when it was a matter of life or death to be able to ride away. The horse fell on him, but struggled up again, and Tony managed to keep hold of it. It was in trying to remount that he discovered, by helplessness and anguish, that one of his legs was crushed and broken, and that no feat of which he was master would get him into the saddle. Not able even to stand alone, awkwardly, agonizingly unable to mount his restive horse, his life was yet so strong within him! And on one side of him rolled the dust and smoke-cloud of his advancing foes, and on the other, that which covered his retreating friends.

He turned one piteous gaze after them, with a bitter twinge, not of reproach, but of loneliness; and then, dragging himself up by the side of his horse, he turned the other way and drew out his pistol, and waited for the end. Whether he waited seconds or minutes he never knew, before some one gripped him by the arm.

'*Jackanapes! GOD bless you!* It's my left leg. If you *could* get me on—'

It was like Tony's luck that his pistol went off at his horse's tail, and made it plunge; but Jackanapes threw him across the saddle.

'Hold on anyhow, and stick your spur in. I'll lead him. Keep your head down, they're firing high.'

And Jackanapes laid his head down—to Lollo's ear.

It was when they were fairly off, that a sudden upspringing of the enemy in all directions had made it necessary to change the gradual retirement of our force into as rapid a retreat as possible. And when Jackanapes became aware of this, and felt the lagging and swerving of Tony's horse, he began to wish he had thrown his friend across his own saddle, and left their lives to Lollo.

When Tony became aware of it, several things came into his head. 1. That the dangers of their ride for life were now more than doubled. 2. That if Jackanapes and Lollo were not burdened with him they would undoubtedly escape. 3. That Jackanapes' life was infinitely valuable, and his—Tony's—was not. 4. That this—if he could seize it—was the supremest of all the moments in which he had tried to assume the virtues which Jackanapes had by nature; and that if he could be courageous and unselfish now—

He caught at his own reins and spoke very loud—

'Jackanapes! It won't do. You and Lollo must go on. Tell the fellows I gave you back to them, with all my heart. Jackanapes, if you love me, leave me!'

There was a daffodil light over the evening sky in front of them, and it shone strangely on Jackanapes' hair and face. He turned with an odd look in his eyes that a vainer man than Tony Johnson might have taken for brotherly pride. Then he shook his mop, and laughed at him.

'*Leave you?* To save my skin? No, Tony, not to save my soul!'

<h2 style="text-align:center">Chapter V</h2>

Coming out of a hospital-tent, at headquarters, the surgeon cannoned against, and rebounded from, another officer; a sallow man, not young, with a face worn more by ungentle experiences than by age: with weary eyes that kept their own counsel, iron-grey hair, and a moustache that was as if a raven had laid its wing across his lips and sealed them.

'Well?'

'Beg pardon, Major. Didn't see you. Oh, compound fracture and bruises, but it's all right. He'll pull through.'

'Thank God.'

It was probably an involuntary expression, for prayer and praise were not much in the Major's line, as a jerk of the surgeon's head would have betrayed to an observer. He was a bright little man, with his feelings showing all over him, but with gallantry and contempt of death enough for both sides of his profession; who took a cool head, a white handkerchief and a case of instruments, where other men went hot-blooded with weapons, and who was the biggest gossip, male or female, of the regiment. Not even the Major's taciturnity daunted him.

'Didn't think he'd as much pluck about him as he has. He'll do all right if he doesn't fret himself into a fever about poor Jackanapes.'

'Whom are you talking about?' asked the Major hoarsely.

'Young Johnson. He—'

'What about Jackanapes?'

'Don't you know? Sad business. Rode back for Johnson, and brought him in; but, monstrous ill-luck, hit as they rode. Left lung—'

'Will he recover?'

'No. Sad business. What a frame—what limbs—what health—and what good looks! Finest young fellow—'

'Where is he?'

'In his own tent,' said the surgeon sadly.

The Major wheeled and left him.

'Can I do anything else for you?'

'Nothing, thank you. Except – Major! I wish I could get you to appreciate Johnson.'

'This is not an easy moment, Jackanapes.'

'Let me tell you, sir—*he* never will—that if he could have driven me from him, he would be lying yonder at this moment, and I should be safe and sound.'

The Major laid his hand over his mouth, as if to keep back a wish he would have been ashamed to utter.

'I've known old Tony from a child. He's a fool on impulse, a good man and a gentleman in principle. And he acts on principle, which it's not every—some water, please! Thank you, sir. It's very hot, and yet one's feet get uncommonly cold. Oh, thank you thank you. He's no fire-eater, but he has a trained conscience and a tender heart, and he'll do his duty when a braver and more selfish man might fail you. But he wants encouragement; and when I'm gone—'

'He shall have encouragement. You have my word for it. Can I do nothing else?'

'Yes, Major. A favour.'

'Thank you, Jackanapes.'

'Be Lollo's master, and love him as well as you can. He's used to it.'

'Wouldn't you rather Johnson had him?'

The blue eyes twinkled in spite of mortal pain.

'Tony *rides* on principle, Major. His legs are bolsters, and will be to the end of the chapter. I couldn't insult dear Lollo, but if you don't care—'

'Whilst I live—which will be longer than I desire or deserve—Lollo shall want nothing, but—you. I have too little tenderness for—my dear boy, you're faint. Can you spare me for a moment?'

'No, stay—Major!'

'What? What?'

'My head drifts so—if you wouldn't mind.'

'Yes! Yes!'

'Say a prayer by me. Out loud please, I am getting deaf.'

'My dearest Jackanapes—my dear boy—'

'One of the Church Prayers—Parade Service, you know—'

'I see. But the fact is—God forgive me, Jackanapes—I'm a very different sort of fellow to some of you youngsters. Look here, let me fetch—'

But Jackanapes' hand was in his, and it wouldn't let go.

There was a brief and bitter silence.

''Pon my soul I can only remember the little one at the end.'

'Please,' whispered Jackanapes.

Pressed by the conviction that what little he could do it was his duty to do, the Major—kneeling—bared his head, and spoke loudly, clearly, and very reverently—

'The Grace of our Lord Jesus Christ—'

Jackanapes moved his left hand to his right one, which still held the Major's—

'—The Love of God.'

And with that—Jackanapes died.

## Chapter VI

Jackanapes' death was sad news for the Goose Green, a sorrow just qualified by honourable pride in his gallantry and devotion. Only the Cobbler dissented, but that was his way. He said he saw nothing in it but foolhardiness and vainglory. They might both have been killed, as easy as not, and then where would ye have been? A man's life was a man's life, and one life was as good as another. No one would catch him throwing his away. And, for that matter, Mrs. Johnson could spare a child a great deal better than Miss Jessamine.

But the parson preached Jackanapes' funeral sermon on the text, 'Whosoever will save his life shall lose it; and whosoever will lose his life for My sake shall find it;' and all the village went and wept to hear him.

Nor did Miss Jessamine see her loss from the Cobbler's point of view. On the contrary, Mrs. Johnson said she never to her dying day should forget how, when she went to condole with her, the old lady came forward, with gentlewomanly self-control, and kissed her, and thanked God that her dear nephew's effort had been blessed with success, and that this sad war had made no gap in her friend's large and happy home circle.

'But she's a noble, unselfish woman,' sobbed Mrs. Johnson, 'and she taught Jackanapes to be the same, and that's how it is that my Tony has been spared to me. And it must be sheer goodness in Miss Jessamine, for what can she know of a mother's feelings? And I'm sure most people seem to think that if you've a large family you don't know one from another any more than they do, and that a lot of children are like a lot of store-apples, if one's taken it won't be missed.'

Lollo – the first Lollo, the Gipsy's Lollo – very aged, draws Miss Jessamine's bath-chair slowly up and down the Goose Green in the sunshine.

The Ex-postman walks beside him, which Lollo tolerates to the level of his shoulder. If the Postman advances any nearer to his head, Lollo quickens his pace, and were the Postman to persist in the injudicious attempt, there is, as Miss Jessamine says, no knowing what might happen.

In the opinion of the Goose Green, Miss Jessamine has borne her troubles 'wonderfully.' Indeed, to-day, some of the less delicate and less intimate of those who see everything from the upper windows, say (well behind her back) that 'the old lady seems quite lively with her military beaux again.'

The meaning of this is, that Captain Johnson is leaning over one side of her chair, whilst by the other bends a brother officer who is staying with him, and who has manifested an extraordinary interest in Lollo. He bends lower and lower, and Miss Jessamine calls to the Postman to request Lollo to be kind enough to stop, while she is fumbling for something which always hangs by her side, and has got entangled with her spectacles.

It is a twopenny trumpet, bought years ago in the village fair, and over it she and Captain Johnson tell, as best they can, between them, the story of Jackanapes' ride across the Goose Green; and how he won Lollo – the Gipsy's Lollo – the racer Lollo – dear Lollo – faithful Lollo – Lollo the never vanquished – Lollo the tender servant of his old mistress. And Lollo's ears twitch at every mention of his name.

Their hearer does not speak, but he never moves his eyes from the trumpet, and when the tale is told, he lifts Miss Jessamine's hand and presses his heavy black moustache in silence to her trembling fingers.

The sun, setting gently to his rest, embroiders the sombre foliage of the oak-tree with threads of gold. The Grey Goose is sensible of an atmosphere of repose, and puts up one leg for the night. The grass glows with a more vivid green, and, in answer to a ringing call from Tony, his sisters, fluttering over the daisies in pale-hued muslins, come out of their ever-open door, like pretty pigeons from a dovecote.

And, if the good gossips' eyes do not deceive them, all the Miss Johnsons, and both the officers, go wandering off into the lanes, where bryony wreaths still twine about the brambles.

A sorrowful story, and ending badly?

Nay, Jackanapes, for the End is not yet.

A life wasted that might have been useful?

Men who have died for men, in all ages, forgive the thought!

There is a heritage of heroic example and noble obligation, not reckoned in the Wealth of Nations, but essential to a nation's life; the contempt of which, in any people, may, not slowly, mean even its commercial fall.

Very sweet are the uses of prosperity, the harvests of peace and progress, the fostering sunshine of health and happiness, and length of days in the land.

But there be things – oh, sons of what has deserved the name of Great Britain, forget it not! – 'the good of' which and 'the use of' which are beyond all calculation of worldly goods and earthly uses: things such as Love, and Honour, and the Soul of Man, which cannot be bought with a price, and which do not die with death. And they who would fain live happily EVER after, should not leave these things out of the lessons of their lives.

# Edward Eggleston (1837–1902)

Eggleston's pair of books, *The Hoosier Schoolmaster* (1871) and *The Hoosier Schoolboy* (1883) ('Hoosier' is a nickname for the people of Indiana) are vivid accounts, which perhaps demonstrate the universality of school life. They were also historical accounts: as Eggleston wrote:

> Happy boys and girls that go to school nowadays! You have to study harder than the generations before you, it is true; you miss the jolly spelling-schools, and the good old games that were not half so scientific as baseball, lawn tennis, or lacrosse, but that had ten times more fun and frolic in them; but all this is made up to you by the fact that you escape the tyrannical old master. Whatever the faults the teachers of this day may have, they do not generally lacerate the backs of their pupils, as did some of their fore-runners. At the time of which I write, thirty years ago, a better race of school-masters was crowding out the old, but many of the latter class, with their terrible switches and cruel beatings, kept their ground until they died off one by one, and relieved the world of their odious ways.

The realistic setting of *The Hoosier Schoolboy* does not prevent Eggleston falling back on the devices of the genre: Jack makes good (he 'was sure to go up to the head of the class') and rescues a small boy, Andy, from drowning. These two chapters show Jack Dudley's arrival at school, and his encounter with the bully, Peewee.

## from *The Hoosier Schoolboy* (1883)

### CHAPTER I

### THE NEW SCHOLAR

While the larger boys in the village school of Greenbank were having a game of 'three old cat' before school-time, there appeared on the playground a strange boy, carrying two books, a slate, and an atlas under his arm.

He was evidently from the country, for he wore a suit of brown jeans, or woollen homespun, made up in the natural color of the 'black' sheep, as we call it. He shyly sidled up to the school-house door, and looked doubtfully at the boys who were playing; watching the familiar game as though he had never seen it before.

The boys who had the 'paddles' were standing on three bases, while three others stood each behind a base and tossed the ball around the triangle from one hole or base to another. The new-comer soon perceived that, if one with a paddle, or bat, struck at the ball and missed it, and the ball was caught directly, or 'at the first bounce,' he gave up his bat to the one who had 'caught him out.' When the ball was struck, it was called a 'tick,' and when there was a tick, all the batters were obliged to run one base to the left, and then the ball thrown between a batter and the base to which he was running 'crossed him out,' and obliged him to give up his 'paddle' to the one who threw the ball.

'Four old cat,' 'two old cat,' and 'five old cat' are, as everybody knows, played in the same way, the number of bases or holes increasing with the addition of each pair of players.

It is probable that the game was once – some hundreds of years ago, maybe – called 'three hole catch,' and that the name was gradually corrupted into 'three hole cat,' as it is still called in the interior States, and then became changed by mistake to 'three old cat.' It is, no doubt, an early form of our present game of base-ball.

It was this game which the new boy watched, trying to get an inkling of how it was played. He stood by the school-house door, and the girls who came in were obliged to pass near him. Each of them stopped to scrape her shoes, or rather the girls remembered the foot-scraper because they were curious to see the new-comer. They cast furtive glances at him, noting his new suit of brown clothes, his geography and atlas, his arithmetic, and, last of all, his face.

'There's a new scholar,' said Peter Rose, or, as he was called, 'Pewee' Rose, a stout and stocky boy of fourteen, who had just been caught out by another.

'I say, Greeny, how did you get so brown?' called out Will Riley, a rather large, loose-jointed fellow.

Of course, all the boys laughed at this. Boys will sometimes laugh at any one suffering torture, whether the victim be a persecuted cat or a persecuted boy. The new boy made no answer, but Joanna Merwin, who, just at that moment, happened to be scraping her shoes, saw that he grew red in the face with a quick flush of anger.

'Don't stand there, Greeny, or the cows'll eat you up!' called Riley, as he came round again to the base nearest to the school-house.

Why the boys should have been amused at this speech, the new scholar could not tell – the joke was neither new nor witty – only impudent and coarse. But the little boys about the door giggled.

'It's a pity something wouldn't eat you, Will Riley – you are good for nothing but to be mean.' This sharp speech came from a rather tall and graceful girl of sixteen, who came up at the time, and who saw the annoyance of the new boy at Riley's insulting words. Of course the boys laughed again. It was rare sport to hear pretty Susan Lanham 'take down' the impudent Riley.

'The bees will never eat you for honey, Susan,' said Will.

Susan met the titter of the playground with a quick flush of temper and a fine look of scorn.

'Nothing would eat you, Will, unless, maybe, a turkey-buzzard, and a very hungry one at that.'

This sharp retort was uttered with a merry laugh of ridicule, and a graceful toss of the head, as the mischievous girl passed into the school-house.

'That settles you, Will,' said Pewee Rose. And Bob Holliday began singing, to a doleful tune:

'Poor old Pidy,
She died last Friday.'

Just then, the stern face of Mr. Ball, the master, appeared at the door; he rapped sharply with his ferule, and called: 'Books, books, books!' The bats were dropped, and the boys and girls began streaming into the school, but some of the boys managed to nudge Riley, saying:

'Poor old creetur,
The turkey-buzzards eat her,'

and such like soft and sweet speeches. Riley was vexed and angry, but nobody was afraid of him, for a boy may be both big and mean and yet lack courage.

The new boy did not go in at once, but stood silently and faced the inquiring looks of the procession of boys as they filed into the school-room with their faces flushed from the exercise and excitement of the games.

'I can thrash him easy,' thought Pewee Rose.

'He isn't a fellow to back down easily,' said Harvey Collins to his next neighbor.

Only good-natured, rough Bob Holliday stopped and spoke to the newcomer a friendly word. All that he said was 'Hello!' But how much a boy can put into that word 'Hello!' Bob put his whole heart into it, and there was no boy in the school that had a bigger heart, a bigger hand, or half so big a foot as Bob Holliday.

The village school-house was a long one built of red brick. It had taken the place of the old log institution in which one generation of Greenbank children had learned reading, writing, and Webster's spelling-book. There were long, continuous writing-tables down the sides of the room, with backless benches, so arranged that when the pupil was writing his face was turned toward the wall – there was a door at each end, and a box stove stood in the middle of the room, surrounded by a rectangle of four backless benches. These benches were for the little fellows who did not write, and for others when the cold should drive them nearer the stove.

The very worshipful master sat at the east end of the room, at one side of the door; there was a blackboard – a 'new-fangled notion' in 1850 – at the other side of the door. Some of the older scholars, who could afford private desks with lids to them, suitable for concealing smuggled apples and maple-sugar, had places at the other end of the room from the master. This arrangement was convenient for quiet study, for talking on the fingers by signs, for munching apples or gingerbread, and for passing little notes between the boys and girls.

When the school had settled a little, the master struck a sharp blow on his desk for silence, and looked fiercely around the room, eager to find a culprit on whom to wreak his ill-humor. Mr. Ball was one of those old-fashioned teachers who gave the impression that he would rather beat a boy than not, and would even like to eat one, if he could find a good excuse. His eye lit upon the new scholar.

'Come here,' he said, severely, and then he took his seat.

The new boy walked timidly up to a place in front of the master's desk. He was not handsome, his face was thin, his eyebrows were prominent, his mouth was rather large and good-humored, and there was that shy twinkle about the corners of his eyes which always marks a fun-loving spirit. But his was a serious, fine-grained face, with marks of suffering in it, and he had the air of having been once a strong fellow; of late, evidently, shaken to pieces by the ague.

'Where do you live?' demanded Mr. Ball.

'On Ferry Street.'

'What do they call you?' This was said with a contemptuous, rasping inflection that irritated the new scholar. His eyes twinkled, partly with annoyance and partly with mischief.

'They *call* me Jack, for the most part,' – then catching the titter that came from the girls' side of the room, and frightened by the rising hurricane on the master's face, he added quickly: 'My name is John Dudley, sir.'

'Don't you try to show your smartness on me, young man. You are a new-comer, and I let you off this time. Answer me that way again, and you will remember it as long as you live.' And the master glared at him like a savage bull about to toss somebody over a fence.

The new boy turned pale, and dropped his head.

'How old are you?' 'Thirteen.'

'Have you ever been to school?'

'Three months.'

'Three months. Do you know how to read?'

'Yes, sir,' with a smile.

'Can you cipher?' 'Yes, sir.'

'In multiplication?' 'Yes, sir.'

'Long division?'

'Yes, sir; I've been half through fractions.'

'You said you'd been to school but three months!' 'My father taught me.'

There was just a touch of pride in his voice as he said this – a sense of something superior about his father. This bit of pride angered the master, who liked to be thought to have a monopoly of all the knowledge in the town.

'Where have you been living?'

'In the Indian Reserve, of late; I was born in Cincinnati.'

'I didn't ask you where you were born. When I ask you a question, answer that and no more.'

'Yes, sir.' There was a touch of something in the tone of this reply that amused the school, and that made the master look up quickly and suspiciously at Jack Dudley, but the expression on Jack's face was as innocent as that of a cat who has just lapped the cream off the milk.

## Chapter VI

## A Battle

One morning, when Jack proposed to play a game of ball with the boys, Riley and Pewee came up and entered the game, and objected.

'It isn't interesting to play with greenhorns,' said Will. 'If Jack plays, little Christopher Columbus Andsoforth will want to play, too; and then there'll be two babies to teach. I can't be always helping babies. Let Jack play two-hole cat or Anthony-over with the little fellows.' To which answer Pewee assented, of course.

That day at noon Riley came to Jack, with a most gentle tone and winning manner, and whiningly begged Jack to show him how to divide 770 by 14.

'It isn't interesting to show greenhorns,' said Jack, mimicking Riley's tone on the playground that morning. 'If I show you, Pewee Rose will want me to show him; then there'll be two babies to teach. I can't be always helping babies. Go and play two-hole cat with the First-Reader boys.'

That afternoon, Mr. Ball had the satisfaction of using his new beech switches on both Riley and Pewee, though indeed Pewee did not deserve to be punished for not getting his lesson. It was Nature's doing that his head, like a goat's, was made for butting and not for thinking.

But if he had to take whippings from the master and his father, he made it a rule to get satisfaction out of somebody else. If Jack had helped him he wouldn't have missed. If he had not missed his lesson badly, Mr. Ball would not have whipped him. It would be inconvenient to whip Mr. Ball in return, but Jack would be easy to manage, and as somebody must be whipped, it fell to Jack's lot to take it.

King Pewee did not fall upon his victim at the school-house door; this would have insured him another beating from the master. Nor did he attack Jack while Bob Holliday was with him. Bob was big and strong – a great fellow of sixteen. But after Jack had passed the gate of Bob's house, and was walking on toward home alone, Pewee came out from behind an alley fence, accompanied by Ben Berry and Will Riley.

'I'm going to settle with you now,' said King Pewee, sidling up to Jack like an angry bull-dog.

It was not a bright prospect for Jack, and he cast about him for a chance to escape a brutal encounter with such a bully, and yet avoid actually running away.

'Well,' said Jack, 'if I must fight, I must. But I suppose you won't let Riley and Berry help you.'

'No, I'll fight fair.' And Pewee threw off his coat, while Jack did the same.

'You'll quit when I say "enough," won't you?' said Jack.

'Yes, I'll fight fair, and hold up when you've got enough.'

'Well, then, for that matter, I've got enough now. I'll take the will for the deed and just say "enough" before you begin,' and he turned to pick up his coat.

'No, you don't get off that way,' said Pewee. 'You've got to stand up and see who is the best man, or I'll kick you all the way home.'

'Didn't you ever hear about Davy Crockett's 'coon?' said Jack. 'When the 'coon saw him taking aim, it said: "Is that you, Crockett? Well, don't fire – I'll come down anyway. I know you'll hit anything you shoot at." Now, I'm that 'coon. If it was anybody but you, I'd fight. But as it's you, Pewee, I might just as well come down before you begin.'

Pewee was flattered by this way of putting the question. Had he been alone, Jack would have escaped. But Will Riley, remembering all he had endured from Jack's retorts, said:

'Oh, give it to him, Pewee; he's always making trouble.'

At which Pewee squared himself off, doubled up his fists, and came at the slenderer Jack. The latter prepared to meet him, but, after all, it was hard for Pewee to beat so good-humored a fellow as Jack. The king's heart failed him, and suddenly he backed off, saying:

'If you'll agree to help Riley and me out with our lessons hereafter, I'll let you off. If you don't, I'll thrash you within an inch of your life.' And Pewee stood ready to begin.

Jack wanted to escape the merciless beating that Pewee had in store for him. But it was quite impossible for him to submit under a threat. So he answered:

'If you and Riley will treat me as you ought to, I'll help you when you ask me, as I always have. But even if you pound me into jelly I won't agree to help you, unless you treat me right. I won't be bullied into helping you.'

'Give it to him, Pewee,' said Ben Berry; 'he's too sassy.'

Pewee was a rather good-natured dog – he had to be set on. He now began to strike at Jack. Whether he was to be killed or not, Jack did not know, but he was resolved not to submit to the bully. Yet he could not do much at defence against Pewee's hard fists. However, Jack was active and had long limbs; he soon saw that he must do something more than stand up to be beaten. So, when King Pewee, fighting in the irregular Western fashion, and hoping to get a decided advantage at once, rushed upon Jack and pulled his head forward, Jack stooped lower than his enemy expected, and, thrusting his head between Pewee's knees, shoved his legs from under him, and by using all his strength threw Pewee over his own back, so that the king's nose and eyes fell into the dust of the village street.

'I'll pay you for that,' growled Pewee, as he recovered himself, now thoroughly infuriated; and with a single blow he sent Jack flat on his back, and then proceeded to pound him. Jack could do nothing now but shelter his eyes from Pewee's blows.

Joanna Merwin had seen the beginning of the battle from her father's house, and feeling sure that Jack would be killed, she had run swiftly down the garden walk to the back gate, through which she slipped into the alley; and then she hurried on, as fast as her feet would carry her, to the blacksmith-shop of Pewee Rose's father.

'Oh, please, Mr. Rose, come quick! Pewee's just killing a boy in the street.'

'Vitin' ag'in,' said Mr. Rose, who was a Pennsylvanian from the limestone country, and spoke English with difficulty. 'He ees a leetle ruffen, dat poy. I'll see apout him right avay a'ready, may be.'

And without waiting to put off his leathern apron, he walked briskly in the direction indicated by Joanna. Pewee was hammering Jack without pity, when suddenly he was caught by the collar and lifted sharply to his feet.

'Wot you doin' down dare in de dirt wunst a'ready? Hey?' said Mr. Rose, as he shook his son with the full force of his right arm, and cuffed him with his left hand. 'Didn't I dells you I'd gill you some day if you didn't gwit vitin' mit oder poys, a'ready?'

'He commenced it,' whimpered Pewee.

'You dells a pig lie a'ready, I beleefs, Peter, and I'll whip you fur lyin' besides wunst more. Fellers like *him*,' pointing to Jack, who was brushing the dust off his clothes, – 'fellers like him don't gommence on such a poy as you. You're such anoder viter I never seed.' And he shook Pewee savagely.

'I won't do it no more,' begged Pewee – ''pon my word and honor I won't.'

'Oh, you don't gits off dat away no more, a'ready. You know what I'll giff you when I git you home, you leedle ruffen. I shows you how to vite, a'ready.'

And the king disappeared down the street, begging like a spaniel, and vowing that he 'wouldn't do it no more.' But he got a severe whipping, I fear; – it is doubtful if such beatings ever do any good. The next morning Jack appeared at school with a black eye, and Pewee had some scratches, so the master whipped them both for fighting.

# George Wilbur Peck (1840–1916)

The 'bad boy' in the work of Aldrich and Twain was still struggling with the respectable world. With G. W. Peck's hugely successful 'Peck's Bad Boy' series, he had become a comic figure, and the drunken father was now the butt of jokes rather than the source of lachrymose tragedy.

There is, however, still the American ideal of self-improvement behind the book. In an introductory 'A Card from the Author', Peck wrote:

> The 'Bad Boy' is not a 'myth', though there may be some stretches of the imagination in the articles. The counterpart of this boy is located in every city, village and country hamlet throughout the land…his coat-tail is oftener touched with a boot than his heart is by kindness. But he shuffles through life until the time comes for him to make a mark on the world, and then he buckles on the harness …and becomes successful.

George Peck's *Peck's Sun*, published in Milwaukee, was advertised as 'The Funniest Paper in America! What vaccination is to smallpox, Peck's Sun is to the Blues. Malice to None, Good Will to All', and there was a Saturday column on the Bad Boy's exploits every week.

Peck's work is obviously at the popular end of the market and was as much for adults as for children, but it rests upon a new attitude: what was previously frightening or sacrosanct is now a source of fun. Comedy only works in a context; the Bad Boy stories work because of the audience's awareness of moralistic and sententious approaches to the poor and badly behaved.

## from *Peck's Bad Boy and his Pa* (1883)

### CHAPTER II

### THE BAD BOY AT WORK AGAIN

THE BEST BOYS FULL OF TRICKS — THE OLD MAN LAYS DOWN THE LAW ABOUT JOKES — RUBBER-HOSE MACARONI — THE OLD MAN'S STRUGGLES — CHEWING VIGOROUSLY BUT IN VAIN — AN INQUEST HELD — REVELRY BY NIGHT — MUSIC IN THE WOOD-SHED — 'TWAS EVER THUS.'

Of course all boys are not full of tricks, but the best of them are. That is, those who are the readiest to play innocent jokes, and who are continually looking for chances to make Rome howl, are the most apt to turn out to be first-class business men. There is a boy in the Seventh Ward who is so full of fun that sometimes it makes him ache. He is the same boy who not long since wrote a note to his father and signed the name 'Daisy' to it, and got the old man to stand on a corner for two hours waiting for the girl. After that scrape the old man told the boy that he had no objection to innocent jokes, such as would not bring reproach upon him, and as long as the boy confined himself to jokes that would simply cause pleasant laughter, and not cause the finger of scorn to be pointed at a parent, he would be the last one to kick. So the boy has been for three weeks trying to think of some innocent joke to play on his father. The old man is getting a little near sighted, and his teeth are not as good as they used to be, but the old man will not admit it. Nothing that anybody can say can make him own up that his eyesight is failing, or that his teeth are poor, and he would bet a hundred dollars that he could see as far as ever. The boy knew the failing, and made up his mind to demonstrate to the old man that he was rapidly getting off his base. The old person is very fond of macaroni, and eats it about three times a week. The other day the boy was in a drug store and noticed in a show case a lot of small rubber hose, about the size of sticks of macaroni, such as is used on nursing bottles, and other rubber utensils. It was white and nice, and the boy's mind was made up at once. He bought a yard of it, and took it home. When the macaroni was cooked and ready to be served, he hired the table girl to help him play it on the old man. They took a pair of shears and cut the rubber hose in pieces about the same length as the pieces of boiled macaroni, and put them in a saucer with a little macaroni over the rubber pipes, and placed the dish at the old man's plate. Well, we suppose if ten thousand people could have had reserved seats and seen the old man struggle with the India rubber macaroni, and have seen the boy's struggle to keep from laughing, they would have had more fun than they would at a circus. First the old delegate attempted to cut the macaroni into small pieces, and failing, he remarked that it was not cooked enough. The boy said his macaroni was cooked too tender, and that his father's teeth were so poor that he would have to eat soup entirely pretty soon. The old man said, 'Never you mind my teeth, young man,' and decided that he would not complain of anything again. He took up a couple of pieces of rubber and one piece of macaroni on a fork and put them in his mouth. The macaroni dissolved easy enough, and went down perfectly easy, but the flat macaroni was too much for him. He chewed on it for a minute or two, and talked about the weather in order that none of the family should see that he was in trouble, and when he found the macaroni would not down, he called their attention to something out of the window and *took* the rubber slyly from his mouth, and laid it under the edge of his plate. He was more than half convinced that his teeth were played out, but went on eating something else for a while, and finally he thought he would just chance the macaroni once more for luck, and he mowed away another fork full in his mouth. It was the same old story. He chewed like a seminary girl chewing gum, and his eyes stuck out and his face became red, and his wife looked at him as though afraid he was going to die of apoplexy, and finally the servant girl burst out laughing, and went out of the room with her apron stuffed in her mouth, and the boy felt as though it was unhealthy to tarry too long at the table and he went out.

Left alone with his wife the old man took the rubber macaroni from his mouth and laid it on his plate, and he and his wife held an inquest over it. The wife tried to spear it with a fork, but couldn't make any impression on it, and then she see it was rubber hose, and told the old man. He was mad and glad, at the same time; glad because he had found that his teeth were not to blame, and mad because the grocer had sold him boarding house macaroni. Then the girl came in and was put on the confessional, and told all, and presently there was a sound of revelry by night, in the wood shed, and the still, small voice was saying, 'O, Pa, don't! you said you didn't care for innocent jokes. Oh!' And then the old man, between the strokes of the piece of clap-board would say, 'Feed you father a hose cart next, won't ye. Be firing car springs and clothes wringers down me next, eh? Put some gravy on a rubber overcoat, probably, and serve it to me for salad. Try a piece of overshoe, with a bone in it, for my beefsteak, likely. Give your poor old father a slice of rubber bib in place of tripe to-morrow, I expect. Boil me a rubber water bag for apple dumplings, pretty soon, if I don't look out. There! You go and split the kindling wood.' 'Twas ever thus. A boy can't have any fun now days.

# CHAPTER XVI

## THE BAD BOY IN LOVE

ARE YOU A CHRISTIAN? — NO GETTING TO HEAVEN ON SMALL POTATOES! — THE BAD BOY HAS TO CHEW COBS — MA SAYS IT'S GOOD FOR A BOY TO BE IN LOVE — LOVE WEAKENS THE BAD BOY — HOW MUCH DOES IT COST TO GET MARRIED? — MAD DOG! — NEVER EAT ICE CREAM.

'Are you a christian?' asked the bad boy of the grocery man, as that gentleman was placing vegetables out in front of the grocery one morning.

'Well, I hope so,' answered the grocery man, 'I try to do what is right, and hope to wear the golden crown when the time comes to close my books.'

'Then how is it that you put out a box of great big sweet potatoes, and when we order some, and they come to the table, they are little bits of things, not bigger than a radish? Do you expect to get to heaven on such small potatoes, when you use big ones for a sign?' asked the boy, as he took out a silk handkerchief and brushed a speck of dust off his nicely blacked shoes.

The grocery man blushed and said he did not mean to take any such advantage of his customers. He said it must have been a mistake of the boy that delivers groceries.

'Then you must hire the boy to make mistakes, for it has been so every time we have had sweet potatoes for five years,' said the boy. 'And about green corn. You have a few ears stripped down to show how nice and plump it is, and if we order a dozen ears there are only two that have got any corn on at all, and Pa and Ma gets them, and the rest of us have to chew cobs. Do you hope to wear a crown of glory on that kind of corn?'

'O, such things will happen,' said the grocery man with a laugh, 'But don't let's talk about heaven. Let's talk about the other place. How's things over to your house? And say, what's the matter with you. You are all dressed up, and have got a clean shirt on, and your shoes blacked, and I notice your pants are not raveled out so at the bottoms of the legs behind. You are not in love are you?'

'Well, I should smile,' said the boy, as he looked in a small mirror on the counter, covered with fly specks. 'A girl got mashed on me, and Ma says it is good for a boy who hasn't got no sister, to be in love with a girl, and so I kind of tumbled to myself and she don't go no where without I go with her. I take her to dancing school, and everywhere, and she loves me like a house afire. Say, was you ever in love? Makes a fellow feel queer, don't it? Well sir, the first time I went home with her I put my arm around her and honest it scared me. It was just like when you take hold of the handles of a lectric battery, and you can't let go till the man turns the knob. Honest, I was just as weak as a cat. I thought she had needles in her belt and was going to take my arm away, but it was just like it was glued on. I asked her if she felt that way too, and she said she used to, but it was nothing when you got used to it. That made me mad. But she is older than me and knows more about it. When I was going to leave her at the gate, she kissed me, and that was worse than putting my arm around her. By gosh, I trembled all over just like I had chills, but I was as warm as toast. She wouldn't let go for much as a minute, and I was tired as though I had been carrying coal up stairs. I didn't want to go home at all, but she said it would be the best way for me to go home, and come again the next day, and the next morning I went to her house before any of them were up, and her Pa came out to let the cat in, and I asked him what time his girl got up, and he laffed and said I had got it bad, and that I had better go home and not be picked till I got ripe. Say, how much does it cost to get married?'

'Well, I should say you had got it bad,' said the grocery man, as he set out a basket of beets. 'Your getting in love will be a great thing for your Pa. You won't have any time to play any more jokes on him.'

'O, I guess we can find time to keep Pa from being lonesome. Have you seen him this morning? You ought to have seen him last night. You see, my chum's Pa has got a setter dog stuffed. It is one that died two years ago, and he thought a great deal of it, and he had it stuffed, for a ornament. Well, my chum and me took the dog and put it on our front steps, and took some cotton and fastened it to the dog's mouth so it looked just like froth, and we got behind the door and waited for Pa to come home from the theatre. When Pa started to come up the steps I growled and Pa looked at the dog and said, "Mad dog, by crimus," and he started down the sidewalk, and my chum barked just like a dog, and I "Ki-yi'd" and growled like a dog that gets licked, and you ought to see Pa run. He went around in the alley and was going to get in the basement window, and my chum had a revolver with some blank cartridges, and we went down in the basement and when Pa was trying to open the window my chum began to fire towards Pa. Pa hollered that it was only him, and not a burglar, but after my chum fired four shots Pa run and climbed over the fence, and then we took the dog home and I stayed with my chum all night, and this morning Ma said Pa didn't get home till four o'clock and then a policeman came with him, and Pa talked about mad dogs and being taken for a burglar and nearly killed, and she said she was afraid Pa had took to drinking again, and she asked me if I heard any firing of guns, and I said no, and then she put a wet towel on Pa's head.'

'You ought to be ashamed,' said the grocery man. 'How does your Pa like your being in love with the girl? Does he seem to encourage you in it?'

'Oh, yes, she was up to our house to borry some tea, and Pa patted her on the cheek and hugged her and said she was a dear little daisy, and wanted her to sit in his lap, but when I wanted him to let me have fifty cents to buy her some ice cream he said that was all nonsense. He said: "Look at your Ma. Eating ice cream when she was a girl was what injured her health for life." I asked Ma about it, and she said Pa never laid out ten cents for ice cream or any luxury for her in all the five years he was sparking her. She says he took her to a circus once but he got free tickets for carrying water for the elephant. She says Pa was tighter than the bark to a tree. I tell you its going to be different with me. If there is anything that girl wants she is going to have it if I have to sell Ma's copper boiler to get the money, What is the use of having wealth if you hoard it up and don't enjoy it? This family will be run on different principles after this, you bet. Say, how much are those yellow wooden pocket combs in the show case? I've a good notion to buy them for her. How would one of them round mirrors, with a zinc cover, do for a present for a girl? There's nothing too good for her.'

# Laura Elizabeth [Howe] Richards (1850–1943)

Few authors have had two voices so widely divergent as Laura Richards, whose fiction was (in Gillian Avery's words) 'preposterously sentimental' (such as *Captain January*, 1890) and whose nonsense verse was cheerfully inconsequential. Both modes found an enthusiastic audience. 'Mrs Snipkin and Mrs Wobblechin' is from *Sketches and Scraps* (1881): 'Skinny Mrs. Snipkin, | With her little pipkin, | Sat by the fireside a-warming of her toes. | Fat Mrs. Wobblechin, | With her little doublechin, | Sat by the window a-cooling of her nose.'

*The Joyous Story of Toto* shows her at her charming, (rather than sentimental) if inconsequential, best. This extract, the opening chapter, has echoes both of the folk-tale and the tall story, all told in a refreshingly unpatronizing deadpan style.

Laura Richards (with her sister Maud Howe Elliot) won a Pulitzer Prize for the biography of their mother, *The Life of Julia Ward Howe* (1916).

## from *The Joyous Story of Toto* (1885)

### CHAPTER I

Toto was a little boy, and his grandmother was an old woman (I have noticed that grandmothers are very apt to be old women); and this story is about both of them. Now, whether the story be true or not you must decide for yourselves; and the child who finds this out will be wiser than I.

Toto's grandmother lived in a little cottage far from any town, and just by the edge of a thick wood; and Toto lived with her, for his father and mother were dead, and the old woman was the only relation he had in the world.

The cottage was painted red, with white window-casings, and little diamond-shaped panes of glass in the windows. Up the four walls grew a red rose, a yellow rose, a woodbine, and a clematis; and they all met together at the top, and fought and scratched for the possession of the top of the chimney, from which there was the finest view; so foolish are these vegetables.

Inside the cottage there was a big kitchen, with a great open fireplace, in which a bright fire was always crackling; a floor scrubbed white and clean; a dresser with shining copper and tin dishes on it; a table, a rocking-chair for the grandmother, and a stool for Toto. There were two bedrooms and a storeroom, and perhaps another room; and there was a kitchen closet, where the cookies lived. So now you know all about the inside of the cottage. Outside there was a garden behind and a bit of green in front, and three big trees; and that is all there is to tell.

As for Toto, he was a curly-haired fellow, with bright eyes and rosy cheeks, and a mouth that was always laughing.

His grandmother was the best grandmother in the world, I have been given to understand, though that is saying a great deal, to be sure. She was certainly a very good, kind old body; and she had pretty silver curls and pink cheeks, as every grandmother should have. There was only *one* trouble about her; but that was a very serious one, – she was blind.

Her blindness did not affect Toto much; for he had never known her when she was not blind, and he supposed it was a peculiarity of grandmothers in general. But to the poor old lady herself it was a great affliction, though she bore it, for the most part, very cheerfully. She was wonderfully clever and industrious; and her fingers seemed, in many ways, to see better than some people's eyes. She kept the cottage always as neat as a new pin. She was an excellent cook, too, and made the best gingerbread and cookies in the world. And she knit – oh! how she *did* knit! – stockings, mittens, and comforters; comforters, mittens, and stockings: all for Toto. Toto wore them out very fast; but he could not keep up with his grandmother's knitting. Clickety click, clickety clack, went the shining needles all through the long afternoons, when Toto was away in the wood; and nothing answered the needles, except the tea-kettle, which always did its best to make things cheerful. But even in her knitting there were often trials for the grandmother. Sometimes her ball rolled off her lap and away over the floor; and then the poor old lady had a hard time of it groping about in all the corners (there never was a kitchen that had so many corners as hers), and knocking her head against the table and the dresser.

The kettle was always much troubled when anything of this sort happened. He puffed angrily, and looked at the tongs. 'If *I* had legs,' he said, 'I would make some use of them, even if they *were* awkward and ungainly. But when a person is absolutely *all* head and legs, it is easy to understand that he should have no heart.'

The tongs never made any reply to these remarks, but stood stiff and straight, and pretended not to hear.

But the grandmother had other troubles beside dropping her ball. Toto was a very good boy, – better, in fact, than most boys, – and he loved his grandmother very much indeed; but he was forgetful, as every child is. Sometimes he forgot this, and sometimes that, and sometimes the other; for you see his heart was generally in the forest, and his head went to look after it; and that often made trouble. He always *meant* to get before he went to the forest everything that his grandmother could possibly want while he was away. Wood and water he never forgot, for he always brought those in before breakfast. But sometimes the brown potatoes sat waiting in the cellar closet, with their jackets all buttoned up, wondering why they were not taken out, as their brothers had been the day before, and put in a wonderful wicker cage, and carried off to see the great world. And the yellow apples blushed with anger and a sense of neglect; while the red apples turned yellow with vexation. And sometimes, – well, sometimes *this* sort of thing would happen: one day the old lady was going to make some gingerbread; for there was not a bit in the house, and Toto could *not* live without gingerbread. So she said, 'Toto, go to the cupboard and get me the ginger-box and the soda, that's a good boy!'

Now, Toto was standing in the doorway when his grandmother spoke, and just at that moment he caught sight of a green lizard on a stone at a little distance. He wanted very much to catch that lizard; but he was an obedient boy, and always did what 'Granny' asked him to do. So he ran to the cupboard, still keeping one eye on the lizard outside, seized a box full of something yellow and a bag full of something white, and handed them to his grandmother. 'There, Granny,' he cried, 'that's ginger, and *that's* soda. Now may I go? There's a lizard –' and he was off like a flash.

Well, Granny made the gingerbread, and at tea-time in came Master Toto, quite out of breath, having chased the lizard about twenty-five miles (so he said, and he ought to know), and hungry as a hunter. He sat down, and ate his bread-and-milk first, like a good boy; and then he pounced upon the gingerbread, and took a huge bite out of it. Oh, oh! what a dreadful face he made! He gave a wild howl, and jumping up from the table, danced up and down the room, crying, 'Oh! what *nasty* stuff! Oh, Granny, how *could* you make such horrid gingerbread? Br-r-rr! oh, dear! I never, never, *never* tasted anything so horrid.'

The poor old lady was quite aghast. 'My dear boy,' she said, 'I made it just as usual. You must be mistaken. Let me –' and then *she* tasted the gingerbread.

Well, she did not get up and dance, but she came very near it. 'What does this mean?' she cried. 'I made it just as usual. What can it be? Ah!' she added, a new thought striking her. 'Toto, bring me the ginger and the soda; bring just what you brought me this afternoon. Quick! don't stop to examine the boxes; bring the same ones.'

Toto, wondering, brought the box full of something yellow, and the bag full of something white.

His grandmother tasted the contents of both, and then she leaned back in her chair and laughed heartily. 'My dear little boy,' she said, 'you think I am a very good cook, and I myself think I am not a very bad one; but I certainly can*not* make good gingerbread with mustard and salt instead of ginger and soda!'

Toto thought there *were* some disadvantages about being blind, after all; and after that his grandmother always tasted the ingredients before she began to cook.

Now, it happened one day that the grandmother was sitting in the sun before the cottage door, knitting; and as she knitted, from time to time she heaved a deep sigh. And one of those sighs is the reason why this story is written; for if the grandmother had not sighed, and Toto had not heard her, none of the funny things that I am going to tell you would have happened. Moral: always sigh when you want a story written.

Toto was just coming home from the wood, where he had been spending the afternoon, as usual. As he came round the corner of the cottage he heard his grandmother sigh deeply, as if she were very sad about something; and this troubled Toto, for he was an affectionate little boy, and loved his grandmother dearly.

'Why, Granny!' he cried, running up to her and throwing his arms round her neck. 'Dear Granny, why do you sigh so? What is the matter? Are you ill?'

The grandmother shook her head, and wiped a tear from her sightless eyes. 'No, dear little boy!' she said. 'No, I am not ill; but I am very lonely. It's a solitary life here, though you are too young to feel it, Toto, and I am very glad of that. But I do wish, sometimes, that I had some one to talk to, who could tell me what is going on in the world. It is a long time since any one has been here. The travelling pedlar comes only once a year, and the last time he came he had a tooth-ache, so that he could not talk. Ah, deary me! it's a solitary life.' And the grandmother shook her head again, and went on with her knitting.

Toto had listened to this with his eyes very wide open, and his mouth very tight shut; and when his grandmother had finished speaking, he went and sat down on a stone at a little distance, and began to think very hard. His grandmother was lonely. The thought had never occurred to him before. It had always seemed as natural for her to stay at home and knit and make cookies, as for him to go to the wood. He supposed all grandmothers did so. He wondered how it felt to be lonely; he thought it must be very unpleasant. *He* was never lonely in the wood.

'But then,' he said to himself, 'I have all my friends in the wood, and Granny has none. Very likely if I had no friends I should be lonely too. I wonder what I can do about it.'

Then suddenly a bright idea struck him. 'Why,' he thought, – 'why should not my friends be Granny's friends too? They are very amusing, I am sure. Why should I not bring them to see Granny, and let them talk to her? She *could n't* be lonely then. I'll go and see them this minute, and tell them all about it. I'm sure they will come.'

Full of his new idea, the boy sprang to his feet, and ran off in the direction of the wood. The grandmother called to him, 'Toto! Toto! where are you going?' but he did not hear her. The good woman shook her head and went on with her knitting. 'Let the dear child amuse himself as much as he can now. There's little enough amusement in life.'

But Toto was not thinking of his own amusement this time. He ran straight to the wood, and entered it, threading his way quickly among the trees, as if he knew every step of the way, which, indeed, he did. At length, after going some way, he reached an open space, with trees all round it. Such a pretty place! The ground was carpeted with softest moss, into which the boy's feet sunk so deep that they were almost covered; and all over the moss were sprinkled little star-shaped pink flowers. The trees stood back a little from this pretty place, as I said; but their long branches met overhead, as they bent over to look down into – what do you think? – the loveliest little pool of water that ever was seen, I verily believe. A tiny pool, as round as if a huge giant had punched a hole for it with the end of his umbrella or walking-stick, and as clear as crystal. The edge of the pool was covered all round with plants and flowers, which seemed all to be trying to get a peep into the clear brown water. I have heard that these flowers growing round the pool had become excessively vain through looking so constantly at their own reflection, and that they gave themselves insufferable airs in consequence; but as this was only said by the flowers which did *not* grow near the pool, perhaps it was a slight exaggeration. They were certainly very pretty flowers, and I never wondered at their wanting to look at themselves. You see I have been in the wood, and know all about it.

It was in this pretty place that Toto stopped. He sat down on a great cushion of moss near the pool, and began to whistle. Presently he heard a rustling in the tree-tops above his head. He stopped whistling and looked up expectantly. A beechnut fell plump on his nose, and he saw the sharp black eyes of a gray squirrel peering at him through the leaves.

'Hello, Toto!' said the squirrel. 'Back again already? What's the matter?'

'Come down here, and I'll tell you,' said Toto.

The squirrel took a flying leap, and alighted on Toto's shoulder. At the same moment a louder rustling was heard, among the bushes this time, a sound of cracking and snapping twigs, and presently a huge black bear poked his nose out of the bushes, and sniffed inquiringly. 'What's up?' he asked. 'I thought you fellows had gone home for the night, and I was just taking a nap.'

'So we had,' said Toto; 'but I came back because I had something important to say. I want to see you all on business. Where are the others?'

'Coon will be here in a minute,' answered the bear. 'He stopped to eat the woodchuck's supper. Chucky was so sound asleep it seemed a pity to miss such an opportunity. The birds have all flown away except the wood-pigeon, and she told me she would come as soon as she had fed her young ones. What's your business, Toto?' and Bruin sat down in a very comfortable attitude, and prepared to listen.

'Well,' said Toto, 'it's about my grandmother. You see, she – oh! here's Coon! I'll wait for him.' As he spoke, a large raccoon came out into the little dell. He was very handsome, with a most beautiful tail, but he looked sly and lazy. He winked at Toto, by way of greeting, and sat down by the pool, curling his tail round his legs, and then looking into the water to see if the effect was good. At the same moment a pretty wood-pigeon fluttered down, with a soft 'Coo!' and settled on Toto's other shoulder.

'Now then!' said the squirrel, flicking the boy's nose with his tail, 'go on, and tell us all about it!'

So Toto began again. 'My grandmother, you see: she is blind; and she's all alone most of the time when I'm out here playing with all of you, and it makes her lonely.'

'Lonely! What's that?' asked the raccoon.

'I know what it is!' said the bear. 'It's when there are n't any blueberries, and you've hurt your paw so that you can't climb. It's a horrid feeling. Is n't that it, Toto?'

'N-no, not exactly,' said Toto, 'for my grandmother never climbs trees, anyhow. She has n't anybody to talk to, or listen to; nobody comes to see her, and she doesn't know what is going on in the world. That's what she means by "lonely."'

'Humph!' said the raccoon, waving his tail thoughtfully. 'Why don't you both come and live in the wood? She couldn't be lonely here, you know; and it would be very convenient for us all. I know a nice hollow tree that I could get for you not far from here. A wild-cat lives in it now, but if your grandmother doesn't like wild-cats, the bear can easily drive him away. He's a disagreeable fellow, and we shall be glad to get rid of him and have a pleasanter neighbor. Does – a – does your grandmother scratch?'

'No, certainly not!' said Toto indignantly. 'She is the best grandmother in the world. She never scratched anybody in her life, I am sure.'

'No offence, no offence,' said the raccoon. '*My* grandmother scratched, and I thought yours might. Most of them do, in my experience.'

'Besides,' Toto went on, 'she wouldn't like at all to live in a hollow tree. She is not used to that way of living, you see. Now, *I* have a plan, and I want you all to help me in it. In the morning Granny is busy, so she has not time to be lonely. It's only in the afternoon, when she sits still and knits. So I say, why shouldn't you all come over to the cottage in the afternoon, and talk to Granny instead of talking here to each other? I don't mean *every* afternoon, of course, but two or three times a week. She would enjoy the stories and things as much as I do; and she would give you gingerbread, I'm sure she would; and perhaps jam too, if you were *very* good.'

'What's gingerbread?' asked the bear. 'And what's jam? You do use such queer words sometimes, Toto.'

'Gingerbread?' said Toto. 'Oh, it's – well, it's – why, it's *gingerbread*, you know. You don't have anything exactly like it, so I can't exactly tell you. But there's molasses in it, and ginger, and things; it's good, anyhow, very good. And jam – well, jam is sweet, something like honey, only better. You will like it, I know, Bruin.

'Well, what do you all say? Will you come and try it?'

The bear looked at the raccoon; the raccoon looked at the squirrel; and the squirrel looked at the wood-pigeon. The pretty, gentle bird had not spoken before; but now, seeing all the other members of the party undecided, she answered quietly and softly, 'Yes, Toto; I will come, and I am sure the others will, for they are all good creatures. You are a dear boy, and we shall all be glad to give pleasure to you or your grandmother.'

The other creatures all nodded approval to the wood-pigeon's little speech, and Toto gave a sigh of relief and satisfaction. 'That is settled, then,' he said. 'Thank you, dear pigeon, and thank you all. Now, when will you come? To-morrow afternoon? The sooner the better, I think.'

The raccoon looked critically at his reflection in the water. 'Chucky bit my ear yesterday,' he said, 'and it doesn't look very well for making visits. Suppose we wait till it is healed over. Nothing like making a good impression at first, you know.'

'Nonsense, Coon!' growled the bear. 'You are always thinking about your looks. I never saw such a fellow. Let us go to-morrow if we are going.'

'Besides,' said Toto, laughing, 'Granny is blind, and will not know whether you have any ears or not, Master Coon. So I shall expect you all to-morrow. Good-by, all, and thank you very much.' And away ran Toto, and away went all the rest to get their respective suppers.

# Robert Louis Stevenson (1850–1894)

Stevenson wrote laconically to Edmund Gosse in 1885 that he had just published '*The Complete Proof of Mr R. L. Stevenson's Incapability to Write Verse*'; most critics have disagreed, seeing *A Child's Garden of Verses* as a new direction, in which the poet was taking the child's viewpoint, rather than imposing a way of thinking on the child.

How far this is true, and how far there is still an element of nostalgia and/or sentimentalization, is debatable. Stevenson cannot, perhaps, be held responsible for the 'beautiful child' cult which produced a good deal of sugary verse on the Stevenson model well into the 1920s, nor the somewhat precious tone of a great deal of twentieth-century poetry for children thereafter. He did, however, focus on the 'small' concerns of childhood, not concerning himself with what was or was not 'consequential', and thus widened the scope of poetry for children.

In any debate about children's poetry (or even the possibility of its existence) *A Child's Garden of Verses* will be pivotal. Stevenson grappled with the central difficulties: the very fact of writing the poem changes the value of the experience it describes; the very fact of the *adult* writing the poem brings an inevitable interference in the transmission of the experience to the child. How successful he was might be judged from this selection.

It may well be that Stevenson came as close to the ideal of what F. J. Harvey Darton described as poetry 'written as a child, given word-skill, might have written it', but the opposing view has been trenchantly put by John Goldthwaite (1996): 'Where Greenaway was giving innocence a look, Stevenson was giving it a voice and things to do and think and hum to oneself while being childlike. No one had ever lied up a stereotype so sweetly or at this artistic level before, and a genteel reading public doted on Stevenson's image of itself "[s]itting safe in nursery nooks, | Reading picture story-books".'

## from *A Child's Garden of Verses* (1885)

### Whole Duty of Children

A child should always say what's true,
And speak when he is spoken to,
And behave mannerly at table:
At least as far as he is able.

### Rain

The rain is raining all around,
    It falls on field and tree,
It rains on the umbrellas here,
    And on the ships at sea.

### Where Go the Boats

Dark brown is the river,
    Golden is the sand.
It flows along for ever,
    With trees on either hand.

Green leaves a-floating,
    Castles of the foam,
Boats of mine a-boating –
    Where will all come home

On goes the river
   And out past the mill,
Away down the valley,
   Away down the hill.

Away down the river,
   A hundred miles or more,
Other little children
   Shall bring my boats ashore.

## System

Every night my prayers I say,
And get my dinner every day;
And every day that I've been good,
I get an orange after food.

The child that is not clean and neat,
With lots of toys and things to eat,
He is a naughty child, I'm sure –
Or else his dear papa is poor.

## Good and Bad Children

Children, you are very little,
And your bones are very brittle;
If you would grow great and stately,
You must try to walk sedately.

You must still be bright and quiet,
And content with simple diet;
And remain, through all bewild'ring,
Innocent and honest children.

Happy hearts and happy faces,
Happy play in grassy places –
That was how, in ancient ages,
Children grew to kings and sages.

But the unkind and the unruly,
And the sort who eat unduly,
They must never hope for glory –
Theirs is quite a different story!

Cruel children, crying babies,
All grow up as geese and gabies,
Hated, as their age increases,
By their nephews and their nieces.

## THE LAMPLIGHTER

My tea is nearly ready and the sun has left the sky;
It's time to take the window to see Leerie going by;
For every night at tea-time and before you take your seat,
With lantern and with ladder he comes posting up the street.

Now Tom would be a driver and Maria go to sea,
And my papa's a banker and as rich as he can be;
But I, when I am stronger and can choose what I'm to do,
O Leerie, I'll go round at night and light the lamps with you!

For we are very lucky, with a lamp before the door,
And Leerie stops to light it as he lights so many more;
And O! before you hurry by with ladder and with light,
O Leerie, see a little child and nod to her tonight!

## THE COW

The friendly cow, all red and white
    I love with all my heart:
She gives me cream with all her might,
    To eat with apple tart.
She wanders lowing here and there,
    And yet she cannot stray,
All in the pleasant open air,
    The pleasant light of day;
And blown by all the winds that pass,
    And wet with all the showers,
She walks among the meadow grass
    And eats the meadow flowers.

## HAPPY THOUGHT

The world is so full of a number of things,
I'm sure we should all be as happy as Kings.

# Lucretia Peabody Hale (1820–1900)

'We are not', Agamemnon Peterkin observes when the whole neighbourhood comes to tea, 'a family for emergencies'. The Peterkins' innocent literal-mindedness works best in small doses, and the first two stories, reprinted here, are in a sense the purest. As the collection develops and the stories become longer there is more room for the reader to question the situation, as when the ceiling has to be elaborately raised because the Christmas tree is too tall.

But, at their best, *The Peterkin Papers* are pure farce, a rare enough item at any stage in the history of children's books (although some critics see them as gentle satires on Bostonian society).

*The Peterkin Papers* first appeared in *Our Young Folks* in 1868 and were republished in *St. Nicholas* from 1874–9. *The Last of the Peterkins and Others of their Kin* was published in 1886.

## from *The Peterkin Papers* (1880)

### THE LADY WHO PUT SALT IN HER COFFEE

This was Mrs. Peterkin. It was a mistake. She had poured out a delicious cup of coffee, and, just as she was helping herself to cream, she found she had put in salt instead of sugar! It tasted bad. What should she do? Of course she couldn't drink the coffee; so she called in the family, for she was sitting at a late breakfast all alone. The family came in; they all tasted, and looked, and wondered what should be done, and all sat down to think.

At last Agamemnon, who had been to college, said, 'Why don't we go over and ask the advice of the chemist?' (For the chemist lived over the way, and was a very wise man.)

Mrs. Peterkin said, 'Yes,' and Mr. Peterkin said, 'Very well,' and all the children said they would go too. So the little boys put on their india-rubber boots, and over they went.

Now the chemist was just trying to find out something which should turn everything it touched into gold; and he had a large glass bottle into which he put all kinds of gold and silver, and many other valuable things, and melted them all up over the fire, till he had almost found what he wanted. He could turn things into almost gold. But just now he had used up all the gold that he had round the house, and gold was high. He had used up his wife's gold thimble and his great-grandfather's gold-bowed spectacles; and he had melted up the gold head of his great-great-grandfather's cane; and, just as the Peterkin family came in, he was down on his knees before his wife, asking her to let him have her wedding-ring to melt up with all the rest, because this time he knew he should succeed, and should be able to turn everything into gold; and then she could have a new wedding-ring of diamonds, all set in emeralds and rubies and topazes, and all the furniture could be turned into the finest of gold.

Now his wife was just consenting when the Peterkin family burst in. You can imagine how mad the chemist was! He came near throwing his crucible – that was the name of his melting-pot – at their heads. But he didn't. He listened as calmly as he could to the story of how Mrs. Peterkin had put salt in her coffee.

At first he said he couldn't do anything about it; but when Agamemnon said they would pay in gold if he would only go, he packed up his bottles in a leather case, and went back with them all.

First he looked at the coffee, and then stirred it. Then he put in a little chlorate of potassium, and the family tried it all round; but it tasted no better. Then he stirred in a little bichlorate of magnesia. But Mrs. Peterkin didn't like that. Then he added some tartaric acid and some hypersulphate of lime. But no; it was no better. 'I have it!' exclaimed the chemist, – 'a little ammonia is just the thing!' No, it wasn't the thing at all.

Then he tried, each in turn, some oxalic, cyanic, acetic, phosphoric, chloric, hyperchloric, sulphuric, boracic, silicic, nitric, formic, nitrous nitric, and carbonic acids. Mrs. Peterkin tasted each, and said the flavor was pleasant, but not precisely that of coffee. So then he tried a little calcium, aluminium, barium, and strontium, a little clear bitumen, and a half of a third of a sixteenth of a grain of arsenic. This gave rather a pretty color; but still Mrs. Peterkin ungratefully said it tasted of anything but coffee. The chemist was not discouraged. He put in a little belladonna and atropine, some granulated hydrogen, some potash, and a very little antimony, finishing off with a little pure carbon. But still Mrs. Peterkin was not satisfied.

The chemist said that all he had done ought to have taken out the salt. The theory remained the same, although the experiment had failed. Perhaps a little starch would have some effect. If not, that was all the time he could give. He should like to be paid, and go. They were all much obliged to him, and willing to give him $1.37 $\frac{1}{2}$ in gold. Gold was now 2.69 $\frac{3}{4}$, so Mr. Peterkin found in the newspaper. This gave Agamemnon a pretty little sum. He sat himself down to do it. But there was the coffee! All sat and thought awhile, till Elizabeth Eliza said, 'Why don't we go to the herb-woman?' Elizabeth Eliza was the only daughter. She was named after her two aunts, – Elizabeth, from the sister of her father; Eliza, from her mother's sister. Now, the herb-woman was an old woman who came round to sell herbs, and knew a great deal. They all shouted with joy at the idea of asking her, and Solomon John and the younger children agreed to go and find her too. The herb-woman lived down at the very end of the street; so the boys put on their india-rubber boots again, and they set off. It was a long walk through the village, but they came at last to the herb-woman's house, at the foot of a high hill. They went through her little garden. Here she had marigolds and hollyhocks, and old maids and tall sunflowers, and all kinds of sweet-smelling herbs, so that the air was full of tansy-tea and elder-blow. Over the porch grew a hop-vine, and a brandy-cherry tree shaded the door, and a luxuriant cranberry-vine flung its delicious fruit across the window. They went into a small parlor, which smelt very spicy. All around hung little bags full of catnip, and peppermint, and all kinds of herbs; and dried stalks hung from the ceiling; and on the shelves were jars of rhubarb, senna, manna, and the like.

But there was no little old woman. She had gone up into the woods to get some more wild herbs, so they all thought they would follow her, – Elizabeth Eliza, Solomon John, and the little boys. They had to climb up over high rocks, and in among huckleberry-bushes and blackberry-vines. But the little boys had their india-rubber boots. At last they discovered the little old woman. They knew her by her hat. It was steeple-crowned, without any vane. They saw her digging with her trowel round a sassafras bush. They told her their story, – how their mother had put salt in her coffee, and how the chemist had made it worse instead of better, and how their mother couldn't drink it, and wouldn't she come and see what she could do? And she said she would, and took up her little old apron, with pockets all round, all filled with everlasting and pennyroyal, and went back to her house.

There she stopped, and stuffed her huge pockets with some of all the kinds of herbs. She took some tansy and peppermint, and caraway-seed and dill, spearmint and cloves, pennyroyal and sweet marjoram, basil and rosemary, wild thyme and some of the other time, – such as you have in clocks, – sappermint and oppermint, catnip, valerian, and hop; indeed, there isn't a kind of herb you can think of that the little old woman didn't have done up in her little paper bags, that had all been dried in her little Dutch-oven. She packed these all up, and then went back with the children, taking her stick.

Meanwhile Mrs. Peterkin was getting quite impatient for her coffee.

As soon as the little old woman came she had it set over the fire, and began to stir in the different herbs. First she put in a little hop for the bitter. Mrs. Peterkin said it tasted like hop-tea, and not at all like coffee. Then she tried a little flagroot and snakeroot, then some spruce gum, and some caraway and some dill, some rue and rosemary, some sweet marjoram and sour, some oppermint and sappermint, a little spearmint and peppermint, some wild thyme, and some of the other tame time, some tansy and basil, and catnip and valerian, and sassafras, ginger, and pennyroyal. The children tasted after each mixture, but made up dreadful faces. Mrs. Peterkin tasted, and did the same. The more the old woman stirred, and the more she put in, the worse it all seemed to taste.

So the old woman shook her head, and muttered a few words, and said she must go. She believed the coffee was bewitched. She bundled up her packets of herbs, and took her trowel, and her basket, and her stick, and went back to her root of sassafras, that she had left half in the air and half out. And all she would take for pay was five cents in currency.

Then the family were in despair, and all sat and thought a great while. It was growing late in the day, and Mrs. Peterkin hadn't had her cup of coffee. At last Elizabeth Eliza said, 'They say that the lady from Philadelphia, who is staying in town, is very wise. Suppose I go and ask her what is best to be done.' To this they all agreed, it was a great thought, and off Elizabeth Eliza went.

She told the lady from Philadelphia the whole story, – how her mother had put salt in the coffee; how the chemist had been called in; how he tried everything but could make it no better; and how they went for the little old herb-woman, and how she had tried in vain, for her mother couldn't drink the coffee. The lady from Philadelphia listened very attentively, and then said, 'Why doesn't your mother make a fresh cup of coffee?' Elizabeth Eliza started with surprise. Solomon John shouted with joy; so did Agamemnon, who had just finished his sum; so did the little boys, who had followed on. 'Why didn't we think of that?' said Elizabeth Eliza; and they all went back to their mother and she had her cup of coffee.

## ABOUT ELIZABETH ELIZA'S PIANO

Elizabeth Eliza had a present of a piano, and she was to take lessons of the postmaster's daughter.

They decided to have the piano set across the window in the parlor, and the carters brought it in, and went away.

After they had gone the family all came in to look at the piano; but they found the carters had placed it with its back turned towards the middle of the room, standing close against the window.

How could Elizabeth Eliza open it? How could she reach the keys to play upon it?

Solomon John proposed that they should open the window, which Agamemnon could do with his long arms. Then Elizabeth Eliza should go round upon the piazza, and open the piano. Then she could have her music-stool on the piazza, and play upon the piano there.

So they tried this; and they all thought it was a very pretty sight to see Elizabeth Eliza playing on the piano, while she sat on the piazza, with the honeysuckle vines behind her.

It was very pleasant, too, moonlight evenings. Mr. Peterkin liked to take a doze on his sofa in the room; but the rest of the family liked to sit on the piazza. So did Elizabeth Eliza, only she had to have her back to the moon.

All this did very well through the summer; but, when the fall came, Mr. Peterkin thought the air was too cold from the open window, and the family did not want to sit out on the piazza.

Elizabeth Eliza practised in the mornings with her cloak on; but she was obliged to give up her music in the evenings the family shivered so.

One day, when she was talking with the lady from Philadelphia, she spoke of this trouble.

The lady from Philadelphia looked surprised, and then said, 'But why don't you turn the piano round?'

One of the little boys pertly said, 'It is a square piano.'

But Elizabeth Eliza went home directly, and, with the help of Agamemnon and Solomon John, turned the piano round.

'Why did we not think of that before?' said Mrs. Peterkin. 'What shall we do when the lady from Philadelphia goes home again?'

# Frances Hodgson Burnett (1849–1924)

Frances Hodgson Burnett's greatest successes as a novelist were, in effect, fairy-tales, incorporating both the trappings of romance and the affecting aspects of the realism developed by the evangelical writers. They were read by adults and children alike: children's and adults' literature – both for males and females – had been growing closer together, and the firm division between the children's book and the adult book which is characteristic of much of the twentieth century had not yet occurred.

*Little Lord Fauntleroy* (1886), which reflected Burnett's transatlantic background (she had been born in England), transformed the 'beautiful child' into a robust, upstanding boy (although a little given to sentimentalism). Brought up in New York City (which he survives despite the long golden curls and velvet suit), Cedric Errol overcomes the prejudices of his aristocratic grandfather, the Earl of Dorincourt, in fine melodramatic scenes that were to be repeated endlessly, most notably in Eleanor Porter's *Pollyanna* (1912). *Sara Crewe, or What Happened at Miss Minchin's* (1887), later revised and expanded as *A Little Princess* (1905), takes the rich Sara down to the level of the street urchins. But this is a fairy-tale, providing wish-fulfilment,

and the starving girl crouching in the baker's doorway to whom Sara (although starving herself) gives the hot buns, is only a dramatic foil, seen only in terms of Sara's inner nobility and as a turning-point in the restoration of her fortune. The same theatricality can be seen in *The Secret Garden* (1911), which borrows with great zest from *Jane Eyre* and the gothic novels of the nineteenth century, athough that is not to underestimate the symbolic complexity of that book.

Many of Burnett's books deal with the solid financial rewards for virtue, the meeting of the commercial and the romantic, yet the underlying messages about imagination and personal freedom give her books their depth. The messages in them operate at symbolic levels, rather than at allegoric or specifically moral ones.

*Editha's Burglar* is an example of the way in which Burnett could manipulate a fashionable (and sentimental) view of childhood – that of innocence overcoming evil. She was a consummately professional writer, and here she walks a tightrope between dangerous realism and whimsical fantasy.

## *Editha's Burglar* (1888)

I will begin by saying that Editha was always rather a queer little girl, and not much like other children. She was not a strong, healthy little girl, and had never been able to run about and play; and, as she had no sisters or brothers, or companions of her own size she was rather old-fashioned, as her aunts used to call it. She had always been very fond of books, and had learned to read when she was such a tiny child, that I should almost be afraid to say how tiny she was when she read her first volume through. Her papa wrote books himself, and was also the editor of a newspaper; and as he had a large library, Editha perhaps read more than was quite good for her. She lived in London; and, as her mamma was very young and pretty, and went out a great deal, and her papa was so busy, and her governess only came in the morning, she was left to herself a good many hours in the day, and when she was left to herself, she spent the greater part of her time in the library reading her papa's big books, and even his newspapers.

She was very fond of the newspapers, because she found so many curious things in them, – stories, for instance, of strange events which happened every day in the great city of London, and yet never seemed to happen anywhere near where she lived. Through the newspapers, she found that there were actually men who lived by breaking into people's houses and stealing all the nice things they could carry away, and she read that such men were called burglars. When she first began to read about burglars, she was very much troubled. In the first place, she felt rather timid about going to bed at night, and, in the second place, she felt rather sorry for the burglars.

'I suppose no one ever taught them any better,' she thought.

In fact, she thought so much about the matter, that she could not help asking her papa some questions one morning when he was at breakfast. He was reading his paper and eating his chops both at once when she spoke to him.

'Papa,' she said, in a solemn little voice, and looking at him in a very solemn manner, 'papa dear, what do you think of burglars – as a class?' (She said 'as a class,' because she had heard one of her papa's friends say it, and as he was a gentleman she admired very much, she liked to talk as he did.) Her papa gave a little jump in his chair, as if she had startled him, and then he pushed his hair off his forehead and stared at her.

'Burglars! As a class!' he said, and then he stared at her a minute again in rather a puzzled way. 'Bless my soul!' he said. 'As a class, Nixie!' (that was his queer pet name for her). 'Nixie, where is your mother?'

'She is in bed, papa dear, and we mustn't disturb her,' said Editha. 'The party last night tired her out. I peeped into her room softly as I came down. She looks so pretty when she is asleep. What *do* you think of burglars, papa?'

'I think they're a bad lot, Nixie,' said her papa, 'a bad lot.'

'Are there no good burglars, papa?'

'Well, Nixie,' answered papa, 'I should say not. As a rule, you know, –' and here he began to smile, as people often smiled at Editha when she asked questions – 'as a rule, burglars are not distinguished for moral perspicuity and blameless character.'

But Editha did not understand what moral perspicuity meant, and besides she was thinking again.

'Miss Lane was talking to me the other day about some poor children who had never been taught anything; they had never had any French or music lessons, and scarcely knew how to read, and she said they had never had any advantages. Perhaps that is the way with the burglars, papa – perhaps they have never had any advantages, – perhaps if they had had advantages they mightn't have been burglars.'

'Lessons in French and music are very elevating to the mind, my dear Nixie,' papa began in his laughing way, which was always a trial to Editha, but suddenly he stopped, and looked at her rather sadly.

'How old are you, Nixie?' he asked.

'I am seven,' answered Editha, 'seven years, going on eight.'

Papa sighed.

'Come here, little one,' he said, holding out his strong white hand to her.

She left her chair and went to him, and he put his arms around her, and kissed her, and stroked her long brown hair.

'Don't puzzle your little brain too much,' he said, 'never mind about the burglars, Nixie.'

'Well,' said Editha, 'I can't help thinking about them a little, and it seems to me that there must be, perhaps, one good burglar among all the bad ones, and I can't help being rather sorry, even for the bad ones. You see, they must have to be up all night, and out in the rain sometimes, and they can't help not having had advantages.'

It was strange that the first thing she heard, when she went up to her mamma's room, was something about burglars.

She was very, very fond of her mamma, and very proud of her. She even tried to take care of her in her small way; she never disturbed her when she was asleep, and she always helped her to dress, bringing her things to her, buttoning her little shoes and gloves, putting the perfume on her handkerchiefs, and holding her wraps until she wanted them.

This morning, when she went into the dressing-room, she found the chamber-maid there before her, and her dear little mamma looking very pale.

'Ah, mem, if you please, mem,' the chamber-maid was saying, 'what a blessing it was they didn't come here!'

'Who, Janet?' Editha asked.

'The burglars, miss, that broke into Number Eighteen last night, and carried off all the silver, and the missus's jewellery.'

'If burglars ever do break in here,' said mamma, 'I hope none of us will hear them, though it would almost break my heart to have my things taken. If I should waken in the night, and find a burglar in my room, I think it would kill me, and I know I should scream, and then there is no knowing what they might do. If ever you think there is a burglar in the house, Nixie, whatever you do, don't scream or make any noise. It would be better to have one's things stolen, than to be killed by burglars for screaming.'

She was not a very wise little mamma, and often said rather thoughtless things; but she was very gentle and loving, and Editha was so fond of her that she put her arms round her waist and said to her,

'Mamma, dearest, I will never let any burglars hurt you or frighten you if I can help it. I do believe I could persuade them not to. I should think even a burglar would listen to reason.'

That made her mamma laugh, so that she forgot all about the burglars and began to get her colour again, and it was not long before she was quite gay, and was singing a song she had heard at the opera, while Editha was helping her to dress.

But that very night Editha met a burglar.

Just before dinner, her papa came up from the city in a great hurry. He dashed up to the front door in a cab, and, jumping out, ran upstairs to mamma, who was sitting in the drawing-room, while Editha read aloud to her.

'Kitty, my dear,' he said, 'I am obliged to go to Glasgow by the "five" train. I must throw a few things into a portmanteau and go at once.'

'Oh, Francis!' said mamma. 'And just after that burglary at the Norris's! I don't like to be left alone.'

'The servants are here,' said papa, 'and Nixie will take care of you; won't you, Nixie? Nixie is interested in burglars.'

'I am sure Nixie could do more than the servants,' said mamma. 'All three of them sleep in one room at the top of the house when you are away, and even if they awakened they would only scream.'

'Nixie wouldn't scream,' said papa, laughing; 'Nixie would do something heroic. I will leave you in her hands.'

He was only joking, but Editha did not think of what he said as a joke; she felt that her mamma was really left in her care, and that it was a very serious matter.

She thought about it so seriously that she hardly talked at all at dinner, and was so quiet afterward that her mamma said, 'Dear me, Nixie, what *are* you thinking of? You look as solemn as a little owl.'

'I am thinking of you, mamma,' the child answered.

And then her mamma laughed and kissed her, and said: 'Well, I must say I don't see why you should look so grave about me. I didn't think I was such a solemn subject.'

At last bed-time came, and the little girl went to her mother's room, because she was to sleep there.

'I am glad I have you with me, Nixie,' said mamma, with a rather nervous little laugh. 'I am sure I shouldn't like to sleep in this big room alone.'

But, after she was in bed, she soon fell asleep, and lay looking so happy and sweet and comfortable that Editha thought it was lovely to see her.

Editha did not go to sleep for a long time. She thought of her papa trying to sleep in the train, rushing through the dark night on its way to Scotland; she thought of a new book she had just begun to read; she thought of a child she had once heard singing in the street; and when her eyes closed at length, her mind had just gone back to the burglars at Number Eighteen. She slept until midnight, and then something wakened her. At first she did not know what it was, but in a few minutes she found that it was a queer little sound coming from downstairs, a sound like a stealthy filing of iron.

She understood in a moment then, because she had heard the chamber-maid say that the burglars broke into Number Eighteen by filing through the bars of the shutters.

'It is a burglar,' she thought, 'and he will awaken mamma.'

If she had been older, and had known more of the habits of burglars, she might have been more frightened than she was. She did not think of herself at all, however, but of her mother.

She began to reason the matter over as quickly as possible, and she made up her mind that the burglar must not be allowed to make a noise.

'I'll go down and ask him to please to be quiet as he can,' she said to herself, 'and I'll tell him why.'

Certainly, this was a queer thing to think of doing, but I told you when I began my story that she was a queer little girl.

She slipped out of bed so quietly that she scarcely stirred the clothes, and then slipped just as quietly out of the room and down the stairs.

The filing had ceased, but she heard a sound of stealthy feet in the kitchen; and, though it must be confessed her heart beat rather faster than usual, she made her way to the kitchen and opened the door.

Imagine the astonishment of that burglar when, on hearing the door open, he turned round and found himself looking at a slender little girl, in a white frilled night-gown, and with bare feet, a little girl whose large brown eyes rested on him in a by no means unfriendly way.

'I'll be polite to him,' Editha had said, as she was coming downstairs. 'I am sure he'll be more obliging if I am very polite. Miss Lane says politeness always wins its way.'

So the first words she spoke were as polite as she could make them.

'Don't be frightened,' she said, in a soft voice. 'I don't want to hurt you; I came to ask a favour of you.'

The burglar was so amazed that he actually forgot he was a burglar, and staggered back against the wall. I think he thought at first that Editha was a little ghost. 'You see I couldn't hurt you if I wanted to,' she went on, wishing to encourage him. 'I'm too little. I'm only seven – and a little over – and I'm not going to scream, because that would waken mamma, and that's just what I don't want to do.'

That did encourage the burglar, but still he was so astonished that he did not know what to do.

'Well, I'm blowed,' he said in a whisper, 'if this ain't a rummy go,' which was extremely vulgar language; but, unfortunately, he was one of those burglars who, as Miss Lane said, 'had not had any advantages,' which is indeed the case with the majority of the burglars of my acquaintance.

Then he began to laugh, in a whisper also, if one can be said to laugh in a whisper. He put his hand over his mouth, and made no noise, but he laughed so hard that he doubled up and rocked himself to and fro.

'The rummiest go,' he said, in his uneducated way. 'An' she hain't a-goin' to 'urt me. Oh, my heye.'

He was evidently very badly educated, indeed, for he not only used singular words, but sounded his h's all in the wrong places. Editha noticed this, even in the midst of her surprise at his laughter. She could not understand what he was laughing at. Then it occurred to her that she might have made a mistake.

'If you please,' she said, with great delicacy, 'are you really a burglar?'

He stopped laughing just long enough to answer her.

'Lor' no, miss,' he said, 'by no manner o' means. I'm a dear friend o' yer par's, come to make a evenin' call, an' not a-wishin' to trouble the servants, I stepped in through the winder.'

'Ah,' said Editha, looking very gravely at him, 'I see you are joking with me, as papa does sometimes. But what I wanted to say to you was this; papa has gone to Scotland, and all our servants are women, and mamma would be so frightened if you were to waken her, that I am sure it would make her ill. And if you are going to burgle, would you please burgle as quietly as you can, so that you won't disturb her.'

The burglar stopped laughing, and, staring at her, once more uttered his vulgar exclamation:

'Well, I'll be blowed!'

'Why don't you say, "I'll be blown"?' asked Editha. 'I'm sure it isn't correct to say you'll be blowed.'

She thought he was going off into one of his unaccountable fits of laughter again, but he did not; he seemed to check himself with an effort.

'There hain't no time to waste,' she heard him mutter.

'No, I suppose there isn't,' she answered. 'Mamma might wake and miss me. What are you going to burgle first?'

'You'd better go upstairs to yer mar,' he said, rather sulkily.

Editha thought deeply for a few seconds.

'You oughtn't to burgle anything,' she said. 'Of course you know that, but if you have really made up your mind to do it, I would like to show you the things you'd better take.'

'What, fer instance?' said the burglar, with interest.

'You mustn't take any of mamma's things,' said Editha, 'because they are all in her room, and you would waken her, and besides, she said it would break her heart; and don't take any of the things papa is fond of. I'll tell you what,' turning rather pale, 'you can take my things.'

'What kind o' things?' asked the burglar.

'My locket, and the little watch papa gave me, and the necklace and bracelets my grandmamma left me, – they are worth a great deal of money, and they are very pretty, and I was to wear them when I grew to be a young lady, but – but you can take them. And – then –' very slowly, and with a deep sigh, 'there are – my books. I'm very fond of them, but —'

'I don't want no books,' said the burglar.

'Don't you?' exclaimed she. 'Ah, thank you.'

'Well,' said the burglar, as if to himself, and staring hard at her brightening face, 'I never see no sich a start afore.'

'Shall I go upstairs and get the other things?' said Editha.

'No,' he said. 'You stay where you are – or stay, come along o' me inter the pantry, an' sit down while I'm occypied.'

He led the way into the pantry, and pushed her down on a step, and then began to open the drawers where the silver was kept.

'It's curious that you should know just where to look for things, and that your key should fit, isn't it?' said Editha.

'Yes,' he answered, 'it's werry sing'lar, indeed. There's a good deal in bein' eddicated.'

'Are you educated?' asked Editha, with a look of surprise.

'Did yer think I wasn't?' said the burglar.

'Well,' said Editha, not wishing to offend him, 'you see, you pronounce your words so very strangely.'

'It's all a matter o' taste,' interrupted the burglar. 'Oxford an' Cambridge 'as different vocabillaries.'

'Did you go to Oxford?' asked Editha, politely.

'No,' said he, 'nor yet to Cambridge.'

Then he laughed again, and seemed to be quite enjoying himself as he made some forks and spoons up into a bundle. 'I 'ope there ain't no plated stuff 'ere,' he said. 'Plate's wulgar, an' I 'ope yer parents hain't wulgar, cos that'd be settin' yer a werry bad example an' sp'ilin' yer morals.'

'I am sure papa and mamma are not vulgar,' said Editha.

The burglar opened another drawer, and chuckled again, and this suggested to Editha's mind another question.

'Is your business a good one?' she suddenly inquired of him.

''Tain't as good as it ought to be, by no manner o' means,' said the burglar. 'Every one hain't as hobligin' as you, my little dear.'

'Oh!' said Editha. 'You know you obliged me by not making a noise.'

'Well,' said the burglar, 'as a rule we don't make a practice o' making' no more noise than we can help. It hain't considered 'ealthy in the profession.'

'Would you mind leaving us a few forks and spoons to eat with, if you please? I beg pardon for interrupting you, but I'm afraid we shall not have any to use at breakfast.'

'Hain't you got no steel uns?' inquired the burglar.

'Mamma wouldn't like to use steel ones, I'm sure,' Editha answered. 'I'll tell you what you can do; please leave out enough for mamma, and I can use steel. I don't care about myself, much.'

The man seemed to think a moment, and then he was really so accommodating as to do as she asked, and even went to the length of leaving out her own little fork and knife and spoon.

'Oh! you are very kind,' said Editha, when she saw him do this.

'That's a reward o' merit, cos yer didn't squeal,' said the burglar.

He was so busy for the next few minutes that he did not speak, though now and then he broke into a low laugh, as if he was thinking of something very funny indeed. During the silence, Editha sat holding her little feet in her night-gown, and watching him very curiously. A great many new thoughts came into her active brain, and at last she could not help asking some more questions.

'Would you really rather be a burglar than anything else?' she inquired, respectfully.

'Well,' said the man, 'p'r'aps I'd prefer to be Lord Mayor, or a member o' the 'Ouse o' Lords, or heven the Prince o' Wales, honly for there being' hobstacles in the way of it.'

'Oh!' said Editha; 'you couldn't be the Prince of Wales, you know. I meant wouldn't you rather be in some other profession? My papa is an editor,' she added. 'How would you like to be an editor?'

'Well,' said the burglar, 'hif yer par ud change with me, or hif he chanced to know hany heditor with a roarin' trade as ud be so hobligin' as to 'and it hover, hit's wot I've allers 'ad a leanin' to.'

'I am sure papa would not like to be a burglar,' said Editha, thoughtfully; 'but perhaps he might speak to his friends about you, if you would give me your name and address, and if I were to tell him how obliging you were, and if I told him you really didn't like being a burglar.'

The burglar put his hand to his pocket and gave a start of great surprise.

'To think o' me a-forgettin' my card-case,' he said, 'an' a-leavin' it on the pianner when I come hout! I'm sich a bloomin' forgetful cove. I might hev knowed I'd hev wanted it.'

'It is a pity,' said Editha; 'but if you told me your name and your number, I think I could remember it.'

'I'm afeared yer couldn't,' said the burglar, regretfully, 'but I'll try yer. Lord Halgernon Hedward Halbert de Pentonwille, Yde Park. Can you think o' that?'

'Are you a lord?' exclaimed Editha. 'Dear me, how strange!'

'It is sing'lar,' said the burglar, shaking his head. 'I've hoften thought so myself. But not wishin' to detain a lady no longer than can be 'elped, s'pose we take a turn in the lib'ery among yer respected par's things.'

'Don't make a noise,' said Editha, as she led the way.

But when they reached the library her loving little heart failed her. All the things her father valued most were there, and he would be sure to be so sorry if one thing was missing when he returned. She stood on the threshold a moment and looked about her.

'Oh,' she whispered, 'please do me another favour, won't you? Please let me slip quietly upstairs and bring down my own things instead. They will be so easy to carry away, and they are very valuable, and – and I will make you a present of them if you will not touch anything that belongs to papa. He is so fond of his things, and, besides that, he is so good.'

The burglar gave a rather strange and disturbed look at her.

'Go an' get yer gimcracks,' he said in a somewhat grumbling voice.

Her treasures were in her own room, and her bare feet made no sound as she crept slowly up the staircase and then down again. But when she handed the little box to the burglar her eyes were wet.

'Papa gave me the watch, and mamma gave me the locket,' she whispered, tremulously; 'and the pearls were grandmamma's, and grandmamma is in heaven.'

It would not be easy to know what the burglar thought; he looked queerer than ever. Perhaps he was not quite so bad as some burglars, and felt rather ashamed of taking her treasures from a little girl who loved other people better than she loved herself. But he did not touch any of papa's belongings, and, indeed, did not remain much longer. He grumbled a little when he looked into the drawing-room, saying something to himself about 'folks never 'avin' no consideration for a cove, an' leavin' nothin' portable 'andy, a expectin' of him to carry off seventy-five pound bronze clocks an' marble stattoos;' but though Editha was sorry to see that he appeared annoyed, she did not understand him.

After that, he returned to the pantry and helped himself to some cold game pie, and seemed to enjoy it, and then poured out a tumbler of wine, which Editha thought a great deal to drink at once.

'Yer 'e'lth, my dear,' he said, "an 'appy returns, an' many on 'em. May yer grow up a hornyment to yer sect, an' a comfort to yer respected mar an' par.'

And he threw his head very far back, and drank the very last drop in the glass, which was vulgar, to say the least of it.

Then he took up his bundles of silver and the other articles he had appropriated, and seeing that he was going away, Editha rose from the pantry step.

'Are you going out through the window?' she asked.

'Yes, my dear,' he answered, with a chuckle, 'it's a little 'abit I've got into. I prefers 'em to doors.'

'Well, good-bye,' she said, holding out her hand politely. 'And thank you, my lord.'

She felt it only respectful to say that, even if he had fallen into bad habits and become a burglar. He shook hands with her in quite a friendly manner, and even made a bow.

'Yer welcome, my dear,' he said. 'An' I must hadd that if I ever see a queerer or better behaved little kid, may I be blowed – or, as yer told me it would be more correcter to say, I'll be blown.'

Editha did not know he was joking; she thought he was improving, and that if he had had advantages he might have been a very nice man.

It was astonishing how neatly he slipped through the window; he was gone in a second, and Editha found herself standing alone in the dark, as he had taken his lantern with him.

She groped her way out and up the stairs, and then, for the first time, she began to feel cold and rather weak and strange; it was more like being frightened than any feeling she had had while the burglar was in the house.

'Perhaps, if he had been a very bad burglar, he might have killed me,' she said to herself, trembling a little. 'I am very glad he did not kill me, for – for it would have hurt mamma so, and papa too, when he came back, and they told him.'

Her mamma wakened in the morning with a bright smile.

'Nobody hurt us, Nixie,' she said. 'We are all right, aren't we?'

'Yes, mamma dear,' said Editha.

She did not want to startle her just then, so she said nothing more, and she even said nothing all through the excitement that followed the discovery of the robbery, and indeed said nothing until her papa came home, and then he wondered so at her pale face, and petted her so tenderly, and thought it so strange that nothing but her treasures had been taken from upstairs, that she could keep her secret no longer.

'Papa,' she cried out all at once in a trembling voice, 'I gave them to him myself.'

'You, Nixie! You!' exclaimed her papa, looking alarmed. 'Kitty, the fright has made the poor little thing ill.'

'No, papa,' said Editha, her hands shaking, and the tears rushing into her eyes, she did not know why. 'I heard him, and – I knew mamma would be so frightened, – and it came into my mind to ask him – not to waken her, – and I crept down stairs – and asked him; – and he was not at all unkind though he laughed. And I stayed with him, and – and told him I would give him all my things if he would not touch yours or mamma's. He – he wasn't such a bad burglar, papa, – and he told me he would rather be something more respectable.'

And she hid her face on her papa's shoulder.

'Kitty!' papa cried out. 'Oh, Kitty!'

Then her mamma flew to her and knelt down by her, kissing her and crying aloud:

'Oh, Nixie! if he had hurt you, – if he had hurt you!'

'He knew I was not going to scream, mamma,' said Editha. 'And he knew I was too little to hurt him. I told him so.'

She scarcely understood why mamma cried so much more at this, and why even papa's eyes were wet as he held her close up to his breast.

'It is my fault, Francis,' wept the poor little mamma, 'I have left her too much to herself, and I have not been a wise mother. Oh, to think of her risking her dear little life just to save me from being frightened, and to think of her giving up the things she loves for our sakes. I will be a better mother to her, after this, and take care of her more.'

But I am happy to say that the watch and locket and pearls were not altogether lost, and came back to their gentle little owner in time. About six months after, the burglar was caught, as burglars are apt to be, and after being tried and sentenced to transportation to the penal settlements (which means that he was to be sent away to be a prisoner in a far country), a police officer came one day to see Editha's papa, and he actually came from that burglar, who was in jail and wanted to see Editha for a special reason. Editha's papa took her to see him, and the moment she entered his cell she knew him.

'How do you do, my lord?' she said, in a gentle tone.

"YER 'E'LTH, MY DEAR," HE SAID, "AN' 'APPY RETÜRNS, AN' MANY ON 'EM.   MAY
YER GROW UP A HORNYMENT TO YER SECT, AND A COMFORT TO YER RESPECTED
MAR AN' PAR."

Plate 6   Editha and the Burglar from *Editha's Burglar*, illustrated by R. B. Birch

'Not as lively as common, miss,' he answered, 'in consekence o' the confinement not bein' good for my 'e'lth.'

'None of your chaff,' said the police officer. 'Say what you have to say.'

And then, strange to say the burglar brought forth from under his mattress a box, which he handed to the little girl.

'One o' my wisitors brought 'em in to me this mornin',' he said. 'I thought yer might as well hev 'em. I kep' 'em partly 'cos it was more convenienter, an' partly 'cos I took a fancy to yer. I've seed a many curi's things, sir,' he said to Editha's papa, 'but never nothin' as bloomin' queer as that little kid a-comin' in an' tellin' me she won't 'urt me, nor yet won't scream, and please won't I burgle quietly so as to not disturb her mar. It brought my 'art in my mouth when first I did see her, an' then, lor', how I larft! I almost made up my mind to give her things back to her afore I left, but I didn't quite do that – it was ag'in' human natur'.'

But they were in the box now, and Editha was so glad to see them that she could scarcely speak for a few seconds. Then she thanked the burglar politely.

'I am much obliged to you,' she said, 'and I'm really very sorry you are to be sent so far away. I am sure papa would have tried to help you if he could, though he says he is afraid you would not do for an editor.'

The burglar closed one eye and made a very singular grimace at the police officer, who turned away suddenly and did not look round until Editha had bidden her acquaintance good-bye.

And even this was not quite all. A few weeks later, a box was left for Editha by a very shabby, queer-looking man, who quickly disappeared as soon as he had given it to the servant at the door; and in this box was a very large old-fashioned silver watch, almost as big as a turnip, and inside the lid were scratched these words:

To the little kid from 'er frind and wel wisher,
Lord halgernon hedward halbert de pentonville ide park

# Frank Richard Stockton (1834–1902)

Arguably the most famous of Stockton's fantasies, *The Bee-man of Orn* is set in the nebulous world of folk-tale, and, in comparison with much of his output, is a gentle and contemplative piece. He had assisted Mary Mapes Dodge in editing *Hearth and Home* in 1868 and continued as her assistant on *St. Nicholas* from 1873. He published in both the *Riverside Magazine* and *St. Nicholas* and his collections include *Ting-a-Ling* (1870) – stories about the eponymous fairy – and *The Floating Prince* (1881).

Both *The Bee-man of Orn* and the rather more sombre *The Griffin and the Minor Canon* have been issued in editions illustrated by Maurice Sendak.

In reprinting the story, I have omitted the secondary (and fairly inconsequential) tale of the languid youth and the Ghastly Griffin.

## from *The Bee-man of Orn* (1887)

In the ancient country of Orn there lived an old man who was called the Bee-man, because his whole time was spent in the company of bees. He lived in a small hut, which was nothing more than an immense beehive, for these little creatures had built their honeycombs in every corner of the one room it contained, on the shelves, under the little table, all about the rough bench on which the old man sat, and even about the headboard and along the sides of his low bed.

All day the air of the room was thick with buzzing insects, but this did not interfere in any way with the old Bee-man, who walked in among them, ate his meals, and went to sleep without the slightest fear of being stung.

He had lived with the bees so long, they had become so accustomed to him, and his skin was so tough and hard that the bees no more thought of stinging him than they would of stinging a tree or a stone. A swarm of bees had made their hive in a pocket of his old leathern doublet; and when he put on his coat to take one of his long walks in the forest in search of wild bees' nests, he was very glad to have this hive with him, for, if he did not find any wild honey, he would put his hand in his pocket and take out a piece of a comb for a luncheon. The bees in his pocket worked very industriously, and he was always certain of having something to eat with him wherever he went. He lived principally upon honey; and when he needed bread or meat, he carried some fine combs to a village not far away and bartered them for other food. He was ugly, untidy, shrivelled, and brown. He was poor, and the bees seemed to be his only friends. But, for all that, he was happy and contented; he had all the honey he wanted, and his bees, whom he considered the best company in the world, were as friendly and sociable as they could be, and seemed to increase in number every day.

One day there stopped at the hut of the Bee-man a Junior Sorcerer. This young person, who was a student of magic, was much interested in the Bee-man, whom he had often noticed in his wanderings, and he considered him an admirable subject for study. He had got a great deal of useful practice by trying to find out, by the various rules and laws of sorcery, exactly why the old Bee-man did not happen to be something that he was not, and why he was what he happened to be. He had studied a long time at this matter, and had found out something.

'Do you know,' he said, when the Bee-man came out of his hut, 'that you have been transformed?'

'What do you mean by that?' said the other, much surprised.

'You have surely heard of animals and human beings who have been magically transformed into different kinds of creatures?'

'Yes, I have heard of these things,' said the Bee-man, 'but what have I been transformed from?'

'That is more than I know,' said the Junior Sorcerer. 'But one thing is certain: you ought to be changed back. If you will find out what you have been transformed from, I will see that you are made all right again. Nothing would please me better than to attend to such a case.'

And, having a great many things to study and investigate, the Junior Sorcerer went his way.

This information greatly disturbed the mind of the Bee-man. If he had been changed from something else, he ought to be that other thing, whatever it was. He ran after the young man and overtook him.

'If you know, kind sir,' he said, 'that I have been transformed, you surely are able to tell me what it is I was.'

'No,' said the Junior Sorcerer, 'my studies have not proceeded far enough for that. When I become a Senior I can tell you all about it. But, in the meantime, it will be well for you to try to find out for yourself your original form; and when you have done that, I will get some of the learned Masters of my art to restore you to it. It will be easy enough to do that, but you could not expect them to take the time and trouble to find out what it was.'

And, with these words, he hurried away, and was soon lost to view.

Greatly disturbed, the Bee-man retraced his steps, and went to his hut. Never before had he heard anything which had so troubled him.

'I wonder what I was transformed from?' he thought, seating himself on his rough bench. 'Could it have been a giant, or a powerful prince, or some gorgeous being whom the magicians or the fairies wished to punish? It may be that I was a dog or a horse, or perhaps a fiery dragon or a horrid snake. I hope it was not one of these. But whatever it was, everyone has certainly a right to his original form, and I am resolved to find out mine. I will start early tomorrow morning; and I am sorry now that I have not more pockets to my old doublet so that I might carry more bees and more honey for my journey.'

He spent the rest of the day in making a hive of twigs and straw; and, having transferred to this a number of honeycombs and a colony of bees which had just swarmed, he rose before sunrise the next day; and, having put on his leathern doublet and having bound his new hive to his back, he set forth on his quest, the bees who were to accompany him buzzing around him like a cloud.

As the Bee-man pressed through the little village the people greatly wondered at his queer appearance, with the hive upon his back. 'The Bee-man is going on a long journey this time,' they said; but no one imagined the strange business on which he was bent. About noon he sat down under a tree, near a beautiful meadow covered with blossoms, and ate a little honey. Then he untied his hive and stretched himself out on the grass to rest. As he gazed upon his bees hovering about him, some going out to the blossoms in the sunshine and some returning laden with the sweet pollen, he said to himself, 'They know just what they have to do, and they do it, but alas for me! I know not what I may have to do. And yet, whatever it may be, I am determined to do it. In some way or other I will find out what was my original form, and then I will have myself changed back to it.'

And now again the thought came to him that perhaps his original form might have been something very disagreeable or even horrid.

'But it does not matter,' he said sturdily. 'Whatever I was, that shall I be again. It is not right for anyone to keep a form which does not properly belong to him. I have no doubt I shall discover my original form in the same way that I find the trees in which the wild bees hive. When I first catch sight of a bee tree I am drawn toward it, I know not how. Something says to me: "That is what you are looking for." In the same way I believe I shall find my original form. When I see it, I shall be drawn toward it. Something will say to me: "That is it." '

When the Bee-man was rested, he started off again, and in about an hour he entered a fair domain. Around him were beautiful lawns, grand trees, and lovely gardens; while at a little distance stood the stately palace of the Lord of the Domain. Richly dressed people were walking about or sitting in the shade of the trees and arbours; splendidly equipped horses were waiting for their riders; and everywhere were seen signs of wealth and gaiety.

'I think,' said the Bee-man to himself, 'that I should like to stop here for a time. If it should happen that I was originally like any of these happy creatures, it would please me much.'

He untied his hive and hid it behind some bushes, and, taking off his old doublet, laid that beside it. It would not do to have his bees flying about him if he wished to go among the inhabitants of this fair domain.

For two days the Bee-man wandered about the palace and its grounds, avoiding notice as much as possible but looking at everything. He saw handsome men and lovely ladies; the finest horses, dogs, and cattle that were ever known; beautiful birds in cages, and fishes in crystal globes; and it seemed to him that the best of all living things were here collected.

At the close of the second day the Bee-man said to himself: 'There is one being here toward whom I feel very much drawn and that is the Lord of the Domain. I cannot feel certain that I was once like him, but it would be a very fine thing if it were so; and it seems impossible for me to be drawn toward any other being in the domain when I look upon him, so handsome, rich, and powerful. But I must observe him more closely, and feel more sure of the matter, before applying to the sorcerers to change me back into a lord of a fair domain.'

The next morning the Bee-man saw the Lord of the Domain walking in his gardens. He slipped along the shady paths and followed him, so as to observe him closely and find out if he were really drawn toward this noble and handsome being. The Lord of the Domain walked on for some time, not noticing that the Bee-man was behind him. But suddenly turning, he saw the little old man.

'What are you doing here, you vile beggar?' he cried, and he gave him a kick that sent him into some bushes that grew by the side of the path.

The Bee-man scrambled to his feet and ran as fast as he could to the place where he had hidden his hive and his old doublet.

'If I am certain of anything,' he thought, 'it is that I was never a person who would kick a poor old man. I will leave this place. I was transformed from nothing that I see here.'

He now travelled for a day or two longer, and then he came to a great black mountain near the bottom of which was an opening like the mouth of a cave.

The Bee-man went by himself through a great part of the mountain, and looked into many of its gloomy caves and recesses, recoiling in horror from most of the dreadful monsters who met his eyes. While he was wandering about, an awful roar was heard resounding through the passages of the mountain, and soon there came flapping along an enormous dragon, with body black as night, and wings and tail of fiery red. In his great foreclaws he bore a little baby.

'Horrible!' exclaimed the Bee-man. 'He is taking that little creature to his cave to devour it.'

He saw the dragon enter a cave not far away, and, following, looked in. The dragon was crouched upon the ground with the little baby lying before him. It did not seem to be hurt, but was frightened and crying. The monster was looking upon it with delight, as if he intended to make a dainty meal of it as soon as his appetite should be a little stronger.

'It is too bad!' thought the Bee-man. 'Somebody ought to do something.' And, turning around, he ran away as fast as he could.

He ran through various passages until he came to the spot where he had left his beehive. Picking it up, he hurried back, carrying the hive in his two hands before him. When he reached the cave of the dragon, he looked in and saw the monster still crouched over the weeping child. Without a moment's hesitation, the Bee-man rushed into the cave and threw his hive straight into the face of the dragon. The bees, enraged by the shock, rushed out in an angry crowd and immediately fell upon the head, mouth, eyes, and nose of the dragon. The great monster, astounded by this sudden attack, and driven almost wild by the numberless stings of the bees, sprang back to the farthest corner of his cave, still followed by the bees, at whom he flapped wildly with his great wings and struck with his paws. While the dragon was thus engaged with the bees, the Bee-man rushed forward, and, seizing the child, he hurried away.

[The Bee-man encounters a languid youth, and they go on together]

They soon entered the village, and after walking a short distance, the Youth exclaimed: 'Do you see that woman over there sitting at the door of her house? She has beautiful hair, and she is tearing it all to pieces. She should not be allowed to do that.'

'No,' said the Bee-man. 'Her friends should tie her hands.'

'Perhaps she is the mother of this child,' said the Youth, 'and if you give it to her, she will no longer think of tearing her hair.'

'But,' said the Bee-man, 'you don't really think this is her child?'

'Suppose you go over and see,' said the other.

The Bee-man hesitated a moment, and then he walked toward the woman. Hearing him coming, she raised her head, and when she saw the child she rushed toward it, snatched it into her arms, and screaming with joy she covered it with kisses. Then, with happy tears, she begged to know the story of the rescue of her child, whom she never expected to see again; and she loaded the Bee-man with thanks and blessings. The friends and neighbours gathered around, and there was great rejoicing. The mother urged the Bee-man and the Youth to stay with her, and rest and refresh themselves, which they were glad to do, as they were tired and hungry.

They remained at the cottage all night, and in the afternoon of the next day the Bee-man said to the Youth: 'It may seem an odd thing to you, but never in all my life have I felt myself drawn toward any living being as I am drawn toward this baby. Therefore, I believe that I have been transformed from a baby.'

'Good!' cried the Youth. 'It is my opinion that you have hit the truth. And now would you like to be changed back to your original form?'

'Indeed I would!' said the Bee-man. 'I have the strongest yearning to be what I originally was.'

The Youth, who had now lost every trace of languid feeling, took a great interest in the matter, and early the next morning started off to tell the Junior Sorcerer that the Bee-man had discovered what he had been transformed from and desired to be changed back to it.

The Junior Sorcerer and his learned Masters were filled with delight when they heard this report; and they at once set out for the mother's cottage. And there, by magic arts, the Bee-man was changed back into a baby. The mother was so grateful for what the Bee-man had done for her that she agreed to take charge of this baby and to bring it up as her own.

'It will be a grand thing for him,' said the Junior Sorcerer, 'and I am glad that I studied his case. He will now have a fresh start in life, and will have a chance to become something better than a miserable old man living in a wretched hut with no friends or companions but buzzing bees.'

The Junior Sorcerer and his Masters then returned to their homes, happy in the success of their great performance; and the Youth went back to his home anxious to begin a life of activity and energy.

Years and years afterward, when the Junior Sorcerer had become a Senior and was very old indeed, he passed through the country of Orn, and noticed a small hut about which swarms of bees were flying. He approached it, and, looking in at the door, he saw an old man in a leathern doublet, sitting at a table, eating honey. By his magic art he knew this was the baby which had been transformed from the Bee-man.

'Upon my word!' exclaimed the Sorcerer. 'He has grown up into the same thing again!'

# Palmer Cox (1840–1924)

Although much of the charm of Palmer Cox's *The Brownies* and its twelve companion volumes exists in the detailed drawings that are integrated into the letterpress of each page, the doggerel verse is simple and good-natured. The Brownies' adventures, initially 'At school', 'At the Gymnasium' and so on, but later around the world, owe nothing to magic, but a great deal to Yankee ingenuity. They are uniformly cheerful and non-violent, and demonstrate the way in which the perception of childhood and its needs was radically changing.

On the opening page, Cox wrote: 'Brownies, like fairies and goblins, are imaginary little sprites, who are supposed to delight in harmless pranks, and helpful deeds. They work and sport while weary households sleep, and never allow themselves to be seen by mortal eyes.'

Cox was born in Canada and worked as an illustrator before beginning his contributions to *St. Nicholas* in 1880.

## from *The Brownies: their Book* (1887)

### THE BROWNIES' GOOD WORK

One time, while Brownies passed around
An honest farmer's piece of ground,
They paused to view the garden fair
And fields of grain that needed care.
'My friends,' said one who often spoke
About the ways of human folk,
'Now here 's a case in point, I claim,
Where neighbors scarce deserve the name:
This farmer on his back is laid
With broken ribs and shoulder-blade,
Received, I hear, some weeks ago;
While at the village here below,
He checked a running team, to save
Some children from an early grave.
Now overripe his harvest stands
In waiting for the reaper's hands;
The piece of wheat we lately passed
Is shelling out at every blast;
Those pumpkins in that corner plot
Begin to show the signs of rot;
The mold has fastened on their skin,
The ripest ones are caving in,
And soon the pig in yonder sty
With scornful grunt would pass them by.
His Early Rose potatoes there
Are much in need of light and air;
The turnip withers where it lies,
The beet and carrot want to rise.
'Oh, pull us up!' they seem to cry
To every one that passes by;
'The frost will finish our repose,
The grubs are working at our toes;
Unless you come and save us soon,

We'll not be worth a picayune!'
The corn is breaking from the stalk,
The hens around the hill can walk,
And with their ever ready bill
May pick the kernels at their will.
His neighbors are a sordid crowd,
Who've such a shameful waste allowed;
So wrapped in self some men can be,
Beyond their purse they seldom see;
'T is left for us to play the friend
And here a helping hand extend.
But as the wakeful chanticleer
Is crowing in the stable near,
Too little of the present night
Is left to set the matter right.
'To-morrow eve, at that dark hour
When birds grow still in leafy bower
And bats forsake the ruined pile
To exercise their wings awhile,

ONE time, while Brownies passed around
An honest farmer's piece of ground,
They paused to view the garden fair
And fields of grain that needed care.
"My friends," said one who often spoke
About the ways of human folk,
"Now here 's a case in point, I claim,
Where neighbors scarce deserve the name:
This farmer on his back is laid
With broken ribs and shoulder-blade,
Received, I hear, some weeks ago;
While at the village here below,
He checked a running team, to save
Some children from an early grave.
Now overripe his harvest stands
In waiting for the reaper's hands;
The piece of wheat we lately passed
Is shelling out at every blast;

Plate 7   'The Brownies' Good Work' from *The Brownies: Their Book*, illustration by Palmer Cox.
Courtesy of the Trustees of the Victoria and Albert Museum, London

In yonder shady grove we'll meet,
With all our active force complete,
Prepared to give this farmer aid
With basket, barrel, hook, and spade.
But, ere we part, one caution more:
Let some invade a druggist's store,
And bring along a coated pill;
We'll dose the dog to keep him still.
For barking dogs, however kind,
Can oft disturb a Brownie's mind.'
– When next the bat of evening flew,
And drowsy things of day withdrew,
When beetles droned across the lea,
And turkeys sought the safest tree
To form aloft a social row
And criticise the fox below, –
Then cunning Brownies might be seen
Advancing from the forest green;
Now jumping fences, as they ran,
Now crawling through (a safer plan);
Now keeping to the roads awhile,
Now 'cutting corners,' country style;
Some bearing hoes, and baskets more,
Some pushing barrows on before,
While others, swinging sickles bright,
Seemed eager for the grain in sight.
But in advance of all the throng
Three daring Brownies moved along,
Whose duty was to venture close
And give the barking dog his dose.
Now soon the work was under way,
Each chose the part he was to play:
While some who handled hoes the best
Brought 'Early Roses' from their nest,
To turnip-tops some laid their hands,
More plied the hook, or twisted bands.
And soon the sheaves lay piled around,
Like heroes on disputed ground.
Now let the eye turn where it might,
A pleasing prospect was in sight;
For garden ground or larger field
Alike a busy crowd revealed:
Some pulling carrots from their bed,
Some bearing burdens on their head,
Or working at a fever heat
While prying out a monster beet.
Now here two heavy loads have met,
And there a barrow has upset,
While workers every effort strain
The rolling pumpkins to regain;
And long before the stars withdrew,
The crop was safe, the work was through.
In shocks the corn, secure and good,
Now like a Sioux encampment stood;
The wheat was safely stowed away;
In bins the 'Early Roses' lay,
While carrots, turnips, beets, and all
Received attention, great and small.

When morning dawned, no sight or sound
Of friendly Brownies could be found;
And when at last old Towser broke
The spell, and from his slumber woke,
He rushed around, believing still
Some mischief lay behind the pill.
But though the fields looked bare and strange,
His mind could hardly grasp the change.
And when the farmer learned at morn
That safe from harm were wheat and corn,
That all his barley, oats, and rye
Were in the barn, secure and dry,
That carrots, beets, and turnips round
Were safely taken from the ground,
The honest farmer thought, of course,
His neighbors had turned out in force
While helpless on the bed he lay,
And kindly stowed his crop away.
But when he thanked them for their aid,
And hoped they yet might be repaid
For acting such a friendly part,
His words appeared to pierce each heart;
For well they knew that other hands
Than theirs had laid his grain in bands,
That other backs had bent in toil
To save the products of the soil.
And then they felt as such folk will
Who fail to nobly act, until
More earnest helpers, stepping in,
Do all the praise and honor win.

# Oscar Wilde (1854–1900)

It is somewhat surprising that the fairy-tale met with such disapproval in the early part of the nineteenth century from evangelical writers, for it is (especially in its 'modern' or 'constructed' form) an ideal vehicle for metaphors and secondary meanings, if not actual moralizing. The folk-tales from which the genre sprang were concerned with specific issues of life, death, fear, sexuality and power, not 'simply' the telling of tales.

Oscar Wilde's venture into the genre was published at a particularly rich period in British interest in the fairy-tale; for example, Andrew Lang began his series of twelve 'colour' fairy books with *The Blue Fairy Book* in 1889 and Joseph Jacobs published *English Fairy Tales* in 1890. In original fantasy and fairy-tale writing, Molesworth, Ewing and Nesbit were using the tales tacitly to explore the female place in the world, and there are examples from Laurence Houseman, Kenneth Grahame (although probably not intended for children) and others, which are implicit critiques of Victorian society.

Wilde's exercises in what John Goldthwaite dismissed as 'quasi-religious bathos' are, in Jack Zipes' (1999) opinion 'finely chiselled gems that have been recognised as among the best of the fairy-tale genre'. They were written, as Wilde put it, 'partly for children, and partly for those who have kept the childlike faculties of wonder and joy', and yet there is little joy in *The Happy Prince*. It is politically motivated, setting out to be an exemplar of both Wilde's artistic–socialist principles and his personal preoccupations with lack of fulfilment, and self-sacrifice.

In *The Selfish Giant* at least, Wilde mixes (if a little crudely) folk-tale and Christianity to provide a satisfactory ending for believers. A sceptic might well argue that children's literature, so often used by the religious Right for their own purposes, was now being hijacked by the aesthetic Left for theirs.

## from *The Happy Prince* (1888)

### THE SELFISH GIANT

Every afternoon, as they were coming from school, the children used to go and play in the Giant's garden.

It was a large lovely garden, with soft green grass. Here and there over the grass stood beautiful flowers like stars, and there were twelve peach-trees that in the spring-time broke out into delicate blossoms of pink and pearl, and in the autumn bore rich fruit. The birds sat on the trees and sang so sweetly that the children used to stop their games in order to listen to them. 'How happy we are here!' they cried to each other.

One day the Giant came back. He had been to visit his friend the Cornish ogre, and had stayed with him for seven years. After the seven years were over he had said all that he had to say, for his conversation was limited, and he determined to return to his own castle. When he arrived he saw the children playing in the garden.

'What are you doing here?' he cried in a very gruff voice, and the children ran away.

'My own garden is my own garden,' said the Giant; 'anyone can understand that, and I will allow nobody to play in it but myself.' So he built a high wall all round it, and put up a notice-board.

TRESPASSERS
WILL BE
PROSECUTED

He was a very selfish Giant.

The poor children had now nowhere to play. They tried to play on the road, but the road was very dusty and full of hard stones, and they did not like it. They used to wander round the high walls when their lessons were over, and talk about the beautiful garden inside. 'How happy we were there!' they said to each other.

Then the Spring came, and all over the country there were little blossoms and little birds. Only in the garden of the Selfish Giant it was still winter. The birds did not care to sing in it as there were no children, and the trees forgot to blossom. Once a beautiful flower put its head out from the grass, but when it saw the notice-board it was so sorry for the children that it slipped back into the ground again, and went off to sleep. The only people who were pleased were the Snow and the Frost. 'Spring has forgotten this garden,' they cried, 'so we will live here all the year round.' The Snow covered up the grass with her great white cloak, and the Frost painted all the trees silver. Then they invited the North Wind to stay with them, and he came. He was wrapped in furs, and he roared all day about the garden, and blew the chimney-pots down. 'This is a delightful spot,' he said, 'we must ask the Hail on a visit.' So the Hail came. Every day for three hours he rattled on the roof of the castle till he broke most of the slates, and then he ran round and round the garden as fast as he could go. He was dressed in grey, and his breath was like ice.

'I cannot understand why the Spring is so late in coming,' said the Selfish Giant, as he sat at the window and looked out at his cold, white garden; 'I hope there will be a change in the weather.'

But the Spring never came, nor the Summer. The Autumn gave golden fruit to every garden, but to the Giant's garden she gave none. 'He is too selfish,' she said. So it was always winter there, and the North Wind and the Hail, and the Frost, and the Snow danced about through the trees.

One morning the Giant was lying awake in bed when he heard some lovely music. It sounded so sweet to his ears that he thought it must be the King's musicians passing by. It was really only a little linnet singing outside his window, but it was so long since he had heard a bird sing in his garden that it seemed to him to be the most beautiful music in the world. Then the Hail stopped dancing over his head, and the North Wind ceased roaring, and a delicious perfume came to him through the open casement. 'I believe the Spring has come at last,' said the Giant; and he jumped out of bed and looked out.

What did he see?

He saw a most wonderful sight. Through a little hole in the wall the children had crept in, and they were sitting in the branches of the trees. In every tree that he could see there was a little child. And the trees were so glad to have the children back again that they had covered themselves with blossoms, and were waving their arms gently above the children's heads. The birds were flying about and twittering with delight, and the flowers were looking up through the green grass and laughing. It was a lovely scene, only in one corner it was still winter. It was the farthest corner of the garden, and in it was standing a little boy. He was so small that he could not reach up to the branches of the tree, and he was wandering all round it, crying bitterly. The poor tree was still covered with frost and snow, and the North Wind was blowing and roaring above it. 'Climb up! little boy,' said the Tree, and it bent its branches down as low as it could; but the boy was too tiny.

And the Giant's heart melted as he looked out. 'How selfish I have been!' he said: 'now I know why the Spring would not come here. I will put that poor little boy on the top of the tree, and then I will knock down the wall, and my garden shall be the children's playground for ever and ever.' He was really very sorry for what he had done.

So he crept downstairs and opened the front door quite softly, and went out into the garden. But when the children saw him they were so frightened that they all ran away, and the garden became winter again. Only the little boy did not run for his eyes were so full of tears that he did not see the Giant coming. And the Giant stole up behind him and took him gently in his hand, and put him up into the tree. And the tree broke at once into blossom, and the birds came and sang on it, and the little boy stretched out his two arms and flung them round the Giant's neck, and kissed him. And the other children when they saw that the Giant was not wicked any longer, came running back, and with them came the Spring. 'It is your garden now, little children,' said the Giant, and he took a great axe and knocked down the wall. And when the people were going to market at twelve o'clock they found the Giant playing with the children in the most beautiful garden they had ever seen.

All day long they played, and in the evening they came to the Giant to bid him good-bye.

'But where is your little companion?' he said: 'the boy I put into the tree.' The Giant loved him the best because he had kissed him.

'We don't know,' answered the children: 'he has gone away.'

'You must tell him to be sure and come tomorrow,' said the Giant. But the children said that they did not know where he lived and had never seen him before; and the Giant felt very sad.

Every afternoon, when school was over, the children came and played with the Giant. But the little boy whom the Giant loved was never seen again. The Giant was very kind to all the children, yet he longed for his first little friend, and often spoke of him. 'How I would like to see him!' he used to say.

Years went over, and the Giant grew very old and feeble. He could not play about any more, so he sat in a huge armchair, and watched the children at their games, and admired his garden. 'I have many beautiful flowers,' he said; 'but the children are the most beautiful flowers of all.'

One winter morning he looked out of his window as he was dressing. He did not hate the Winter now, for he knew that it was merely the Spring asleep, and that the flowers were resting.

Suddenly he rubbed his eyes in wonder, and looked and looked. It certainly was a marvellous sight. In the farthest corner of the garden was a tree quite covered with lovely white blossoms. Its branches were golden, and silver fruit hung down from them, and underneath it stood the little boy he had loved.

Downstairs ran the Giant in great joy, and out into the garden. He hastened across the grass, and came near to the child. And when he came quite close his face grew red with anger, and he said, 'Who hath dared to wound thee?' For on the palms of the child's hands were the prints of two nails, and the prints of two nails were on the little feet.

'Who hath dared to wound thee?' cried the Giant, 'tell me, that I may take my big sword and slay him.'

'Nay,' answered the child: 'but these are the wounds of Love.'

'Who art thou?' said the Giant, and a strange awe fell on him, and he knelt before the little child.

And the child smiled on the Giant, and said to him, 'You let me play once in your garden, today you shall come with me to my garden, which is Paradise.'

And when the children ran in that afternoon, they found the Giant lying dead under the tree, all covered with white blossoms.

# Thomas Nelson Page (1853–1922)

Edmund Wilson once observed, rather unkindly, that 'It was hard to make the Civil War seem cosy, but Thomas Nelson Page did his best'. Page, from Virginia, certainly attempted to produce a sympathetic account of the South and the Confederacy, and the view given in *Two Little Confederates* seems to be well balanced. The book was originally another *St. Nicholas* serial.

The two little Confederates are Frank and Willy, who live in Virginia; for part of the book, General Marshall and Hugh, their elder brother (who is seventeen), are in hiding from the Yankees. In the first of these extracts, what the twenty-first century observer might regard as the improbable idea of the benevolence of slavery is stressed: Lucy Ann fools the Yankees by *pretending* to wish to be free. In the second, Frank and Willy have been visiting Hugh and the General when they are caught by Yankee troops. The idea of common decency on both sides is emphasized, although the superior courtesy of the Southerners (quite apart from the 'stiff-upper-lip' behaviour of the boys) is quietly implied.

## from *Two Little Confederates* (1888)

## CHAPTER XIV

The next day was Sunday. The General and Hugh had but one day to stay. They were to leave at day-break the following morning. They thoroughly enjoyed their holiday; at least the boys knew that Hugh did. They had never known him so affable with them. They did not see much of the General, after breakfast. He seemed to like to stay 'stuck up in the house' all the time, talking to Cousin Belle; the boys thought this due to his lameness. Something had occurred, the boys didn't understand just what; but the General was on an entirely new footing with all of them, and their Cousin Belle was in some way concerned in the change. She did not any longer run from the General, and it seemed to them as though everyone acted as if he belonged to her. The boys did not altogether like the state of affairs. That afternoon, however, he and their Cousin Belle let the boys go out walking with them, and he was just as hearty as he could be; he made them tell him all about capturing the deserter, and about catching the hogs, and everything they did. They told him all about their 'Robbers' Cave,' down in the woods near where an old house had stood. It was between two ravines near a spring they had found. They had fixed up the 'cave' with boards and old pieces of carpet 'and everything,' and they told him, as a secret, how to get to it through the pines without leaving a trail. He had to give the holy pledge of the 'Brotherhood' before this could be divulged to him; but he took it with a solemnity which made the boys almost forgive the presence of their Cousin Belle. It was a little awkward at first that she was present; but as the 'Constitution' provided only as to admitting men to the mystic knowledge, saying nothing about women, this difficulty was, on the General's suggestion, passed over, and the boys fully explained the location of the spot, and how to get there by turning off abruptly from the path through the big woods right at the pine thicket, – and all the rest of the way.

''Tain't a "sure-enough" cave,' explained Willy; 'but it's 'most as good as one. The old rock fire-place is just like a cave.'

'The gullies are so deep you can't get there except that one way,' declared Frank.

'Even the Yankees could n't find you there,' asserted Willy.

'I don't believe anybody could, after that; but I trust they will never have to try,' laughed their Cousin Belle, with an anxious look in her bright eyes at the mere thought.

That night they were at supper, about eight o'clock, when something out-of-doors attracted the attention of the party around the table. It was a noise, – a something indefinable, but the talk and mirth stopped suddenly, and everybody listened.

There was a call, and the hurried steps of some one running, just outside the door, and Lucy Ann burst into the room, her face ashy pale.

'The yard's full o' mens – Yankees,' she gasped, just as the General and Hugh rose from the table.

'How many are there?' asked both gentlemen.

'They's all "roun" the house ev'y which a-way.'

The General looked at his sweetheart. She came to his side with a cry.

'Go up stairs to the top of the house,' called the boys' mother.

'We can hide you; come with us,' said the boys.

'Go up the back way, Frank 'n' Willy, to you-all's den,' whispered Lucy Ann.

'That's where we are going,' said the boys as she went out.

'You all come on!' This to the General and Hugh.

'The rest of you take your seats,' said the boys' mother.

All this had occupied only a few seconds. The soldiers followed the boys out by a side-door and dashed up the narrow stairs to the second-story just as a thundering knocking came at the front door. It was as dark as pitch, for candles were too scarce to burn more than one at a time.

'You run back,' said Hugh to the boys, as they groped along. 'There are too many of us. I know the way.'

But it was too late; the noise down stairs told that the enemy was already in the house!

As the soldiers left the supper-room, the boys' mother had hastily removed two plates from the places and set two chairs back against the wall; she made the rest fill up the spaces, so that there was nothing to show that the two men had been there.

She had hardly taken her seat again, when the sound of heavy footsteps at the door announced the approach of the enemy. She herself rose and went to the door; but it was thrown open before she reached it and an officer in full Federal uniform strode in, followed by several men.

The commander was a tall young fellow, not older than the General. The lady started back somewhat startled, and there was a confused chorus of exclamations of alarm from the rest of those at the table. The officer, finding himself in the presence of ladies, removed his cap with a polite bow.

'I hope, madam, that you ladies will not be alarmed,' he said. 'You need be under no apprehension, I assure you.' Even while speaking, his eye had taken a hasty survey of the room.

'We desire to see General Marshall, who is at present in this house, and I am sorry to have to include your son in my requisition. We know that they are here, and if they are given us, I promise you that nothing shall be disturbed.'

'You appear to be so well instructed that I can add little to your information,' said the mistress of the house, haughtily. 'I am glad to say, however, that I hardly think you will find them.'

'Madam, I know they are here,' said the young soldier positively, but with great politeness. 'I have positive information to that effect. They arrived last evening and have not left since. Their horses are still in the stable. I am sorry to be forced to do violence to my feelings, but I must search the house. Come, men.'

'I doubt not you have found their horses,' began the lady, but she was interrupted by Lucy Ann, who entered at the moment with a plate of fresh corn-cakes, and caught the last part of the sentence.

'Come along, Mister,' she said, 'I 'll show you myself,' and she set down her plate, took the candle from the table, and walked to the door, followed by the soldiers.

'Lucy Ann!' exclaimed her mistress; but she was too much amazed at the girl's conduct to say more.

'I know whar dey is!' Lucy Ann continued, taking no notice of her mistress. They heard her say, as she was shutting the door, 'Y' all come with me; I 'feared they gone; ef they ain't, I know whar they is!'

'Open every room,' said the officer.

'Oh, yes, sir; I gwine ketch 'em for you,' she said, eagerly opening first one door, and then the other, 'that is, ef they ain' gone. I mighty 'feared they gone. I seen 'em goin' out the back way about a little while befo' you all come, – but I thought they might 'a' come back. Mister, ken y' all teck me 'long with you when you go?' she asked the officer, in a low voice. 'I want to be free.'

'I don't know; we can some other time, if not now. We are going to set you all free.'

'Oh, glory! Come 'long, Mister; let's ketch 'em. They ain't heah, but I know whar dey is.'

The soldiers closely examined every place where it was possible a man could be concealed, until they had been over all the lower part of the house.

Lucy Ann stopped. 'Dey's gone!' she said positively.

The officer motioned to her to go up stairs.

'Yes, sir, I wuz jes' goin' tell you we jes' well look upstairs, too,' she said, leading the way, talking all the time, and shading the flickering candle with her hand.

The little group, flat on the floor against the wall in their dark retreat, could now hear her voice distinctly. She was speaking in a confidential undertone, as if afraid of being overheard.

'I wonder I did n't have sense to get somebody to watch 'em when they went out,' they heard her say.

'She's betrayed us!' whispered Hugh.

The General merely said, 'Hush,' and laid his hand firmly on the nearest boy to keep him still. Lucy Ann led the soldiers into the various chambers one after another. At last she opened the next room, and, through the wall, the men in hiding heard the soldiers go in and walk about.

They estimated that there were at least half-a-dozen.

'Is n't there a garret?' asked one of the searching party.

'Nor, sir, 't ain't no garret, jes' a loft; but they ain't up there,' said Lucy Ann's voice.

'We'll look for ourselves.' They came out of the room. 'Show us the way.'

'Look here, if you tell us a lie, we'll hang you!'

The voice of the officer was very stern.

'I ain' gwine tell you no lie, Mister. What you reckon I wan' tell you lie for? Dey ain' in the garret, I know, – Mister, please don't p'int dem things at me. I 's 'feared o' dem things,' said the girl in a slightly whimpering voice; 'I gwine show you.'

She came straight down the passage toward the recess where the fugitives were huddled, the men after her, their heavy steps echoing through the house. The boys were trembling violently. The light, as the searchers came nearer, fell on the wall, crept along it, until it lighted up the whole alcove, except where they lay. The boys held their breath. They could hear their hearts thumping.

Lucy Ann stepped into the recess with her candle, and looked straight at them.

'They ain't in here,' she exclaimed, suddenly putting her hand up before the flame, as if to prevent it flaring, thus throwing the alcove once more into darkness. 'The trap-door to the garret 's 'roun' that a-way,' she said to the soldiers, still keeping her position at the narrow entrance, as if to let them pass. When they had all passed, she followed them.

The boys began to wriggle with delight, but the General's strong hand kept them still.

Naturally, the search in the garret proved fruitless, and the hiding-party heard the squad swearing over their ill-luck as they came back; while Lucy Ann loudly lamented not having sent some one to follow the fugitives, and made a number of suggestions as to where they had gone, and the probability of catching them if the soldiers went at once in pursuit.

'Did you look in here?' asked a soldier approaching the alcove.

'Yes, sir; they ain't in there.' She snuffed the candle out suddenly with her fingers. 'Oh, oh! – my light done gone out! Mind! Let me go in front and show you the way,' she said; and, pressing before, she once more led them along the passage.

'Mind yo' steps; ken you see?' she asked.

They went down stairs, while Lucy Ann gave them minute directions as to how they might catch 'Marse Hugh an' the Gen'l' at a certain place a half-mile from the house (an unoccupied quarter), which she carefully described.

A further investigation ensued downstairs, but in a little while the searchers went out of the house. Their tone had changed since their disappointment, and loud threats floated up the dark stairway to the prisoners still crouching in the little recess.

In a few minutes the boys' Cousin Belle came rushing up stairs.

'Now's your time! Come quick,' she called; 'they will be back directly. Is n't she an angel!' The whole party sprang to their feet, and ran down to the lower floor.

'Oh, we were so frightened!' 'Don't let them see you.' 'Make haste,' were the exclamations that greeted them as the two soldiers said their good-byes and prepared to leave the house.

'Go out by the side-door; that's your only chance. It's pitch-dark, and the bushes will hide you. But where are you going?'

'We are going to the boys' cave,' said the General, buckling on his pistol; 'I know the way, and we'll get away as soon as these fellows leave, if we cannot before.'

'God bless you!' said the ladies, pushing them away in dread of the enemy's return.

'Come on, General,' called Hugh in an undertone. The General was lagging behind a minute to say good-bye once more. He stooped suddenly and kissed the boys' Cousin Belle before them all.

'Good-bye. God bless you!' and he followed Hugh out of the window into the darkness. The girl burst into tears and ran up to her room.

A few seconds afterward the house was once more filled with the enemy, growling at their ill-luck in having so narrowly missed the prize.

'We'll catch 'em yet,' said the leader.

## Chapter XVI

[Frank and Willy have been visiting Hugh and the General.]
After crossing the gully, and walking on through the woods for what they thought a safe distance, they turned into the path.

They were talking very merrily about the General and Hugh and their friend Mills, and were discussing some romantic plan for the recapture of their horses from the enemy, when they came out of the path into the road, and found themselves within twenty yards of a group of Federal soldiers, quietly sitting on their horses, evidently guarding the road.

The sight of the blue-coats made the boys jump. They would have crept back, but it was too late – they caught the eye of the man nearest them. They ceased talking as suddenly as birds in the trees stop chirruping when the hawk sails over; and when one Yankee called to them, in a stern tone, 'Halt there!' and started to come toward them, their hearts were in their mouths.

'Where are you boys going?' he asked, as he came up to them.

'Going home.'

'Where do you belong?'

'Over there – at Oakland,' pointing in the direction of their home, which seemed suddenly to have moved a thouand miles away.

'Where have you been?' The other soldiers had come up now.

'Been down this way.' The boys' voices were never so meek before. Each reply was like an apology.

'Been to see your brother?' asked one who had not spoken before – a pleasant looking fellow. The boys looked at him. They were paralyzed by dread of the approaching question.

'Now, boys, we know where you have been,' said a small fellow, who wore a yellow chevron on his arm. He had a thin moustache and a sharp nose, and rode a wiry, dull sorrel horse. 'You may just as well tell us all about it. We know you 've been to see 'em, and we are going to make you carry us where they are.'

'No, we ain't,' said Frank, doggedly.

Willy expressed his determination also.

'If you don't it's going to be pretty bad for you,' said the little corporal. He gave an order to two of the men, who sprang from their horses, and, catching Frank, swung him up behind another cavalryman. The boy's face was very pale, but he bit his lip.

'Go ahead,' – continued the corporal to a number of his men, who started down the path. 'You four men remain here till we come back,' he said to the men on the ground, and to two others on horseback. 'Keep him here,' jerking his thumb toward Willy, whose face was already burning with emotion.

'I 'm going with Frank,' said Willy. 'Let me go.' This to the man who had hold of him by the arm. 'Frank, make him let me go,' he shouted, bursting into tears, and turning on his captor with all his little might.

'Willy, he's not goin' to hurt you, – don't you tell!' called Frank, squirming until he dug his heels so into the horse's flanks that the horse began to kick up.

'Keep quiet, Johnny; he 's not goin' to hurt him,' said one of the men, kindly. He had a brown beard and shining white teeth.

They rode slowly down the narrow path, the dragoon holding Frank by the leg. Deep down in the woods, beyond a small branch, the path forked.

'Which way?' asked the corporal, stopping and addressing Frank.

Frank set his mouth tight and looked him in the eyes.

'Which is it?' the corporal repeated.

'I ain't going to tell,' said he, firmly.

THE BOY FACED HIS CAPTOR, WHO HELD A STRAP IN ONE HAND.

Plate 8  'The Bay Faced His Capton', from *Two Little Confederates*, illustration by E. W. Kemble. Courtesy of the Trustees of the Victoria and Albert Museum, London

'Look here, Johnny; we 've got you, and we are going to make you tell us; so you might just as well do it, easy. If you don't, we 're goin' to make you.'

The boy said nothing.

'You men dismount. Stubbs, hold the horses.' He himself dismounted, and three others did the same, giving their horses to a fourth.

'Get down' – this to Frank and the soldier behind whom he was riding. The soldier dismounted, and the boy slipped off after him and faced his captor, who held a strap in one hand.

'Are you goin' to tell us?' he asked.

'No.'

'Don't you know?' He came a step nearer, and held the strap forward. There was a long silence. The boy's face paled perceptibly, but took on a look as if the proceedings were indifferent to him.

'If you say you don't know' – said the man, hesitating in face of the boy's resolution. 'Don't you know where they are?'

'Yes, I know; but I ain't goin' to tell you,' said Frank, bursting into tears.

'The little Johnny's game,' said the soldier who had told him the others were not going to hurt Willy. The corporal said something to this man in an undertone, to which he replied:

'You can try, but it is n't going to do any good. I don't half like it, anyway.'

Frank had stopped crying after his first outburst.

'If you don't tell, we are going to shoot you,' said the little soldier, drawing his pistol.

The boy shut his mouth close, and looked straight at the corporal. The man laid down his pistol, and, seizing Frank, drew his hands behind him, and tied them.

'Get ready, men,' he said, as he drew the boy aside to a small tree, putting him with his back to it.

Frank thought his hour had come. He thought of his mother and Willy, and wondered if the soldiers would shoot Willy, too. His face twitched and grew ghastly white. Then he thought of his father, and of how proud he would be of his son's bravery when he should hear of it. This gave him strength.

'The knot – hurts my hands,' he said.

The man leaned over and eased it a little.

'I was n't crying because I was scared,' said Frank.

The kind looking fellow turned away.

'Now, boys, get ready,' said the corporal, taking up his pistol.

How large it looked to Frank. He wondered where the bullets would hit him, and if the wounds would bleed, and whether he would be left alone all night out there in the woods, and if his mother would come and kiss him.

'I want to say my prayers,' he said, faintly.

The soldier made some reply which he could not hear, and the man with the beard started forward; but just then all grew dark before his eyes.

Next, he thought he must have been shot, for he felt wet about his face, and was lying down. He heard some one say, 'He's coming to;' and another replied, 'Thank God!'

He opened his eyes. He was lying beside the little branch with his head in the lap of the big soldier with the beard, and the little corporal was leaning over him throwing water in his face from a cap. The others were standing around.

'What's the matter?' asked Frank.

'That's all right,' said the little corporal, kindly. 'We were just a-foolin' a bit with you, Johnny.'

'We never meant to hurt you,' said the other. 'You feel better now?'

'Yes, where 's Willy?' He was too tired to move.

'He 's all right. We 'll take you to him.'

'Am I shot?' asked Frank.

'No! Do you think we 'd have touched a hair of your head – and you such a brave little fellow? We were just trying to scare you a bit and carried it too far, and you got a little faint, – that 's all.'

The voice was so kindly that Frank was encouraged to sit up.

'Can you walk now?' asked the corporal, helping him and steadying him as he rose to his feet.

'I'll take him,' said the big fellow, and before the boy could move, he had stooped, taken Frank in his arms, and was carrying him back toward the place where they had left Willy, while the others followed after with the horses.

'I can walk,' said Frank.

'No, I'll carry you, b-bless your heart!'

The boy did not know that the big dragoon was looking down at the light hair resting on his arm, and that while he trod the Virginia wood-path, in fancy he was home in Delaware; or that the pressure the boy felt from his strong arms, was a caress given for the sake of another boy far away on the Brandywine. A little while before they came in sight Frank asked to be put down.

The soldier gently set him on his feet, and before he let him go kissed him.

'I've got a curly-headed fellow at home, just the size of you,' he said softly.

Frank saw that his eyes were moist. 'I hope you'll get safe back to him,' he said.

'God grant it!' said the soldier.

When they reached the squad at the gate, they found Willy still in much distress on Frank's account; but he wiped his eyes when his brother reappeared, and listened with pride to the soldiers' praise of Frank's 'grit' as they called it. When they let the boys go, the little corporal wished Frank to accept a five-dollar gold piece; but he politely declined it.

# Edward B. Kennedy (?–?)

*Blacks and Bushrangers* is a fascinating combination of the new world and the old, in terms of both structure and content. Structurally it is a traditional British adventure story: a boy is caught poaching (in the New Forest) and he escapes abroad (his brother stows away to be with him). They are shipwrecked (with their dog, Jumper), have adventures in the wild, live with the natives and prove their manhood. Returning to more civilized areas, they meet the heroine who is kidnapped by outlaws; they rescue her (with the help of the natives). And there is a conventional ending: the last chapter is described on the contents page thus: 'Back in the old Forest – Jumper's last home – Return of our hero and heroine for good and all to Bulinda Creek – Conclusion and farewell.' In content, there is a detailed picture of the Australian outback and an empathetic view of the Aboriginal people (although the author could not avoid a certain paternalistic racial superiority).

Kennedy, who came to Australia in 1864, also wrote an autobiographical novel, *Out of the Groove: A Romance of Aus-*
*tralian Life* (1892) and *The Black Police of Queensland* (1902), which describes his varied experiences across Australia. In the Preface to *Blacks and Bushrangers* he makes it clear that the book is based on fact, the knowledge of Aborigine customs coming from 'one "Jimmy Morrill"' who 'had been wrecked on the northern coast of Queensland' and had been protected and cared for by tribes for seventeen years. Indeed, Kennedy establishes the veracity of his account by his description of the voyage to Australia as mundane: 'The emigrant-ship has no battles to recount, no running down of slavers.... The emigrant-ship, though just useful in her line, runs the same humdrum voyage year after year, unrelieved by any adventure.... In fact, a little world, of no interest scarcely to any one excepting those on board.'

In the chapter reprinted here, Tim and Mat, having been shipwrecked, encounter the native people. The incident with the giant clam shell, *Tridacna gigas*, Kennedy insists, is true.

## from *Blacks and Bushrangers: Adventures in Queensland* (1889)

### CHAPTER V

The island – The gigantic cockle-shell – Amongst the blacks – The *Corroboree*

After getting out of the water, Mat and Tim remained stretched on the sand without moving a limb, enjoying the sense of perfect security from the sea; but at length they felt that they must commence to look for water, their thirst was so great after all the salt water that they had swallowed. On trying to rise, they found they could scarcely stand, so numbed and weary were their limbs; but by stamping and running, they caused the blood to flow through their veins, and were thus enabled to start on a small voyage of discovery.

The island, as it proved to be, consisted of large rocks full of caves with a few bushes and ferns growing here and there. There was no lack of water in the crevices of the rocks, and astringent though it was, it seemed like nectar to the thirsty lads. In one of the caves they found that the sand was deep, dry, and even warm, and in this spot they determined to take a good long rest, which they felt themselves sadly in need of. Tim had proceeded to explore one of these caves, when Mat heard him call, 'Look here,' and proceeding to the spot, found his brother examining the floor of the cave, which was covered with oyster shells; a further search showed the remains of several small fires with more shells round them.

'Some one has had a good feast here, Mat; let us have a nap, and then *we'll* look for oysters.'

So without more ado, they buried themselves in the sand up to their necks, and fell into a sound sleep.

How long they slept neither of them knew, but Mat was awakened by a cold feeling about his nose, and jumping up, found to his astonishment and delight, his faithful dog, which greeted him with short, sharp barks of delight; the noise woke Tim, who perceiving his favourite, seized him, and the two rolled over together with joy. They found to their surprise that Jumper's coat was quite dry, and on emerging from the cave, perceived that whilst they had been sleeping, the storm had abated, and the sun was now shining, also that the tide had run out, leaving their island connected with the mainland by a spit of sand. The tracks of the dog plainly showed that, having landed farther down the coast, he had been trying along the edge of the water for his masters, until led to them by this streak of sand.

Congratulating themselves upon the recovery of their dog, which they had given up for lost, Mat and Tim proceeded to gather a supply of oysters – these being rock oysters were easily detached by the tap of a stone.

In the pools, left by the receding tide, amongst the rocks and coral, many kinds of fish were imprisoned, and there were quantities of crabs in a muddy belt of mangroves, so that there was no lack of food, which, however, had to be eaten raw.

'We've always eaten oysters raw,' quoth Mat, 'and why not fish that swim?'

But Tim was too much engaged to answer, he had seen some large mullet endeavouring to escape out of a channel in the rocks, and was wading about amongst the green weed, piling stones across the outlet of this creek, previous to pursuing the fish, when suddenly under water, in a cleft of the rocks, he felt his foot seized, and held in a vice-like grasp. The shock nearly threw him down, but recovering himself, he shouted, –

'Mat! *here*, quick!'

The latter rushed up at once, crying, –

'Got a rock on your foot?'

'No,' gasped Tim, 'it's more like a dozen rat-traps, and it's pinching fearful.'

Mat by this time had cleared away the weed, and at length, through the dark water could be seen the outlines of a gigantic double-shell, with his brother's leg imprisoned in its jaws.

'Look, how awful!' cried Tim; 'I can never get loose from that big brute of a cockle.'

Mat tugged and tore at the shell, and, being a powerful lad, he expected to be able to rip one side off by the hinge, but he could no more move it than he could the rocks to which it was attached.

'It's no good, old man, it's too far for me to reach it yet, but, thank God, the water's falling; if 'twere rising we'd be done. Do you feel you can last out an hour or so?'

'I don't know, Mat, I feel awful queer and sick, but I can find the pain is out of my foot, for I can't feel the limb at all.'

The first thing that Mat did was to pile up rocks under his brother, by this means getting him into a more restful position, he then wedged stones into the jaws of the fish, hoping thus to take some of the frightful pressure off the foot, and, bidding Tim be of good cheer, started for the shore, returning presently with a heavy, waterlogged piece of wreckage, and –

'See here, Tim!' he cried, as he approached him, and triumphantly held up an iron spike, 'I knocked this out of the old timber, this'll do the job.'

The water had now fallen so much that the jaws of the huge shell were well exposed.

First scraping the mud and stones, so as to get down to the base of the fish, Mat placed the heavy spike against the shell, which Tim had graphically enough described as a huge cockle; such, indeed, it exactly resembled, but on a gigantic scale, measuring along the jaws over three feet; he then dealt his piece of iron a heavy blow with the piece of timber, but the iron would not penetrate – flew off at a tangent: recovering it, he proceeded to examine the shell more closely, and for this purpose baled out most of the remaining water with his hands, then inserted the end of the spike at another angle; the next time he essayed he drove the bolt right through the shell up to the hilt; this, however, had no effect upon the clasping powers of the monster, the foot was jammed as tight as ever.

'Oh! for my axe!' said Mat, 'but never fear. Now to get the spike out. I'll kill this devil *somehow*.'

It seemed a long time before the spike could be released, but at length, succeeding in this, Mat drove it in every direction through the living, leathery substance of the creature itself.

It would *not* relax.

He then rammed the piece of timber in, and, exerting his full strength, attempted to prise open the shell, he felt that the enemy was slowly opening, when snap went his rotten lever, broken short off.

'It's too "brow"' (brittle), gasped Tim.

Nothing discouraged, Mat set to work with the remaining bit of his stick, but after another hard struggle, and sweating at every pore, he had to sit down a moment to recover; literally a moment, for he had hardly settled himself in a position to catch the breeze, turning towards the open sea for this purpose, when his ear caught the dull moaning of the tide, which had turned!!

Without a word, but with an agonized feeling in his heart, Mat jumped up, and driving his lever far down into the mutilated fish, and planting his feet against the opposite rock, gave one long and frantic 'prise;' when, oh, joy! through the blinding streams of perspiration that ran over his face, he first saw the stones falling in, and he plainly *felt* the double shell slowly give.

'Pull, Tim!' he yelled; and his brother was free, being, however, forced to lift his crippled foot with both hands out of the jaws of the fish, whilst Mat never relaxed his hold of the lever.

The instant that the foot was released, and the timber thrown aside, the stones fell completely in, and the shell closed with a sudden snap. Mat, however, did not wait to see more, for merely administering a furious blow on to the beast, which only had the effect of splintering the lips, he seized the almost unconscious Tim, hoisted him on his shoulders, and hurried as fast as he could over cruelly sharp rocks to the shore, somewhere about a quarter of a mile distant. With a couple of rests he got over the distance, and at length sank down with his burden under some shady trees, through which a little stream of water flowed on its way to the sea.

'I believe that pure water has saved my life,' said Tim, after he had drunk his fill, and had his leg, which was terribly swollen and cut, swathed in some soft bark, which was hanging down in ragged tatters on a large tree close by, and which Mat wetted in the sweet water before applying.

Our foresters, it must be borne in mind, were in a woeful plight. True, they had escaped the one great danger which they shared during that terrible swim; but what had been their experience, so far, on the shore? In the first place, they were aware that savages were about, for they had seen their lately-used camping-places, at all events their fishing resorts, and remains of their recent fires. Then the action of the salt water and wind on their skins; still worse, the powerful rays of a tropical sun, subsequently, had caused a sort of boiling-peeling process to set in. Added to this, Tim, as we have seen, had had his ankle-bone nearly crushed through, and Mat, now that he had a moment of leisure, found that his old wound – that one inflicted by the blood-hound – had broken open, a fact which he was aware of during the last two hours from the pain he felt. It is doubtful, had they not found shade and *good* water, whether our lads would not have left their bones on the strand.

After Mat had made up a soft bed of grass and bark for his brother, and covered him over with the same material, he stepped outside the timber to have a look round.

Having finished his survey, he was returning to doctor his own leg when he descried a thin column of smoke, which seemed suddenly to shoot up in the distance. Hastening to Tim, he told him what he had just seen, and that he believed the fire must have been just lit, for that there was no appearance of smoke when he first quitted him to look round.

'Now, Tim,' he continued, 'men have lit that fire, and, be they friends or foes, we'd better seek them out when we can travel; for I know we can't last long without fire or clothes, and both of us wounded; but I'll strap up my leg tight with this soft bark stuff, and then after a bit I'll be able to carry you. I can easily do it, with rests; anyhow, we'll get away from this salt water, there's too much danger in it.'

Tim answered wearily enough, –

'Let's rest here a day or so, and then, I think, with your help, in a cool night or early morning, I can get along.'

So Mat brought up a heap of shell-fish to the camp, and by evening had made their sleeping quarters a little more comfortable by means of boughs and bark.

The night passed without further incident; but it was a period of feverish nightmare to both brothers; lie how they would, their skins were so blistered that the pain was almost unendurable, and Mat, besides, was up many times to cool his brother's wounded leg with water.

At daylight they were awakened from a doze by the barking of Jumper. Mat was on his legs in a moment, and, proceeding cautiously to the spot, discovered the dog trying to claw up a tree, evidently striving to get at something in the branches. This proved to be a huge lizard, which was lying out on a limb a few feet from the ground.

Being an adept at 'squirrelling' at his old home in the Forest, Mat knocked the animal off his perch with sticks; and Jumper, who had been intently watching the proceedings, had it in his jaws almost before it reached the ground.

Near this spot Mat observed lying on the ground some tempting-looking fruits, in colour and shape somewhat resembling an orange, which had evidently fallen off a kind of stunted palm-tree. These he gathered up, and, together with the lizard, carried them back to their camp. With a sharp shell he cut out the fat from the lizard, and put it by to dress their wounds with; but the raw flesh of the beast proved quite uneatable by reason of its utter want of taste; whilst the delicious-looking fruit was far worse from the opposite reason – it was so intensely bitter and acrid that they quickly spat it out again. However, Jumper made a hearty meal off the lizard, the poor dog not having had anything but raw fish up to this time.

The view from their camp was a calm and peaceful one. The Pacific Ocean, which had so lately belied its name, now stretched, as far as the eye could reach, in one unruffled surface; beautiful bays indented the coast both north and south, whilst huge grey-looking forests seemed to mingle with the now blue waters, growing apparently to their very edge. Not a sail of any description had the brothers seen upon the ocean; the only sign of man was the smoke, or rather smokes, for by the second day the fires had evidently increased in numbers.

Our foresters found that the fat of the lizard well rubbed in did them more good than cold water bandages, and one afternoon Tim said he thought he could travel. They both agreed that it would be a relief even to move camp, though they might take a long time before they reached the strange fires. Mat procured a couple of stout sticks to lean upon, remarking, as he gave one to his brother with a smile, 'We've no call to trouble about the luggage;' which, indeed, so far, was lucky.

As long as they travelled quite slowly, with long rests, they found they could 'keep going' very well. Mat – by far the most able man, though they were both cripples – carried Tim over bad bits of ground; but on level country the latter managed well enough by resting one hand on his brother's shoulder. Having thus covered some miles of country, they came to a water-hole with several small tracks leading to it; round the margin were prints of numerous feet freshly stamped in the sand.

'Here they be,' whispered Mat, pointing to the signs, 'big feet and little feet, a whole tribe of 'em, and can't be far off neither. We must go careful like.'

Resuming their journey, they crossed a plain of treeless waste, and then entered a country thickly overgrown with scrub.

Jumper, who was ahead, and had entered the thicket, returned growling, with bristles erect, and at the same moment some dark forms could be seen rushing into a lagoon, which now appeared in a sort of clearing. Then all was still.

Mat, whose eyesight was specially sharp, whispered,—

'I can see what looks like a black nose shaking the water by that great water-leaf.'

The brothers stood quietly, hesitating what to do next.

Suddenly Jumper commenced growling again, with his gaze fixed on one side of the lagoon. At the same instant more than one black fellow could be seen stealthily approaching through the long grass, their bodies glistening with beads of water.

'Some have got behind us,' again whispered Mat.

And indeed the white men appeared to be surrounded.

'You hold the dog tight, Tim, and I'll try and make friends.'

Perceiving that Jumper was held, an old black fellow, armed with club, spear, and shield, walked boldly up to Mat, jabbering loudly the whole time, with chin in the air, and after feeling him all over, was about to do the same to Tim; but this Jumper would not stand, and Tim, by signs, implored the native to keep back.

The old man understood, and called to the other blacks, who immediately flocked up, and, hearing the white men talk, were evidently relieved to find that they were human beings like themselves, and thereupon made signs to know from whence they came. Mat, for answer, pointed to the sea, imitating the action of swimming. One of the blacks, who seemed to be the chief, comprehended at once; and the brothers saw by his gestures that he was explaining to the others what was meant, at which there was much jabbering and guttural ejaculations.

Mat pointed out how blistered and wounded their bodies and legs were, and explained by pantomime that they were hungry.

The natives now seemed satisfied, and led them by the hand, or rather conducted Mat in this manner – for they were afraid to approach Tim again, on account of the furious growls of Jumper – to the camp fires, where they intimated to the white men they should lie down; they then gave them a couple of cloaks of 'possum skin to cover their bodies with, and a quantity of roasted roots and fish to eat; this fare seemed to put new life in the brothers as they reclined on their soft rugs.

A black fellow then cooe'ed loudly, and several women and children seemed to spring up from the long grass around, where they had doubtless been hiding until the men knew with whom they had to deal.

Mat so far knew, as the whole tribe had now surrounded them, that he and his brother had fallen amongst blacks of the mainland of Australia, for he not only recognized types of visage, pictures of which he had seen in the squire's museum in the Forest, but also most of the camp equipment, of which the squire had many specimens. Thus he was able to point out and name to Tim spears, woomeras, yelamans, boomerangs, stone tomahawks, and nullah-nullahs; also their dilly bags, large and small, containing fish and roots, and many small articles wrapt up in 'possum skins.

Whilst they were regaling themselves the tribe kept up an incessant jabbering, as they pointed out the white men to each other.

One of the blacks showed by signs that there were other white men, but men clothed; he seemed to imply far, far away to the west. This gave the brothers hope that there might be a settlement in that direction, until by repeated signs they surmised that they must be white men travelling to the north.

It was almost night when our gipsies encountered the natives, and by the time that they had finished their meal, the camp was wrapped in darkness, save for the light given out by the tiny fires.

Seeing that the white men had eaten up all their food, the blacks gave them a gourd of water, and then, taking Mat by the hand again, and signing to Tim to follow, conducted them to a gunyah, or hut, which was made of saplings and covered with bark. It contained a tiny upper story, also made of sheets of bark, just large enough for two men to lie down in. Pointing to this, they intimated that the white men might sleep there, which, indeed, they were nothing loth to do.

Mat, having first placed some cool green leaves on his brother's ankles, pulled the rugs over them, for the night was chilly, and prepared to sleep.

Before darkness had quite set in they had observed two blacks start off on their back trail towards the coast, which caused Mat to remark that he 'had read that blacks never travelled at night. However,' he added, 'we shall know more about it in the morning. If I'd a pipe of 'baccy now, I'd be all right, but we can't have everything, and these chaps don't seem a bad lot, though they're rum 'uns to look at.'

'That they be,' said Tim; 'we shall know all about 'em in a day or two. If they'd meant badly you said as they'd have killed us at once.'

'Yes, from what I've been told, it was a good sign their bringing up the women and children so soon. We might get them to take us to the white men they spoke about, who knows?'

The conversation, which took place as they were lying in their hut, was at this point interrupted by the sound of a high-pitched voice singing a sort of mournful ditty, presently other voices joined in.

'Hullo! let's see what's up,' said Tim; and from the opening in their gunyah they witnessed a curious sight.

Three or four women, or 'jins,' were seated on the ground, singing and beating time with pieces of stick; a dozen little freshly-lit fires were burning in a circle, and in the midst of them were some fifteen painted warriors, white paint and red paint was daubed in regular lines over their faces and jaws, causing them to resemble so many death's heads, whilst their bodies were streaked with broad white stripes, each rib being distinctly marked.

These white lines followed the course of their limbs, giving them the appearance of so many skeletons, as they appeared in the flickering light cast upon them.

'What a rum sight!' said Tim, who, with his brother, was intently watching these proceedings, as we have said.

'Yes, a sort of free-and-easy, I should fancy, but, look!' for as Mat spoke each warrior took up the refrain of the 'jins,' and, whilst singing a hoarse chant, sprang high into the air, descending so heavily that the earth seemed to shake under them; then shaking their spears with a quivering motion, and uttering tremendous yells, they sprang again into the air and ran 'amuck' against each other.

As they pursued these ferocious antics, the sight made the white men's blood curdle, for they thought that this must be the prelude to a rush upon themselves.

The 'Corroboree,' as they afterwards found was the right name for this peculiar form of black-fellow recreation, waxed louder and fiercer, each man working himself up to a perfect frenzy, now darting in and out of the fires, and even in some cases plunging *into* them, and scattering the blazing embers, till exhausted, they would here and there 'fall out' and beat time to recover.

Their aspect appeared terrible and unearthly, the brothers were spell-bound, not knowing whether fury or joy was the cause of this extraordinary scene. Then the infernal din died away, only to be renewed louder than ever, as fresh warriors took the places of those pumped out, until the exhibition reached, as it seemed, a fight in terrible reality, as man closed with man, fending off each other's spears and clubs with their 'yelamans,' showing surprising feats of agility as they sprang high into the air, shouting fiercely a sort of war-cry the whole time.

The ceremony was brought to a close by all stamping their feet with heavy thuds on the ground, and then each coiled himself up by his fire, exhausted.

Our foresters breathed again.

'Well, if they ain't the most bloodthirsty-looking devils I ever seed,' said Tim; 'but I suppose it's all sham; the women don't dance, and ain't painted, they're what's called the "Orkistry" in the play-house, I suppose.'

'Just *about* a rum go,' joined in Mat; 'I reckon we're all right to sleep now, though.'

It was about midnight when the whole camp had retired to rest, so the brothers followed the general example.

# Eugene Field (1850–1895)

The sentimentalization of childhood which had been an undercurrent of Victorian children's literature slowly transmuted into the cult of the 'beautiful child'. Field, a newspaper columnist in Chicago, was one of the primary American practitioners of this form. A good deal of his verse is marked (if not marred) by a now unfashionable cosiness, bathos and affected diction. In form, he might be seen as a follower of Lear; in content, of Stevenson. As with other writers of the period, such as Rossetti, he often writes from an adult point of view ('So come, little child, cuddle closer to me') rather than a child's. Other collections by Field included *With Trumpet and Drum* (1892) and *Love Songs of Childhood* (1896).

## from *A Little Book of Western Verse* (1889)

### Wynken, Blynken, and Nod

Wynken, Blynken, and Nod one night
   Sailed off in a wooden shoe –
Sailed on a river of crystal light,
   Into a sea of dew.
   'Where are you going, and what do you wish?'
   The old moon asked the three.
   'We have come to fish for the herring fish
   That live in this beautiful sea;
   Nets of silver and gold have we!'
      Said Wynken,
      Blynken,
      And Nod.

The old moon laughed and sang a song,
   As they rocked in the wooden shoe,
And the wind that sped them all night long
   Ruffled the waves of dew.
The little stars were the herring fish
   That lived in that beautiful sea –
   'Now cast your nets wherever you wish –
   Never afeard are we';
   So cried the stars to the fishermen three:
      Wynken,
      Blynken,
      And Nod.

All night long their nets they threw
   To the stars in the twinkling foam –
Then down from the skies came the wooden shoe,
   Bringing the fishermen home;
'Twas all so pretty a sail it seemed
   As if it could not be,
And some folks thought 'twas a dream they'd dreamed

Of sailing that beautiful sea —
But I shall name you the fishermen three:
    Wynken,
    Blynken,
    And Nod.

Wynken and Blynken are two little eyes,
    And Nod is a little head,
And the wooden shoe that sailed the skies
    Is the wee one's trundle-bed.
So shut your eyes while mother sings
    Of wonderful sights that be,
And you shall see the beautiful things
    As you rock in the misty sea,
    Where the old shoe rocked the fishermen three:
    Wynken,
    Blynken,
    And Nod.

# Andrew Lang (1844–1912)

Andrew Lang was a major authority on the fairy-tale, and his series of twelve 'Colour' *Fairy Books* (1889–1910) collected hundreds of stories in an accessible, profusely illustrated format. These books both reflected and influenced the considerable interest in the form towards the end of the century. Perhaps the most ingenious of his original work was *The Princess Nobody* (1884), which was based around an existing set of illustrations by Richard Doyle.

*Prince Prigio* is at once a celebration of, and a gentle satire on the traditional fairy-tale, and the change in narrative voice and attitude to the relationships between adults and children that was occurring across children's literature can be seen by comparing this book with *The Hope of the Katzekopfs* (see p. 75) and *The Rose and the Ring* (see p. 120). How far Lang's tone is genuinely directed at children and how far he is winking at adult readers, might be debated: he certainly takes an obvious delight in adult anachronisms and the Prince's final wish 'to SEEM no cleverer than other people' is at best ambiguous in its implications.

Prince Prigio, born into a royal house whose motto is (as Lang explains in the preface) 'Anything for a Quiet Life', is brought up as a rationalist, and the gifts that the fairies bring to his christening are 'tossed . . . away into a dark lumber-room; for [the Queen] thought that they were *all nonsense*, and merely old rubbish out of books, or pantomime "properties" '. He grows up hated by everyone because he is cleverer than anyone else, and when he refuses to believe in the Firedrake that is ravaging the country, he is shunned as a coward. The finding of the fairy's gifts transforms him and there is a happy ending: the 'message' (if there is one) is clearly more romantic than moral.

Lang also produced a successful sequel, *Prince Ricardo of Pantouflia* (1893), and some lesser stories about Pantouflia.

## from *Prince Prigio* (1889)

### CHAPTER V

### WHAT PRINCE PRIGIO FOUND IN THE GARRET

The Prince walked from room to room of the palace; but, unless he wrapped himself up in a curtain, there was nothing for him to wear when he went out in the rain. At last he climbed up a turret-stair in the very oldest part of the castle, where he had never been before; and at the very top was a little round room, a kind of garret. The Prince pushed in the door with some difficulty – not that it was locked, but the handle was rusty, and the wood had swollen with the damp. The room was very dark; only the last grey light of the rainy evening came through a slit of a window, one of those narrow windows that they used to fire arrows out of in old times.

But in the dusk the Prince saw a heap of all sorts of things lying on the floor and on the table. There were two caps; he put one on – an old, grey, ugly cap it was, made of felt. There was a pair of boots; and he kicked off his slippers, and got into *them*. They were a good deal worn, but fitted as if they had been made for him. On the table was a purse with just three gold coins – old ones too – in it; and this, as you may fancy, the Prince was very well pleased to put in his pocket. A sword, with a sword-belt, he buckled about his waist; and the rest of the articles, a regular collection of odds and ends, he left just where they were lying. Then he ran downstairs and walked out of the hall door.

### CHAPTER VI

### WHAT HAPPENED TO PRINCE PRIGIO IN TOWN

By this time the Prince was very hungry. The town was just three miles off; but he had such a royal appetite that he did not like to waste it on bad cookery, and the people of the royal town were bad cooks.

'I wish I were in the Bear, at Gluckstein,' said he to himself; for he remembered that there was a very good cook there. But then the town was twenty-one leagues away – sixty-three long miles!

No sooner had the Prince said this, and taken just three steps, than he found himself at the door of the Bear Inn at Gluckstein!

'This is the most extraordinary dream,' said he to himself; for he was far too clever of course to believe in seven-league boots. Yet he had a pair on at that very moment, and it was they which had carried him in three strides from the palace to Gluckstein!

The truth is that the Prince, in looking about the palace for clothes, had found his way into the very old lumber-room where the magical gifts of the fairies had been thrown by his clever mother, who did not believe in them. But this of course the prince did not know.

Now you should be told that seven-league boots only take those prodigious steps when you say you *want* to go a long distance. Otherwise they would be very inconvenient – when you only want to cross the room, for example. Perhaps this has not been explained to you by your governess?

Well, the Prince walked into the Bear, and it seemed odd to him that nobody took any notice of him. And yet his face was as well known as that of any man in Pantouflia; for everybody had seen it, at least in pictures. He was so puzzled by not being attended to as usual that *he quite forgot to take off his cap*. He sat down at a table, however, and shouted 'Kellner!' at which all the waiters jumped, and looked round in every direction, but nobody came to him. At first he thought they were too busy, but presently another explanation occurred to him.

'The King,' said he to himself, 'has threatened to execute anybody who speaks to me, or helps me in any way. Well, I don't mean to starve in the midst of plenty, anyhow; here goes!'

The Prince rose, and went to the table in the midst of the room, where a huge roast turkey had just been placed. He helped himself to half the breast, some sausages, chestnut stuffing, bread sauce, potatoes and a bottle of red wine – Burgundy. He then went back to a table in a corner, where he dined very well, nobody taking any notice of him. When he had finished, he sat watching the other people dining, and smoking his cigarette. As he was sitting thus, a very tall man, an officer in the uniform of the Guards, came in, and, walking straight to the Prince's table, said: 'Kellner, clean this table, and bring in the bill of fare.'

With these words, the officer sat down suddenly in the Prince's lap, as if he did not see him at all. He was a heavy man, and the Prince, enraged at the insult, pushed him away and jumped to his feet. As he did so, *his cap dropped off*. The officer fell on his knees at once, crying:

'Pardon, my Prince, pardon! I never saw you!'

This was more than the Prince could be expected to believe.

'Nonsense! Count Frederick von Matterhorn,' he said, 'you must be intoxicated. Sir! you have insulted your prince and your superior officer. Consider yourself under arrest! You shall be sent to a prison tomorrow.'

On this, the poor officer appealed piteously to everybody in the tavern. They all declared that they had not seen the Prince, nor even had an idea that he was doing them the honour of being in the neighbourhood of their town.

More and more offended, and convinced that there was a conspiracy to annoy and insult him, the prince shouted for the landlord, called for his bill, threw down his three pieces of gold without asking for change and went into the street.

'It is a disgraceful conspiracy,' he said. 'The King shall answer for this! I shall write to the newspapers at once!'

He was not put in a better temper by the way in which people hustled him in the street. They ran against him exactly as if they did not see him, and then staggered back in the greatest surprise, looking in every direction for the person they had jostled. In one of these encounters, the Prince pushed so hard against a poor old beggar woman that she fell down. As he was usually most kind and polite he pulled off his cap to beg her pardon, when, behold, the beggar woman gave one dreadful scream, and fainted! A crowd was collecting, and the Prince, forgetting that he had thrown down all his money in the tavern, pulled out his purse. Then he remembered what he had done, and expected to find it empty; but, lo, there were three pieces of gold in it! Overcome with surprise, he thrust the money into the woman's hand, and put on his cap again. In a moment the crowd, which had been staring at him, rushed away in every direction, with cries of terror, declaring that there was a magician in the town, and a fellow who could appear and disappear at pleasure!

By this time, you or I, or anyone who was not so extremely clever as Prince Prigio, would have understood what was the matter. He had put on, without knowing it, not only the seven-league boots, but the cap of darkness, and had taken Fortunatus's purse, which could never be empty, however often you took all the money out. All those and many other delightful wares the fairies had given him at his christening, and the Prince had found them in the dark garret. But the Prince was so extremely wise, and learned, and scientific, that he did not believe in fairies nor in fairy gifts.

'It is indigestion,' he said to himself: 'those sausages were not of the best; and that Burgundy was extremely strong. Things are not as they appear.'

Here, as he was arguing with himself, he was nearly run over by a splendid carriage and six, the driver of which never took the slightest notice of him. Annoyed at this, the Prince leaped up behind, threw down the two footmen, who made no resistance, and so was carried to the door of a magnificent palace. He was determined to challenge the gentleman who was in the carriage; but noticing that he had a very beautiful young lady with him, whom he had never seen before, he followed them into the house, not wishing to alarm the girl, and meaning to speak to the gentleman when he found him alone.

A great ball was going on; but, as usual, nobody took any notice of the Prince. He walked among the guests, being careful not to jostle them, and listening to their conversation.

It was all about himself! Everyone had heard of his disgrace, and almost everyone cried 'Serve him right!' They said that the airs he gave himself were quite unendurable – that nothing was more rude than to be always in the right – that cleverness might be carried far too far – that it was better even to be born stupid ('Like the rest of you,' thought the Prince); and, in fact, nobody had a good word for him.

Yes, one had! It was the pretty lady of the carriage. I never could tell you how pretty she was. She was tall, with cheeks like white roses blushing, she had dark hair, and very large dark-grey eyes, and her face was the kindest in the world! The Prince first thought how nice and good she looked, even before he thought how pretty she looked. *She* stood up for Prince Prigio when her partner would speak ill of him. She had never seen the Prince, for she was but newly come to Pantouflia; but she declared that it was his *misfortune*, not his fault, to be so clever. 'And then, think how hard they made him work at school! Besides,' said this kind young lady, 'I hear he is extremely handsome, and very brave; and he has a good heart, for he was kind, I have heard, to a poor boy, and did all his examination papers for him, so that the boy passed first in *everything*. And now he is Minister of Education, though he can't do a line of Greek prose!'

The Prince blushed at this, for he knew his conduct had not been honourable. But he at once fell over head and ears in love with the young lady, a thing he had never done in his life before, because – he said – 'women were so stupid!' You see he was so clever!

Now, at this very moment – when the Prince, all of a sudden, was as deep in love as if he had been the stupidest officer in the room – an extraordinary thing happened! Something seemed to give a whirr! in his brain, and in one instant *he knew all about it*! He believed in fairies and fairy gifts, and understood that his cap was the cap of darkness, and his shoes the seven-league boots, and his purse the purse of Fortunatus! He had read about those things in historical books: but now he believed in them.

# CHAPTER VII

## THE PRINCE FALLS IN LOVE

He understood all this, and burst out laughing, which nearly frightened an old lady near him out of her wits. Ah! how he wished he was only in evening dress, that he might dance with the charming young lady. But there he was, dressed just as if he were going out to hunt, if anyone could have seen him. So, even if he took off his cap of darkness and became visible, he was no figure for a ball. Once he would not have cared, but now he cared very much indeed.

But the Prince was not clever for nothing. He thought for a moment, then went out of the room, and in three steps of the seven-league boots was at his empty, dark, cold palace again. He struck a light with a flint and steel, lit a torch and ran upstairs to the garret. The flaring light of the torch fell on the pile of 'rubbish', as the Queen would have called it, which he turned over with eager hands. Was there – yes, there was another cap! There it lay, a handsome green one with a red feather. The Prince pulled off the cap of darkness, put on the other and said:

'*I wish I were dressed in my best suit of white and gold, with the royal Pantouflia diamonds!*'

In one moment there he was in white and gold, the greatest and most magnificent dandy in the whole world, and the handsomest man!

'How about my boots, I wonder,' said the Prince; for his seven-league boots were stout riding-boots, not good to dance in, whereas now he was in elegant shoes of silk and gold.

He threw down the wishing cap, put on the other – the cap of darkness – and made three strides in the direction of Gluckstein. But he was only three steps nearer it than he had been, and the seven-league boots were standing beside him on the floor!

'No,' said the Prince; 'no man can be in two different pairs of boots at one and the same time! That's mathematics!'

He then hunted about in the lumber-room again till he found a small, shabby, old Persian carpet, the size of a hearthrug. He went to his own room, took a portmanteau in his hand, sat down on the carpet, and said:

'I wish I were in Gluckstein.'

In a moment there he found himself; for this was that famous carpet which Prince Hussein bought long ago, in the market at Bisnagar, and which the fairies had brought with the other presents to the christening of Prince Prigio.

When he arrived at the house where the ball was going on, he put the magical carpet in the portmanteau, and left it in the cloakroom, receiving a numbered ticket in exchange. Then he marched in all his glory (and of course without the cap of darkness) into the room where they were dancing. Everybody made place for him, bowing down to the ground, and the loyal band struck up *The Prince's March*:

> Heaven bless our Prince Prigio!
> What is there he doesn't know?
>    Greek, Swiss, German (High and Low),
> And the names of the mountains in Mexico,
>    Heaven bless the Prince!

He used to be very fond of this march, and the words – some people said he had made them himself. But now, somehow, he didn't much like it. He went straight to the Duke of Stumpfelbahn, the Hereditary Master of the Ceremonies, and asked to be introduced to the beautiful young lady. She was the daughter of the new English Ambassador, and her name was Lady Rosalind. But she nearly fainted when she heard who it was that wished to dance with her, for she was not at all particularly clever; and the Prince had such a bad character for snubbing girls, and asking them difficult questions. However, it was impossible to refuse, and so she danced with the Prince, and he danced very well. Then they sat out in the conservatory, among the flowers, where nobody came near them; and then they danced again, and then the Prince took her down to supper. And all the time he never once said: 'Have you read *this*?' or 'Have you read *that*?' or 'What! you never heard of Alexander the Great?' or Julius Caesar, or Michael Angelo, or whoever it might be – horrid, difficult questions he used to ask. That was the way he *used* to go on: but now he only talked to the young lady about *herself*; and she quite left off being shy or frightened, and asked him all about his own country, and about the Firedrake shooting, and said how fond she was of hunting herself. And the Prince said:

'Oh, if *you* wish it, you shall have the horns and tail of a Firedrake to hang up in your hall, tomorrow evening!'

Then she asked if it was not very dangerous work, Firedrake hunting; and he said it was nothing, when you knew the trick of it: and he asked her if she would not give him a rose out of her bouquet; and, in short, he made himself so agreeable and *unaffected* that she thought him very nice indeed.

For even a clever person can be nice when he likes – above all when he is not thinking about himself. And now the Prince was thinking of nothing in the world but the daughter of the English Ambassador, and how to please her. He got introduced to her father too, and quite won his heart; and at last he was invited to dine next day at the embassy.

In Pantouflia, it is the custom that a ball must not end while one of the royal family goes on dancing. *This* ball lasted till the light came in, and the birds were singing out of doors, and all the mothers present were sound asleep. Then nothing would satisfy the Prince but that they all should go home singing through the streets: in fact, there never had been so merry a dance in all Pantouflia. The Prince had made a point of dancing with almost every girl there: and he had suddenly become the most beloved of the royal family. But everything must end at last; and the Prince, putting on the cap of darkness and sitting on the famous carpet, flew back to his lonely castle.

# James Macdonald Oxley (1855–1907)

The theme of survival in the Canadian wastes, seen in Traill's *Canadian Crusoes* (see p. 104), is at the forefront of *Up Among the Ice Flows*. In many ways a conventional sea-adventure – the book features a stowaway, and a mutiny in which one of the seamen is shot ('a sharp crack split the air, and with a bullet in his brain the ill-starred wretch pitched forward at the Captain's feet – stone-dead') – there is much that makes it distinctively Canadian.

Captain Marling and his son Hal are on an expedition on the *Narwhal* and spend the winter in the ice; there is a great deal of information, skilfully disguised, on the hunting and killing of seals, whales, walruses and reindeer.

There is also a good deal of contact with the Esquimaux, whose 'good nature' and superior survival skills are acknowledged. The narrator's attitude to the 'Innuit', however, only just avoids the patronizing ('there is nothing they crave more than farinaceous food') and the boys' rudeness to them passes without comment.

'A Good Day's Work' describes a day's whaling and the excitement and authenticity of the description needs no artificial elaboration.

Oxley wrote over twenty boys' stories, including *The Boy Tramps, or, Across Canada* (1896).

## from *Up Among the Ice Floes* (1890)

### Chapter IX

### A Good Day's Work

During the next week whales were seen constantly, and the deck of the *Narwhal* was a scene of bustle and excitement from daybreak till dark, the whole fleet of eight boats being at times sent out in pursuit of the great creatures that showed themselves in the distance. But so far success had held aloof. The whales seemed unusually wary, and after a hard pull of two or three miles a boat would get perhaps almost within striking distance, only to have its intended victim make off under the ice, where pursuit was impossible. All sailors are more or less superstitious, and if there is one class of them more superstitious than any other, it is the whaler.

Accordingly, they set themselves diligently to seek out the cause of their ill-luck, and resorted to many absurd expedients in their endeavours to avert the evil chance. As one day followed another without bringing better fortune, they began to show signs of depression, causing Captain Marling to feel as anxious to break this spell of failure for the sake of his men as for his own sake.

At length the tide turned. Pushing her way through the ice, the *Narwhal* reached a wide bay or inlet which was entirely clear of pack or floe, and here the captain felt sure there would be fish to take. Two boats were ordered to keep 'on bran' – that is, manned and ready to start off at a moment's notice – the steamer being brought to a stand-still, and the boats drifting about in her immediate neighbourhood. Captain Marling himself spent much of his time in the crow's nest, Harold often being with him, as he swept the circle of his vision with his glass, alert to discover the first sign of the presence of whales. One fine, clear morning, when father and son were thus employed, the captain happened to be looking due north, while Harold was looking due south, when Harold suddenly grasped his arm, and pulling him around, pointed away off, about three miles distant, exclaiming breathlessly, 'There, father! what's that?'

Captain Marling brought his glass to bear upon the spot to which Harold pointed, and the moment he looked his face became radiant, and turning toward the boats 'on bran,' he shouted joyfully, 'A fish! a fish! a whole school of them, right off to the south! Make ready every boat on board.'

The excitement that followed was indescribable. Every man on board the *Narwhal* was in motion, and to an unpractised eye it might have seemed a scene of hopeless confusion. But this was not the case at all. Each man knew his place and his work. The confused crowd soon resolved itself into groups gathered about each boat, and with a quickness hardly credible the boats were dropped into the water, the men into their seats, and with a hearty 'Good-luck to you, my boys,' they were off to meet the approaching whales.

In the stern of the second mate's boat sat Harold, scarcely able to keep his seat for the fever of excitement that possessed him. The instant his father had confirmed his hope that the black spots far to the south were possible prey, he had slipped out of the crow's nest, and not missing his footing this time, scuttled down to the deck, where he posted himself in close proximity to Frank Lewis, determined that the boat should not go off without him.

The whales were coming directly towards the ship, there being at least a dozen of the monsters, ploughing their way through the water rippled by a gentle breeze, and sending up little fountains from the blow-holes in their mighty heads. As they would soon become aware of the steamer's presence, and in all probability take to the depths at once, it was necessary to meet them before they came too near, and accordingly the men bent to their oars with an energy that called for every ounce of muscle in their sturdy frames. Yet not a word was spoken. Neither did the oars, vigorously as they were being pulled, make the slightest sound beyond a faint splashing, for thick thrum mats lay on the gunwale between the thole pins. These precautions were necessary because of the exceeding quick hearing of the whales.

Dividing into two groups of four each, the boats spread out so as to allow the procession of whales to pass between them, thus affording the best possible opportunities for attack, and thus they shot over the waves toward their gigantic prey.

Lewis's boat led the group to the right, and Harold felt as though he could hardly breathe as they drew nearer and nearer to the big fish without their presence being observed by them. The steersman stood high in his place, one hand grasping the great oar, to every movement of which the swift boat responded like a thing of life, and the other keeping time to the strokes of the rowers. A few minutes more, and at a signal from him Lewis drew in his oar, laid it carefully fore and aft, then turned his face toward the bow, and put his hands upon the harpoon-gun. They were now almost within striking distance. A few strokes more, and the critical moment would come. The oarsmen strained yet a little harder: the boat fairly leaped over the water. The second mate having given one sharp glance along the line to make sure that all was clear, pointed the gun at the unconscious whale: there was an instant's pause, then a loud report, and then the glad cry of 'A fall! a fall!' rang out over the waves, for Frank Lewis's luck had once more asserted itself, and he was fast to a fine big whale.

But the luck was not with him only. Scarcely had his shout of triumph reached the ship, when it was followed by the same inspiring sound from others of the boats, until, before the school of terrified whales sank out of sight, no less than four boats were fast, and the men of the *Narwhal* were in for a most exciting and exhausting struggle. This time the fates seemed altogether favourable. The bay was entirely clear of ice; only a gentle breeze stirred the surface of the blue waters. The whale-hunters had the whole day before them, and no reason appeared why they should not make prizes of all four of the huge creatures in which their harpoons were now fastened. Two of the fish were rather small, but the other two – one of them being Frank Lewis's – were of great size, and worth perhaps almost two thousand pounds apiece.

The instant the whale to which the second mate was fast felt the keen harpoon boring into its vitals, it threw up its tail and dived into the depths, the line running out at such a rate that the smoke arose in clouds from the bollard head, half shrouding Lewis, who, lance in hand, stood up in the bow, ready to give his captive its *coup de grace* so soon as he could get near enough. The men drew in their oars, and the light boat fled like a shadow over the waters, as the stricken monster vainly sought safety in flight. So desperate were its efforts to free itself, that nearly a mile of line was taken before the running out ceased. Harold's heart was palpitating with delight. He thought that in all his life he had never experienced anything half so glorious as this, being towed along at the speed of an express train by a giant fish. Not a mite of fear or nervousness had he. He had no time for that. The struggle was too absorbing to allow him to think of anything else.

'My, but this is grand!' he exclaimed to the steersman. 'I never had so much fun in my life.'

The steersman gave him a pleasant smile, to show that he heard him, but was too engrossed in his work to make any reply; which, however, made little difference to Harold.

'Take in line,' called out Lewis; and with the speed and skill that come only from long practice, the men drew in the dripping line, and coiled it away in its nest, ready to run out again should it be required. Fathom after fathom it came swiftly in, until at least one-half of it had been recovered.

'Stand by now, and be ready to give way,' was Lewis's next order; and the men put their oars in position, while all waited with bated breath for the reappearance of the whale, which must soon come to the surface to breathe. One, two, three minutes passed, and then suddenly, so close to the boat that the commotion it caused set it to rocking, the huge black, glistening back of the whale rose out of the water, and a stream of water deeply dyed with blood shot up in the air.

'There she blows! there she blows! Give away on your left there, hard!' shouted Lewis, grasping the long, keen lance in his right hand; and round swept the boat in the direction he desired. 'Now, then, all together,' he cried again. The men bent to their oars. The stout ash blades bent beneath the strain upon them, and the boat almost sprang out of the water in response. Three mighty strokes, and Lewis was close beside the whale's forefin. For an instant the polished lance flashed in the sunlight, then it sank up to its haft in the soft flesh.

'Back water, for your lives!' shouted the second mate, dropping down into the bottom of the boat, and the oarsmen sent the boat backward. They did so just in time. Maddened by this fresh attack, the whale lifted its terrible tail high in the air, and brought it down with awful force upon the very spot where the boat had been the moment before. The spray from the blow drenched every one on board, and the boat rocked as though in a whirlpool.

'No, you don't,' cried Lewis joyously. 'That was a close shave. But a miss is as good as a mile.'

As if disgusted at its failure to crush its tormentors, the whale sent up a spout that was nearly all blood this time, and then 'sounded' once more. But evidently its end was near. The line did not run out at all so fast as before, and only a few hundred yards had been taken ere the creature returned to the surface a short distance from the boat.

'We've got our fish right enough this time,' said Lewis, smiling broadly. 'We'll just stand off until she "kicks the bucket."'

For a few minutes the whale lay still upon the water, as though resting, and the tired men were glad to rest also. Then came the final flurry. The huge frame trembled all over, the deadly tail was lifted and brought down upon the water with resounding blows, spout after spout of dark heart's blood incarnadined the sea, and then all was still.

'Pull up now, men; it's all over,' ordered Lewis, after waiting a little while to make sure it was the case.

The boat drew alongside of the mighty carcass, a hole was cut in each fin, the fin tow passed through them, and the big fins lashed tight to the sides, so as to offer no obstruction to towing. The tail was then secured to the stern of the boat, and the prize in this manner towed to the steamer, which, happily, was not far away.

When they got time to look about them, those on the second mate's boat saw with delight that one of the other boats had already killed its fish, and was making toward the ship, while the other two were still fast, with good prospects of like success.

The towing of such an unwieldy prize was no easy task, but they had only half a mile to go, and their hearts were light; so with cheery songs they tugged away, and in due time were alongside of the *Narwhal*. Approaching at the port side, the fish was brought between the fore and main rigging, and made fast by a rope around its tail that passed through a block on the fore-mast, and another rope through a hole in the under jaw that was rove through a tackle on the main-mast. The whale was on its back, and the right fin, which was next the ship, was dragged taut up, and secured by a chain to the upper deck. A stout wire rope, stretching from the main-mast to the foremast, and known as the 'blubber guy,' held four large blocks, through which were rove the fore and main 'spek' tackles, whose use was for hoisting on board the huge layers of blubber, some of which would weigh between one and two tons. The 'kent' or cant tackle having been rigged, the object of which is to turn the fish over as it is being flinched, everything was in readiness for this interesting operation. The men were duly refreshed from the ship's stores, and then the work of flinching the whale began.

Harold looked forward to this with intense curiosity, and posted himself in his favourite eyrie in the main cross-tree, where he could overlook everything without getting in anybody's way. He did not expect it to be as interesting as the chase of the whale, but it could hardly help being well worth seeing; and such, indeed, it proved to be.

In the port main rigging was the captain, superintending the whole business; at the gangway stood Peter Strum, with eye watchful to see that every command of the captain was minutely carried out. Upon the upturned belly of the whale jumped the eight harpooners, their boots being armed with iron spikes, to prevent their slipping, and at it they went with their keen blubber spades and knives.

First of all, a strip of blubber, nearly a yard in width, was cut from the neck, just abaft the fin; and a large hole being cut in the end, the strap of the cant tackle was passed through it, and by this means the fish could be turned over as desired. With spade and knife the men cut big strips of blubber from the belly, which were one by one hoisted on board the steamer, where they were received by the boat-steerers, who with long knives cut them into pieces about two feet square, and passed these pieces over to the line-managers, whose work was to seize them with pick haaks, or pickies, as they are called for short, and send them shooting through a small hole in the main hatchway to the deck below. Here they were taken charge of by the 'skeeman,' and by another man, oddly denominated as the 'king,' and stowed away between decks until a favourable opportunity should come for the final operation of 'making off.'

When the blubber had all been removed, the precious whalebone, worth between two and three thousand pounds a ton, and of which the whale would yield a good part of a ton by itself, was carefully detached from the vast mouth, and lifted on board by special tackle. Then the great tail was cut off for a purpose that will be afterwards explained; and thus stripped of everything of value, the 'kreng' or carcass was released, disappearing with a plunge into the green water, which it turned to blood for some distance, while the men sent up a lusty cheer by way of a farewell.

The men had worked hard and well, only two hours being required to dispose of the first whale, and were allowed a brief rest and another 'lunch all around' before attacking the second. For the *Narwhal* had been wonderfully fortunate, three out of the four whales having been secured – the two big fellows and one of the small ones; and the day's work would 'pan out' at least six thousand pounds: so that it is safe to say that from Captain Marling down there was not a merrier – nor a dirtier – crew afloat than toiled and laughed and joked and shouted on board the steamer all through that long mid-summer afternoon.

Harold found abundant amusement for a long time in watching all the bustle and noise, and then after it became somewhat monotonous he discovered another way of entertaining himself, which proved so diverting that he felt bound to call Patsy up to share it with him. No sooner had the process of flinching begun than the steamer was surrounded by hundreds of fulmar petrels, or 'mollies,' as the whalers call them – noisy, greedy, quarrelsome birds, in appearance much resembling the ordinary sea-gull, that clamoured and fought over the numerous pieces of kreng and blubber wherewith the water about the ship was liberally sprinkled. So fearless did their insatiable voracity render them, that they would even alight upon the whale within reach of the men, who would often catch one of them and fling it back into the midst of the flock swimming eagerly alongside, producing a disturbance that very soon subsided. They were not worth killing, and Captain Marling would not suffer Harold to shoot them; but they were a great nuisance, so he had no objection to his making a mark of them in throwing. Accordingly, the two lads brought up a bucket of small lumps of coal, and had fine fun seeing which could make the better shots, using the coal for ammunition. The 'mollies' were pretty cute, and could dodge the missiles with good success; but their voracity often betrayed them, for they would run the risk of being hit rather than lose some choice morsel upon which they had decided, so that as between hitting and missing, honours were about even.

Just before darkness infolded the ship in its soft embrace for the night, the work of flinching was finished, and to the accompaniment of a lusty cheer that actually terrified the mollies, and went echoing out over the still water, the third and last kreng sank into the depths, while the tired men, all smeared with blood and blubber, indulged in a grand clear up before tumbling into their berths.

Harold soon followed their example, and his dreams were full of whales and mollies and exciting incidents, but they contained no prophecy of what awaited him on the morrow, and in blissful ignorance of coming peril he slept as only a weary boy can sleep.

# Thomas Hardy (1840–1928)

A good many major authors for adults have also written children's books, but Hardy seems to be an unlikely candidate, and *Our Exploits at West Poley* must have one of the most curious publishing histories of any book. Hardy, already an important novelist, wrote it for the American magazine *Youth's Companion* in 1883 (between *The Return of the Native* (1878) and *The Mayor of Casterbridge* (1886)). It was not published and the editor passed on the manuscript to his son-in-law, who ran an unsuccessful magazine, *The Household* ('devoted to the interests of the American housewife'), in which the story was published in six parts (without Hardy's knowledge).

This is a robust tale, set in Hardy's Mendip hills, which centres on a moral dilemma. Two cousins, Leonard the narrator and Steve, while exploring some caves, divert the West Poley mill-stream to East Poley, to the despair of the first village and the delight of the second. Their efforts to restore the status quo lead them into danger; ulti-

mately, all returns to normal and although the issues involved are difficult, a straightforward moral is supplied: 'Quiet perseverance in clearly defined courses is, as a rule, better than the erratic exploits that may do much harm'. This observation comes from the dour (and characteristically Hardyesque) figure of the Man who had Failed, who comments on the action at key points. However, his attitude is so solipsistic as to suggest that moralizing is quite irrelevant to high-spirited youth, whatever Hardy's intention. In terms of the children's literature of the time, *Our Exploits at West Poley* is rather old-fashioned in its manner, but remarkable in terms of its intellectual content.

The tale was exhumed from *The Household* by Richard L. Purdy and reprinted in 1952. This extract shows Steve and Leonard, with the help of Job the Miller's apprentice, at work.

## from *Our Exploits at West Poley* (1892–3)

'First, we'll go to Job,' said Steve. 'Take him into the secret: show him the cave; give him a spade and pickaxe; and tell him to turn off the water from East Poley at, say, twelve o'clock, for a little while. Then we'll go to the East Poley boys and declare ourselves to be magicians.'

'Magicians?' I said.

'Magicians, able to dry up rivers, or to make 'em run at will,' he repeated.

'I see it!' I almost screamed, in my delight.

'To show our power, we'll name an hour for drying up theirs, and making it run again after a short time. Of course, we'll say the hour we've told Job to turn the water in the cave. Won't they think something of us then?'

I was enchanted. The question of mischief or not mischief was as indifferent to me now as it was to Steve – for which indifference we got rich deserts, as will be seen in the sequel.

'And to look grand and magical,' continued he, 'we'll get some gold lace that I know of in the garret, on an old coat my grandfather wore in the Yeomanry Cavalry, and put it round our caps, and make ourselves great beards with horse-hair. They will look just like real ones at a little distance off.'

'And we must each have a wand!' said I, explaining that I knew how to make excellent wands, white as snow, by peeling a couple of straight willows; and that I could do all that in the morning while he was preparing the beards.

Thus we discussed and settled the matter, and at length fell asleep – to dream of tomorrow's triumphs among the boys of East Poley, till the sun of that morrow shone in upon our faces and woke us. We arose promptly and made our preparations, having *carte blanche* from my Aunt Draycot to spend the days of my visit as we chose.

Our first object on leaving the farmhouse was to find Job Tray, apprise him of what it was necessary that he should know, and induce him to act as confederate. We found him outside the garden of his lodging; he told us he had nothing to do till the following Monday, when a farmer had agreed to hire him. On learning the secret of the river-head, and what we proposed to do, he expressed his glee by a low laugh of amazed delight, and readily promised to assist as bidden. It took us some little time to show him the inner cave, the tools, and to arrange candles for him, so that he might enter without difficulty just after eleven and do the trick. When this was all settled we put Steve's watch on a ledge in the cave, that Job might know the exact time, and came out to ascend the hills that divided the eastern from the western village.

For obvious reasons we did not appear in magician's guise till we had left the western vale some way behind us. Seated on the limestone ridge, removed from all observation, we set to work at preparing ourselves. I peeled the two willows we had brought with us to be used as magic wands, and Steve pinned the pieces of old lace round our caps, congratulating himself on the fact of the lace not being new, which would thus convey the impression that we had exercised the wizard's calling for some years. Our last adornments were the beards; and, finally equipped, we descended on the other side.

Our plan was now to avoid the upper part of East Poley, which we had traversed on the preceding day, and to strike into the parish at a point farther down, where the humble cottages stood, and where we were both absolutely unknown. An hour's additional walking brought us to this spot, which, as the crow flies, was not more than half so far from West Poley as the road made it.

The first boys we saw were some playing in an orchard near the new stream, which novelty had evidently been the attraction that had brought them there. It was an opportunity for opening the campaign, especially as the hour was long after eleven, and the cessation of water consequent on Job's performance at a quarter past might be expected to take place as near as possible to twelve, allowing the five and forty minutes from eleven-fifteen, as the probable time that would be occupied by the stream in travelling to the point we had reached.

I forget at this long distance of years the exact words used by Steve in addressing the strangers; but to the best of my recollection they were, 'How d'ye do, gentlemen, and how does the world use ye?' I distinctly remember the sublimity he threw into his gait, and how slavishly I imitated him in the same.

The boys made some indifferent answer, and Steve continued, 'You will kindly present us with some of those apples, I presume, considering what we are?'

They regarded us dubiously, and at last one of them said, 'What are you, that you should expect apples from us?'

'We are travelling magicians,' replied Steve. 'You may have heard of us, for by our power this new river has begun to flow. Rhombustas is my name, and this is my familiar, Balcazar.'

'I don't believe it,' said an incredulous one from behind.

'Very well, gentlemen; we can't help that. But if you give us some apples we'll prove our right to the title.'

'Be hanged if we will give you any apples,' said the boy who held the basket; 'since it is already proved that magicians are impossible.'

'In that case,' said Steve, 'we – we—'

'Will perform just the same,' interrupted I, for I feared Steve had forgotten that the time was at hand when the stream would be interrupted by Job, whether he willed it or not.

'We will stop the water of your new river at twelve o'clock this day, when the sun crosses the meridian,' said Rhombustas, 'as a punishment for your want of generosity.'

'Do it!' said the boys incredulously.

'Come here, Balcazar,' said Steve. We walked together to the edge of the stream; then we muttered, *Hi, hae, haec, horum, harum, horum,* and stood waving our wands.

'The river do run just the same,' said the strangers derisively.

'The spell takes time to work,' said Rhombustas, adding in an aside to me, 'I hope that fellow Job has not forgotten, or we shall be hooted out of the place.'

There we stood, waving and waving our white sticks, hoping and hoping that we should succeed; while still the river flowed. Seven or ten minutes passed thus; and then, when we were nearly broken down by ridicule, the stream diminished its volume. All eyes were instantly bent on the water, which sank so low as to be in a short time but a narrow rivulet. The faithful Job had performed his task. By the time that the clock of the church tower struck twelve the river was almost dry.

The boys looked at each other in amazement, and at us with awe. They were too greatly concerned to speak except in murmurs to each other.

'You see the result of your conduct, unbelieving strangers,' said Steve, drawing boldly up to them. 'And I seriously ask that you hand over those apples before we bring further troubles upon you and your village. We give you five minutes to consider.'

'We decide at once!' cried the boys. 'The apples be yours and welcome.'

'Thank you, gentlemen,' said Steve, while I added, 'For your readiness the river shall run again in two or three minutes' time.'

'Oh – ah, yes,' said Steve, adding heartily in undertones, 'I had forgotten that!'

Almost as soon as the words were spoken we perceived a little increase in the mere dribble of water which now flowed, whereupon he waved his wand and murmured more words. The liquid thread swelled and rose; and in a few minutes was the same as before. Our triumph was complete; and the suspension had been so temporary that probably nobody in the village had noticed it but ourselves and the boys.

At this acme of our glory who should come past but a hedger whom Steve recognized as an inhabitant of West Poley; unluckily for our greatness the hedger also recognized Steve.

'Well, Maister Stevey, what be you doing over in these parts then? And yer little cousin, too, upon my word! And beards – why ye've made yerselves ornamental! haw, haw!'

In great trepidation Steve moved on with the man, endeavouring, thus, to get him out of hearing of the boys.

'Look here,' said Steve to me on leaving that outspoken rustic; 'I think this is enough for one day. We'd better go farther before they guess all.'

'With all my heart,' said I. And we walked on.

'But what's going on here?' said Steve, when, turning a corner of the hedge, we perceived an altercation in progress hard by. The parties proved to be a poor widow and a corn-factor, who had been planning a water-wheel lower down the stream. The latter had dammed the water for his purpose to such an extent as to submerge the poor woman's garden, turning it into a lake.

'Indeed, sir, you need not ruin my premises so!' she said with tears in her eyes. 'The mill-pond can be kept from overflowing my garden by a little banking and digging; it will be just as well for your purpose to keep it lower down, as to let it spread out into a great pool here. The house and garden are yours by law, sir; that's true. But my father built the house, and, oh, sir, I was born here, and I should like to end my days under its roof!'

'Can't help it, mis'ess,' said the corn-factor. 'Your garden is a mill-pond already made, and to get a hollow farther down I should have to dig at great expense. There is a very nice cottage up the hill, where you can live as well as here. When your father died the house came into my hands; and I can do what I like with my own.'

The woman went sadly away indoors. As for Steve and myself, we were deeply moved, as we looked at the pitiable sight of the poor woman's garden, the tops of the gooseberry bushes forming small islands in the water, and her few apple-trees standing immersed half-way up their stems.

'The man is a rascal,' said Steve. 'I perceive that it is next to impossible, in this world, to do good to one set of folks without doing harm to another.'

'Since we have not done all good to these people of East Poley', said I, 'there is a reason for restoring the river to its old course through West Poley.'

'But then,' said Steve, 'if we turn back the stream, we shall be starting Miller Griffin's mill; and then, by the terms of his 'prenticeship, poor Job will have to go back to him and be beaten again! It takes good brains no less than a good heart to do what's right towards all.'

Quite unable to solve the problem into which we had drifted, we retraced our steps, till, at a stile, within half a mile of West Poley, we beheld Job awaiting us.

'Well, how did it act?' he asked with great eagerness. 'Just as the hands of your watch got to a quarter past eleven, I began to shovel away, and turned the water in no time. But I didn't turn it where you expected – not I – 'twould have started the mill for a few minutes, and I wasn't going to do that.'

'Then where did you turn it?' cried Steve.

'I found another hole,' said Job.

'A third one?'

'Ay, hee, hee! a third one! So I pulled the stones aside from this new hole, and shovelled the clay, and down the water went with a gush. When it had run down there a few minutes, I turned it back to the East Poley hole, as you ordered me to do. But as to getting it back to the old West Poley hole, that I'd never do.'

Steve then explained that we no more wished the East village to have the river than the West village, on account of our discovery that equal persecution was going on in the one place as in the other. Job's news of a third channel solved our difficulty. 'So we'll go at once and send it down this third channel,' concluded he.

We walked back to the village, and, as it was getting late, and we were tired, we decided to do nothing that night, but told Job to meet us in the cave on the following evening, to complete our work there.

All next day my cousin was away from home, at market for his mother, and he had arranged with me that if he did not return soon enough to join me before going to Nick's Pocket, I should proceed thither, where he would meet me on his way back from the market-town. The day passed anxiously enough for me, for I had some doubts of a very grave kind as to our right to deprive two parishes of water on our own judgement, even though that should be, as it was, honestly based on our aversion to tyranny. However, dusk came on at last, and Steve not appearing from market, I concluded that I was to meet him at the cave's mouth.

To this end I strolled out in that direction, and there being as yet no hurry, I allowed myself to be tempted out of my path by a young rabbit, which, however, I failed to capture. This divergence had brought me inside a field, behind a hedge, and before I could resume my walk along the main road, I heard some persons passing along the other side. The words of their conversation arrested me in a moment.

''Tis a strange story if it's true,' came through the hedge in the tones of Miller Griffin, 'We know that East Poley folk will say queer things; but the boys wouldn't say that it was the work of magicians if they hadn't some ground for it.'

'And how do they explain it?' asked the shoemaker.

'They say that these two young fellows passed down their lane about twelve o'clock, dressed like magicians, and offered to show their power by stopping the river. The East Poley boys challenged 'em; when, by George, they did stop the river! They said a few words, and it dried up like magic. Now mark my words, my suspicion is this: these two gamesters have somehow got at the river-head, and been tampering with it in some way. The water that runs down East Poley bottom is the water that ought, by rights, to be running through my mill.'

'A very pretty piece of mischief, if that's the case!' said the shoemaker, 'I've never liked them lads, particularly that Steve – for not a boot or shoe hev he had o' me since he's been old enough to choose for himself – not a pair, or even a mending. But I don't see how they could do all this, even if they had got at the river-head. 'Tis a spring out of the hill, isn't it? And how could they stop the spring?'

It seemed that the miller could offer no explanation, for no answer was returned. My course was clear: to join Job and Steve at Nick's Pocket immediately; tell them that we were suspected, and to get them to give over further proceeding, till we had stated our difficulties to some person of experience – say the Man who had Failed.

I accordingly ran like a hare over the clover inside the hedge, and soon was far away from the interlocutors. Drawing near the cave, I was relieved to see Steve's head against the sky. I joined him at once, and recounted to him, in haste, what had passed.

He meditated. 'They don't even now suspect that the secret lies in the cavern,' said he.

'But they will soon,' said I.

'Well, perhaps they may,' he answered, 'But there will be time for us to finish our undertaking, and turn the stream down the third hole. When we've done that we can consider which of the villages is most worthy to have the river, and act accordingly.'

'Do let us take a good wise man into our confidence,' I said.

After a little demurring, he agreed that as soon as we had completed the scheme we would state the case to a competent adviser, and let it be settled fairly. 'And now,' he said, 'where's Job? Inside the cave, no doubt, as it is past the time I promised to be here.'

Stepping inside the cave's mouth, we found that the candles and other things which had been deposited there were removed. The probability being that Job had arrived and taken them in with him, we groped our way along in the dark, helped by an occasional match which Steve struck from a box he carried. Descending the gallery at the farther end of the outer cavern, we discerned a glimmer at the remote extremity, and soon beheld Job working with all his might by the light of one of the candles.

'I've almost got it to the hole that leads to neither of the Poleys, but I wouldn't actually turn it till you came,' he said, wiping his face.

We told him that the neighbours were on our track, and might soon guess that we performed our tricks in Nick's Pocket, and come there, and find that the stream flowed through the cave before rising in the spring at the top of the village; and asked him to turn the water at once, and be off with us.

'Ah!' said Job, mournfully, 'then 'tis over with me! They will be here tomorrow, and will turn back the stream, and the mill will go again, and I shall have to finish my time as 'prentice to the man who did this!' He pulled up his shirt sleeve, and showed us on his arm several stripes and bruises – black and blue and green – the tell-tale relics of old blows from the miller.

Steve reddened with indignation. 'I would give anything to stop up the channels to the two Poleys so close that they couldn't be found again!' he said, 'Couldn't we do it with stones and clay? Then, if they come here 'twould make no difference, and the water would flow down the third hole for ever, and we should save Job and the widow after all.'

'We can but try it,' said Job, willing to fall in with anything that would hinder his recall to the mill. 'Let's set to work.'

Steve took the spade, and Job the pickaxe. First they finished what Job had begun – the turning of the stream into the third tunnel or crevice, which led to neither of the Poleys. This done, they set to work jamming stones into the other two openings, treading earth and clay around them, and smoothing over the whole in such a manner that nobody should notice they had ever existed. So intent were we on completing it that – to our utter disaster – we did not notice what was going on behind us.

I was the first to look round, and I well remember why. My ears had been attracted by a slight change of tone in the purl of the water down the new crevice discovered by Job, and I was curious to learn the reason of it. The sight that met my gaze might well have appalled a stouter and older heart than mine. Instead of pouring down out of sight, as it had been doing when we last looked, the stream was choked by a rising pool into which it boiled, showing at a glance that what we had innocently believed to be another outlet for the stream was only a blind passage or cul-de-sac, which the water, when first turned that way by Job, had not been left long enough to fill before it was turned back again.

'Oh, Steve – Job!' I cried, and could say no more.

They gazed round at once, and saw the situation. Nick's Pocket had become a cauldron. The surface of the rising pool stood, already, far above the mouth of the gallery by which we had entered, and which was our only way out – stood far above the old exit of the stream to West Poley, now sealed up; far above the second outlet to East Poley, discovered by Steve, and also sealed up by our fatal ingenuity. We had been spending the evening in making a closed bottle of the cave, in which the water was now rising to drown us.

'There is one chance for us – only one,' said Steve in a dry voice.

'What one?' we asked in a breath.

'To open the old channel leading to the mill,' said Steve.

'I would almost as soon be drowned as do that,' murmured Job gloomily. 'But there's more lives than my own, so I'll work with a will. Yet how be we to open any channel at all?'

The question was, indeed, of awful aptness. It was extremely improbable that we should have power to reopen either conduit now. Both those exits had been funnel-shaped cavities, narrowing down to mere fissures at the bottom; and the stones and earth we had hurled into these cavities had wedged themselves together by their own weight. Moreover – and here was the rub – it might have been possible to pull the stones out while they remained unsubmerged, but the whole mass was now under water, which enlarged the task of reopening the channel to Herculean dimensions.

But we did not know my cousin Steve as yet, 'You will help me here,' he said authoritatively to Job, pointing to the West Poley conduit. 'Lenny, my poor cousin,' he went on, turning to me, 'we are in a bad way. All you can do is to stand in the niche, and make the most of the candles by keeping them from the draught with your hat, and burning only one at a time. How many have we, Job?'

'Ten ends, some long, some short,' said Job.

'They will burn many hours,' said Steve. 'And now we must dive, and begin to get out the stones.'

They had soon stripped off all but their drawers, and, laying their clothes on the dry floor of the niche behind me, stepped down into the middle of the cave. The water here was already above their waists, and at the original gulley-hole leading to West Poley spring was proportionately deeper. Into this part, nevertheless, Steve dived. I have recalled his appearance a hundred – aye, a thousand times since that day, as he came up – his crown bobbing into the dim candlelight like a floating apple. He stood upright, bearing in his arms a stone as big as his head.

'That's one of 'em!' he said as soon as he could speak. 'But there are many, many more!'

He threw the stone behind; while Job, wasting no time, had already dived in at the same point. Job was not such a good diver as Steve, in the sense of getting easily at the bottom; but he could hold his breath longer, and it was an extraordinary length of time before his head emerged above the surface, though his feet were kicking in the air more than once. Clutched to his chest, when he rose, was a second large stone, and a couple of small ones with it. He threw the whole to a distance; and Steve, having now recovered breath, plunged again into the hole.

But I can hardly bear to recall this terrible hour even now, at a distance of many years. My suspense was, perhaps, more trying than that of the others, for, unlike them, I could not escape reflection by superhuman physical efforts. My task of economizing the candles, by shading them with my hat, was not to be compared, in difficulty, to theirs; but I would gladly have changed places, if it had been possible to such a small boy, with Steve and Job, so intolerable was it to remain motionless in the desperate circumstances.

Thus I watched the rising of the waters, inch by inch, and on that account was in a better position than they to draw an inference as to the probable end of the adventure.

There were a dozen, or perhaps twenty, stones to extract before we could hope for an escape of the pent mass of water; and the difficulty of extracting them increased with each successive attempt, in two ways, by the greater actual remoteness of stone after stone, and by its greater relative remoteness through the rising of the pool. However, the sustained, gallant struggles of my two comrades succeeded, at last, in raising the number of stones extracted to seven. Then we fancied that some slight passage had been obtained for the stream; for, though the terrible pool still rose higher, it seemed to rise less rapidly.

After several attempts, in which Steve and Job brought up nothing, there came a declaration from them that they could do no more. The lower stones were so tightly jammed between the sides of the fissure that no human strength seemed able to pull them out. ·

Job and Steve both came up from the water. They were exhausted and shivering, and well they might be. 'We must try some other way,' said Steve.

'What way?' asked I.

Steve looked at me. 'You are a very good little fellow to stand this so well!' he said, with something like tears in his eyes.

They soon got on their clothes; and, having given up all hope of escape downward, we turned our eyes to the roof of the cave, on the chance of discovering some outlet there.

There was not enough light from our solitary candle to show us all the features of the vault in detail; but we could see enough to gather that it formed anything but a perfect dome. The roof was rather a series of rifts and projections, and high on one side, almost lost in the shades, there was a larger and deeper rift than elsewhere, forming a sort of loft, the back parts of which were invisible, extending we knew not how far. It was through this overhanging rift that the draught seemed to come which had caused our candle to gutter and flare.

To think of reaching an opening so far above our heads, so advanced into the ceiling of the cave as to require a fly's power of walking upside down to approach it, was mere waste of time. We bent our gaze elsewhere. On the same side with the niche in which we stood there was a small narrow ledge quite near at hand, and to gain it my two stalwart companions now exerted all their strength.

By cutting a sort of step with the pickaxe, Job was enabled to obtain a footing about three feet above the level of our present floor, and then he called to me.

'Now, Leonard, you be the lightest. Do you hop up here, and climb upon my shoulder, and then I think you will be tall enough to scramble to the ledge, so as to help us up after you.'

I leapt up beside him, clambered upon his stout back as he bade me, and, springing from his shoulder, reached the ledge. He then handed up the pickaxe, directed me how to make its point firm into one of the crevices on the top of the ledge; next, to lie down, hold on to the handle of the pickaxe and gave him my other hand. I obediently acted, when he sprang up, and turning, assisted Steve to do likewise.

We had now reached the highest possible coign of vantage left to us, and there remained nothing more to do but wait and hope that the encroaching water would find some unseen outlet before reaching our level.

Job and Steve were so weary from their exertions that they seemed almost indifferent as to what happened, provided they might only be allowed to rest. However, they tried to devise new schemes, and looked wistfully over the surface of the pool.

'I wonder if it rises still?' I said. 'Perhaps not, after all.'

'Then we shall only exchange drowning for starving,' said Steve.

Job, instead of speaking, had endeavoured to answer my query by stooping down and stretching over the ledge with his arm. His face was very calm as he rose again. 'It will be drowning,' he said almost inaudibly, and held up his hand, which was wet.

# [Margaret] Marshall Saunders (1861–1947)

There is nothing subtle about *Beautiful Joe*; it ends: 'My last words are, "Boys and girls, be kind to dumb animals, not only because you will lose nothing by it, but because you ought to; for they were placed on the earth by the same Kind Hand that made all living creatures"'. This is the canine version of *Black Beauty* and it uses much the same set of tactics, although Joe gets off to a much less felicitous start than Black Beauty – Jenkins the milkman kills Joe's siblings, and then chops off his ears and tail – and the whole book is more given to melodrama.

Like Black Beauty, Joe is the observer of human foibles, and as in the case of the hotel fire described here, human tragedy. The inherent power of the device of the animal narrative may account for the book's survival, together with its incidental Canadian background; its mode was soon to be superseded by realistic animal stories, notably those of Ernest Thompson Seton (see p. 448).

Apart from his avowed purpose of writing a book, Joe stays within the character of an animal, as constructed by Anna Sewell. It was not until Kipling's *Thy Servant, a Dog* (1930) that a serious attempt was made to approximate to an animal's actual perceptions.

## from *Beautiful Joe, The Autobiography of a Dog* (1894)

### CHAPTER XXXI

### A FIRE IN FAIRPORT

I had several times run to a fire with the boys and knew that there was always a great noise and excitement. There was a light in the house, so I knew that somebody was getting up. I don't think – indeed, I know, for they were good boys – that they ever wanted anybody to lose property, but they did enjoy seeing a blaze, and one of their greatest delights, when there hadn't been a fire for some time, was to build a bonfire in the garden.

Jim and I ran around to the front of the house and waited. In a few minutes, some one came rattling at the front door, and I felt sure it was Jack. However, it was Mr. Morris, and without a word to us, he set off running toward the town. As we hurried after him, other men ran out from the houses along the streets, and either joined him, or dashed ahead. They seemed to have dressed in a hurry, and were thrusting their arms in their coats, and buttoning themselves up as they went. Some of them had hats and some of them had none, and they all had their faces toward the great, red light ahead of us that kept getting brighter and brighter.

'Where's the fire?' they shouted to each other. 'Don't know – afraid it's the hotel, or the town hall – hope not. What a blaze! How's the water supply now? Bad time for a fire.'

It was the hotel. We saw that as soon as we got on the main street. There were people all about, and a great noise and confusion, and smoke and blackness, and up above, bright tongues of flame were leaping against the sky. Jim and I kept close to Mr. Morris' heels, as he pushed his way through the crowd. When we got nearer the burning building, we saw men carrying ladders and axes, and others were shouting directions, and rushing out of the hotel, carrying boxes and bundles and furniture in their arms. From the windows above came a steady stream of articles, thrown among the crowd. A mirror struck Mr. Morris on the arm, and a whole package of clothes fell on his head and almost smothered him; but he brushed them aside and scarcely noticed them.

There was something the matter with Mr. Morris – I knew by the worried sound of his voice when he spoke to any one. I could not see his face, though it was as light as day about us, for we had got jammed in the crowd, and if I had not kept between his feet, I should have been trodden to death. Jim, being larger than I was, had got separated from us.

Presently Mr. Morris raised his voice above the uproar, and called, 'Is every one out of the hotel?' A voice shouted back, 'I'm going up to see.'

'It's Jim Watson, the fireman,' cried some one near. 'He's risking his life to go into that pit of flame. Don't go, Watson.'

I don't think the brave fireman paid any attention to this warning, for an instant later the same voice said, 'He's planting his ladder against the third story. He's bound to go. He'll not get any farther than the second, anyway.'

'Where are the Montagues?' shouted Mr. Morris. 'Has any one seen the Montagues?'

'Mr. Morris! Mr. Morris!' cried a frightened voice, and young Charlie Montague pressed through the people to us. 'Where's papa?'

'I don't know. Where did you leave him?' said Mr. Morris, taking his hand and drawing him closer. 'I was sleeping in his room,' said the boy, 'and a man knocked at the door, and said, "Hotel on fire. Five minutes to dress and get out," and papa told me to put on my clothes and go downstairs, and he ran up to mamma.'

'Where was she?' asked Mr. Morris quickly.

'On the fourth floor. She and her maid Blanche were up there. You know, mamma hasn't been well and couldn't sleep, and our room was so noisy that she moved upstairs where it was quiet.' Mr. Morris gave a kind of groan. 'Oh, I'm so hot, and there's such a dreadful noise,' said the little boy bursting into tears, 'and I want mamma.' Mr. Morris soothed him as best he could, and drew him a little to the edge of the crowd.

While he was doing this, there was a piercing cry. I could not see the person making it, but I knew it was the Italian's voice. He was screaming in broken English that the fire was spreading to the stables, and his animals would be burned. Would no one help him to get them out? There was a great deal of confused language. Some voices shouted, 'Look after the people first. Let the animals go.' Others said, 'For shame. Get the horses out.' But no one seemed to do anything, for the Italian went on crying for help. I heard a number of people who were standing near us say that it had just been found out that several persons who had been sleeping in the top of the hotel had not got out. They said that at one of the attic windows a poor housemaid was shrieking for help. Here in the street we could see no one at the upper windows for smoke was pouring from them.

The air was very hot and heavy, and I didn't wonder that Charlie Montague felt ill. He would have fallen on the ground if Mr. Morris hadn't taken him in his arms, and carried him out of the crowd. He put him down on the brick sidewalk, and unfastened his shirt, and left me to watch him, while he held his hands under a leak in a hose that was fastened to a hydrant near us. He got enough water to dash on Charlie's face and chest, and then seeing that the boy was reviving, he sat down on the curbstone and took him on his knee. Charlie lay in his arms and moaned. He was a delicate boy, and he could not stand rough usage as the Morris boys could.

Mr. Morris was terribly uneasy. His face was deathly white, and he shuddered whenever there was a cry from the burning building. 'Poor souls – God help them. Oh, this is awful!' he said, and then he turned his eyes from the great sheets of flame and strained the little boy to his breast. At last there were wild shrieks that I knew came from no human throats. The fire must have reached the horses. Mr. Morris sprang up, then sank back again. He wanted to go, yet he could be of no use. There were hundreds of men standing about, but the fire had spread so rapidly, and they had so little water to put on it, that there was not much they could do. I wondered whether I could do anything for the poor animals. I was not as much afraid of fire as most dogs, for one of the tricks that the Morris boys had taught me was to put out a blaze with my paws. They would throw a piece of lighted paper on the floor, and I would crush it with my forepaws; and if the blaze was too large for that, I would drag a bit of old carpet over it and jump on it.

I left Mr. Morris, and ran around the corner of the street to the back of the hotel. It was not burned as much here as in the front, and people were spreading wet blankets on the roofs of the near-by houses, and some were standing at the windows watching the fire, or packing up their belongings ready to move if it should spread to them.

There was a narrow lane running up behind the hotel, and I had just started up this lane, when in front of me I heard such a wailing, piercing noise, that I shuddered and stood still. The Italian's animals were going to be burned up and they were calling to their master to come and let them out. Their voices sounded like the voices of children in mortal pain. I could not stand it. I was suddenly seized with such an awful horror of the fire, that I turned and ran, feeling so thankful that I was not in it. As I got into the street, I stumbled over something. It was a large bird – a parrot, and at first I thought it was Bella. Then I remembered hearing Jack say that the Italian had a parrot. It was not dead, but seemed stupid with the smoke. I seized it in my mouth, and ran and laid it at Mr. Morris' feet. He wrapped it in his handkerchief, and laid it beside him.

I sat and trembled, and did not leave him again. I shall never forget that dreadful night. It seemed as if we were there for hours, but in reality it was only a short time. The hotel soon got to be all red flames, and there was very little smoke. The inside of the building had burned away, and nothing more could be taken out. The firemen and all the people drew back, and there was no noise. Everybody stood gazing silently at the flames. A man stepped quietly up to Mr. Morris, and looking at him, I saw that it was Mr. Montague. He was usually a well-dressed man, with a kind face, and a head of thick greyish-brown hair. Now his face was black and grimy, his hair was burnt from the front of his head, and his clothes were half torn from his back.

Mr. Morris sprang up when he saw him, and said, 'Where is your wife?'

The gentleman did not say a word, but pointed to the burning building.

'Impossible!' cried Mr. Morris. 'Is there no mistake? Your beautiful young wife, Montague? Can it be so?' Mr. Morris was trembling from head to foot.

'It is true,' said Mr. Montague quietly. 'Give me the boy.' Charlie had fainted again, and his father took him in his arms, and turned away.

'Montague!' cried Mr. Morris, 'my heart is sore for you. Can I do nothing?'

'No, thank you,' said the gentleman without turning around; but there was more anguish in his voice than in Mr. Morris', and though I am only a dog, I knew that his heart was breaking.

# Ethel Sybil Turner (1872–1958)

Ethel Turner's Woolcot family stories show a marked break from their British (and to a lesser extent American) counterparts. They depict a tightly knit group of children, and as Turner says at the outset of *Seven Little Australians*, 'Not one of the seven is really good, for the very excellent reason that Australian children never are'. The books were, in all probability, a conscious reaction to the sentimental spirit of so much Victorian fiction, such as *The Daisy Chain* (see p. 130), partly ironic parody, and partly something quite new.

Turner has often been compared to Louisa Alcott, and there are many echoes of *Little Women* (for example, there are Megs in both books who have very similar lapses into vanity, and there is even an echo in the Alcott/Woolcot names). But *Seven Little Australians* reads almost as a realistic gloss on *Little Women* (see p. 205): the father, rather than being saintly, is downright unpleasant; the supportive mother has been replaced by a young stepmother who does very little. Things are much tougher: Jo March may

rebel, but she does not run away from boarding school and walk over seventy miles home; and, far from the whole story being circumscribed by religious principles, Judy dies uncomforted by religion and without a protracted deathbed scene.

The attitude of self-reliance and group interdependence among the children goes very deep, and was reflected later in the family stories of Edith Nesbit and other writers. *Seven Little Australians*, therefore, is not only, or merely, one of the first books to make use of an authentic Australian setting in children's fiction. It is almost a statement of national intent, that the literary ways of the old world are no longer ours.

Ethel Turner came to Australia when she was eight; of her twenty-seven books, three others were about the Woolcots: *The Family at Misrule* (1895), which was a success, and the lesser *Little Mother Meg* (1902) and *Judy and Punch* (1902) which were produced, with some reluctance, at the request of Turner's publishers.

## from *Seven Little Australians* (1894)

### CHAPTER 20

### LITTLE JUDY

Across the grass came a little flying figure, Judy in a short pink frock with her wild curls blowing about her face.

'Are you a candidate for sunstroke – where *is* your hat, Miss Judy?' Mr Gillet asked.

Judy shook back her dark tangle.

'Sorrow a know I knows,' she said – 'it's a banana the General is afther dyin' for, and sure it's a dead body I shall live to see misself if you've eaten all the oranges.'

Meg pushed the bag of fruit across the cloth to her, and tried to tilt her hat over her tell-tale eyes. But the bright dark ones had seen the wet lashes the first moment.

'I s'pose you've been reading stupid poetry and making Meg cry?' she said, with an aggressive glance from Mr Gillet to the book on the grass. 'You really ought to be ashamed of yourselves, *sich* behaviour at a picnic. It's been a saving in oranges though, that's a mercy.'

She took half-a-dozen great fat ones from the bag, as well as four or five bananas, and went back with flying steps to the belt of trees, where the General in his holland coat could just be seen.

He was calmly grubbing up the earth and putting it in his little red mouth when she arrived with the bananas.

He looked up at her with an adorable smile.

'*Baby!*' she said, swooping down upon him with one of her wild rushes. '*Baby!*'

She kissed him fifty times. It almost hurt her sometimes, the feeling of love for this little fat, dirty boy.

Then she gathered him up on her knee and wiped as much of the dirt as possible from his mouth with the corner of his coat.

'Narna,' he said, struggling on to the ground again, so she took the skin from a great yellow one and put it in his small, chubby hand.

He ate some of it, and squeezed the rest up tightly in his hands, gleefully watching it come up between his wee fingers in little worm-like morsels.

Then he smeared it over his dimpled face, and even rubbed it on his hair, while Judy was engrossed with her fifth orange.

So, of course, she had to whip him for doing it, or pretend to, which came to the same thing. And then he had to whip her, which did not only mean pretence.

He beat her with a stick he found near, he smacked her face and pulled her hair and bumped himself up and down on her chest, and all in such solemn, painstaking earnestness that she could only laugh even when he really hurt her.

'Dood now?' he said at last anxiously. And she began to weep noisily, with covered face and shaking shoulders, in the proper, penitent way. And then he put his darling arms round her neck and hugged her, and said 'Ju-Ju' in a choking little voice, and patted her cheeks, and gave her a hundred eager, wide, wet kisses till she was better.

Then they played chasings, and the General fell down twenty times, and scratched his little knees and hands, and struggled up again and staggered on.

Presently Judy stood still in a hurry – there was a tick working its slow way into her wrist. Only its two back legs were left out from under the skin, and for a long time she pulled and pulled without any success. Then it broke in two, and she had to leave one half in for little Grandma and kerosene to extract on their return.

Two or three minutes it had taken her to try to move it, and when she looked up the General had toddled some distance away, and was travelling along as fast as ever his little fat legs would carry him, thinking he was racing her. Just as she started after him he looked back, his eyes dancing, his face dimpled and mischievous, and, oh so dirty.

And then – ah, God!

It is so hard to write it. My pen has had only happy writing to do so far, and now!

'You rogue!' Judy called, pretending to run very quickly. Then the whole world seemed to rise up before her.

There was a tree falling, one of the great, gaunt, naked things that had been ringbarked long ago. All day it had swayed to and fro, rotten through and through; now there came up across the plain a puff of wind, and down it went before it. One wild ringing cry Judy gave, then she leaped across the ground, her arms outstretched to the little lad with the laughing eyes and lips straight to death.

The crash shook the trees around, the very air seemed splintered.

They had heard it – all the others – heard the wild cry and then the horrible thud.

How their knees shook! What blanched faces they had as they rushed towards the sound!

They lifted it off the little bodies – the long, silvered trunk with the gum dead and dried in streaks upon it. Judy was face downwards, her arms spread out.

And underneath her was the General, a little shaken, mightily astonished, but quite unhurt.

Meg clasped him for a minute, but then laid him down, and gathered with the others close around Judy.

Oh, the little dark, quiet head, the motionless body, in its pink crushed frock, the small, thin, out-spread hands!

'Judy!' Pip said, in a voice of beseeching agony.

But the only answer was the wind at the tree-tops and the frightened breathings of the others.

Mr Gillet remembered there was no one to act but himself. He went with Pip to the stockman's hut, and they took the door off its leather hinges and carried it down the hill.

'I will lift her,' he said, and passed his arms around the little figure, raising her slowly, slowly, gently upwards, laying her on the door with her face to the sky.

But she moaned – oh, how she moaned!

Pip, whose heart had leapt to his throat at the first sign of life, almost went mad as the little sounds of agony burst from her lips.

They raised the stretcher, and bore her up the hill to the little brown hut at the top.

Then Mr Gillet spoke, outside the doorway, to Meg and Pip, who seemed dazed, stunned.

'It will be hours before we can get help, and it is five now,' he said. 'Pip, there is a doctor staying at Boolagri, ten miles along the road. Fetch him – run all the way. I will go back home – fourteen miles. Miss Meg, I can't be back all at once. I will bring a buggy – the bullock-dray is too slow and jolting, even when it comes back. You must watch by her, give her water if she asks – there is nothing else you can do.'

'She is dying?' Meg said. 'Dying?'

He thought of all that might happen before he brought help, and dare not leave her unprepared.

'I think her back is broken,' he said, very quietly. 'If it is, it means death.'

Pip fled away down the road that led to the doctor's.

Mr Gillet gave a direction or two, then he looked at Meg.

'Everything depends on you. You must not even think of breaking down,' he said. 'Don't move her, watch all the time.'

He moved away towards the lower road.

She sprang after him.

'Will she die while you are away? – no one but me – '

Her eyes were wild, terrified.

'God knows!' he said, and turned away.

It was almost more than he could bear to go and leave this little girl alone to face so terrible a thing.

'God help me!' she moaned, hurrying back, but not looking at the hot, low-hanging sky. 'Help me, God! God, help me, help me!'


## CHAPTER 21

### WHEN THE SUN WENT DOWN

Such a sunset!

Down at the foot of the grass hill there was a flame-coloured sky, with purple, soft clouds massed in banks high up where the dying glory met the paling blue. The belt of trees had grown black, and stretched sombre, motionless arms against the orange background. All the wind had died, and the air hung hot and still, freighted with the strange silence of the bush.

And at the top of the hill, just within the doorway of the little brown hut, her wide eyes on the wonderful heavens, Judy lay dying. She was very quiet now, though she had been talking – talking of all sorts of things. She told them she had no pain at all.

'Only I shall die when they move me,' she said.

Meg was sitting in a little heap on the floor beside her. She had never moved her eyes from the face on the pillow of mackintoshes, she had never opened her white lips to say one word.

Outside the bullocks stood motionless against the sky – Judy said they looked like stuffed ones having their portrait taken. She smiled the least little bit, but Meg said, 'Don't', and writhed.

Two of the men had gone on superfluous errands for help, the others stood some distance away, talking in subdued voices.

There was nothing for them to do. The brown man had been talking – a rare thing for him.

He had soothed the General off to sleep, and laid him in the bunk with the blue blanket tucked around him. And he had made a billy of hot, strong tea, and asked the children, with tears in his eyes, to drink some, but none of them would.

Baby had fallen to sleep on the floor, her arms clasped tightly around Judy's lace-up boot.

Bunty was standing, with a stunned look on his white face, behind the stretcher. His eyes were on his sister's hair, but he did not dare to let them wander to her face, for fear of what he should see there. Nellie was moving all the time: now to the fence to strain her eyes down the road, where the evening shadows lay heavily, now to fling herself face downward behind the hut and say, 'Make her better, God! God, make her better, make her better! Oh, *can't* You make her better?'

Greyer grew the shadows round the little hut, the bullocks' outlines had faded, and only an indistinct mass of soft black loomed across the light. Behind the trees the fire was going out, here and there were yellow, vivid streaks yet, but the flaming sun-edge had dipped beyond the world, and the purple, delicate veil was dropping down.

A curlew's note broke the silence, wild, mournful, unearthly. Meg shivered, and sat up straight. Judy's brow grew damp, her eyes dilated, her lips trembled.

'Meg!' she said, in a whisper that cut the air. 'Oh, Meg, I'm frightened! *Meg,* I'm so frightened!'

'God!' said Meg's heart.

'Meg, say something. Meg, help me! Look at the dark, Meg. *Meg,* I can't die! Oh, why don't they be quick?'

Nellie flew to the fence again – then to say, 'Make her better, God – oh, please, God!'

'Meg, I can't think of anything to say. Can't you say something, Meg? Aren't there any prayers about the dying in the Prayer Book? I forget. Say something, Meg!'

Meg's lips moved, but her tongue uttered no word.

'Meg, I'm so frightened! I can't think of anything but "For what we are about to receive" and that's grace, isn't it? And there's nothing in Our Father that would do either. Meg, I wish we'd gone to Sunday school and learnt things. Look at the dark, Meg! Oh, Meg, hold my hands!'

'Heaven won't – be – dark,' Meg's lip said.

Even when speech came, it was only a halting, stereotyped phrase that fell from them.

'If it's all gold and diamonds, I don't want to go!' The child was crying now. 'Oh, Meg, I want to be alive! How'd you like to die, Meg, when you're only thirteen? Think how lonely I'll be without you all. Oh, Meg! Oh, Pip, Pip! Oh, Baby! Nell!'

The tears streamed down her cheeks, her chest rose and fell.

'Oh, say something, Meg – hymns – anything!'

Half the book of *Hymns Ancient and Modern* danced across Meg's brain. Which one could she think of that would bring quiet into those feverish eyes that were fastened on her face with such a frightening, imploring look?

Then she opened her lips:

> 'Come unto Me, ye weary,
> And I will give you rest,
> Oh, bl –'

'I'm not weary, I don't *want* to rest,' Judy said, in a fretful tone.

Again Meg tried:

> 'My God, my Father, while I stray
> Far from my home on life's rough way,
> Oh, teach me from my heart to say –
> Thy will be done!'

'That's for old people,' said the little tired voice. 'He won't expect *me* to say it.'

Then Meg remembered the most beautiful hymn in the world, and said the first and last verses without a break in her voice:

> 'Abide with me, fast falls the eventide,
> The darkness deepens; Lord, with me abide.
> When other helpers fail, and comforts flee,
> Help of the helpless, oh, abide with me!
>
> Hold Thou Thy Cross before my closing eyes,
> Shine through the gloom and point me to the skies.

Heaven's morning breaks, and earth's vain shadows flee
In life, in death, O Lord, abide with me!'

'Oh – and Judy, dear, we are forgetting – there's Mother. Judy, dear – you won't be lonely! Can't you remember Mother's eyes, little Judy?'

Judy grew quiet, and still more quiet. She shut her eyes so she could not see the gathering shadows.

Meg's arms were round her, Meg's cheek was on her brow, Nell was holding her hands, Baby her feet, Bunty's lips were on her hair. Like that they went with her right to the Great Valley, where there are no lights even for stumbling, childish feet.

The shadows were cold, and smote upon their hearts; they could feel the wind from the strange waters on their brows; but only she who was about to cross heard the low lapping of the waves.

Just as her feet touched the water there was a figure in the doorway.

'Judy!' said a wild voice, and Pip brushed them aside and fell down beside her.

'Judy, Judy, *Judy*!'

The light flickered back in her eyes. She kissed him with pale lips once, twice; she gave him both her hands, and her last smile.

Then the wind blew over them all, and, with a little shudder, she slipped away.

## Chapter 22

## And Last

*'She seemed a thing that could not feel
The touch of earthly years.'*

*'No motion has she now – no force;
She neither hears nor sees;
Rolled round in earth's diurnal course,
With rocks and stones and trees.'*

They went home again, the six of them, and Esther, who, all her days, 'would go the softlier, sadlier' because of the price that had been paid for the life of her little sweet son. The very air of Yarrahappini seemed to crush them and hang heavy on their souls.

So when the Captain, who had hurried up to see the last of his poor little girl, asked if they would like to go home, they all said 'Yes'.

There was a green space of ground on a hill-top behind the cottage, and a clump of wattle trees, dark-green now, but gold-crowned and gracious in the spring.

This is where they left little Judy. All around it Mr Hassal had white tall palings put – the short grave was in the shady corner of it.

The place looked like a tiny churchyard in a children's country where there had only been one death.

Or a green fair field, with one little garden bed.

Meg was glad the little mound looked to the east, the suns died behind it – the orange and yellow and purple suns she could not bear to watch ever again while she lived.

But away in the east they rose tenderly always, and the light crept up across the sky to the hill-top in delicate pinks and trembling blues and brightening greys, but never fiery, yellow streaks, that made the eyes ache with hot tears.

There was a moon making it white and beautiful when they said goodbye to it on the last day.

They plucked a blade or two of grass each from the fresh turfs, and turned away. Nobody cried; the white stillness of the far moon, the pale, hanging stars, the faint wind stirring the wattles, held back their tears till they had closed the little gate behind them and left her alone on the quiet hill-top.

Then they went back to Misrule, each to pick up the thread of life and go on with the weaving that, thank God, must be done, or hearts would break every day.

Meg had grown older; she would never be quite so young again as she had been before that red sunset sank into her soul.

There was a deeper light in her eyes; such tears as she had wept clear the sight till life becomes a thing more distinct and far-reaching.

Nellie and she went to church the first Sunday after their return. Aldith was a few pews away, light-souled as ever, dressed in gay attire, flashing smiling, coquettish glances across to the Court-neys' pew, and the Grahams sitting just behind.

How far away Meg had grown from her! It seemed years since she had been engrossed with the latest mode in hat trimming, the dip of 'umbrella' skirts, and the best method of making the hands white. Years since she had tried a trembling 'prentice hand at flirtations. Years, almost, since she had given the little blue ribbon at Yarrahappini, that was doing more good than she dreamed of.

Alan looked at her from his pew – the little figure in its sorrowful black, the shining hair hanging in a plait no longer frizzed at the end, the chastened droop of the young lips, the wistful sadness of the blue eyes. He could hardly realise it was the little scatterbrain girl who had written that letter, and stolen away through the darkness to meet his graceless young brother.

He clasped her hand when church was over; his grey eyes, with the quick moisture in them, made up for the clumsy, stumbling words of sympathy he tried to speak.

'Let us be friends always, Miss Meg,' he said, as they parted at the Misrule gate.

'Yes, let us,' said Meg.

And the firm, frank friendship became a beautiful thing in both their lives, strengthening Meg and making the boy gentler.

Pip became his laughing, high-spirited self again, as even the most loving boy will, thanks to the merciful making of young hearts; but he used to get sudden fits of depression at times, and disap-pear all at once, in the midst of a game of cricket or football, or from the table when the noise was at its highest.

Bunty presented to the world just as grimy a face as of old, and hands even more grubby, for he had taken a mechanical turn of late, and spent his spare moments in manufacturing printing machines – so called – and fearful and wonderful engines, out of an old stove and some pots and rusty frying-pans rescued from the rubbish heap.

But he did not tell so many stories in these days. That deep sunset had stolen even into his young heart, and whenever he felt inclined to say 'I never, 'twasn't me, 'twasn't my fault', a tangle of dark curls rose before him, just as they had lain that night when he had not dared to move his eyes away from them.

Baby's legs engrossed her very much at present, for she had just been promoted from socks to stockings, and all who remember the occasion in their own lives will realise the importance of it to her.

Nell seemed to grow prettier every day. Pip had his hands full with trying to keep her from growing conceited; if brotherly rubs and snubs availed anything, she ought to have been as lowly minded as if she had had red hair and a nose of heavenward bent.

Esther said she wished she could buy a few extra years, a stern brow, and dignity in large quan-tities from some place or other – there might be some chance, then, of Misrule resuming its bap-tismal and unexciting name of The River House.

But, oddly enough, no one echoed the wish.

The Captain never smoked at the end of the side verandah now: the ill-kept lawn made him see always a little figure in a pink frock and battered hat mowing the grass in a blaze of sunlight. Judy's death made his six living children dearer to his heart, though he showed his affection very little more.

The General grew chubbier and more adorable every day he lived. It is no exaggeration to say that they all worshipped him now in his little kingly babyhood, for the dear life had been twice given, and the second time it was Judy's gift, and priceless therefore.

My pen has been moving heavily, slowly, for these last two chapters. It refuses to run lightly, freely again just yet, so I will lay it aside, or I shall sadden you.

Some day, if you would care to hear it, I should like to tell you of my young Australians again, slipping a little space of years.

Until then, farewell and adieu.

# [Joseph] Rudyard Kipling (1865–1936)

Rudyard Kipling acquired major reputations in several areas of children's literature, partly because he examined his own preoccupations within broad forms rather than following any of the dominant trends. Similarly, he had a tough-minded respect for the intelligence of childhood and made few modifications (if any) to the intricacy of his style or the subtlety of his content.

Kipling had had a highly successful career as poet and short-story writer with work based on his experiences in India, such as *Departmental Ditties* (1886) and *Plain Tales from the Hills* (1888). *The Jungle Books* were written when the Kiplings were living in Vermont and the stories were initially read to his children.

*The Jungle Book* has been classified among animal stories, but Kipling does not draw on established fables beyond – in the Mowgli stories – the generalized idea of the child brought up with wolves. The book concentrates on Kipling's preoccupations: it is about power, initiation and codes of behaviour, and it is driven by fundamental motivations such as love, revenge and rejection. Thus Mowgli's education by Baloo the bear and Bagheera the black panther is an education into the highly stratified law of the jungle, which has metaphorical implications for the education of the child in the British empire.

Many of these themes are apparent in this extract from the story 'Kaa's Hunting'. Any reader coming to Kipling from the Walt Disney version of the book will be surprised to learn that Baloo the bear is the wise old law-master, who teaches Mowgli the words of power and protection of all the jungle peoples. Baloo's teaching ultimately leads to the situation, as Kipling puts it in the story 'Red Dog' in *The Second Jungle Book* (1895), that 'all the jungle was [Mowgli's] friend, and just a little afraid of him'. The laws are complex and profound, but there is one group who are outside the law, the *Bandar-log*, the monkeys, who have no leaders, no discipline and no aim; Baloo and the rest of the animals despise them. The monkeys capture Mowgli, who, as he is carried across the jungle, appeals to Rann the kite to mark his trail. Meanwhile Baloo and Bagheera turn to Kaa, the Rock-python, for help and Rann hails them.

## from *The Jungle Book* (1894)

Baloo looked up to see where the voice came from, and there was Rann the Kite, sweeping down with the sun shining on the upturned flanges of his wings. It was near Rann's bed-time, but he had ranged all over the jungle looking for the Bear and missed him in the thick foliage.

'What is it?' said Baloo.

'I have seen Mowgli among the *Bandar-log*. He bade me tell you. I watched. The *Bandar-log* have taken him beyond the river to the monkey city – to the Cold Lairs. They may stay there for a night, or ten nights, or an hour. I have told the bats to watch through the dark time. That is my message. Good hunting, all you below!'

'Full gorge and a deep sleep to you, Rann,' cried Bagheera. 'I will remember thee in my next kill, and put aside the head for thee alone, O best of kites!'

'It is nothing. It is nothing. The boy held the Master Word. I could have done no less,' and Rann circled up again to his roost.

'He has not forgotten to use his tongue,' said Baloo, with a chuckle of pride. 'To think of one so young remembering the Master Word for the birds too while he was being pulled across-trees!'

'It was most firmly driven into him,' said Bagheera. 'But I am proud of him, and now we must go to the Cold Lairs.'

They all knew where that place was, but few of the Jungle-People ever went there, because what they called the Cold Lairs was an old deserted city, and lost and buried in the jungle, and beasts seldom use a place that men have once used. The wild boar will, but the hunting-tribes do not. Besides, the monkeys lived there as much as they could be said to live anywhere, and no self-respecting animal would come within eye-shot of it except in times of drouth, when the half-ruined tanks and reservoirs held a little water.

'It is half a night's journey — at full speed,' said Bagheera, and Baloo looked very serious. 'I will go as fast as I can,' he said, anxiously.

'We dare not wait for thee. Follow, Baloo. We must go on the quick-foot — Kaa and I.'

'Feet or no feet, I can keep abreast of all thy four,' said Kaa, shortly. Baloo made one effort to hurry, but had to sit down panting, and so they left him to come on later, while Bagheera hurried forward, at the quick panther-canter. Kaa said nothing, but, strive as Bagheera might, the huge Rock-python held level with him. When they came to a hill-stream, Bagheera gained, because he bounded across while Kaa swam, his head and two feet of his neck clearing the water, but on level ground Kaa made up the distance.

'By the Broken Lock that freed me,' said Bagheera, when twilight had fallen, 'thou art no slow goer!'

'I am hungry,' said Kaa. 'Besides, they called me speckled frog.'

'Worm — earth-worm, and yellow to boot.'

'All one. Let us go on,' and Kaa seemed to pour himself along the ground, finding the shortest road with his steady eyes, and keeping to it.

In the Cold Lairs the Monkey-People were not thinking of Mowgli's friends at all. They had brought the boy to the Lost City, and were very pleased with themselves for the time. Mowgli had never seen an Indian city before, and though this was almost a heap of ruins it seemed very wonderful and splendid. Some king had built it long ago on a little hill. You could still trace the stone causeways that led up to the ruined gates where the last splinters of wood hung to the worn, rusted hinges. Trees had grown into and out of the walls; the battlements were tumbled down and decayed, and wild creepers hung out of the windows of the towers on the walls in bushy hanging clumps.

A great roofless palace crowned the hill, and the marble of the courtyards and the fountains was split, and stained with red and green, and the very cobble-stones in the courtyard where the king's elephants used to live had been thrust up and apart by grasses and young trees. From the palace you could see the rows and rows of roofless houses that made up the city looking like empty honeycombs filled with blackness; the shapeless block of stone that had been an idol, in the square where four roads met; the pits and dimples at street-corners where the public wells once stood, and the shattered domes of temples with wild figs sprouting on their sides. The monkeys called the place their city, and pretended to despise the Jungle-People because they lived in the forest. And yet they never knew what the buildings were made for nor how to use them. They would sit in circles on the hall of the king's council chamber, and scratch for fleas and pretend to be men; or they would run in and out of the roofless houses and collect pieces of plaster and old bricks in a corner, and forget where they had hidden them, and fight and cry in scuffling crowds, and then break off to play up and down the terraces of the king's garden, where they would shake the rose trees and the oranges in sport to see the fruit and flowers fall. They explored all the passages and dark tunnels in the palace and the hundreds of little dark rooms, but they never remembered what they had seen and what they had not; and so drifted about in ones and twos or crowds telling each other that they were doing as men did. They drank at the tanks and made the water all muddy, and then they fought over it, and then they would all rush together in mobs and shout: 'There is no one in the jungle so wise and good and clever and strong and gentle as the *Bandar-log*.' Then all would begin again till they grew tired of the city and went back to the tree-tops, hoping the Jungle-People would notice them.

Mowgli, who had been trained under the Law of the Jungle, did not like or understand this kind of life. The monkeys dragged him into the Cold Lairs late in the afternoon, and instead of going to sleep, as Mowgli would have done after a long journey, they joined hands and danced about and sang their foolish songs. One of the monkeys made a speech and told his companions that Mowgli's capture marked a new thing in the history of the *Bandar-log*, for Mowgli was going to show them how to weave sticks and canes together as a protection against rain and cold. Mowgli picked up some creepers and began to work them in and out, and the monkeys tried to imitate; but in a very few minutes they lost interest and began to pull their friends' tails or jump up and down on all fours, coughing.

'I wish to eat,' said Mowgli. 'I am a stranger in this part of the jungle. Bring me food, or give me leave to hunt here.'

Twenty or thirty monkeys bounded away to bring him nuts and wild pawpaws; but they fell to fighting on the road, and it was too much trouble to go back with what was left of the fruit. Mowgli was sore and angry as well as hungry, and he roamed through the empty city giving the Strangers' Hunting Call from time to time, but no one answered him, and Mowgli felt that he had reached a very bad place indeed. 'All that Baloo has said about the *Bandar-log* is true,' he thought to himself. 'They have no Law, no Hunting Call, and no leaders – nothing but foolish words and little picking thievish hands. So if I am starved or killed here, it will be all my own fault. But I must try to return to my own jungle. Baloo will surely beat me, but that is better than chasing silly rose leaves with the *Bandar-log*.'

No sooner had he walked to the city wall than the monkeys pulled him back, telling him that he did not know how happy he was, and pinching him to make him grateful. He set his teeth and said nothing, but went with the shouting monkeys to a terrace above the red sandstone reservoirs that were half-full of rain water. There was a ruined summer-house of white marble in the centre of the terrace, built for queens dead a hundred years ago. The domed roof had half fallen in and blocked up the underground passage from the palace by which the queens used to enter; but the walls were made of screens of marble tracery – beautiful milk-white fret-work, set with agates and cornelians and jasper and lapis lazuli, and as the moon came up behind the hill it shone through the open work, casting shadows on the ground like black velvet embroidery. Sore, sleepy, and hungry as he was, Mowgli could not help laughing when the *Bandar-log* began, twenty at a time, to tell him how great and wise and strong and gentle they were, and how foolish he was to wish to leave them. 'We are great. We are free. We are wonderful. We are the most wonderful people in all the jungle! We all say so, and so it must be true,' they shouted. 'Now as you are a new listener and can carry our words back to the Jungle-People so that they may notice us in future, we will tell you all about our most excellent selves.' Mowgli made no objection, and the monkeys gathered by hundreds and hundreds on the terrace to listen to their own speakers singing the praises of the *Bandar-log*, and whenever a speaker stopped for want of breath they would all shout together: 'This is true; we all say so.' Mowgli nodded and blinked, and said 'Yes' when they asked him a question, and his head spun with the noise. 'Tabaqui the Jackal, must have bitten all these people,' he said to himself, 'and now they have the madness. Certainly this is *dewanee*, the madness. Do they never go to sleep? Now there is a cloud coming to cover that moon. If it were only a big enough cloud I might try to run away in the darkness. But I am tired.'

That same cloud was being watched by two good friends in the ruined ditch below the city wall, for Bagheera and Kaa, knowing well how dangerous the Monkey-People were in large numbers, did not wish to run any risks. The monkeys never fight unless they are a hundred to one, and few in the jungle care for those odds.

'I will go to the west wall,' Kaa whispered, 'and come down swiftly with the slope of the ground in my favour. They will not throw themselves upon *my* back in their hundreds, but –'

'I know it,' said Bagheera. 'Would that Baloo were here; but we must do what we can. When that cloud covers the moon I shall go to the terrace. They hold some sort of council there over the boy.'

'Good hunting,' said Kaa, grimly, and glided away to the west wall. That happened to be the least ruined of any, and the big snake was delayed awhile before he could find a way up the stones. The cloud hid the moon, and as Mowgli wondered what would come next he heard Bagheera's light feet on the terrace. The Black Panther had raced up the slope almost without a sound and was striking – he knew better than to waste time in biting – right and left among the monkeys, who were seated round Mowgli in circles fifty and sixty deep. There was a howl of fright and rage, and then as Bagheera tripped on the rolling, kicking bodies beneath him, a monkey shouted: 'There is only one here! Kill him! Kill.' A scuffling mass of monkeys, biting, scratching, tearing, and pulling, closed over Bagheera, while five or six laid hold of Mowgli, dragged him up the wall of the summer-house and pushed him through the hole of the broken dome. A man-trained boy would have been badly bruised, for the fall was a good fifteen feet, but Mowgli fell as Baloo had taught him to fall, and landed on his feet.

'Stay there,' shouted the monkeys, 'till we have killed thy friends, and later we will play with thee – if the Poison-People leave thee alive.'

'We be of one blood, ye and I,' said Mowgli, quickly giving the Snake's Call. He could hear rustling and hissing in the rubbish all round him and gave the Call a second time, to make sure.

'Even sso! Down hoods all!' said half a dozen low voices (every ruin in India becomes sooner or later a dwelling-place of snakes, and the old summer-house was alive with cobras). 'Stand still, Little Brother, for thy feet may do us harm.'

Mowgli stood as quietly as he could, peering through the open work and listening to the furious din of the fight round the Black Panther – the yells and chatterings and scufflings, and Bagheera's deep, hoarse cough as he backed and bucked and twisted and plunged under the heaps of his enemies. For the first time since he was born, Bagheera was fighting for his life.

'Baloo must be at hand; Bagheera would not have come alone,' Mowgli thought; and then he called aloud: 'To the tank, Bagheera. Roll to the water-tanks. Roll and plunge! Get to the water!'

Bagheera heard, and the cry that told him Mowgli was safe gave him new courage. He worked his way desperately, inch by inch, straight for the reservoirs, hitting in silence. Then from the ruined wall nearest the jungle rose up the rumbling war-shout of Baloo. The old Bear had done his best, but he could not come before. 'Bagheera,' he shouted, 'I am here. I climb! I haste! *Ahuwora!* The stones slip under my feet! Wait my coming, O most infamous *Bandar-log!*' He panted up the terrace only to disappear to the head in a wave of monkeys, but he threw himself squarely on his haunches, and, spreading out his forepaws, hugged as many as he could hold, and then began to hit with a regular *bat-bat-bat*, like the flipping strokes of a paddle-wheel. A crash and a splash told Mowgli that Bagheera had fought his way to the tank where the monkeys could not follow. The Panther lay gasping for breath, his head just out of water, while the monkeys stood three deep on the red steps, dancing up and down with rage, ready to spring upon him from all sides if he came out to help Baloo. It was then that Bagheera lifted up his dripping chin, and in despair gave the Snake's Call for protection – 'We be of one blood, ye and I' – for he believed that Kaa had turned tail at the last minute. Even Baloo, half smothered under the monkeys on the edge of the terrace, could not help chuckling as he heard the Black Panther asking for help.

Kaa had only just worked his way over the west wall, landing with a wrench that dislodged a coping-stone into the ditch. He had no intention of losing any advantage of the ground, and coiled and uncoiled himself once or twice, to be sure that every foot of his long body was in working order. All that while the fight with Baloo went on, and the monkeys yelled in the tank round Bagheera, and Mang, the Bat, flying to and fro, carried the news of the great battle over the jungle, till even Hathi the Wild Elephant trumpeted, and, far away, scattered bands of the Monkey-Folk woke and came leaping along the tree-roads to help their comrades in the Cold Lairs, and the noise of the fight roused all the day-birds for miles round. Then Kaa came straight, quickly, and anxious to kill. The fighting-strength of a python is in the driving blow of his head backed by all the strength and weight of his body. If you can imagine a lance, or a battering ram, or a hammer weighing nearly half a ton driven by a cool, quiet mind living in the handle of it, you can roughly imagine what Kaa was like when he fought. A python four or five feet long can knock a man down if he hits him fairly in the chest, and Kaa was thirty feet long, as you know. His first stroke was delivered into the heart of the crowd round Baloo – was sent home with shut mouth in silence, and there was no need of a second. The monkeys scattered with cries of – 'Kaa! It is Kaa! Run! Run!'

Generations of monkeys had been scared into good behaviour by the stories their elders told them of Kaa, the night-thief, who could slip along the branches as quietly as moss grows, and steal away the strongest monkey that ever lived; of old Kaa, who could make himself look so like a dead branch or a rotten stump that the wisest were deceived, till the branch caught them. Kaa was everything that the monkeys feared in the jungle, for none of them knew the limits of his power, none of them could look him in the face, and none had ever come alive out of his hug. And so they ran, stammering with terror, to the walls and the roofs of the houses, and Baloo drew a deep breath of relief. His fur was much thicker than Bagheera's, but he had suffered sorely in the fight. Then Kaa opened his mouth for the first time and spoke one long hissing word, and the far-away monkeys, hurrying to the defence of the Cold Lairs, stayed where they were, cowering, till the loaded branches bent and crackled under them. The monkeys on the walls and the empty houses stopped their cries, and in the stillness that fell upon the city Mowgli heard Bagheera shaking his wet sides as he came up from the tank. Then the clamour broke out again. The monkeys leaped higher up the walls; they clung round the necks of the big stone idols and shrieked as they skipped along the battlements, while Mowgli, dancing in the summer-house, put his eye to the screen work and hooted owl-fashion between his front teeth, to show his derision and contempt.

'Get the man-cub out of that trap; I can do no more,' Bagheera gasped. 'Let us take the man-cub and go. They may attack again.'

'They will not move till I order them. Stay you ssso!' Kaa hissed, and the city was silent once more. 'I could not come before, Brother, but I *think* I heard thee call' – this was to Bagheera.

'I – I may have cried out in the battle,' Bagheera answered. 'Baloo, art thou hurt?'

'I am not sure that they have not pulled me into a hundred little bearlings,' said Baloo gravely, shaking one leg after the other. 'Wow! I am sore. Kaa, we owe thee, I think, our lives – Bagheera and I.'

'No matter. Where is the manling?'

'Here, in a trap. I cannot climb out,' cried Mowgli. The curve of the broken dome was above his head.

'Take him away. He dances like Mao the Peacock. He will crush our young,' said the cobras inside.

'Hah!' said Kaa, with a chuckle, 'he has friends everywhere, this manling. Stand back, Manling; and hide you, O Poison People. I break down the wall.'

Kaa looked carefully till he found a discoloured crack in the marble tracery showing a weak spot, made two or three light taps with his head to get the distance, and then lifting up six feet of his body clear of the ground, sent home half-a-dozen full-power, smashing blows, nose-first. The screen-work broke and fell away in a cloud of dust and rubbish, and Mowgli leaped through the opening and flung himself between Baloo and Bagheera – an arm round each big neck.

'Art thou hurt?' said Baloo, hugging him softly.

'I am sore, hungry, and not a little bruised; but, oh, they have handled ye grievously, my Brothers! Ye bleed.'

'Others also,' said Bagheera, licking his lips, and looking at the monkey-dead on the terrace and round the tank.

'It is nothing, it is nothing, if thou are safe, O my pride of all little frogs!' whimpered Baloo.

'Of that we shall judge later,' said Bagheera, in a dry voice that Mowgli did not at all like. 'But here is Kaa, to whom we owe the battle and thou owest thy life. Thank him according to our customs, Mowgli.'

Mowgli turned and saw the great python's head swaying a foot above his own.

'So this is the manling,' said Kaa. 'Very soft is his skin, and he is not so unlike the *Bandar-log*. Have a care, Manling, that I do not mistake thee for a monkey some twilight when I have newly changed my coat.'

'We be one blood, thou and I,' Mowgli answered. 'I take my life from thee, to-night. My kill shall be thy kill if ever thou art hungry, O Kaa.'

'All thanks, Little Brother,' said Kaa, though his eyes twinkled. 'And what may so bold a hunter kill? I ask that I may follow when next he goes abroad.'

'I kill nothing, – I am too little, – but I drive goats toward such as can use them. When thou are empty come to me and see if I speak the truth. I have some skill in these (he held out his hands), and if ever thou art in a trap, I may pay the debt which I owe to thee, to Bagheera, and to Baloo, here. Good hunting to ye all, my masters.'

'Well said,' growled Baloo, for Mowgli had returned thanks very prettily. The python dropped his head lightly for a minute on Mowgli's shoulder. 'A brave heart and a courteous tongue,' said he. 'They shall carry thee far through the jungle, Manling. But now go hence quickly with thy friends. Go and sleep, for the moon sets, and what follows it is not well that thou shouldst see.'

The moon was sinking behind the hills, and the lines of trembling monkeys huddled together on the walls and battlements looked like ragged, shaky fringes of things. Baloo went down to the tank for a drink, and Bagheera began to put his fur in order, as Kaa glided out into the centre of the terrace and brought his jaws together with a ringing snap that drew all the monkeys' eyes upon him.

'The moon sets,' he said. 'Is there yet light to see?'

From the walls came a moan like the wind in the tree-tops: 'We see, O Kaa.'

'Good. Begins now the Dance – the Dance of the Hunger of Kaa. Sit still and watch.'

He turned twice or thrice in a big circle, weaving his head from right to left. Then he began making loops and figures of eight with his body, and soft, oozy triangles that melted into squares and five-sided figures, and coiled mounds, never resting, never hurrying, and never stopping his low, humming song. It grew darker and darker, till at last the dragging, shifting coils disappeared, but they could hear the rustle of the scales.

Baloo and Bagheera stood still as stone, growling in their throats, their neck-hair bristling, and Mowgli watched and wondered.

'*Bandar-log*', said the voice of Kaa at last, 'can ye stir foot or hand without my order? Speak!'

'Without thy order we cannot stir foot or hand, O Kaa!'

'Good! Come all one pace nearer to me.'

The lines of the monkeys swayed forward helplessly, and Baloo and Bagheera took one stiff step forward with them.

'Nearer!' hissed Kaa, and they all moved again.

Mowgli laid his hands on Baloo and Bagheera to get them away, and the two great beasts started as though they had been waked from a dream.

'Keep thy hand on my shoulder,' Bagheera whispered. 'Keep it there, or I must go back – must go back to Kaa. *Aah!*'

'It is only old Kaa making circles on the dust,' said Mowgli; 'let us go'; and the three slipped off through a gap in the walls to the jungle.

'*Whoof!*' said Baloo, when he stood under the still trees again. 'Never more will I make an ally of Kaa,' and he shook himself all over.

'He knows more than we,' said Bagheera, trembling. 'In a little time, had I stayed, I should have walked down his throat.'

'Many will walk by that road before the moon rises again,' said Baloo. 'He will have good hunting – after his own fashion.'

'But what was the meaning of it all?' said Mowgli, who did not know anything of a python's powers of fascination. 'I saw no more than a big snake making foolish circles till the dark came. And his nose was all sore. Ho! Ho!'

'Mowgli,' said Bagheera angrily, 'his nose was sore on *thy* account; as my ears and sides and paws and Baloo's neck and shoulders are bitten on *thy* account. Neither Baloo nor Bagheera will be able to hunt with pleasure for many days.'

'It is nothing,' said Baloo; 'we have the man-cub again.'

'True; but he has cost us heavily in time which might have been spent in good hunting, in wounds, in hair – I am half plucked along my back, – and last of all, in honour. For, remember, Mowgli, I, who am the Black Panther, was forced to call upon Kaa for protection, and Baloo and I were both made stupid as little birds by the Hunger-Dance. All this, Man-cub, came of thy playing with the *Bandar-log*.'

'True; it is true,' said Mowgli, sorrowfully. 'I am an evil man-cub, and my stomach is sad in me.'

'*Mf!* What says the Law of the Jungle, Baloo?'

Baloo did not wish to bring Mowgli into any more trouble, but he could not tamper with the Law, so he mumbled: 'Sorrow never stays punishment. But remember, Bagheera, he is very little.'

'I will remember; but he has done mischief, and blows must be dealt now. Mowgli, hast thou anything to say?'

'Nothing. I did wrong. Baloo and thou are wounded. It is just.'

Bagheera gave him half a dozen love-taps; from a panther's point of view they would hardly have waked one of his own cubs, but for a seven-year-old boy they amounted to as severe a beating as you could wish to avoid. When it was all over Mowgli sneezed, and picked himself up without a word.

'Now,' said Bagheera, 'jump on my back, Little Brother, and we will go home.'

One of the beauties of Jungle Law is that punishment settles all scores. There is no nagging afterward.

Mowgli laid his head down on Bagheera's back and slept so deeply that he never waked when he was put down by Mother Wolf's side in the home-cave.

# George Edward Farrow (1862–?1920)

The tenor of *The Wallypug* is evident from the preface:

(For specially nice boys and girls only). Dear Children, Listen! One day Girlie and Boy, their two brothers and myself were sitting by an open window in Broadstairs. I had been telling them fairy-tales, and they had been so eager and interested and had asked so many questions that when I shut my eyes . . . I seemed to see hundreds of other bright eyes, and to hear hundreds of other happy children's voices asking 'Won't you please tell us a story, too?' Perhaps – who knows? – I may have seen your bright eyes amongst the rest . . . . Did I?

Farrow was the most popular of Carroll's imitators, and as we are now moving into the era of the 'beautiful child' cult, Farrow is imitating the fey side of Carroll, not his intellectualism. *The Wallypug* is cast as a dream ('"Had she been asleep or not?" that was the question') and is full of word-play, although this is much more superficial than Carroll's ('it's called a menu for two reasons; first, because it's what they *mean you* to have, and, secondly, because it's between *me and you*.').

The difference between Farrow and Carroll is, however, more fundamental. Carroll was able to empathize with the child and manipulate a narrative voice that was essentially on the child's side and relating to the child's consciousness; Farrow is very often writing down to his audience and across at other adults (see, for example, the microscope joke about jokes in this extract).

Nevertheless, *The Wallypug* was popular, with sequels such as *The Wallypug in the Moon* (1898) which borrows folk-tale characters, and *The Wallypug in Fog Land* (1904); the device of the dream was soon abandoned.

## from *The Wallypug of Why* (1895)

### CHAPTER IV

### GIRLIE SEES THE WALLYPUG

'Late again!' called out the Hall Porter when Girlie hurried up the broad stone steps leading to a great building opposite to the little green gate.

'How can I be late *again*,' asked Girlie angrily, 'when I've never been here at all before?'

'If you've not been here *before*, then you must have been *behind*,' said the Hall Porter; 'and, if one is behind, they are late, don't you know? You are fined sixpence,' he added, taking sixpence from his pocket and handing it to Girlie.

'What is this?' she asked.

'The sixpence that I fined you, of course,' replied the Hall Porter.

'But what am I to do with it?' asked Girlie in surprise.

'Oh! findings', keepings,' muttered the Hall Porter, walking away. 'Put it in your pocket; you'll want it soon.'

And, sure enough, before she had gone many steps along the stone corridor, Girlie came to a great door with the words 'Admission, sixpence' written on it.

After knocking timidly, she waited awhile, till it was, at last, opened by a policeman, who, silently taking the sixpence which she offered him, motioned her to a seat near the door.

'Well, it's a good thing that I *was* fined, or I should never have got in here,' thought Girlie; and she sat down and looked about her curiously.

She found herself in a long Gothic hall with low seats against the wall on each side. At one end was a raised dais, on which was a throne with a canopy over it. The centre of the room was quite bare. On the seats against the wall were sitting a number of animals, and Girlie could see that the Fish with a cold and his companion the Calf were sitting near the throne. The Fish had his tail in a tub of hot mustard-and-water; and by his side was a small table, on which were a basin of gruel, some cough mixture and a packet of lozenges. And near him, at a low desk, sat a Lobster writing rapidly; Girlie afterwards discovered that he was a Reporter. None of the animals had taken the slightest notice of her on her entrance, except an old white Cockatoo in a Paisley shawl, carrying a huge market-basket, and who, as soon as Girlie sat down, made some remark to two Monkeys who were sitting near her. The Monkeys laughed, and one of them, leaning forward so that he could see Girlie more distinctly, made a grimace at her.

'Don't take any notice of them, dear,' said a motherly-looking Penguin, who sat next to her knitting a very curiously-shaped stocking. 'They are always rude to strangers; and I think you have not been here before, have you?' she asked smilingly.

'No, never,' replied Girlie, smiling back again, for she quite took to this kindly-looking creature.

'You're what they call a Proper Noun, aren't you?' asked the Penguin after a pause.

Girlie thought the matter over, and then replied that she supposed she was, although usually spoken of as a little girl.

'It's all the same, my dear,' said the Penguin. 'All girls are nouns, you know, although all nouns are not girls, which is very funny when you come to think of it, because—'

Before she could finish the sentence, there was a stir amongst the animals, when a severe-looking gentleman in black velvet and steel buckles and buttons entered, carrying a long wand.

'Silence!' he cried in a loud voice, and the talking, which had been going on all over the room, immediately ceased.

'The Husher,' whispered the Penguin, hastily putting away her knitting.

'Silence!' again called out the Husher, glaring fiercely at Girlie.

'I didn't speak, sir,' said Girlie nervously.

'Yes, she did! yes, she did!' screamed the Cockatoo. 'She's been talking ever since she came in,' she went on noisily.

'Silence, both of you!' said the Husher, frowning severely first at Girlie and then at the Cockatoo, and then walking to the other end of the room, as a door at the top of some steps near the throne opened, and two Heralds entered, blowing a blast on their trumpets.

'Here comes the Wallypug!' said the Penguin, and everybody stood up as a kind of procession filed into the room.

Girlie and the Penguin moved a little nearer the door, in order to see more distinctly.

First in the procession came the Doctor-in-law, smiling blandly; then the King's Minstrel came strutting in, looking more conceited than ever, and carrying a large roll of music under his arm. He was followed by an elderly gentleman carrying a microscope.

'The Royal Microscopist,' said the Penguin in answer to an inquiring glance that Girlie gave her.

'What is the microscope for?' asked Girlie in a whisper.

'To see the jokes with,' replied the Penguin. 'Some of them cannot be seen at all without it.'

Following the Royal Microscopist came an old lady in a poke bonnet and black lace shawl, who turned out to be the Head Mistress of the High School at Why. She was a very sharp-featured person and wore blue glasses.

There was a slight pause, and then the Wallypug entered. He was a meek-looking little creature, splendidly dressed in royal robes, which, however, fitted him very badly, and his crown was so much too big that it came quite over his head and just rested on the tip of his nose. He carried an orb in one hand and a sceptre in the other. His long velvet cloak, lined with ermine, was held by two pages, who were giggling and occasionally giving the cloak a tug which nearly upset the poor Wallypug, who seemed to have great difficulty in getting along as it was.

'Now then, Wallypug, sparkle up!' called out the Husher, giving him a poke with his wand as soon as he entered the door.

Girlie was greatly surprised to see him treated so disrespectfully, and was quite indignant when, the Wallypug having reached the steps of the dais, the pages gave an extra hard pull at his cloak and caused him to fall awkwardly forward on to his hands and knees, dropping his orb and sceptre and knocking his crown further over his face than ever.

Everybody else, however, seemed to think it a great joke, and even the Wallypug smiled apologetically while he scrambled nervously up to the throne.

During the time that the animals were settling into their places, Girlie found out from the Penguin that the Wallypug was a *kind of King*, governed by the people instead of governing them. He was obliged to spend his money as *they* decided, and was not allowed to do *anything* without their permission. He had to address every one as 'Your Majesty,' and had even to wear such clothes as the people directed. The state robes he now wore had belonged to the previous Wallypug, who had been a much larger man, and that was why they fitted him so badly.

So soon as the room was quiet, the Husher announced in a loud voice, 'The Speech from the Throne'; and the Wallypug immediately stood up, nervously fumbling at a sheet of parchment which he held in his hand. His crown being quite over his eyes, he had to hold the parchment nearly up to his nose in order to see what was written on it. However, he soon began in a feeble voice,—

'May it please your Majesties –' when he was immediately interrupted by the Cockatoo, who screamed out,—

'We don't want to hear all that rubbish! Let's get to business.'

'Yes, yes,' cried several voices; 'business first.'

The Husher called out 'Silence! silence!' in a dignified way. 'I think you *had* better sit down, though,' he added, turning to the Wallypug.

'Very well, your Majesty,' said the Wallypug, looking greatly relieved and sitting down immediately.

The Husher then walked over to the Fish and seemed to be asking him some question, to which the Fish evidently replied in the affirmative, for the Husher looked very pleased and immediately announced, –

'Ladies and gentlemen—'

'What about us?' screamed the Cockatoo.

'And others,' continued the Husher, giving a glance in her direction. 'You will be pleased to hear that the Lecture to-day will be given by A. Fish, Esq., and the subject is one which will no doubt interest you all. It is "*The Whichness of the What as compared to the Thatness of the Thus.*"'

A storm of applause followed this announcement, in the midst of which the Fish arose, assisted by his friend the Calf, who, so soon as he had helped him to stand, ran hurriedly out of the room, returning almost immediately with a large kettle of boiling water and some more mustard. These he poured hastily into the tub, stirring it round and round and gazing up anxiously into the Fish's face.

The Fish gasped once or twice, and then, after swallowing a little gruel, he began in a very choky voice:

'O-o-o-b, o-o-o-b, o-o-o-b, Ladles ad Geddlebed—'

The Reporter looked up with a puzzled air. 'May I trouble you to repeat that?' he asked, putting his claw to his head. 'I didn't quite catch the last part of the sentence.'

'O-o-o-b, o-o-o-b, I said, Ladles ad Geddlebed,' repeated the Fish, looking rather put out.

'Latin quotation?' asked the Reporter of the Doctor-in-law, who stood near him.

'Partly,' replied the Doctor-in-law. '"Ladles" is English, "ad" is Latin, and "Geddlebed" is Dutch, I think. It's a very clever remark,' he continued.

The Reporter looked greatly impressed, and made a note of what the Doctor-in-law had said, and then waited for the Fish to go on.

The Fish, however, was taking some more gruel, and saying 'O-o-o-b' between every spoonful. Presently he choked dreadfully, and, amidst great excitement, had to be helped from the room by the Calf and the Doctor-in-law, who kept thumping him violently on the back all the way to the door.

So soon as they had gone out, the King's Minstrel jumped up and rapidly began undoing his roll of music.

'I will now oblige you with one of my charming songs,' he said.

There was immediately a great commotion in all parts of the room.

'No, you won't!' 'Turn him out!' 'We don't want to hear it,' was heard on all sides, while the old Cockatoo got positively frantic, jumping madly up and down, and screaming out as loudly as she could, 'Down with him! *Down with him*! Down with him!'

The Husher rushed wildly about calling out 'Silence! silence!' and it was not until the King's Minstrel had sulkily rolled up his music and sat down again that order was restored.

# Bertha Upton (1849–1912); illustrated by Florence K. Upton (1873–1922)

This is the first appearance of the 'Golliwogg', which, transmuted into a toy, had a major vogue at the beginning of the century, and then many years of success (and other literary manifestations). The verses were written by Bertha Upton in the USA and sent to England where her daughter illustrated them.

At midnight on Christmas Eve, Peg Deutchland and her doll friends come alive and begin to play. They soon meet the amiable Golliwogg who joins them; in this book he is something of the hero: it was only much later (in books by writers such as Enid Blyton) that his character acquired sinister overtones. However, it remains a matter for debate how far the Golliwogg, like Helen Bannerman's *Little Black Sambo* (1899) is, or could be, the product of racial innocence, rather than subconscious racism.

The Golliwogg is the first of a group of creations from this period, among them the Teddy Bear, Peter Rabbit and Peter Pan, that in one way or another became an integral part of twentieth-century childhood.

### from *The Adventures of Two Dutch Dolls and a 'Golliwogg'* (1895)

But soon they hear the clock strike 'two'
The hours are flying fast!
  With much to do
  Ere night be thro'
Its pleasures overpast!

'Just one leap more!' cries Sarah Jane,
'This fills my wildest dream!'
  E'en as she spoke,
  Peg Deutchland broke
Into a piercing scream.

Then all look round, as well they may
To see a horrid sight!
  The blackest gnome
  Stands there alone,
They scatter in their fright.

With kindly smile he nearer draws:
Begs them to feel no fear
  'What is your name?'
  Cries Sarah Jane;
'The "Golliwogg" my dear.'

Their fears allayed – each takes an arm,
While up and down they walk;
  With sidelong glance
  Each tries her chance
And charms him with 'small talk.'

       *

But even wooden limbs get tired
And want a change of play,
  So 'Golliwogg'
  A 'jolly dog'
Suggests they run away.

The big shop door is bolted fast,
But through the yard behind,
  Peggy has spied
  One open wide,
Which she will shortly find.

Nor stop until they reach a field,
And find a lovely slide;
  No fear has Peg,
  But Meg and Weg
Cling screaming as they glide.

The 'Golliwogg' with flying hair,
Takes the first lead you see,
  Nor minds at all
  The 'Midget' small,
Her arms outstretched in glee.

The sliders never dreamed of harm.
They sailed like ships at sea:
  'Twas Meg and Weg,
  Who tripped up Peg,
And brought to grief their spree.

The wrong man often gets the blame
'Twas just so in this case,
  And balls of snow
  They madly throw
At 'Golliwogg's' kind face.

Anon all reached the valley safe,
And skating longed to try;
  The ice seemed good,
  As each one stood
Upon the bank hard by.

While 'Golliwogg', with cautious steps,
Toward the middle skates;
  They hear a crack!
  They cry, 'come back
To your devoted mates!'

Too late! alas their call is vain!
He swiftly disappears!
  His kind forethought
  Is dearly bought,
It melts them unto tears.

But sturdy Peg is quick to act,
She gives an order clear,
  'Creep on your knees,
  And by degrees
We to the hole will steer.'

They reach in time, Peg drags him out
With all her might and main;
  Poor 'Golliwogg',
  A dripping log,
Must be got home again.

Behold sure signs of early dawn,
As down the field they start;
   A leaden weight,
   This living freight,
With faintly beating heart.

# Annie Fellows Johnston (1863–1913)

Frances Hodgson Burnett's work has survived as the exemplar of the sentimental–romantic wish-fulfilment novel, and a character like Cedric Errol, who could stand up to, and face down, angry adults was highly popular, as in L. M. Montgomery's *Anne of Green Gables* (1908) and Eleanor H. Porter's *Pollyanna* (1913). Annie Fellows Johnston's *The Little Colonel* is *Little Lord Fauntleroy* in the deep South, with certain inversions. The Little Colonel is just as stubborn and tough as her grandfather and she overcomes his prejudices (although with rather more ease than does Cedric).

There is, however, more than a fairy-tale here. The reuniting of a fragmented family by the little girl, Lloyd Sherman (her mother had married a Northerner), is a symbolic reuniting of a whole country, and this symbolism extends to racial integration. Lloyd plays with black children, and the white 'mistress', Elizabeth Lloyd Sherman, has a close relationship with the black servant, Mom Beck.

Johnston was obviously limited by her context in what she could achieve and what she could express. Thus while she also emphasized the virtues of the 'new woman', strong and independent, all her heroines marry.

But, as Burnett had found, the elements brought together here were a potent mixture, and it is not surprising to find that the novel was followed by twelve sequels, and spread out to include *Mary Ware, the Little Colonel's Chum* (1908). *The Little Colonel* was filmed in 1935, starring Shirley Temple and Lionel Barrymore.

This extract relates a memorable encounter between the Little Colonel and her grandfather.

## from *The Little Colonel* (1896)

### CHAPTER III

Two hours later, Colonel Lloyd, riding down the avenue under the locusts, was surprised by a novel sight on his stately front steps.

Three little darkies and a big flop-eared hound were crouched on the bottom step, looking up at the Little Colonel, who sat just above them.

She was industriously stirring something in an old rusty pan with a big battered spoon.

'Now, May Lilly,' she ordered, speaking to the largest and blackest of the group, 'you run an' find some nice 'mooth pebbles to put in for raisins. Henry Clay, you go get me some moah sand. This is 'most too wet.'

'Here, you little pickaninnies!' roared the Colonel as he recognized the cook's children. 'What did I tell you about playing around here, tracking dirt all over my premises? You just chase back to the cabin where you belong!'

The sudden call startled Lloyd so that she dropped the pan, and the great mud pie turned upside down on the white steps.

'Well, you're a pretty sight!' said the Colonel as he glanced with disgust from her soiled dress and muddy hands to her bare feet.

He had been in a bad humor all morning. The sight of the steps covered with sand and muddy tracks gave him an excuse to give vent to his cross feelings.

It was one of his theories that a little girl should always be kept as fresh and dainty as a flower. He had never seen his own little daughter in such a plight as this, and she had never been allowed to step outside of her own room without her shoes and stockings.

'What does your mother mean,' he cried savagely, 'by letting you run barefooted around the country just like poor white trash? An' what are you playing with low-flung niggers for? Haven't you ever been taught any better? I suppose it's some of your father's miserable Yankee notions.'

May Lilly, peeping around the corner of the house, rolled her frightened eyes from one angry face to the other. The same temper that glared from the face of the man, sitting erect in his saddle, seemed to be burning in the eyes of the child who stood so defiantly before him.

The same kind of scowl drew their eyebrows together darkly.

'Don't you talk that way to me,' cried the Little Colonel, trembling with a wrath she did not know how to express.

Suddenly she stooped, and snatching both hands full of mud from the overturned pie, flung it wildly over the spotless white coat.

Colonel Lloyd gasped with astonishment. It was the first time in his life he had ever been openly defied. The next moment his anger gave way to amusement.

'By George!' he chuckled admiringly. 'The little thing has got spirit, sure enough. She's a Lloyd through and through. So that's why they call her the "Little Colonel," is it?'

There was a tinge of pride in the look he gave her haughty little head and flashing eyes.

'There, there, child!' he said soothingly. 'I didn't mean to make you mad, when you were good enough to come and see me. It isn't often I have a little lady like you to pay me a visit.'

'I didn't come to see you, suh,' she answered indignantly as she started toward the gate. 'I came to see May Lilly. But I nevah would have come inside yo' gate if I'd known you was goin' to hollah at me an' be so cross.'

She was walking off with the air of an offended queen, when the Colonel remembered that if he allowed her to go away in that mood she would probably never set foot on his grounds again. Her display of temper had interested him immensely.

Now that he had laughed off his ill humor, he was anxious to see what other traits of character she possessed.

He wheeled his horse across the walk to bar her way, and quickly dismounted.

'Oh, now, wait a minute,' he said in a coaxing tone. 'Don't you want a nice big saucer of strawberries and cream before you go? Walker's picking some now. And you haven't seen my hothouse. It's just full of the loveliest flowers you ever saw. You like roses, don't you, and pinks and lilies and pansies?'

He saw he had struck the right chord as soon as he mentioned the flowers. The sullen look vanished as if by magic. Her face changed as suddenly as an April day.

'Oh, yes!' she cried, with a beaming smile. 'I loves 'm bettah than anything!'

He tied his horse, and led the way to the conservatory. He opened the door for her to pass through, and then watched her closely to see what impression it would make on her. He had expected a delighted exclamation of surprise, for he had good reason to be proud of his rare plants. They were arranged with a true artist's eye for color and effect.

She did not say a word for a moment, but drew a long breath, while the delicate pink in her cheeks deepened and her eyes lighted up. Then she began going slowly from flower to flower, laying her face against the cool velvety purple of the pansies, touching the roses with her lips, and tilting the white lily-cups to look into their golden depths.

As she passed from one to another as lightly as a butterfly might have done, she began chanting in a happy undertone.

Ever since she had learned to talk she had a quaint little way of singing to herself. All the names that pleased her fancy she strung together in a crooning melody of her own.

There was no special tune. It sounded happy, although nearly always in a minor key.

'Oh, the jonquils an' the lilies!' she sang. 'All white an' gold an' yellow. Oh, they're all a-smilin' at me, an' a-sayin' howdy! howdy!'

She was so absorbed in her intense enjoyment that she forgot all about the old Colonel. She was wholly unconscious that he was watching or listening.

'She really does love them,' he thought complacently. 'To see her face one would think she had found a fortune.'

It was another bond between them.

After a while he took a small basket from the wall and began to fill it with his choicest blooms.

'You shall have these to take home,' he said. 'Now come into the house and get your strawberries.'

She followed him reluctantly, turning back several times for one more long sniff of the delicious fragrance.

She was not at all like the Colonel's ideal of what a little girl should be, as she sat in one of the high, stiff chairs, enjoying her strawberries. Her dusty little toes wriggled around in the curls on Fritz's back, as she used him for a foot-stool. Her dress was draggled and dirty, and she kept leaning over to give the dog berries and cream from the spoon she was eating with herself.

He forgot all this, however, when she began to talk to him.

'My great-aunt Sally Tylah is to ou' house this mawnin',' she announced confidentially. 'That's why we came off. Do you know my Aunt Sally Tylah?'

'Well, slightly!' chuckled the Colonel. 'She was my wife's half sister. So you don't like her, eh? Well, I don't like her either.'

He threw back his head and laughed heartily. The more the child talked the more entertaining he found her. He did not remember when he had ever been so amused before as he was by this tiny counterpart of himself.

When the last berry had vanished, she slipped down from the tall chair.

'Do you 'pose it's very late?' she asked in an anxious voice. 'Mom Beck will be comin' for me soon.'

'Yes, it is nearly noon,' he answered. 'It didn't do much good to run away from your Aunt Tyler; she'll see you after all.'

'Well, she can't 'queeze me an' kiss me, 'cause I've been naughty, an' I'll be put to bed like I was the othah day, just as soon as I get home. I 'most wish I was there now,' she sighed. 'It's so fa' an' the sun's so hot. I lost my sunbonnet when I was comin' heah, too.'

Something in the tired, dirty face prompted the old Colonel to say, 'Well, my horse hasn't been put away yet. I'll take you home on Maggie Boy.'

The next moment he repented making such an offer, thinking what the neighbors might say if they should meet him on the road with Elizabeth's child in his arm.

But it was too late. He could not unclasp the trusting little hand that was slipped in his. He could not cloud the happiness of the eager little face by retracting his promise.

He swung himself into the saddle, with her in front.

Then he put his one arm around her with a firm clasp, as he reached forward to take the bridle.

'You couldn't take Fritz on behin', could you?' she asked anxiously. 'He's mighty ti'ed too.'

'No,' said the Colonel with a laugh. 'Maggie Boy might object and throw us all off.'

Hugging her basket of flowers close in her arms, she leaned her head against him contentedly as they cantered down the avenue.

'Look!' whispered all the locusts, waving their hands to each other excitedly. 'Look! The master has his own again. The dear old times are coming back to us.'

'How the trees blow!' exclaimed the child, looking up at the green arch overhead. 'See! They's all a-noddin' to each othah.'

'We'll have to get my shoes an' 'tockin's,' she said presently, when they were nearly home. 'They're in that fence cawnah behin' a log.'

The Colonel obediently got down and handed them to her. As he mounted again he saw a carriage coming toward them. He recognized one of his nearest neighbors. Striking the astonished Maggie Boy with his spur, he turned her across the railroad track, down the steep embankment, and into an unfrequented lane.

'This road is just back of your garden,' he said. 'Can you get through the fence if I take you there?'

'That's the way we came out,' was the answer. 'See that hole where the palin's are off?'

Just as he was about to lift her down, she put one arm around his neck, and kissed him softly on the cheek.

'Good by, gran'fatha',' she said in her most winning way. 'I've had a mighty nice time.' Then she added in a lower tone, 'Kuse me fo' throwin' mud on you' coat.'

He held her close a moment, thinking nothing had ever before been half so sweet as the way she called him grandfather.

From that moment his heart went out to her as it had to little Tom and Elizabeth. It made no difference if her mother had forfeited his love. It made no difference if Jack Sherman was her father, and that the two men heartily hated each other.

It was his own little grandchild he held in his arms.

She had sealed the relationship with a trusting kiss.

'Child,' he said huskily, 'you will come and see me again, won't you, no matter if they do tell you not to? You shall have all the flowers and berries you want, and you can ride Maggie Boy as often as you please.'

She looked up into his face. It was very familiar to her. She had looked at his portrait often, unconsciously recognizing a kindred spirit that she longed to know.

Her ideas of grandfathers gained from stories and observation led her to class them with fairy god-mothers. She had always wished for one.

The day they moved to Lloydsborough, Locust had been pointed out to her as her grandfather's home. From that time on she slipped away with Fritz on every possible occasion to peer through the gate, hoping for a glimpse of him.

'Yes, I'll come suah!' she promised. 'I likes you just lots, gran'fathah!'

He watched her scramble through the hole in the fence. Then he turned his horse's head slowly homeward.

# Samuel Rutherford Crockett (1860–1914)

Although *Sir Toady Lion* supposed itself to be a children's book, it is in a similar vein to Kenneth Grahame's highly influential *The Golden Age* (1895) and *Dream Days* (1898), which were books *about* childhood, rather than *for* children. Thus although *Sir Toady Lion* is an exciting account of rural childhood and not-too-friendly battles between children, it remains somewhat ambivalent about its true audience. It is a characteristically transitional text, as British writers negotiated their way towards a mode of address that accounted for the rapidly changing nature of childhood.

Here we have the formula family of the end of the century: the absent father, the dead mother and three children,

brought up by the good-hearted housekeeper. The elder boy, Hugh John, has assumed, for their playing, the name of General Napoleon Smith, and the younger, the five-year-old Arthur George, is Sir Toady Lion. This name comes from his attempt to say 'Coeur-de-Lion': Arthur George is given to fashionable lisping and at one point delivers the memorable encomium 'Oo is a bwick. Us likes 'oo!' but, like his siblings, he is a good British fighter.

In this extract, the mainspring of the plot is set up: at the end of the book, it is the independent (and landed) family which triumphs.

from *The Surprising Adventures of Sir Toady Lion... with those of General Napoleon Smith. An Improving History for Old Boys, Young Boys, Little Boys, Cow Boys and Tom-Boys* (1897)

## CHAPTER IV

## CASTLE PERILOUS

In one corner of the property of Hugh John's father stood an ancient castle – somewhat doubtfully of it, however, for it was claimed as public property by the adjoining abbey town, now much decayed and fallen from its high estate, but desirous of a new lease of life as a tourist and manufacturing centre. The castle and the abbey had for centuries been jealous neighbours, treacherous friends, embattled enemies, according to the fluctuating power of those who possessed them. The lord of the castle harried the abbot and his brethren. The abbot promptly retaliated by launching, in the name of the Church, the dread ban of excommunication against the freebooter. The castle represented feudal rights, the abbey popular and ecclesiastical authority.

And so it was still. Mr. Picton Smith had, indeed, only bought the property a few years before the birth of our hero; but, among other encumbrances, he had taken over a lawsuit with the town concerning the castle, which for years had been dragging its slow length along. Edam Abbey was a show-place of world-wide repute, and the shillings of the tourist constituted a very important item in the finances of the overburdened municipality. If the Council and magistrates of the good town of Edam could add the Castle of Windy Standard to their attractions, the resultant additional sixpence a head would go far toward making up the ancient rental of the town parks, which now let for exactly half of their former value.

But Mr. Picton Smith was not minded thus tamely to hand over an ancient fortress, secured to him by deed and charter. He declared at once that he would resist the claims of the town by every means in his power. He would, however, refuse right-of-way to no respectable sightseer. The painter, all unchallenged, might set up his easel there, the poet meditate, even the casual wanderer in search of the picturesque and romantic, have free access to these gloomy and desolate halls. The townspeople would be at liberty to conduct their friends and visitors thither. But Mr. Smith was resolved that the ancient fortalice of the Windy Standard should not be made a vulgar show. Sandwich papers and ginger-beer bottles would not be permitted to profane the green sward of the courtyard, across which had so often ridden all the chivalry of the dead Lorraines.

'Those who want sixpenny shows will find plenty at Edam Fair,' was Mr. Picton Smith's ulti-matum. And when he had once committed himself, like most of his stalwart name, Mr. Smith had the reputation of being very set in his mind.

But in spite of this the town asserted its right-of-way through the courtyard. A footpath was said to have passed that way by which persons might go to and fro to kirk and market.

'I have no doubt a footpath passed through my dining-room a few centuries ago,' said Mr. Smith, 'but that does not compel me to keep my front and back doors open for all the rabble of Edam to come and go at their pleasure.'

And forthwith he locked his lodge gates and bought the largest mastiff he could obtain. The castle stood on an island rather more than a mile long, a little below the mansion-house. A wooden bridge led over the deeper, narrower, and more rapid branch of the Edam River from the direction of the abbey and town. Across the broader and shallower branch there could be traced, from the house of Windy Standard, the remains of an ancient causeway. This, in the place where the stream was to be crossed, had become a series of stepping-stones over which Hugh John and Priscilla could go at a run (without falling in and wetting themselves more than once in three or four times), but which still constituted an impregnable barrier to the short fat legs of Toady Lion – who usually stood on the shore and proclaimed his woes to the world at large till somebody carried him over and deposited him on the Castle Island.

Affairs were in this unsettled condition when, at twelve years of age, Hugh John ceased to be Hugh John, and became, without, however, losing his usual surname of Smith, one of the august and imperial race of the Buonapartes.

It was a clear June evening, the kind of night when the whole landscape seems to have been newly swept, washed down, and generally spring-cleaned. All nature spoke peace to Janet Sheep-shanks, housekeeper, nurse, and general responsible female head of the house of Windy Standard, when a procession came towards her across the stepping-stones over the broad Edam water from the direction of the Castle Island. Never had such a disreputable sight presented itself to the eyes of Janet Sheepshanks. At once douce and severe, sharp-tongued and covertly affectionate, she represented the authority of a father who was frequently absent from them, and the memory of a dead mother which remained to the three children in widely different degrees. To Priscilla her mother was a loving being, gracious alike by the tender sympathy of her voice and by the magic of a touch which healed all childish troubles with the kiss of peace upon the place 'to make it well.' To Hugh John she had been a confidante to whom he could rush, eager and dishev-elled, with the tale of the glorious defeat of some tin enemy (for even in those prehistoric days Hugh John had been a soldier), and who, smoothing back his ruffled hair, was prepared to join as eagerly as himself in all his tiny triumphs. But to Toady Lion, though he hushed the shrill per-sistence of his treble to a reverent murmur when he talked of 'muvver,' she was only an imagina-tion, fostered mostly by Priscilla – his notion of motherhood being taken from his rough-handed loving Janet Sheepshanks; while the tomb in the village churchyard was a place to which he had no desire to accompany his mother, and from whose gloomy precincts he sought to escape as soon as possible.

## CHAPTER V

## THE DECLARATION OF WAR

But, meanwhile, Janet Sheepshanks stands at the end of the stepping-stones, and Janet is hardly a person to keep waiting anywhere near the house of Windy Standard.

Over the stepping-stones came as leader Priscilla Smith, her head thrown back, straining in every nerve with the excitement of carrying Sir Toady Lion, whose scratched legs and shoeless feet dangled over the stream. Immediately beneath her, and wading above the knee in the rush of the water, there staggered through the shallows Hugh John, supporting his sister with voice and hand – or, as he would have said, 'boosting her up' whenever she swayed riverward with her burden, pushing her behind when she hesitated, and running before to offer his back as an additional stepping-stone when the spaces were wide between the boulders.

Janet Sheepshanks waited grimly for her charges on the bank, and her eyes seemed to deceive her, words to fail her, as the children came nearer. Never had such a sight been seen near the decent house of Windy Standard. Miss Priscilla and her pinafore were represented by a ragged tinkler's lass with a still more ragged frill about her neck. Her cheeks and hands were as variously scratched as if she had fallen into a whole thicket of brambles. Her face, too, was pale, and the tattooed places showed bright scarlet against the whiteness of her skin. She had lost a shoe, and her dress was ripped to the knee by a great ragged triangular tear, which flapped wet about her ankles as she walked.

Sir Toady Lion was somewhat less damaged, but still showed manifold signs of rough usage. His lace collar, the pride of Janet Sheepshanks' heart, was torn nearly off his shoulders, and now hung jagged and unsightly down his back. Several buttons of his well-ordered tunic were gone, and as to his person he was mud as far above the knees as could be seen without turning him upside down.

But Hugh John – words are vain to describe the plight of Hugh John. One eye was closed, and began to be discoloured, taking on above the cheekbone the shot green and purple of a half-ripe plum. His lip was cut, and a thin thread of scarlet stealing down his brow told of a broken head. What remained of his garments presented a ruin more complete, if less respectable, than the ancient castle of the Windy Standard. Neither shoe nor shoe-string, neither stocking nor collar, remained intact upon him. On his bare legs were the marks of cruel kicks, and for ease of transport he carried the *débris* of his jacket under his arm. He had not the remotest idea where his cap had gone to.

No wonder that Janet Sheepshanks awaited this sorry procession with a grim tightening of the lips, or that her hand quivered with the desire of punishment, even while her kind and motherly heart yearned to be busy repairing damages and binding up the wounded. Of this feeling, however, it was imperative that for the present, in the interests of discipline, she should show nothing.

It was upon Priscilla, as the eldest in years and senior responsible officer in charge, that Janet first turned the vials of her wrath.

'Eh, Priscilla Smith, but ye are a ba-a-ad, bad lassie. Ye should ha'e your bare back slashit wi' nettles! Where ha'e ye been, and what ha'e ye done to these twa bairns? Ye shall be marched straight to your father, and if he doesna gar ye loup when ye wad raither stand still, and claw where ye are no yeuky, he will no be doing his duty to the Almichty, and to your puir mither that's lang syne in her restin' grave in the kirk-yaird o' Edom.'

By which fervent address in her native tongue, Janet meant that Mr. Smith would be decidedly spoiling the child if on this occasion he spared the rod. Janet could speak good enough formal English when she chose, for instance to her master on Sabbath, or to the minister on visitation days; but whenever she was excited she returned to that vigorous ancient Early English which some miscall a dialect, and of which she had a noble and efficient command.

To Janet's attack, Priscilla answered not a word either of explanation or apology. She recognised that the case had gone far beyond that. She only set Sir Toady Lion on his feet, and bent down to brush the mud from his tunic with her usual sisterly gesture. Janet Sheepshanks thrust her aside without ceremony.

'My wee man,' she said, 'what have they done to you?'

Toady Lion began volubly, and in his usual shrill piping voice, to make an accusation against certain bad boys who had 'hit him,' and 'hurted him,' and 'kicked him.' And now when at last he was safely delivered and lodged in the well-proven arms of Janet Sheepshanks his tears flowed apace, and made clean furrows down the woebegone grubbiness of his face.

Priscilla walked by Janet's side, white and silent, nerving herself for the coming interview. At ordinary times Janet Sheepshanks was terrible enough, and her word law in all the precincts of Windy Standard. But Priscilla knew that she must now face the anger of her father; and so, with this in prospect, the railing accusations of her old nurse scarcely so much as reached her ears.

John Hugh, stripped of all military pomp, limped behind – a short, dry, cheerless sob shaking him at intervals. But in reality this was more the protest of ineffectual anger than any concession to unmanly weakness.


## CHAPTER VI

### FIRST BLOOD

Ten minutes later, and without, as Janet Sheepshanks said, 'so muckle as a sponge or a brush-and-comb being laid upon them,' the three stood before their father. Silently Janet had introduced them, and now as silently she stood aside to listen to the evidence – and, as she put it, 'keep the maister to his duty, and mind him o' his responsibilities to them that's gane.'

Janet Sheepshanks never forgot that she had been maid for twenty years to the dead mother of the children, nor that she had received 'the bits o' weans' at her hand as a dying charge. She considered herself, with some reason, to be the direct representative of the missing parent, and referred to Priscilla, Toady Lion, and Hugh John as 'my bairns,' just as, in moments of affection, she would still speak to them of 'my bonnie lassie your mither,' as if the dead woman were still one of her flock.

For a full minute Mr. Picton Smith gazed speechless at the spectacle before him. He had been writing something that crinkled his brow and compressed his lips, and at the patter of the children's feet in the passage outside his door, as they ceremoniously marshalled themselves to enter, he had turned about on his great office chair with a smile of expectation and anticipation. The door opened, and Janet Sheepshanks pushed in first Sir Toady Lion, still voluble and calling for vengeance on the 'bad, bad boys at the castle that had striked him and hurted his dear Prissy.' Priscilla herself stood white-lipped and dumb, and through the awful silence pulsed the dry, recurrent, sobbing catch in the throat of Hugh John.

Mr. Picton Smith was a stern man, whose great loss had caused him to shut up the springs of his tenderness from the world. But they flowed the sweeter and the rarer underneath; and though his grave and dignified manner daunted his children on the occasion of any notable evil-doing, they had no reason to be afraid of him.

'Well, what is the meaning of this?' he said, his face falling into a greyer and graver silence at the sound of Hugh John's sobs, and turning to Priscilla for explanation.

Meanwhile Sir Toady Lion was pursuing the subject with his usual shrill alacrity.

'Be quiet, sir,' said his father. 'I will hear you all one by one, but let Priscilla begin – she is the eldest.'

'We went to the castle after dinner, over by the stepping-stones,' began Priscilla, fingering nervously the frill of the torn pinafore about her throat, 'and when we got to the castle we found out that our pet lamb Donald had come after us by the ford; and he was going everywhere about the castle, trying to rub his bell off his neck on the gate-posts and on the stones at the corners.'

'Yes, and I stooded on a rock, and Donald he butted me over behind!' came the voice of Sir Toady Lion in shrill explanation of his personal share in the adventure.

'And then we played on the grass in the inside of the castle. Toady Lion and I were plaiting daisy-chains and garlands for Donald, and Hugh John was playing at being the Prisoner of Chilly-on: he had tied himself to the gate-post with a rope.'

''T wasn't,' muttered Hugh John, who was a stickler for accuracy; 'it was a plough chain!'

'And it rattled,' added Sir Toady Lion, not to be out of the running.

'And just when we were playing nicely, a lot of horrid boys from the town came swarming and clambering in. They had run over the bridge and climbed the gate, and then they began calling us names and throwing mud. So Hugh John said he would tell on them.'

'Didn't,' interrupted Hugh John indignantly. 'I said I'd knock the heads off them if they didn't stop and get out; and they only laughed and said things about father. So I hit one of them with a stone.'

'Then,' continued Priscilla, gaining confidence from a certain curious spark of light which began to burn steadily in her father's eyes, 'after Hugh John threw the stone, the horrid boys all came and said that they would kill us, and that we had no business there anyway.'

'They frowed me down the well, and I went splass! Yes, indeedy!' interrupted Toady Lion, who had imagination.

'Then Donald, our black pet lamb, that is, came into the court, and they all ran away after him and caught him. First he knocked down one or two of them, and then they put a rope round his neck and began to take rides on his back.'

'Yes, and he bleated and "kye-kyed" just feeful!' whimpered Toady Lion, beginning to weep all over again at the remembrance.

But the Smith of the imperial race only clenched his torn hands and looked at his bruised knuckles.

'So Hugh John said he would kill them if they did not let Donald go, and that he was a soldier. But they only laughed louder, and one of them struck him across the lip with a stick – I know him, he's the butch – '

'Shut up, Pris!' shouted Hugh John, with sudden fierceness; 'it's dasht mean to tell names.'

'Be quiet, sir,' said his father severely; 'let your sister finish her story in her own way.'

But for all that there was a look of some pride on his face. At that moment Mr. Picton Smith was not sorry to have Hugh John for a son.

'Well,' said Priscilla, who had no such scruples as to telling on her enemies, 'I won't tell if you say not. But that was the boy who hurt Donald the worst.'

'Well, I smashed him for that!' muttered Napoleon Smith.

'And then when Hugh John saw them dragging Donald away and heard him bleating – '

'And "kye-kying" big, big tears, big as cherries!' interjected Toady Lion, who considered every narrative incomplete to which he did not contribute.

'He was overcome with rage and anger' – at this point Priscilla began to talk by the book, the dignity of the epic tale working on her, 'and he rushed upon them fearlessly, though they were ten to one; and they all struck him and kicked him. But Hugh John fought like a lion.'

'Yes, like Wichard Toady Lion,' cried the namesake of that hero, 'and I helped him and bited a bad boy on the leg, and didn't let go though he kicked and hurted feeful! Yes, indeedy!'

'And I went to their assistance and fought as Hugh John showed me. And – I forget the rest,' said Priscilla, her epic style suddenly failing her. Also she felt she must begin to cry very soon, now the strain was over. So she made haste to finish. 'But it was dreadful, and they swore, and said they would cut Donald's throat. And one boy took out a great knife and said he knew how to do it. He was the butch – '

'Shut up, Pris! Now don't you dare!' shouted Hugh John, in his most warning tones.

'And when Hugh John rushed in to stop him, he hit him over the head with a stick, and Hugh John fell down. And, oh! I thought he was dead, and I didn't know what to do' (Priscilla was crying in good earnest now); 'and I ran to him and tried to lift him up. But I could not – he was so wobbly and soft.'

'I bited the boy's leg. It was dood. I bited hard!' interrupted Toady Lion, whose mission had been vengeance.

'And when I looked up again they had taken away p-p-poor Donald,' Priscilla went on spasmodically between her tears, 'and I think they killed him because he belonged to you, and – they said he had no business there! Oh, they were such horrid cruel boys, and much bigger than us. And I can't bear that Don should have his throat cut. I was promised that he should never be sold for mutton, but only clipped for wool. And he had such a pretty throat to hang daisy-chains on, and was such a dear, dear thing.'

'I don't think they would dare to kill him,' said Mr. Smith gravely; 'besides, they could not lift him over the gate. I will send at once and see. In fact I will go myself!'

There was only anger against the enemy now, and no thought of chastisement of his own in the heart of Mr. Picton Smith. He was rising to reach out his hand to his riding-whip, when General Napoleon Smith, who, like most great makers of history, had taken little part in the telling of it, created a diversion which put all thought of immediate action out of his father's head. He had been standing up, shoulders squared, arms dressed to his side, head erect, as he had seen Sergeant Steel do when he spoke to his Colonel. Once or twice he had swayed slightly, but the heart of the Buonapartes, which beat bravely in his bosom, brought him up again all standing. Nevertheless he grew ever whiter and whiter, till, all in a moment, he gave a little lurch forward, checked himself, and again looked straight before him. Then he sobbed out once suddenly and helplessly, said 'I couldn't help getting beaten, father – there were too many of them!' and fell over all of a piece on the hearthrug.

At which his father's face grew very still and angry as he gathered the great General gently in his arms and carried him upstairs to his own little white cot.

# Albert Bigelow Paine (1861–1937)

*The Arkansas Bear* is a fine tall story, owing, perhaps, something to *Toby Tyler* (see p. 303). Bo[sephus] has run away from home where he had been ill-treated, and meets [Hor]Ratio, the fiddle-playing, acrobatic bear. The bear had also run away from his parents, been trapped and taught the first half of the tune 'The Arkansaw Traveller' before eating his (Italian) master. Bo teaches him the rest of the tune, and together they travel into Louisiana. In each chapter they have an adventure; generally the bear tries to steal something – corn, melon, honey – but they escape by playing and singing, even from a creek full of alligators. Finally Ratio rescues a bear cub from another wicked Italian; the cub turns out to be his brother; he finds his long-lost family, and sets up his bear colony in the Arkansas woods, with Bo as Prime Minister. But Bo misses people, and heads south again. Ratio joins him.

Clearly and simply told, with neat rhymes and fiddle-tunes in the text, *The Arkansas Bear* contrives to build engaging characters – notably Ratio, the cowardly comic, who is still a savage bear. However, the encounters that Bo and Ratio have with niggers, darkys, and pickaninnies, one of whom is caught doing a 'hoo-doo' dance, and whose dialect is strong ('Oh, Mars Debbil... lemme go dis time, an' I nevah do so no mo') might well move the book out of what is now acceptable.

Paine was Mark Twain's secretary and wrote Twain's authorized biography (three volumes, 1912). He is also noted for coining the phrase 'Great White Way' for Broadway (as the title of a play).

## from *The Arkansas Bear, a Tale of Fanciful Adventure told in Song and Story* (1898)

### CHAPTER II

### THE FIRST PERFORMANCE

*'Oh, 't was down in the woods of the Arkansaw*
*I met an Old Bear with a very nimble paw;*
*He could dance and he could fiddle at the only tune he knew,*
*And he fiddled and he fiddled, but he never played it through.'*

Bo was awake first, and Horatio still lay sound asleep. As the boy paused, the Bear opened one eye sleepily and reached lazily toward his fiddle, but dropped asleep again before his paw touched it. They had found a very cosy place in a big heap of dry leaves under some spreading branches, and Horatio, though fond of music, was still more fond of his morning nap. Bosephus looked at him a moment and began singing again, in the same strain: –

'Then there came a little boy who could whistle all the tune,
And he whistled and he sang it by the rising of the moon;
And he whistled and he whistled, and he sang it o'er and o'er,
Till Horatio learned the music that he never learned before.'

The Bear opened the other eye, and once more reached for his fiddle. This time he got hold of it, but before his other paw touched the bow he was asleep again. Bo waited a moment. Then he suddenly began singing the other part of the tune:–

'Yes, he learned it all so neatly and he played it all so sweetly
That he fell in love completely with the boy without a home;
And he said, "No matter whether it is dark or sunny weather,
We will travel on together till the cows – come – home."'

Before Bosephus finished the first two lines of this strain Horatio was sitting up straight and fiddling for dear life.

'Once more, Bo, once more!' he shouted, as they finished.

They repeated the music, and Horatio turned two handsprings without stopping.

'Now,' he said, 'we will go forth and conquer the world.'

'I could conquer some breakfast first,' said Bo.

'Do you like roasting ears?'

'Oh, yes,' said Bo.

'Well, I have an interest in a little patch near here – that is, I take an interest, I should say, and you can take part of mine, or one of your own, if you like. It really doesn't make any difference which you do, just so you take it before the man that planted it gets up.'

'Why,' exclaimed the boy, as they came out into a little clearing, 'that is old Zack Todd's field!'

'It is, is it? Well, how did old Zack Todd get it, I'd like to know.'

'Why – why, I don't know,' answered Bo, puzzled.

'Of course not,' said the Bear. 'And now, Bosephus, let me tell you something. The bears owned that field long before old Zack Todd was ever thought of. We're just renting it to him on shares. This is rent day. We don't need to wake Zack up. You get over the fence and hand me a few of the best ears you can get quick and handy, and you might bring one of those water-melons I see in the corn there, and we'll find a quiet place that I know of, and have our breakfast.'

Bo hopped lightly over the rail fence, and, gathering an armful of green corn, handed it to Horatio. Then he turned to select a melon.

'Has Zack Todd got a gun, Bosephus?' asked the Bear.

'Yes, sir-ee. The best gun in Arkansaw, and he's a dead shot with it.'

'Oh, he is! Well, maybe you better not be quite so slow picking out that melon. Just take the first big one you see and come on.'

'Why, Zack would n't care for us collecting rent, would he?'

'Well, I don't know. You see, some folks are peculiar that way. Zack might forget it was rent day, and a man with a bad memory and a good gun can't be trusted. Especially when he 's a dead shot. There, that one will do. Never mind about leaving a receipt – we 'll mail it to him.'

Bo scrambled back over the fence with the melon, and hastened as fast as he could after Horatio, who was already moving across the clearing with his violin under one arm and the green ears under the other.

'Wait, Ratio,' called the little boy. 'This melon is heavy.'

'Is that a long-range gun, Bo?' called back the Bear.

'Carries a mile and a half.'

'Can't you move up a little faster, Bo? I'm afraid, after all, that melon is bigger than we needed.'

The boy was fat and he panted after his huge companion.

Suddenly there was a sharp report, and Bosephus saw a little tuft of fur fly from one of his companion's ears. Horatio dodged frantically and dropped part of his corn.

'Run zigzag, Bo!' he called, 'and don't drop the melon. Run zigzag. He can't hit you so well then,' and Horatio himself began such a performance of running first one way and then the other that Bo was almost obliged to laugh in spite of their peril.

'Is this what you call conquering the world, Ratio?' he called. Then, as he followed the Bear's example, he caught a backward glimpse out of the corner of his eye.

'Oh, Ratio, the whole family is after us. Zack Todd, and old Mis' Todd, and Jim, and the girls.'

'How many times does that gun shoot?'

'Only once without loading.'

'Muzzle loader?'

'Yep,' panted Bo. 'Old style.'

'Good! Hold on to that melon. We'll get to the woods yet.'

But Horatio was mistaken, for just as they dashed into the edge of the timber, with the pursuers getting closer every moment, right in front of them was a high barbed-wire fence which the Todd family had built around the clearing but a few days before. The Bear dropped his corn, and the boy,

"IN A SECOND MORE HE WAS PLAYING AND DANCING."

Plate 9   Illustration from *The Arkansas Bear*

with some haste, put down the melon. They then turned. The Todd family was entering the woods – old Zack and the gun in front. He had loaded it, and was putting on the cap as he ran.

'What shall we do, Bo? what shall we do now?' groaned Horatio.

They were in a fix, sure enough. Their enemy was upon them, and in a moment more the deadly gun would be leveled. Suddenly a bright thought occurred to Bo.

'I know,' he shouted; 'dance, Horatio! dance!'

Horatio still had his fiddle under his arm. He threw it into position and ran the bow over the strings. In a second more he was playing and dancing, and Bo was singing as though it were a matter of life and death, which, perhaps, it was: –

> 'Oh, there was a fine man and a mighty fine gun
> And a Bear that played the fiddle and a boy that could n't run,
> And the boy was named Bosephus and Horatio was the Bear,
> And they could n't find a bite to eat for breakfast anywhere.'

The Todd family stood still at this unexpected performance and stared at the two musicians. Old man Todd leaned his gun against a tree.

'Now they could n't buy their breakfast for their money all was spent,
So they dropped into a cornfield to collect a little rent;
But they only took a melon and an ear of corn or so,
And were going off to eat them where the butter blossoms grow.'

The Todd family were falling into the swing of the music. Old Mis' Todd and the girls were swaying back and forth and the men were beating time with their feet. Suddenly Bosephus changed to the second part of the tune.

'But the old man got up early with a temper rather surly,
And he chased them with his rifle and to catch them he was bound;
Till he heard the ridy-diddle of Horatio and his fiddle,
Then he shouted, "Hallelujah, girls, and all – hands – 'round!"' '

The first line of this had started the Todd family. Old Zack swung old Mis' Todd, and Jim swung the girls. Then all joined hands and circled to the left. They circled around Bosephus and Horatio, who kept on with the music, faster and faster. Then there was a grand right and left and balance all – every one for himself – until they were breathless and could dance no more. Horatio stopped fiddling and when old man Todd could catch his breath he said to Bo: –

'Look a-here; that Bear of yours is a whole show by himself, and you're another. Anybody that can play and sing like that can have anything I've got. There's my house and there's my cornfield; help yourselves.'

Bo thanked him and said that the corn and the melon already selected would do for the time. To please them, however, he would take up a modest collection. He passed his hat and received a silver twenty-five cent piece, a spool of thread with a needle in it, a one-bladed jack-knife, and two candy hearts with mottoes on them – the last being from the girls, who blushed and giggled as they dropped them in. Then he said good-by, and the Todd family showed them a gate that led into the thick woods. As the friends passed out of sight and hearing Bosephus paused and waved his handkerchief to the girls. A little later Horatio turned to him and said, gravely:

'That is what I call conquering the world, Bosephus. We began a little sooner and more abruptly than I had expected, but it was not badly done, and, all things considered, you did your part very well, Bosephus; very well indeed.'

# John Meade Falkner (1858–1932)

*Moonfleet* was a popular boys' story for a hundred years, latterly becoming a text read in schools, and it is now available in a scholarly edition for adults. It is in the same vein as Stevenson's *Treasure Island* (by which it was influenced), in that it is both a full-blooded adventure and an affectionate pastiche of the genre. It is centred on the smuggling community of Moonfleet in eighteenth-century Dorset, described with an enthusiasm that masks its debt to the penny-dreadful tradition.

Like Stevenson, Falkner blurs, or even reverses, the customary moral order. The real hero is the grizzled giant, Elzevir Block, chief smuggler of the district; the villain is the rich magistrate, Maskew, who early in the book shoots Block's son in a dastardly fashion during a smuggling raid. Also like Stevenson, Falkner makes his narrator, John Trenchard, less than heroic and not much given to self-criticism. Indeed, much of the plot hinges on Trenchard's foolish actions, which are partly due to ingenuousness

and partly to weakness. The plot becomes somewhat expedient towards the end: after years of imprisonment and slavery in the east, Block and Trenchard happen to be shipwrecked on Moonfleet beach.

However, the novel's great strengths are its set pieces, such as John being trapped in the crypt under the church, or retrieving Blackbeard's treasure from eighty feet down a well shaft. It is also notable for its element of romance: Trenchard is in love with Maskew's beautiful daughter, Grace, who is a girl of considerable spirit. (In fact, for me, one of the flaws in the book is how she continues to admire such an unsatisfactory character as Trenchard.)

In this extract, Maskew has attempted to catch Elzevir and his smuggling gang, but has been caught himself. The smugglers leave him to Elzevir's mercy, not knowing that the Revenue Troops are about to appear. Elzevir is about to shoot him when Trenchard (thinking of Grace) knocks his arm up into the air, and Elzevir's pistol goes off.

## from *Moonfleet* (1898)

## from Chapters IX and X

But now a new thing happened; for before the echoes of that pistol-shot had died on the keen morning air, I thought I heard a noise of distant shouting, and looked about to see whence it could come. Elzevir looked round too, forgetting to upbraid me for making him miss his aim, but Maskew still kept his face turned up towards the cliff. Then the voices came nearer, and there was a mingled sound as of men shouting to one another, and gathering in from different places. 'Twas from the cliff-top that the voices came, and thither Elzevir and I looked up, and there too Maskew kept his eyes fixed. And in a moment there were a score of men stood on the cliff's edge high above our heads. The sky behind them was pink flushed with the keenest light of the young day, and they stood out against it sharp cut and black as the silhouette of my mother that used to hang up by the parlour chimney. They were soldiers, and I knew the tall mitre-caps of the 13th, and saw the shafts of light from the sunrise come flashing round their bodies, and glance off the barrels of their matchlocks.

I knew it all now; it was the Posse who had lain in ambush. Elzevir saw it too, and then all shouted at once.

'Yield at the King's command: you are our prisoners!' calls the voice of one of those black silhouettes, far up on the cliff-top.

'We are lost,' cries Elzevir; 'it is the Posse; but if we die, this traitor shall go before us,' and he makes towards Maskew to brain him with the pistol.

'Shoot, shoot, in the Devil's name,' screams Maskew, 'or I am a dead man.'

Then there came a flash of fire along the black line of silhouettes, with a crackle like a near peal of thunder, and a fut, fut, fut, of bullets in the turf. And before Elzevir could get at him, Maskew had fallen over on the sward with a groan and with a little red hole in the middle of his forehead.

'Run for the cliff-side,' cried Elzevir to me; 'get close in, and they cannot touch thee,' and he made for the chalk wall. But I had fallen on my knees like a bullock felled by a pole-axe, and had a scorching pain in my left foot. Elzevir looked back. 'What, have they hit thee too?' he said, and ran and picked me up like a child. And then there is another flash and fut, fut, in the turf; but the shots find no billet this time, and we are lying close against the cliff, panting but safe.

The white chalk was a bulwark between us and the foe; and though one or two of them loosed off their matchlocks, trying to get at us sideways, they could not even see their quarry, and 'twas only shooting at a venture. We were safe. But for how short a time! Safe just for so long as it should please the soldiers not to come down to take us, safe with a discharged pistol in our grasp, and a shot man lying at our feet.

Elzevir was the first to speak: 'Can you stand, John? Is the bone broken?'

'I cannot stand,' I said; 'there is something gone in my leg, and I feel blood running down into my boot.'

He knelt, and rolled down the leg of my stocking; but though he only moved my foot ever so little, it caused me sharp pain, for feeling was coming back after the first numbness of the shot.

'They have broke the leg, though it bleeds little,' Elzevir said. 'We have no time to splice it here, but I will put a kerchief round, and while I wrap it, listen to how we lie, and then choose what we shall do.'

I nodded, biting my lips hard to conceal the pain he gave me, and he went on: 'We have a quarter of an hour before the Posse can get down to us. But come they will, and thou canst judge what chance we have to save liberty or life with that carrion lying by us' – and he jerked his thumb at Maskew – 'though I am glad 'twas not my hand that sent him to his reckoning, and therefore do not blame thee if thou didst make me waste a charge in air. So one thing we can do is to wait here until they come, and I can account for a few of them before they shoot me down; but thou canst not fight with a broken leg, and they will take thee alive, and then there is a dance on air at Dorchester Gaol.'

I felt sick with pain and bitterly cast down to think that I was like to come so soon to such a vile end; so only gave a sigh, wishing heartily that Maskew were not dead, and that my leg were not broke, but that I was back again at the *Why Not?* or even hearing one of Dr. Sherlock's sermons in my aunt's parlour.

Elzevir looked down at me when I sighed, and seeing, I suppose, that I was sorrowful, tried to put a better face on a bad business. 'Forgive me, lad,' he said, 'if I have spoke too roughly. There is yet another way that we may try; and if thou hadst but two whole legs, I would have tried it, but now 'tis little short of madness. And yet, if thou fear's not, I will still try it. Just at the end of this flat ledge, furthest from where the bridle-path leads down, but not a hundred yards from where we stand, there is a sheep-track leading up the cliff. It starts where the under-cliff dies back again into the chalk face, and climbs by slants and elbow-turns up to the top. The shepherds call it the Zigzag, and even sheep lose their footing on it; and of men I never heard but one had climbed it, and that was lander Jordan, when the Excise was on his heels, half a century back. But he that tries it stakes all on head and foot, and a wounded bird like thee may not dare that flight. Yet, if thou art content to hang thy life upon a hair, I will carry thee some way and where there is no room to carry, thou must down on hands and knees and trail thy foot.'

It was a desperate chance enough, but came as welcome as a patch of blue through lowering skies. 'Yes,' I said, 'dear Master Elzevir, let us get to it quickly; and if we fall, 'tis better far to die upon the rocks below than to wait here for them to hale us off to gaol.' And with that I tried to stand, thinking I might go dot-and-carry even with a broken leg. But 'twas no use, and down I sank with a groan. Then Elzevir caught me up, holding me in his arms, with my head looking over his back, and made off for the Zigzag. And as we slunk along, close to the cliff-side, I saw, between the brambles, Maskew lying with his face turned up to the morning sky. And there was the little red hole in the middle of his forehead, and a thread of blood that welled up from it and trickled off on to the sward.

It was a sight to stagger any man, and would have made me swoon perhaps, but that there was no time, for we were at the end of the under-cliff, and Elzevir set me down for a minute, before he buckled to his task. And 'twas a task that might cow the bravest, and when I looked upon the Zig-zag, it seemed better to stay where we were and fall into the hands of the Posse than set foot on that awful way, and fall upon the rocks below. For the Zigzag started off as a fair enough chalk path, but in a few paces narrowed down till it was but a whiter thread against the grey-white cliff-face, and afterwards turned sharply back, crossing a hundred feet direct above our heads. And then I smelt an evil stench, and looking about, saw the blown-out carcass of a rotting sheep lie close at hand.

'Faugh,' said Elzevir, 'tis a poor beast has lost his foothold.'

It was an ill omen enough, and I said as much, beseeching him to make his own way up the Zigzag and leave me where I was, for that they might have mercy on a boy.

'Tush!' he cried; 'it is thy heart that fails thee, and 'tis too late now to change counsel. We have fifteen minutes yet to win or lose with, and if we gain the cliff-top in that time we shall have an hour's start, or more, for they will take all that to search the under-cliff. And Maskew, too, will keep them in check a little, while they try to bring the life back to so good a man. But if we fall, why, we shall fall together, and outwit their cunning. So shut thy eyes, and keep them tight until I bid thee open them.' With that he caught me up again, and I shut my eyes firm, rebuking myself for my faint-heartedness, and not telling him how much my foot hurt me.

In a minute I knew from Elzevir's steps that he had left the turf and was upon the chalk. Now I do not believe that there were half a dozen men beside in England who would have ventured up that path, even free and untrammelled, and not a man in all the world to do it with a full-grown lad in his arms. Yet Elzevir made no bones of it, nor spoke a single word; only he went very slow, and I felt him scuffle with his foot as he set it forward, to make sure he was putting it down firm.

I said nothing, not wishing to distract him from his terrible task, and held my breath, when I could, so that I might lie quieter in his arms. Thus he went on for a time that seemed without end, and yet was really but a minute or two; and by degrees I felt the wind, that we could scarce perceive at all on the under-cliff, blow fresher and cold on the cliff-side. And then the path grew steeper and steeper, and Elzevir went slower and slower, till at last he spoke:

'John, I am going to stop; but open not thy eyes till I have set thee down and bid thee.'

I did as bidden, and he lowered me gently, setting me on all fours upon the path; and speaking again:

'The path is too narrow here for me to carry thee, and thou must creep round this corner on thy hands and knees. But have a care to keep thy outer hand near to the inner, and the balance of thy body to the cliff, for there is no room to dance hornpipes here. And hold thy eyes fixed on the chalk-wall, looking neither down nor seaward.'

'Twas well he told me what to do, and well I did it; for when I opened my eyes, even without moving them from the cliff-side, I saw that the ledge was little more than a foot wide, and that ever so little a lean of the body would dash me on the rocks below. So I crept on, but spent much time that was so precious in travelling those ten yards to take me round the first elbow of the path; for my foot was heavy and gave me fierce pain to drag, though I tried to mask it from Elzevir. And he, forgetting what I suffered, cried out, 'Quicken thy pace, lad, if thou canst, the time is short.' Now so frail is man's temper, that though he was doing more than any ever did to save another's life, and was all I had to trust to in the world; yet because he forgot my pain and bade me quicken, my choler rose, and I nearly gave him back an angry word, but thought better of it and kept it in.

Then he told me to stop, for that the way grew wider and he would pick me up again. But here was another difficulty, for the path was still so narrow and the cliff-wall so close that he could not take me up in his arms. So I lay flat on my face, and he stepped over me, setting his foot between my shoulders to do it; and then, while he knelt down upon the path, I climbed up from behind upon him, putting my arms round his neck; and so he bore me 'pickaback.' I shut my eyes firm again, and thus we moved along another spell, mounting still and feeling the wind still freshening.

At length he said that we were come to the last turn of the path, and he must set me down once more. So down upon his knees and hands he went, and I slid off behind, on to the ledge. Both were on all fours now; Elzevir first and I following. But as I crept along, I relaxed care for a moment, and my eyes wandered from the cliff-side and looked down. And far below I saw the blue sea twinkling like a dazzling mirror, and the gulls wheeling about the sheer chalk wall, and then I thought of that bloated carcass of a sheep that had fallen from this very spot perhaps, and in an instant felt a sickening qualm and swimming of the brain, and knew that I was giddy and must fall.

Then I called out to Elzevir, and he, guessing what had come over me, cries to turn upon my side, and press my belly to the cliff. And how he did it in such a narrow strait I know not; but he turned round, and lying down himself, thrust his hand firmly in my back, pressing me closer to the cliff. Yet it was none too soon, for if he had not held me tight, I should have flung myself down in sheer despair to get quit of that dreadful sickness.

'Keep thine eyes shut, John,' he said, 'and count up numbers loud to me, that I may know thou art not turning faint.' So I gave out, 'One, two, three,' and while I went on counting, heard him repeating to himself, though his words seemed thin and far off: 'We must have taken ten minutes to get here, and in five more they will be on the under-cliff; and if we ever reach the top, who knows but they have left a guard! No, no, they will not leave a guard, for not a man knows of the Zigzag; and, if they knew, they would not guess that we should try it. We have but fifty yards to go to win, and now this cursed giddy fit has come upon the child, and he will fall and drag me with him; or they will see us from below, and pick us off like sitting guillemots against the cliff-face.'

So he talked to himself, and all the while I would have given a world to pluck up heart and creep on farther; yet could not, for the deadly sweating fear that had hold of me. Thus I lay with my face to the cliff, and Elzevir pushing firmly in my back; and the thing that frightened me most was that there was nothing at all for the hand to take hold of, for had there been a piece of string, or even a thread of cotton, stretched along to give a semblance of support, I think I could have done it; but there was only the cliff wall, sheer and white, against that narrowest way, with never cranny to put a finger into. The wind was blowing in fresh puffs, and though I did not open my eyes, I knew that it was moving the little tufts of bent grass, and the chiding cries of the gulls seemed to invite me to be done with fear and pain and broken leg, and fling myself off on to the rocks below.

Then Elzevir spoke. 'John,' he said, 'there is no time to play the woman; another minute of this and we are lost. Pluck up thy courage, keep thy eyes to the cliff, and forward.'

Yet I could not, but answered: 'I cannot, I cannot; if I open my eyes, or move hand or foot, I shall fall on the rocks below.'

He waited a second, and then said: 'Nay, move thou must, and 'tis better to risk falling now, than fall for certain with another bullet in thee later on.' And with that he shifted his hand from my back and fixed it in my coat collar, moving backwards himself, and setting to drag me after him.

Now, I was so besotted with fright that I would not budge an inch, fearing to fall over if I opened my eyes. And Elzevir, for all he was so strong, could not pull a helpless lump backwards up that path. So he gave it up, leaving go hold on me with a groan; and at that moment there rose from the under-cliff below a sound of voices and shouting.

'By God, they are down already!' cried Elzevir, 'and have found Maskew's body; it is all up; another minute and they will see us.'

But so strange is the force of mind on body, and the power of a greater to master a lesser fear, that when I heard those voices from below, all fright of falling left me in a moment, and I could open my eyes without a trace of giddiness. So I began to move forward again on hands and knees. And Elzevir, seeing me, thought for a moment I had gone mad, and was dragging myself over the cliff; but then saw how it was, and moved backwards himself before me, saying in a low voice, 'Brave lad! Once creep round this turn, and I will pick thee up again. There is but fifty yards to go, and we shall foil these devils yet!'

Then we heard the voices again, but farther off, and not so loud; and knew that our pursuers had left the under-cliff and turned down on to the beach, thinking that we were hiding by the sea.

Five minutes later Elzevir stepped on to the cliff-top, with me upon his back.

'We have made something of this throw,' he said, 'and are safe for another hour, though I thought thy giddy head had ruined us.'

Then he put me gently upon the springy turf, and lay down himself upon his back, stretching his arms out straight on either side, and breathing hard to recover from the task he had performed.

The day was still young, and far below us was stretched the moving floor of the Channel, with a silver-grey film of night mists not yet lifted in the offing. A hummocky up-and-down line of cliffs, all projections, dents, bays, and hollows, trended southward till it ended in the great bluff of St. Alban's Head, ten miles away. The cliff-face was gleaming white, the sea tawny inshore, but purest blue outside, with the straight sun-path across it, spangled and gleaming like a mackerel's back.

The relief of being once more on firm ground, and the exultation of an escape from immediate danger, removed my pain and made me forget that my leg was broken. So I lay for a moment basking in the sun; and the wind, which a few minutes before threatened to blow me from that narrow ledge, seemed now but the gentlest of breezes, fresh with the breath of the kindly sea. But this was only for a moment, for the anguish came back and grew apace, and I fell to thinking dismally of the plight we were in. How things had been against us in these last days! First, there was losing the *Why Not?*, and that was bad enough; second, there was the being known by the Excise for smugglers, and perhaps for murderers; third and last, there was the breaking of my leg, which made escape so difficult. But, most of all, there came before my eyes that grey face turned up against the morning sun, and I thought of all it meant for Grace, and would have given my own life to call back that of our worst enemy.

# Ernest [Evan] Thompson Seton (1860–1946)

Seton was a self-taught naturalist who revolutionized the animal story: he was concerned with the real lives of individual animals in natural settings without sentimentalization or romanticism. For him, as for Richard Jefferies, violent death was a normal part of animal life: he gives his subjects respect, rather than human characteristics. Seton came to Canada from England when he was six, and later moved to the USA, where he was a co-founder of the Boy Scouts of America. *Wild Animals I Have Known*

was the first of his books; others included *The Biography of a Grizzly* (1900) and *Two Little Savages* (1903).

'The Springfield Fox' opens with a long account of the ways in which the Vixen trains her cubs, until the dog Fox, Scarface, is killed. This extract demonstrates how Seton was able to describe the most trying scenes, which many of his predecessors might have milked for sentimental effect, in a sympathetic but realistic way.

## from *Wild Animals I Have Known* (1898)

## from 'The Springfield Fox'

But still the hens were disappearing. My uncle was wrathy. He determined to conduct the war himself, and sowed the woods with poison baits, trusting to luck that our own dogs would not get them. He indulged in contemptuous remarks on my by-gone woodcraft, and went out evenings with a gun and the two dogs, to see what he could destroy.

Vix knew right well what a poisoned bait was; she passed them by or else treated them with active contempt, but one she dropped down the hole of an old enemy, a skunk, who was never afterward seen. Formerly old Scarface was always ready to take charge of the dogs, and keep them out of mischief. But now that Vix had the whole burden of the brood, she could no longer spend time in breaking every track to the den, and was not always at hand to meet and mislead the foes that might be coming too near.

The end is easily foreseen. Ranger followed a hot trail to the den, and Spot, the fox-terrier, announced that the family was at home, and then did his best to go in after them.

The whole secret was now out, and the whole family doomed. The hired man came around with pick and shovel to dig them out, while we and the dogs stood by. Old Vix soon showed herself in the near woods, and led the dogs away off down the river, where she shook them off when she thought proper, by the simple device of springing on a sheep's back. The frightened animal ran for several hundred yards, then Vix got off, knowing that there was now a hopeless gap in the scent, and returned to the den. But the dogs, baffled by the break in the trail, soon did the same, to find Vix hanging about in despair, vainly trying to decoy us away from her treasures.

Meanwhile Paddy plied both pick and shovel with vigor and effect. The yellow, gravelly sand was heaping on both sides, and the shoulders of the sturdy digger were sinking below the level. After an hour's digging, enlivened by frantic rushes of the dogs after the old fox, who hovered near in the woods, Pat called:

'Here they are, sor!'

It was the den at the end of the burrow, and cowering as far back as they could, were the four little woolly cubs.

Before I could interfere, a murderous blow from the shovel, and a sudden rush for the fierce little terrier, ended the lives of three. The fourth and smallest was barely saved by holding him by his tail high out of reach of the excited dogs.

He gave one short squeal, and his poor mother came at the cry, and circled so near that she would have been shot but for the accidental protection of the dogs, who somehow always seemed to get between, and whom she once more led away on a fruitless chase.

The little one saved alive was dropped into a bag, where he lay quite still. His unfortunate brothers were thrown back into their nursery bed, and buried under a few shovelfuls of earth.

We guilty ones then went back into the house, and the little fox was soon chained in the yard. No one knew just why he was kept alive, but in all a change of feeling had set in, and the idea of killing him was without a supporter.

He was a pretty little fellow, like a cross between a fox and a lamb. His woolly visage and form were strangely lamb-like and innocent, but one could find in his yellow eyes a gleam of cunning and savageness as unlamb-like as it possibly could be.

As long as anyone was near he crouched sullen and cowed in his shelter-box, and it was a full hour after being left alone before he ventured to look out.

My window now took the place of the hollow basswood. A number of hens of the breed he knew so well were about the cub in the yard. Late that afternoon as they strayed near the captive there was a sudden rattle of the chain, and the youngster dashed at the nearest one and would have caught him but for the chain which brought him up with a jerk. He got on his feet and slunk back to his box, and though he afterward made several rushes he so gauged his leap as to win or fail within the length of the chain and never again was brought up by its cruel jerk.

As night came down the little fellow became very uneasy, sneaking out of his box, but going back at each slight alarm, tugging at his chain, or at times biting it in fury while he held it down with his fore paws. Suddenly he paused as though listening, then raising his little black nose he poured out a short quavering cry.

Once or twice this was repeated, the time between being occupied in worrying the chain and running about. Then an answer came. The far-away *Yap-yurrr* of the old fox. A few minutes later a shadowy form appeared on the wood-pile. The little one slunk into his box, but at once returned and ran to meet his mother with all the gladness that a fox could show. Quick as a flash she seized him and turned to bear him away by the road she came. But the moment the end of the chain was reached the cub was rudely jerked from the old one's mouth, and she, scared by the opening of a window, fled over the wood-pile.

An hour afterward the cub had ceased to run about or cry. I peeped out, and by the light of the moon saw the form of the mother at full length on the ground by the little one, gnawing at something – the clank of iron told what, it was that cruel chain. And Tip, the little one, meanwhile was helping himself to a warm drink.

On my going out she fled into the dark woods, but there by the shelter-box were two little mice, bloody and still warm, food for the cub brought by the devoted mother. And in the morning I found the chain was very bright for a foot or two next the little one's collar.

On walking across the woods to the ruined den, I again found signs of Vixen. The poor heartbroken mother had come and dug out the bedraggled bodies of her little ones.

There lay the three little baby foxes all licked smooth now, and by them were two of our hens fresh killed. The newly heaved earth was printed all over with tell-tale signs – signs that told me that here by the side of her dead she had watched like Rizpah. Here she had brought their usual meal, the spoil of her nightly hunt. Here she had stretched herself beside them and vainly offered them their natural drink and yearned to feed and warm them as of old; but only stiff little bodies under their soft wool she found, and little cold noses still and unresponsive.

A deep impress of elbows, breast, and hocks showed where she had laid in silent grief and watched them for long and mourned as a wild mother can mourn for its young. But from that time she came no more to the ruined den, for now she surely knew that her little ones were dead.

# Ethel C. Pedley (?1860–1898)

With *Dot and the Kangaroo* we return to the Australian relationship with the outback, at a time when Australian children's literature was becoming gradually urbanized, as with Louise Mac's *Teens* (1897 and sequels). The book begins abruptly: 'Little Dot had lost her way in the bush. She knew it, and was very frightened. She was too frightened to cry.' But the Australian world is more settled now, and there is educative fantasy at work here. Dorothy can understand what the animals say, and there is much material on conservation and on the way in which humans affect the bush, before the Kangaroo bravely escorts her home to a not-over-sentimentalized meeting (and a responsible coda).

There are points at which Pedley wavers between satire, comedy and serious observation, both social and semimystical, and the effect (rather as in Jefferies' *Wood Magic*, p. 312, this volume) can be to reduce the impact of the narrative. When Dot is brought to trial by the birds 'for the

wrongs we Bush creatures have suffered from the cruelties of white Humans', the proceedings follow human law, as picked up by the Welcome Swallow, who has nested in the eaves of the Gabblebabble Court House. He explains, for example, the purpose of the jury: '"The Swallow says that's the Jury" [said] the Magpie. "Their business is to do just what they like with you when all the talking is done, and whether they find you guilty or not, will depend on if they are tired, or hungry, or feel cross; or if the trial only lasts a short time.... If this is human law...it isn't funny at all."'

*Dot and the Kangaroo* is at its best when it ignores any European influences, as Australian literature generally was now increasingly – and increasingly successfully – to do. This is the final chapter, when for the first time the focus moves to the bereft parents (although earlier Dot has remembered the tragedy of a little boy who died in the bush) and fantasy and reality merge.

## from *Dot and the Kangaroo* (1899)

### CHAPTER 13

Two men were walking near a cottage in the winter sunlight of the early morning.

There came to the door a young woman, who looked pale and tired. She carried a bowl of milk to a little calf, and on her way back to the cottage she paused, and shading her eyes, that were red with weeping, lingered awhile, looking far and near. Then, with a sigh, she returned indoors and worked restlessly at her household duties.

'It breaks my heart to see my wife do that,' said the taller man, who carried a gun. 'All day long she comes out and looks for the child. One knows, now, that the poor little one can never come back to us,' and as the big man spoke there was a queer choking in his voice.

The younger man did not speak, but he patted his friend's shoulder in a kindly manner, which showed that he too was very sorry.

'Even you have lost heart, Jack,' said the big bushman, 'but we shall find her yet; the wife shall have that comfort.'

'You'll never do it now,' said the young fellow with a mournful shake of the head. 'There is not an inch of ground that so young a child could reach that we have not searched. The mystery is, what could have become of her?'

'That's what beats me,' said the tall man, who was Dot's father. 'I think of it day and all night. There is the track of the dear little mite as clear as possible for five miles, as far as the dry creek. The trackers say she rested her poor weary legs by sitting under the black-butt tree. At that point she vanishes completely. The blacks say there isn't a trace of man, or beast, beyond that place excepting the trail of a big kangaroo. As you say, it's a mystery!'

As the men walked towards the bush, close to the place where Dot had run after the hare the day she was lost, neither of them noticed the fuss and scolding made by a Willy Wagtail; although the little bird seemed likely to die of excitement.

Willy Wagtail was really saying, 'Dot and her Kangaroo are coming this way. Whatever you do, don't shoot them with that gun.'

Presently the young man, Jack, noticed the little bird. 'What friendly little chaps those wagtails are,' he said. 'See how tame and fearless this one is. Upon my word, he nearly flew in your face that time!'

Dot's father did not notice the remark, for he stopped suddenly, and was peering into the bush whilst he quietly shifted his gun into position, ready to raise it and fire.

'By jove!' he said, 'I saw the head of a Kangaroo a moment ago behind that iron-bark. Fancy its coming so near the house. Next time it shows, I'll get a shot at it.'

Both men waited for the moment when the Kangaroo should be seen again.

The next instant the Kangaroo bounded out of the Bush into the open paddock. Swift as lightning up went the cruel gun, but, as it exploded with a terrible report, the man, Jack, struck it upwards, and the fatal bullet lodged in the branch of a tall gum-tree.

'Great Scott!' exclaimed Jack pointing at the Kangaroo.

'Dot!' cried her father, dropping his gun, and stumbling blindly forward with outstretched arms, towards his little girl, who had just tumbled out of the Kangaroo's pouch in her hurry to reach her father.

'Hoo, hoo, ho, ho, he, he, ha, ha, ha, ha!' laughed a Kookaburra on a tree, as he saw Dot clasped in her father's great strong arms, and the little face hidden in his big brown beard.

'Wife! wife!' shouted Dot's father, 'Dot's come back! Dot's come back!'

'Dot's here!' yelled the young man, as he ran like mad to the house. And all the time the good Kangaroo sat up on her haunches, still panting with fear from the sound of the gun, and a little afraid to stay, yet so interested in all the excitement and delight, that she couldn't make up her mind to hop away.

'Dadda,' said Dot, 'You nearly killed Dot and her Kangaroo! Oh! if you'd killed my Kangaroo, I'd never have been happy any more!'

'But I don't understand,' said her father. 'How did you come to be in the Kangaroo's pouch?'

'Oh! I've got lots and lots to tell you!' said Dot; 'but come and stroke dear Kangaroo, who saved little Dot and brought her home.'

'That I will!' said Dot's father, 'and never more will I hurt a Kangaroo!'

'Nor any of the Bush creatures,' said Dot. 'Promise Dadda!'

'I promise,' said the big man, in a queer-sounding voice, as he kissed Dot over and over again, and walked towards the frightened animal.

Dot wriggled down from her father's arms, and said to the Kangaroo, 'It's all right; no one's ever going to be shot or hurt here again!' and the Kangaroo looked delighted at the good news.

'Dadda,' said Dot, holding her father's hand, and, with her disengaged hand touching the Kangaroo's little paw. 'This is my own dear Kangaroo.' Dot's father, not knowing quite how to show his gratitude, stroked the Kangaroo's head, and said 'How do you do?' which, when he came to think of it afterwards, seemed rather a foolish thing to say. But he wasn't used, like Dot, to talking to Bush creatures, and had not eaten the berries of understanding.

The Kangaroo saw that Dot's father was grateful, and so she was pleased, but she did not like to be stroked by a man who let off guns, so she was glad that Dot's mother had run to where they were standing, and was hugging and kissing the little girl, and crying all the time; for then Dot's father turned and watched his wife and child, and kept doing something to his eyes with a handkerchief, so that there was no attention to spare for Kangaroos.

The good Kangaroo, seeing how happy these people were, and knowing that her life was quite safe, wanted to peep about Dot's home and see what it was like – for kangaroos can't help being curious. So presently she quietly hopped off towards the cottage, and then a very strange thing happened. Just as the Kangaroo was wondering what the great iron tank by the kitchen door was meant for, there popped out of the open door a joey Kangaroo. Now, to human beings, all joey Kangaroos look alike, but amongst Kangaroos there are no two the same, and Dot's Kangaroo at once recognized in the little Joey her own baby Kangaroo. The Joey knew its mother directly, and, whilst Dot's Kangaroo was too astonished to move, and not being able to think, was trying to get at a conclusion why her Joey was coming out of a cottage, the little Kangaroo, with a hop-skip-and-a-jump, had landed itself comfortably in the nice pouch Dot had just vacated.

Then Dot's mother, rejoicing over the safe return of her little girl, was not more happy than the Kangaroo with her Joey once more in her pouch. With big bounds she leaped towards Dot, and the little girl suddenly looking round for her Kangaroo friend, clapped her hands with delight as she saw a little grey nose, a pair of tiny black paws, and the point of a little black tail, hanging out of the pouch that had carried her so often.

'Why!' exclaimed Dot's mother, 'if she hasn't got the little Joey Jack brought me yesterday! He picked it up after a Kangaroo hunt some time ago.'

'It's her Joey; her lost Joey!' cried Dot running to the Kangaroo. 'Oh, dear Kangaroo, I am so glad!' she said, 'for now we are all happy; as happy as can be!' Dot hugged her Kangaroo, and kissed the little Joey, and they all three talked together, so that none of them understood what the others were saying, only that they were all much pleased and delighted.

'Wife,' said Dot's father, 'I'll tell you what's mighty queer: our little girl is talking away to those animals, and they're all understanding one another, as if it was the most natural thing in the world to treat Kangaroos as if they were human beings!'

'I expect,' said his wife, 'that their feelings are not much different from ours. See how that poor animal is rejoicing in getting back its little one, just as we are over having our little Dot again.'

'To think of all the poor things I have killed,' said Dot's father sadly, 'I'll never do it again.'

'No,' said his wife, 'we must try and get everyone to be kind to the Bush creatures, and protect them all we can.'

This book would never come to an end if it told all that passed that day. How Dot explained the wonderful power of the berries of understanding, and how she told the Kangaroos all that her parents wanted her to say on their behalf, and what kind things the Kangaroo said in return.

All day long the Kangaroo stayed near Dot's home, and the little girl persuaded her to eat bread, which she said was 'most delicious, but one would get tired of it sooner than of grass.'

Every effort was made by Dot and her parents to get the Kangaroo to live on their selection, so that they might protect her from harm. But she said that she liked her own free life best, only she would never go far away and would come often to see Dot. At sunset she said goodbye to Dot, a little sadly, and the child stood in the rosy light of the afterglow, waving her hand, as she saw her kind animal friend hop away and disappear into the dark shadow of the bush.

She wandered about for some time listening to the voices of birds and creatures, who came to tell her how glad everyone was that her way had been found, and that no harm was to befall them in future. The news of her safe return, and of the Kangaroo's finding her Joey, had been spread far and near, by Willy Wagtail and the Kookaburra; and she could hear the shouts of laughter from kookaburras telling the story until nearly dark.

Quite late at night she was visited by the Opossum, the Native Bear, and the Nightjar, who entered by the open window, and, sitting in the moonlight conversed about the day's events. They said that their whole rest and sleep had been disturbed by the noise and excitement of the day creatures spreading the news through the bush. The Mopoke wished to sing a sad song because Dot was feeling happy, but the Opossum warned it that it was sitting in a draught on the window sill and might spoil its beautiful voice, so it flew away and only sang in the distance. The Native Bear said that the story of Dot's return and the finding of Kangaroo's Joey was so strange that it made its head feel quite empty. The Opossum inspected everything in Dot's room, and tried to fight itself in the looking-glass. It then got the Koala to look into the mirror also, and said it would get an idea into its little empty head if it did. When the Koala had taken a timid peep at itself, the Opossum said that the Koala now had an idea of how stupid it looked, and the little bear went off to get used to having an idea in its head. The Opossum was so pleased with its spiteful joke that it hastily said good-night, and hurried away to tell it to the other possums.

Gradually the voices of the creatures outside became more and more faint and indistinct; and then Dot slept in the grey light of the dawn.

When she went out in the morning, the kookaburras were gurgling and laughing, the magpies were warbling, the parakeets made their twittering, and Willy Wagtail was most lively; but Dot was astonished to find that she could not understand what any of the creatures said, although they were all very friendly towards her. When the Kangaroo came to see her she made signs that she wanted some berries of understanding, but, strange as it may seem, the Kangaroo pretended not to understand. Dot has often wondered why the Kangaroo would not understand, but, remembering what that considerate animal had said when she first gave her the berries, she is inclined to think that the Kangaroo is afraid of her learning too much, and thereby getting indigestion. Dot and her parents have often sought for the berries, but up to now they have failed to find them. There is something very mysterious about those berries!

During that day every creature Dot had known in the bush came to see her, for they all knew that their lives were safe now, so they were not afraid. It greatly surprised Dot's parents to see such numbers of birds and animals coming around their little girl, and they thought it very pretty when in the evening a flock of Native Companions settled down and danced their graceful dance with the little girl joining in the game.

'It seems to me, wife,' said Dot's father, with a glad laugh, 'that the place has become a regular menagerie!'

Later on, Dot's father made a dam on a hollow piece of ground near the house, which soon became full of water, and is surrounded by beautiful willow-trees. There all the thirsty creatures come to drink in safety. And very pretty it is, to sit on the veranda of that happy home, and see Dot playing near the water surrounded by her Bush friends, who come and go as they please, and play with the little girl beside the pretty lake. And no one in all the Gabblebabble district hurts a Bush creature, because they are all called 'Dot's friends'.

Before putting away the pen and closing the inkstand, now that Dot has said all she wishes to be recorded of her bewildering adventures, the writer would like to warn little people, that the best thing to do when one is lost in the bush, is to sit still in one place, and not to try to find one's way home at all. If Dot had done this, and had not gone off in the Kangaroo's pouch, she would have been found almost directly. As the more one tries to find one's way home, the more one gets lost, and as helpful Kangaroos like Dot's are very scarce, the best way to get found quickly is to wait in one place until the search parties find one. Don't forget this advice! And don't eat any strange berries in the bush, unless a Kangaroo brings them to you.

# [Joseph] Rudyard Kipling (1805–1936)

The major exception to Kipling's forging of new materials without direct reference to established genres is *Stalky and Co*, which goes some way to undercutting the by-now clichéd school story. The book, a fictionalized account of Kipling's own experiences at the minor public school, the United Services College at Westward Ho, explores the subtle mores of boyhood, as well as the rituals of school. Although overlaid with Kipling's customary complex ironies, there is an implication that such an education produces just the tricksters who will hold the empire.

Kipling's characters are scathing about fictional schools. In the story 'An Unsavoury Interlude', a maiden aunt of Stalky's sends him *Eric, or Little By Little*, and another school story by Farrar, *St. Winifred's, or, the World of School* (both of which the boys cannot sell as they are a 'drug' on the market). M'Turk reads an extract from *Eric* and comments 'oh, naughty Eric! Let's get to where he goes in for drink.' As Stalky says, 'Golly, what we've missed – not going to St. Winifred's!' (Kipling had to apologize to the aged Farrar for these comments). But this spirit of realism is the spirit of the new century, at least in children's books; moral imperatives are still there, but they are now implicit, discussible and discussed. The old fictions are there to be questioned.

In the first half of the story, 'The Moral Reformers', Stalky and his friends M'Turk and Beetle (a self-portrait of Kipling) of Study Number 5 discuss bullying with the Chaplain, who wants them to exercise their 'authority' to stop a small boy from being bullied. He thinks that 'most bullying is thoughtlessness' but M'Turk disagrees: 'Not one little bit of it, Padre.…Bullies like bullyin''. There is no hint of the pious words of the team captain in *Tom Brown's Schooldays*, (see p. 139) that being bullied is ultimately good for you.

The rest of the story, reprinted here, is a remarkable example of pure literary revenge: Kipling's rage at his own treatment comes out as a savage catharsis, very rarely equalled in a literature dominated by various forms of control. Kipling, the exponent of the modern, brings a passion that is the passion of the child, not, as with Farrar (and even Hughes), the passion of the adult, to children's books.

## from *Stalky and Co* (1899)

## from 'The Moral Reformers'

'Well, what are we goin' to do?' Number Five stared at each other.

'Young Clewer would give his eyes for a place to be quiet in. *I* know that,' said Beetle. 'If we made him a study fag, eh?'

'No!' said M'Turk firmly. 'He's a dirty little brute, and he'd mess up everything. Besides, we ain't goin' to have any beastly Erickin'. D'you want to walk about with your arm round his neck?'

'He'd clean out the jam-pots, anyhow; an' the burnt-porridge saucepan – it's filthy now.'

'Not good enough,' said Stalky, bringing up both heels with a crash on the table. 'If we find the merry jester who's been bullyin' him an' make him happy, that'll be all right. Why didn't we spot him when we were in the form-rooms, though?'

'Maybe a lot of fags have made a dead set at Clewer. They do that sometimes.'

'Then we'll have to kick the whole of the lower school in our house – on spec. Come on,' said M'Turk.

'Keep your hair on! We mustn't make a fuss about the biznai. Whoever it is, he's kept quiet or we'd have seen him,' said Stalky. 'We'll walk round and sniff about till we're sure.'

They drew the house form-rooms, accounting for every junior and senior against whom they had suspicions – investigated, at Beetle's suggestion, the lavatories and box-rooms, but without result. Everybody seemed to be present save Clewer.

'Rum!' said Stalky, pausing outside a study door. 'Golly!'

A thin piping mixed with tears came muffled through the panels.

'As beautiful Kitty one morning was tripping –'

'Louder, you young devil, or I'll buzz a book at you!'

'With a pitcher of milk –

Oh, Campbell, please don't!

To the fair of –'

A book crashed on something soft, and squeals arose.

'Well, I never thought it was a study-chap, anyhow. That accounts for our not spotting him,' said Beetle. 'Sefton and Campbell are rather hefty chaps to tackle. Besides, one can't go into their study like a form-room.'

'What swine!' M'Turk listened. 'Where's the fun of it? I suppose Clewer's faggin' for them.'

'They aren't prefects. That's one good job,' said Stalky, with his war-grin. 'Sefton and Campbell! Um! Campbell and Sefton! Ah! One of 'em's a crammer's pup.'

The two were precocious hairy youths between seventeen and eighteen, sent to the school in despair by parents who hoped that six months' steady cram might, perhaps, jockey them into Sandhurst. Nominally they were in Mr Prout's house; actually they were under the Head's eye; and since he was very careful never to promote strange new boys to prefectships, they considered they had a grievance against the school. Sefton had spent three months with a London crammer, and the tale of his adventures there lost nothing in the telling. Campbell, who had a fine taste in clothes and a fluent vocabulary, followed his lead in looking down loftily on the rest of the world. This was only their second term, and the school, used to what it profanely called 'crammers' pups', had treated them with rather galling reserve. But their whiskers – Sefton owned a real razor – and their moustaches were beyond question impressive.

'Shall we go in an' dissuade 'em?' M'Turk asked. 'I've never had much to do with 'em, but I'll bet my hat Campbell's a funk.'

'No – o! That's *oratio directa*,' said Stalky, shaking his head. 'I like *oratio obliqua*. 'Sides, where'd our moral influence be then? Think o' that!'

'Rot! What are you goin' to do?' Beetle turned into Lower Number Nine form-room, next door to the study.

'Me?' The lights of war flickered over Stalky's face. 'Oh, I want to jape with 'em. Shut up a bit!'

He drove his hands into his pockets and stared out of the window at the sea, whistling between his teeth. Then a foot tapped the floor; one shoulder lifted; he wheeled, and began the short quick double-shuffle – the war-dance of Stalky in meditation. Thrice he crossed the empty form-room, with compressed lips and expanded nostrils, swaying to the quick-step. Then he halted before the dumb Beetle and softly knuckled his head, Beetle bowing to the strokes. M'Turk nursed one knee and rocked to and fro. They could hear Clewer howling as though his heart would break.

'Beetle is the sacrifice,' Stalky said at last. 'I'm sorry for you, Beetle. 'Member Galton's *Art of Travel* (one of the forms had been studying that pleasant work) an' the kid whose bleatin' excited the tiger?'

'Oh, curse!' said Beetle uneasily. It was not his first season as a sacrifice. 'Can't you get on without me?'

'"Fraid not, Beetle, dear. You've got to be bullied by Turkey an' me. The more you howl, o' course, the better it'll be. Turkey, go an' covet a stump and a box-rope from somewhere. We'll tie him up for a kill – *à la* Galton. 'Member when "Molly" Fairburn made us cockfight with our shoes off, an' tied up our knees?'

'But that hurt like sin.'

'Course it did. What a clever chap you are, Beetle! Turkey 'll knock you all over the place, 'Member we've had a big row all round, an' I've trapped you into doin' this. Lend us your wipe.'

Beetle was trussed for cock-fighting; but, in addition to the transverse stump between elbow and knee, his knees were bound with a box-rope. In this posture, at a push from Stalky he rolled over sideways, covering himself with dust.

'Ruffle his hair, Turkey. Now you get down, too. "The bleatin' of the kid excites the tiger." You two are in such a sweatin' wax with me that you only curse. 'Member that. I'll tickle you up with a stump. You'll have to blub, Beetle.'

'Right-o! I'll work up to it in half a shake,' said Beetle.

'Now begin – and remember the bleatin' o' the kid.'

'Shut up, you brutes! Let me up! You've nearly cut my knees off. Oh, you *are* beastly cads! Do shut up. 'Tisn't a joke!' Beetle's protest was, in tone, a work of art.

'Give it to him, Turkey! Kick him! Roll him over! Kill him! Don't funk, Beetle, you brute. Kick him again, Turkey.'

'He's not blubbin' really. Roll up, Beetle, or I'll kick you into the fender,' roared M'Turk.

They made a hideous noise among them, and the bait allured their quarry.

'Hullo. What's the giddy jest?' Sefton and Campbell entered to find Beetle on his side, his head against the fender, weeping copiously, while M'Turk prodded him in the back with his toes.

'It's only Beetle,' Stalky explained. 'He's shammin' hurt. I can't get Turkey to go for him properly.'

Sefton promptly kicked both boys, and his face lighted. 'All right, I'll attend to 'em. Get up an' cock-fight, you two. Give me the stump. I'll tickle 'em. Here's a giddy jest! Come on, Campbell. Let's cook 'em.'

Then M'Turk turned on Stalky and called him very evil names.

'You said you were goin' to cock-fight too, Stalky. Come on!'

'More ass you for believin' me, then!' shrieked Stalky.

'Have you chaps had a row?' said Campbell.

'Row?' said Stalky. 'Huh! I'm only educatin' them. D'you know anythin' about cock-fighting, Seffy?'

'Do I know? Why, at Maclagan's, where I was crammin' in town, we used to cock-fight in his drawing-room, and little Maclagan daren't say anything. But we were just the same as men there, of course. Do I know? I'll show you.'

'Can't I get up?' moaned Beetle, as Stalky sat on his shoulder.

'Don't jaw, you fat piffler. You're going to fight Seffy.'

'He'll slay me!'

'Oh, lug 'em into our study,' said Campbell. 'It's nice an' quiet in there. I'll cock-fight Turkey. This is an improvement on young Clewer.'

'Right-o! I move it's shoes-off for them an' shoes-on for us,' said Sefton joyously, and the two were flung down on the study floor. Stalky rolled them behind an armchair.

'Now I'll tie you two up an' direct the bullfight. Golly, what wrists you have, Seffy. They're too thick for a wipe; got a box-rope?' said he.

'Lots in the corner,' Sefton replied. 'Hurry up! Stop blubbin', you brute, Beetle. We're goin' to have a giddy campaign. Losers have to sing for the winners – sing odes in honour of the conqueror. You call yourself a beastly poet, don't you, Beetle? I'll poet you.' He wriggled into position by Campbell's side.

Swiftly and scientifically the stumps were thrust through the natural crooks, and the wrists tied with well-stretched box-ropes to an accompaniment of insults from M'Turk, bound, betrayed, and voluble behind the chair.

Stalky set away Campbell and Sefton, and strode over to his allies, locking the door on the way.

'And that's all right,' said he in a changed voice.

'What the devil –?' Sefton began. Beetle's false tears had ceased; M'Turk, smiling, was on his feet. Together they bound the knees and ankles of the enemy even more straitly.

Stalky took the armchair and contemplated the scene with his blandest smile. The man trussed for cock-fighting is, perhaps, the most helpless thing in the world.

'The bleatin' of the kid excites the tiger. Oh, you frabjous asses!' He lay back and laughed till he could no more. The victims took in the situation but slowly.

'We'll give you the finest lickin' you ever had in your young lives when we get up!' thundered Sefton from the floor. 'You'll laugh the other side of your mouth before you've done. What the deuce d'you mean by this?'

'You'll see in two shakes,' said M'Turk. 'Don't swear like that. What we want to know is, why you two hulkin' swine have been bullyin' Clewer?'

'It's none of your business.'

'What did you bully Clewer for?' The question was repeated with maddening iteration by each in turn. They knew their work.

'Because we jolly well chose,' was the answer at last. 'Let's get up.' Even then they could not realize the game.

'Well, now we're goin' to bully you because we jolly well choose. We're goin' to be just as fair to you as you were to Clewer. He couldn't do anything against you. You can't do anything to us. Odd, ain't it?'

'Can't we? You wait an' see.'

'Ah,' said Beetle reflectively, 'that shows you've never been properly jested with. A public lickin' ain't in it with a gentle jape. Bet a bob you'll weep an' promise anything.'

'Look here, young Beetle, we'll half kill you when we get up. I'll promise you that, at any rate.'

'You're going to be half killed first, though. Did you give Clewer head-knuckles?'

'Did you give Clewer head-knuckles?' M'Turk echoed. At the twentieth repetition – no boy can stand the torture of one unvarying query, which is the essence of bullying – came confession.

'We did, confound you!'

'Then you'll be knuckled'; and knuckled they were, according to ancient experience. Head-knuckling is no trifle; 'Molly' Fairburn of the old days could not have done better.

'Did you give Clewer brush-drill?'

This time the question was answered sooner, and brush-drill was dealt out for the space of five minutes by Stalky's watch. They could not even writhe in their bonds. No brush is employed in brush-drill.

'Did you give Clewer the key?'

'No; we didn't. I swear we didn't!' from Campbell, rolling in agony.

'Then we'll give it to you, so you can see what it would be like if you had.'

The torture of the key – which has no key at all – hurts excessively. They endured several minutes of it, and their language necessitated the gag.

'Did you give Clewer corkscrews?'

'Yes. Oh, curse your silly souls! Let us alone, you cads.'

They were corkscrewed, and the torture of the corkscrew – this has nothing to do with corkscrews – is keener than the torture of the key.

The method and silence of the attacks was breaking their nerves. Between each new torture came the pitiless, dazing rain of questions, and when they did not answer to the point, Isabella-coloured handkerchiefs were thrust into their mouths.

'Now are those all the things you did to Clewer? Take out the gag, Turkey, and let 'em answer.'

'Yes, I swear that was all. Oh, you're killing us, Stalky!' cried Campbell.

'Pre-cisely what Clewer said to you. I heard him. Now we're goin' to show you what real bullyin' is. What I don't like about you, Sefton, is, you come to the Coll. with your stick-up collars an' patent-leather boots, an' you think you can teach us something about bullying. *Do* you think you can teach us anything about bullying? Take out the gag and let him answer.'

'No!' – ferociously.

'He says no. Rock him to sleep. Campbell can watch.'

It needs three boys and two boxing-gloves to rock a boy to sleep. Again the operation has nothing to do with its name. Sefton was 'rocked' till his eyes set in his head and he gasped and crowed for breath, sick and dizzy.

'My aunt!' said Campbell, appalled, from his corner, and turned white.

'Put him away,' said Stalky. 'Bring on Campbell. Now this *is* bullyin'. Oh, I forgot! I say, Campbell, what did you bully Clewer for? Take out his gag and let him answer.'

'I – I don't know. Oh, let me off! I swear I'll make it *pax*. Don't "rock" me!'

' "The bleatin' of the kid excites the tiger." He says he don't know. Set him up, Beetle. Give me the glove an' put in the gag.'

In silence Campbell was 'rocked' sixty-four times.

'I believe I'm goin' to die!' he gasped.

'He says he is goin' to die. Put him away. Now, Sefton! Oh, I forgot! Sefton, what did you bully Clewer for?'

The answer is unprintable; but it brought not the faintest flush to Stalky's downy cheek.

'Make him an Ag Ag, Turkey!'

And an Ag Ag was he made, forthwith. The hard-bought experience of nearly eighteen years was at his disposal, but he did not seem to appreciate it.

'He says we are sweeps. Put him away! Now, Campbell! Oh, I forgot! I say, Campbell, what did you bully Clewer for?'

Then came the tears – scalding tears; appeals for mercy and abject promises of peace. Let them cease the tortures and Campbell would never lift hand against them. The questions began again – to an accompaniment of keen persuasions.

'You seem hurt, Campbell. Are you hurt?'

'Yes. Awfully!'

'He says he is hurt. Are you broke?'

'Yes, yes! I swear I am. Oh, stop!'

'He says he is broke. Are you humble?'

'Yes!'

'He says he is humble. Are you devilish humble?'

'Yes!'

'He says he is devilish humble. Will you bully Clewer any more?'

'No. No – ooh!'

'He says he won't bully Clewer. Or any one else?'

'No. I swear I won't!'

'Or any one else. What about that lickin' you and Sefton were goin' to give us?'

'I won't! I won't! I swear I won't!'

'He says he won't lick us. Do you esteem yourself to know anything about bullyin'?'

'No, I don't!'

'He says he doesn't know anything about bullyin'. Haven't we taught you a lot?'

'Yes – yes!'

'He says we've taught him a lot. Aren't you grateful?'

'Yes!'

'He says he is grateful. Put him away. Oh, I forgot! I say, Campbell, what did you bully Clewer for?'

He wept anew; his nerves being raw. 'Because I was a bully. I suppose that's what you want me to say?'

'He says he is a bully. Right he is. Put him in the corner. No more japes for Campbell. Now, Sefton!'

'You devils! You young devils!' This and much more as Sefton was punted across the carpet by skilful knees.

' "The bleatin' of the kid excites the tiger." We're goin' to make you beautiful. Where does he keep his shaving-things? (Campbell told.) Beetle, get some water. Turkey, make the lather. We're goin' to shave you, Seffy, so you'd better lie jolly still, or you'll get cut. I've never shaved any one before.'

'Don't! Oh, don't! Please don't!'

'Gettin' polite, eh? I'm only goin' to take off one ducky little whisker —'

'I'll – I'll make it *pax*, if you don't. I swear I'll let you off your lickin' when I get up!'

'And half that moustache we're so proud of. He says he'll let us off our lickin'. Isn't he kind?'

M'Turk laughed into the nickel-plated shaving-cup, and settled Sefton's head between Stalky's vice-like knees.

'Hold on a shake,' said Beetle, 'you can't shave long hairs. You've got to cut all that moustache short first, an' then scrope him.'

'Well, I'm not goin' to hunt about for scissors. Won't a match do? Chuck us the match-box. He is a hog, you know; we might as well singe him. Lie still!'

He lit a vesta, but checked his hand. 'I only want to take off half, though.'

'That's all right.' Beetle waved the brush. 'I'll lather up to the middle — see? and you can burn off the rest.'

The thin-haired first moustache of youth fluffed off in flame to the lather line in the centre of the lip, and Stalky rubbed away the burnt stumpage with his thumb. It was not a very gentle shave, but it abundantly accomplished its purpose.

'Now the whisker on the other side. Turn him over!' Between match and razor this, too, was removed. 'Give him his shaving-glass. Take the gag out. I want to hear what he'll say.'

But there were no words. Sefton gazed at the lop-sided wreck in horror and despair. Two fat tears rolled down his check.

'Oh, I forgot! I say, Sefton, what did you bully Clewer for?'

'Leave me alone! Oh, you infernal bullies, leave me alone! Haven't I had enough!'

'He says we must leave him alone,' said M'Turk.

'He says we are bullies, an' we haven't even begun yet,' said Beetle. 'You're ungrateful, Seffy. Golly! You do look an atrocity and a half!'

'He says he has had enough,' said Stalky. 'He errs!'

'Well, to work, to work!' chanted M'Turk, waving a stump. 'Come on, my giddy Narcissus. Don't fall in love with your own reflection!'

'Oh, let him off,' said Campbell from his corner; 'he's blubbing, too.'

Sefton cried like a twelve-year-old with pain, shame, wounded vanity, and utter helplessness.

'You'll make it *pax*, Sefton, won't you? You can't stand up to those young devils—'

'Don't be rude, Campbell, de-ah,' said M'Turk, 'or you'll catch it again!'

'You *are* devils, you know,' said Campbell.

'What? for a little bullyin' – same as you've been givin' Clewer! How long have you been jestin' with him?' said Stalky. 'All this term?'

'We didn't always knock him about, though!'

'You did when you could catch him,' said Beetle, cross-legged on the floor, dropping a stump from time to time across Sefton's instep. 'Don't I know it!'

'I – perhaps we did.'

'And you went out of your way to catch him? Don't I know it! Because he was an awful little beast, eh? Don't I know it! Now, you see *you're* awful beasts, and you're gettin' what he got – for bein' a beast. Just because we choose.'

'We never really bullied him – like you've done us.'

'Yah!' said Beetle. 'They never really bully – "Molly" Fairburn didn't. Only knock 'em about a little bit. That's what they say. Only kick their souls out of 'em, and they go and blub in the box-rooms. Shove their heads into the ulsters an' blub. Write home three times a day – yes, you brute, I've done that – askin' to be taken away. You've never been bullied properly, Campbell. I'm sorry you made *pax*.'

'I'm not!' said Campbell, who was a humorist in a way. 'Look out, you're slaying Sefton!'

In his excitement Beetle had used the stump unreflectingly, and Sefton was now shouting for mercy.

'An' you!' he cried, wheeling where he sat. 'You've never been bullied, either. Where were you before you came here?'

'I – I had a tutor.'

'Yah! You would. You never blubbed in your life. But you're blubbin' now, by gum. Aren't you blubbin'?'

'Can't you see, you blind beast?' Sefton fell over sideways, tear tracks furrowing the dried lather. Crack came the cricket-stump on the curved latter-end of him.

'Blind, am I,' said Beetle, 'and a beast? Shut up, Stalky. I'm goin' to jape a bit with our friend, *à la* "Molly" Fairburn. *I* think I can see. Can't I see, Sefton?'

'The point is well taken,' said M'Turk, watching the stump at work. 'You'd better say that he sees, Seffy.'

'You do – you can! I swear you do!' yelled Sefton, for strong arguments were coercing him.

'Aren't my eyes lovely?' The stump rose and fell steadily throughout this catechism.

'Yes.'

'A gentle hazel, aren't they?'

'Yes – oh yes!'

'What a liar you are! They're sky-blue. Ain't they sky-blue?'

'Yes – oh yes!'

'You don't know your mind from one minute to another. You must learn – you must learn.'

'What a bait you're in!' said Stalky. 'Keep your hair on, Beetle.'

'I've had it done to me,' said Beetle. 'Now – about my being a beast.'

'*Pax* – oh, *pax!*' cried Sefton; 'make it *pax*. I'll give up! Let me off! I'm broke! I can't stand it!'

'Ugh! Just when we were gettin' our hand in!' grunted M'Turk. 'They didn't let Clewer off, I'll swear.'

'Confess – apologize – quick!' said Stalky.

From the floor Sefton made unconditional surrender, more abjectly even than Campbell. He would never touch any one again. He would go softly all the days of his life.

'We've got to take it, I suppose?' said Stalky. 'All right, Sefton. You're broke? Very good. Shut up, Beetle! But before we let you up, you an' Campbell will kindly oblige us with "Kitty of Coleraine" – *à la* Clewer.'

'That's not fair,' said Campbell; 'we've surrendered.'

'Course you have. Now you're goin' to do what we tell you – same as Clewer would. If you hadn't surrendered you'd ha' been really bullied. Havin' surrendered – do you follow, Seffy? – you sing odes in honour of the conquerors. Hurry up!'

They dropped into chairs luxuriously. Campbell and Sefton looked at each other, and, neither taking comfort from that view, struck up 'Kitty of Coleraine'.

'Vile bad,' said Stalky, as the miserable wailing ended. 'If you hadn't surrendered it would have been our painful duty to buzz books at you for singin' out o' tune. Now then.'

He freed them from their bonds, but for several minutes they could not rise. Campbell was first on his feet, smiling uneasily. Sefton staggered to the table, buried his head in his arms, and shook with sobs. There was no shadow of fight in either – only amazement, distress, and shame.

'Ca – can't he shave clean before tea, please?' said Campbell. 'It's ten minutes to bell.'

Stalky shook his head. He meant to escort the half-shaved one to that meal.

M'Turk yawned in his chair and Beetle mopped his face. They were all dripping with excitement and exertion.

'If I knew anything about it, I swear I'd give you a moral lecture,' said Stalky severely.

'Don't jaw; they've surrendered,' said M'Turk. 'This moral suasion biznai takes it out of a chap.'

'Don't you see how gentle we've been?' We might have called Clewer in to look at you,' said Stalky. 'The bleatin' of the tiger excites the kid. But we didn't. We've only got to tell a few chaps in Coll. about this and you'd be hooted all over the shop. Your life wouldn't be worth havin'. But we aren't goin' to do that, either. We're strictly moral suasers, Campbell; so, unless you or Seffy split about this no one will.'

'I swear you're a brick,' said Campbell. 'I suppose I was rather a brute to Clewer.'

'It looked like it,' said Stalky. 'But I don't think Seffy need come into hall with cock-eye whiskers. Horrid bad for the fags if they saw him. He can shave. Ain't you grateful, Sefton?'

The head did not lift. Sefton was deeply asleep.

'That's rummy,' said M'Turk, as a snore mixed with a sob. 'Cheek, *I* think; or else he's shammin'.'

'No, 'tisn't,' said Beetle. 'When "Molly" Fairburn had attended to me for an hour or so I used to go bung off to sleep on a form sometimes. Poor devil! But he called me a beastly poet, though.'

'Well, come on.' Stalky lowered his voice. 'Good-bye, Campbell. 'Member, if you don't talk, nobody will.'

There should have been a war-dance, but that all three were so utterly tired that they almost went to sleep above the tea-cups in their study, and slept till prep.

# Edith Nesbit (1858–1924)

In *The Story of the Treasure Seekers* one can hear the authentic voice of the twentieth century: child-centred (as far as is possible for an adult writer), allowing the child reader a certain superiority over the child-narrator, and deriving its moral position not from some externally imposed criteria, but from some inwardly absorbed codes.

Nesbit spent much of her writing career in finding a voice by which to address the new child reader. She had begun as a hack writer producing versions of Shakespeare (heavily dependent on the Lambs) for children and forgotten pieces such as *Doggy Tales* (1895); became a highly successful children's writer (from *The Story of the Treasure Seekers* through to, perhaps, *Harding's Luck* (1909)) and then returned to hack work. She was both helped and hindered by her political views: she was an 'advanced' woman with radical ideas on the role of women, and as a founder of the Fabian Society could be described as a middle-class socialist. Although, unlike Kipling, she made many modifications to her style when writing for children, like Kipling she accorded her readership a great deal of intellectual respect.

Nesbit's pivotal position in literary history as the *first* twentieth-century voice has been exaggerated, as this anthology has demonstrated. The change of tone exemplified in her best books and which she was instrumental in passing on, had been a preoccupation of writers from Carroll to Ewing and from Page to Burnett. She was also not original in what has come to be known as 'domestic fantasy' – Molesworth is an obvious precursor – nor in the family story – she clearly owes a great deal to Ethel Turner, Louisa Alcott and their distinguished foremothers. Even in her historical position as a writer, she was but one of a formidably distinguished line of strong, independent women, who supported their families (and weaker or less provident menfolk) by the pen.

But she did write at a pivotal moment in the development of British childhood (the USA and 'the colonies' had, on the whole, a concept of childhood perhaps thirty years in advance of the British), when families were (relatively) smaller, when parental attitudes were laxer and fonder. There is an inherent paradox in her family stories, in that they portray the clichés of the dead mother and the absent father, while giving the children a positive independence. At the beginning of *The Treasure Seekers* the modest narrator, Oswald, says 'Our mother is dead, and if you think we don't care about her you only show that you do not understand people at all': a more succinct summary of the difference between the nineteenth-century situation and the twentieth-century attitude would be difficult to find. Children have a voice: they are still children, bounded by, but no longer intellectually controlled by, adult value systems.

Nesbit allowed children to satirize adults, rather than the other way around. This is engineered partly by the literary awareness of her characters. This is also nothing new: children in children's fiction, from Tom Sawyer to Jo March and on into the twentieth century, have children's literature as part of their psyche. Oswald is a particularly biting literary critic, describing *Sir Toady Lion* as 'the only decent book I have ever read by *Toady Lion*'s author. The others are mere piffle'. A good cross-section of Victorian reading, from *The Daisy Chain* to Dickens, are neatly pinned down by the children's beady eyes.

Nesbit's domestic fantasies, notably *Five Children and It* (1902), have retained their popularity for a century; her 'realistic' social novel, *The Railway Children* (1906), her ultimate assertion of female superiority and nineteenth-century contrivance, was filmed by Lionel Jeffries in 1970, and remains a classic.

*The Treasure Seekers* is a collection of short stories in which the Bastable children do their best to restore the family fortunes.

## from *The Story of the Treasure Seekers* (1899)

### LORD TOTTENHAM

Oswald is a boy of firm and unswerving character, and he had never wavered from his first idea. He felt quite certain that the books were right, and that the best way to restore fallen fortunes was to rescue an old gentleman in distress. Then he brings you up as his own son; but if you preferred to go on being your own father's son I expect the old gentleman would make it up to you some other way. In the books the least thing does it – you put up the railway carriage window – or you pick up his purse when he drops it – or you say a hymn when he suddenly asks you to, and then your fortune is made.

The others, as I said, were very slack about it, and did not seem to care much about trying the rescue. They said there wasn't any deadly peril, and we should have to make one before we could rescue the old gentleman from it, but Oswald didn't see that that mattered. However, he thought he would try some of the easier ways first, by himself.

So he waited about the station, pulling up railway carriage windows for old gentlemen who looked likely – but nothing happened, and at last the porters said he was a nuisance. So that was no go. No one ever asked him to say a hymn, though he had learned a nice short one, beginning 'New every morning' – and when an old gentleman did drop a two-shilling piece just by Ellis's the hairdresser's, and Oswald picked it up, and was just thinking what he should say when he returned it, the old gentleman caught him by the collar and called him a young thief. It would have been very unpleasant for Oswald if he hadn't happened to be a very brave boy, and knew the policeman on that beat very well indeed. So the policeman backed him up, and the old gentleman said he was sorry, and offered Oswald sixpence. Oswald refused it with polite disdain, and nothing more happened at all.

When Oswald had tried by himself and it had not come off, he said to the others, 'We're wasting our time, not trying to rescue the old gentleman in deadly peril. Come – buck up! Do let's do something!'

It was dinner-time, and Pincher was going round getting the bits off the plates. There were plenty because it was cold-mutton day. And Alice said –

'It's only fair to try Oswald's way – he has tried all the things the others thought of. Why couldn't we rescue Lord Tottenham?'

Lord Tottenham is the old gentleman who walks over the Heath every day in a paper collar at three o'clock – and when he gets halfway, if there is no one about, he changes his collar and throws the dirty one into the furze-bushes.

Dicky said, 'Lord Tottenham's all right – but where's the deadly peril?'

And we couldn't think of any. There are no highwaymen on Blackheath now, I am sorry to say. And though Oswald said half of us could be highwaymen and the other half rescue party, Dora kept on saying it would be wrong to be a highwayman – and so we had to give that up.

Then Alice said, 'What about Pincher?'

And we all saw at once that it could be done.

Pincher is very well bred, and he does know one or two things, though we never could teach him to beg. But if you tell him to hold on – he will do it, even if you only say 'Seize him!' in a whisper.

So we arranged it all. Dora said she wouldn't play; she said she thought it was wrong, and she knew it was silly – so we left her out, and she went and sat in the dining-room with a goody-book, so as to be able to say she didn't have anything to do with it, if we got into a row over it.

Alice and H. O. were to hide in the furze-bushes just by where Lord Tottenham changes his collar, and they were to whisper, 'Seize him!' to Pincher; and then when Pincher had seized Lord Tottenham we were to go and rescue him from his deadly peril. And he would say, 'How can I reward you, my noble young preservers?' and it would be all right.

So we went up to the Heath. We were afraid of being late. Oswald told the others what Procrastination was – so they got to the furze-bushes a little after two o'clock, and it was rather cold. Alice and H. O. and Pincher hid, but Pincher did not like it any more than they did, and as we three walked up and down we heard him whining. And Alice kept saying, 'I *am* so cold! Isn't he coming yet?' And H. O. wanted to come out and jump about to warm himself. But we told him he must learn to be a Spartan boy, and that he ought to be very thankful he hadn't got a beastly fox eating his inside all the time. H. O. is our little brother, and we are not going to let it be our fault if he grows up a milksop. Besides, it was not really cold. It was his knees – he wears socks. So they stayed where they were. And at last, when even the other three who were walking about were beginning to feel rather chilly, we saw Lord Tottenham's big black cloak coming along, flapping in the wind like a great bird. So we said to Alice –

'Hist! he approaches. You'll know when to set Pincher on by hearing Lord Tottenham talking to himself – he always does while he is taking off his collar.'

Then we three walked slowly away whistling to show we were not thinking of anything. Our lips were rather cold, but we managed to do it.

Lord Tottenham came striding along, talking to himself. People call him the mad Protectionist. I don't know what it means – but I don't think people ought to call a Lord such names.

As he passed us he said, 'Ruin of the country, sir! Fatal error, fatal error!' And then we looked back and saw he was getting quite near where Pincher was, and Alice and H. O. We walked on – so that he shouldn't think we were looking – and in a minute we heard Pincher's bark, and then nothing for a bit; and then we looked round, and sure enough good old Pincher had got Lord Tottenham by the trouser leg and was holding on like billy-ho, so we started to run.

Lord Tottenham had got his collar half off – it was sticking out sideways under his ear – and he was shouting, 'Help, help, murder!' exactly as if some one had explained to him beforehand what he was to do. Pincher was growling and snarling and holding on. When we got to him I stopped and said –

'Dicky, we must rescue this good old man.'

Lord Tottenham roared in his fury, 'Good old man be –' something or othered. 'Call the dog off!'

So Oswald said, 'It is a dangerous task – but who would hesitate to do an act of true bravery?'

And all the while Pincher was worrying and snarling, and Lord Tottenham shouting to us to get the dog away. He was dancing about in the road with Pincher hanging on like grim death; and his collar flapping about, where it was undone.

Then Noël said, 'Haste, ere yet it be too late.' So I said to Lord Tottenham –

'Stand still, aged sir, and I will endeavour to alleviate your distress.'

He stood still, and I stooped down and caught hold of Pincher and whispered, 'Drop it, sir; drop it!'

So then Pincher dropped it, and Lord Tottenham fastened his collar again – he never does change it if there's any one looking – and he said –

'I'm much obliged, I'm sure. Nasty vicious brute! Here's something to drink my health.'

But Dicky explained that we are teetotallers, and do not drink people's healths. So Lord Tottenham said, 'Well, I'm much obliged any way. And now I come to look at you – of course, you're not young ruffians, but gentlemen's sons, eh? Still, you won't be above taking a tip from an old boy – I wasn't when I was your age,' and he pulled out half a sovereign.

It was very silly; but now we'd done it I felt it would be beastly mean to take the old boy's chink after putting him in such a funk. He didn't say anything about bringing us up as his own sons – so I didn't know what to do. I let Pincher go, and was just going to say he was very welcome, and we'd rather not have the money, which seemed the best way out of it, when that beastly dog spoiled the whole show. Directly I let him go he began to jump about at us and bark for joy, and try to lick our faces. He was so proud of what he'd done. Lord Tottenham opened his eyes and he just said, 'The dog seems to know you.'

And then Oswald saw it was all up, and he said, 'Good morning,' and tried to get away. But Lord Tottenham said –

'Not so fast!' And he caught Noël by the collar. Noël gave a howl, and Alice ran out from the bushes. Noël is her favourite. I'm sure I don't know why. Lord Tottenham looked at her, and he said –

'So there are more of you!' And then H. O. came out.

'Do you complete the party?' Lord Tottenham asked him. And H. O. said there were only five of us this time.

Lord Tottenham turned sharp off and began to walk away, holding Noël by the collar. We caught up with him, and asked him where he was going, and he said, 'To the Police Station.' So then I said quite politely, 'Well, don't take Noël; he's not strong, and he easily gets upset. Besides, it wasn't his doing. If you want to take any one take me – it was my very own idea.'

Dicky behaved very well. He said, 'If you take Oswald I'll go too, but don't take Noël; he's such a delicate little chap.'

Lord Tottenham stopped, and he said, 'You should have thought of that before.' Noël was howling all the time, and his face was very white, and Alice said –

'Oh, do let Noël go, dear, good, kind Lord Tottenham; he'll faint if you don't, I know he will, he does sometimes. Oh, I wish we'd never done it! Dora said it was wrong.'

'Dora displayed considerable common sense,' said Lord Tottenham, and he let Noël go. And Alice put her arm round Noël and tried to cheer him up, but he was all trembly, and as white as paper.

Then Lord Tottenham said –

'Will you give me your word of honour not to try to escape?'

So we said we would.

'Then follow me,' he said, and led the way to a bench. We all followed, and Pincher too, with his tail between his legs – he knew something was wrong. Then Lord Tottenham sat down, and he made Oswald and Dicky and H. O. stand in front of him, but he let Alice and Noël sit down. And he said –

'You set your dog on me, and you tried to make me believe you were saving me from it. And you would have taken my half-sovereign. Such conduct is most – No – you shall tell me what it is, sir, and speak the truth.'

So I had to say it was most ungentlemanly, but I said I hadn't been going to take the half-sovereign.

'Then what did you do it for?' he asked. 'The truth, mind.'

So I said, 'I see now it was very silly, and Dora said it was wrong, but it didn't seem so till we did it. We wanted to restore the fallen fortunes of our house, and in the books if you rescue an old gentleman from deadly peril, he brings you up as his own son – or if you prefer to be your father's son, he starts you in business, so that you end in wealthy affluence; and there wasn't any deadly peril, so we made Pincher into one – and so –' I was so ashamed I couldn't go on, for it did seem an awfully mean thing. Lord Tottenham said –

'A very nice way to make your fortune – by deceit and trickery. I have a horror of dogs. If I'd been a weak man the shock might have killed me. What do you think of yourselves, eh?'

We were all crying except Oswald, and the others say he was; and Lord Tottenham went on –

'Well, well, I see you're sorry. Let this be a lesson to you; and we'll say no more about it. I'm an old man now, but I was young once.'

Then Alice slid along the bench close to him, and put her hand on his arm: her fingers were pink through the holes in her woolly gloves, and said, 'I think you're very good to forgive us, and we are really very, very sorry. But we wanted to be like the children in the books – only we never have the chances they have. Everything they do turns out all right. But we *are* sorry, very, very. And I know Oswald wasn't going to take the half-sovereign. Directly you said that about a tip from an old boy I began to feel bad inside, and I whispered to H. O. that I wished we hadn't.'

Then Lord Tottenham stood up, and he looked like the Death of Nelson, for he is clean shaved and it is a good face, and he said –

'Always remember never to do a dishonourable thing, for money or for anything else in the world.'

And we promised we would remember. Then he took off his hat, and we took off ours, and he went away, and we went home. I never felt so cheap in all my life! Dora said, 'I told you so,' but we didn't mind even that so much, though it was indeed hard to bear. It was what Lord Tottenham had said about ungentlemanly. We didn't go on to the Heath for a week after that; but at last we all went, and we waited for him by the bench. When he came along Alice said, 'Please, Lord Tottenham, we have not been on the Heath for a week, to be a punishment because you let us off. And we have brought you a present each if you will take them to show you are willing to make it up.'

He sat down on the bench, and we gave him our presents. Oswald gave him a sixpenny compass – he bought it with my own money on purpose to give him. Oswald always buys useful presents. The needle would not move after I'd had it a day or two, but Lord Tottenham used to be an admiral, so he will be able to make that go all right. Alice had made him a shaving-case, with a rose worked on it. And H. O. gave him his knife – the same one he once cut all the buttons off his best suit with. Dicky gave him his prize, *Naval Heroes*, because it was the best thing he had, and Noël gave him a piece of poetry he had made himself:

When sin and shame bow down the brow
Then people feel just like we do now.
We are so sorry with grief and pain
We never will be so ungentlemanly again.


Lord Tottenham seemed very pleased. He thanked us, and talked to us for a bit, and when he said good-bye he said —

'All's fair weather now, mates,' and shook hands.

And whenever we meet him he nods to us, and if the girls are with us he takes off his hat, so he can't really be going on thinking us ungentlemanly now.

# Lyman Frank Baum (1856–1919)

The 'facts' surrounding *The Wonderful Wizard of Oz* have just that combination of utilitarianism and unlikeliness that the book exudes. Baum himself epitomizes a free-wheeling, pragmatic spirit; by turns an actor, an oil sales-man, storekeeper, journalist and travelling salesman, and Secretary of the National Association of Window Trim-mers, he named his book (it is said) after a drawer in his filing cabinet. Having found the golden goose, he pro-ceeded to encourage its output of golden eggs in the form of at least fourteen sequels (a bewildering number of further sequels have been produced by other hands). Like *Mary Poppins*, the book did not merely receive a new lease of life by being made into a film: rather, the 1939 Judy Garland film has *become The Wizard of Oz* in the mind of popular culture. L. Frank Baum would have been, one feels, delighted at the success of the product.

However, few 'classics' have been given such a bad cri-tical press: it is regarded as clumsy and styleless. At its cen-tre is a crude paradox, for while the theme of the book seems to be self-reliance (the lion is really brave, the tin woodman really does have a heart, and the scarecrow has brains), the characters actually succeed in the end through the random application of magic. And it has been widely maintained that W. W. Denslow's illustrations were a key factor in the book's initial success.

A more charitable reading might describe the prose as simple and the plotting expedient – characteristics, after all, of the folk-tale, to the status of which *The Wizard of Oz* has undoubtedly risen (or fallen).

Recent critics have explored the psychological implica-tions of the text. The land of Oz has been seen as a uto-pian dream, in direct contrast to the dry land of Kansas, or simply as a map of the USA; Dorothy's journey is seen as a parallel exploration of her personal problems, or a disturbing reflection of the (sometimes very) disturb-ing elements in Oz. As far as Baum was concerned, this was to be a modern 'wonder tale' to replace the outdated nineteenth-century fairy-tales, in which 'the wonderment and joy are retained and the heartache and nightmares left out'.

## from *The Wonderful Wizard of Oz* (1900)

## Chapter XII

## The Search for the Wicked Witch

The soldier with the green whiskers led them through the streets of the Emerald City until they reached the room where the Guardian of the Gates lived. This officer unlocked their spectacles to put them back in his great box, and then he politely opened the gate for our friends.

'Which road leads to the Wicked Witch of the West?' asked Dorothy.

'There is no road,' answered the Guardian of the Gates. 'No one ever wishes to go that way.'

'How then are we to find her?' inquired the girl.

'That will be easy,' replied the man; 'for when she knows you are in the Country of the Winkies she will find you and make you all her slaves.'

'Perhaps not,' said the Scarecrow, 'for we mean to destroy her.'

'Oh, that is different,' said the Guardian of the Gates. 'No one has ever destroyed her before, so I naturally thought she would make slaves of you as she has of all the rest. But take care: for she is wicked and fierce, and may not allow you to destroy her. Keep to the West, where the sun sets, and you cannot fail to find her.'

They thanked him and bade him goodbye, and turned towards the West, walking over fields of soft grass dotted here and there with daisies and buttercups. Dorothy still wore the pretty silk dress she had put on in the palace, but now to her surprise she found it was no longer green, but pure white. The ribbon around Toto's neck had also lost its green colour and was as white as Dorothy's dress.

The Emerald City was soon left far behind. As they advanced the ground became rougher and hillier, for there were no farms nor houses in this country of the West, and the ground was untilled.

In the afternoon the sun shone hot in their faces, for there were no trees to offer them shade; so that before night Dorothy and Toto and the Lion were tired, and lay down upon the grass and fell asleep, with the Woodman and the Scarecrow keeping watch.

Now the Wicked Witch of the West had but one eye, yet that was as powerful as a telescope, and could see everywhere. So, as she sat in the door of her castle, she happened to look around and saw Dorothy lying asleep with her friends all about her. They were a long distance off, but the Wicked Witch was angry to find them in her country; so she blew upon a silver whistle that hung around her neck.

At once there came running to her from all directions a pack of great wolves. They had long legs and fierce eyes and sharp teeth.

'Go to those people', said the Witch, 'and tear them to pieces.'

'Are you not going to make them your slaves?' asked the leader of the wolves.

'No,' she answered. 'One is of tin, and one of straw; one is a girl and another a lion. None of them is fit to work, so you may tear them into small pieces.'

'Very well,' said the Wolf, and he dashed away at full speed followed by the others.

It was lucky the Scarecrow and the Woodman were wide awake and heard the wolves coming.

'This is my fight,' said the Woodman; 'so get behind me and I will meet them as they come.'

He seized his axe, which he had made very sharp, and as the leader of the wolves came on the Tin Woodman swung his arm and chopped the Wolf's head from his body, so that he immediately died. As soon as he could raise his axe another wolf came up, and he also fell under the sharp edge of the Tin Woodman's weapon. There were forty wolves, and forty times a wolf was killed; so that at last they all lay dead in a heap before the Woodman.

Then he put down his axe and sat beside the Scarecrow, who said: 'It was a good fight, friend.'

They waited until Dorothy awoke the next morning. The little girl was quite frightened when she saw the great pile of shaggy wolves, but the Tin Woodman told her all. She thanked him for saving them and sat down to breakfast, after which they started again upon their journey.

Now this same morning the Wicked Witch came to the door of her castle and looked out with her one eye that could see afar off. She saw all her wolves lying dead, and the strangers still travelling through her country. This made her angrier than before, and she blew her whistle twice.

Straightway a great flock of wild crows came flying towards her, enough to darken the sky. And the Wicked Witch said to the King Crow: 'Fly at once to the strangers; peck out their eyes and tear them to pieces.'

The wild crows flew in one great flock towards Dorothy and her companions. When the little girl saw them coming she was afraid. But the Scarecrow said: 'This is my battle; so lie down beside me and you will not be harmed.'

So they all lay upon the ground except the Scarecrow, and he stood up and stretched out his arms. And when the crows saw him they were frightened, as these birds always are by scarecrows, and did not dare to come any nearer. But the King Crow said: 'It is only a stuffed man. I will peck his eyes out.'

The King Crow flew at the Scarecrow, who caught it by the head and twisted its neck until it died. And then another crow flew at him, and the Scarecrow twisted its neck also. There were forty crows and forty times the Scarecrow twisted a neck, until at last all were lying dead beside him. Then he called to his companions to rise, and again they went upon their journey.

When the Wicked Witch looked out again and saw all her crows lying in a heap she got into a terrible rage, and blew three times upon her silver whistle.

Forthwith there was heard a great buzzing in the air, and a swarm of black bees came flying towards her.

'Go to the strangers and sting them to death!' commanded the Witch, and the bees turned and flew rapidly until they came to where Dorothy and her friends were walking. But the Woodman had seen them coming and the Scarecrow had decided what to do.

'Take out my straw and scatter it over the little girl and the dog and the Lion,' he said to the Woodman, 'and the bees cannot sting them.' This the Woodman did, and as Dorothy lay close beside the Lion and held Toto in her arms the straw covered them entirely.

The bees came and found no one but the Woodman to sting, so they flew at him and broke off all their stings against the tin, without hurting the Woodman at all. And as bees cannot live when their stings are broken, that was the end of the black bees, and they lay scattered thick about the Woodman like little heaps of fine coal.

Then Dorothy and the Lion got up, and the girl helped the Tin Woodman put the straw back into the Scarecrow again, until he was as good as ever. So they started upon their journey once more.

The Wicked Witch was so angry when she saw her black bees in little heaps like fine coal that she stamped her foot and tore her hair and gnashed her teeth. And then she called a dozen of her slaves, who were the Winkies, and gave them sharp spears, telling them to go to the strangers and destroy them.

The Winkies were not a brave people, but they had to do as they were told; so they marched away until they came near to Dorothy. Then the Lion gave a great roar and sprang towards them, and the poor Winkies were so frightened that they ran back as fast as they could.

When they returned to the castle the Wicked Witch beat them well with a strap, and sent them back to their work, after which she sat down to think what she should do next. She could not understand how all her plans to destroy these strangers had failed; but she was a powerful witch as well as a wicked one, and she soon made up her mind how to act.

There was in her cupboard a Golden Cap, with a circle of diamonds and rubies running round it. This Golden Cap had a charm. Whoever owned it could call three times upon the Winged Monkeys, who would obey any order they were given. But no person could command these strange creatures more than three times. Twice already the Wicked Witch had used the charm of the Cap. Once was when she had made the Winkies her slaves and set herself to rule over their country. The Winged Monkeys had helped her to do this. The second time was when she had fought against the Great Oz himself, and driven him out of the land of the West. The Winged Monkeys had also helped her in doing this. Only once more could she use this Golden Cap, for which reason she did not like to do so until all her other powers were exhausted. But now that her fierce wolves and her wild crows and her stinging bees were gone, and her slaves had been scared away by the Cowardly Lion, she saw there was only one way left to destroy Dorothy and her friends.

So the Wicked Witch took the Golden Cap from her cupboard and placed it upon her head. Then she stood upon her left foot and said slowly: 'Ep-pe, pep-pe, kak-ke!'

Next she stood upon her right foot and said: 'Hil-lo, hol-lo, hel-lo!'

After this she stood upon both feet and cried in a loud voice: 'Ziz-zy, zuz-zy, zik!'

Now the charm began to work. The sky was darkened, and a low rumbling sound was heard in the air. There was a rushing of many wings; a great chattering and laughing; and the sun came out of the dark sky to show the Wicked Witch surrounded by a crowd of monkeys, each with a pair of immense and powerful wings on his shoulders.

One, much bigger than the others, seemed to be their leader. He flew close to the Witch and said: 'You have called us for the third and last time. What do you command?'

'Go to the strangers who are within my land and destroy them all except the Lion,' said the Wicked Witch. 'Bring that beast to me, for I have a mind to harness him like a horse and make him work.'

'Your commands shall be obeyed,' said the leader; and then, with a great deal of chattering and noise, the Winged Monkeys flew away to the place where Dorothy and her friends were walking.

Some of the Monkeys seized the Tin Woodman and carried him through the air until they were over a country thickly covered with sharp rocks. Here they dropped the poor Woodman, who fell a great distance to the rocks, where he lay so battered and dented that he could neither move nor groan.

Others of the Monkeys caught the Scarecrow, and with their long fingers pulled all of the straw out of his clothes and head. They made his hat and boots and clothes into a small bundle and threw it into the top branches of a tall tree.

The remaining Monkeys threw pieces of stout rope around the Lion and wound many coils about his body and head and legs, until he was unable to bite or scratch or struggle in any way.

Then they lifted him up and flew away with him to the Witch's castle, where he was placed in a small yard with a high iron fence around it, so that he could not escape.

But Dorothy they did not harm at all. She stood, with Toto in her arms, watching the sad fate of her comrades and thinking it would soon be her turn. The leader of the Winged Monkeys flew up to her, his long hairy arms stretched out and his ugly face grinning terribly; but he saw the mark of the Good Witch's kiss upon her forehead and stopped short, motioning the others not to touch her.

'We dare not harm this little girl,' he said to them, 'for she is protected by the Power of Good, and that is greater than the Power of Evil. All we can do is to carry her to the castle of the Wicked Witch and leave her there.'

So, carefully and gently, they lifted Dorothy in their arms and carried her swiftly through the air until they came to the castle, where they set her down upon the front doorstep.

Then the leader said to the Witch: 'We have obeyed you as far as we were able. The Tin Woodman and the Scarecrow are destroyed, and the Lion is tied up in your yard. The little girl we dare not harm, nor the dog she carries in her arms. Your power over our band is now ended and you will never see us again.'

Then all the Winged Monkeys, with much laughing and chattering and noise, flew into the air and were soon out of sight.

The Wicked Witch was both surprised and worried when she saw the mark on Dorothy's forehead, for she knew well that neither the Winged Monkeys nor she herself dare hurt the girl in any way. She looked down at Dorothy's feet, and seeing the silver shoes began to tremble with fear, for she knew what a powerful charm belonged to them. At first the Witch was tempted to run away from Dorothy; but she happened to look into the child's eyes and saw how simple the soul behind them was, and that the little girl did not know of the wonderful power the silver shoes gave her. So the Wicked Witch laughed to herself and thought: 'I can still make her my slave, for she does not know how to use her power.'

Then she said to Dorothy, harshly and severely: 'Come with me; and see that you mind everything I tell you, for if you do not I will make an end of you, as I did of the Tin Woodman and the Scarecrow.'

Dorothy followed her through many of the beautiful rooms in her castle until they came to the kitchen, where the Witch bade her clean the pots and kettles and sweep the floor and keep the fire fed with wood.

Dorothy went to work meekly, with her mind made up to work as hard as she could; for she was glad the Wicked Witch had decided not to kill her.

With Dorothy hard at work the Witch thought she would go into the courtyard and harness the Cowardly Lion like a horse; it would amuse her, she was sure, to make him draw her chariot whenever she wished to go to drive. But as she opened the gate the Lion gave a loud roar and bounded at her so fiercely that the Witch was afraid, and ran out and shut the gate again.

'If I cannot harness you,' said the Witch to the Lion, speaking through the bars of the gate, 'I can starve you. You shall have nothing to eat until you do as I wish.'

So after that she took no food to the imprisoned Lion; but every day she came to the gate at noon and asked: 'Are you ready to be harnessed like a horse?'

And the Lion would answer: 'No. If you come in this yard I will bite you.'

The reason the Lion did not have to do as the Witch wished was that every night, while the woman was asleep, Dorothy carried him food from the cupboard. After he had eaten he would lie down on his bed of straw, and Dorothy would lie beside him and put her head on his soft shaggy mane, while they talked of their troubles, and tried to plan some way to escape. But they could find no way to get out of the castle, for it was constantly guarded by the yellow Winkies, who were the slaves of the Wicked Witch and too afraid of her not to do as she told them.

The girl had to work hard during the day, and often the Witch threatened to beat her with the same old umbrella she always carried in her hand. But in truth she did not dare to strike Dorothy, because of the mark upon her forehead. The child did not know this, and was full of fear for herself and Toto. Once the Witch struck Toto a blow with her umbrella and the brave little dog flew at her and bit her leg in return. The Witch did not bleed where she was bitten, for she was so wicked that the blood in her had dried up many years before.

Dorothy's life became very sad as she grew to understand that it would be harder than ever to get back to Kansas and Aunt Em again. Sometimes she would cry bitterly for hours, with Toto sitting at her feet and looking into her face, whining dismally to show how sorry he was for his little mistress. Toto did not really care whether he was in Kansas or the Land of Oz so long as Dorothy was with him; but he knew the little girl was unhappy, and that made him unhappy too.

Now the Wicked Witch had a great longing to have for her own the silver shoes which the girl always wore. Her bees and her crows and her wolves were lying in heaps and drying up, and she had used up all the power of the Golden Cap; but if she could only get hold of the silver shoes they would give her more power than all the other things she had lost. She watched Dorothy carefully, to see if she ever took off her shoes, thinking she might steal them. But the child was so proud of her pretty shoes that she never took them off except at night and when she took her bath. The Witch was too much afraid of the dark to dare go in Dorothy's room at night to take the shoes, and her dread of water was greater than her fear of the dark, so she never came near when Dorothy was bathing. Indeed the old Witch never touched water, nor ever let water touch her in any way.

But the wicked creature was very cunning, and she finally thought of a trick that would give her what she wanted. She placed a bar of iron in the middle of the kitchen floor and then by her magic arts made the iron invisible to human eyes, so that when Dorothy walked across the floor she stumbled over the bar, not being able to see it, and fell at full length. She was not much hurt, but in her fall one of the silver shoes came off and before she could reach it the Witch had snatched it away and put it on her own skinny foot.

The wicked woman was greatly pleased with the success of her trick, for as long as she had one of the shoes she owned half the power of their charm, and Dorothy could not use it against her even had she known how to do so.

The little girl, seeing she had lost one of her pretty shoes, grew angry and said to the Witch: 'Give me back my shoe!'

'I will not,' retorted the Witch, 'for it is now my shoe and not yours.'

'You are a wicked creature!' cried Dorothy. 'You have no right to take my shoe from me.'

'I shall keep it just the same,' said the Witch, laughing at her, 'and some day I shall get the other one from you too.'

This made Dorothy so very angry that she picked up the bucket of water that stood near and dashed it over the Witch, wetting her from head to foot.

Instantly the wicked woman gave a loud cry of fear; and then, as Dorothy looked at her in wonder, the Witch began to shrink and fall away.

'See what you have done!' she screamed. 'In a minute I shall melt away!'

'I'm very sorry indeed,' said Dorothy, who was truly frightened to see the Witch actually melting away like brown sugar before her very eyes.

'Didn't you know water would be the end of me?' asked the Witch, in a wailing despairing voice.

'Of course not,' answered Dorothy. 'How should I?'

'Well, in a few minutes I shall be all melted and you will have the castle to yourself. I have been wicked in my day, but I never thought a little girl like you would ever be able to melt me and end my wicked deeds. Look out – here I go!'

With these words the Witch fell down in a brown melted shapeless mass and began to spread over the clean boards of the kitchen floor. Seeing that she had really melted away to nothing, Dorothy drew another bucket of water and threw it over the mess. She then swept it all out the door. After picking out the silver shoe, which was all that was left of the old woman, she cleaned and dried it with a cloth, and put it on her foot again. Then, being at last free to do as she chose, she ran out to the courtyard to tell the Lion that the Wicked Witch of the West had come to an end, and that they were no longer prisoners in a strange land.

# L'Envoi
# [Joseph] Rudyard Kipling (1865–1936)

There are several early twentieth-century children's books that could fitly end this anthology. There are those, like Alice Heagan's *Mrs Wiggs of the Cabbage Patch* (1901) or L. M. Montgomery's *Anne of Green Gables* (1908) which carry on (perhaps even perfect) nineteenth-century genres – the cheerful poor family, the powerful individualistic female, respectively. There are books like Angela Brazil's *The Fortunes of Philippa* (1906) which consolidate a fledgling genre (the school story for girls), or individualistic books which nevertheless became icons for the century, such as Beatrix Potter's *The Tale of Peter Rabbit* (1902) or J. M. Barrie's *Peter Pan* (first performed 1904). Or perhaps suitable books to end with might be those that consciously looked backwards and forwards, such as Kipling's *Puck of Pook's Hill* (1906), or Kenneth Grahame's *The Wind in the Willows* (1908). But, for all Kipling's celebration of the modern, *Puck of Pook's Hill* is deeply rooted in nineteenth-century thinking, and *The Wind in the Willows* is very arguably not a children's book at all – and all Grahame's views are profoundly regressive. A temptation is to end with Hilaire Belloc's *Cautionary Tales* (1907), for the fact that Belloc was able to satirize the work of the moralists of nearly a hundred years before (as Carroll had done) demonstrates the lasting influence of those writers. A final fire, perhaps: the case of Matilda, 'Who told Lies, and was Burned to Death.'

> That Night a Fire *did* break out –
> You should have heard Matilda Shout!

> You should have heard her Scream and Bawl,
> And throw the window up and call
> To People passing in the Street –
> (The rapidly increasing Heat
> Encouraging her to obtain
> Their confidence) – but all in vain!
> For every time she shouted 'Fire!'
> They only answered 'Little Liar!'
> And therefore when her Aunt returned,
> Matilda, and the House, were Burned.

It has to be said, however, that Belloc generally had at least one eye on an adult audience. His contemporary, Harry Graham, also a possibility, might be said to have had both eyes on them, with *Ruthless Rhymes for Heartless Homes* (1899): 'Billy, in one of his nice new sashes, | Fell in the fire and was burnt to ashes; | Now, although the room grows chilly, | I haven't the heart to poke poor Billy.'

And so I would like to end with a rarity: a masterpiece which does not seem to lead anywhere. Its form, the transcribed, ritualized, personal, family and child-orientated oral tale is very hard to find in written texts. It may, of course, have its roots and derive its humour from a century of tales, but that is not relevant. In Rudyard Kipling's *Just-So Stories* (1902) we come as close as it is perhaps possible to come to 'pure' children's literature, and the pursuit of *that* would be a central theme of any anthology of twentieth-century children's literature.

## from *Just-So Stories* (1902)

### How the Rhinoceros Got His Skin

Once upon a time, on an uninhabited island on the shores of the Red Sea, there lived a Parsee from whose hat the rays of the sun were reflected in more-than-oriental splendour. And the Parsee lived by the Red Sea with nothing but his hat and his knife and a cooking-stove of the kind that you must particularly never touch. And one day he took flour and water and currants and plums and sugar and things, and made himself one cake which was two feet across and three feet thick. It was indeed a Superior Comestible (*that's* Magic), and he put it on the stove because *he* was allowed to cook on that stove, and he baked it and he baked it till it was all done brown and smelt most sentimental. But just as he was going to eat it there came down to the beach from the Altogether Uninhabited Interior one Rhinoceros with a horn on his nose, two piggy eyes, and few manners. In those days the Rhinoceros's skin fitted him quite tight. There were no wrinkles in it anywhere. He looked exactly like a Noah's Ark Rhinoceros, but of course much bigger. All the same, he had no manners then, and he has no manners now, and he never will have any manners. He said, 'How!' and the Parsee left that cake and climbed to the top of a palm-tree with nothing on but his hat, from which the rays of the sun were always reflected in more-than-oriental splendour. And the Rhinoceros upset the oil-stove with his nose, and the cake rolled on the sand, and he spiked that cake on the horn of his nose, and he ate it, and he went away, waving his tail, to the desolate and Exclusively Uninhabited Interior which abuts on the islands of Mazanderan, Socotra, and the Promontories of the Larger Equinox. Then the Parsee came down from his palm-tree and put the stove on its legs and recited the following *Sloka*, which, as you have not heard, I will now proceed to relate –

> 'Them that takes cakes
> Which the Parsee-man bakes
> Makes dreadful mistakes.'

And there was a great deal more in that than you would think.

Plate 10   Illustration by Rudyard Kipling *Just So Stories*

*Because*, five weeks later, there was a heatwave in the Red Sea, and everybody took off all the clothes they had. The Parsee took off his hat; but the Rhinoceros took off his skin and carried it over his shoulder as he came down to the beach to bathe. In those days it buttoned underneath with three buttons and looked like a waterproof. He said nothing whatever about the Parsee's cake, because he had eaten it all; and he never had any manners, then, since, or henceforward. He waddled straight into the water and blew bubbles through his nose, leaving his skin on the beach.

Presently the Parsee came by and found the skin, and he smiled one smile that ran all round his face two times. Then he danced three times round the skin and rubbed his hands. Then he went to his camp and filled his hat with cake-crumbs, for the Parsee never ate anything but cake, and never swept out his camp. He took that skin, and he shook that skin, and he scrubbed that skin, and he rubbed that skin just as full of old, dry, stale, tickly cake-crumbs and some burned currants as ever it could *possibly* hold. Then he climbed to the top of his palm-tree and waited for the Rhinoceros to come out of the water and put it on.

And the Rhinoceros did. He buttoned it up with the three buttons, and it tickled like cake-crumbs in bed. Then he wanted to scratch, but that made it worse; and then he lay down on the sands and rolled and rolled and rolled, and every time he rolled the cake-crumbs tickled him worse and worse and worse. Then he ran to the palm-tree and rubbed and rubbed and rubbed himself against it. He rubbed so much and so hard that he rubbed his skin into a great fold over his shoulders, and another fold underneath, where the buttons used to be (but he rubbed the buttons off), and he rubbed some more folds over his legs. And it spoiled his temper, but it didn't make the least difference to the cake-crumbs. They were inside his skin and they tickled. So he went home, very angry indeed and horribly scratchy; and from that day to this every rhinoceros has great folds in his skin and a very bad temper, all on account of the cake-crumbs inside.

But the Parsee came down from his palm-tree, wearing his hat, from which the rays of the sun were reflected in more-than-oriental splendour, packed up his cooking-stove, and went away in the direction of Orotavo, Amygdala, the Upland Meadows of Anantarivo, and the Marshes of Sonaput.

# Select Bibliography

Auerbach, Nina and U. C. Knoepflmacher (eds) *Forbidden Journeys: Fairy Tales and Fantasies by Victorian Women Writers*. Chicago: University of Chicago Press, 1992.

Avery, Gillian. *Childhood's Pattern: A Study of the Heroes and Heroines of Children's Fiction, 1770 1950*. London: Hodder and Stoughton, 1975.

Avery, Gillian. 'A Sense of History.' *Signal: Approaches to Children's Books*, 55, 1988, 53–72.

Avery, Gillian. *Behold the Child: American Children and their Books, 1621 1922*. London: Bodley Head, 1994.

Avery, Gillian and Julia Briggs (eds) *Children and their Books*. Oxford: Clarendon Press, 1989.

Battiscombe, Georgina. *Charlotte Mary Yonge: The Story of an Uneventful Life*. London: Constable, 1943.

Berry, Jani L. 'Discipline and (Dis)order: Paternal Socialization in Jacob Abbott's Rollo Books.' *Children's Literature Association Quarterly*, 18, 3, 1993, 100–6.

Bixler, Phyllis. *Frances Hodgson Burnett*. Boston: Twayne, 1984.

Blount, Margaret. *Animal Land: The Creatures of Children's Fiction*. London: Hutchinson, 1974.

Bratton, J. S. *The Impact of Victorian Children's Fiction*. London: Croom Helm, 1981.

Briggs, Julia. *A Woman of Passion: The Life of E. Nesbit*. London: Penguin, 1987.

Bristow, Joseph. *Empire Boys: Adventures in a Man's World*. London: Harper Collins Academic, 1991.

Butts, Dennis. *Mistress of our Tears: A Literary and Biographical Study of Barbara Hofland*. Aldershot: Scolar Press, 1992.

Butts, Dennis (ed.) *Stories and Society: Children's Literature in its Social Context*. London: Macmillan, 1992.

Butts, Dennis. 'How Children's Literature Changed: What Happened in the 1840s?' *The Lion and the Unicorn*, 21, 1997, 153–62.

Cadogan, Mary and Patricia Craig. *You're a Brick, Angela! A New Look at Girls' Fiction from 1839 to 1975*. London: Gollancz, 1976.

Carpenter, Humphrey. *Secret Gardens: A Study of the Golden Age of Children's Literature*. London: Allen and Unwin, 1985.

Carpenter, Humphrey and Mari Prichard. *The Oxford Companion to Children's Literature*. Oxford: Oxford University Press, 1984.

Carpenter, Kevin. *Penny Dreadfuls and Comics: English Periodicals for Children from Victorian Times to the Present Day*. London: Victoria and Albert Museum, 1983.

Chitty, Susan. *The Beast and the Monk: A Life of Charles Kingsley*. London: Hodder and Stoughton, 1974.

Clark, Beverly Lyon. *Regendering the School Story: Sassy Sissies and Tattling Tomboys*. New York: Garland, 1996.

Cooper, Jane. ' "Just Really What They Do", or, Re-reading Mrs Molesworth.' *Signal: Approaches to Children's Books*, 57, 1988, 181–96.

Cutt, M. Nancy. *Mrs Sherwood and Her Books for Children*. Oxford: Oxford University Press, 1974.

Cutt, Margaret N. *Ministering Angels: A Study of Nineteenth-century Evangelical Writing for Children*. Wormley: Five Owls Press, 1979.

Darton, F. J. Harvey. *Children's Books in England: Five Centuries of Social Life*, 3rd edn, revd by Brian Alderson. Cambridge: Cambridge University Press, 1982.

Demers, Patricia (ed.) *A Garland from the Golden Age: An Anthology of Children's Literature from 1850 to 1900*. Toronto: Oxford University Press, 1983.

Demers, Patricia and Gordon Moyles (eds) *From Instruction to Delight: An Anthology of Children's Literature to 1850*. Toronto: Oxford University Press, 1982.

Dennis, Barbara. *Charlotte Yonge (1823–1901): Novelist of the Oxford Movement*. Lampeter: Edwin Mellen, 1992.

Drotner, Kirsten. *English Children and their Magazines*. New Haven, Conn.: Yale University Press, 1988.

Dusinberre, Juliet. *Alice to the Lighthouse: Children's Books and Radical Experiments in Art*. London: Macmillan, 1987.

Egoff, Sheila. *The Republic of Childhood: A Critical Guide to Canadian Children's Literature in English*, 2nd edn. Toronto: Oxford University Press, 1975.

Estes, Angela M. and Kathleen Margaret Lane. 'Dismembering the Text: The Horror of Louisa May Alcott's *Little Women.'* *Children's Literature*, 17, 1989, 98–123.

Fisher, Margery. *Classics for Children and Young People*. South Woodchester: Thimble Press, 1986.

Fisher, Margery. 'Perspectives in Prose: Re-reading Some of Mrs Ewing's Stories.' *Signal: Approaches to Children's Books*, 59, 1989, 118–26.

Fisher, Margery. 'A Bear in the Nursery: Richard Hengist Horne Writing for Children.' *Signal: Approaches to Children's Books*, 61, 1990, 27–41.

Foster, Shirley and Judy Simons. *What Katy Read: Feminist Re-readings of 'Classic' Stories for Girls*. London: Macmillan, 1995.

Gardner, Martin. *The Annotated Alice: The Definitive Edition*. New York: Norton, 2000.

Gilderdale, Betty. *A Sea Change: 145 Years of New Zealand Junior Fiction*. Auckland: Longman Paul, 1982.

Gilderdale, Betty. *The Seven Lives of Lady Barker*. Auckland: David Bateman, 1996.

Goldthwaite, John. *The Natural History of Make-Believe*. New York: Oxford University Press, 1996.

Griswold, Jerry. *Audacious Kids: Coming of Age in America's Classic Children's Books*. New York: Oxford University Press, 1992.

Haviland, Virginia (ed.) *Yankee Doodles's Literary Sampler of Prose, Poetry and Pictures before 1900*. Washington: Library of Congress, 1974.

Hearne, Michael Patrick (ed.) *The Wizard of Oz*. The Critical Heritage Series. New York: Schocken, 1983.

Hilton, Mary, Morag Styles and Victor Watson (eds) *Opening the Nursery Door: Reading, Writing and Childhood 1600–1900*. London: Routledge, 1997.

Howarth, Patrick. *Play Up and Play the Game: The Heroes of Popular Fiction*. Eyre Methuen, 1972.

Hunt, Peter (ed.) *Children's Literature: An Illustrated History*. Oxford: Oxford University Press, 1995.

Hunt, Peter (ed.) *International Companion Encyclopedia of Children's Literature*. London: Routledge, 1996.

Inglis, Fred. *The Promise of Happiness: Value and Meaning in Children's Fiction*. Cambridge: Cambridge University Press, 1981.

Jackson, Mary V. *Engines of Instruction, Mischief, and Magic: Children's Literature in England from its Beginnings to 1839*. Lincoln, Nebr.: Nebraska University Press, 1989.

Jones, Jo Elwyn and J. Francis Gladstone. *The Alice Companion*. London: Macmillan, 1998.

Kearney, Anthony. 'Savage and Barbaric Themes in Victorian Children's Writing.' *Children's Literature in Education*, 17, 4, 1986, 233–40.

Keyser, Elizabeth Lennox. *Whispers in the Dark: The Fiction of Louisa May Alcott*. Knoxville: University of Tennessee Press, 1993.

Kieley, Robert. *Robert Louis Stevenson and The Fiction of Adventure*. Cambridge, Mass.: Harvard University Press, 1964.

Kincaid, James R. *Child-Loving: The Erotic Child and Victorian Culture*. New York: Routledge, 1992.

Knoepflmacher, U. C. 'Resisting Growth Through Fairy Tale in Ruskin's *The King of the Golden River.'* *Children's Literature*, 13. New Haven, Conn.: Yale University Press, 1985, 3–30.

Laski, Marghanita. *Mrs Ewing, Mrs Molesworth and Mrs Hodgson Burnett*. London: Arthur Barker, 1950.

Lees, Stella and Pam Macintyre. *The Oxford Companion to Australian Children's Literature*. Melbourne: Oxford University Press, 1993.

Levi, Peter. *Edward Lear: A Biography.* New York: Scribner, 1995.

MacLeod, Anne Scott. *A Moral Tale: Children's Fiction and American Culture, 1829–1860.* Hamden, Conn.: Shoe String Press, 1975.

MacLeod, Anne Scott. *American Childhood: Essays on Children's Literature of the Nineteenth and Twentieth Centuries.* Athens, Ga.: University of Georgia Press, 1994.

McGavran, James Holt (ed.) *Literature and the Child: Romantic Constructions, Postmodern Contestations.* Iowa City: University of Iowa Press, 1999.

McGavran, James Holt, Jr (ed.) *Romanticism and Children's Literature in Nineteenth-century England.* Athens, Ga.: University of Georgia Press, 1991.

McGillis, Roderick (ed.) *Voices of the Other: Children's Literature and the Postcolonial Context.* New York: Garland, 2000.

Manlove, Colin (ed.) *Modern Fantasy.* Cambridge: Cambridge University Press, 1975.

Moore, Opal and Donnarae MacCann. 'The Uncle Remus Travesty.' *Children's Literature Association Quarterly*, 11, 2, 1986, 96–9.

Muir, Marcie and Kerry White. *Australian Children's Books: A Bibliography. Volume 1, 1742–1972.* Melbourne: Melbourne University Press, 1992.

Muir, Percy. *English Children's Books 1600 to 1900.* London: Batsford, 1954.

Musgrave, P. W. *From Brown to Bunter: The Life and Death of the School Story.* London: Routledge and Kegan Paul, 1985.

Nelson, Claudia. *Boys will be Girls: The Feminine Ethic and British Children's Fiction, 1857–1917.* New Brunswick, NJ: Rutgers University Press, 1991.

Niall, Brenda. *Seven Little Billabongs.* Ringwood, Victoria: Penguin, 1982.

Nikolajeva, Maria (ed.) *Aspects and Issues in the History of Children's Literature.* Westport, Conn.: Greenwood, 1995.

Opie, Iona and Peter Opie. *The Oxford Book of Children's Verse.* Oxford: Oxford University Press, 1973.

Phillips, Robert (ed.) *Aspects of Alice.* Harmondsworth: Penguin, 1974.

Pickering, Samuel F., Jr. *Moral Instruction and Fiction for Children, 1749–1820.* Athens, Ga.: University of Georgia Press, 1993.

Plotz, Judith (guest ed.) 'Kipling Issue.' *Children's Literature*, 20. New Haven, Conn.: Yale University Press, 1992.

Quayle, Eric. *Early Children's Books: A Collector's Guide.* Newton Abbott: David and Charles; Totowa, NJ: Barnes and Noble, 1983.

Quigley, Isabel. *The Heirs of Tom Brown: The English School Story.* London: Chatto and Windus, 1982.

Reis, Richard. *George MacDonald.* New York: Twayne.

Reynolds, Kimberley. *Girls Only? Gender and Popular Children's Fiction in Britain 1880–1910.* Hemel Hempstead: Harvester, 1990.

Reynolds, Kimberley. *Children's Literature in the 1890s and the 1990s.* Plymouth: Northcote House, 1994.

Richards, Jeffrey. *Happiest Days: The Public Schools in English Fiction.* Manchester: Manchester University Press, 1988.

Richards, Jeffrey (ed.) *Imperialism and Juvenile Literature.* Manchester: Manchester University Press, 1989.

Rieder, John. 'Edward Lear's Limericks: The Function of Children's Nonsense Poetry.' *Children's Literature*, 26. New Haven, Conn.: Yale University Press, 1998, 47–60.

Rowbotham, Judith. *Good Girls make Good Wives: Guidance for Girls in Victorian Fiction.* Oxford: Blackwell Publishers, 1989.

Salway, Lance (ed.) *A Peculiar Gift: Nineteenth-century Writings on Books for Children.* Harmondsworth: Penguin, 1976.

Saxby, Maurice. *A History of Australian Children's Literature.* Sydney: Wentworth, Vol. 1, 1969; Vol. 2, 1971.

Sircar, Sanjay. 'The Victorian Auntly Narrative Voice and Mrs Molesworth's *Cuckoo Clock.*' *Children's Literature*, 17. New Haven, Conn.: Yale University Press, 1989, 1–24.

Styles, Morag. *From the Garden to the Street: An Introduction to 300 Years of Poetry for Children*. London: Cassell, 1998.

Tatar, Maria. *Off With Their Heads! Fairy Tales and the Culture of Childhood*. Princeton, NJ: Princeton University Press, 1992.

Thomas, Donald. *Lewis Carroll: A Portrait with Background*. London: John Murray, 1996.

Thwaite, Ann. *Waiting for the Party: The Life of Frances Hodgson Burnett*. London: Secker and Warburg, 1974.

Thwaite, Mary F. *From Primer to Pleasure in Reading*, 2nd edn. London: Library Association, 1972.

Tuer, Andrew W. (ed.) *Old Fashioned Children's Books*. London: Bracken, 1985.

Turner, E. S. *Boys Will Be Boys*. Harmondsworth: Penguin, 1976.

Vallone, Lynne. *Disciplines of Virtue: Girls' Culture in the Eighteenth and Nineteenth Centuries*. New Haven, Conn.: Yale University Press, 1995.

Wall, Barbara. *The Narrator's Voice: The Dilemma of Children's Fiction*. London: Macmillan, 1991.

Warner, Philip (ed.) *The Best of British Pluck: The Boy's Own Paper*. London: Macdonald and Janes, 1976.

West, Mark I. (ed.) *Before Oz: Juvenile Fantasy Stories from Nineteenth-century America*. Hamden, Conn.: Archon, 1989.

West, Mark I. (ed.) *A Wondrous Menagerie: Animal Fantasy Stories from American Children's Literature*. Hamden, Conn.: Archon, 1994.

Westbrook, M. David. 'Readers of Oz: Young and Old, Old and New Historicist.' *Children's Literature Association Quarterly*, 21, 3, 1996, 111–19.

Whalley, Joyce Irene and Tessa Rose Chester. *A History of Children's Book Illustration*. London: John Murray with the Victoria and Albert Museum, 1988.

Wolfe, Robert Lee. *The Golden Key: A Study of the Fiction of George MacDonald*. New Haven, Conn.: Yale University Press, 1961.

Zipes, Jack. *When Dreams Came True: Classical Fairy Tales and Their Tradition*. New York and London: Routledge, 1999.

# Index